Experience **Physics**

ISBN-13: 978-1-4183-3396-6
ISBN-10: 1-4183-3396-4

Geraldine Cochran is an Assistant Professor of Professional Practice in the School of Arts and Sciences and the Department of Physics and Astronomy at Rutgers University, and she is a physics education researcher. She earned her Ph.D. in curriculum and instruction with a cognate in physics and her Ed.S. in science education with a specialization in teacher preparation from Florida International University in Miami. She earned her M.A.T. with a specialization in secondary school physics, her B.S. degree in physics, and her B.S. degree in mathematics from Chicago State University in Chicago, IL.

Christopher Moore is the Dr. George F. Haddix Community Chair in Physical Science and associate professor of physics at the University of Nebraska Omaha. Holding a M.S. in applied physics and a Ph.D. in chemistry from Virginia Commonwealth University, Dr. Moore has worked as a physical science teacher at several secondary schools in Virginia, as a professional materials scientist, and as a scholar of and consultant on science education. Dr. Moore is author of the book *Creating Scientists: Teaching and Assessing Science Practice for the NGSS.*

Jason Sterlace is a former high school physics and chemistry teacher from Virginia who is currently employed at James Madison University, where he is both the Physics Coordinator for the Learning Center and an Instructor for the Department of Physics and Astronomy. Mr. Sterlace is a STEP-UP Ambassador for APS and a Nanoscience Fellow at the MathScience Innovation Center in Richmond. He was named the Physics Teacher of the Year in 2013 by Virginia Association of Science Teachers. Mr. Sterlace is a veteran of the United States Navy.

Michael Wysession is a Professor of Earth and Planetary Sciences and Executive Director of The Teaching Center at Washington University in St. Louis. Author of more than 100 science and science education publications, Dr. Wysession was awarded the National Science Foundation Presidential Faculty Fellowship and Packard Foundation Fellowship for his research in geophysics. Dr. Wysession is also a leader in geoscience literacy and education; he is the chair of the Earth Science Literacy Initiative, author of several popular video lectures on geoscience, and a lead writer of the Next Generation Science Standards.

Program Consultant

Alison Hapka is a physics, chemistry, and computer science educator who is passionate about getting people excited about discovering how their world works. Ms. Hapka has published notes in The Physics Teacher and served as President for the Maryland Association of Physics Teachers. She also worked on the state committee for the NGSS and served as a curator of NGSS resources for National Science Teachers Association for several years.

Academic Reviewers

Daniel Bardayan, Ph.D.
Professor
Department of Physics
University of Notre Dame
Notre Dame, IN

Tengiz Bibilashvili, Ph.D.
Senior Lecturer, Physics Instruction
University of California Santa Barbara
Santa Barbara, CA

Duncan Carlsmith, Ph.D.
Professor
Department of Physics
University of Wisconsin–Madison
Madison, WI

E. Dan Dahlberg, Ph.D.
Professor
School of Physics and Astronomy
University of Minnesota
Minneapolis, MN

Jacek K. Furdyna, Ph.D.
Professor
Department of Physics
University of Notre Dame
Notre Dame, IN

Umesh Garg, Ph.D.
Professor
Department of Physics
University of Notre Dame
Notre Dame, IN

Colin Jessop, Ph.D.
Professor
Department of Physics and Astronomy
University of Notre Dame
Notre Dame, IN

Zosia Krusberg, Ph.D.
Director of Graduate Studies and Senior Lecturer
Department of Physics
University of Chicago
Chicago, IL

David W. Miller, Ph.D.
Associate Professor
Department of Physics
University of Chicago
Chicago, IL

James Schombert, Ph.D.
Professor
Department of Physics
University of Oregon
Eugene, OR

David Weintraub, Ph.D.
Professor
Physics & Astronomy Department
Vanderbilt University
Nashville, TN

Teacher Reviewers

Ekaterina Denisova, Ph.D.
National Board Certified Teacher (Physics, Adolescence and Young Adulthood)
Assistant Principal
Western HS, Baltimore City Public Schools
Baltimore, MD

David Downing
Adjunct Professor
School of Engineering, Technology, Mathematics and Science
Dallas College
Dallas, TX

Bradford Hill
Teacher and Science Specialist
Beaverton School District
Beaverton, OR

Scott Hertting
Physics Teacher
Neenah High School
Neenah, WI

Harvey Mamrus
Principles of Engineering Teacher
St. Joseph High School
Trumbull, CT

Jeffrey Mann
Science Department
Valley Central School District
Montgomery, New York

Don Pata
Physics Teacher
Grosse Pointe North High School
Grosse Pointe Woods, MI

Heena Patel, M.S.
Chemistry and Physics Teacher
West Aurora High School
Aurora, IL

Melissa L. Shirley, Ph.D.
Science Teacher
Valley View High School
Germantown, OH

Lab Review

All labs in the program were developed and tested by **FLINN SCIENTIFIC**

TABLE OF CONTENTS

STORYLINE 1

Forces and Motion 2

 **ANCHORING PHENOMENON** How will we get to Mars?

 GO ONLINE to find hands-on and virtual labs, CER and modeling activities, and other resources—videos, animations, and simulations—that complete the Experiences.

STORYLINE 2
Forces at a Distance 112

ANCHORING PHENOMENON How does the moon shape our coastline?

Energy Conversion

278

STORYLINE 4

Waves and Electromagnetic Radiation   462

ANCHORING PHENOMENON How do waves transfer energy?

GO ONLINE to find hands-on and virtual labs, CER and modeling activities, and other resources—videos, animations, and simulations—that complete the Experiences.

GO ONLINE to find hands-on and virtual labs, CER and modeling activities, and other resources—videos, animations, and simulations— that complete the Experiences.

STORYLINE 4
- Mechanical Waves
- Interference of Sound Waves
- Reflection and Refraction
- Diffraction
- Particle Nature of Light
- Electromagnetic Radiation and Matter
- Binary Logic
- Converting Electrical Signals to Sounds
- Converting Sunlight to Electricity

STORYLINE 5
- Subatomic Particles
- Forces and Atomic Nuclei
- Nuclear Reactions and Critical Mass
- Half-Life Simulation
- Radiometric Dating of Rocks
- Plate Tectonics and Seafloor Spreading
- Sunlight Intensity and Solar Flares
- Elemental Composition of Stars
- The Expansion of the Universe

FLINN
SCIENTIFIC
ENGINEERING WORKBENCH PROJECTS

STORYLINE 1
- Design an Airdrop System
- Landslide Prevention

STORYLINE 2
- Defy Gravity
- Design an Electronic Quiz Board
- Build a Flashlight Without Batteries
- Earthquake-Resistant Structures

STORYLINE 3
- Design a Roller Coaster
- Egg Supply Drop
- Build an Efficient Travel Mug
- Energy Sources: Costs and Benefits

STORYLINE 4
- Waves and Erosion
- Solar Panel Art
- Rover

STORYLINE 5
- Energy Production
- Build a Glove Box
- The Colors of Light

VIRTUAL LAB PERFORMANCE-BASED ASSESSMENTS

STORYLINE 1
- Coin Drop
- Sliding Down

STORYLINE 2
- Gravitational Forces on Satellites
- Oil Drop Experiment
- Generator Testing
- Properties of Materials

STORYLINE 3
- Rocket Launch
- Minimizing Car Crash Injuries
- Meltdown at the Pool
- Junkyard Electromagnet

STORYLINE 4
- Making Waves
- Particle-Wave Duality of Light
- Music Storage for Home Recording

STORYLINE 5
- Operate a Nuclear Fission Reactor
- Rock Clocks
- Build a Star!

VIDEOS

STORYLINE 1
- Velocity and Speed Are Different
- Common Free-Fall Pitfalls
- Demonstrating the Components of Projectile Motion
- Newton's Third Law of Motion
- Introduction to Static and Kinetic Friction
- What Forces Are Acting On You?
- How Tall Can Mountains Be?

STORYLINE 2
- Newton's Universal Law of Gravitation
- Tides
- Kepler's Laws and Beyond
- Introduction to Coulomb's Law
- How to Survive a Lightning Strike
- Series and Parallel Circuits
- Where Is the True North Pole?
- World's First Electric Generator
- Induction: An Introduction
- The 2,400-year Search for the Atom
- Is Glass a Liquid?
- 20 MILLION Year-Old Spider! Unweaving Spider Silk
- How Do Geckos Defy Gravity?

STORYLINE 3
- Introduction to Kinetic Energy
- All of the Energy in the Universe
- Conservation of Energy
- Demonstrating How Helmets Affect Impulse and Impact Force
- Elastic and Inelastic Collisions
- Why Are Earthquakes So Hard to Predict?
- Celsius Didn't Invent Celsius
- Misconceptions About Heat
- Why is it Hot Underground
- How Batteries Work
- Electric Power, Current, and Resistance
- How Power Gets to Your Home
- A Guide to the Energy of the Earth

STORYLINE 4
- Understanding Waves, Wavelength, and Period Using Graphs
- Research on Harnessing Wave Energy from the World's Oceans
- Refraction in Animals
- The Original Double Slit Experiment
- Single Photon Interference
- How Microwaving Grapes Makes Plasma
- Amazing Hard Drives of the Future
- The Wow! Signal
- Do Cell Phones Cause Brain Tumors?

STORYLINE 5
- Atomic Nucleus
- Strong Nuclear Force
- Nuclear Reactions, Radioactivity, Fission, and Fusion
- Half-Life and Radioactive Decay
- Radiometric Dating
- A Brief History of Geologic Time
- How Epic Solar Winds Make Brilliant Polar Lights
- How to Detect a Supernova
- The Genesis of the Universe

ADDITIONAL RESOURCES
- Claim-Evidence-Reasoning
- Modeling
- Analyzing Data
- Discussion Rubric
- Peer Review Rubric
- Writing About Science
- Problem-Based Learning
- Practice Problems
- PhET Simulations

End-of-Book Resources

Forces and Motion

How will we get to Mars?

Investigation 1
Modeling Motion

Investigation 2
Forces

ANCHORING PHENOMENON

Inquiry Launch Humans have been to the moon, but we have not yet been to Mars. To get there, a rocket has to travel tens of millions of kilometers and reach enormous speeds. The photograph suggests the scale of the task and the size of the forces involved. The bright arc might remind you of a graph of the rocket's trajectory.

What questions would you need to answer in order to plan a trip to Mars?

GO ONLINE to engage with real-world phenomena. Watch the **anchoring phenomenon video** and preview the optional **problem-based learning** experience.

INVESTIGATIVE PHENOMENON

 GO ONLINE to engage with real-world phenomena by watching a **phenomenon video** and completing a **modeling worksheet**.

How did this rock move across the valley?

Modeling Motion

Long trails terminated by heavy rocks were discovered along smooth valley floors in Nevada and California in the early 1900s. No trace of human involvement, such as footprints or other tracks, could be seen. Called "sailing stones," such rocks are often too large to be reasonably moved by wind alone, and similar rock trails have recently been discovered on the surface of Mars.

The trails left by the sailing stones vary in length and often change direction. Rocks that seem to have started their journey next to each other often appear to travel along parallel paths, until something causes one to abruptly change direction.

What could move such heavy rocks across the desert floor? A mystery for decades, the causes of the stones' motion have only recently become understood through scientists' research. Using time-lapse photography and global positioning system (GPS) tracking units attached to the rocks, scientists have been able to describe and analyze their motion.

1. **SEP Plan an Investigation** What experiments would you do to learn more about how sailing stones move across the valley?

2. **SEP Define Problems** What variables can you identify that could be used to model a stone's motion?

3. **CCC Cause and Effect** What do you think might cause the stones to move across the valley?

EXPERIENCE 1

Displacement and Velocity

 GO ONLINE to do a **hands-on lab** to model and investigate the differences between displacement and distance traveled.

Displacement

Position and Displacement The **position** of an object is a measure of where the object is at a particular time with respect to some reference point. You will use units of meters (m) for position, but other units include miles and inches. **Displacement** is the change in position of an object. **Distance traveled** is the total length of the path traveled between two positions. In any given scenario, the distance traveled is greater than or equal to the displacement.

Displacement
$$\Delta d = d_f - d_i$$
Δd = displacement d_i = initial position
d_f = final position

The Greek letter Δ means "change in." Therefore, Δd means "change in position."

Displacement and Distance Traveled A cyclist travels from one position to another, turns around, and begins to ride back toward his original position. The distance he traveled is greater than his displacement.

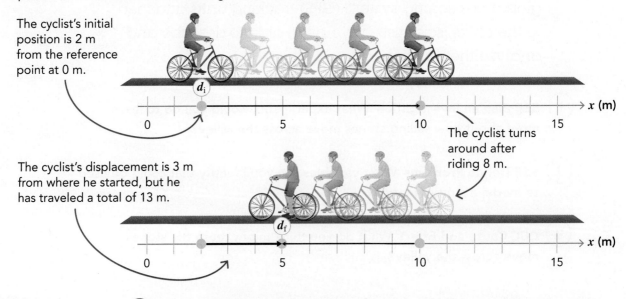

The cyclist's initial position is 2 m from the reference point at 0 m.

d_i

The cyclist turns around after riding 8 m.

The cyclist's displacement is 3 m from where he started, but he has traveled a total of 13 m.

d_f

(4) **SEP Use Mathematics** A cyclist rides 3 km west and then turns around and rides 2 km east. What is her displacement? What total distance does she ride?

Representing Displacement Distance traveled is an example of a **scalar quantity,** a quantity with magnitude or size, but no defined direction. Displacement is an example of a **vector quantity,** a quantity having both magnitude and direction. You can refer to such quantities more simply as vectors and scalars. You can represent a vector using an arrow, with the length of the arrow indicating the magnitude. A vector can also be represented mathematically as a set of components. A **vector component,** or simply a component, is the projection of a vector quantity along an axis in a coordinate system. When representing a component, use x to represent horizontal motion and y to represent vertical motion.

EXPERIENCE IT!

Use a piece of tape to mark your position. Take four steps forward. Then turn to your right and take three steps. Count how many steps it takes to get back to where you started, following a straight line.

Vector Representations Suppose you cut through your backyard to get to a friend's house. Your motion can be represented both as a displacement vector and as components.

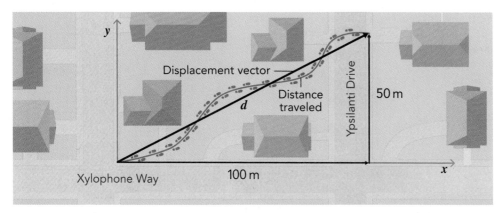

Components A coordinate system is defined with the x-direction parallel to Xylophone Way and the y-direction parallel to Ypsilanti Drive. The distances you would have walked along the two roads are the components.

Magnitude The components make a right triangle with the displacement vector. You can use the Pythagorean theorem to determine the magnitude of the displacement from the components.

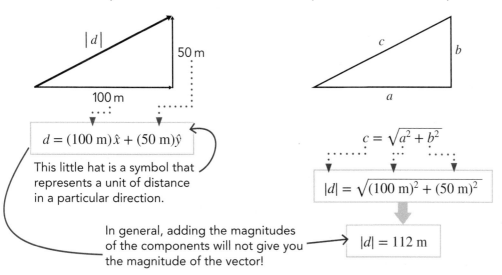

$$d = (100 \text{ m})\hat{x} + (50 \text{ m})\hat{y}$$

This little hat is a symbol that represents a unit of distance in a particular direction.

In general, adding the magnitudes of the components will not give you the magnitude of the vector!

$$c = \sqrt{a^2 + b^2}$$

$$|d| = \sqrt{(100 \text{ m})^2 + (50 \text{ m})^2}$$

$$|d| = 112 \text{ m}$$

(5) SEP Develop a Model Changing classes, you walk 20.0 m down a hall, turn left, and then walk 10.0 m down another hall. Define a coordinate system and sketch the displacement vector. Also, sketch the displacement components, and then determine the vector's magnitude.

Vector Mathematics

You will often need to add or subtract vectors. The **resultant** is a vector that is the sum of two or more vectors. There are two methods for determining resultants: graphical (the head-to-tail method) and analytical.

Head-to-Tail Method

How do you graphically **add multiple vectors** to solve problems?

Problem A person walks 22.0 m in a direction 43.0° with respect to the x-direction. She then walks 20.0 m at a 20.0° angle above the x-direction. Finally, she turns and walks 29.0 m at an angle of 68.0° below the x-direction. What is her total displacement?

Step 1 Graphically represent the data, using a ruler and a protractor.

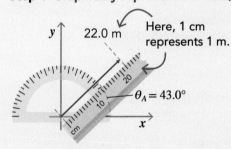

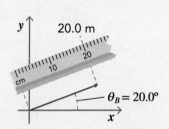

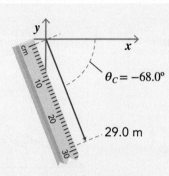

Step 2 Place the vectors head to tail. Retain each vector's initial magnitude and direction.

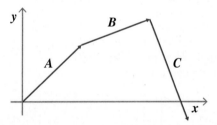

Step 3 Draw a line from the tail of the first vector to the head of the last vector. This is the resultant vector.

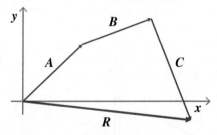

Step 4 Measure the magnitude and angle of the resultant vector, using a ruler and a protractor.

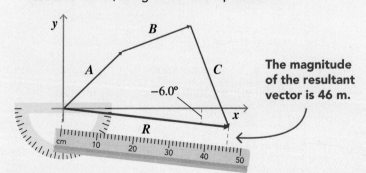

The magnitude of the resultant vector is 46 m.

NOTE: If you are subtracting vectors, use an arrow that points in the opposite direction and change the sign of the vector.

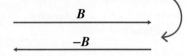

 SEP Use a Model Using the head-to-tail method, determine the magnitude of the displacement for $A - B$ using the vectors shown in the figure. Use a ruler and protractor.

GO ONLINE to do a PhET **simulation** that allows you to explore vector addition.

Analytical Method The horizontal and vertical components of any two-dimensional motion are independent of each other. Motion in one direction does not affect motion in the other direction. You use that independence to add and subtract vectors analytically.

When adding two vectors, add the x-component of one vector to the x-component of the other vector. The result is the x-component of the resultant vector. In the same way, add the y-components of two vectors to determine the y-component of the resultant vector. Once you have the x- and y-components of the resultant vector, use the Pythagorean theorem to determine the magnitude of the displacement.

Adding Components To add vectors analytically, represent each vector as the hypotenuse of a right triangle. Then, add the respective x-components and y-components.

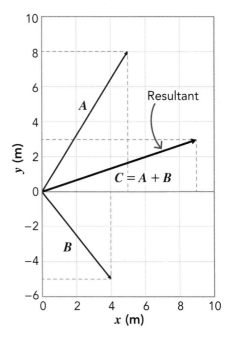

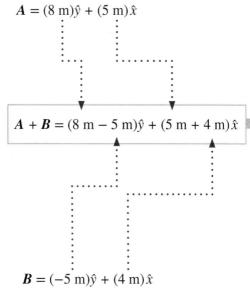

$$A = (8 \text{ m})\hat{y} + (5 \text{ m})\hat{x}$$

$$A + B = (8 \text{ m} - 5 \text{ m})\hat{y} + (5 \text{ m} + 4 \text{ m})\hat{x}$$

$$B = (-5 \text{ m})\hat{y} + (4 \text{ m})\hat{x}$$

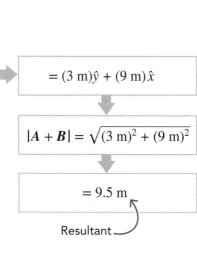

$$= (3 \text{ m})\hat{y} + (9 \text{ m})\hat{x}$$

$$|A + B| = \sqrt{(3 \text{ m})^2 + (9 \text{ m})^2}$$

$$= 9.5 \text{ m}$$

Resultant

⑦ **SEP Use Mathematics** Two displacement vectors A and B are shown. Determine the component representation for the sum of the two vectors $C = A + B$. Sketch vector C and determine its magnitude.

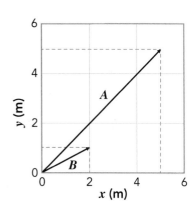

Row, Row, Row Your Boat

Starting from one shore, you row a boat across a narrow river to the other shore. The river is 22.0 m wide. As you row, the river current moves your boat down the river a distance of 35.0 m. What is the resultant displacement of your boat? Express your answer in components, and then determine the magnitude.

1. DRAW A PICTURE Sketch a picture of the situation.

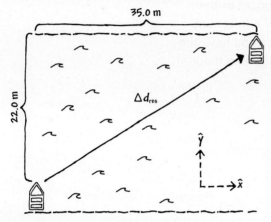

35.0 m

22.0 m

Δd_{res}

$\hat{y}$

$\hat{x}$

2. DEFINE THE PROBLEM List knowns and unknowns, and assign values to variables.

$\Delta d_{boat} = (0\ \text{m})\hat{x} + (22.0\ \text{m})\hat{y}$

$\Delta d_{river} = (35.0\ \text{m})\hat{x} + (0\ \text{m})\hat{y}$

$\Delta d_{res} = ?$

3. PLAN AND EXECUTE Use mathematical relationships, the picture, and your definitions to plan and execute a solution.

Write the simplified equation.	$\Delta d_{res} = \Delta d_{boat} + \Delta d_{river}$
Use the analytical method to determine the components of the resultant displacement.	$\Delta d_{res} = (0\ \text{m} + 35.0\ \text{m})\hat{x} + (22.0\ \text{m} + 0\ \text{m})\hat{y}$ $\Delta d_{res} = (35.0\ \text{m})\hat{x} + (22.0\ \text{m})\hat{y}$
Use the Pythagorean theorem to determine the magnitude of the displacement.	$\lvert \Delta d_{res} \rvert = \sqrt{(35.0\ \text{m})^2 + (22.0\ \text{m})^2} = 41.3\ \text{m}$

4. EVALUATE Reflect on your answer.
The units are appropriate for displacement. The displacement is larger than both of the components, which is a requirement for the hypotenuse of a right triangle.

 GO ONLINE for more **math support.**

Math Practice Problems

(8) Starting from one shore, you row a boat across a narrow river to the other shore. The river is 30.0 m wide. As you row, the river current moves your boat down the river a distance of 15.0 m. What is the resultant displacement of your boat? Express your answer in components, and then determine the magnitude.

📖 **NEED A HINT?** Go online to your **eText Sample Problem** for stepped out support.

(9) Your friend rows a canoe across a river 44.0 m wide. Using the GPS on her phone, she determines that her total displacement is 66.0 m. How far down the river did the current move her canoe?

Motion Diagram Individual frames from a video of a skier are layered on top of each other. The composite image shows the skier's position at several equally spaced moments in time.

Dot Diagrams

Motion is a change in position. You can use video to measure change in position with time. A video camera captures images at a fixed rate, typically 30 images every second. Each individual image is a frame. Individual frames can be layered on top of each other, producing a motion diagram. A **motion diagram** shows an object's position at several equally spaced moments in time.

To simplify a motion diagram, you can model the object as a dot. A **dot diagram** is a motion diagram in which each position of the moving object of interest is represented as a single point. A key feature of a dot diagram is that the time interval, or step, between successive dots is constant.

Dot Diagram The velociraptor's position is represented as a dot. Modeling the position as a dot simplifies the motion diagram, since you don't need to draw several velociraptors.

The times t_1, t_2, t_3, and t_4 show the order of the frames. The time interval between frames and dots is constant.

Equally spaced dots mean that the velociraptor moves the same distance in each time interval.

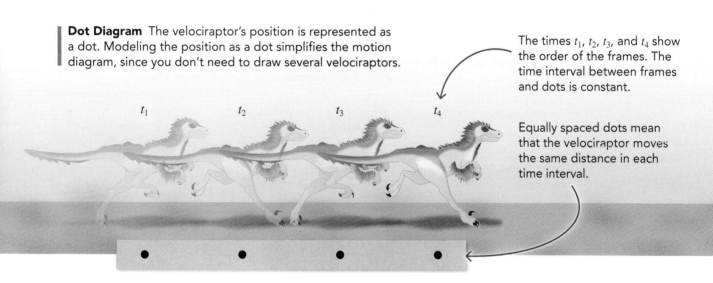

⑩ **SEP Ask Questions** The two dot diagrams show an object getting faster (left diagram) and an object getting slower (right diagram). What features about each dot diagram can you use to determine increasing vs. decreasing speed? How do you think speed is defined?

Position Graphs

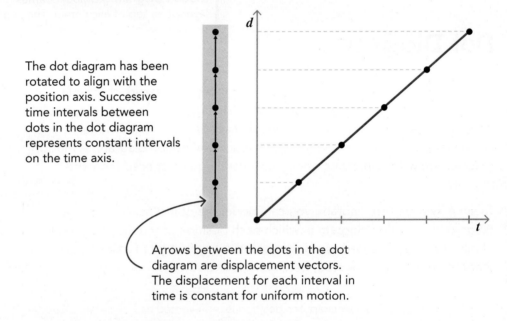

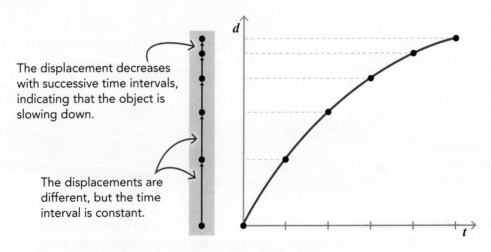

VOCABULARY

The word *uniform* comes from the Latin word *uniformis*, which means "having only one form or shape." **Uniform motion** means motion that stays the same.

Straight-line motion in which the position changes the same amount in each time interval is called **uniform motion.** Motion in which the position does not change the same amount in each time interval is called **nonuniform motion.** You can graph either sort of motion by starting with a dot diagram. You then convert the dot diagram into a graph of position as a function of time, called a position vs. time graph, or a **position graph.**

Uniform Motion Equally spaced dots in a dot diagram indicate uniform motion. A linear (meaning following a straight line) position graph also indicates uniform motion.

The dot diagram has been rotated to align with the position axis. Successive time intervals between dots in the dot diagram represents constant intervals on the time axis.

Arrows between the dots in the dot diagram are displacement vectors. The displacement for each interval in time is constant for uniform motion.

Nonuniform Motion Unequally spaced dots indicate nonuniform motion. A curved position graph also indicates nonuniform motion.

The displacement decreases with successive time intervals, indicating that the object is slowing down.

The displacements are different, but the time interval is constant.

⑪ **SEP Develop a Model** Sketch a dot diagram and a position vs. time graph for an object starting at rest and speeding up.

Speed and Velocity

Velocity is a measure of how much an object's position changes in a specified amount of time. **Speed** is a measure of how much distance an object travels in a specified amount of time. Since velocity is defined by the displacement, a vector quantity, then velocity is also a vector quantity. Speed is defined as the distance traveled, which is a scalar quantity, so speed is also a scalar quantity. Both measurements have units of m/s.

Velocity
$$v = \frac{\Delta d}{\Delta t} = \frac{(d_f - d_i)}{(t_f - t_i)}$$
v = velocity $\qquad$ Δt = change in Δd = displacement $\qquad\quad$ the time

For one-dimensional uniform motion, the velocity can also be determined from analysis of a position vs. time graph. The slope of the line is the velocity.

> **Slope of a Position Graph** Uniform motion results in a linear position vs. time graph. The slope of the line is the velocity. The steeper the slope, the greater the velocity.

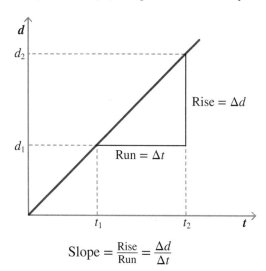

$$\text{Slope} = \frac{\text{Rise}}{\text{Run}} = \frac{\Delta d}{\Delta t}$$

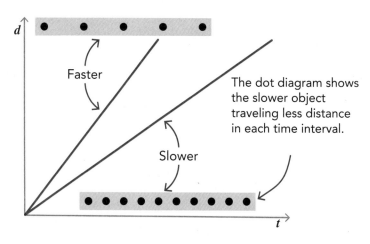

The dot diagram shows the slower object traveling less distance in each time interval.

(12) **SEP Analyze and Interpret Data** The table shows data for the position of two animals as a function of time. Plot the data for each animal and determine which animal is going faster.

Animal 1		Animal 2	
t (s)	d (m)	t (s)	d (m)
1.0	13.5	1.0	0.09
2.0	27.0	2.0	0.18
3.0	40.5	3.0	0.27

An Ant on a Meter Stick

You time an ant's movement as it walks along a meter stick. You record the following data: {(0 s, 0.10 m), (1.0 s, 0.18 m), (2.0 s, 0.26 m)}. Determine the ant's velocity from the slope of the position vs. time graph.

1. DRAW A PICTURE Sketch a picture of the situation.

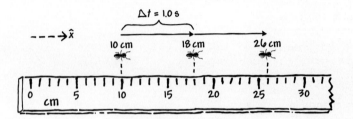

2. DEFINE THE PROBLEM List knowns and unknowns, and assign values to variables.

t (s)	d (m)
0.0	0.10
1.0	0.18
2.0	0.26

$$v = ?$$

3. PLAN AND EXECUTE Use mathematical relationships, the picture, and your definitions to plan and execute a solution.

Graph the position as a function of time using the data provided. Since the graph is a straight line, you know the motion is uniform.

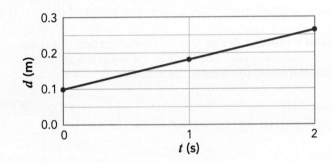

For uniform motion, choose any two points to determine the slope.

$$v = \frac{\text{rise}}{\text{run}} = \frac{0.26 \text{ m} - 0.18 \text{ m}}{2.0 \text{ s} - 1.0 \text{ s}} = 0.08 \text{ m/s}$$

4. EVALUATE Reflect on your answer.
All of the units are appropriate for the given quantities. The answer is reasonable, since you know that an ant can only move a small fraction of a meter each second.

 GO ONLINE for more **math support**.

    📶 **Math Practice Problems**

---

(13) You time an ant's movement as it walks along a meter stick. You record the following data: {(0.0 s, 0.00 m), (1.0 s, 0.08 m), (2.0 s, 0.16 m)}. Determine the ant's velocity from the slope of the position vs. time graph.

📖 **NEED A HINT?** Go online to your **eText Sample Problem** for stepped out support.

(14) You stop the stopwatch at 4.0 s, but you notice a short time later that the same ant is at 0.81 m on the meter stick. Assuming the ant keeps going at the same velocity, how much time has passed since you stopped the stopwatch?

Speed and Velocity Graphs

 GO ONLINE to watch a **video** about the difference between speed and velocity.

You probably use the words *velocity* and *speed* interchangeably in everyday conversation. However, in physics, speed and velocity are not the same quantities, in the same way that displacement and distance traveled are different quantities. Unlike velocity, speed has no direction. This can result in the speed being greater than the velocity when averaged over a trip.

As an example, suppose you make a trip to the store and back. You have an average speed greater than zero, because you travel some distance. However, since your position at the beginning and end of the trip is the same, your displacement and your average velocity are zero. Sometimes it is more useful to determine a speed, while other times it is more useful to determine a velocity.

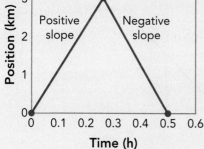 **Differentiating Speed and Velocity** Suppose you ride your bicycle to pick up a few items at the neighborhood grocery store, which is 3 km away. You realize you have forgotten to bring any money, so you turn around and arrive back home 30 minutes later.

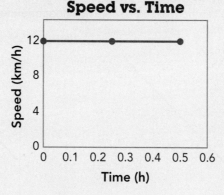

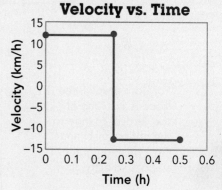

The position vs. time graph shows your position relative to your home. For the entire trip, your displacement is zero.

Your speed has no direction, so you go 12 km/h both going to and returning from the store.

Your velocity going toward the store is 12 km/h. Your velocity coming back home is −12 km/hr.

(15) **SEP Argue from Evidence** There are many ways to graph data. Make a claim about whether a line graph is better than a circle graph for representing motion data. Use evidence to support your claim.

(16) **CCC Scale, Proportion, and Quantity** If you wanted to know how long it would take you to get to the store and back, which would be more useful, average speed or average velocity? Explain why.

How Far? Highway distance signs show you how far away different locations are from your current position.

Modeling Uniform Motion

Position vs. Time You have seen that the slope of a position vs. time graph is the velocity. You can also use a position graph to write an equation for the position as a function of time for uniform motion. The general equation for a line is $y(x) = mx + b$, where m is the slope, and b is the y-intercept. When the position graph is a line, you can write the general equation in terms of the specific variables for initial position, final position, velocity, and time.

In much the same way, you can go in the other direction and sketch a position graph when you are provided the equation for the position as a function of time. You can and will convert graphs to equations and equations to graphs.

> **Position Graph to Equation** The general equation for a line can be used to generate an equation for position.

For both graphs, the slope is the ratio of the vertical change to the horizontal change. On a position graph, slope is velocity, v.

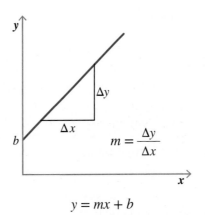

$$m = \frac{\Delta y}{\Delta x}$$

$$y = mx + b$$

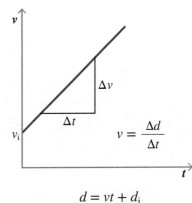

$$v = \frac{\Delta d}{\Delta t}$$

$$d = vt + d_i$$

The table shows the corresponding variables in the graphs.

	Horizontal	Vertical	Slope	Intercept
y vs. x	x	y	m	b
d vs. t	t	d	v	d_i

(17) **SEP Develop a Model** The following is an equation describing the motion of an object: $d(t) = (1.0 \text{ m/s})t + 2.0 \text{ m}$. Sketch the position vs. time graph for the motion from 0 to 4 seconds.

Velocity vs. Time You can use a velocity vs. time graph to write an equation for the displacement. The area under the line is the displacement for the time period highlighted. If the function is above the t-axis, the area is positive. If it is below the t-axis, the area is negative.

When you compare the equation derived using the position vs. time graph to the equation derived using the velocity vs. time graph, keep in mind that d represents position and Δd represents displacement. The area under the line does not tell you about position, only about displacement.

Velocity Graph and Displacement A velocity vs. time graph for uniform motion is flat, since velocity is constant.

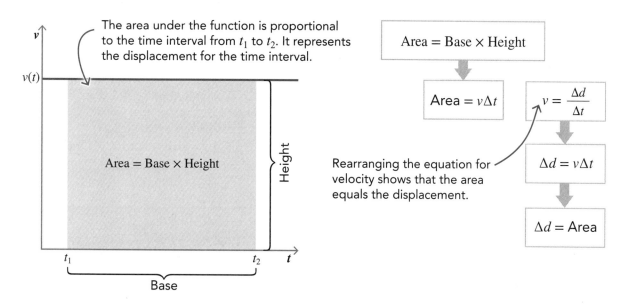

The area under the function is proportional to the time interval from t_1 to t_2. It represents the displacement for the time interval.

Area = Base × Height

Area = $v\Delta t$

$v = \dfrac{\Delta d}{\Delta t}$

Rearranging the equation for velocity shows that the area equals the displacement.

$\Delta d = v\Delta t$

Δd = Area

(18) **SEP Construct an Explanation** Sketch a velocity graph with a negative constant velocity and shade the area defining the displacement. Construct an explanation for why a negative velocity graph results in a negative displacement.

How Fast? The number on a speed limit sign tells you the maximum speed you can drive legally.

SPEED LIMIT 30

Driving Distance

As you drive, a passenger in your car records your speed at 10-second intervals. The passenger records the following data: {(0 s, 15 m/s), (10 s, 15 m/s), (20 s, 15 m/s), (30 s, 15 m/s), (40 s, 15 m/s)}. Using a graph of the velocity as a function of time, determine your displacement between $t = 5$ s and $t = 25$ s.

1. DRAW A PICTURE Sketch a picture of the situation.

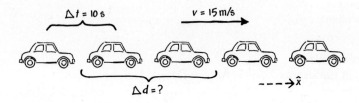

2. DEFINE THE PROBLEM List knowns and unknowns, and assign values to variables.

t (s)	v (m/s)
0	15
10	15
20	15
30	15
40	15

$\Delta d(t = 5 \text{ s} \rightarrow 25 \text{ s}) = \, ?$

3. PLAN AND EXECUTE Use mathematical relationships, the picture, and your definitions to plan and execute a solution.

> Graph the velocity as a function of time using the provided data.

> Shade the area under the line between $t = 5$ s and $t = 25$ s.

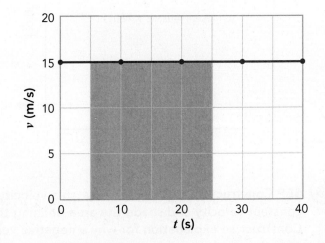

> Calculate the area of the shaded region.

$\Delta d = \text{base} \times \text{height}$

$\Delta d = (25 \text{ s} - 5 \text{ s}) \times 15 \text{ m/s}$

$\Delta d = 300 \text{ m}$

4. EVALUATE Reflect on your answer.

All of the units are appropriate for the given quantities. Since your maximum speed was 15 m/s, and the time was 40 s, you could not have traveled any more than 600 m. The answer 300 m is reasonable.

 GO ONLINE for more **math support**.

▶ **Math Tutorial Video**

🖥 **Math Practice Problems**

(19) As you drive, a passenger in your car records your speed at 15-second intervals. The passenger records the following data: {(0 s, 25 m/s), (15 s, 25 m/s), (30 s, 25 m/s), (45 s, 25 m/s), (60 s, 25 m/s)}. Using a graph of the velocity as a function of time, determine your displacement between $t = 10$ s and $t = 40$ s.

📖 **NEED A HINT?** Go online to your **eText Sample Problem** for stepped out support.

(20) As you drive, a passenger in your car records the following speeds at 8-second intervals: {(0 s, 20 m/s), (8 s, 20 m/s), (16 s, 20 m/s), (24 s, 20 m/s), (32 s, 20 m/s)}. Using a graph of the velocity as a function of time, determine your displacement between $t = 0$ s and $t = 30$ s.

(21) The graph shows velocity vs. time for an object in uniform motion. Determine the total displacement between $t = 3$ s and $t = 5$ s.

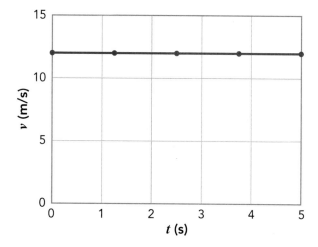

(22) The graph shows position vs. time for an object in uniform motion. Write an equation that describes the motion and determine the object's velocity.

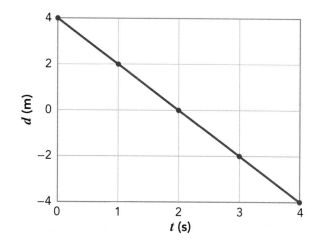

(23) The following is an equation describing the motion of an object: $d(t) = (-5.0 \text{ m/s})t + 10.0 \text{ m}$. Sketch the position vs. time graph for the motion from 0 to 4 seconds.

INVESTIGATIVE PHENOMENON

 GO ONLINE to revisit your **Investigative Phenomenon modeling activity** with the new information you have learned about Displacement and Velocity.

These questions will help you apply what you learned in this experience to the Investigative Phenomenon.

(24) **SEP Develop and Use a Model** Scientists photographed a sailing stone during its motion. Their camera took photos once every 10 seconds. The stone moved 4 meters per minute. Draw a motion diagram of the stone's motion over 40 seconds and construct a dot diagram. Assume the motion is uniform. How should you label the spacing between successive dots?

(25) **SEP Analyze and Interpret Data** Scientists attached GPS trackers to several sailing stones in Racetrack Playa in Death Valley, California. On December 4, 2013, at approximately 7:00 P.M., the stone named Eos began to move. The table shows data for the first 4 minutes of the motion. Graph the data and determine the average velocity of the stone during the interval. Was the motion uniform?

Time (s)	Distance (m)
0	0
60	5.175
120	10.625
180	16.505
240	22.290

(26) **SEP Use Mathematics** Assume Eos moved uniformly for 240 seconds at the average velocity you determined from your graph. Sketch a graph of the stone's velocity as a function of time from $t = 0$ s to $t = 300$ s. Using the graph, determine Eos's total displacement between 240 s and 300 s.

 GO ONLINE for a **quiz** to evaluate what you learned about Displacement and Velocity.

EXPERIENCE 2

Acceleration

  GO ONLINE to do a **hands-on lab**, to investigate acceleration, and to do a PhET **simulation** that allows you to explore acceleration with a mass on a spring.

Instantaneous Velocity

Instantaneous velocity is the average velocity over an infinitesimally small time interval. To find that velocity, think of zooming in on a position vs. time graph. As you look at smaller and smaller time intervals, a curved line will appear more and more to be straight. That straight line through a pair of infinitely close points on a curve is the **tangent line,** or tangent, for short. The slope of the tangent line on a position vs. time graph is the instantaneous velocity.

Determining Instantaneous Velocity Look at the dot diagram and position graph for an object with nonuniform motion. The more you zoom in on a region of the graph, the more uniform the motion looks.

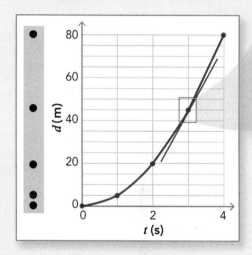

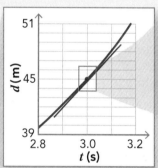

Extending the line of the zoomed-in motion gives a line tangent to the function.

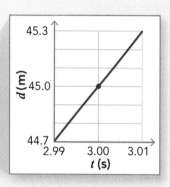

The slope of the zoomed-in line of uniform motion is the instantaneous velocity.

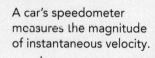

A car's speedometer measures the magnitude of instantaneous velocity.

(27) **SEP Analyze and Interpret Data** The graph shows data for an object's position as a function of time. The tangent line at Point A, has been drawn for you. Determine the instantaneous velocity at Point A, where $t = 2.5$ s. In which direction is the object moving? How do you know?

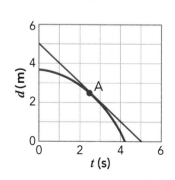

2 Acceleration   **21**

Increasing Velocity The velociraptor's velocity is increasing. The vectors drawn between the dots in a dot diagram represent the average velocity between successive points, because the time interval is constant.

Graphs of Changing Velocity

VOCABULARY

The word *derivative* comes from the Latin word *derivatus*, which means "to draw off." When you find the **time derivative,** you are drawing the tangent line off the function at a single point.

When you look at how the tangent's slope changes on a position vs. time graph, you are finding the time derivative of the position. The **time derivative** of a function is the rate at which the value of the function changes with time. You can see that the time derivative at any point is the slope of the curve at that point.

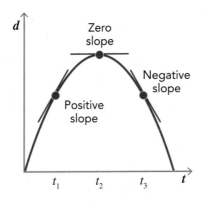

Position vs. Time A positive tangent slope indicates positive velocity, a negative slope indicates negative velocity, and a flat tangent line indicates zero velocity.

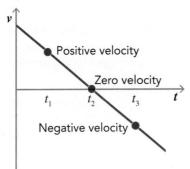

Velocity vs. Time The slope of the tangent at each instant on the position vs. time graph can be used to construct a velocity vs. time graph.

28 **SEP Communicate Information** The position graph shown represents an object's motion. Write a sentence that describes that motion. Sketch the velocity as a function of time. Then act out the motion.

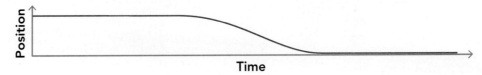

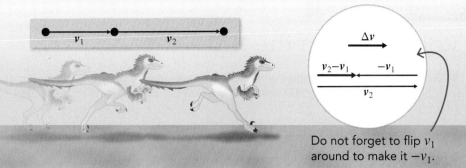

Change in Velocity The head-to-tail method can be used to find Δv, the change in velocity.

Do not forget to flip v_1 around to make it $-v_1$.

Acceleration

Acceleration is a vector that is the time derivative of velocity, and it is measured in m/s². Use the head-to-tail method and the velocity vectors from a dot diagram to determine the direction of the acceleration. **Constant accelerated motion** is motion with a constant acceleration.

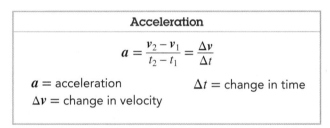

Acceleration
$a = \dfrac{v_2 - v_1}{t_2 - t_1} = \dfrac{\Delta v}{\Delta t}$
a = acceleration $\qquad$ Δt = change in time
Δv = change in velocity

Slope of a Velocity Graph Constant accelerated motion results in a linear graph of velocity vs. time. The slope of the line is the acceleration.

The steeper the slope, the greater the acceleration.

$$\text{Slope} = \frac{\text{Rise}}{\text{Run}} = \frac{\Delta v}{\Delta t}$$

Greater

Lesser

The dot diagrams show the lesser acceleration as a smaller change in velocity for each time interval.

(29) **SEP Develop a Model** The diagram shows a ball rolling at a constant speed along a horizontal track. It comes to a hill and has enough velocity to get over the hill. Sketch a dot diagram and a velocity graph for the ball's motion.

Rolling Down the Hill

As your friend skateboards down a hill, you measure their velocity at 1-second intervals. You record the following data: {(0.00 s, 0.55 m/s), (1.00 s, 1.80 m/s), (2.00 s, 3.05 m/s)}. Determine your friend's acceleration.

1. DRAW A PICTURE Sketch a picture of the situation.

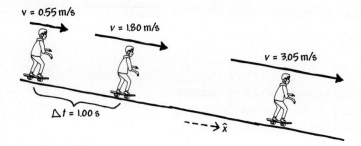

2. DEFINE THE PROBLEM List knowns and unknowns, and assign values to variables.

$t =$ (s)	v (m/s)
0.00	0.55
1.00	1.80
2.00	3.05

$$a = ?$$

3. PLAN AND EXECUTE Use mathematical relationships, the picture, and your definitions to plan and execute a solution.

> Graph the velocity as a function of time, using the provided data.

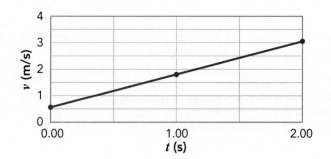

> For motion where the velocity vs. time graph is a line with a constant slope, choose any two points to determine the slope.

$$a = \frac{\text{Rise}}{\text{Run}} = \frac{3.05 \text{ m/s} - 1.80 \text{ m/s}}{2.00 \text{ s} - 1.00 \text{ s}} = 1.25 \text{ m/s}^2$$

4. EVALUATE Reflect on your answer. All of the units are appropriate for the given quantities. The answer is reasonable, because the acceleration is relatively low, which you would expect for a skateboarder.

 GO ONLINE for more **math support**.

 Math Practice Problems

---

30 As your friend skateboards down a hill, you measure their velocity at 1.0-second intervals. You record the following data: {(0.0 s, 0.0 m/s), (1.0 s, 2.3 m/s), (2.0 s, 4.6 m/s)}. Determine your friend's acceleration.

 NEED A HINT? Go online to your **eText Sample Problem** for stepped out support.

31 You stop recording velocity data at $t = 4.0$ *s*, but you notice a short time later that your friend is going a very fast 13.8 m/s. Assuming your friend keeps the same acceleration, how much time has passed since you stopped recording data?

| **Sudden Acceleration** In a car crash, a sudden change in the acceleration can have disastrous effects.

Instantaneous Acceleration

Like instantaneous velocity, **instantaneous acceleration** is the average acceleration over an infinitesimally small time interval. The slope of the tangent line, or the time derivative, at each instant on a velocity vs. time graph is the instantaneous acceleration. The time derivative of the acceleration is called jerk. The time derivative of the jerk is called snap, with the next two time derivatives called crackle and pop, respectively.

| **Acceleration vs. Time** The graph shows acceleration data from a crash test. A large positive jerk becomes a large negative jerk in a very short time. The change can lead to a condition called whiplash.

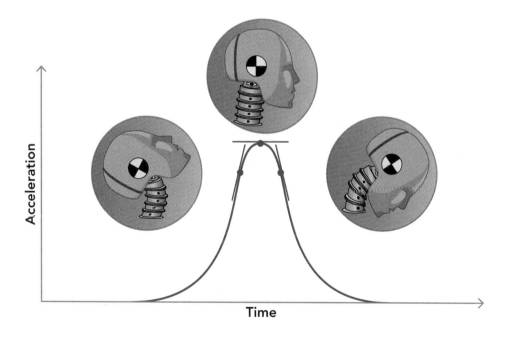

(32) **CCC Patterns** The area under a velocity vs. time graph is the displacement. What do you think the area under an acceleration vs. time graph would represent? What would you suppose about the area under a jerk vs. time graph?

Constant Acceleration

You can construct two equations for constant accelerated motion through analysis of the graph of an object's velocity vs. time. The two equations that describe an object's velocity and displacement are called **equations of motion.**

Velocity Equation As you did with the position graph for uniform motion, you can write an equation for velocity as a function of time for constant accelerated motion.

Equation of Motion (Velocity)
$v = v_i + at$
v = velocity $\quad\quad a$ = acceleration
v_i = initial velocity $\quad\quad t$ = time

Velocity Graph to Velocity Equation The general equation for a line can be used to produce a mathematical expression for the velocity.

For both graphs, the slope is the ratio of the vertical change to the horizontal change. On a velocity graph, slope is acceleration.

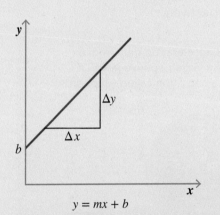

$$y = mx + b$$

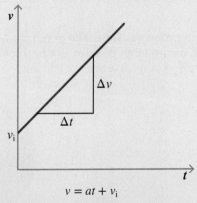

$$v = at + v_i$$

The table shows the correspondence between the variables in the two graphs.

	Horizontal	Vertical	Slope	Intercept
y vs. x	x	y	m	b
v vs. t	t	v	a	v_i

(33) **SEP Develop a Model** An equation describing the velocity of an object is $v = (-2.0 \text{ m/s}^2)t + 2.0 \text{ m/s}$. Sketch the velocity vs. time graph for that motion from 0.0 second to 2.0 seconds.

(34) **CCC Patterns** The equations of motion can only be used when acceleration is treated as constant. For comparison, sketch and label example velocity vs. time graphs for the two cases—constant accelerated motion and accelerated motion that is not constant.

Displacement Equation When you calculate the tangent slope, you are finding the time derivative. When you calculate the area under a curve on a graph, you are finding the **integral.** The resulting integral of the velocity vs. time graph for constant accelerated motion provides an equation for displacement as a function of time.

Equation of Motion (Displacement)
$$\Delta d = v_i t + \frac{1}{2} a t^2$$
Δd = displacement $\qquad t$ = time
v_i = initial velocity $\qquad a$ = acceleration

Velocity Graph to Displacement Equation A velocity vs. time graph for constant accelerated motion is a straight line. The sum of the area of the rectangle and the area of the triangle is the displacement for the time period highlighted.

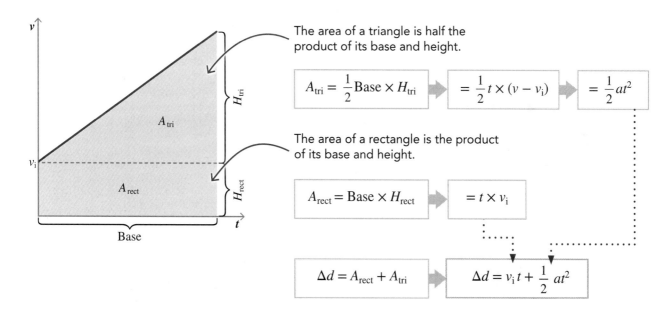

The area of a triangle is half the product of its base and height.

$$A_{tri} = \frac{1}{2} \text{Base} \times H_{tri} \quad\Rightarrow\quad = \frac{1}{2} t \times (v - v_i) \quad\Rightarrow\quad = \frac{1}{2} a t^2$$

The area of a rectangle is the product of its base and height.

$$A_{rect} = \text{Base} \times H_{rect} \quad\Rightarrow\quad = t \times v_i$$

$$\Delta d = A_{rect} + A_{tri} \quad\Rightarrow\quad \Delta d = v_i t + \frac{1}{2} a t^2$$

The two equations of motion (velocity and displacement) describe the motion of any object that has a constant acceleration. Those two equations will also help you to solve problems that involve motion with constant acceleration.

35. **SEP Use Mathematics** Some steps in determining the area of the triangle are missing. Use the velocity equation of motion to show that $v - v_i$ is equal to at. Then, show that the area of the triangle can be written as $\frac{1}{2} a t^2$.

36. **SEP Construct an Explanation** Go online to find a graph for accelerated motion that is not constant. Use the graph to explain why the displacement equation of motion is not appropriate for analyzing accelerated motion that is not constant.

Solving Nonuniform Motion Problems

What methods can you use to **solve problems** that involve nonuniform motion?

Graphical Method For velocity graphs, use the **area under the function to determine the displacement.** Use the **slope of the function to determine the acceleration.**

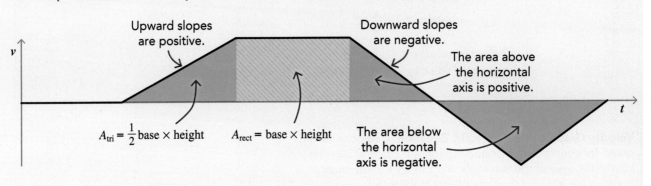

Upward slopes are positive.

Downward slopes are negative.

The area above the horizontal axis is positive.

$A_{tri} = \frac{1}{2}$ base × height

A_{rect} = base × height

The area below the horizontal axis is negative.

Mathematical Method Combine the two equations of motion to mathematically solve **constant acceleration problems.** They come from **graphical analysis of the velocity graph.**

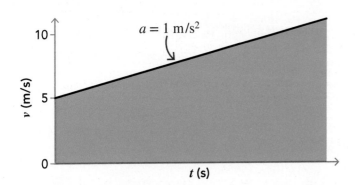

$a = 1\ \text{m/s}^2$

The equations contain five different variables. **If you know three variables, then you can find the others.** Place a check over known values and a question mark over unknown values.

$$\overset{\checkmark}{v} = \overset{\checkmark}{v_i} + \overset{\checkmark ?}{at}$$

$$\overset{?}{\Delta d} = \overset{\checkmark ?}{v_i t} + \frac{1}{2} \overset{\checkmark ?}{at^2}$$

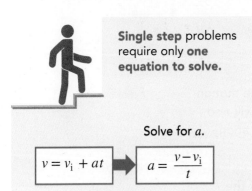

Single step problems require only **one equation** to solve.

Solve for a.

$$v = v_i + at \quad\longrightarrow\quad a = \frac{v - v_i}{t}$$

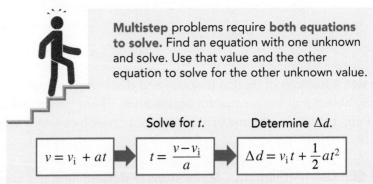

Multistep problems require **both equations to solve.** Find an equation with one unknown and solve. Use that value and the other equation to solve for the other unknown value.

Solve for t.

$$v = v_i + at \quad\longrightarrow\quad t = \frac{v - v_i}{a}$$

Determine Δd.

$$\Delta d = v_i t + \frac{1}{2} at^2$$

37) SEP Obtain and Evaluate Information Often, a third equation of motion is used when solving constant acceleration problems: $v^2 = v_i^2 + 2a\Delta d$. Go online to find how the equation is derived. Does it come directly from analyzing the motion graphs, or is it derived from the other two equations of motion? When would it be useful?

A Scared Bunny

At $t = 0$ s, a bunny is hopping along at 1.0 m/s. It continues at that speed, until at $t = 10$ s, when the bunny begins to slow down with a constant acceleration. It comes to a complete stop at $t = 12$ s. What is the bunny's displacement at $t = 12$ s? What is the bunny's acceleration when slowing down?

1. DRAW A PICTURE Sketch a picture of the situation.

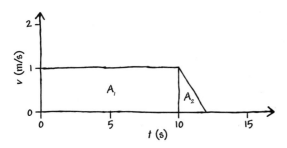

2. DEFINE THE PROBLEM List knowns and unknowns, and assign values to variables.

t (s)	v (m/s)	a (m/s^2)
0	1.0	0
10	1.0	?
12	0.0	?

$$\Delta d(t = 0\ \text{s} \rightarrow 12\ \text{s}) = ?$$

3. PLAN AND EXECUTE Use mathematical relationships, the picture, and your definitions to plan and execute a solution.

Calculate the areas of the rectangle and the triangle.

$$A_1 = (10\ \text{s}) \times (1.0\ \text{m/s}) = 10\ \text{m}$$
$$A_2 = \frac{1}{2}(2\ \text{s}) \times (1.0\ \text{m/s}) = 1\ \text{m}$$

Determine the total area under the function to find the displacement.

$$\Delta d = 10\ \text{m} + 1\ \text{m} = 11\ \text{m}$$

Determine the slope of the line from 10 seconds to 12 seconds to find the acceleration.

$$a = \frac{\text{Rise}}{\text{Run}} = \frac{0.0\ \text{m/s} - 1.0\ \text{m/s}}{12\ \text{s} - 10\ \text{s}} = -0.5\ \text{m/s}^2$$

4. EVALUATE Reflect on your answer.

All of the units are appropriate for the given quantities. The answer provides reasonably small displacement and acceleration.

 GO ONLINE for more **math support**.

▶ **Math Tutorial Video**

🖥 **Math Practice Problems**

---

(38) At $t = 0$ s, a bunny is hopping along at 2.0 m/s. It continues at that speed, until at $t = 20$ s, when the bunny begins to slow down with a constant acceleration. It comes to a complete stop at $t = 25$ s. What is the bunny's displacement at 25 seconds? What is the bunny's acceleration when slowing down?

📖 **NEED A HINT?** Go online to your **eText Sample Problem** for stepped out support.

(39) At $t = 0$ s, a ball is launched straight upward with a velocity of 19.6 m/s. The ball slows with constant acceleration until it stops at $t = 2.00$ s. The ball falls back to the ground with the same acceleration until it hits the ground with velocity −19.6 m/s at $t = 4.00$ s. What is the ball's total displacement after 2.00 s? What is the ball's acceleration during its entire motion?

Hitting the Brakes

You are driving at 14 m/s when you suddenly slam on the brakes to avoid a collision. You come to a complete stop. When you stop, your acceleration is determined by your tires and the road conditions, and it is a constant -8.2 m/s^2. The skid marks you leave behind can be measured to determine your displacement. How long will your skid marks be?

1. DRAW A PICTURE Sketch a picture of the situation.

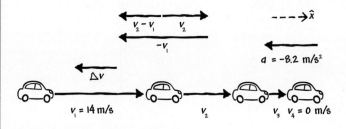

2. DEFINE THE PROBLEM List knowns and unknowns, and assign values to variables.

$v_i = 14$ m/s $\quad\quad t = ?$

$a = -8.2$ m/s^2 $\quad\quad \Delta d = ?$

$v_f = 0$ m/s

3. PLAN AND EXECUTE Use mathematical relationships, the picture, and your definitions to plan and execute a solution.

Determine the time using the velocity equation of motion.

$v = v_i + at \rightarrow t = \dfrac{v - v_i}{a}$

$t = \dfrac{0 - 14 \text{ m/s}}{-8.2 \text{ m/s}^2} = 1.7$ s

Determine the displacement from the displacement equation of motion and the calculated time.

$\Delta d = v_i t + \dfrac{1}{2} at^2$

$\Delta d = (14 \text{ m/s})(1.7 \text{ s}) + \dfrac{1}{2}(-8.2 \text{ m/s}^2)(1.7 \text{ s})^2$

$\Delta d = 12$ m

4. EVALUATE Reflect on your answer.
The units are appropriate for both time and displacement. The answers are reasonable time and displacement values.

 GO ONLINE for more **math support**.

📄 **Math Practice Problems**

---

40 You are driving at 10.0 m/s when you suddenly slam on the brakes to avoid a collision. You come to a complete stop. When you stop, your acceleration is determined by your tires and the road conditions, and it is a constant -4.1 m/s^2. The skid marks you leave behind can be measured to determine your displacement. How long will your skid marks be?

📖 **NEED A HINT?** Go online to your **eText Sample Problem** for stepped out support.

41 To determine a car's maximum acceleration, you start from rest, press down hard on the accelerator pedal, and time how long it takes to get up to 26.8 m/s (about 60 miles per hour). It takes a powerful new electric car only 3.50 s to reach 26.8 m/s. What is the car's acceleration?

Acceleration Due to Gravity

▶ **GO ONLINE** to watch a **video** about objects in free fall.

An object falling without resistance under the influence of Earth's gravity is in **free fall.** A body in free fall experiences a constant acceleration toward the center of Earth, which is known as the **acceleration due to gravity.** That acceleration is represented by the letter g and has a constant magnitude of 9.8 m/s^2 toward the ground. You can rewrite the equations of motion for the specific case of free fall.

> **Equations of Motion (Free Fall)**
>
> $$\Delta y = v_i t + \frac{1}{2} g t^2 \quad \text{and} \quad v = v_i + gt$$
>
> Δy = displacement in the y-direction
> g = acceleration due to gravity

Bouncing When the woman leaves the trampoline, her acceleration is a constant 9.8 m/s^2 in the downward direction. The acceleration slows her down as she goes up, and it increases her speed as she comes back down. Her motion is completely described by position, velocity, and acceleration graphs.

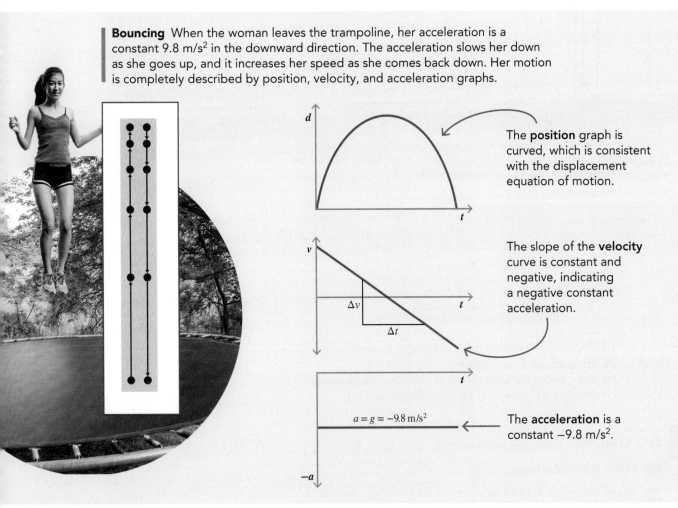

The **position** graph is curved, which is consistent with the displacement equation of motion.

The slope of the **velocity** curve is constant and negative, indicating a negative constant acceleration.

$$a = g = -9.8 \text{ m/s}^2$$

The **acceleration** is a constant -9.8 m/s^2.

42 **SEP Develop a Model** Using the velocity vectors from the dot diagram for a woman jumping on a trampoline, show that the acceleration vector is downward for both her upward and downward motions.

Smashing Watermelons

Your physics teacher takes your class outdoors to a stand of bleachers. You climb to the top and drop a watermelon to the ground below. One of your classmates measures the height from which the watermelon is dropped to be 4.3 m above the ground. How long should it take the watermelon to hit the ground? How fast will it be going just before it lands?

1. DRAW A PICTURE Sketch a picture of the situation.

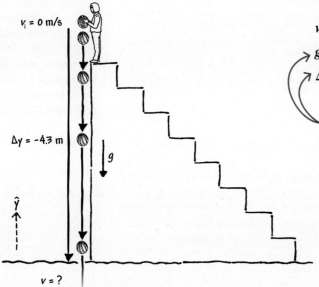

2. DEFINE THE PROBLEM List knowns and unknowns, and assign values to variables.

$$v_i = 0 \text{ m/s} \qquad t = ?$$
$$g = -9.8 \text{ m/s}^2 \qquad v = ?$$
$$\Delta y = -4.3 \text{ m}$$

Note that these two values are negative because they point in the negative y-direction.

3. PLAN AND EXECUTE Use mathematical relationships, the picture, and your definitions to plan and execute a solution.

Determine the time using the displacement equation of motion.

$$\Delta y = v_i t + \frac{1}{2} g t^2 = 0t + \frac{1}{2} g t^2 \rightarrow t = \sqrt{\frac{2\Delta y}{g}}$$

$$t = \sqrt{\frac{2(-4.3 \text{ m})}{-9.8 \text{ m/s}^2}} = 0.94 \text{ s}$$

Determine the final velocity from the velocity equation of motion and the calculated time.

$$v = v_i + gt = 0 \text{ m/s} + (-9.8 \text{ m/s}^2)(0.94 \text{ s})$$

$$v = -9.2 \text{ m/s}$$

4. EVALUATE Reflect on your answer.

The units are appropriate for both time and velocity. The velocity is negative, indicating it is downward, as it should be.

 GO ONLINE for more **math support**.

▶ **Math Tutorial Video**

🖥 **Math Practice Problems**

43 Your physics teacher crumples a piece of paper into a ball and releases it from rest 1.5 m from the ground. How long does the ball take to hit the ground?

📖 **NEED A HINT?** Go online to your **eText Sample Problem** for stepped out support.

44 Your friend throws a rock off of a cliff straight down with an initial speed of 10.0 m/s. Using a stopwatch, you determine it takes the rock 3.2 s to hit the ground below. How high is the cliff?

45 Kangaroos are strong jumpers and can leap over an object 1.8 m high. Calculate a kangaroo's minimum vertical speed when it leaves the ground.

46 A girl tosses up a ball vertically in the air with an initial velocity of 13.1 m/s. How high will the ball rise above its initial height?

47 An astronaut on the moon dropped an object at rest from a height of 3.0 meters. The table shows data from a sensor used to measure position as a function of time. Complete the table by determining the velocity at each time. Determine the acceleration due to gravity on the moon.

Time (s)	Position (m)	Velocity (m/s)
0.0000	0.0000	
0.1000	−0.0081	
0.2000	−0.0326	
0.3000	−0.0733	
0.4000	−0.1304	

48 The graph shows the velocity as a function of time for an object dropped on a planet in the solar system. On which planet was the object dropped?

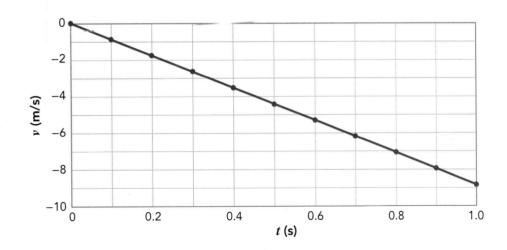

INVESTIGATIVE PHENOMENON

GO ONLINE to revisit your **Investigative Phenomenon modeling activity** with the new information you have learned about Acceleration.

These questions will help you apply what you learned in this experience to the Investigative Phenomenon.

49 **SEP Analyze and Interpret Data** At approximately 7:20 P.M. on December 4, 2013, the sailing stone Eos began to slow down, coming to rest four minutes later. The table shows the GPS velocity data for that time period. Graph the data and determine Eos's average acceleration. Was the acceleration approximately constant?

Time (s)	Velocity (m/s)
0	0.0584
60	0.0481
120	0.0344
180	0.0136
240	0

50 **SEP Develop a Model** Using the graph that you constructed in the previous problem of Eos's velocity vs. time, write two equations, one that approximates the velocity as a function of time and one that approximates the displacement as a function of time. Use your answer to the previous question to determine if you can model the acceleration as a constant.

51 **SEP Use Mathematics** From the graph of velocity vs. time, determine Eos's approximate displacement between times $t = 60$ s and $t = 180$ s.

GO ONLINE for a **quiz** to evaluate what you learned about Acceleration.

Circular and Projectile Motion

 GO ONLINE to do a **hands-on lab** to investigate projectile motion and to do a PhET **simulation** that allows you to explore how different variables affect the motion of a projectile.

Representing Velocity

So far, you have only learned about velocity in one dimension. However, an object's velocity can be defined in more than one dimension and can even change directions with time. Vector representations allow you to explore motion in two or more dimensions.

Like displacement, velocity can be represented mathematically as a set of vector components. The components of velocity represent how fast an object is moving in the directions defined by a coordinate system. As before, x represents horizontal motion, and y represents vertical motion. The Pythagorean theorem is used to determine the magnitude.

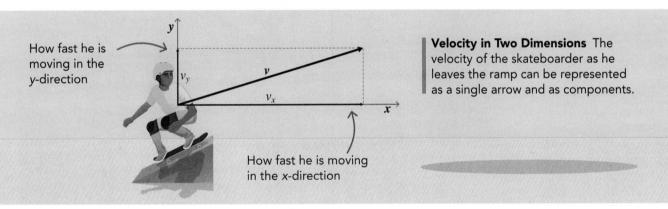

How fast he is moving in the y-direction

Velocity in Two Dimensions The velocity of the skateboarder as he leaves the ramp can be represented as a single arrow and as components.

How fast he is moving in the x-direction

Components A coordinate system is defined with the x-direction parallel to the ground and the y-direction perpendicular to the ground.

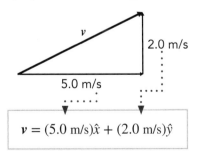

$$v = (5.0 \text{ m/s})\hat{x} + (2.0 \text{ m/s})\hat{y}$$

Magnitude The components make a right triangle with the velocity vector. You use the Pythagorean theorem to determine the magnitude of the velocity from its components.

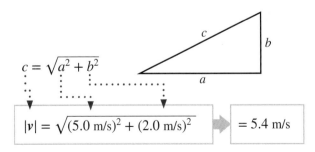

$$c = \sqrt{a^2 + b^2}$$

$$|v| = \sqrt{(5.0 \text{ m/s})^2 + (2.0 \text{ m/s})^2} \quad = 5.4 \text{ m/s}$$

52 **SEP Develop a Model** At a point in time, the velocity of Titan, one of Saturn's moons, is represented as the components $v = (2.7 \text{ km/s})\hat{x} + (5.1 \text{ km/s})\hat{y}$. Sketch a vector representation and determine the magnitude of Titan's velocity.

Adding Velocities in Two Dimensions

As with displacement in two dimensions, the horizontal and vertical components of velocity are independent of each other. The component of velocity in one direction does not affect the component in the other direction. You use that independence to add and subtract velocity vectors analytically.

When adding two velocity vectors, the x-component of one velocity is added to the x-component of the other velocity. The result is the x-component of the resultant vector. You similarly add the y-components to determine the y-component of the resultant vector. Once you have the x- and y-components of the resultant velocity vector, you can use the Pythagorean theorem to determine the magnitude.

River Crossing A person rows a boat across a river with a constant velocity. The river current pushes the boat downstream with a different constant velocity.

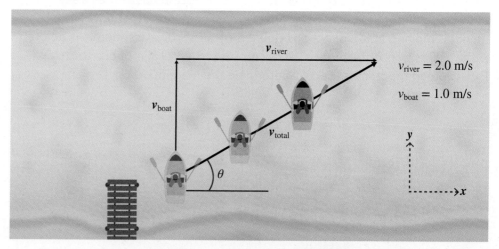

v_{river}

$v_{river} = 2.0$ m/s

$v_{boat} = 1.0$ m/s

v_{boat}

v_{total}

θ

Add the x-components. Add the y-components. The results are the x-component and the y-component of the resultant.

$$v_{boat} = (0.0 \text{ m/s})\hat{x} + (1.0 \text{ m/s})\hat{y}$$

$$v_{river} = (2.0 \text{ m/s})\hat{x} + (0.0 \text{ m/s})\hat{y}$$

$$v_{total} = (0.0 \text{ m/s} + 2.0 \text{ m/s})\hat{x} + (1.0 \text{ m/s} + 0.0 \text{ m/s})\hat{y}$$

The resultant can be written in components or as a magnitude.

$$v_{total} = (2.0 \text{ m/s})\hat{x} + (1.0 \text{ m/s})\hat{y}$$

$$|v_{total}| = \sqrt{(2.0 \text{ m/s})^2 + (1.0 \text{ m/s})^2}$$

$$\approx 2.2 \text{ m/s}$$

(53) **SEP Use Mathematics** Determine the sum of the following two vectors: $v_1 = (3.0 \text{ m/s})\hat{x} + (5.0 \text{ km/s})\hat{y}$ and $v_2 = (1.0 \text{ m/s})\hat{x} + (-2.0 \text{ km/s})\hat{y}$. Write the resultant vector in components, and then determine the magnitude.

The Ant and the Moving Sidewalk

While at an airport, you notice an ant walking across a moving sidewalk perpendicular to the sidewalk's motion. Curious about how fast the ant could be going, you find out that the sidewalks move at a constant velocity of 0.60 m/s. The ant is walking with a velocity of 0.078 m/s. Determine the ant's resultant velocity.

1. DRAW A PICTURE Sketch a picture of the situation.

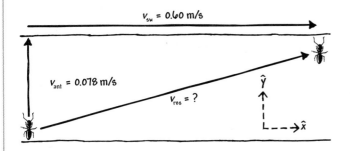

2. DEFINE THE PROBLEM List knowns and unknowns, and assign values to variables.

$$v_{ant} = (0\ \text{m/s})\hat{x} + (0.078\ \text{m/s})\hat{y}$$
$$v_{sw} = (0.60\ \text{m/s})\hat{x} + (0\ \text{m/s})\hat{y}$$
$$v_{res} = ?$$

3. PLAN AND EXECUTE Use mathematical relationships, the picture, and your definitions to plan and execute a solution.

Add the x- and y-components of the ant and sidewalk velocities.	$v_{res} = v_{ant} + v_{sw}$ $v_{res} = (0\ \text{m/s} + 0.60\ \text{m/s})\hat{x} + (0.078\ \text{m/s} + 0\ \text{m/s})\hat{y}$
The sum is the components of the resultant velocity.	$v_{res} = (0.60\ \text{m/s})\hat{x} + (0.078\ \text{m/s})\hat{y}$
Use the Pythagorean theorem to determine the magnitude of the resultant velocity.	$|v_{res}| = \sqrt{(0.60\ \text{m/s})^2 + (0.078\ \text{m/s})^2} = 0.61\ \text{m/s}$

4. EVALUATE Reflect on your answer.
The units are appropriate for velocity. The resultant velocity is larger than both of the components, which is a requirement for the hypotenuse of a right triangle.

 GO ONLINE for more **math support**.

Math Practice Problems

(54) While at an airport, you notice an ant walking across a moving sidewalk perpendicular to the sidewalk's motion. Curious about how fast the ant could be going, you find out that the sidewalks move at a constant velocity of 0.60 m/s. The ant is walking with a velocity of 0.25 m/s. Determine the ant's resultant velocity.

📖 **NEED A HINT?** Go online to your **eText Sample Problem** for stepped out support.

(55) A child walks at 0.9 m/s in the direction opposite the moving sidewalk, which is still moving at 0.6 m/s. What is the child's resultant velocity?

Projectile Motion

 GO ONLINE to watch a **video** about the horizontal and vertical components of projectile motion.

EXPERIENCE IT!

Crumple up two pieces of paper. Standing side-by-side with a friend, have your friend throw one ball horizontally at the same time you drop your ball from the same height. Which ball hits the ground first?

Independent Motions A **projectile** is an object that is moving through the air affected only by gravity. **Projectile motion** is the combination of uniform motion parallel to Earth's surface and free-fall motion, which has a constant acceleration perpendicular to Earth's surface. Common examples of projectile motion include a softball after it has left the hand of the pitcher, a stream of water from a hose, and you as you fly through the air during a long jump.

You analyze two-dimensional projectile motion by separating the motion into two independent one-dimensional motions, one along the horizontal axis and the other along the vertical axis. The horizontal motion is uniform. The vertical motion is free-fall motion with constant acceleration g directed downward.

Motion Diagram in Two Dimensions Once the rock leaves your hand, the only acceleration is the acceleration due to gravity, which is downward. There is no horizontal acceleration.

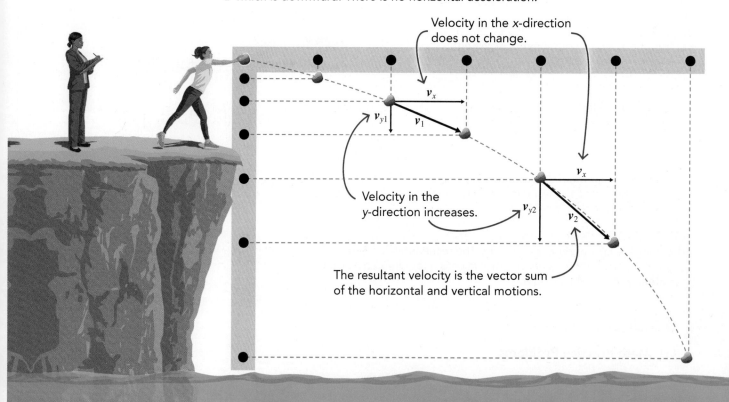

56 **SEP Use Computational Thinking**
The table contains motion data for a football during the kickoff in a professional game. Using a computer spreadsheet program or graph paper, plot the x- and y-positions of the football as functions of time. How are the x- and y-motions different?

Time (s)	x (m)	y (m)
1.0	24.5	19.6
2.0	49.0	29.4
3.0	73.5	29.4
4.0	98.0	19.6

Graphing Projectile Motion The path a projectile takes is called its **trajectory.** A two-dimensional dot diagram that shows the object's total trajectory is called a **trajectory graph.** The graph can be drawn as a line or as a two-dimensional dot diagram. Be careful! Trajectory graphs are often confused with position graphs, since they look very similar for the *y*-directed motion.

A projectile trajectory follows a curved path called a *parabola*. It can be represented mathematically using a second-degree polynomial, called a quadratic function, which has the form $y(x) = ax^2 + bx + c$.

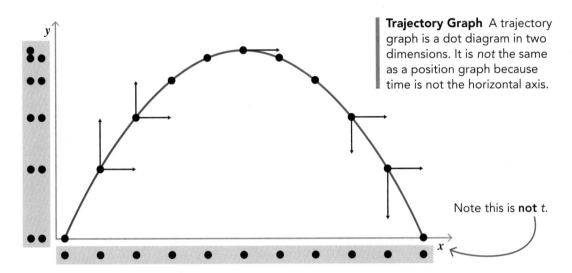

Trajectory Graph A trajectory graph is a dot diagram in two dimensions. It is *not* the same as a position graph because time is not the horizontal axis.

Note this is **not** *t*.

Uniform Motion The horizontal motion is uniform because there is no acceleration.

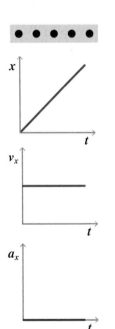

Accelerated Motion Vertical motion has a negative acceleration, *g*. Do not confuse the parabolic graph of *y* versus *t* with the parabolic trajectory graph of *y* versus *x*. Both graphs are parabolic, one in space and one in time.

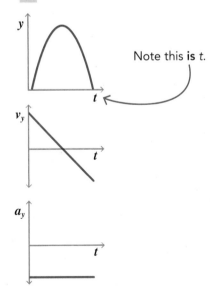

Note this **is** *t*.

51 **SEP Develop and Use a Model** Sketch the position, velocity, and acceleration graphs for the *y*-motion of a projectile, one on top of the other. The time axes should align. Where on all three graphs is the velocity zero? Is the acceleration ever zero?

Modeling Projectile Motion

Equations of Motion in Two Dimensions As you have done in previous experiences, you can construct three equations that describe projectile motion through analysis of graphs of an object's horizontal and vertical velocity vs. time. The equations of motion describe the horizontal and vertical components of an object's velocity and displacement at all times, and they can be used to solve projectile problems.

Horizontal Equation of Motion	Vertical Equations of Motion
$\Delta x = v_x t$	$v_y = v_{iy} + gt$ and $\Delta y = v_{iy}t + \frac{1}{2}gt^2$
Δx = horizontal displacement component v_x = horizontal velocity component	v_y = vertical velocity component v_{iy} = initial vertical velocity component Δy = vertical displacement component

Graphs to Math Equations are constructed from the velocity vs. time graphs for both the horizontal and vertical motions.

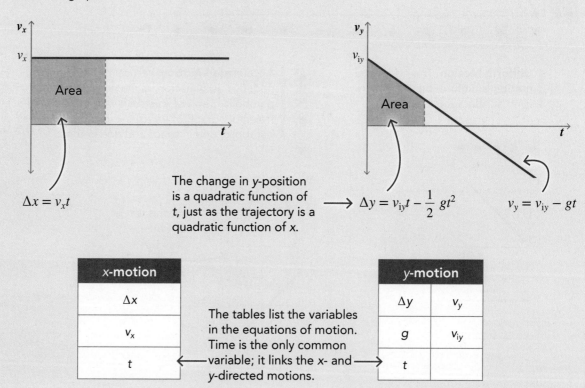

$\Delta x = v_x t$

The change in y-position is a quadratic function of t, just as the trajectory is a quadratic function of x. $\longrightarrow \Delta y = v_{iy}t - \frac{1}{2}gt^2$

$v_y = v_{iy} - gt$

x-motion
Δx
v_x
t

The tables list the variables in the equations of motion. Time is the only common variable; it links the x- and y-directed motions.

y-motion	
Δy	v_y
g	v_{iy}
t	

(58) CCC Patterns Earlier, you investigated the following equation of motion: $v^2 = v_i^2 + 2a\Delta d$. Write equivalent equations for the y-motion and the x-motion of a projectile by using appropriate variable substitutions.

Solving Projectile Motion Problems

How can you **solve projectile motion problems?**

Step 1 Draw a **trajectory graph,** using a useful coordinate system, that describes the problem and **label all the relevant variables.**

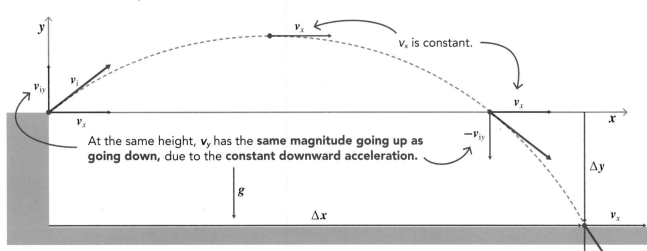

v_x is constant.

At the same height, v_y has the **same magnitude going up as going down,** due to the **constant downward acceleration.**

Step 2 Make a table of the knowns and unknowns for the time of interest. There are six variables in the 2D equations of motion. **You always know the value of g.**

Knowns	Unknowns
Δx	Δy
v_{iy}	t
v_x	v_y

Step 3 Write the 2D equations of motion. Place a check over the knowns and a question mark over the unknowns.

$$\overset{?}{\Delta y} = \overset{\checkmark}{v_{iy}}\overset{?}{t} + \frac{1}{2}\overset{\checkmark}{g}t^2$$

$$\overset{?}{v_y} = \overset{\checkmark}{v_{iy}} + \overset{?}{gt}$$

$$\overset{\checkmark}{\Delta x} = \overset{\checkmark}{v_x}\overset{?}{t}$$

Look for equations with only one unknown value. Solve for the unknown. Then, **use this value to find another unknown value.** Often, you will solve for time and use the value in another equation.

$v_y = 0$ at this point $v_y = 0$ at this point

For objects launched horizontally off a table, $v_{iy} = 0$. Similarly, for an object tossed upward, the **y-velocity at the maximum height is 0,** even if it is not explicitly given.

Hang Time

A professional football punter kicks a football with an initial velocity $v = (12.0 \text{ m/s})\hat{x} + (22.0 \text{ m/s})\hat{y}$. How long the football stays in the air is known as the hang time. Determine the hang time, as well as the horizontal and maximum vertical displacements.

1. DRAW A PICTURE Sketch a picture of the situation.

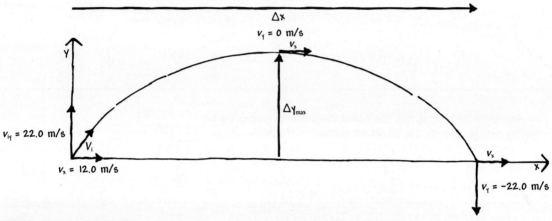

2. DEFINE THE PROBLEM List knowns and unknowns, and assign values to variables.

$v_{iy} = 22.0$ m/s	$t = ?$
$v_y = -22.0$ m/s	$\Delta x = ?$
$g = -9.80$ m/s^2	$\Delta y_{max} = ?$
$v_x = 12.0$ m/s	

3. PLAN AND EXECUTE Use mathematical relationships, the picture, and your definitions to plan and execute a solution.

Determine the time using the vertical velocity equation of motion.

$$v_y = v_{iy} + gt \rightarrow t = \frac{v_y - v_{iy}}{g}$$
$$t = \frac{-22.0 \text{ m/s} - 22.0 \text{ m/s}}{-9.80 \text{ m/s}^2} = 4.49 \text{ s}$$

Determine the horizontal displacement using the horizontal displacement equation of motion.

$$\Delta x = v_x t = (12.0 \text{ m/s})(4.49 \text{ s}) = 53.9 \text{ m}$$

The maximum vertical displacement happens halfway through the motion. Use the vertical displacement equation of motion and half the time.

$$\Delta y_{max} = v_{iy}(t_{\frac{1}{2}})^2 + \frac{1}{2}g(t_{\frac{1}{2}})^2$$
$$\Delta y_{max} = (22.0 \text{ m/s})(2.25 \text{ s}) + \frac{1}{2}(-9.80 \text{ m/s}^2)(2.25 \text{ s})^2$$
$$\Delta y_{max} = 24.7 \text{ m}$$

4. EVALUATE Reflect on your answer.

The units are appropriate for both time and displacement. The actual average hang time for a professional kick is about 4.4 s, so the answer is reasonable.

 GO ONLINE for more **math support**.

▶ **Math Tutorial Video**

🖳 **Math Practice Problems**

(59) A professional football player kicks a football with an initial velocity $v = (6.0\ \text{m/s})\hat{x} + (20.0\ \text{m/s})\hat{y}$. Determine how long the football stays in the air, as well as the horizontal displacement.

📖 **NEED A HINT?** Go online to your **eText Sample Problem** for stepped out support.

(60) A friend kicks a soccer ball into the air with an initial velocity $v = (9.0\ \text{m/s})\hat{x} + (18\ \text{m/s})\hat{y}$. Determine the hang time for the ball and how far away it will land from its initial position.

(61) If the average hang time of a professional football kick is 4.4 s, then determine the average maximum height.

(62) While on a vacation in Kenya, you visit the port city of Mombassa on the Indian Ocean. On the coast is an old Portuguese fort with large stone walls rising vertically from the shore. An inscription on a plaque states that the walls are an impressive 44 m high. You find the fort's cannons mounted so that they fire horizontally out of openings near the top of the walls facing the ocean. Calculate the muzzle velocity necessary to hit a ship 300.0 meters from the base of the fort.

(63) You crumple up two pieces of paper and throw one piece with a horizontal velocity of 2.2 m/s. At the same time, a friend releases the other piece from rest. Both pieces start 1.5 m from the floor. How long does it take each piece of paper to hit the ground?

(64) A professional baseball pitcher throws a baseball horizontally across a field. The graphs show velocity vs. time for the horizontal and vertical motions of the baseball. What were the baseball's total horizontal and vertical displacements during the 0.5-s motion?

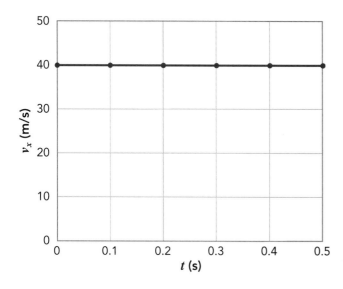

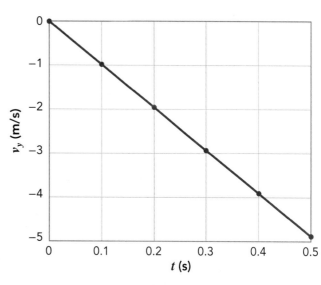

Star Trails Captured using a long exposure time, the photo shows the apparent circular motion of stars due to Earth's rotation.

Circular Motion

VOCABULARY

The word **centripetal** comes from the Latin words *centrus* and *petus*, which mean "center" and "seeking," respectively.

Changing Direction When an object travels in a circular path at a constant speed, the motion is called **uniform circular motion.** Uniform circular motion is a unique type of two-dimensional motion in which the magnitude of the velocity remains constant, but the direction of the velocity continually changes. You can still use the term *uniform* because the change in velocity has a constant magnitude and acts uniformly toward the center of the circular motion. A vector quantity that is always directed toward the center of a circle is called a **centripetal vector.**

You can show that the change in velocity is center-seeking by looking at the velocity at two instants in time during the circular motion. You then use the head-to-tail method to determine the direction of the change in velocity.

Changing Velocity A woman swings a rock in a circle. The overhead view shows that the direction of the velocity changes even though the magnitude stays the same.

The change in velocity is always toward the center of the circle.

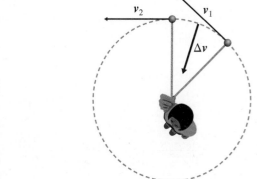

65 **SEP Argue from Evidence** If the woman lets go of the rope, what do you think the motion of the rock will look like? Make a claim and argue from evidence.

Centripetal Acceleration The acceleration of an object in uniform circular motion is called **centripetal acceleration.** The acceleration is in the direction of the change in velocity and is therefore also center-seeking. Like velocity, the acceleration also has a constant magnitude. However, you cannot use the equations of motion for constant accelerated motion, since the direction changes.

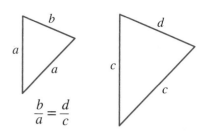

Similar Triangles Triangles are similar if the only difference is in size or orientation. The ratios of the corresponding sides are equal.

$$\frac{b}{a} = \frac{d}{c}$$

Centripetal Acceleration
$$a_c = \frac{v^2}{R}$$

a_c = magnitude of centripetal acceleration
v = magnitude of velocity
R = radius of circle

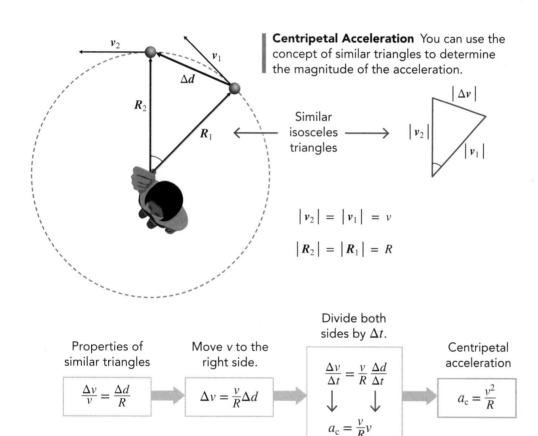

Centripetal Acceleration You can use the concept of similar triangles to determine the magnitude of the acceleration.

Similar isosceles triangles

$$|v_2| = |v_1| = v$$
$$|R_2| = |R_1| = R$$

Properties of similar triangles

$$\frac{\Delta v}{v} = \frac{\Delta d}{R}$$

➡ Move v to the right side.

$$\Delta v = \frac{v}{R}\Delta d$$

➡ Divide both sides by Δt.

$$\frac{\Delta v}{\Delta t} = \frac{v}{R}\frac{\Delta d}{\Delta t}$$

$$\downarrow \qquad \downarrow$$

$$a_c = \frac{v}{R}v$$

➡ Centripetal acceleration

$$a_c = \frac{v^2}{R}$$

66 SEP Design a Solution A rotating space station such as the one in the figure could generate artificial gravity. Design a solution for producing *g* in space.

Artificial Gravity

A large, doughnut-shaped section of a spacecraft is being designed for long-term space flight. The outer wall of the rotating section will become the floor for the astronauts, and the centripetal acceleration produced by the floor will simulate gravity. If this section of the spacecraft has a radius of 200.0 m, what speed will produce an acceleration of 9.81 m/s²?

1. DRAW A PICTURE Sketch a picture of the situation.

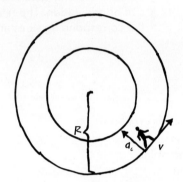

2. DEFINE THE PROBLEM List knowns and unknowns, and assign values to variables.

$R = 200.0$ m $\qquad$ $v = ?$

$a_c = 9.81$ m/s²

3. PLAN AND EXECUTE Use mathematical relationships, the picture, and your definitions to plan and execute a solution.

Write the equation for the centripetal acceleration and solve for v^2.	$a_c = \dfrac{v^2}{R} \rightarrow v^2 = a_c R$
Take the square root of both sides to solve for v.	$v = \sqrt{a_c R}$
Determine the magnitude of the velocity.	$v = \sqrt{(9.81 \text{ m/s}^2)(200.0 \text{ m})} = 44.3$ m/s

4. EVALUATE Reflect on your answer.
The units are appropriate for velocity. The speed of rotation is reasonable, about 160 kilometers per hour.

 GO ONLINE for more **math support**.

    📶 **Math Practice Problems**

---

67 The spacecraft designers have decided that the 200-meter-radius spacecraft only needs to produce an acceleration of 0.5*g*. What speed will produce that acceleration?

    📖 **NEED A HINT?** Go online to your **eText Sample Problem** for stepped out support.

68 A fairground ride spins its occupants inside a large teacup. If the radius of the circular path is 10.0 m and the acceleration is 1.5*g*, what is the speed of the riders?

Graphing Circular Motion

The trajectory graph for uniform circular motion is a circle. However, the graphs of position vs. time for the horizontal and vertical motions appear to oscillate. An **oscillatory motion** is any motion in which an object repeats the same movement over and over. Oscillatory motion can be described mathematically using either a sine wave or a cosine wave, which are trigonometric curves that describe smooth periodic oscillation. When a sine wave is at its maximum, the corresponding cosine wave is at its zero, and vice versa.

Oscillatory Motion
$x = R \cos\left(\frac{v}{R}t\right)$ and $y = R \sin\left(\frac{v}{R}t\right)$

Circular Trajectory Not surprisingly, the trajectory graph for an object moving counterclockwise in a circle is circular. However, the position vs. time graphs are sinusoidal.

The position graph for the vertical motion is a sine wave.

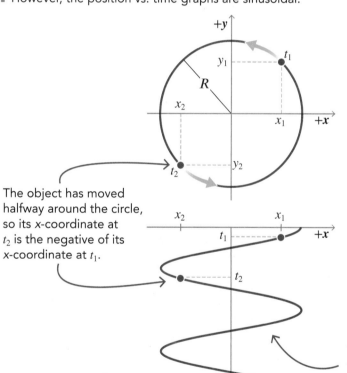

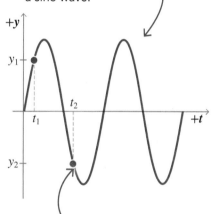

The object has moved halfway around the circle, so its x-coordinate at t_2 is the negative of its x-coordinate at t_1.

As the object moves in a circle, its y-coordinate oscillates between positive and negative values.

The position graph for the horizontal motion is a cosine wave.

69 **SEP Argue from Evidence** A friend looks at the trajectory graph for a person riding a Ferris wheel and says that the velocity of the person in the y-direction is zero at the top and bottom of the circular motion. Construct an argument for that claim using the position graph in the y-direction. Sketch the velocity vectors at the top and bottom.

70 **SEP Develop a Model** Using the position graph in the x-direction, sketch a velocity graph for the person's x-motion. When is the person going the fastest? The slowest?

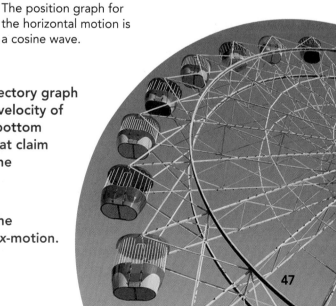

47

INVESTIGATIVE PHENOMENON

GO ONLINE to revisit your **Investigative Phenomenon modeling activity** with the new information you have learned about Circular and Projectile Motion.

These questions will help you apply what you learned in this experience to the Investigative Phenomenon.

71 **SEP Develop a Model** A sailing stone sliding with constant acceleration directed down an incline would have both horizontal and vertical components of motion. Draw a side view of the motion for the situation, labeling the acceleration vector and its components. Sketch graphs of position, velocity, and acceleration vs. time for both the horizontal and vertical motions.

72 **SEP Use Mathematics** Bottomless Pit Canyon in Death Valley National Park is an informal name given to a steep canyon in the Grapevine Mountains. The canyon has a cliff face 116 m high. Assuming the cliff face is exactly vertical, how far from the face would a stone land if it fell from the top of the canyon moving with a horizontal velocity of 0.9 m/s?

73 **CCC Cause and Effect** Think about the motion of a sailing stone. Would you consider its motion a cause or an effect? Does explaining *how* a sailing stone moves help explain *why* it moves? Which of these two questions were you answering during this investigation?

GO ONLINE
for a **quiz** to evaluate what you learned about Circular and Projectile Motion.

These questions will help you apply what you learned in this investigation to the Anchoring Phenomenon.

74) **SEP Define a Problem** Space travel using constant acceleration requires the propulsion system to operate continuously. For the first half of the journey, the spacecraft accelerates toward its destination, and for the second half, it accelerates in the opposite direction. The result is that the spacecraft slows to a stop as it reaches its destination. Such a system has the benefit of generating its own artificial gravity. Sketch a motion diagram for a mission to Mars using constant acceleration. What variables would you need to define in order to further plan the mission?

75) **SEP Design a Solution** Design a mission to Mars that acclimates the astronauts to the acceleration due to gravity on Mars during the trip. Supposing that Mars is approximately 54 million km away, how long would the trip take?

✓ INVESTIGATION ASSESSMENT

 GO ONLINE for activities that will give you an opportunity to **demonstrate what you have learned:**

☑ **Science Performance-Based Assessment** Analyze the motion of an object and graph the relationship between mass and acceleration.

📄 **Engineering Workbench** Design a device to affect motion.

🖥 **Career Connections** Learn about how a mechanical engineer applies knowledge of physics.

☑ **Investigation Test** Take this test to evaluate your understanding of motion.

🖥 **Virtual Lab Performance-Based Assessment** Explain whether a penny dropped from a specified height could break your skin.

INVESTIGATIVE PHENOMENON

GO ONLINE to engage with real-world phenomena by watching a **phenomenon video** and completing a **CER worksheet**.

What caused this rockslide?

Forces

When an object pushes or pulls on another object, it is exerting a force. When you push a door closed, for example, you are exerting a force on the door. When you pull a drawer open, you are exerting a force on the drawer. Often multiple forces act on an object at the same time. The strength and direction of each of these forces can cause an object's motion to change.

Geologists study the forces that change Earth's surface. Some of these changes are difficult to observe because they happen on a very small scale or gradually over long periods of time, such as the movement of Earth's tectonic plates. Other changes are extensive or very sudden, such as the rockslide pictured here.

What causes large masses of rock and debris to quickly move down a steep slope? How do factors such as precipitation, weathering, erosion, and temperature affect rockslides? Answering these questions requires an understanding of the forces acting on Earth's surface.

1. **CCC Cause and Effect** What kinds of forces do you think act on Earth's surface to cause rockslides?

2. **SEP Develop and Use a Model** How do you think geologists use models to study and make predictions about the forces acting on Earth's surface?

3. **SEP Ask Questions** Reread the last paragraph. What are some other questions that geologists might ask to better understand the role that forces acting on Earth's surface play in rockslides?

Force, Mass, and Acceleration

 GO ONLINE to do a **hands-on lab** to investigate the relationships between force, mass, and acceleration.

Changing Motion

An object's motion does not change unless there is some cause. **Newton's first law of motion** states that objects remain at rest or continue with uniform motion in a straight line unless some action causes a change in motion. In the previous investigation, you modeled acceleration, or a change in velocity. In this investigation, you will model the causes of acceleration.

Cause and Effect A soccer goalie changes the ball's motion by striking it with her hands. The ball's acceleration is the effect of the impact.

Cause

v_1

a

v_2

Effect

v_2 Δv $-v_1$

The change in velocity points in the same direction as the acceleration.

(4) **CCC Cause and Effect** Think back to the sailing stones. What do you think causes the change in motion of sailing stones? Is the acceleration of a stone a cause or an effect?

Inertia

Some objects accelerate more easily than others. It is easier to push a lawnmower across the ground than to push a car. The car resists the change in motion more, which means you have to push it harder to achieve the same acceleration. An object's resistance to a change in its motion is called **inertia.**

The **mass** of an object is a measure of its inertia, and the SI unit of mass is the kilogram (kg). The car has more mass; therefore it has more inertia, making it harder to accelerate than the lawnmower. Mass can also be thought of as the amount of "stuff," determined by the number and types of atoms in the object. That amount does not change with location, meaning that the mass of an object is the same on Earth, on the moon, or floating in space.

Mass and Acceleration
The hovercraft's fan produces equal causes in both scenarios. However, the effects on the hovercraft's motion are different because of the different masses.

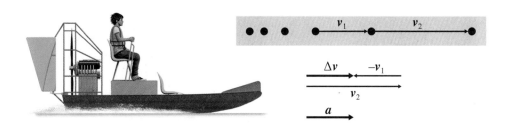

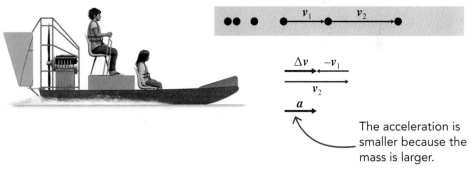

The acceleration is smaller because the mass is larger.

Inversely Proportional
An object's acceleration is inversely proportional to its mass when the cause is the same.

$$a \propto \frac{1}{m}$$

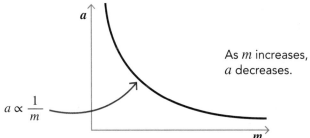

As m increases, a decreases.

(5) **SEP Argue from Evidence** If you kick a large bowling ball on Earth, it will hurt your foot. What will happen if you kick the same bowling ball in space? Make a claim and construct an argument from evidence.

(6) **CCC Patterns** Imagine you put a third person in the hovercraft. Sketch the resulting dot diagram. How does it differ from the two shown?

Force Causes an Acceleration

📄 **GO ONLINE** to do a PhET **simulation** that allows you to explore the relationship between force and acceleration.

A **force** is the cause of a change in motion or change in shape resulting from the unopposed interaction between objects. The interaction between a goalie's hand and a soccer ball results in a force that causes the acceleration of the ball. Force is measured in the SI unit of newtons (N) and is a vector quantity. Multiple forces can act on an object at any time. The vector sum of all of the forces acting on an object is called the **net force.** The mathematical relationship between the net force (cause) and the change in motion (effect) is known as **Newton's second law of motion.**

Newton's Second Law of Motion (Acceleration)
$\Sigma F = ma$
ΣF = net force m = mass a = acceleration

Mass and Force A larger net force (the cause) results in greater acceleration (the effect).

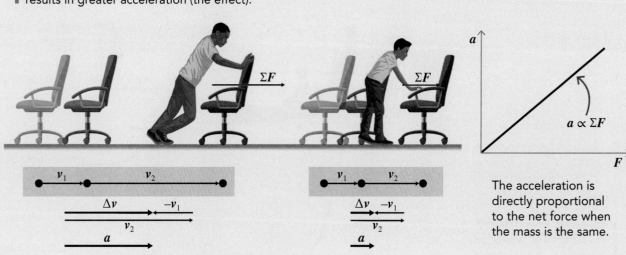

The acceleration is directly proportional to the net force when the mass is the same.

⑦ **SEP Plan an Investigation** You are conducting an experiment to investigate the relationship between force and acceleration. What would the independent and dependent variables be? How are those variables related through cause and effect?

⑧ **CCC Scale, Proportion, and Quantity** Suppose that two spaceships have engines that produce the same constant force. However, one of the spaceships has a much smaller mass. Which spaceship would have the greater acceleration?

Mowing the Lawn

A battery-powered lawn mower has a mass of 52.0 kg. If the net external force on the lawn mower, including both your push and any resistance, is 44.5 N (about 10 pounds), then what will be the magnitude of the mower's acceleration?

1. DRAW A PICTURE Sketch a picture of the situation.

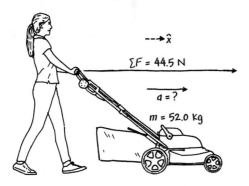

2. DEFINE THE PROBLEM List knowns and unknowns, and assign values to variables.

$m = 52.0$ kg $\quad\Big|\quad a = ?$

$\Sigma F = 44.5$ N $\quad\Big|$

3. PLAN AND EXECUTE Use mathematical relationships, the picture, and your definitions to plan and execute a solution.

Write Newton's second law of motion.	$\Sigma F = ma$
Solve for the acceleration.	$a = \dfrac{\Sigma F}{m} = \dfrac{44.5 \text{ N}}{52.0 \text{ kg}}$
Convert the unit newtons to kilograms, meters, and seconds.	$1 \text{ N} = 1 \text{ kg·m/s}^2$ $44.5 \text{ N} = 44.5 \text{ kg·m/s}^2$
Substitute for newtons and complete the calculation.	$a = \dfrac{44.5 \text{ N}}{52.0 \text{ kg}} = \dfrac{44.5 \text{ kg·m/s}^2}{52.0 \text{ kg}} = 0.856 \text{ m/s}^2$

4. EVALUATE Reflect on your answer.
The units are appropriate for acceleration. The acceleration of a real lawn mower should be relatively small, as determined in this problem.

 GO ONLINE for more **math support**.

Math Practice Problems

9 A battery-powered lawn mower has a mass of 48.0 kg. If the net external force on the lawn mower, including both your push and any resistance, is 40.5 N, then what is the mower's acceleration?

📖 NEED A HINT? Go online to your **eText Sample Problem** for stepped-out support.

10 A soccer ball is kicked with a force of 28 N. If the ball accelerates at 62.2 m/s², then what is its mass?

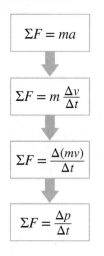

Newton's Second Law
The second law of motion can be written in terms of the acceleration or the momentum.

$$\Sigma F = ma$$

$$\Sigma F = m\frac{\Delta v}{\Delta t}$$

$$\Sigma F = \frac{\Delta(mv)}{\Delta t}$$

$$\Sigma F = \frac{\Delta p}{\Delta t}$$

Momentum

Momentum is the product of the mass and velocity of an object, and it represents an object's total quantity of motion. An object moving quickly is harder to bring to a stop than the same object moving slowly. This is because an object moving quickly has more momentum. Newton's second law of motion can also be expressed in terms of the change in an object's momentum. A force causes a change in motion, where the quantity of motion is defined as the momentum. The momentum form of Newton's second law is useful when you know an object's velocity but not its acceleration, or when you investigate collisions.

Momentum	Newton's Second Law (Momentum)
$p = mv$ p = momentum m = mass v = velocity	$\Sigma F = \frac{\Delta p}{\Delta t}$ ΣF = net force Δp = change in momentum Δt = change in time

Momentum Graphs The slope of a velocity graph gives you the acceleration. Similarly, the slope of a momentum graph gives you the force.

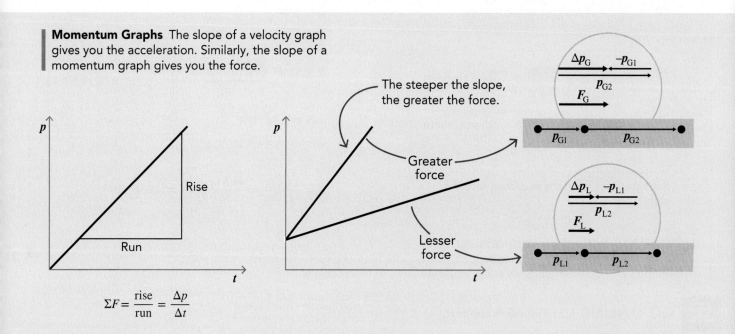

$$\Sigma F = \frac{\text{rise}}{\text{run}} = \frac{\Delta p}{\Delta t}$$

(11) **SEP Use Models** Sketch velocity vs. time graphs for two objects that have the same acceleration. Then, sketch momentum vs. time graphs, assuming the objects have different masses. Use your graphs to show that two objects can have the same acceleration but experience different forces.

(12) **CCC Patterns** The area under an acceleration vs. time graph is the change in velocity. What do you think is represented by the area under a force vs. time graph?

I Push You, and You Push Back

 GO ONLINE to watch a **video** about Newton's third law of motion.

Force results from the interaction between objects, which means that it takes two objects interacting in some way to produce a force. **Newton's third law of motion** states that the interaction between two objects can be represented as two forces having equal magnitudes and opposite directions. If object A exerts a force on object B, then object B exerts an equal and opposite force on object A.

To help make the law clear, you will use a special subscript notation to keep track of objects and their interactions. The force exerted by object A on object B is written as F_{AB}, and the force exerted by object B on object A is written as F_{BA}. The two related action-reaction forces described by Newton's third law are called a **third-law pair.** A third-law pair of forces represents the interaction, whereas each individual force represents how that interaction will affect an individual object.

EXPERIENCE IT!

Have a classmate take your hand and gently pull it. Can you feel the stretch in the muscles in your arm? Can your classmate feel a similar stretch? In which direction do you feel the pull? In which direction does your classmate feel it?

| **Third-Law Pairs** Forces come in pairs because they result from interactions. The forces on the interacting objects are equal and opposite.

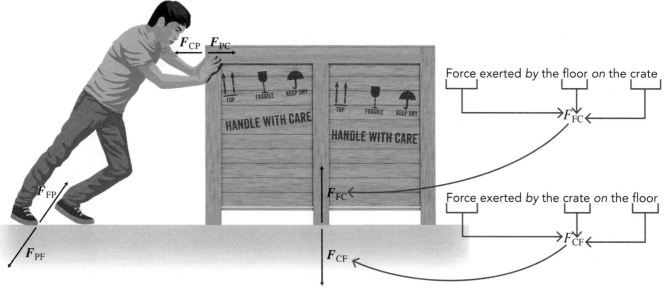

13) **SEP Communicate Information** Two forces are written as follows: F_{HD} and F_{DH}. H symbolizes your hand and D symbolizes a dog. Sketch your hand petting a dog, and represent the two forces on your sketch. How would you describe the two forces in words?

14) **SEP Develop and Use a Model** Sketch a model of the "push" force between the two skaters shown. How do the sizes of the forces experienced by the two skaters compare? What happens if one person pushes harder?

Tug-of-War In which direction will the rope accelerate? Who will win this tug-of-war?

Representing Forces

Force as a Vector When you evaluate how a specific interaction or set of interactions will affect a single object, you model all of the forces acting on that object to determine the net force. For example, to model how the motion of a piece of rope might change when two people pull on it, you only consider the forces the people exert on the rope. The third-law pairs are the forces the rope exerts on the people, which tell you how they move and not how the rope moves; so you leave those out of your model.

Summing Forces Forces are vectors. The net force is the vector sum of all of the forces acting on an object.

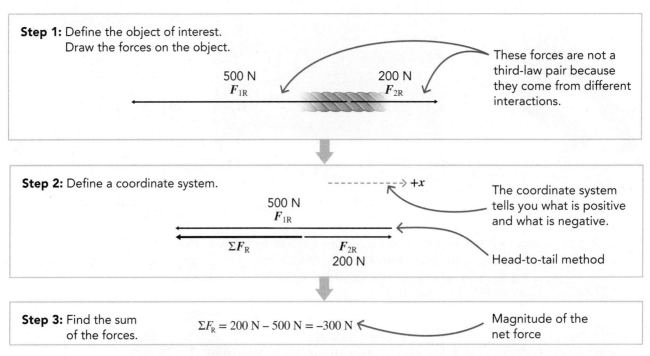

Step 1: Define the object of interest. Draw the forces on the object.

500 N F_{1R} 200 N F_{2R}

These forces are not a third-law pair because they come from different interactions.

Step 2: Define a coordinate system.

500 N F_{1R} $+x$

ΣF_R F_{2R} 200 N

The coordinate system tells you what is positive and what is negative.

Head-to-tail method

Step 3: Find the sum of the forces.

$\Sigma F_R = 200\ N - 500\ N = -300\ N$

Magnitude of the net force

(15) **SEP Use Mathematics** A force of 20 N is applied to an object in the positive x-direction. A force of 12 N is applied to the same object in the negative x-direction. Sketch the two force vectors and determine the magnitude and direction of the resultant vector.

Free-Body Diagrams Sometimes you will be interested in modeling the forces acting on multiple objects arranged in a system. A **system** is whatever pieces of the universe you are interested in studying, and it can be composed of many objects. Typically, you define systems as objects coupled together either mechanically or via some common interaction. A stack of books on a cart is an example of a system.

A **free-body diagram** is a graphical representation of all of the forces and resulting effects on an object or a system. It is composed of a coordinate system and vector diagrams representing all the forces and the acceleration. The coordinate system defines the directions in which the forces are oriented. The way a vector arrow points indicates the direction of a force, and the length of the arrow indicates its relative magnitude. The vector diagram for the rope is an example of a free-body diagram.

Systems and Free-Body Diagrams There are several forces involved in this situation. However, suppose you are only interested in the forces *on* the cart and its contents. Not all forces are shown for simplicity.

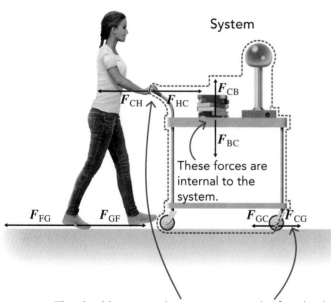

System

F_{CB}

F_{CH} F_{HC}

F_{BC}

These forces are internal to the system.

F_{FG} F_{GF}

F_{GC} F_{CG}

The third-law pairs do not appear in the free-body diagram because they represent forces on other systems, specifically the ground and the hand.

Free-body diagram for system

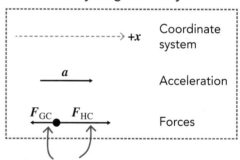

$+x$ — Coordinate system

a — Acceleration

F_{GC} F_{HC} — Forces

The last subscript is the same, indicating forces *on* the cart.

16. **CCC System Models** You look at a classmate's notes and see the following equation: $\Sigma F_A = F_{BA} - F_{CA} + F_{DA}$. Sketch the free-body diagram that the equation might represent.

17. **SEP Develop a Model** Think about a swimmer making a turn by pushing off the wall in a pool. In your notebook, make a sketch of the situation, circle the system of interest, and sketch a free-body diagram for the swimmer. Then, make a sketch for the wall. If you wanted to know about the forces on the swimmer's knee, how would you define the system?

Modeling Force

Statics and Dynamics The study of balanced forces on objects or systems that are at rest is called **statics.** Since the objects or systems do not move, the acceleration and the net force are always zero. **Dynamics** is the study of the forces on objects or systems that are in motion, whether that motion is uniform or nonuniform. Dynamic systems can be moving at a constant velocity or accelerating. For each case, you use Newton's second law to write an equation that represents the system, called a **force-acceleration equation.**

Statics	Dynamics
$\Sigma F = 0$	$\Sigma F = ma$
Acceleration, a, always equals zero.	Acceleration, a, sometimes equals zero.

Statics Static systems are not moving. The acceleration and net force are always zero.

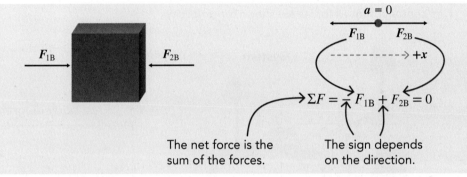

The net force is the sum of the forces.

The sign depends on the direction.

Accelerated

Dynamics Dynamic systems are moving. The net force is equal to the mass times the acceleration. The acceleration is sometimes zero.

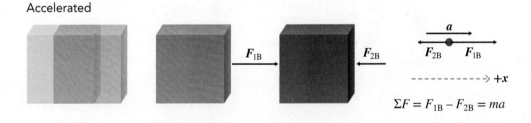

$$\Sigma F = F_{1B} - F_{2B} = ma$$

Constant velocity

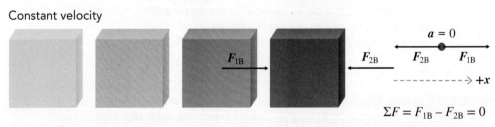

$$\Sigma F = F_{1B} - F_{2B} = 0$$

(18) **SEP Develop and Use a Model** Sketch the momentum graph of an object moving at constant velocity. Use your sketch to make a claim about whether or not a moving object can experience zero net force.

(19) **SEP Construct an Explanation** You notice that a friend of yours is pushing a box across a room at a constant velocity. Your friend exerts a force, and yet the box does not accelerate. Construct an explanation for how that can be.

Solving Force Problems Students often think that solving physics problems involves finding an equation on a list and plugging in numbers. However, different situations require different mathematical models, so you need to write a different force-acceleration equation for each problem you solve. A **general equation** is one that is applicable across a large number of situations but typically requires more analysis. A **specific equation** is one that is applicable to the specific problem that concerns you. Newton's second law is an example of a general equation. You will use it and a free-body diagram to write specific force-acceleration equations for every problem.

Writing Force-Acceleration Equations

How do you **write Newton's second law force-acceleration equations** for specific problems?

Step 1 Determine the system of interest. If you want to know the acceleration or force on a box, then the system is the box. **Consider only the forces acting on the system.**

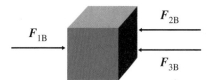

Step 2 Draw the free-body diagram for the system of interest. Include the coordinate system and the acceleration vector. If the acceleration is 0, label it as 0.

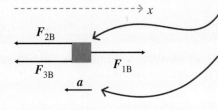

Draw the force vectors starting from the system.

Draw the acceleration vector separately from the system so that you do not confuse it with a force.

Step 3 Use the diagram in Step 2 to **write the specific equation.** Use the coordinate system to determine the sign for each term.

General Equation

Use the free-body diagram to write the left side of the equation.

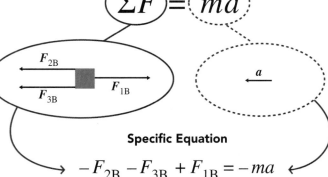

$$\Sigma F = ma$$

Use the acceleration vector to write the right side of the equation.

Specific Equation

$$-F_{2B} - F_{3B} + F_{1B} = -ma$$

The + and − signs indicate the direction because all vectors point along the same axis.

(20) **SEP Argue from Evidence** Write the force-acceleration equation for a coordinate system with positive x defined as to the left. Does a change in coordinate system affect the specific equation? Make a claim and argue from evidence for your claim.

Will the Wire Break?

A designer is trying to determine the type of wire to use for a pendant light that will hang from the ceiling of an elevator. The wire can withstand a force of 66 N before breaking. Therefore, the upward force on the lamp, called tension, cannot exceed 66 N. The lamp also experiences a 52-N gravitational force, called weight, in the downward direction. What is the maximum upward acceleration the elevator can have before the wire breaks? The lamp's mass is 5.3 kg.

1. **DRAW A PICTURE** Sketch a picture of the situation.

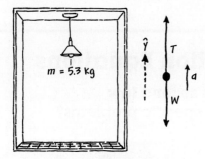

2. **DEFINE THE PROBLEM** List knowns and unknowns, and assign values to variables.

$T = 66$ N	$a = ?$
$W = 52$ N	
$m = 5.3$ kg	

3. **PLAN AND EXECUTE** Use mathematical relationships, the picture, and your definitions to plan and execute a solution.

Write Newton's second law of motion as the general equation.	$\Sigma F = ma$
Write a specific force-acceleration equation for the problem, using the free-body diagram.	$T - W = ma$
Solve for the acceleration.	$a = \dfrac{T - W}{m}$
Complete the calculation.	$a = \dfrac{(66 \ \text{kg·m/s}^2 - 52 \ \text{kg·m/s}^2)}{5.3 \ \text{kg}} = 2.6 \ \text{m/s}^2$

4. **EVALUATE Reflect on your answer.**
   The units are appropriate for acceleration. The acceleration is positive, which is consistent with the free-body diagram. The magnitude of the acceleration is also less than the magnitude of the free-fall acceleration, $-9.8 \ \text{m/s}^2$.

 GO ONLINE for more **math support**.

   ▶ **Math Tutorial Video**

   🖥 **Math Practice Problems**

(21) A designer is trying to determine the type of wire to use for a pendant light that will hang from the ceiling of an elevator. The wire can withstand a force of 82 N before breaking. Therefore, the upward directed force on the lamp, called tension, cannot exceed 82 N. The lamp also experiences a 45-N gravitational force, called weight, in the downward direction. What is the maximum upward acceleration the elevator can have before the wire breaks? The lamp has a mass of 4.6 kg.

📖 **NEED A HINT?** Go online to your **eText Sample Problem** for stepped out support.

(22) A designer is trying to determine the type of wire to use for a pendant light that will hang from the ceiling of an elevator. The wire can withstand a force of 70.0 N before breaking. Therefore, the upward directed force on the lamp, called tension, cannot exceed 70.0 N. The lamp also experiences a 60.0-N gravitational force, called weight, in the downward direction. What is the maximum upward acceleration the elevator can have before the wire breaks? The lamp has a mass of 6.1 kg.

(23) Two friends are pushing an 18-kg crate across the floor. One of them applies a force of 75.0 N to the left, and the crate moves at a constant speed. What force must the other person be applying, and in what direction does the force act?

(24) A trapeze is a short, horizontal bar held up by two vertical ropes on either side. An acrobat with a mass of 60.0 kg provides a 588-N downward force on the bar. Each of the two trapeze ropes provides an upward force of 349 N. What is the upward acceleration of the acrobat?

(25) A horse is dragging a crate behind it. The horse applies a force of 60.0 N to accelerate the crate to the right, and the crate experiences a 10.0-N force in the opposite direction due to a force called friction from the ground. The crate's acceleration is 0.67 m/s^2. Determine the crate's mass.

(26) Marco and his sister are rummaging through a large box of books. Their younger brother also wants to see what's inside the box. Marco pulls the box away from his brother, applying a force of 38 N to the left. His sister helps him by applying an additional force of 36 N to the left. Their brother applies a force of 35 N to pull the box in the opposite direction. The box weighs 22 kg. Determine the acceleration of the box.

(27) Two dogs are pulling on either end of a toy rope. One dog has a mass of 12 kg and pulls to the left with a force of 12 N. The other dog has a mass of 18 kg and pulls to the right with a force of 12 N. Determine the acceleration of the rope.

INVESTIGATIVE PHENOMENON

GO ONLINE to revisit your **Investigative Phenomenon CER** with the new information you have learned about Force, Mass, and Acceleration.

These questions will help you apply what you have learned in this experience to the Investigative Phenomenon.

(28) **SEP Develop and Use a Model** Model a boulder sliding down an icy incline with no friction and constant acceleration. Sketch a free-body diagram, a dot diagram, a distance graph, a velocity graph, and a momentum graph. How does the momentum graph show a constant force down the incline?

(29) **SEP Analyze and Interpret Data** The table shows the velocities of two rocks as they slide down a hill. Their masses are $m_1 = 4.5$ kg and $m_2 = 7$ kg. Sketch velocity and momentum graphs, and determine the force on each rock. How do the forces and accelerations compare?

Time (s)	v_1 (m/s)	v_2 (m/s)
0.50	1.50	2.00
1.00	2.73	3.23
1.50	3.95	4.45
2.00	5.18	5.68

(30) **SEP Use Mathematics** A helicopter is used to rescue a skier trapped by an avalanche on the side of a mountain. A cable attached to the helicopter is lowered and attached to the skier. The downward force on the skier due to gravity is 700 N. If the skier is lifted at a constant velocity, then what is the magnitude of the force exerted by the cable on the skier?

GO ONLINE for a **quiz** to evaluate what you learned about Force, Mass, and Acceleration.

Types of Forces

 GO ONLINE to do a **hands-on lab** to investigate different types of forces.

Contact and Noncontact Forces

There are two fundamental types of interactions between objects that can cause a change in motion: contact forces and noncontact forces. A **contact force** represents the interaction between objects due to direct contact with each other. A **noncontact force** represents the interaction between two objects that are separated by some distance. Noncontact forces are also called field forces because they result from objects exerting influence through the space around themselves.

Contact Forces The surface force between the hand and rope keeps the orangutan attached. The spring forces between the atoms in the rope cause a stretch.

Noncontact Forces Gravitational force tries to pull the orangutan down. The electric force holds the electrons to the nucleus of the atom, and nuclear forces keep the nucleus from flying apart.

(31) **CCC Scale, Proportion, and Quantity** As you move from macroscopic to microscopic scales, the relevance of the different types of forces changes. Make a diagram showing a distance scale that ranges from the size of the solar system to the size of the proton, with a few points in between. Specify on your diagram the range where each force is most relevant.

Weight

The **gravitational force,** or gravity, is the noncontact attractive interaction between two objects having mass. Gravity keeps the moon in orbit around Earth and results in you having weight. **Weight** is the downward force experienced by objects resulting from their gravitational attraction to Earth. You can write weight as the force exerted by Earth on the mass (F_{EM}), or simply as W. You can model weight as a force vector acting at the **center of mass** of the object, defined as a point representing the mean position of an object's matter.

Weight
$$F_{EM} = W = mg$$
W = force exerted by Earth on a mass m = mass $g = -9.8$ m/s^2

Gravitational Force The gravitational force between massive objects such as Earth and the moon is inversely proportional to the distance between them.

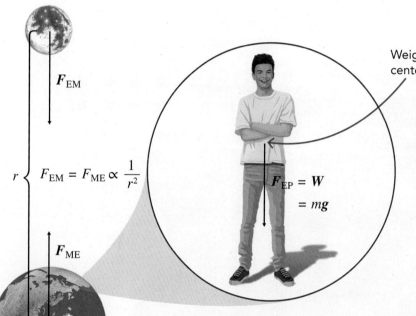

Weight, W, acts at the center of mass.

Weight Objects much less massive than Earth and near the surface experience a constant force proportional to mass because the distance to the center of Earth is approximately constant.

$$F_{EM} = F_{ME} \propto \frac{1}{r^2}$$

$$F_{EP} = W$$
$$= mg$$

(32) **SEP Analyze and Interpret Data** An apple has a mass of 0.10 kg. The velocity as a function of time for an apple falling from a tree is shown in the table. Using the data, plot a momentum graph and determine the force on the apple as it falls. Does the force change, or is it constant? Determine whether the data support Newton's second law of motion.

Time (s)	Velocity (m/s)
0.10	−0.98
0.30	−2.94
0.50	−4.90
0.70	−6.86

(33) **SEP Construct an Explanation** If weight is the force exerted by Earth on a mass, then what would be the Newton's third-law pair and where would it be applied?

Spring Force

GO ONLINE to do a PhET **simulation** that allows you to explore the forces acting on a mass hanging from a spring.

When you bounce a basketball against the floor, the ball's motion changes, but the floor's motion does not seem to change. However, the floor does experience an effect called **deformation,** a change in shape due to the application of a force. A simple example of a deformation resulting from a change in shape is the compression or stretching of a spring. **Hooke's law** states that the size of a spring's deformation is proportional to the applied force; and that when no force acts, the spring returns to its original length. The constant of proportionality is called the **spring constant,** which represents the spring's resistance to deformation.

Hooke's Law
$$F_{SO} = -k\Delta L$$

F_{SO} = force exerted by a spring on an object

k = spring constant
ΔL = change in length

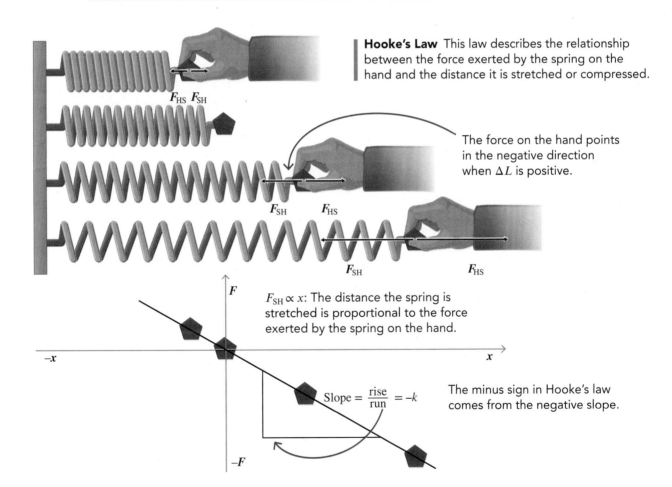

Hooke's Law This law describes the relationship between the force exerted by the spring on the hand and the distance it is stretched or compressed.

F_{HS} F_{SH}

The force on the hand points in the negative direction when ΔL is positive.

F_{SH} F_{HS}

F_{SH} F_{HS}

$F_{SH} \propto x$: The distance the spring is stretched is proportional to the force exerted by the spring on the hand.

$$\text{Slope} = \frac{\text{rise}}{\text{run}} = -k$$

The minus sign in Hooke's law comes from the negative slope.

(34) **SEP Plan an Investigation** Explain how to measure a spring constant using a set of five small masses. What are the independent and dependent variables? How can you determine the spring constant?

Determining Springiness

You are handed a spring that is 0.30 m long. You hang the spring from a hook on the ceiling and then attach a 0.50-kg mass to the other end of the spring. You measure the stretched spring length to be 0.35 m. What is the spring constant?

1. DRAW A PICTURE Sketch a picture of the situation.

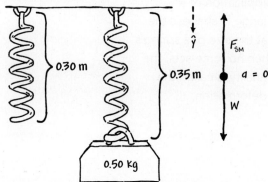

2. DEFINE THE PROBLEM List knowns and unknowns, and assign values to variables.

$L_i = 0.30$ m	$\Delta L = ?$
$L_f = 0.35$ m	$W = ?$
$m = 0.50$ kg	$k = ?$

3. PLAN AND EXECUTE Use mathematical relationships, the picture, and your definitions to plan and execute a solution.

Determine the magnitude of the hanging mass's weight.

$$W = mg = (0.50 \text{ kg})(9.8 \text{ m/s}^2) = 4.9 \text{ N}$$

Determine the change in the spring's length.

$$\Delta L = L_f - L_i = 0.35 \text{ m} - 0.30 \text{ m} = 0.05 \text{ m}$$

Write a force-acceleration equation using the free-body diagram.

$$\Sigma F = ma \rightarrow W - F_{SM} = 0$$
$$W - k\Delta L = 0 \rightarrow k\Delta L = W \rightarrow k = \frac{W}{\Delta L}$$
$$k = \frac{4.9 \text{ N}}{0.05 \text{ m}} = 98 \text{ N/m}$$

4. EVALUATE Reflect on your answer.

The units are appropriate for both weight and spring force. The weight is positive, which agrees with the free-body diagram.

 GO ONLINE for more **math support.**

▶ **Math Tutorial Video**

🖥 **Math Practice Problems**

(35) You are handed a spring that is 0.30 m long. You hang the spring from a hook on the ceiling and attach a 0.50-kg mass to the other end of the spring. The stretched spring length is 0.32 m. What is the spring constant?

📖 **NEED A HINT?** Go online to your **eText Sample Problem** for stepped-out support.

(36) A spring scale is a device that uses a spring with a known spring constant to measure the weight of objects. You have a spring scale with a spring constant of 10.0 N/m. How much will the spring stretch when a 15-N weight is hung from one end?

Tension

A rope is composed of atoms arranged in a uniform manner. The chemical bonds between the atoms behave somewhat like a spring. Therefore, you can model a rope as atoms connected to their neighbors by springs. When you pull on a piece of rope, the rope deforms in order to produce the equal and opposite third-law force on you called tension. **Tension** is the pulling force a rope, cable, or chain exerts along its length. The cause of the spring-like nature of the chemical bonds is a combination of attractive electric forces and a repulsive quantum effect. The **electric force** is a noncontact interaction between two objects having electric charge.

Understanding Tension The force along the length of the rope is tension. Microscopically, tension is the result of spring-like forces on atoms due to chemical bonds.

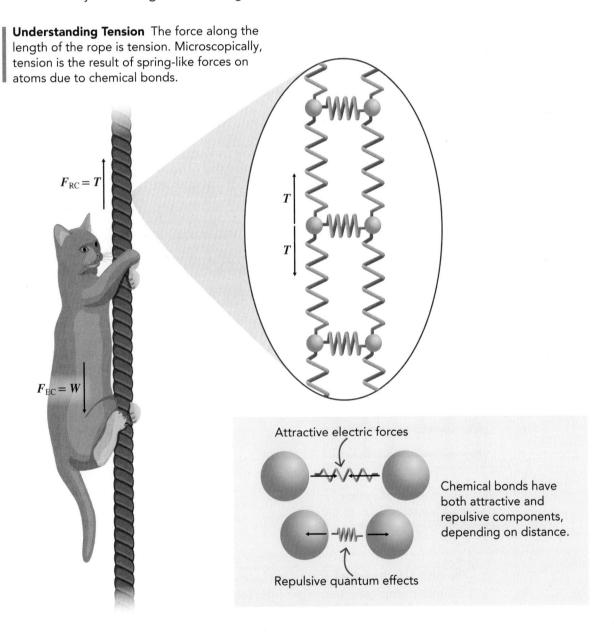

Attractive electric forces

Chemical bonds have both attractive and repulsive components, depending on distance.

Repulsive quantum effects

$F_{RC} = T$

$F_{EC} = W$

T

T

(37) **SEP Interpret Data** Copper is significantly easier to stretch than steel. What does that suggest about the strength of the electric forces (the metallic bond strength) between atoms in the two materials?

Surface Forces

A Box on a Table A model of a solid that has atoms connected to their neighbors by springs is called an **Einstein solid.** As with tension in a rope, this model describes the interaction between objects touching each other. The spring-like interaction between two surfaces in contact with each other results in **surface forces.** The atoms at the surface of the box interact with the atoms at the surface of the table, microscopically compressing each other in opposite directions. When the surfaces do not move relative to each other, the surface forces are perpendicular to the interface. When the surfaces move past each other, the forces have both a perpendicular and a parallel component, dependent on the roughness of the two surfaces.

Surface Force Touching objects experience a perpendicular surface force. The force is caused by spring-like interactions among surface atoms.

Relative Motion When the surfaces move relative to each other, the surface force has both a parallel and a perpendicular component.

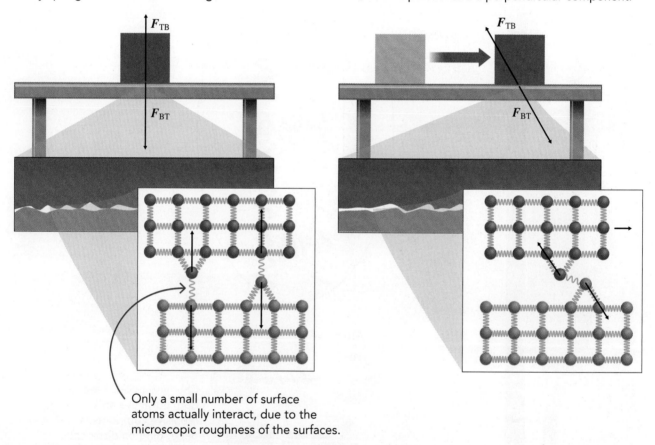

Only a small number of surface atoms actually interact, due to the microscopic roughness of the surfaces.

(38) **SEP Use a Model** If two surfaces are polished to produce a microscopically smoother interface, then would the result be an increase, a decrease, or no change to the parallel component of the surface force?

(39) **CCC Cause and Effect** What causes a rock on the side of a hill to remain in place? During a heavy rainstorm, rainwater can get underneath the rock. What might be the effect, and why might this occur?

GO ONLINE to watch a **video** about static and kinetic friction.

Friction The perpendicular component of the surface force is called the **normal.** The parallel component of the surface force is called **friction.** Friction is partially caused by attractive electric forces between the surface atoms of the two objects. Once the surfaces start to move relative to each other, there are fewer points of contact and so less friction. Therefore, the magnitude of the friction depends on whether or not the surfaces are moving. **Static friction** describes the parallel response to attempted motion between two surfaces. **Kinetic friction** describes the friction for surfaces moving relative to each other. The **coefficient of friction** describes the amount of resistance and depends on the properties of the two materials and whether or not they are moving.

Static Friction	Kinetic Friction
$f \leq \mu_s N$	$f = \mu_k N$
f = friction component of the surface force μ_s = coefficient of static friction N = normal component of the surface force	f = friction component of the surface force μ_k = coefficient of kinetic friction N = normal component of the surface force

Surface Force Components Surface forces have a perpendicular component called the normal and a parallel component called friction.

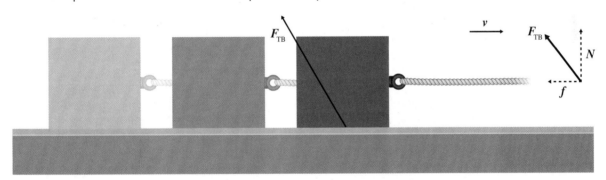

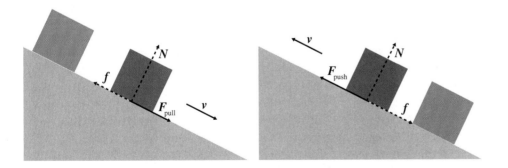

Friction and Normal The normal component always acts perpendicular to the surface. Friction always acts parallel and in the direction opposite the direction of motion—or, for bodies at rest, opposite the direction of any force.

(40) SEP Argue from Evidence A classmate finds the static friction between two objects to be 40 N by multiplying the normal and the coefficient of static friction. You claim that the actual static friction depends on what it is responding to. Argue your claim with evidence by describing two situations in which the static friction would be less than 40 N.

Modeling Force in Two Dimensions

Independent Directions As you have discovered about surface forces, forces that are applied in more than one direction are represented mathematically as a set of vector components. The components of force represent how much of the force is being applied in the directions defined by the coordinate system. As with motion vectors such as velocity and acceleration, x represents the horizontal direction and y represents vertical direction. The Pythagorean theorem is used to determine the magnitude of the force.

Just as for projectile problems, you analyze two-dimensional force problems by separating all of the forces into two independent one-dimensional components along the vertical and horizontal axes. You then use Newton's second law and a free-body diagram to write a force-acceleration equation for each direction.

Modeling Leash Force
The tension force exerted by the leash on the dog can be modeled using components or magnitude. To solve two-dimensional force problems, you need to write the force in its components.

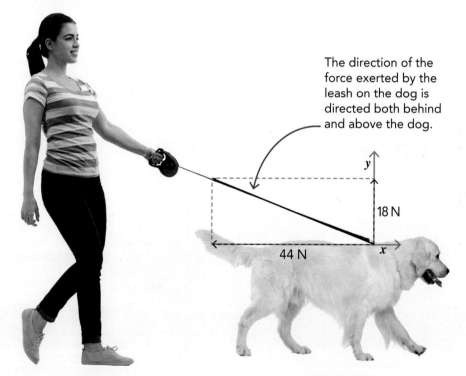

The direction of the force exerted by the leash on the dog is directed both behind and above the dog.

18 N

44 N

Components

$$F_{LD} = (-44 \text{ N})\hat{x} + (18 \text{ N})\hat{y}$$

Force in the   Force in the
x-direction   y-direction

Magnitude

$$c = \sqrt{a^2 + b^2}$$

$$F_{LD} = \sqrt{(-44 \text{ N})^2 + (18 \text{ N})^2} = 47.5 \text{ N}$$

41 **SEP Use Mathematics** Suppose the surface force exerted by the ground on the dog's paw is broken into its components. Write F_{GP} in the component representation.

42 **SEP Develop a Model** Surface forces can be drawn as having a perpendicular component called the normal and a parallel component called friction. Sketch a model for a book sliding across a table showing the surface force and its components. Write a mathematical expression for the surface force in component form.

Solving Two-Dimensional Force Problems

How do you write **Newton's second law force-acceleration equations in two dimensions** and solve problems?

Problem A box with mass m is **pulled across a floor at a constant velocity** with a force T. Determine μ_k.

Constant velocity

T

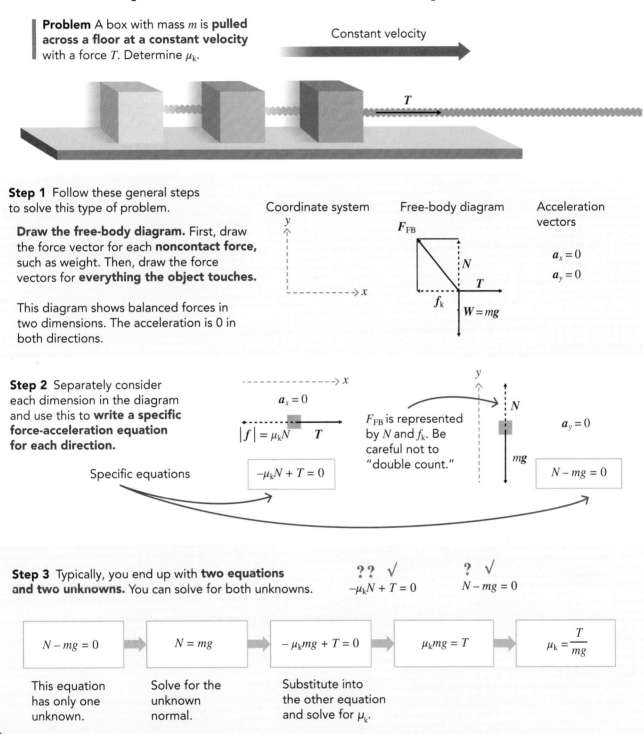

Step 1 Follow these general steps to solve this type of problem.

Draw the free-body diagram. First, draw the force vector for each **noncontact force,** such as weight. Then, draw the force vectors for **everything the object touches.**

This diagram shows balanced forces in two dimensions. The acceleration is 0 in both directions.

Coordinate system

Free-body diagram

F_{FB}

N

T

f_k

$W = mg$

Acceleration vectors

$a_x = 0$

$a_y = 0$

Step 2 Separately consider each dimension in the diagram and use this to **write a specific force-acceleration equation for each direction.**

$a_x = 0$

$|f| = \mu_k N \quad T$

F_{FB} is represented by N and f_k. Be careful not to "double count."

N

mg

$a_y = 0$

Specific equations

$-\mu_k N + T = 0$

$N - mg = 0$

Step 3 Typically, you end up with **two equations and two unknowns.** You can solve for both unknowns.

$?? \checkmark$
$-\mu_k N + T = 0$

$? \checkmark$
$N - mg = 0$

$N - mg = 0$	$N = mg$	$-\mu_k mg + T = 0$	$\mu_k mg = T$	$\mu_k = \dfrac{T}{mg}$

This equation has only one unknown.

Solve for the unknown normal.

Substitute into the other equation and solve for μ_k.

43 **SEP Use Mathematics** Rewrite the force-acceleration equations for the box accelerating in the positive *x*-direction. Does the *y*-direction force-acceleration equation change? Explain.

Pulling a Sled

You are pulling a sled with a constant velocity using a rope held horizontally in the snow. Using a spring scale attached to the rope, you measure the tension to be 8.8 N. The sled's mass is 4.50 kg. Write the surface force the ground exerts on the sled in component form, and determine its magnitude.

1. DRAW A PICTURE Sketch a picture of the situation.

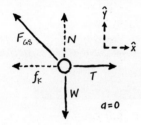

2. DEFINE THE PROBLEM List knowns and unknowns, and assign values to variables.

$m = 4.50$ kg	$N = ?$	$F_{GS} = ?$
$T = 8.8$ N	$f_k = ?$	
$a = 0$ m/s^2	$W = ?$	

3. PLAN AND EXECUTE Use mathematical relationships, the picture, and your definitions to plan and execute a solution.

Determine the sled's weight.	$W = mg = (4.50$ kg$)(9.8$ m/s$^2) = 44.1$ N
Write a force-acceleration equation for the x-direction.	$\Sigma F_x = -f_k + T = 0$ $f_k = T = 8.8$ N
Write a force-acceleration equation for the y-direction.	$\Sigma F_y = N - W = 0$ $N = W = 44.1$ N
Write the surface force in component form. Remember that the friction component points in the negative x-direction.	$F_{GS} = (-8.8$ N$)\hat{x} + (44.1$ N$)\hat{y}$
Determine the magnitude using the Pythagorean theorem.	$\|F_{GS}\| = \sqrt{(8.8 \text{ N})^2 + (44.1 \text{ N})^2} = 45.0$ N

4. EVALUATE Reflect on your answer.

The units are appropriate for the forces involved. The component form has directions consistent with the free-body diagram.

GO ONLINE for more **math support**.

▶ **Math Tutorial Video**

🔊 **Math Practice Problems**

(44) You are pulling a sled with a constant velocity using a rope held horizontally in the snow. Using a spring scale attached to the rope, you measure the tension to be 0.96 N. The sled's mass is 0.58 kg. Write the surface force the ground exerts on the sled in component form, and determine its magnitude.

📖 **NEED A HINT?** Go online to your **eText Sample Problem** for stepped out support.

(45) You are pulling a friend on a sled with a constant velocity using a rope held horizontally in the snow. Using a spring scale attached to the rope, you measure the tension to be 112 N. The combined mass of the sled and your friend is 57.4 kg. Write the surface force the ground exerts on the sled in component form, and determine its magnitude.

(46) A dog is pulling an empty sled attached by a harness that is parallel to the ground in the snow. The sled is moving with constant velocity. The mass of the sled is 1.2 kg, and the coefficient of static friction is 0.20. Determine the harness tension.

(47) A team of dogs is pulling a person in a sled in the snow. The dogs are attached by a harness that is parallel to the ground. The combined mass of the person and the sled is 62.5 kg. The coefficient of kinetic friction is 0.190, and the harness tension is 180.0 N. Determine the sled's acceleration.

(48) During an experiment in physics class, a student places a large block on a plank. The student raises one end of the plank to form an incline until just before the block starts to slide down. The block experiences a force of 26 N parallel to the incline and 42 N perpendicular to the incline. What is the coefficient of static friction such that the block stays at rest?

(49) During another experiment, a student places the same large block on a plank. The student raises one end of the plank until the block starts to slide down. Another classmate explains that the block begins to slide because the parallel component of the surface force exerted on the block by the plank increases as the plank is lifted higher. Use mathematical reasoning to explain why the classmate is incorrect.

(50) A large painting hangs motionless from two wires attached to the same point at the top of the frame. The wires are attached to equidistant points on the wall above the painting. Each wire has a tension force of 108 N in the y-direction and 80.0 N in the x-direction. Determine the mass of the painting.

(51) A child is pulling an empty cart attached by a rope that is parallel to the ground. The cart is moving with constant velocity, and its mass is 1.5 kg. Suppose a mass of 7.5 kg is added to the sled, and its velocity stays the same. By what factor does the tension in the rope change?

Centripetal Force

Try to roll a ball on the floor in a circular path. In which direction do you have to keep hitting it for it to follow a circular path?

You have investigated linear accelerations as the effects of forces. However, forces can also cause centripetal accelerations. A **centripetal force** is any force that causes an object to move in a circular path. Many types of forces can cause a circular motion, such as tension in a rope attached to a ball, gravity exerted by Earth on the moon, or friction on a car's tires as it travels around a circular track. Like centripetal acceleration, the centripetal force is directed toward the center of the circular path and has a magnitude equal to the product of the mass and the centripetal acceleration.

Centripetal Force
$$F_C = ma_c = m\frac{v^2}{R}$$
F_C = centripetal force m = mass
v = speed R = radius

Racetrack The figure shows top and side views of a car driving at a constant speed around a circular racetrack. Static friction is the centripetal force. How can you find the minimum coefficient of friction needed?

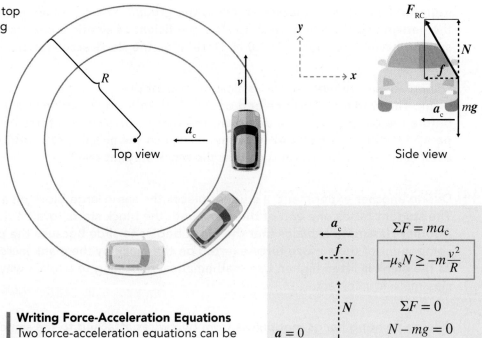

Top view

Side view

Writing Force-Acceleration Equations
Two force-acceleration equations can be written, with one for each dimension in the free-body diagram.

$$\Sigma F = ma_c$$
$$-\mu_s N \geq -m\frac{v^2}{R}$$

$$\Sigma F = 0$$
$$N - mg = 0$$
$$N = mg$$

Static friction is used because the tires are not moving in the direction of the force.

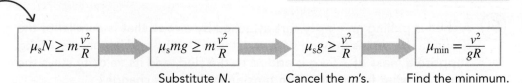

$\mu_s N \geq m\frac{v^2}{R}$ → $\mu_s mg \geq m\frac{v^2}{R}$ → $\mu_s g \geq \frac{v^2}{R}$ → $\mu_{min} = \frac{v^2}{gR}$

Substitute N.   Cancel the m's.   Find the minimum.

52 CCC Cause and Effect Any force can cause a centripetal acceleration and corresponding circular motion. Give an example that has not already been mentioned of a gravitational force and a tension force causing a centripetal acceleration.

Sticking to the Wall

In an amusement park ride called "The Rotor," riders stick to the wall of a spinning cylinder with a radius of 2.5 m. During the ride, the floor drops from beneath the riders, but they do not fall. The average coefficient of static friction between the rider and the wall is 0.70. At what minimum speed must the cylinder spin so that the riders do not slip down when the floor drops away?

1. DRAW A PICTURE Sketch a picture of the situation.

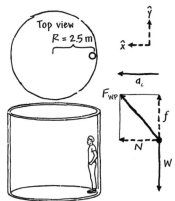

2. DEFINE THE PROBLEM List knowns and unknowns, and assign values to variables.

$R = 2.5$ m	$N = ?$
$\mu_s = 0.70$	$v = ?$

3. PLAN AND EXECUTE Use mathematical relationships, the picture, and your definitions to plan and execute a solution.

Write a force-acceleration equation for the x-direction. The normal component of the surface force is the centripetal force.	$\Sigma F_x = ma_c$ $N = m\dfrac{v^2}{R}$
Write a force-acceleration equation for the y-direction.	$\Sigma F_y = 0 \rightarrow f - W = 0 \rightarrow \mu_s N - mg = 0$ $\mu_s N \geq mg$
Substitute the first force-acceleration equation into the second equation. The mass can be divided out on both sides.	$\mu_s \left(\dfrac{mv^2}{R}\right) > mg \rightarrow \mu_s \left(\dfrac{v^2}{R}\right) > g$
Set the equation to the minimum value for speed and solve.	$v = \sqrt{\dfrac{gR}{\mu_s}} = \sqrt{\dfrac{(9.8\ \text{m/s}^2)(2.5\ \text{m})}{0.70}} = 5.9$ m/s

4. EVALUATE Reflect on your answer.
The units for speed are correct, and the size of the speed is reasonable. The speed did not depend on the mass of the rider, which is important for a ride that has riders with varying masses.

 GO ONLINE for more **math support.**

Math Practice Problems

(53) Riders stick to the wall of a spinning cylinder with a radius of 3.0 m. The average coefficient of static friction between the rider and the wall is 0.50. At what minimum speed must the cylinder spin so that the riders do not slip down when the floor drops away?

📖 **NEED A HINT?** Go online to your **eText Sample Problem** for stepped out support.

Revisit

INVESTIGATIVE PHENOMENON

GO ONLINE to revisit your **Investigative Phenomenon CER** with the new information you have learned about Types of Forces.

These questions will help you apply what you have learned in this experience to the Investigative Phenomenon.

(54) **SEP Develop a Model** Sketch a free-body diagram for a stationary boulder on a hill. Define your coordinate system so that the positive *x*-direction is down the incline and the positive *y*-direction is perpendicular to the incline. How might rotating the coordinate system in this way help you simplify writing force-acceleration equations involving the surface force?

(55) **SEP Use Mathematics** In the tilted coordinate system, the weight of the boulder can be written as $W = (40 \text{ N})\hat{x} - (30 \text{ N})\hat{y}$. Determine the coefficient of static friction necessary to keep the boulder from sliding down the side of the hill.

(56) **SEP Construct an Explanation** Rainwater and the removal of vegetation by fire or drought are two major causes of rockslides. Construct an explanation for how those two causes could result in a previously stationary rock beginning to slide.

(57) **SEP Develop and Use a Model** In a previous investigation, you modeled the motion of a sailing stone accelerating across the flat desert. The changing motion of the stones was an effect. However, you now know that forces are required to cause the change in motion. Construct a model for an accelerating sailing stone by drawing a free-body diagram. Include all of the contact and noncontact forces. Use your model to describe what you think causes their motion. What could provide the push? How might friction be reduced? Using information from online sources, learn more about the cause of a sailing stone's motion to improve your model.

GO ONLINE

for a **quiz** to evaluate what you learned about Types of Forces.

Forces on Systems

 GO ONLINE to do a **hands-on lab** to investigate coefficients of friction and to watch a **video** about free-body diagrams.

Systems with Multiple Objects

So far, you have modeled forces on individual objects or simple systems of directly interacting objects. However, real systems often have multiple interactions that happen among a large number of objects. When you push an elevator button, you start a process that involves a motor generating tension in a cable that passes over a pulley and pulls up on the elevator. The floor of the elevator then pushes up on you. All of the objects experience gravitational forces exerted by Earth. How might you model systems with multiple objects?

Going Up! A system of motors, counterweights, cables, and pulleys moves an elevator quickly up or down dozens of stories.

(58) **CCC System Models** Based on how you have modeled systems with single objects, how do you think you might be able to model systems with multiple objects?

Forces in Systems

Delivering Packages You can investigate the forces acting on the entire grouping of packages or just one package.

 GO ONLINE to do a PhET **simulation** that allows you to see how forces affect the motion of an object and a system of objects.

Defining a System When you push a cart full of boxes, you only interact directly with the cart itself. However, the cart interacts with the boxes and the boxes interact with each other. How does the cart move? How do the boxes move? Do the boxes undergo significant deformations if you push the cart too hard? Answering such questions requires a systems approach to forces.

Newton's second law can be applied to individual objects, entire systems of objects that are connected in some way, or even subsystems of a system. You can write a separate and independent force-acceleration equation for each object in the system, as well as an equation for the system as a whole. You have a powerful tool for modeling how forces will affect the motion and deformations of multiple objects at one time.

Systems There are a few options for defining a system of two blocks on a frictionless surface. A free-body diagram can be drawn for each option. Ignore the weight of the blocks and the upward force exerted by the ground.

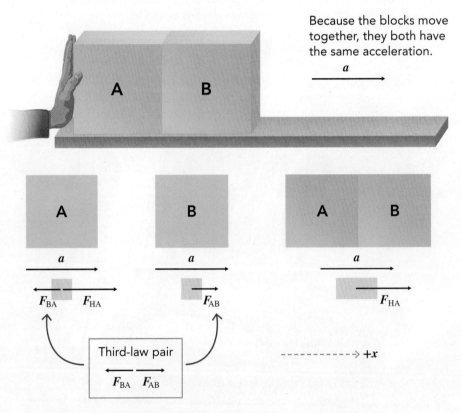

Because the blocks move together, they both have the same acceleration.

59) **CCC Systems and System Models** Imagine a third block C is placed to the right of block B. Can you easily draw a free-body diagram for a system that includes blocks A and C and not block B? Explain.

60) **CCC Cause and Effect** What type of force is F_{AB}? What effect might a large magnitude of F_{AB} have if the two boxes are made of thin cardboard?

Internal vs. External Forces If you define your system as the entire cart of boxes, then the force your hand exerts on the cart is a force that is external to the system. An **external force** is any force exerted by an object outside the system acting on the system. The cart pushes on the boxes and the boxes push on each other. Those forces are called internal forces. An **internal force** is any force exerted by an object in the system on another object within the system.

Only external forces affect the motion of a system. Due to Newton's third law of motion, the internal forces cancel each other out. However, internal forces are important, since large ones could cause deformations that crush the boxes!

External and Internal Forces A hand pushes three 10-kg blocks with an acceleration of 1.0 m/s². The push is external. The forces between the blocks are internal.

External force on the system

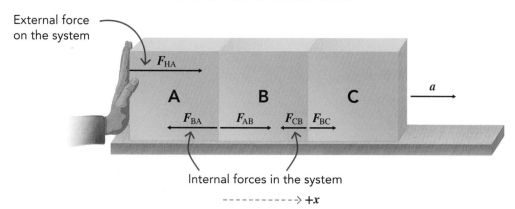

Internal forces in the system

$------\rightarrow +x$

Net force on the system

a

F_{HA}

$$F_{HA} = (m_A + m_g + m_c)a$$
$$= (30 \text{ kg}) (1.0 \text{ m/s}^2) = 30 \text{ N}$$

Internal force on block A

a

$F_{BA} \qquad F_{HA}$

$$F_{HA} - F_{BA} = m_A a$$
$$F_{BA} = 30 \text{ N} - (10 \text{ kg}) (1.0 \text{ m/s}^2)$$
$$= 20 \text{ N}$$

61. **SEP Use Mathematics** Using the figure of the three blocks, determine the internal force block C exerts on block B.

62. **SEP Argue from Evidence** A force is applied on a system consisting of a flatbed truck and car, causing an acceleration. One of your classmates makes the claim that the larger flatbed truck experiences a larger net force than the smaller car on the truck. Use evidence to argue for or against that claim.

Determining Internal Forces

Two blocks, each with a mass of 10.0 kg, are placed on a frictionless horizontal surface and are connected by a massless spring with a spring constant of $k = 250$ N/m. If you apply a horizontal force of 15 N to one of the blocks, then how much will the spring compress as the boxes accelerate?

1. DRAW A PICTURE Sketch a picture of the situation.

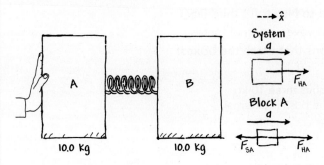

2. DEFINE THE PROBLEM List knowns and unknowns, and assign values to variables.

$m_A = m_B = 10.0$ kg	$\Delta L = ?$
$k = 250$ N/m	$a = ?$
$F_{HA} = 15$ N	

3. PLAN AND EXECUTE Use mathematical relationships, the picture, and your definitions to plan and execute a solution.

Write a force-acceleration equation for the system and calculate the acceleration.

$$\Sigma F_S = (m_A + m_B)a \rightarrow F_{HA} = (m_A + m_B)a$$
$$a = \frac{F_{HA}}{m_A + m_B} = \frac{15 \text{ kg·m/s}^2}{10.0 \text{ kg} + 10.0 \text{ kg}} = 0.75 \text{ m/s}^2$$

Write a force-acceleration equation for block A. The force by the spring on block A can be described by Hooke's law.

$$\Sigma F_A = m_A a \rightarrow F_{HA} - F_{SA} = m_A a \rightarrow F_{HA} - k\Delta L = m_A a$$
$$k\Delta L = F_{HA} - m_A a \rightarrow \Delta L = \frac{F_{HA} - m_A a}{k}$$

Solve for ΔL.

$$\Delta L = \frac{(15 \text{ kg·m/s}^2) - (10 \text{ kg})(0.75 \text{ m/s}^2)}{250 \text{ N/m}} = 0.030 \text{ m}$$

4. EVALUATE Reflect on your answer.
The units are correct for a change in length. The compression is reasonable for a small force.

 GO ONLINE for more **math support**.

Math Practice Problems

63 Two blocks, each with a mass of 12 kg, are placed on a frictionless horizontal surface and are connected by a massless spring with a spring constant of $k = 220$ N/m. If you apply a horizontal force of 18 N to one of the blocks, then how much will the spring compress as the boxes accelerate?

📖 **NEED A HINT?** Go online to your **eText Sample Problem** for stepped out support.

64 A 10.0-kg block is pulled behind a 12-kg block on a frictionless horizontal surface using a massless inelastic rope. The acceleration of both blocks is 1.25 m/s². What is the tension in the rope?

Why Do You Move When You Walk?

Internal forces in a system cancel out due to Newton's third law, and only external forces affect the motion of a system. If that is the case, then why do you move when you walk? To understand why you move, imagine walking in a small rowboat. You apply a surface force with a friction component on the boat, and the boat applies an equal and opposite force on you. As a result, you should accelerate forward, and the boat should accelerate backward. That is exactly what happens!

However, there is no net external force on the system composed of you and the boat because the surface force is an internal force. The system as a whole does not accelerate. The acceleration of a system is defined by the acceleration of the system's center of mass. As you accelerate forward, the boat accelerates backward in such a way that the center of mass of the entire system does not accelerate at all.

Forces in Systems A 70-kg person walks forward in a 35-kg rowboat. The person moves forward and the boat moves backward due to internal friction between them.

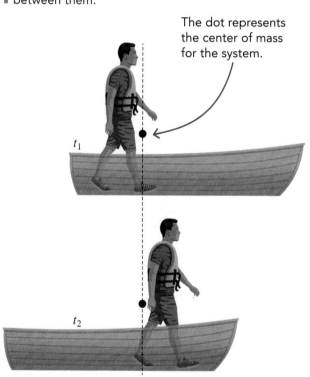

The dot represents the center of mass for the system.

t_1

t_2

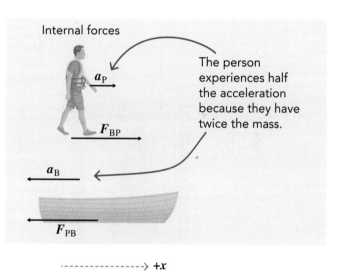

Internal forces

a_P

F_{BP}

a_B

F_{PB}

The person experiences half the acceleration because they have twice the mass.

$\dashrightarrow +x$

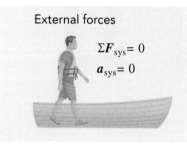

External forces

$\Sigma F_{sys} = 0$

$a_{sys} = 0$

There are no net external forces on the person and boat system. The system's center of mass does not accelerate.

65 **SEP Develop a Model** Develop a model for you and Earth as you walk forward. Does your model suggest that Earth should accelerate backward? If so, then why do you not notice that acceleration?

66 **SEP Construct an Explanation** Seismic noise is the persistent vibration of the ground, a significant part of it due to human activity. The COVID-19 pandemic in 2020 resulted in millions of people staying indoors. Construct an explanation for why scientists recorded less seismic noise during that time.

Modeling Systems

Systems in One Dimension When you travel in an elevator from a high floor to a lower floor, you feel heavier as the elevator comes to a stop. The **apparent weight** of an object is the upward force that opposes gravity. In the elevator, that upward force is the normal component of the surface force by the elevator floor on your feet. If you stand on a scale in the elevator, then the apparent weight it measures changes as you accelerate. You can model the situation using the systems approach discussed.

For systems with forces acting in one dimension, you write a force-acceleration equation for each object in the system. When objects are connected, they experience the same acceleration. That acceleration is what links the independent force-acceleration equations and allows you to solve more complex force problems.

Elevator Model An elevator slows down as it goes from a top floor to the ground floor. If you know the masses and the acceleration, then you can determine the cable tension and the apparent weight.

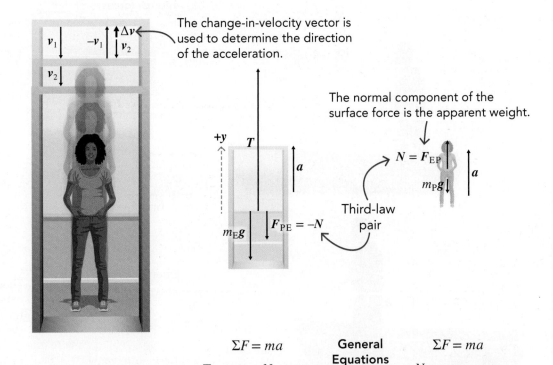

The change-in-velocity vector is used to determine the direction of the acceleration.

The normal component of the surface force is the apparent weight.

$N = F_{EP}$

$m_P g$

Third-law pair

$F_{PE} = -N$

$$\Sigma F = ma$$

$$T - m_E g - N = m_E a$$

General Equations

$$\Sigma F = ma$$

$$N - m_P g = m_P a$$

$$T = N + m_E g + m_E a$$

Specific Equations

$$N = m_P g + m_P a$$

67 **SEP Construct an Explanation** Construct an explanation for why you feel lighter just before an elevator stops going upward.

68 **SEP Design a Solution** If the tension in an elevator cable becomes too great, then the cable can break. What variables can you control in an elevator design to ensure the cable does not break?

Systems in Two Dimensions Most objects experience forces in more than one dimension. In a simple pulley system, the vertically directed weight of an object such as a sandbag can be used to pull another object horizontally via the tension in a rope or cable. As with systems in one dimension, you model a two-dimensional system by drawing a free-body diagram for each object in the system. For each free-body diagram, you can write a force-acceleration equation for each direction.

Objects in systems are typically coupled together in some way, such as via direct contact, a rope, or a spring. The connection typically causes the magnitudes of the objects' accelerations to be the same. The forces resulting from the coupling interactions can also be used to link the independent force-acceleration equations.

Pulley System Model A sandbag is used to pull a dolly. Because the dolly and bag are connected, they have the same magnitude of acceleration. If you know the masses, then you can find the acceleration. Ignore friction for now.

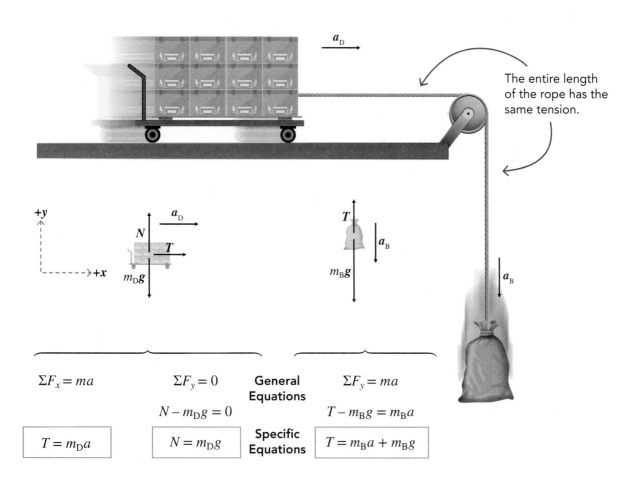

The entire length of the rope has the same tension.

$\Sigma F_x = ma$	$\Sigma F_y = 0$	**General Equations**	$\Sigma F_y = ma$
	$N - m_D g = 0$		$T - m_B g = m_B a$
$\boxed{T = m_D a}$	$\boxed{N = m_D g}$	**Specific Equations**	$\boxed{T = m_B a + m_B g}$

69 **SEP Develop a Model** Draw the free-body diagram and write the force-acceleration equations without ignoring the friction between the dolly and the ground.

70 **SEP Construct an Explanation** A classmate suggests that you could reduce the tension in the rope by removing mass from the dolly. Is your classmate correct? Explain.

Solving System Problems

How do you use Newton's laws to **solve problems involving systems?**

| **Problem** What is the **minimum coefficient of friction** if **block A does not move?**

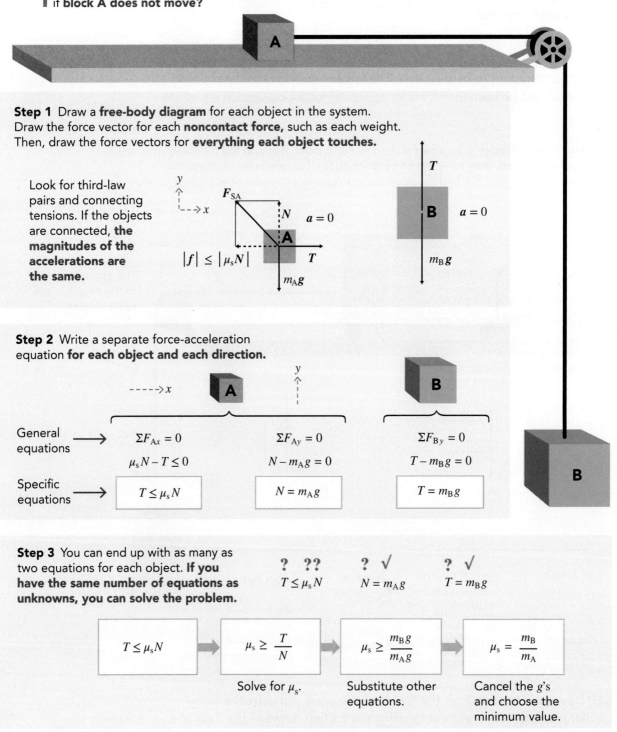

Step 1 Draw a **free-body diagram** for each object in the system. Draw the force vector for each **noncontact force,** such as each weight. Then, draw the force vectors for **everything each object touches.**

Look for third-law pairs and connecting tensions. If the objects are connected, **the magnitudes of the accelerations are the same.**

$|f| \leq |\mu_s N|$

F_{SA} N $a = 0$

A T

$m_A g$

T

B $a = 0$

$m_B g$

Step 2 Write a separate force-acceleration equation **for each object and each direction.**

General equations

$\Sigma F_{Ax} = 0$ $\Sigma F_{Ay} = 0$ $\Sigma F_{By} = 0$

$\mu_s N - T \leq 0$ $N - m_A g = 0$ $T - m_B g = 0$

Specific equations

$T \leq \mu_s N$ $N = m_A g$ $T = m_B g$

Step 3 You can end up with as many as two equations for each object. **If you have the same number of equations as unknowns, you can solve the problem.**

? ??   ? √   ? √
$T \leq \mu_s N$ $N = m_A g$ $T = m_B g$

$T \leq \mu_s N$ → $\mu_s \geq \dfrac{T}{N}$ → $\mu_s \geq \dfrac{m_B g}{m_A g}$ → $\mu_s = \dfrac{m_B}{m_A}$

Solve for μ_s.   Substitute other equations.   Cancel the g's and choose the minimum value.

(71) **CCC Patterns** You have solved force problems involving one object and systems with multiple objects. In your own words, explain this process.

Atwood Machine

An Atwood machine is a mechanical system consisting of two objects connected via a rope over a pulley. Suppose object A has a mass of 15 kg, and object B has a mass of 12 kg. Suppose object A is released from rest. Determine the magnitude of the acceleration for both objects. Assume the rope and pulley are massless.

1. DRAW A PICTURE Sketch a picture of the situation.

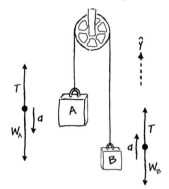

2. DEFINE THE PROBLEM List knowns and unknowns, and assign values to variables.

$$m_A = 15 \text{ kg} \qquad T = ?$$
$$m_B = 12 \text{ kg} \qquad a = ?$$

3. PLAN AND EXECUTE Use mathematical relationships, the picture, and your definitions to plan and execute a solution.

Write a force-acceleration equation for object A. Solve for T.	$\Sigma F = ma \rightarrow T - W_A = -m_A a \rightarrow T = W_A - m_A a$ $T = m_A g - m_A a$
Write a force-acceleration equation for object B. Solve for T.	$\Sigma F = ma \rightarrow T - W_B = m_B a \rightarrow T = W_B + m_B a$ $T = m_B g + m_B a$
Set the two force-acceleration expressions equal to each other. Collect terms with a on one side of the equation.	$m_A g - m_A a = m_B g + m_B a$ $m_A g - m_B g = m_A a + m_B a$
Solve for a.	$a = g \dfrac{m_A - m_B}{m_A + m_B} = (9.8 \text{ m/s}^2) \left(\dfrac{15 \text{ kg} - 12 \text{ kg}}{15 \text{ kg} + 12 \text{ kg}} \right)$ $= 1.1 \text{ m/s}^2$

4. EVALUATE Reflect on your answer.
The units are correct for acceleration. The acceleration is smaller than g.

 GO ONLINE for more **math support**.

Math Practice Problems

---

72 An Atwood machine consists of 40-kg object A and 43-kg object B. Suppose object A is released from rest. Determine the magnitude of the acceleration for both objects. Assume the rope and pulley are massless.

📖 **NEED A HINT?** Go online to your **eText Sample Problem** for stepped out support.

73 An elevator accelerates as it begins to move downward. Suppose the elevator car has a mass of 1100 kg, and the passengers have a mass of 250 kg. Given that the elevator accelerates at 0.49 m/s², what is the tension in the cable?

Disappearing Actor

You are designing a system for your school's theater that will pull a dolly holding an actor off the stage. You have decided to use a rope, a pulley, and a sandbag dropped from the side of the stage out of view of the audience. However, you are concerned that the acceleration will be too great. The mass of the dolly and actor combined is 82 kg, and the mass of the sandbag is 23 kg. The coefficient of kinetic friction between the dolly and the stage floor is 0.20. What is the acceleration?

1. DRAW A PICTURE Sketch a picture of the situation.

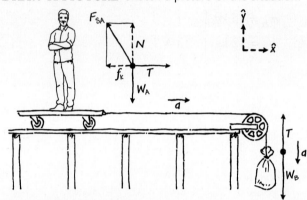

2. DEFINE THE PROBLEM List knowns and unknowns, and assign values to variables.

$$m_A = 82 \text{ kg} \qquad T = ?$$
$$m_B = 23 \text{ kg} \qquad a = ?$$
$$\mu_k = 0.20$$

3. PLAN AND EXECUTE Use mathematical relationships, the picture, and your definitions to plan and execute a solution.

Write a force-acceleration equation for the dolly-and-actor system in the x-direction.	$T - \mu_k N = m_A a \rightarrow T = \mu_k N + m_A a$
Write a force-acceleration equation for the dolly-and-actor system in the y-direction.	$N - m_A g = 0 \rightarrow N = m_A g$
Write a force-acceleration equation for the sandbag.	$T - m_B g = -m_B a \rightarrow T = m_B g - m_B a$
Combine the first two force-acceleration equations.	$T = \mu_k (m_A g) + m_A a$
Set the two expressions for T equal to each other. Collect terms with a on one side of the equation.	$\mu_k m_A g + m_A a = m_B g - m_B a$ $m_A a + m_B a = m_B g - \mu_k m_A g$
Solve for a.	$a = g \left(\dfrac{m_B - \mu_k m_A}{m_A + m_B} \right)$ $= (9.8 \text{ m/s}^2) \left(\dfrac{(23 \text{ kg}) - 0.20(82 \text{ kg})}{(82 \text{ kg}) + (23 \text{ kg})} \right)$ $= 0.62 \text{ m/s}^2$

4. EVALUATE Reflect on your answer.
The units are correct for acceleration. The acceleration is smaller than g.

 GO ONLINE for more **math support**.

▶ **Math Tutorial Video**

🖥 **Math Practice Problems**

74. You are designing another dolly-sandbag system for a different actor in the performance. The mass of the dolly and actor combined is 76 kg, and the mass of the sandbag is 18 kg. The coefficient of kinetic friction between the dolly and the stage floor is 0.20. What is the acceleration?

   📖 **NEED A HINT?** Go online to your **eText Sample Problem** for stepped out support.

75. You are designing one last sandbag-dolly system for the performance. This time, two actors will be on the dolly. The mass of the dolly and actors combined is 94 kg, and the mass of the sandbag is 35 kg. The coefficient of kinetic friction between the dolly and the stage floor is 0.20. What is the acceleration?

76. You decide to change the mass of the sandbag for the two actors to reduce the acceleration. The mass of the dolly and actors combined is still 94 kg, and the coefficient of kinetic friction between the dolly and the stage floor is 0.20. If you want the dolly to accelerate at 1.9 m/s^2, what should the mass of the sandbag be?

77. A truck is pulling an 85-kg rock attached by a rope. The coefficient of friction between the rock and the ground is 0.32. The truck applies 295 N of force to the rock. Determine the net force and the acceleration.

78. For a physics experiment, you stand on a scale in an elevator. You observe that the scale only registers 88 percent of your actual weight as the elevator begins to descend to a lower floor. Based on the data, determine the acceleration of the elevator.

79. An Atwood machine is used in a stage production to make an actress appear to fly up and out of view of the audience. The system consists of a 52-kg actress and a 58-kg sandbag connected via a rope over a pulley. The sandbag is released from rest. Determine the magnitude of the acceleration for both the actress and sandbag. Assume the rope and pulley are massless.

80. You are pulling on a rope to move two boxes, box 1 and box 2, that are connected by a spring. The rope is connected to box 1, which is moving on rollers; so you can ignore friction. The spring connects it to box 2, which is on a surface with a coefficient of friction μ. If the boxes move with a constant velocity, how much does the spring stretch?

81. You are pulling on a rope to move two boxes, box 1 and box 2, that are connected by a spring. The rope is connected to box 1, which is on a surface with a coefficient of friction μ. The spring connects it to box 2, which is moving on rollers, so you can ignore friction. If the boxes move with a constant velocity, how much does the spring stretch?

Static Equilibrium Rock balancing is an art form that requires problem solving and patience.

Forces on Extended Systems

EXPERIENCE IT!

Place a pencil on a table. Have a friend push one end while you push the other end in the opposite direction. How does the pencil move?

A system is in **static equilibrium** if all of the forces on the system add up in such a way that the object does not move. A surface force counteracting the weight of a book on a table is an example of a system in static equilibrium because the forces acting on the book sum to zero. However, forces summing to zero is not a sufficient condition for achieving static equilibrium. Forces applied at different locations on an extended system can cause a type of motion called rotation. The center of mass of the object might not accelerate ($a = 0$), but there is still motion.

Rotation Forces can be balanced; but if their points of application are separated, they can cause a rotation.

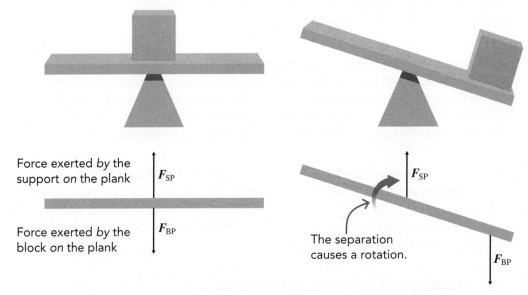

Force exerted *by the* support *on the plank* F_{SP}

Force exerted *by the* block *on the plank* F_{BP}

F_{SP}

The separation causes a rotation.

F_{BP}

(82) **SEP Construct an Explanation**
Construct an explanation for why one of the blocks shown topples over but the other block does not. Develop a basic rule for determining whether an object will topple over.

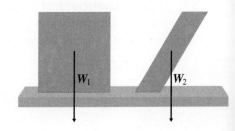

W_1 W_2

Torque

Whether an extended system rotates or not depends on how the forces acting on it are applied. The **line of action** for a force is a line through the point of application of the force in the direction of the force vector. **Torque** is the measure of how effective a force is at producing a rotation, and it is the product of the magnitude of the force and the lever arm. A **lever arm** is the perpendicular distance from the point of rotation to the line of action.

VOCABULARY

Torque comes from the Latin word *torquere*, which means "to twist." Torque is sometimes referred to as "twisting force," though it is not technically a force.

Torque
$\tau = r_{\text{perp}}F$
τ = torque $\qquad r_{\text{perp}}$ = lever arm
F = force

Torque Causes Rotation The magnitude of a torque is determined by the size of the force and the distance from the point of rotation to the line of action.

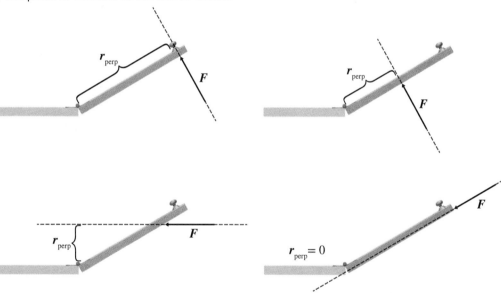

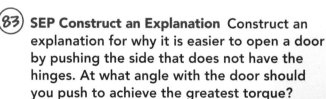

(83) **SEP Construct an Explanation** Construct an explanation for why it is easier to open a door by pushing the side that does not have the hinges. At what angle with the door should you push to achieve the greatest torque?

Torque Balancing

Stability is the ability of a system to restore itself to its original static equilibrium after being displaced. There are two conditions that must be satisfied for a system to be in static equilibrium: (1) the external forces on the system must sum to zero, and (2) the external torques on the system must sum to zero. You use the defined coordinate system to determine positive and negative forces. For torque, a common convention is that torques that would cause a counterclockwise rotation are positive, and those that would cause a clockwise rotation are negative.

Conditions for Static Equilibrium
$\Sigma F = 0$
$\Sigma \tau = 0$

Balancing Torques For systems in static equilibrium, the forces and the torques must balance.

The normal does not produce a torque because the lever arm is zero.

N

r_S

r_L

W_{Small}

W_{Large}

Balance Forces

$\Sigma F = 0$

$N - W_S - W_L = 0$

Balance Torques

$\Sigma \tau = 0$

$+ W_S r_S - W_L r_L = 0$

Counterclockwise rotation is indicated with a "+."

Clockwise rotation is indicated with a "−."

(84) **CCC Stability and Change** The same pencil is shown in two orientations, each with the center of mass labeled. Why is one more stable than the other? Use a series of free-body diagrams and the conditions for static equilibrium to argue your case.

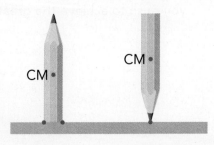

CM

CM

Balancing a Meter Stick

A meter stick is balanced on a support at its center. A 0.20-N weight is hung on the meter stick a distance 0.30 m to the left of the center. Where should you place a 0.50-N weight so that the meter stick is in static equilibrium? Determine the force exerted by the support on the meter stick.

1. DRAW A PICTURE Sketch a picture of the situation.

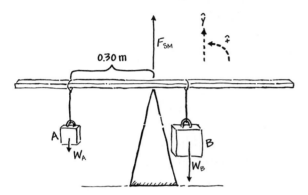

2. DEFINE THE PROBLEM List knowns and unknowns, and assign values to variables.

$W_A = 0.20$ N

$W_B = 0.50$ N

$r_{perpA} = 0.30$ m

$r_{perpB} = ?$

$F_{SM} = ?$

3. PLAN AND EXECUTE Use mathematical relationships, the picture, and your definitions to plan and execute a solution.

Write a force-acceleration equation for the system.	$F_{SM} - W_A - W_B = 0$ $F_{SM} = W_A + W_B = 0.20$ N $+ 0.50$ N $= 0.70$ N
Write a torque-balance equation for the system with the center of the meter stick as the point of rotation. Since weight A causes a counterclockwise rotation, then weight B must cause a clockwise rotation.	$+\tau_A - \tau_B = 0 \rightarrow \tau_A = \tau_B$ $W_A r_{perpA} = W_B r_{perpB}$
Solve for weight B's lever arm.	$r_{perpB} = \dfrac{W_A r_{perpA}}{W_B} = \dfrac{(0.20 \text{ N})(0.30 \text{ m})}{(0.50 \text{ N})} = 0.12$ m

4. EVALUATE Reflect on your answer.
The answer has units of meters, which is correct. The heavier weight should be closer to the support than the lighter one.

 GO ONLINE for more **math support**.

▶ **Math Tutorial Video**

🖥 **Math Practice Problems**

---

85 A meter stick is balanced on a support at its center. A 0.70-N weight is hung on the meter stick a distance 0.25 m to the left of the center. Where should you place a 0.40-N weight so that the meter stick is in static equilibrium? Determine the force exerted by the support on the meter stick.

📖 **NEED A HINT?** Go online to your **eText Sample Problem** for stepped-out support.

INVESTIGATIVE PHENOMENON

GO ONLINE to revisit your **Investigative Phenomenon CER** with the new information you have learned about Forces on Systems.

These questions will help you apply what you have learned in this experience to the Investigative Phenomenon.

86. **SEP Develop and Use a Model** Model the beginning of a rockslide, when one rock begins to slide and collides with another rock, overcoming its static friction. Use your model to explain why rockslides can be considered cascading events.

87. **SEP Construct an Explanation** The steeper the slope of a rocky hill, the less stable the rocks are. Construct an explanation by sketching models for a rock on a steep hill and a rock on a hill that is less steep. Consider the effects on stability from both torques and from the components of the surface force.

88. **SEP Design a Solution** Design a solution for preventing a rockslide. Model your solution using a free-body diagram for a system of rocks prevented from sliding by your solution. Using information from online sources, estimate how much force your solution will need to withstand.

89. **CCC Cause and Effect** In 2018 during the World Cup, earthquake sensors in Mexico City showed activity after the Mexican national team scored a game-winning goal against the Germans. Some scientists speculated this could have resulted from the celebrations. Describe how humans could cause the effect of small earthquakes.

GO ONLINE for a **quiz** to evaluate what you have learned about Forces on Systems.

EXPERIENCE 4

Earth's Surface Forces

 GO ONLINE to do a **hands-on lab** to investigate why Earth's surface looks the way it does.

Earth Systems

Opposing Forces What you have learned about forces can be seen in the motions of the world around you. The surface processes that you know about, such as chemical reactions, rainfall, and landslides, are driven by gravity and sunlight. Now you will learn that Earth's surface is a battleground between two major systems of forces. Opposing the destructive forces on Earth's surface are the internal forces associated with plate tectonics, which move continents and build mountain ranges. Those constructive processes are driven by the motions of rock within Earth's interior as the planet cools down. However, as fast as forces that are part of plate tectonics build up mountains, the forces associated with weather and water wear them down.

Exchanges The atmosphere, geosphere, hydrosphere, and biosphere continuously exchange tremendous amounts of matter and energy. Events that occur in one sphere can have effects on all the others.

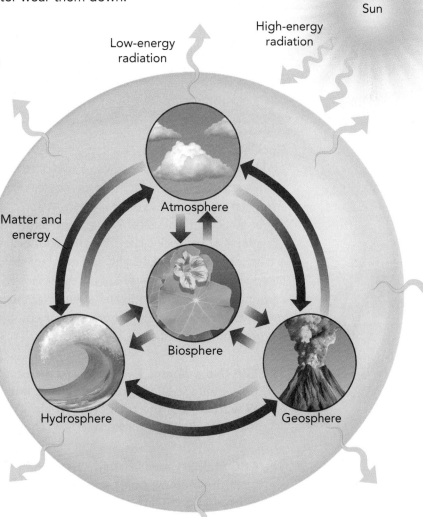

Sun

High-energy radiation

Low-energy radiation

Matter and energy

Atmosphere

Biosphere

Hydrosphere

Geosphere

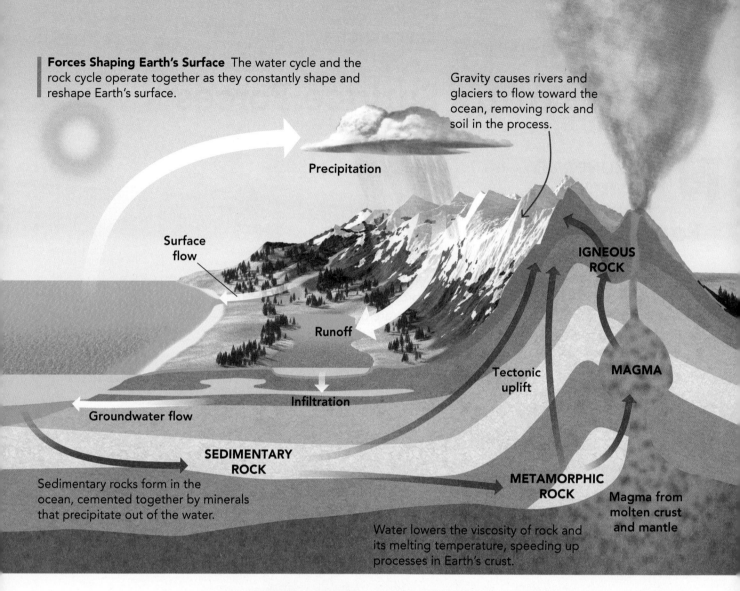

Forces Shaping Earth's Surface The water cycle and the rock cycle operate together as they constantly shape and reshape Earth's surface.

Gravity causes rivers and glaciers to flow toward the ocean, removing rock and soil in the process.

Precipitation

Surface flow

Runoff

IGNEOUS ROCK

Infiltration

Tectonic uplift

MAGMA

Groundwater flow

SEDIMENTARY ROCK

METAMORPHIC ROCK

Magma from molten crust and mantle

Sedimentary rocks form in the ocean, cemented together by minerals that precipitate out of the water.

Water lowers the viscosity of rock and its melting temperature, speeding up processes in Earth's crust.

Rock and Water Cycles You may already have learned about the rock cycle and the water cycle as if they were two different things. They aren't. As with many systems on Earth, multiple processes occur together at the same time. Every part of the rock cycle involves water in one way or another. Each year, about 40,000 km^3 of water falls on land as rain and snow, and that water affects all aspects of the rock cycle. The effects of glaciers and rivers on Earth's surface are apparent. But out of sight, sedimentary rocks form beneath the ocean. Deep in Earth's crust, water lowers the viscosity, or resistance to flow, of rock, allowing mantle convection and speeds up the metamorphic alteration of buried rock. Water also lowers the melting temperatures of rock, helping to form magma underground.

(90) **SEP Use a Model** Early on in its history, Earth's surface was too hot for water vapor to have condensed into liquid, so there was no ocean. Which parts of the rock cycle would likely have been the most different from the way they are now?

(91) **CCC Stability and Change** Given the role that water plays in lowering both the melting point and viscosity of rock, infer how the surface of Earth might be different if the large amount of water within the rock of Earth's mantle were much less than it is.

Forces at Earth's Surface

Gravity Two of the forces you already know about, gravity and electric forces, dominate the processes that change Earth's surface. Those two forces work at scales that range in size from molecules to entire mountains.

Many of Earth's large-scale geologic processes, including precipitation, stream flow, glacial movement, avalanches, and landslides, are driven by gravity. Even wind is a result of differences in pressure caused by gravity. The acceleration due to gravity at Earth's surface is 9.8 m/s^2, and its overall effect is that the rock of Earth's continents eventually is carried down to the ocean.

Electric Forces The wearing down of land by gravity would be much slower without the electric forces that simultaneously break down rock into smaller pieces. During the chemical weathering of rocks, electric forces break minerals into small pieces that are easily washed away by rain and rivers. Because of the electrical structure of the water molecule, water is the most powerful agent for the weathering of rocks.

Gravitational Force Mountains get lower as they age. The force of gravity pulls them down, rock by rock.

Weathering of Rocks The positive and negative ends of water molecules efficiently dissolve rocks, atom by atom. Rivers often carry more dissolved sediment than solid sand, silt, and pebbles.

Gravity

(92) **CCC Cause and Effect** Suppose a boulder rolls down a steep hill and knocks other rocks off the hill along its way. Explain how the process involves both gravitational and electric forces.

Time Scales of Geologic Processes

Erosion is derived from the Latin word *erodere*, which means "to gnaw away or consume." You may have heard of eroding confidence when people say they no longer trust something.

Gradual Processes Changes to Earth's surface occur not only over a wide range of spatial scales, but also over a wide range of time scales, known as **geologic time.** Nearly all geologic processes occur on a spectrum that ranges from continual and small to infrequent and catastrophic.

A key to understanding geology is that processes that are observed today, such as erosion and sedimentation, also occurred the same way in the past. Sedimentation and erosion are examples of geologic processes that are typically gradual. **Erosion** is the combination of the weathering and removal of rock. Streams that run continuously for many years never stop eroding the land. After the eroded sediment is transported to a new location, the process of **sedimentation** compacts and cements the buried particles into new rock.

Other examples of gradual processes include the thousands of small earthquakes that occur around the world every day, most too small to be felt and doing no damage. Even meteor impacts occur ceaselessly. Millions of tiny pieces of comets and meteoroids enter Earth's atmosphere every day, and you see some of them as shooting stars.

Gradual Geologic Change The beautiful layers of red and orange rock visible in the Vermilion Cliffs National Monument are the result of two kinds of continual geologic processes. The layers formed from hundreds of millions of years of accumulated sand and gravel. Tens of millions of years of erosion were then needed to create the shapes seen in the photo.

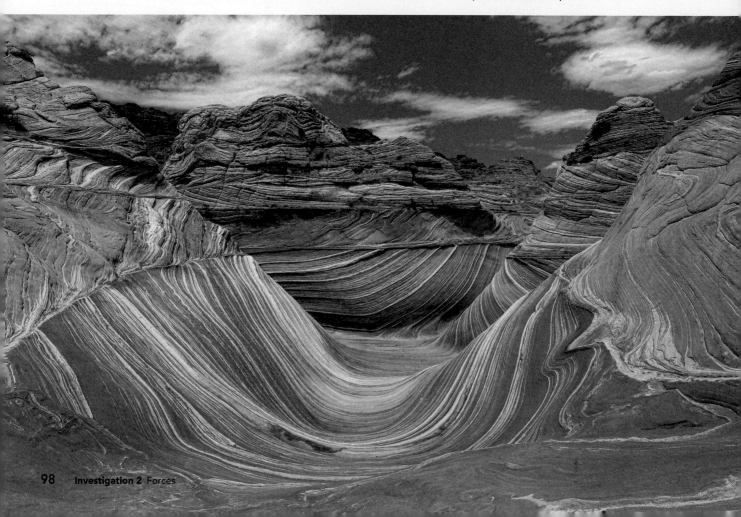

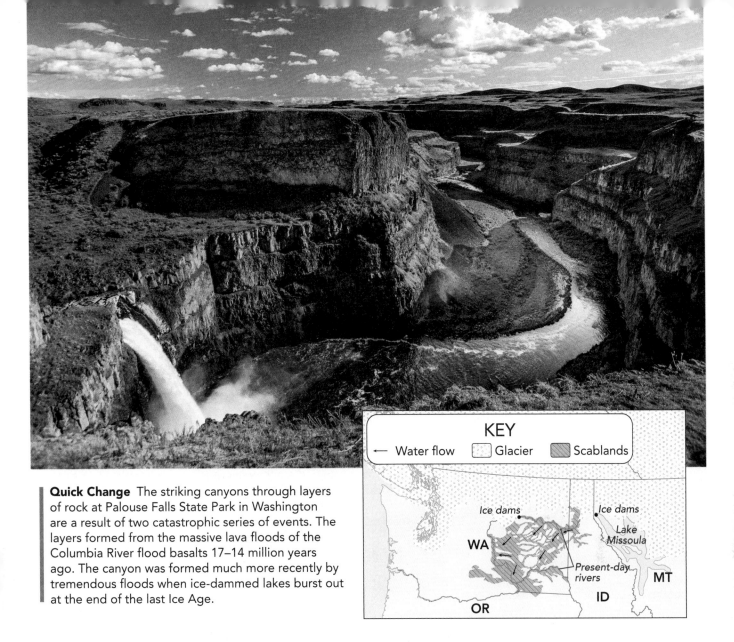

Quick Change The striking canyons through layers of rock at Palouse Falls State Park in Washington are a result of two catastrophic series of events. The layers formed from the massive lava floods of the Columbia River flood basalts 17–14 million years ago. The canyon was formed much more recently by tremendous floods when ice-dammed lakes burst out at the end of the last Ice Age.

KEY

← Water flow ▢ Glacier ▨ Scablands

Ice dams Ice dams
Lake Missoula
WA
Present-day rivers
MT
ID
OR

Catastrophic Change At the other end of the geologic time scale are sudden catastrophic events, such as volcanic eruptions and immense floods. Volcanism can add large amounts of rock to Earth's surface in a short amount of time, obliterating everything in its path. Catastrophic floods have produced such dramatic landforms as the English Channel. Large earthquakes, such as very rare magnitude-9 events, can rearrange landscapes and kill millions of people. And large meteor impacts are rarer still, but it was a meteor impact that killed all remaining dinosaurs on Earth 66 million years ago. Catastrophic processes such as those that occurred thousands or millions of years ago are still possible today, but people are lucky that they are so infrequent—you are unlikely ever to experience one.

93 **CCC Scale, Proportion, and Quantity** A landslide can pull down a mountainside in about a minute. The erosion of a large mountain range can go on for 500 million years. Calculate the orders of magnitude difference between those time frames.

94 **CCC Patterns** Describe how volcanism follows the same pattern of continuous-catastrophic activity as does flooding.

Weathering

The first step in the erosion of landscapes is weathering, which involves the breakdown of minerals and rocks into smaller pieces. Weathering occurs both mechanically, by physically breaking rock into small solid particles, and chemically, by wearing away rock one atom or molecule at a time. Globally, mechanical and chemical weathering produce roughly the same amount of sediment, but the ratio varies greatly with climate, environment, and rock type. Chemical weathering is very active where there is plenty of water present because of the structure of the water molecule. Weathering is controlled by electric forces at either the microscopic scale in chemical reactions, or at the macroscopic scale in processes such as abrasion and frost wedging. Weathering is critically important to humans because it breaks down rock to form soil, which is needed to grow the global food supply.

Weathering Rock is weathered in several ways. Weathering is generally a very slow and gradual process; but over geologic time, it completely reshapes landscapes.

Oxidation (rusting)

Dissolution

Hydrolysis

Chemical weathering primarily occurs through rusting (oxidation), dissolving (dissolution), and changing certain minerals into clay (hydrolysis).

Frost Wedging

Plant Roots

Pressure Release

Mechanical weathering includes the expansion of ice (frost wedging) and plant roots, which pry rocks apart, and the expansion of rock during pressure release, which causes rock to peel off in sheets.

95) **SEP Construct an Explanation** Explain why frost wedging is a much greater problem for roads in a place that experiences both hot and cold seasons, such as Chicago, than it is in a much colder place, such as McMurdo Station in Antarctica.

96) **CCC Stability and Change** Soil forms in place through the chemical weathering of bedrock. Explain why soil layer thickness is much greater in the tropical jungles of the Amazon than in the Mojave Desert.

Mass Wasting

Mass wasting is the removal of rock from its location as a result of gravitational forces. It occurs over a range of scales in time and space and can involve individual rocks falling down a cliff or whole hillsides slowly creeping downhill. There are several factors that affect the type and amount of mass wasting. First, it occurs more easily on steeper slopes. Also, plant roots hold soil in place, so mass wasting often occurs after forest fires. Water has a complex role in mass wasting. A moderate amount of water holds soil grains together in the same way it holds together a sandcastle, so it decreases mass wasting. Too much water, however, can cause mudflows and increase mass wasting.

> **Modes of Mass Wasting** Rock can be removed from hillsides in many different ways that range from sudden (rockfalls and landslides) to gradual (creep).

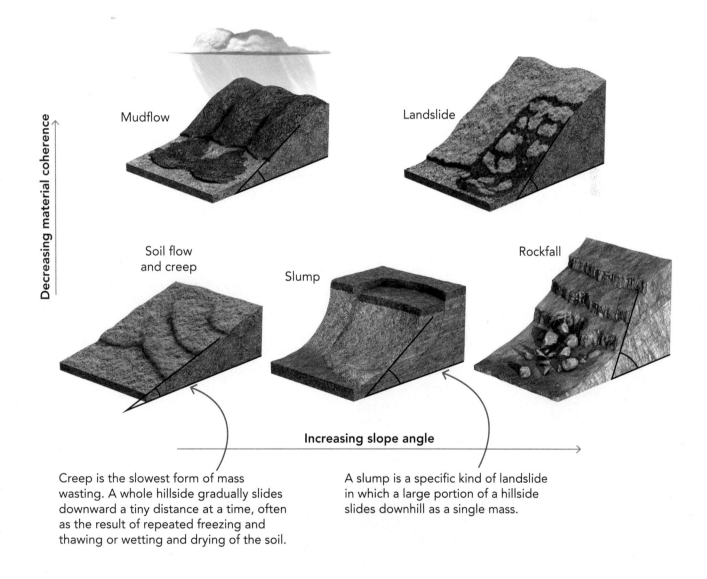

Mudflow

Landslide

Soil flow and creep

Slump

Rockfall

Decreasing material coherence

Increasing slope angle

Creep is the slowest form of mass wasting. A whole hillside gradually slides downward a tiny distance at a time, often as the result of repeated freezing and thawing or wetting and drying of the soil.

A slump is a specific kind of landslide in which a large portion of a hillside slides downhill as a single mass.

97 **SEP Construct an Explanation** Most large landslides occur immediately after nearby earthquakes. Explain why that is the case.

Stream Systems

Drainage Streams form complex systems of branches and channels that can carry the water from rain and snow to the ocean, wherever it falls, pulled downhill by the force of gravity. Such networks form distinct and separate basins, and rain anywhere within a basin ends up at a single location. For example, the largest stream in North America, the Mississippi River, drains the interior of much of the continent and discharges the water all in one place: the delta south of New Orleans, Louisiana, in the Gulf of Mexico.

Erosion The total amount of water in all of the world's streams is not large compared to the ocean—it is only a millionth. However, 40,000 km^3 of water flow through the world's streams each year, and streams are the major natural cause of erosion on continents. Water flows into streams on the surface as runoff, and under the surface as groundwater, where it also erodes rock. Vast networks of caves are a result of such erosion.

Discharge and Sediment Load Small streams can only carry silt. Larger streams can carry sand; and big rivers, especially during floods, can even carry large boulders. The amount of water that a stream carries is called the discharge. The amount of sediment a stream carries is the **sediment load.** Both of these characteristics vary greatly with weather and climate. For example, the Mississippi River sediment load typically varies between 90 and 540 million metric tons per year. The variation is often tied to large-scale atmosphere and ocean current patterns such as the El Niño cycle.

Mountain Stream As rock is carried away by flowing water, deep V-shaped valleys are cut into the land. Most erosion on continents occurs in high mountain areas where slopes are steepest.

Dendritic Stream Pattern Stream systems tend to develop tree-like, or dendritic, patterns that cover most of the land so that rain anywhere can eventually find its way to the ocean.

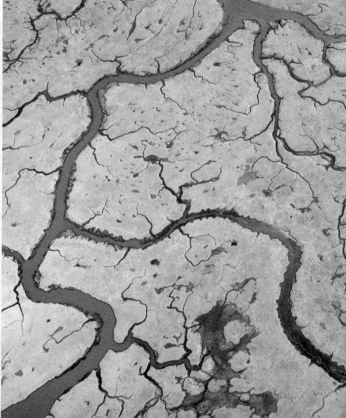

Stream Profile Streams tend to follow a general pattern of being steepest at their headwaters, often in mountains, and shallowest where they flow into a body of water. The typical shape is called the stream profile.

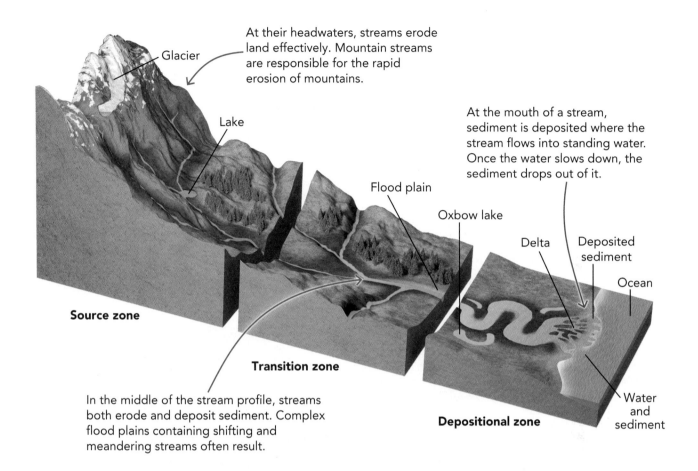

At their headwaters, streams erode land effectively. Mountain streams are responsible for the rapid erosion of mountains.

Glacier

Lake

At the mouth of a stream, sediment is deposited where the stream flows into standing water. Once the water slows down, the sediment drops out of it.

Flood plain

Oxbow lake

Delta

Deposited sediment

Ocean

Source zone

Transition zone

Depositional zone

Water and sediment

In the middle of the stream profile, streams both erode and deposit sediment. Complex flood plains containing shifting and meandering streams often result.

Stream Profiles The slope of a stream follows a profile from steep at the start to flat at the end. A stream erodes sediment when it is steep and moving quickly, and it deposits sediment when it is flat and moving slowly.

Floods Flooding along streams is one of the most damaging and deadliest natural hazards for humans. In some cases, particularly in Asia, single floods have killed millions of people. Flood plains and deltas, rich in sediment, are some of the most fertile lands on Earth, so many people live there. Because the lands are flat, however, natural flooding makes them especially dangerous.

98) **SEP Construct an Explanation** When dams are placed on rivers, they have the effect of resetting the stream profile above and below. As a result, the stream above the dam begins depositing more sediment, and the stream just below the dam begins eroding more sediment. Explain why the change happens and what the implications might be for the dam.

99) **CCC Scale, Proportion, and Quantity** Some streams contain giant boulders, particularly in mountainous regions, that don't ever seem to move. Explain how those boulders move downstream.

Glacial Systems

Alpine Glaciers Glaciers are powerful agents of erosion. Glaciers are analogous to streams in many ways, but orders of magnitude slower, moving only 1 to 100 meters per day. Glaciers that form in mountains are called alpine glaciers. They efficiently carve valleys out of the rock of mountains because the hard ice is in contact with the walls of the entire valley, and not just the bottom, as with water in a stream. Glaciers often have rock fragments embedded along the bottom, which also help grind away Earth's surface. There are about 200,000 alpine glaciers in the world, and their meltwater is an important source of drinking water for many people.

Glaciers lose mass through melting, sublimation, and calving, when large pieces break off. The icy end of the glacier can be stationary, advance forward, or melt quickly enough to cause it to recede. However, the overall mass of the glacier always flows downhill, pulled by the force of gravity. The eroded rock is deposited at the front of the glacier, forming a deposit called a terminal moraine. Most alpine glaciers are entirely on land, but some, called tidewater glaciers, empty directly into the ocean. Because of rising global temperatures, alpine glaciers around the world are thinning and receding.

Alpine Glaciers Like mountain streams, glaciers flow downhill, driven by gravity, and have multiple tributaries that flow into one main channel. Both have a profile in which rock is eroded from the top and deposited at the bottom.

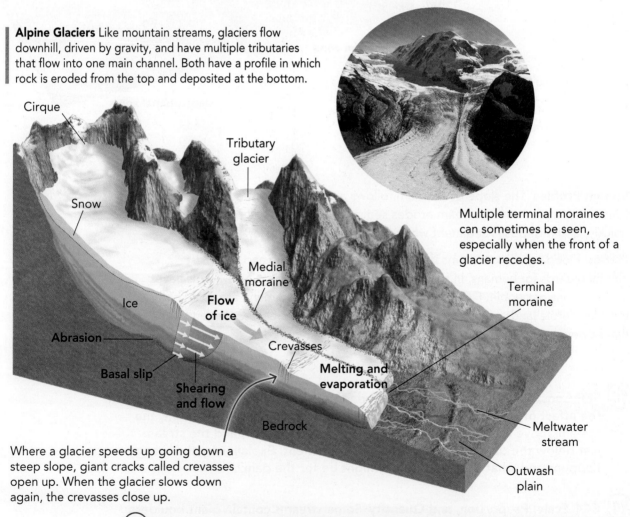

Multiple terminal moraines can sometimes be seen, especially when the front of a glacier recedes.

Cirque

Tributary glacier

Snow

Ice

Flow of ice

Medial moraine

Abrasion

Basal slip

Shearing and flow

Crevasses

Melting and evaporation

Bedrock

Terminal moraine

Meltwater stream

Outwash plain

Where a glacier speeds up going down a steep slope, giant cracks called crevasses open up. When the glacier slows down again, the crevasses close up.

(100) SEP Communicate Scientific Information Communicate two ways that alpine glaciers and streams are similar and two ways that they are different.

Continental Ice Sheet Continental glaciers, also referred to as continental ice sheets, can alter Earth's surface through erosion and deposition in many different ways.

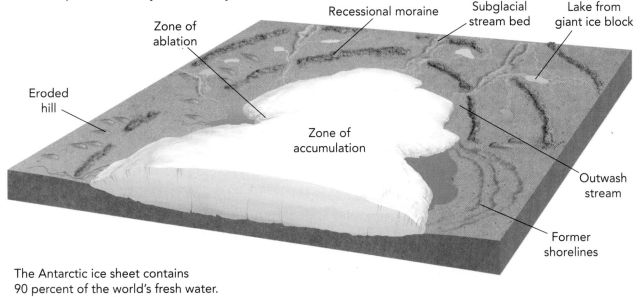

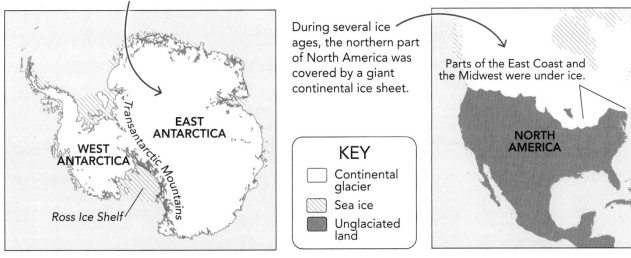

The Antarctic ice sheet contains 90 percent of the world's fresh water.

During several ice ages, the northern part of North America was covered by a giant continental ice sheet.

Parts of the East Coast and the Midwest were under ice.

KEY
☐ Continental glacier
▨ Sea ice
▦ Unglaciated land

Continental Glaciers A continental glacier covers a far larger area than an alpine glacier. The two continental glaciers that now cover Antarctica and Greenland contain 99.4 percent of the world's ice. For most of the past million years, however, large parts of North America and Europe were covered with the kilometers-thick glaciers of multiple ice ages. The last ice age ended just 12 thousand years ago. Continental glaciers significantly erode Earth's surface as they flow outward from their centers. They sculpt many unique landforms that are a result of either erosion or deposition. The rich soils of the Midwest of the United States are largely made of pulverized Canadian rock that was dragged from the north by glaciers. The North American ice sheet was so big that it pushed the crust down into the mantle. When the ice age ice sheets melted, so much water was released that global sea levels rose about 125 m.

(101) **CCC Patterns** Diamonds have occasionally been found on the ground in Illinois and Indiana, but there are no known diamond-bearing geologic formations in those states. Where else might you look for the source of those diamonds?

Aeolian Systems

An **aeolian system** is a system related to the action of wind forces. Much like water, wind can transport sediment from one place to another. Wind can only carry small particles such as dust and sand, although faster wind can carry more and larger particles. Wind erodes rock through abrasion, as high-speed sediments gradually tear away at rock surfaces. Wind can also deposit sediments in several ways. Fine dust is blown all around the globe by atmospheric air currents such as the jet streams. Old ocean seafloor contains accumulations of millions of years of wind-blown dust, which can be several kilometers deep. Immense dust storms or large volcanic eruptions can move a tremendous amount of dust or ash long distances in short periods of time.

Wind plays many roles in shaping desert landscapes. The force of wind moves sand around to form ever-shifting sand dunes. Wind can produce a feature called desert pavement by blowing sand and dust off the dry ground and leaving larger rocks behind. Erosion in deserts is still primarily the result of water, particularly from occasional flash floods.

(102) **CCC Patterns** With the process of how sand dunes form and move in mind, infer how sandy ripples on streambeds form and move.

Saltation in Sand Dunes The force of wind causes sand dunes to move across the surface of a desert. It often appears as if the dunes are moving as a single mass, but in fact they move one sand grain at a time.

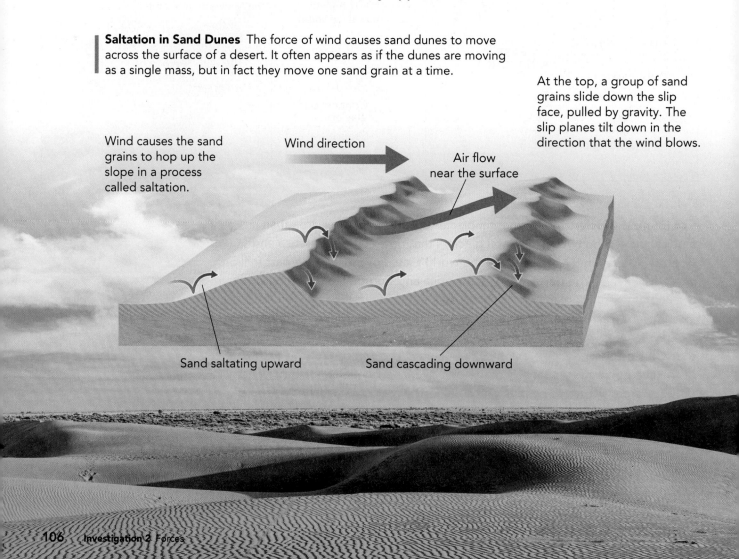

Wind causes the sand grains to hop up the slope in a process called saltation.

Wind direction

Air flow near the surface

At the top, a group of sand grains slide down the slip face, pulled by gravity. The slip planes tilt down in the direction that the wind blows.

Sand saltating upward

Sand cascading downward

Shoreline Systems

Shorelines are shaped by the action of ocean waves, which use the tremendous amount of energy they collect from wind to break down the shore. As well as waves, longshore currents, which are water currents that move parallel to the shore, pick up and transport sediment. You know from studying streams that water picks up sediment when it speeds up and drops sediment when it slows down. The force of waves erode headlands, and longshore currents deposit the sediments into bays, where the water slows down. The end result is that coastlines tend to become straighter over time.

Of course, there are processes that make coastlines irregular. Deposition of sediments at river deltas, changes in global or regional sea levels, and disruptive erosion or deposition due to storms may produce new headlands and bays. But very soon, the straightening actions of waves and longshore currents will start all over again.

New and Mature Coastlines
Global and regional sea levels routinely rise and fall. When they do, a new coastline forms. The new coastline starts off jagged, with bays that fold in and headlands that stick out.

Over time, the jagged coastline becomes straight. Wave action erodes the headlands, bays fill in with silt, and longshore currents carry sand along the shore to make bars and barrier islands.

Headlands

Bay

Longshore current

Beach deposits

Cliff

Baymouth bar

(103) **CCC Cause and Effect** Globally, rates of coastal erosion have increased as more hydroelectric dams have been installed across rivers. Propose an explanation for that increase.

Isostasy and Rebound

 GO ONLINE to watch a **video** about the forces that affect the height of Earth's mountains and to do a PhET **simulation** that allows you to explore the relationship between force and pressure.

EXPERIENCE IT!

Take a pile of books and place them on a spring mattress. What happens as you increase the number of books in the stack? What happens if you then remove the books from the mattress, one at a time?

If you visit old mountains such as the Appalachians or the Alps, you see dramatically folded metamorphic rocks at the surface. Erosion of the mountains alone cannot explain those rocks, for this kind of metamorphism only occurs deep underground. A remarkable process called isostatic rebound is required to explain their presence. **Isostasy** is the principle that thicker crust floats more deeply in Earth's mantle, and thinner crust floats less deeply.

Earth's continental crust is less dense than the mantle; and, because both crust and mantle deform in a fluid manner, the crust ends up floating at an appropriately balanced height. You can think of it as something like the behavior of different sizes of ice cubes floating in water. A bigger ice cube will float a bit higher in the water than a smaller ice cube, but it will also extend much farther down. In geology, the result is that, when mountains form during a tectonic plate collision, continental crust gets pushed down into the mantle at the same time that mountains rise. Later, as the mountains gradually erode, the isostatic pressure becomes imbalanced and the whole crust rebounds upward. As the mountains continue to erode, the crust continues to rebound. After many millions of years, metamorphic rocks such as marble, slate, and gneiss, which formed deep underground at high pressures, are exposed at the surface.

Uplift and Erosion Because continental crust is less dense than the mantle underneath, the mass of mountains is balanced by a root of crust that is pushed down into the mantle—isostasy!

Deep within mountains, high temperatures and pressures cause layers of the crust to fold and new metamorphic rocks to form. Without erosion, you would never see those rocks.

Over millions of years, mountains are eroded. As that happens, the crust rises up to stay in isostatic balance. Eventually, metamorphic rocks once deep underground become exposed at the surface.

 SEP Construct an Explanation Geologists can tell how old a mountain is just by observing the kinds of rocks found at the surface. How does understanding the processes of erosion and isostatic rebound make that possible?

Humans as a Geologic Force

Humans have impacted more than three-fourths of Earth's land (excluding Antarctica), and human activities cause erosion at a rate six times faster than all other natural causes combined. Some of the major ways that human-caused erosion occurs include agriculture, surface mining, deforestation, acid rain, and land development.

Earth and Human Activity

How do **human activities** affect **Earth's surface?**

Agriculture
40% of Earth's surface is used for **growing crops** and **grazing livestock.** Constant irrigation and overgrazing can **cause rapid erosion of topsoil.**

Surface Mining
25 billion metric **tons of material** are mined on Earth's surface each year. **Large sections of land are removed** to extract minerals, coal, and other resources.

Deforestation
1% of the **world's total forests are removed** by deforestation each decade, primarily to make room **to grow more crops.**

Acid Rain
4.2–4.4 is the **pH range of acid rain,** compared to 5.6 for "clean" rain. **Industrial pollutants** which make rain increasingly acidic and cause the **chemical weathering and erosion of rock** to increase.

Development
1.5 million square kilometers of land on Earth's surface is categorized as **urban or built-up land.** As the population increases, **more of Earth's surface is developed** to meet the need for growing towns and cities.

(105) **SEP Design a Solution** Choose one of the five categories of human-induced erosion and propose a change in practice that would reduce the amount of erosion.

INVESTIGATIVE PHENOMENON

 GO ONLINE to revisit your **Investigative Phenomenon CER** with the new information you have learned about Earth's Surface Forces.

These questions will help you apply what you learned in this experience to the Investigative Phenomenon.

106) SEP Construct an Explanation In 1929, a large earthquake occurred off the coast of Labrador, Canada. At that point, communication between North America and Europe was done with underwater seafloor cables. For many minutes following the end of the earthquake, one cable after another stopped carrying a signal. Construct an explanation for what might have happened.

107) CCC Stability and Change Choose and explain one way that human activities can affect the likelihood of a rockslide occurring.

108) CCC Stability and Change As a stream cuts down into the side of a mountain, the slope of the stream valley changes. Explain how that can affect the occurrence of rockslides.

109) CCC Cause and Effect The largest landslide ever recorded was along the north face of Mount Saint Helens, in the state of Washington, moments after a magnitude-5 earthquake and moments before the giant volcanic eruption in May of 1980. Explain how those three phenomena were likely related.

110) SEP Construct an Explanation During an El Niño climate period, southern California typically receives much more rain than normal. Explain why the risks of landslides in the mountains of southern California are greater during El Niño periods.

 GO ONLINE for a **quiz** to evaluate what you learned about Earth's Surface Forces.

These questions will help you apply what you learned in this investigation to the Anchoring Phenomenon.

111 **SEP Construct Explanations** To reach space, a rocket must overcome the force of gravity acting on it. Rocket engines burn fuel to provide thrust, or an upward force. Identify the forces acting on a rocket before liftoff and compare these forces to the ones acting on the rocket as it begins to lift off. Explain how the rocket is able to leave Earth and why the rocket continues to move upward after thrust has finished.

112 **CCC Cause and Effect** Aerospace engineers design and build spacecraft. Think about the different forces acting on a spacecraft during liftoff. What do you think are the most important considerations when choosing materials to build spacecraft? Explain your answer.

☑INVESTIGATION ASSESSMENT

 GO ONLINE for activities that will give you an opportunity to **demonstrate what you have learned:**

☑ **Science Performance-Based Assessment** Analyze experimental data to find relationships between net force, acceleration, and mass.

📄 **Engineering Workbench** Design a system to help protect a structure.

💻 **Career Connections** Learn about how a forest ranger applies knowledge of physics.

🛜 **Investigation Test** Take this test to evaluate your understanding of forces.

☑ **Virtual Lab Performance-Based Assessment** Use experimental evidence to identify the factors that determine whether an object will slide down a hill.

Forces at a Distance

How does the moon shape our coastline?

Investigation 3
Gravitational Forces

Investigation 4
Electric Forces

Investigation 5
Magnetic Forces

Investigation 6
Forces in Materials

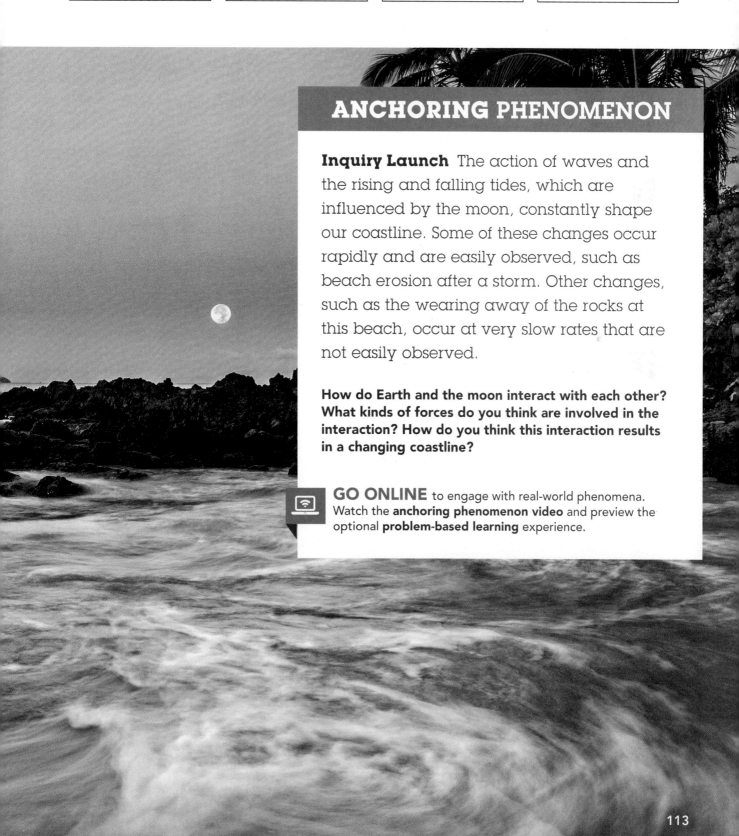

ANCHORING PHENOMENON

Inquiry Launch The action of waves and the rising and falling tides, which are influenced by the moon, constantly shape our coastline. Some of these changes occur rapidly and are easily observed, such as beach erosion after a storm. Other changes, such as the wearing away of the rocks at this beach, occur at very slow rates that are not easily observed.

How do Earth and the moon interact with each other? What kinds of forces do you think are involved in the interaction? How do you think this interaction results in a changing coastline?

GO ONLINE to engage with real-world phenomena. Watch the **anchoring phenomenon video** and preview the optional **problem-based learning** experience.

INVESTIGATIVE PHENOMENON

GO ONLINE to engage with real-world phenomena by watching a **phenomenon video** and completing a **CER worksheet**.

What causes the seasons?

Gravitational Forces

Many of the sciences began as attempts to understand simple observations of the world around us. The change in seasons was one such observation, and it turned out to be connected to gravity. But gravity itself took a long time to explain because it cannot be observed directly. We can see its effects when objects fall to the ground, but what does the pulling? It wasn't until the seventeenth century that Newton was able to identify and describe gravity. Almost 300 years later, Einstein was able to explain it. However, many aspects of gravity still remain a scientific mystery.

For many years, astronomers couldn't even imagine that planets orbited the sun. What would have held them in orbit? We now know that most of the changes we see in the sky—the movements of the sun, moon, and planets; the phases of the moon; the rare occurrences of eclipses; the brilliant flashes of meteors; and even the cycle of the seasons—are all a result of these invisible gravitational forces.

1. **CCC Cause and Effect** Based on your experience, what do you think causes the effect of Earth's seasons?

2. **SEP Develop a Model** Sketch a model that represents your ideas for the causes of the seasons. Be sure to include any relevant objects, distances, and any other information that will communicate your ideas.

3. **SEP Use a Model** Use your model to answer the following question: Is it winter at the same time everywhere on Earth?

EXPERIENCE 1

Universal Gravitation

GO ONLINE to do a **hands-on lab** to examine the factors that affect the period of a pendulum.

What Causes Free Fall?

VOCABULARY

The English word **gravity** comes from the Latin word *gravitas*, which means "weight, seriousness."

Mass and Weight Newton's first law of motion states that an object's motion does not change unless there is some cause. **Gravity** is the noncontact attractive interaction between any two objects having mass. A force due to gravity is what causes free fall, the effect of objects accelerating toward the ground. Specifically, a type of gravitational force called weight is the force experienced by objects, resulting from their gravitational attraction to Earth.

Proportional to Mass An object's weight is proportional to its mass. Weight is the gravitational force exerted by Earth on an object.

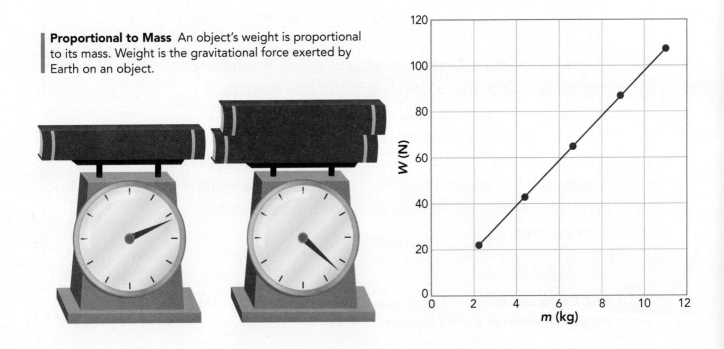

(4) **SEP Analyze and Interpret Data** Find the slope of the line shown in the figure. What does the slope represent?

(5) **CCC Scale, Proportion, and Quantity** Suppose one rollercoaster car has two people riding in it, while a second car has four people riding in it. Assume all the people have approximately the same mass. Which car has a greater gravitational force acting on it? Why?

Position and Weight The magnitude of the gravitational force is inversely proportional to the square of the distance between the centers of mass of Earth and of the object. Near the surface of Earth, weight is approximately constant.

When you stand on the ground, the distance between your center of mass and Earth's is approximately Earth's radius. Even if you stood on the top floor of the tallest building in the world, the distance from the center of Earth to the ground would be 35,000 times greater than the distance from the ground to you.

For space missions, the scale is changed. The distance from the ground to the International Space Station (ISS) is about one-sixteenth the radius of Earth. Astronauts experience a small yet measurable change in the force of gravity.

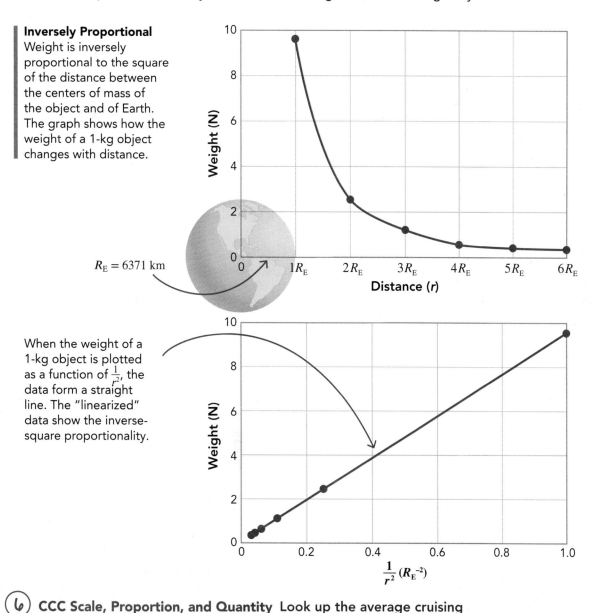

Inversely Proportional Weight is inversely proportional to the square of the distance between the centers of mass of the object and of Earth. The graph shows how the weight of a 1-kg object changes with distance.

$R_E = 6371$ km

When the weight of a 1-kg object is plotted as a function of $\frac{1}{r^2}$, the data form a straight line. The "linearized" data show the inverse-square proportionality.

6 **CCC Scale, Proportion, and Quantity** Look up the average cruising altitude for a commercial airplane. How much larger is Earth's radius than that altitude above Earth's surface?

7 **SEP Ask Questions** In your notebook, recreate the graph of weight versus distance. Draw a dot on the curve at the approximate location and weight of a book on board the ISS. Would the book be weightless?

Gravitational Force

Magnitude of Gravitational Force The gravitational interaction between any two objects having mass is expressed mathematically by **Newton's law of universal gravitation.** Gravitational force is proportional to the product of the masses involved and inversely proportional to the square of the distance between them. The constant of proportionality is called the **gravitational constant.**

Newton's Law of Universal Gravitation
$$F = G\frac{m_1 m_2}{r_{12}^2}\,\hat{r}$$
G = gravitational constant = 6.674×10^{-11} m^3/(kg·s^2)
m_1 = mass 1 $\qquad\qquad m_2$ = mass 2
r_{12} = distance between centers of mass of m_1 and m_2
$\hat{r}$ = unit vector that points to the center of mass

Magnitude of the Gravitational Force

What **affects the strength** of the gravitational force?

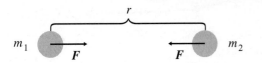

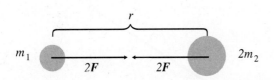

Mass If the mass of **one of the objects doubles,** then the **magnitude of the force on both objects doubles.**

The gravitational force is **directly proportional to the product of the masses.**

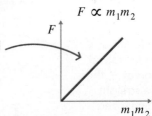

$F \propto m_1 m_2$

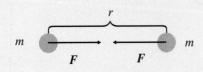

Distance The gravitational force is **inversely proportional to the square of the distance** between the masses.

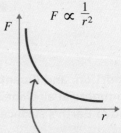

$F \propto \dfrac{1}{r^2}$

Because the **distance is squared,** it has a greater effect on the force.

GO ONLINE to do a PhET **simulation** and to watch a **video** about gravitational force.

Gravitational Force Vectors Two objects are required for every gravitational interaction. The interaction is represented as a pair of force vectors of equal magnitude and pointing in opposite directions, each vector acting on one object. To model the gravitational force on a particular object, draw a free-body diagram for the object. The direction of the gravitational force vector, as experienced by the object, is determined by the position of the other object and by the coordinate system defined.

> **Force Pairs** A vector pair represents the noncontact gravitational attraction between two masses. The vectors always point toward each other.

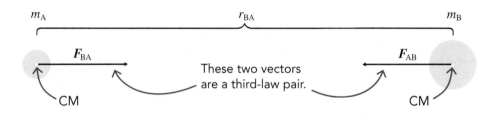

Free-body diagram with m_A defined as the system

$$\Sigma F = \left(G \frac{m_B m_A}{r_{BA}^2} \right) \hat{x}$$

Free-body diagram with m_B defined as the system

$$\Sigma F = \left(-G \frac{m_A m_B}{r_{AB}^2} \right) \hat{x}$$

8 **SEP Use a Model** If the mass of one of the masses in a two-body system were decreased by a third, what would be the change in the magnitude of the gravitational force?

9 **SEP Develop a Model** If the distance between two masses were increased by a factor of 3, what would be the change in the magnitude of the gravitational force?

10 **SEP Develop a Model** The force vectors for a set of masses are shown. On paper, sketch the force vectors for the remaining two sets of masses. Describe the relative directions of the vectors that are third-law pairs.

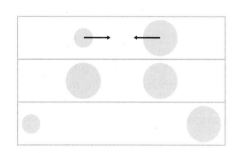

Earth and the Moon

Calculate the force exerted by Earth on the moon and the force exerted by the moon on Earth. The mass of Earth is 5.97×10^{24} kg, and the mass of the moon is 7.35×10^{22} kg. The distance between Earth's and the moon's centers of mass is 3.80×10^8 m. Express your answers as vectors.

1. DRAW A PICTURE Sketch a picture of the situation.

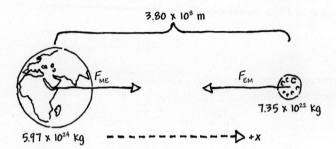

2. DEFINE THE PROBLEM List knowns and unknowns and assign values to variables.

$m_E = 5.97 \times 10^{24}$ kg　　　$F_{EM} = ?$

$m_M = 7.35 \times 10^{22}$ kg　　　$F_{ME} = ?$

$r_{EM} = 3.80 \times 10^8$ m

$G = 6.67 \times 10^{-11}$ m³/(kg · s²)

3. PLAN AND EXECUTE Use mathematical relationships, the picture, and your definitions to plan and execute your solution.

Calculate the magnitude of the force exerted by the moon on Earth.

$$F_{ME} = G\frac{m_M m_E}{r_{EM}^2}$$
$$= [6.67 \times 10^{-11} \text{ m}^3/(\text{kg} \cdot \text{s}^2)]$$
$$\frac{(7.35 \times 10^{22} \text{ kg}) (5.97 \times 10^{24} \text{ kg})}{(3.80 \times 10^8 \text{ m})^2} = 2.02 \times 10^{20} \text{ N}$$

Calculate the magnitude of the force exerted by Earth on the moon. Due to the commutative property of multiplication, the magnitude is the same.

$$F_{EM} = G\frac{m_E m_M}{r_{EM}^2}$$
$$= [6.67 \times 10^{-11} \text{ m}^3/(\text{kg} \cdot \text{s}^2)]$$
$$\frac{(5.97 \times 10^{24} \text{ kg}) (7.35 \times 10^{22} \text{ kg})}{(3.80 \times 10^8 \text{ m})^2} = 2.02 \times 10^{20} \text{ N}$$

Write the force vectors using the magnitudes and the free-body diagram.

$$\mathbf{F}_{ME} = (2.02 \times 10^{20} \text{ N})\hat{x}$$
$$\mathbf{F}_{EM} = (-2.02 \times 10^{20} \text{ N})\hat{x}$$

4. EVALUATE Reflect on your answer.
All of the units are appropriate for the given quantities. The directions are consistent with the free-body diagram.

 GO ONLINE for more **math support**.

▶ **Math Tutorial Video**

▣ **Math Practice Problems**

⑪ Calculate the force exerted by Jupiter on its moon Europa and the force exerted by Europa on Jupiter. The mass of Jupiter is about 1.90×10^{27} kg, and the mass of Europa is about 4.80×10^{22} kg. The distance between their centers of mass is 7.43×10^8 km.

📖 **NEED A HINT?** Go online to your **eText Sample Problem** for stepped out support.

Gravitational Fields

What Is a Field? A vector field is a field in which a vector quantity can be assigned to every point in space. A vector field is used to represent an individual object's influence over the space surrounding it. A **gravitational field** is a vector field in which the physical quantity is the gravitational force per unit mass. The field represents the potential acceleration of a tiny mass placed in the field. Earth's mass produces a gravitational field.

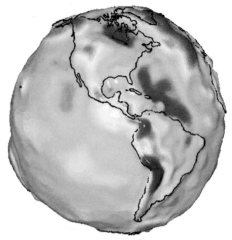

Lumpy Geoid A map of anomalies in Earth's gravitational field produced by the GRACE mission shows the nonuniform distribution of mass. The different colors represent slightly different values for g.

Gravitational Field
$$\boldsymbol{g} = G\frac{M}{r^2}\hat{\boldsymbol{r}}$$

g = gravitational field G = gravitational constant
M = mass of object r = distance from center of object
$\hat{r}$ = unit vector that points to the center of mass M

However, since the mass of Earth is not uniformly distributed, the strength of the field varies over Earth's surface. NASA's Gravity Recovery and Climate Experiment (GRACE) uses twin satellites to measure anomalies in Earth's gravitational field. A gravity anomaly is the amount Earth's actual local field differs from the field of a hypothetical uniform spheroidal Earth.

Twin Satellites NASA's GRACE mission uses a pair of twin satellites orbiting Earth to make precise measurements of gravity anomalies.

d_1

$m\boldsymbol{g}_{\text{Left1}}$ $m\boldsymbol{g}_{\text{Right1}}$

As the two GRACE satellites pass above a large mass, they experience slightly different gravitational forces.

Resulting changes in orbital velocity cause the satellites to move closer or farther apart.

d_2

$m\boldsymbol{g}_{\text{Left2}}$ $m\boldsymbol{g}_{\text{Right2}}$

Precise measurement of the distance between the satellites is used to obtain field data.

Mass

Field Lines Vectors are typically used to represent the gravitational field at a point in space. However, to show how the field potentially influences objects across large regions of space, field lines are used. **Field lines** are graphical representations consisting of lines directed by and tangent to the field vectors at each point. For systems containing multiple objects, field lines at every point in space represent the vector sum of the field lines due to each object.

Gravitational field lines are directed toward mass, since they represent the potential acceleration of a small object released within the field. The magnitude of the mass is represented by the number of field lines entering it. The magnitude of the field at any point in space is represented by the distance between field lines.

Earth–Moon System The gravitational effects on a hypothetical spacecraft placed between Earth and the moon can be represented by field lines.

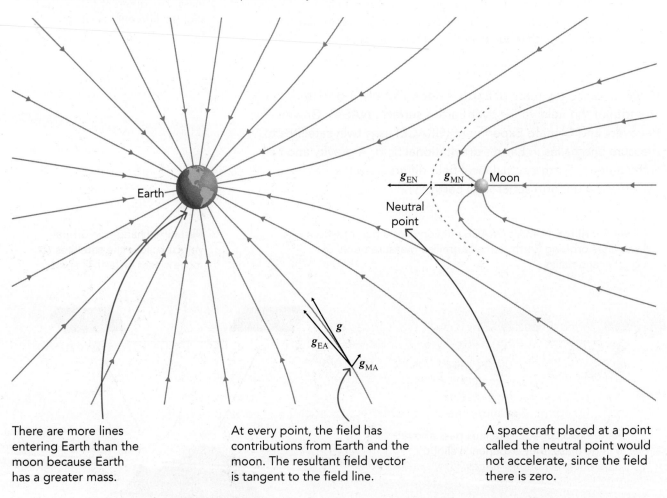

There are more lines entering Earth than the moon because Earth has a greater mass.

At every point, the field has contributions from Earth and the moon. The resultant field vector is tangent to the field line.

A spacecraft placed at a point called the neutral point would not accelerate, since the field there is zero.

(12) **SEP Construct an Explanation** Construct an explanation for why the neutral point is closer to the moon than to Earth.

(13) **SEP Use Mathematics** Using the field equation, determine the units for g. Why do you think g is used to represent the gravitational field? Is the gravitational field a representation of a cause or an effect?

Inverse Square Laws The equation for the magnitude of the gravitational field around a uniformly distributed spherical mass is an example of an inverse-square law. An **inverse-square law** is a mathematical description of any physical quantity that is inversely proportional to the square of the distance from its source. The inverse-square dependency occurs when any quantity radiates outward from a source in all directions. Examples are the gravitational and electric fields, light, and sound. As an emitted quantity gets farther from its source, it spreads out over a spherical surface, the area of which is proportional to the square of the radius, $A = 4\pi r^2$.

Surface Area The surface area of a sphere is proportional to the square of its radius. The farther away the gravitational field is, the more it spreads out.

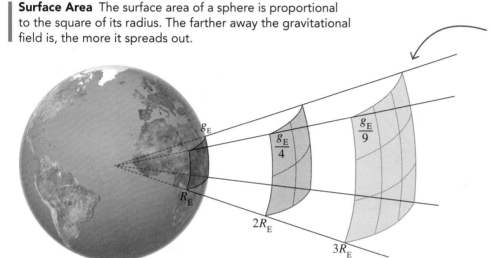

The gravitational field is spread across an area that is nine times larger at a distance three times greater. The field at any point on this area will therefore be one-ninth its size at R_E.

$$g = G\frac{M}{r^2}$$

Gravitational fields and forces

$$E = k\frac{q}{r^2}$$

Electric fields and forces

$$I = \frac{P}{4\pi r^2}$$

Intensity of light and sound

(14) **SEP Define Problems** The figure shows that there is a large difference in the amount of light reflected from the two vases closest to the light. There is a much smaller difference in the amounts of light reflected from the two vases farthest from the light, in spite of the fact that both pairs of vases are separated by the same distance. Explain the effect and how it might cause problems for someone photographing multiple objects at one time.

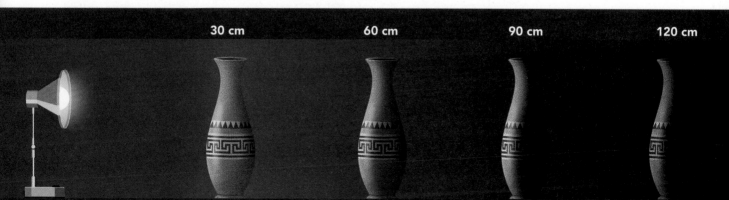

Gravity Near the Surface of Earth

Uniform Fields Vector fields with evenly spaced field lines and a constant magnitude throughout space are called **uniform fields.** Gravitational field lines are perpendicular to the surface of masses. Therefore, a large, flat sheet of mass would generate a uniform gravitational field. In such a field, the force experienced by a small nearby object would not depend on distance.

When viewed from space, Earth's field radiates spherically outward. Close to the surface, Earth looks almost flat, resulting in an approximately uniform gravitational field. This is one reason why your weight near Earth's surface is close to constant and objects fall with nearly the same acceleration.

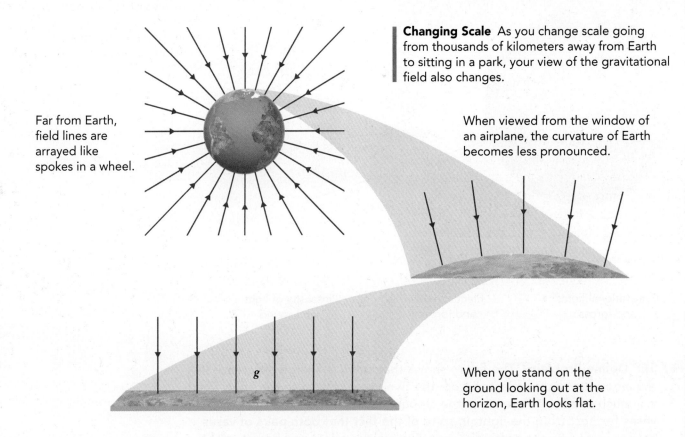

Changing Scale As you change scale going from thousands of kilometers away from Earth to sitting in a park, your view of the gravitational field also changes.

Far from Earth, field lines are arrayed like spokes in a wheel.

When viewed from the window of an airplane, the curvature of Earth becomes less pronounced.

When you stand on the ground looking out at the horizon, Earth looks flat.

(15) **CCC Scale, Proportion, and Quantity** Gravitational anomalies like those measured by the GRACE mission are measured in units called milligals. Look up what the unit represents. Then use the information to determine whether the variations in gravitational field due to nonuniform mass distribution in Earth would have any noticeable effect on your everyday life.

(16) **SEP Design a Solution** A level is an instrument that is used to determine whether a surface is horizontal. Design a solution for determining how horizontal a surface is using only a protractor, string, and a paperclip.

Distance to the Center The total distance between the center of the apple and the center of Earth is the sum of the radius of Earth, R_E, and the apple's distance above the ground, h_A.

R_E

The radius of Earth is 10,630,000 times greater.

$R_E = 6371$ km
$h_A = 0.0006$ km

g h_A

Acceleration Due to Gravity Near the surface of Earth, the gravitational field (and, therefore, the acceleration due to gravity) is approximately constant. Since the heights above the surface of Earth that you experience every day are significantly smaller than the radius of Earth, the distance between centers of mass is approximately constant. Even the height of the tallest mountain, Mount Everest, 8.85 km above sea level, is still only 0.14% of Earth's radius.

Because such heights are so much smaller than Earth's radius, you can make an approximation for the acceleration due to gravity near Earth's surface using Newton's law of universal gravitation, the gravitational constant, and the mass and radius of Earth.

Acceleration Due to Gravity The value of g is constant near the surface of Earth since R_E is significantly greater than any possible height h_A.

$$\Sigma F = m_A g = G \frac{m_E m_A}{(R_E + h_A)^2}$$

$$m_A g \approx G \frac{m_E m_A}{(R_E)^2}$$

$$g \approx G \frac{m_E}{R_E^2}$$

The net force on the apple is equal to the gravitational force.

$R_E \gg h_A$
Ignore h_A.

Cancel m_A.

(17) **SEP Use Mathematics** Calculate the acceleration due to gravity near Earth's surface using G, Earth's mass, and Earth's average radius of 6371 km. Is your result consistent with previous investigations?

(18) **SEP Argue from Evidence** The International Space Station (ISS) is 409 km above the surface of Earth. Would astronauts in the ISS experience an acceleration due to gravity? Make a claim and argue from evidence.

The International Space Station

The International Space Station (ISS) is 4.09×10^5 m above the surface of Earth. Calculate the magnitude of Earth's gravitational field. That will tell you the acceleration due to gravity on the ISS.

1. DRAW A PICTURE Sketch a picture of the situation.

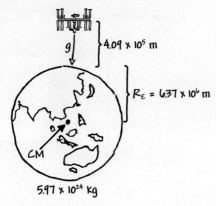

2. DEFINE THE PROBLEM List knowns and unknowns and assign values to variables.

$m_E = 5.97 \times 10^{24}$ kg

$R_E = 6.37 \times 10^6$ m

$h_{ISS} = 4.09 \times 10^5$ m

$g_{ISS} = ?$

3. PLAN AND EXECUTE Use mathematical relationships, the picture, and your definitions to plan and execute your solution.

Calculate the distance between the centers of mass of Earth and of the ISS.

$r = R_E + h_{ISS} = 6.37 \times 10^6$ m $+ 4.09 \times 10^5$ m

$r = 6.78 \times 10^6$ m

Calculate the magnitude of the gravitational field and acceleration due to gravity on the ISS.

$g = G\dfrac{m_E}{r^2} = [6.67 \times 10^{-11} \text{ m}^3/(\text{kg·s}^2)]$

$\dfrac{(5.97 \times 10^{24} \text{ kg})}{(6.78 \times 10^6 \text{ m})^2}$

$g = 8.66$ m/s^2

4. EVALUATE Reflect on your answer.
All of the units are appropriate for the given quantities. The calculated acceleration is less than 9.81 m/s^2, which you expect.

 GO ONLINE for more **math support**.

▶ **Math Tutorial Video**

🖥 **Math Practice Problems**

---

(19) Suppose a spacecraft is orbiting 3.92×10^5 m above the surface of Mars. Calculate the magnitude of Mars' gravitational field and the approximate acceleration due to gravity experienced by the spacecraft. (The mass of Mars is 6.39×10^{23} kg, and its radius is 3.40×10^6 m.)

📖 **NEED A HINT?** Go online to your **eText Sample Problem** for stepped out support.

(20) Approximate the acceleration due to gravity near the surface of Mars.

Why Do Astronauts Feel Weightless? If there is acceleration due to gravity on the ISS, then why do astronauts appear to float in the air as if they are weightless? You can answer that question by modeling the forces on astronauts as they train on a reduced-gravity airplane. The plane follows a parabolic path, simulating the experience of weightlessness. You feel lighter when an elevator begins to move down due to a reduction in the force exerted by the floor on you. In the same way, the apparent weight of the astronaut goes to zero when the plane's downward acceleration matches the acceleration due to gravity.

Free Fall The NASA Reduced Gravity Research Program operated several airplanes that simulated the experience of space flight.

Apparent Weight An astronaut's apparent weight changes during the flight of a reduced-gravity aircraft.

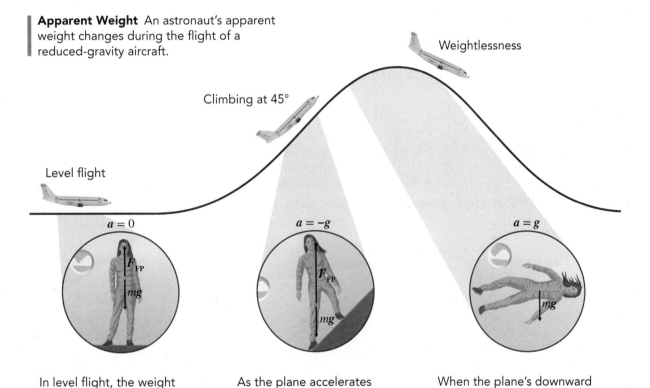

In level flight, the weight and the surface force are the same. The surface force is the apparent weight.

As the plane accelerates upward, the surface force increases. Apparent weight is roughly twice normal weight.

When the plane's downward acceleration matches the acceleration due to gravity, the surface force goes to zero. The astronauts are in free fall with the plane.

(21) **SEP Argue from Evidence** The planes are called "reduced-gravity" aircraft and are said to simulate "zero-g." Are these names technically accurate? Argue your claim using evidence from this learning experience.

(22) **SEP Develop a Model** The ISS and its astronaut occupants are constantly in free fall toward Earth—they just never manage to hit the ground. Sketch a model for how something can keep falling in that way. What type of path is required?

INVESTIGATIVE PHENOMENON

GO ONLINE to revisit your **Investigative Phenomenon CER** with the new information you have learned about Universal Gravitation.

These questions will help you apply what you learned in this experience to the Investigative Phenomenon.

23 **SEP Use Mathematics** Earth revolves around the sun in an elliptical orbit, which means that the distance between Earth and the sun, and the force between them, changes throughout the year. Perihelion is the point where Earth is closest to the sun, at a distance of 146.10 million km. Aphelion is the point where Earth is farthest from the sun, at a distance of 152.10 million km. Calculate the magnitude of the force exerted by the sun on Earth at perihelion and aphelion. Look up any information that you need.

24 **SEP Analyze and Interpret Data** Your friend claims that the seasons are the result of the changing distance between Earth and the sun. They claim that Earth is warmer when closest to the sun and cooler when farthest from the sun, based on the inverse-square law for radiation. Look up when perihelion and aphelion occur in the United States. Does the data support your friend's hypothesis?

25 **SEP Argue from Evidence** Energy is transmitted from the sun to Earth primarily through radiation, which, like gravitational force, obeys an inverse-square law. Show that the energy input at aphelion is 92% the intensity at perihelion. Does that difference explain the difference in surface temperature from winter to summer? Make a claim and argue from evidence.

26 **SEP Construct an Explanation** The difference between high tide and low tide is smallest during a neap tide and largest during a spring tide. Look up the orientation of the sun, moon, and Earth during both. Construct an explanation for the difference between spring tides and neap tides, based on the net gravitational forces experienced by Earth's oceans.

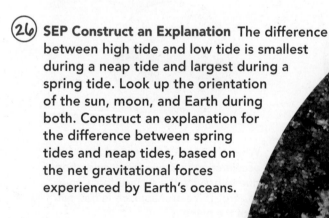

GO ONLINE
for a **quiz** to evaluate what you learned about Universal Gravitation.

Orbital Motion

 GO ONLINE to do a **hands-on lab** to model and explore the forces that keep the planets in orbit around the sun.

Launching a Satellite

In 1665, bubonic plague struck England, and schools shut down. Isaac Newton, a 23-year-old student at Cambridge University, went home for two years. It was during that time of physical distancing that Newton worked out much of his theory of gravitation. He later wrote about his discoveries in terms of a thought experiment: How fast would you have to fire a cannonball for it to orbit Earth indefinitely? An **orbit** is a continuous path of an object going around a star, planet, or moon. Newton realized that the force of gravity would have to provide the centripetal acceleration needed to keep an object moving in a continuous orbit. Expanding upon Newton's discoveries about gravity and motion has allowed space and planetary scientists to launch and maintain networks of thousands of orbiting satellites in space.

VOCABULARY

The word **orbit** is derived from the Latin word *orbis*, meaning "ring." In anatomy, the term *orbit* refers to the circular socket in the skull where the eye is situated.

Putting a Cannonball in Orbit If you could fire a cannonball fast enough, it would never fall to the ground—it would circle the planet and stay in orbit. In a circular orbit, the acceleration needed to keep the a body on its path exactly matches the acceleration due to gravity.

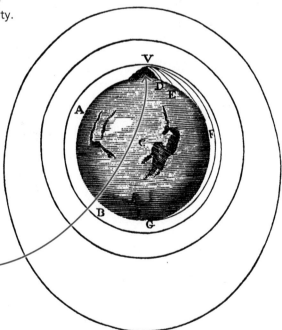

Newton's diagram represents a cannon fired from a mountaintop. The arcs of increasing size represent paths the cannonball would travel if you fired it with greater and greater speed. The innermost circle represents a circular orbit.

(27) **SEP Argue from Evidence** Using evidence, argue for or against the following claim: An object orbits Earth when it falls toward Earth but misses the ground.

Motions in Orbit

As Earth rotates, in one day, a person at the equator travels the entire length of the equator, more than 40,000 km. This person's velocity is much greater than that of a person near the North Pole, who travels a very small circle around the pole during that same day. However, in a different sense, both people have the same velocity, for both make a single revolution around Earth's axis in a day. They both have the same angular velocity, ω, measured in radians per unit time. Both the period of an orbit and the angular acceleration can be written in terms of ω.

Period and Centripetal Acceleration

$$T = \frac{C}{v} = \frac{2\pi r}{v} = \frac{2\pi}{\omega} \qquad\qquad a_c = \frac{v^2}{r} = \omega^2 r$$

T = period $\qquad\qquad\qquad$ v = velocity
C = circumference $\qquad\qquad$ r = radius
ω = angular velocity = $\frac{v}{r}$ $\qquad$ a_c = centripetal acceleration

Period The period is the time to complete one revolution.

$$v = \frac{2\pi r}{T}$$

Angular Motion on a Circle
One radian is $\frac{360°}{2\pi}$, or about 57.3°.

2 radians

1 radian

3 radians
π radians

180°

radius

ω

v

A radian is the angle subtended by an arc of a circle with length equal to the circle's radius.

0, 2π radians, 4π radians,...

0°, 360°, 720°, 1080°,...

Half a circle, or 180°, is π radians.

Linear velocity, v, increases in direct proportion with radius.

Angular velocity, ω, is measured in radians per second.

28 **CCC Scale, Proportion, and Quantity** At the equator, where Earth's radius is 6378 km, calculate your angular and linear velocities both at sea level and at the top of a 1-km mountain. Find the difference in your linear and angular velocities at sea level and at the top of the mountain.

Forces in Orbit

Circular Orbits According to Newton's first law of motion, an object travels in a straight line when no force acts on it. But the motion of a satellite orbiting Earth can be approximately circular, very similar to that of a ball twirled on a string. For the motion of an object to curve continuously, a force must be acting on it. For both the ball and the satellite, the acceleration is centripetal, or toward the center of the circle, and perpendicular to the instantaneous velocity. In the case of the ball, the force is applied by the hand and the string; for the satellite, the force is gravity.

Ball on a String When you swing a ball around on a string with a fixed length, the ball travels in a circular orbit. The force from the string is what keeps the ball moving in a circle. You can feel the equal and opposite force exerted by the string on your hand.

The instantaneous orbital velocity is always tangential to the circle.

The centripetal force acting on the ball is $F = ma = \frac{mv^2}{r}$.

The centripetal acceleration of the ball is $a_c = \frac{v^2}{r}$.

Satellite in a Circular Orbit It is the force of gravity that keeps a satellite moving in a circle. Earth moves very slightly in response to the equal and opposite gravitational force from the satellite.

The instantaneous orbital velocity, v, is always tangential to the orbit.

The centripetal force acting on the satellite is $F = mg = \frac{mv^2}{r}$.

The centripetal acceleration of the satellite is $a_c = \frac{v^2}{r}$.

(29) **SEP Use Mathematics** Imagine that there is no force of gravity acting on you and you are at the equator at sea level (R = 6378 km). Using your answer to the previous question, calculate the centripetal force needed to keep you from flying off into space due to Earth's rotation if your mass is 50 kg.

(30) **SEP Use Mathematics** Calculate the force of Earth's gravity acting on you at the equator at sea level if your mass is 50 kg. How many times larger is this than the centripetal force you calculated in the previous question?

Velocity for a Circular Orbit For a satellite to remain in a circular orbit, the force of gravity exerted by Earth must be equal to the centripetal force of the circular motion. That is the conclusion Newton reached about his mountaintop cannon. As the cannonball falls to Earth, it must also move far enough ahead that it always stays the same distance away from the center of the planet. That is also the reason that astronauts in orbit feel weightless, even though Earth's gravity is still acting on them: they are in constant free-fall. Setting equal the gravitational and centripetal forces provides an equation that connects the velocity and radius, *r*, of the satellite's orbit.

Orbital Velocity

$$v = \left(\frac{GM_E}{r}\right)^{\frac{1}{2}}$$

v = orbital velocity
G = gravitational constant = 6.674×10^{-11} m³/(kg·s²)
M_E = mass of Earth = 5.972×10^{24} kg
r = radius of satellite orbit, measured from the center of Earth (m)

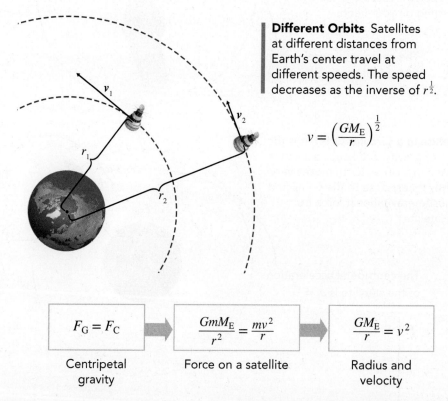

Different Orbits Satellites at different distances from Earth's center travel at different speeds. The speed decreases as the inverse of $r^{\frac{1}{2}}$.

$$v = \left(\frac{GM_E}{r}\right)^{\frac{1}{2}}$$

$F_G = F_C$	$\frac{GmM_E}{r^2} = \frac{mv^2}{r}$	$\frac{GM_E}{r} = v^2$
Centripetal gravity	Force on a satellite	Radius and velocity

Solving the above equation for the velocity shows that the velocity is only a function of the distance from Earth. The velocity decreases with the inverse of the square root of the radius, so when the radius increases by a factor of four, the velocity decreases by half.

(31) **CCC Scale, Proportion, and Quantity** Measuring the gravitational constant, *G*, has been called "weighing Earth." Using the equation for the acceleration of gravity at Earth's surface, explain what that means.

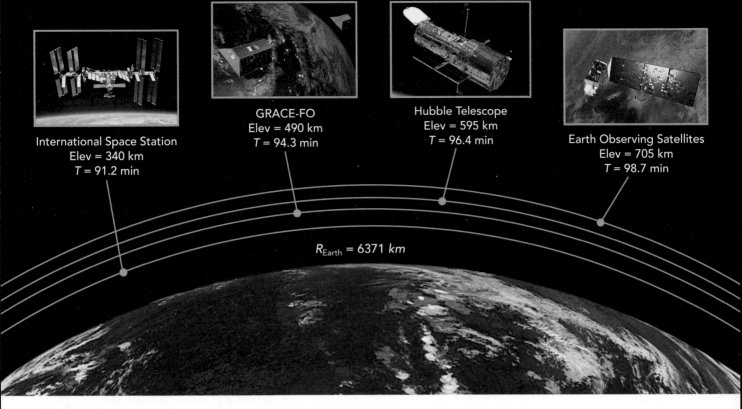

International Space Station
Elev = 340 km
T = 91.2 min

GRACE-FO
Elev = 490 km
T = 94.3 min

Hubble Telescope
Elev = 595 km
T = 96.4 min

Earth Observing Satellites
Elev = 705 km
T = 98.7 min

R_{Earth} = 6371 km

Satellite Orbits Satellites have many possible orbits. Low Earth orbits, like those of the four satellites shown in the figure, extend out to 2000 km above Earth's surface. Medium Earth orbits extend from 2000 km out to the geosynchronous orbit of about 36,000 km above Earth. High Earth orbits extend even beyond that.

Period Knowing the velocity of an object in orbit also allows you to determine the period of the orbit, because the velocity for constant circular motion is $v = \frac{2\pi r}{T}$. If you set the two expressions for velocity equal, you can then solve the equation for both the radius and the period of the orbit:

$$v = \left(\frac{GM_E}{r}\right)^{\frac{1}{2}} = \frac{2\pi r}{T}$$

$$r = \left(\frac{GM_E T^2}{4\pi^2}\right)^{\frac{1}{3}}$$

$$T = 2\pi \left(\frac{r^3}{GM_E}\right)^{\frac{1}{2}}$$

The radius is a function only of the period, and the period is a function only of the radius. The period decreases with increased radius for two reasons. First, the length of the orbit increases directly with the radius. Second, the satellite also goes more slowly with a greater radius. One very useful sort of orbit is a **geosynchronous orbit,** which has a period of exactly 24 hours. A satellite in a geosynchronous orbit always stays above the same place at Earth's equator.

32 **SEP Use Mathematics** Using $v = \left(\frac{GM_E}{r}\right)^{\frac{1}{2}} = \frac{2\pi r}{T}$, show that $r = \left(\frac{GM_E T^2}{4\pi^2}\right)^{\frac{1}{3}}$.

33 **SEP Use Mathematics** Suppose that the radius of an orbit is doubled. Calculate the change to the period of the orbit.

Geosynchronous Orbits

Find how far above Earth's surface a satellite in a geosynchronous orbit must be.

1. DRAW A PICTURE Sketch a picture of the situation.

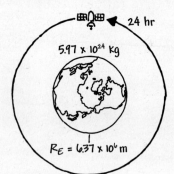

(Approximate the length of a day as 24 hours. A sidereal day, which will be defined soon, is closer to 23.934 hours.)

2. DEFINE THE PROBLEM List knowns and unknowns and assign values to variables.

$M_E = 5.97 \times 10^{24}$ kg $\quad h_{GS} = ?$

$R_E = 6.37 \times 10^6$ m $\quad r_{GS} = ?$

$T_{GS} = 24$ hours

$G = 6.67 \times 10^{-11}$ m^3/(kg·s^2)

3. PLAN AND EXECUTE Use mathematical relationships, the picture, and your definitions to plan and execute your solution.

Convert the geosynchronous period to seconds.

$$24 \text{ hours} \cdot \frac{60 \text{ minutes}}{\text{hour}} \cdot \frac{60 \text{ seconds}}{\text{minute}} = 86,400 \text{ s}$$

Substitute the period into the equation that relates radius and period, and solve for r.

$$r_{GS} = \left(\frac{GM_E T^2}{4\pi^2}\right)^{\frac{1}{3}}$$

$$= \left[\left(6.67 \times 10^{-11} \text{ m}^3/(\text{kg·s}^2)\right) \frac{(5.97 \times 10^{24} \text{ kg})}{4\pi^2} \cdot (86,400 \text{ s})^2\right]^{\frac{1}{3}}$$

$$= 4.22 \times 10^7 \text{ m}$$

Subtract Earth's radius to find how far above Earth's surface the orbit is.

$$h_{GS} = r_{GS} - R_E = 4.22 \times 10^7 \text{ m} - 6.4 \times 10^6 \text{ m} = 3.58 \times 10^7 \text{ m}$$

4. EVALUATE Reflect on your answer.

The distance of 35,800 km makes sense. It is much larger than Earth's radius, yet it is much smaller than the orbit of the moon.

 GO ONLINE for more **math support**.

▶ **Math Tutorial Video**

🖥 **Math Practice Problems**

---

(34) The moon's mass is 7.342×10^{22} kg, its radius is 1734 km, and its period of rotation is 27.32 days. How far above the surface of the moon would a satellite have to orbit to be synchronized with the moon's rotation?

📖 **NEED A HINT?** Go online to your **eText Sample Problem** for stepped out support.

(35) GPS (global positioning system) satellites have a very special mid-Earth orbit with a period that is exactly one half of geosynchronous orbit. GPS satellites orbit Earth twice a day instead of every day. Find the radius of such an orbit.

The Earth–Moon System

Earth's largest satellite is the moon, which is a rocky sphere with a diameter that is 27% of Earth's diameter and a mass 1.2% that of Earth. The moon orbits Earth with a special characteristic: its period of revolution around Earth (approximately 1 month) is exactly the same as its rotation around its axis, so the same side of the moon always faces Earth. The moon's elliptical orbit around Earth is close to a circle, but it varies enough that the apparent size of the moon seen from Earth fluctuates noticeably over time.

Because every action has an equal and opposite reaction, the moon pulls on Earth with the same force that Earth pulls on the moon. The result is that both bodies orbit around a single point called the *barycenter*. Because Earth is so much more massive than the moon, the location of the barycenter is actually within the radius of Earth. The moon's gravity causes tides on Earth (a slight stretching of the planet and a rise and fall of sea levels). Earth's gravity causes much greater tides on the moon, generating large numbers of moonquakes.

The Lunar Orbit The moon's elliptical orbit varies slightly from a circle. The moon is closest to Earth at perigee and farthest from Earth at apogee. The differences between those distances is more than 50,000 km.

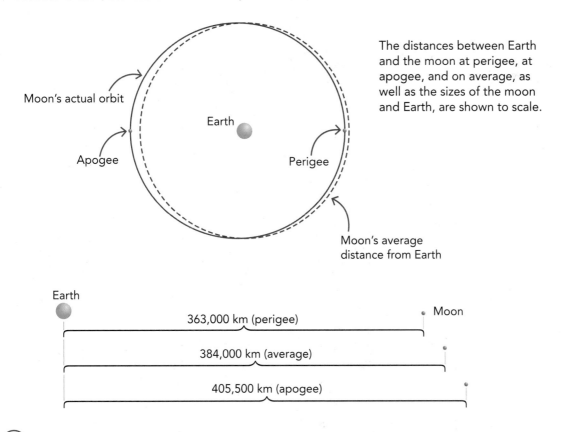

The distances between Earth and the moon at perigee, at apogee, and on average, as well as the sizes of the moon and Earth, are shown to scale.

Moon's actual orbit

Earth

Apogee

Perigee

Moon's average distance from Earth

Earth

363,000 km (perigee)

Moon

384,000 km (average)

405,500 km (apogee)

㊱ **CCC Scale, Proportion, and Quantity** Calculate the percent change in the apparent size of the moon from apogee to perigee, as observed from Earth.

㊲ **SEP Use Mathematics** Find the period of the moon's orbit around Earth, measured in both hours and days. (Use the equation for a circular orbit and the moon's mean orbital radius of 384,400 km.)

The Earth-Sun System

Earth makes one full rotation around its axis, with respect to the stars, in 84,164 seconds, or 23.934 hours. This is called a sidereal day. During this time, Earth has also traveled 1/365 of the way in its orbit around the sun, which takes one year. Earth has to rotate about 4 minutes more each day so that it can make up for its revolution around the sun. This allows the sun to appear at the same point in the sky each day. This day is called the synodic day, and it is exactly 24 hours, or 86,400 seconds.

Earth is 5 million km farther from the sun at the farthest point in its orbit, or aphelion, than it is at its closest point, or perihelion. However, Earth's seasons are the result of its tilted axis, not orbital eccentricity. Earth's axis is currently tilted 23.4° with respect to the ecliptic, the plane of Earth's orbit around the sun.

Earth's Seasons Earth is closest to the sun around January 4, during winter in the Northern Hemisphere.

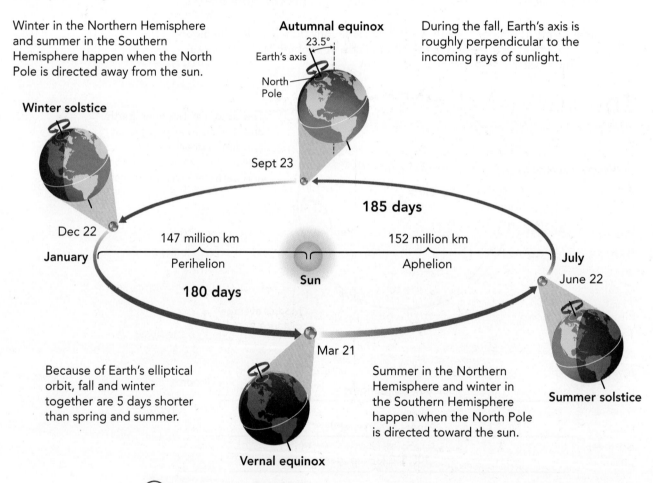

Winter in the Northern Hemisphere and summer in the Southern Hemisphere happen when the North Pole is directed away from the sun.

Autumnal equinox

23.5°

Earth's axis

North Pole

During the fall, Earth's axis is roughly perpendicular to the incoming rays of sunlight.

Winter solstice

Sept 23

185 days

Dec 22

January

147 million km

Perihelion

152 million km

Aphelion

July
June 22

Sun

180 days

Summer solstice

Mar 21

Because of Earth's elliptical orbit, fall and winter together are 5 days shorter than spring and summer.

Summer in the Northern Hemisphere and winter in the Southern Hemisphere happen when the North Pole is directed toward the sun.

Vernal equinox

(38) **SEP Develop and Use Models** Explain why Earth receives more energy from the sun during a day in the northern winter than during a day in the northern summer.

(39) **CCC Cause and Effect** Land reflects much more sunlight than ocean, which absorbs nearly all sunlight that hits it. Given that most of Earth's land is in the Northern Hemisphere, explain whether the entire planet absorbs more solar energy during northern winters or northern summers.

Phases of the Moon The half of the moon that faces the sun is brightly lit. The changing amounts of that lit face as seen from Earth are known as the phases of the moon. During new and full moons, all three bodies are lined up.

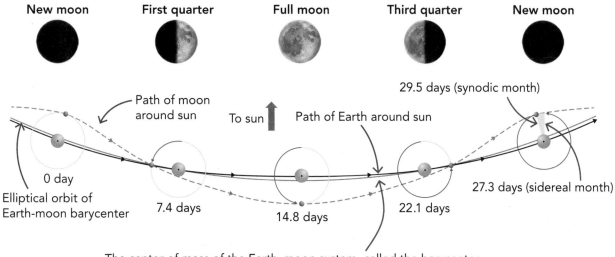

The center of mass of the Earth–moon system, called the barycenter, orbits the sun in an elliptical path. Both the moon and Earth wobble about the barycenter as they revolve around each other.

The Earth–Moon–Sun System

The moon's orbit around Earth and Earth's orbit around the sun are elliptical and slightly misaligned, so the three bodies do a continuous and complex dance around one another. Predicting phenomena such as tides, eclipses, and the phases of the moon requires a thorough understanding of that dance.

Phases of the Moon When the moon is between Earth and the sun, the sunlit face is the far side of the moon, and the new moon is entirely dark. Two weeks later, when Earth is in between the sun and the moon, nearly all of the moon's sunlit face is visible as the circle of the full moon.

Similar to the sidereal and synodic days, there are two ways to define a month. The moon takes 27.321661 days to make one full revolution with respect to the stars, and that is called the **sidereal month.** However, during that month, Earth travels about 7.5% of its orbit around the sun, so the moon must revolve a bit more to complete one cycle with respect to the sun and return to the same position in Earth's sky. As a result, the time from one new moon to the next new moon, which is known as the **synodic month,** is about 29.5 days. The moon's orbit around Earth and Earth's orbit around the sun are elliptical, and the elliptical orbits themselves rotate over time in a process called *precession*. The combined effects produce a synodic month that varies from 29.18 to 29.93 days.

40 **SEP Develop and Use Models** Explain why the number of sidereal months each year is one more than the number of synodic months.

41 **CCC Patterns** From what you know of the planet Venus, describe how the pattern of its path around the sun is different than Earth's path.

Lunar and Solar Eclipses When the Earth, sun, and moon align, an eclipse occurs. A **solar eclipse** occurs when the moon casts it shadow on Earth. A **lunar eclipse** is an event that occurs when Earth casts its shadow on the moon. Because Earth's shadow is much larger than the moon's, lunar eclipses are more common than solar eclipses. A **total eclipse** is an eclipse that occurs when the three bodies are perfectly lined up; a **partial eclipse** occurs when Earth or the moon only partly enters the other's shadow. You might expect eclipses to occur each month, but because of the tilt of the moon's orbit with respect to the ecliptic, eclipses are quite rare. By a remarkable coincidence, the moon and the sun are almost the same size when viewed from Earth. However, because of the eccentricity of the moon's orbit, there are two sorts of eclipses. A total solar eclipse is an eclipse that occurs when the moon is closer to Earth and totally blocks the sun. An **annular solar eclipse** occurs when the moon is farther from Earth. Then, a ring of sun can still be seen around the moon.

Eclipses and the Lunar Orbit Total eclipses are very rare. The plane of the moon's orbit around Earth is tilted by 5.15° with respect to the ecliptic, so during most months, the new and full moons are above or below the ecliptic. The three bodies do not line up, so there is no eclipse.

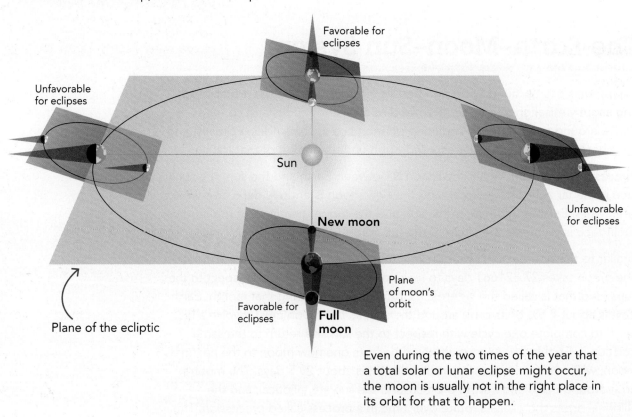

Favorable for eclipses

Unfavorable for eclipses

Sun

Unfavorable for eclipses

New moon

Plane of moon's orbit

Plane of the ecliptic

Favorable for eclipses

Full moon

Even during the two times of the year that a total solar or lunar eclipse might occur, the moon is usually not in the right place in its orbit for that to happen.

㊷ **CCC Systems and System Models** Explain what phase the moon must always be in for a lunar eclipse to occur.

㊸ **CCC Patterns** The moon's orbit always crosses the ecliptic plane in two places. However, at most times of the year, it is impossible to have an eclipse. Explain why.

Tides and Tidal Forces

What **causes solid and ocean tides** on Earth?

Tidal Factors Many factors affect Earth's tides, most importantly **the geography of Earth's surface** and **the gravitational forces of the sun and the moon.**

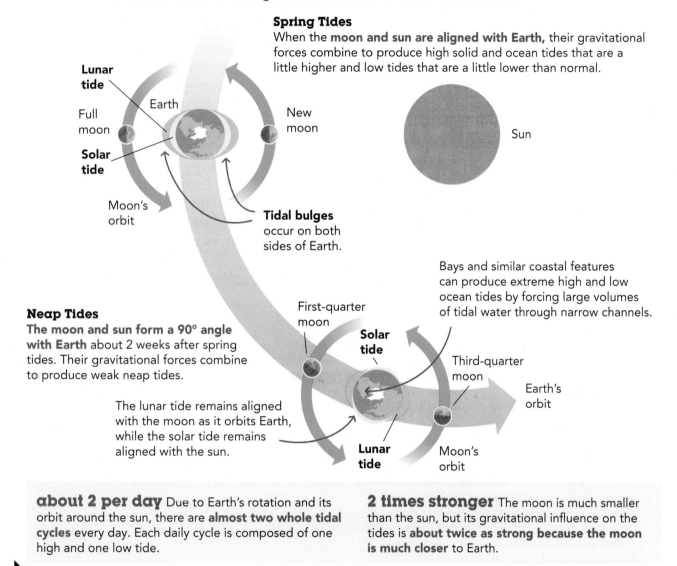

Spring Tides
When the **moon and sun are aligned with Earth,** their gravitational forces combine to produce high solid and ocean tides that are a little higher and low tides that are a little lower than normal.

Lunar tide

Full moon

Earth

New moon

Solar tide

Moon's orbit

Tidal bulges occur on both sides of Earth.

Sun

Bays and similar coastal features can produce extreme high and low ocean tides by forcing large volumes of tidal water through narrow channels.

Neap Tides
The moon and sun form a 90° angle with Earth about 2 weeks after spring tides. Their gravitational forces combine to produce weak neap tides.

The lunar tide remains aligned with the moon as it orbits Earth, while the solar tide remains aligned with the sun.

First-quarter moon

Solar tide

Third-quarter moon

Earth's orbit

Lunar tide

Moon's orbit

about 2 per day Due to Earth's rotation and its orbit around the sun, there are **almost two whole tidal cycles** every day. Each daily cycle is composed of one high and one low tide.

2 times stronger The moon is much smaller than the sun, but its gravitational influence on the tides is **about twice as strong because the moon is much closer** to Earth.

Tides The tidal stretching of Earth is due to differences in the strength of the moon's and sun's gravity on the near and far sides of Earth. The effect is less than 1 meter for the solid Earth, but ocean tides can be much larger because the flow of seawater is constrained by the contours of the coastline. If water from a broad bay flows into a narrow channel, ocean tides can be more than 10 meters high. Due to the friction of tides, Earth loses angular momentum, and its rotation is slowing—620 million years ago, Earth completed 400 daily rotations in a year, instead of 365. The moon, on the other hand, has gained angular momentum, and its orbit is now much farther from Earth than it was in the past.

44 **SEP Use Mathematics** Explain why spring high tides are generally about three times greater than neap high tides.

The Shape and Gravity of Earth

 GO ONLINE to do a PhET **simulation** to investigate orbital motion and to watch a **video** to explore tides.

Just as an apparent centrifugal force seems to pull you away from the center of a spinning carnival ride, Earth's rotation flattens the globe into a shape called an *oblate ellipsoid*. Earth's cross section is *also* an ellipse, like its orbit. The amount of flattening is what you would expect for a fluid body rotating once per day: the equator is 21 km farther from Earth's center than the poles are. Consequently, the point on Earth farthest from Earth's center is not Mt. Everest, but Mt. Chimborazo in Ecuador, which is at the equatorial bulge.

Earth's value of g also varies with latitude. It is least at the equator, 9.78 m/s^2, and greatest at the poles, 9.83 m/s^2. There are two factors contributing to the difference. First, points at the equator are farther from the center, and gravity decreases as the inverse square of that distance. Second, the reactive centripetal acceleration, or centrifugal force, from Earth's rotation is also greatest at the equator. The international reference gravity formula combines the two effects, expressing gravity as a function of latitude, q.

$$g(q) \approx 9.780327 \, [1 + 0.0052792 \sin^2(q) + 0.0000232 \sin^4(q)]$$

Effect of Rotation on Earth's Shape If Earth did not rotate, its radius would be 6,371.01 km, but the rotation stretches Earth into an oblate ellipsoid. Earth's radius is 7 km greater all around the equator and 14 km smaller at the North Pole and South Pole.

Down, the direction of gravity, is always perpendicular to the tangent to Earth's surface. Earth's ellipsoidal shape means that, anywhere except at the equator and poles, Earth's gravity does not pull you toward the center of the planet, but to a point slightly closer to the equator.

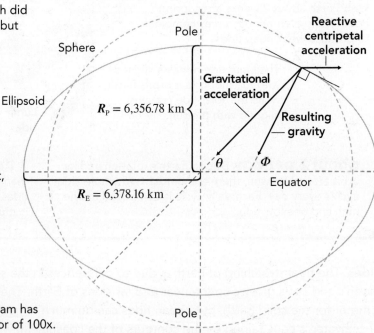

The eccentricity in this diagram has been exaggerated by a factor of 100x.

(45) **SEP Use Mathematics** Suppose you measure your weight at the equator and find it is 650 newtons. Calculate how much you would weigh at the North Pole.

(46) **SEP Use Mathematics** Use vector addition to show that, in the diagram, the resulting gravity is the sum of the gravitational acceleration and the reactive centripetal acceleration.

INVESTIGATIVE PHENOMENON

GO ONLINE to revisit your **Investigative Phenomenon CER** with the new information you have learned about Orbital Motion.

These questions will help you apply what you learned in this experience to the Investigative Phenomenon.

(47) **SEP Use Mathematics** Calculate the instantaneous velocity with which the moon is orbiting Earth.

(48) **SEP Develop and Use Models** Earth completes one complete rotation with respect to the stars in 23 hours, 56 minutes, and 4 seconds. Explain why this sidereal day is not exactly 24 hours.

(49) **SEP Use Mathematics** Jupiter's mass is 1.898×10^{27} kg, its radius is 69,911 km, and its rotational period is 9.925 hours. Using those data, calculate how far above Jupiter's surface a satellite in synchronous orbit would have to be.

(50) **SEP Use Mathematics** Use the international reference gravity formula to show that g at both the North Pole and the South Pole is 9.832 m/s.

(51) **SEP Obtain and Communicate Information** The acceleration of gravity is approximated as 9.81 m/s^2 at Earth's surface. Find the latitude of your school and then use the international reference gravity formula to calculate g for that latitude at sea level. How close to 9.81 is it?

(52) **SEP Develop and Use Models** Knowing the latitude of your school, calculate the height that the sun reaches in the sky at noon on the summer solstice and on the winter solstice.

GO ONLINE for a **quiz** to evaluate what you learned about Orbital Motion.

EXPERIENCE 3

Kepler's Laws

GO ONLINE to do a **hands-on lab** to model and explore elliptical planetary motion.

Kepler's First Law

EXPERIENCE IT!

Carefully draw or trace a circle on a piece of paper and set it on a flat surface. Look at it from different angles, including edge-on and directly from above. How does the shape of the circle appear to change as your point of view changes?

Defining an Ellipse Every orbiting object follows an elliptical path. The object orbited is located not at the center of the ellipse, however, but at a point called the focus. That fact is called Kepler's first law, named for the astronomer who first discovered it in 1605. An **ellipse** is an oval shape with this equation:

Ellipse Equation
$$\frac{x^2}{a^2} + \frac{y^2}{b^2} = 1$$
a = semimajor axis b = semiminor axis

Properties of an Ellipse The length of an ellipse is the major axis, and the width is the minor axis. Half of the length, a, is the semimajor axis, and half of the width, b, is the semiminor axis.

In this example, $a = 7$ and $b = 3$, so the equation for the ellipse is $\frac{x^2}{49} + \frac{y^2}{9} = 1$.

An ellipse can be drawn by pinning the ends of a string at both foci and keeping the string taut.

The two foci are at $(c, 0)$ and $(-c, 0)$, where $c = \sqrt{a^2 - b^2}$. For this ellipse, $c = \sqrt{7^2 - 3^2} = \sqrt{40}$.

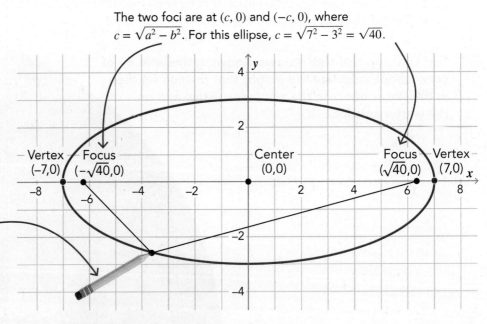

(53) **SEP Use Mathematics** Draw an ellipse with the center at the origin, $a = 5$, and $b = 4$, assuming that both foci are along the x-axis. Write the equation and compute the location of each focus.

(54) **SEP Use Mathematics** For the previous problem, suppose that the sun is at one focus. Compute the locations of aphelion and perihelion.

142   Investigation 3 Gravitational Forces

Eccentricity of Orbits The degree to which an orbit's elliptical shape is flattened is called the **eccentricity.** The eccentricity ranges from 0 to 1.

Ellipse Eccentricity
$$e = \sqrt{\left(1 - \frac{b^2}{a^2}\right)}$$
a = semimajor axis $\quad$ b = semiminor axis $\quad$ e = eccentricity

An orbit that is nearly circular has an eccentricity close to 0, and an orbit that is extremely flattened has an eccentricity close to 1. The orbits of most planets in the solar system are nearly circular, so they have very low eccentricities. Some planets observed around other stars, however, have highly eccentric orbits. Smaller solar system bodies, such as asteroids and comets, often have highly eccentric orbits. Comets are mostly found at the outer edges of the solar system, part of a vast collection of millions of small icy bodies called the Oort cloud. The Oort cloud is hundreds to thousands of times farther from the sun than Earth. Comets, which are visible when they come close to the sun, have very eccentric orbits.

Orbits of Solar System Objects The eccentricities of solar system objects vary greatly. Most planets, with the exception of Mercury, have nearly circular orbits and low eccentricities. Many asteroids, such as Icarus, and comets, such as Halley, have very eccentric orbits.

The orbits are ellipses, and the sun is located at one of the foci.

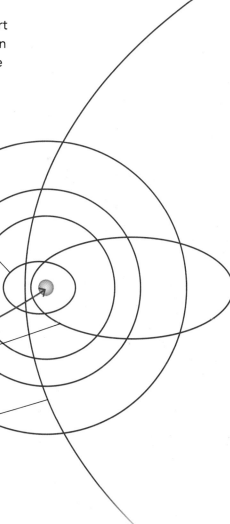

Mercury
$e = 0.21$

Venus
$e = 0.01$

Earth
$e = 0.02$

Mars
$e = 0.09$

Icarus
$e = 0.83$

Halley
$e = 0.97$

VOCABULARY

The word **eccentric** (from Greek *ekkentros*, from *ek* 'out of' + *kentron* 'center') generally refers to unconventional or strange behavior. In geometry, it refers to circles with centers that do not coincide. An *eccentric orbit* does not coincide with the geometric center of the orbital path.

55 **CCC Patterns** In the solar system, there are no planets with highly eccentric orbits. Construct an explanation for why that might be so.

56 **SEP Use Mathematics** Earth has a cross–section that is elliptical, with its major axis in the plane of the equator and its minor axis from pole to pole. Use those axes to compute the eccentricity of Earth's shape and how far each focus is from Earth's center.

Kepler's Second Law

A planet's speed in orbit is not constant; the planet moves fastest when it is closest to the sun and slowest when it is farthest away. As Kepler's second law expresses the relation, the line from a planet to the sun sweeps out equal areas of an ellipse during equal times. A planet's instantaneous velocity can always be calculated from the following relation:

Instantaneous Velocity of an Object in an Elliptical Orbit

$$v = \left[GM\left(\frac{2}{r} - \frac{1}{a}\right) \right]^{\frac{1}{2}}$$

v = instantaneous velocity of orbiting object
r = distance between two bodies
a = semimajor axis
G = gravitational constant
M = mass of the object being orbited

The time from Earth's fall equinox to its spring equinox is about 5 days shorter than the time from the spring equinox to the fall equinox. Earth is closest to the sun at its perihelion, which is about January 4, so Kepler's second law tells you that it travels faster in its orbit during the fall and winter.

The effect of Kepler's second law is more noticeable for more eccentric orbits. Mercury swings past the sun fast enough that the same side of the planet faces the sun for most of its time near perihelion. However, the planet slows down enough that it does half a rotation during its slow aphelion swing. Then, the opposite side of Mercury faces the sun as it swings through the next perihelion.

Kepler's Second Law A planet in an elliptical orbit sweeps out equal parts of the area of an ellipse during equal time intervals. The points along the ellipse are equally spaced in time, and all of the eight shaded regions have the same area.

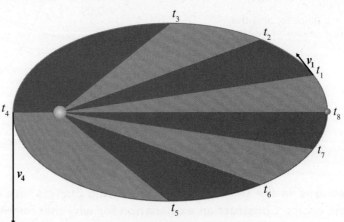

The vectors show the instantaneous velocity of the planet at two points in its orbit. Notice that its velocity is greater when the planet is closer to the sun.

 SEP Use Mathematics For Earth's orbit around the sun, the semimajor axis is 149.60 × 10⁶ km, the distance at perihelion is 147.10 × 10⁶ km, and the distance at aphelion is 152.10 × 10⁶ km. Calculate how much faster Earth is moving in its orbit at perihelion than at aphelion.

Milankovitch Cycles

How does **Earth's orbit change** over time?

Factors Influencing Earth's Orbit Earth's **orbit does not remain constant** over long periods of time. Many **other objects exert gravitational forces on Earth,** primarily Jupiter, Saturn, Venus, and Mars. This causes long-term periodic changes to Earth's orbital parameters of **obliquity, axial precession, and orbital precession.** These cycles were first discovered by the Serbian geophysicist Milutin Milanković in the 1920s.

The shape of Earth's orbit, known as **eccentricity,** changes over a cycle spanning between 100,000 and 400,000 years.*

Future orbit

Current orbit

* Not to scale

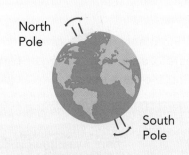

Earth's tilt, or **obliquity,** changes over a cycle of about 41,000 years from 22.1° to 24.5° relative to a line perpendicular to its orbital plane. Currently, Earth's tilt is approximately 23.5°.

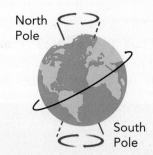

The direction of Earth's axis changes over a cycle spanning about 26,000 years, known as **axial precession.** This means the North Pole will not always point to Polaris, the "North Star."

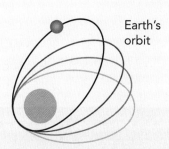

The orientation of Earth's orbit relative to the fixed stars in the sky also slowly changes over a cycle of about 112,000 years. This is known as **orbital precession.**

58 **SEP Analyze Data** Examine the graph of Earth's temperatures. Over the past 2 million years, ice ages have correlated with the 41,000-yr obliquity cycle or the 100,000-yr eccentricity cycle. Determine the difference in the range of variation of average global temperatures during those two periods.

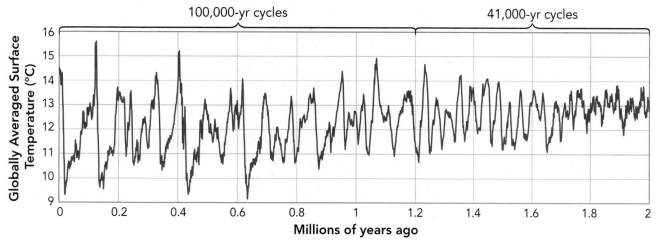

Based on Hansen J, et al., 2013 *Climate sensitivity, sea level and atmospheric carbon dioxide.* Phil Trans R Soc A 371: 20120294

Kepler's Third Law

 GO ONLINE to do a PhET **simulation** and to watch a **video** to investigate Kepler's laws.

The period of a circular orbit is a function only of the radius. Kepler's third law extends that relation to noncircular orbits, replacing the radius of a circle with the semimajor axis of an ellipse. Kepler lived before Newton, so he didn't know about gravity. He knew that the ratio $a^3{:}T^2$ was constant, but he didn't yet know what the constant value was.

Period of an Elliptical Orbit
$$T^2 = 4\pi^2\left(\frac{a^3}{GM}\right) \qquad T = 2\pi\left(\frac{a^3}{GM}\right)^{\frac{1}{2}}$$
T = period of the orbit $\qquad a$ = semimajor axis G = gravitational constant $\quad M$ = mass of the orbited object

Weighing the Sun The ratio $a^3{:}T^2$ for all orbiting planets is $\frac{GM_S}{4\pi^2}$, which is proportional to the mass of the sun, M_S. Therefore, from the shape of Earth's orbit and the length of Earth's year, you can find the sun's mass.

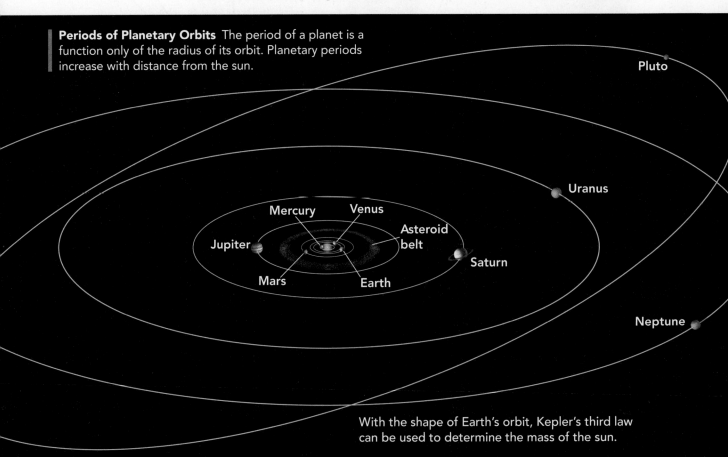

Periods of Planetary Orbits The period of a planet is a function only of the radius of its orbit. Planetary periods increase with distance from the sun.

With the shape of Earth's orbit, Kepler's third law can be used to determine the mass of the sun.

59 **SEP Use Mathematics** Suppose the semimajor axis of a satellite's orbit is increased by a factor of 10. Calculate the increase in its period.

Measuring Distances to the Planets Kepler's third law also applies to many other planetary objects and orbits. For example, because the ratio $a^3 : T^2$ is the same for all planets, knowing a planet's period allows you to calculate its distance from the sun. All you need is a telescope powerful enough to track the path of the planet and measure the period of its orbit. Distances to the planets are typically measured in astronomical units (AU)—one AU is the length of Earth's semimajor axis, or 149.60 million kilometers. Planetary orbits range from Mercury's, with a radius 0.39 AU and a period of 88.0 Earth days, to Neptune's, with a radius of 30.1 AU and a period of 164.8 Earth years. Comets in the Oort cloud can be as far away from the sun as 200,000 AU.

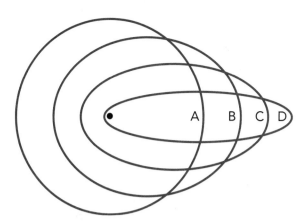

Orbits With Equal Periods The shapes of these orbits are very different, but they all have the same semimajor axis, and they all revolve around the same mass. Therefore, Kepler's third law tells you that they all have the same period.

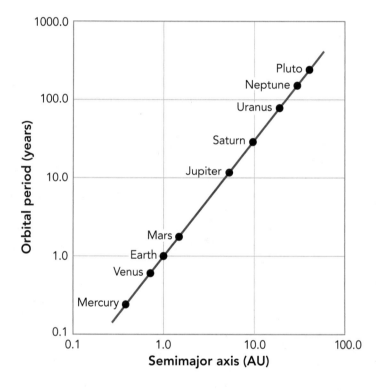

Kepler's Third Law for the Planets A log-log graph compares the periods of planetary orbits (and the orbit of the dwarf planet Pluto) to their semimajor axes. Because the ratio $a^3 : T^2$ is constant, the plot forms a line with a slope equal to the ratio of the exponents, which is 3:2.

Weighing the Planets If a planet has moons, then you can use Kepler's third law to find the mass of the planet. First, use a telescope to measure the radii and periods of the orbits of the moons. Then, calculate the mass of the planet, M_P, using the relation $\frac{a^3}{T^2} = \frac{GM_P}{2\pi}$. It is from the orbits of Jupiter's moons that we know Jupiter's mass to be the largest of the planets, 318 times greater than Earth's. Jupiter contains approximately 70% of all of the mass of the solar system that isn't in the sun.

60 **CCC Patterns** In the graph of the different ellipses that share the same period, describe the patterns you observe in their shapes.

61 **SEP Analyze and Interpret Data** Suppose a comet in the Oort cloud has a semimajor axis of 200,000 AU. Calculate the period of its orbit in Earth years.

Jupiter's Distance From the Sun

Jupiter has an orbital period of 4333 Earth days. Find the semimajor axis of its orbit. Remember that the mass of the sun is 1.988×10^{30} kg.

1. DRAW A PICTURE Sketch a picture of the situation.

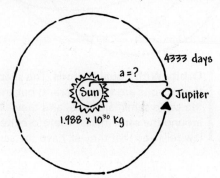

2. DEFINE THE PROBLEM List knowns and unknowns and assign values to variables.

$M = 1.988 \times 10^{30}$ kg $\qquad a = ?$

$T = 4333$ days

$G = 6.674 \times 10^{-11}$ m³/(kg·s²)

3. PLAN AND EXECUTE Use mathematical relationships, the picture, and your definitions to plan and execute your solution.

Convert Jupiter's orbital period to seconds.

$$4333 \text{ days}\left(\frac{86{,}400 \text{ seconds}}{1 \text{ day}}\right) = 3.744 \times 10^{8} \text{ s}$$

Substitute the period into the equation that relates semimajor axis and period, and solve for *a*.

$$a = \left(\frac{GMT^2}{4\pi^2}\right)^{\frac{1}{3}}$$

$$= \left[(6.674 \times 10^{-11} \text{ m}^3/(\text{kg·s}^2)) \frac{(1.988 \times 10^{30} \text{ kg})}{4\pi^2} \cdot (3.744 \times 10^{8} \text{ s})^2\right]^{\frac{1}{3}}$$

$$= (4.711 \times 10^{35} \text{ m}^3)^{\frac{1}{3}}$$

$$= 7.781 \times 10^{11} \text{ m}$$

4. EVALUATE Reflect on your answer.

The distance of 778.1 million km makes sense. It is much larger than Earth's orbit around the sun.

 GO ONLINE for more **math support**.

▶ **Math Tutorial Video**

🖥 **Math Practice Problems**

62 Saturn has an orbital period of 10,759 Earth days. Find the semimajor axis of its orbit.

📖 **NEED A HINT?** Go online to your **eText Sample Problem** for stepped out support.

63 Phobos, one of Mars's moons, has an orbital period of 0.3189 days and a semimajor axis of 9376 km. Use those data to calculate the mass of Mars.

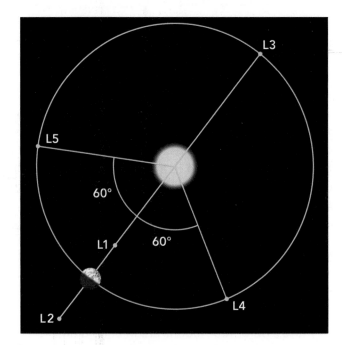

Earth's Lagrange Points Earth's five Lagrange points are L1, L2, and L3, along the line that connects the sun and Earth, and L4 and L5, which are 60° ahead of and behind Earth in its orbit. The figure is not to scale, since L1 is really located only 1.5 million kilometers from Earth.

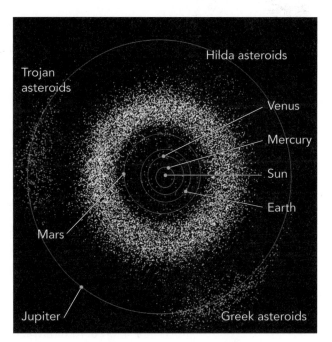

Greeks and Trojans Because of Jupiter's large mass, it has captured many asteroids around its L4 and L5 Lagrange points. Those asteroids, called Greeks and Trojans, are on opposing sides of Jupiter, 60° ahead of and 60° behind the planet in its orbit. Other SSSBs, called Hildas, move among the L3, L4, and L5 points.

Lagrange Points of Gravitational Stability

When the gravitational fields of three or more bodies are considered, the dynamics get much more complicated. For a planet orbiting the sun, there are five stable gravitational points, called Lagrange points. Natural small solar system bodies (SSSBs) or human-made satellites that reach those regions can remain there for long periods of time.

For example, the L1 Lagrange point for Earth sits at the neutral point between Earth and the sun, analogous to the neutral point you observed for Earth and the moon previously. Without Earth, an object at L1 would orbit faster than Earth does, because it is closer to the sun. With Earth, however, that object is trapped between the gravity fields of Earth and the sun. Several NASA satellites have been located at L1, such as the Solar and Heliospheric Observatory. Earth's L2 Lagrange point, on the side of Earth that faces away from the sun, is a good location for satellite telescopes that observe deep space, always pointing away from Earth and avoiding sunlight, such as NASA's Wilkinson Microwave Anisotropy Probe (WMAP).

All of the large planets have trapped many SSSBs near their Lagrange points, but none more than Neptune.

 SEP Develop a Model Imagining that the location of L1 actually was drawn to scale, create a drawing of the combined Earth-sun gravity field lines using the diagram of the Earth-moon gravity system from Universal Gravitation as a guide.

Orbital Resonance

A common and geologically important phenomenon within the solar system is for systems of bodies to lock into resonance. **Orbital resonance** is a situation in which there are integer ratios among the periods of either revolutions only or of both revolutions and rotations of orbiting bodies. For example, you know that the rotation and revolution of Earth's moon are in a 1:1 resonance. The moon makes one rotation around its axis for each revolution around Earth, so the same side of the moon always faces Earth. For Mercury, the rotation and revolution are in a 3:2 resonance.

Resonance also results in gaps in the asteroid belt, called Kirkwood gaps, where asteroids with simple fractions of Jupiter's period, for instance, $\frac{1}{2}$, $\frac{1}{4}$, $\frac{2}{3}$, and so on, are gravitationally unstable. They are flung out of the asteroid belt, leaving gaps. Many other bodies are in near-resonant orbits. Earth and Venus are in an 8:13 near-resonance, Pluto's outer four moons are in 3:4:5:6 near-resonances, and many trans-Neptunian bodies are near a 2:3 resonance with Neptune's period. Over time, such orbits may evolve into resonant orbits. In addition, many of the planets around other stars observed by NASA's Kepler Telescope are in resonant orbits within their solar systems.

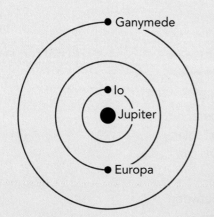

Resonance of Jupiter's Moons The three large inner moons of Jupiter—Io, Europa, and Ganymede—are locked in a 4:2:1 orbital resonance. Io orbits 4 times for every 2 orbits of Europa and 1 orbit of Ganymede. The resonance among the moons and Jupiter causes tidal stretching within them that generates a significant amount of heat.

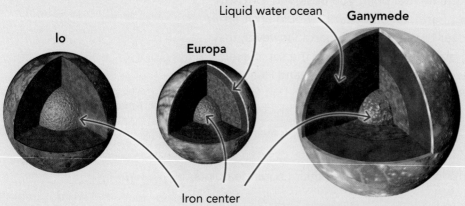

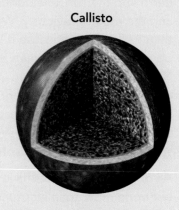

Io is the most volcanically active body in the solar system, with more than 400 volcanoes active at any given time.

The tidal heat has allowed the material of the moons to separate out into individual layers, including liquid water oceans on Europa and Ganymede.

The other large moon of Jupiter, Callisto, is not in a resonant orbit. The interior of Callisto has not been heated enough to stratify.

Resonance and Tidal Heating When two or more orbiting objects go into a resonant orbit, their orbits stretch out and become more eccentric. The result is to gravitationally destabilize the orbits of objects nearby and also to produce large tidal stresses within them. This can determine the geology of moons. The best example is the 4:2:1 orbital resonance of the 3 large inner moons of Jupiter—Io, Europa, and Ganymede. The extreme volcanic activity on Io and liquid saltwater oceans on Europa and Ganymede are likely results of the orbital resonance. Another example is the geysers of ice that shoot out of Saturn's moon Enceladus, the result of internal tidal heating from a 2:1 orbital resonance with another of Saturn's moons, Dione.

Late Heavy Bombardment The single most important instance of orbital resonance may have occurred around 3.9 billion years ago, when the periods of Jupiter and Saturn apparently drifted into a 2:1 orbital resonance. That resonance gravitationally destabilized and reorganized the entire solar system. It pushed Uranus and Neptune outward, removed most of the asteroid belt, pushed the Kuiper belt away from the sun, and sent asteroids crashing into the inner planets, erasing parts of their surfaces.

Late Heavy Bombardment About 3.9 billion years ago, there was a violent period of large impacts called the late heavy bombardment. All of the large impact basins on the moon, Mars, and Mercury formed during this bombardment.

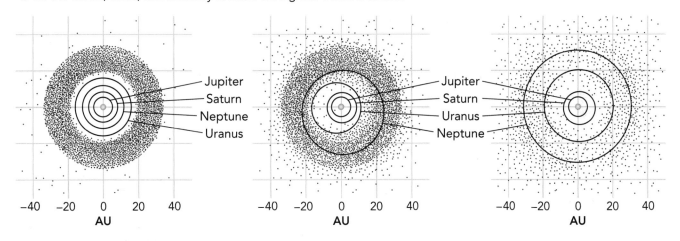

Early in the history of the solar system, all four large planets — Jupiter, Saturn, Neptune, and Uranus— were much closer to the sun, and there were large numbers of smaller bodies just beyond them.

When the periods of Jupiter and Saturn became resonant, their orbits became increasingly eccentric, distorting the orbits of Neptune and Uranus and flinging them farther from the sun.

The eccentric orbits flung most smaller bodies either out of the solar system or to the outer regions, where they formed the Kuiper belt and the Oort Cloud. Note that the order of the planets Uranus and Neptune has reversed.

65) **CCC Scale, Proportion, and Quantity** The periods of the four inner Galilean moons, in Earth days, are 1.769 for Io, 3.551 for Europa, 7.155 for Ganymede, and 16.689 for Callisto. Show that the first three are in orbital resonance with one another, but not with Callisto.

66) **CCC Scale, Proportion, and Quantity** Find the period of the planet Venus's orbit around the sun and show that Earth and Venus are nearly, but not exactly, in an 8:13 orbital resonance.

INVESTIGATIVE PHENOMENON

GO ONLINE to revisit your **Investigative Phenomenon CER** with the new information you have learned about Kepler's Laws.

These questions will help you apply what you learned in this experience to the Investigative Phenomenon.

67 **CCC Patterns** Any location on Earth's surface will receive different amounts of energy from the sun over the course of one day over the course of a year. Explain the two different factors that contribute to this.

68 **SEP Construct Explanations** The shape of Earth's orbit does not play a significant role in affecting the occurrence of seasons. However, the shape of Mars's orbit does play an important role in determining its seasons. Use the difference in the eccentricities of their orbits (Earth: 0.0167; Mars: 0.0934) to explain this.

69 **SEP Use Mathematics** The location of the Lagrange point L1, as a percentage of the distance from the orbiting body, can be approximated as $D = 100\% \times \sqrt[3]{\frac{M_2}{3M_1}}$. For the Earth–moon and sun–Earth systems, find the locations of L1 (as a percentage of the distance) to complete this table.

System	M_1 (mass of object being orbited)	M_2 (mass of orbiting object)	Distance Percentage
Sun–Earth	1.989×10^{30} kg (sun)	5.9722×10^{24} kg (Earth)	
Earth–moon	5.9722×10^{24} kg (Earth)	7.348×10^{22} kg (moon)	

70 **SEP Develop and Use Models** At high latitudes in the Northern Hemisphere, the sun is highest in the sky at the summer solstice, in June. For a location at the equator, determine when the sun is highest in the sky (directly overhead) and explain why.

GO ONLINE
for a **quiz** to evaluate what you learned about Kepler's Laws.

These questions will help you apply what you learned in this investigation to the Anchoring Phenomenon.

71 **SEP Construct an Explanation** Explain what would happen to the tidal force exerted by the moon on Earth if the moon were twice its mass. Apply Newton's law of universal gravitation to support your explanation.

72 **CCC Cause and Effect** In this investigation, you learned that there are almost two complete tidal cycles on Earth each day. How do you think this periodic change in water level might affect the shape of a coastline?

☑ INVESTIGATION ASSESSMENT

 GO ONLINE for activities that will give you an opportunity to **demonstrate what you have learned:**

☑ **Science Performance-Based Assessment** Model the causes of seasons.

📄 **Engineering Workbench** Determine the optimal fuel mixture to propel a model rocket.

💻 **Career Connections** Learn about how an astronaut applies knowledge of physics.

☑ **Investigation Test** Take this test to demonstrate your understanding of gravitational forces.

☑ **Virtual Lab Performance-Based Assessment** Analyze factors that affect the orbit of a satellite.

GO ONLINE to engage with real-world phenomena by watching a **phenomenon video** and completing a **modeling worksheet**.

Why can't we **walk** through walls?

Electric Forces

Atoms are composed of electrons whizzing around a central nucleus of protons and neutrons. The radius of an atom is more than 10,000 times larger than the radius of its tiny nucleus. That means the volume of empty space in an atom is 1 trillion times larger than the volume of the particles that make up the atom!

Like the atoms that it is made of, your body is mostly empty space. Yet, everything about you seems very solid. When you sit in a chair, you don't fall through the chair. When you stand on a floor, you don't fall through the floor.

Why is it that you do not fall through a chair or the floor? Why is it that you cannot effortlessly climb walls, but geckos can? Answering these questions requires an understanding of electric forces and the particle-level interactions that are a result of these electric forces.

1. **SEP Ask Questions** You have learned that atoms contain positive and negative charges and that like charges repel and opposite charges attract. Most atoms have equal numbers of positive and negative charges. What questions could you ask about what happens when two solids, such as you and a wall, get very close together?

2. **SEP Develop a Model** If you rub a balloon on a sweater and bring the balloon close to a wall, the balloon sometimes sticks. Sketch a free-body diagram to model this phenomenon.

EXPERIENCE 1

Coulomb's Law

 GO ONLINE to do a **hands-on lab** to investigate the factors that affect the magnitude of the electric force between charges.

Electric Charge

EXPERIENCE IT!

Charge two strips of tape as shown. See how the strips interact with each other and with different objects, such as hair, clothing, and balloons.

Electric charge is a physical property of matter that causes it to experience an electric force. Two charged objects experience a force when brought near each other, similar to the gravitational force two masses experience. Unlike mass, electric charge can be one of two types, positive and negative. Having two types of charge results in two types of interactions. Like charges (i.e., charges that are alike) repel each other. Opposite charges attract each other.

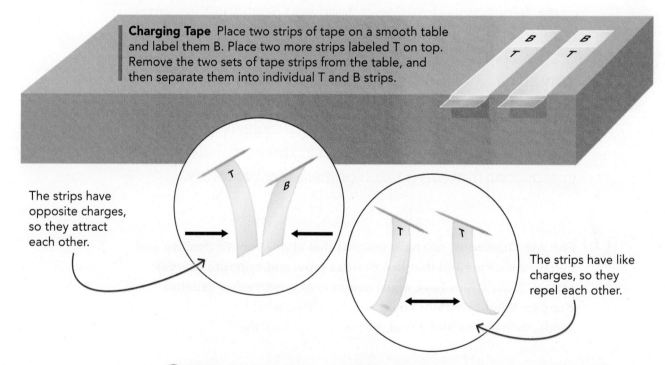

Charging Tape Place two strips of tape on a smooth table and label them B. Place two more strips labeled T on top. Remove the two sets of tape strips from the table, and then separate them into individual T and B strips.

The strips have opposite charges, so they attract each other.

The strips have like charges, so they repel each other.

(3) **SEP Interpret Data** The table shows interactions between the two types of tape strips, a negatively charged balloon, and a positively charged wool sweater. Using the data in the table, determine the charge on the top and bottom tapes.

	Top Strip	Bottom Strip	Balloon	Wool
Top Strip	Repel	Attract	Repel	Attract
Bottom Strip	Attract	Repel	Attract	Repel

Electrons, Protons, and Neutrons

In the Bohr model of the atom, negatively charged electrons orbit a nucleus composed of positively charged protons and uncharged neutrons. Electric force keeps the atom together, much as gravitational force keeps the moon orbiting Earth. The strong nuclear force keeps the nucleus from blowing apart. When you charge a macroscopic object, you are adding or removing electrons. The SI unit for electric charge (q) is called the **coulomb** (C).

Unit Charges
charge (q) of electron $= -e = -1.60 \times 10^{-19}$ C
charge (q) of proton $= +e = +1.60 \times 10^{-19}$ C

VOCABULARY

The SI unit called the **coulomb** is named after physicist Charles-Augustin de Coulomb. He discovered the relationships between electric force, charge, and distance between charged objects.

Bohr Model of the Atom Negatively charged electrons whizz around the positively charged nucleus. There are 6.24×10^{18} electrons in 1 coulomb of charge!

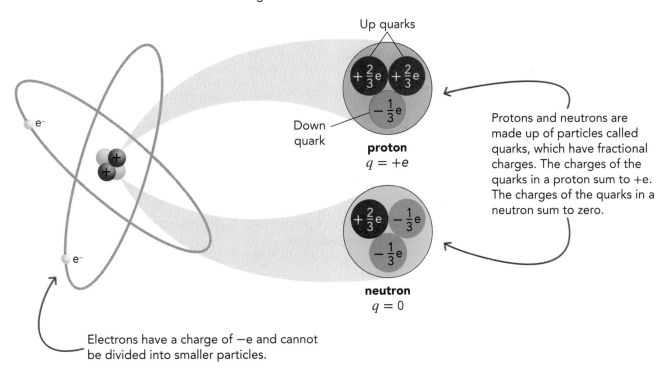

Up quarks

Down quark

proton
$q = +e$

neutron
$q = 0$

Protons and neutrons are made up of particles called quarks, which have fractional charges. The charges of the quarks in a proton sum to +e. The charges of the quarks in a neutron sum to zero.

Electrons have a charge of −e and cannot be divided into smaller particles.

(4) **SEP Develop a Model** When you peel two strips of tape apart, you transfer something from one strip to the other. What do you think is transferred? Sketch a model for the bottom and top strips as they are separated, and include the transfer.

(5) **SEP Argue from Evidence** Construct an argument from evidence for the claim that all the charges that you experience in your day-to-day life are produced by the removal or addition of electrons.

Electric Force

Coulomb's Law The magnitude of the electric force between two charged objects is represented mathematically by **Coulomb's law.** The electric force is proportional to the product of the charges and is inversely proportional to the square of the distance between the charges. The constant of proportionality, k_e, is called the **Coulomb constant.** The letter q represents the quantity of charge.

Coulomb's Law (Magnitude)

$$F_e = k_e \frac{|q_1 q_2|}{r_{12}^2}$$

F_e = magnitude of electric force
$k_e = 8.99 \times 10^9 \ \text{N·m}^2/\text{C}^2$
q_1 = charge of object 1

q_2 = charge of object 2
r_{12} = distance between objects 1 and 2

Electric Force The paired vectors represent the interaction between two charged objects. For like charges, the vectors point away from each other. For opposite charges, they point toward each other.

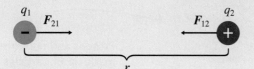

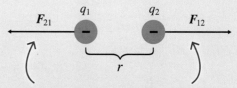

Note the subscripts. These are third-law pairs.

Electric force is a vector. To model the electric force on a particular object, you draw a free-body diagram of the object. The direction of the electric force vector acting on the object is determined by the charges of both objects and by the coordinate system you define.

Modeling a Hydrogen Atom A hydrogen atom typically consists of one electron orbiting one proton. Coulomb's law determines the electric force on the electron.

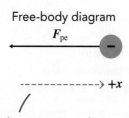

Free-body diagram

In this coordinate system, the positive direction is to the right, so the force acts in the negative direction.

Proton, $q = +e$

Electron, $q = -e$

5.29×10^{-11} m

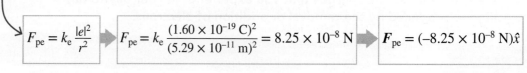

$$F_{pe} = k_e \frac{|e|^2}{r^2} \quad\blacktriangleright\quad F_{pe} = k_e \frac{(1.60 \times 10^{-19} \ \text{C})^2}{(5.29 \times 10^{-11} \ \text{m})^2} = 8.25 \times 10^{-8} \ \text{N} \quad\blacktriangleright\quad F_{pe} = (-8.25 \times 10^{-8} \ \text{N})\hat{x}$$

GO ONLINE to do a PhET **simulation** and to watch a **video** about Coulomb's law.

Force and Distance Like universal gravitation, electric force is inversely proportional to the square of the distance between charged particles. Increasing the distance between particles by a factor of 2 reduces the force to $\frac{1}{4}$ its value.

Inverse-Square Law				
Distance	r	$2r$	$3r$	$4r$
Force	F	$\frac{F}{4}$	$\frac{F}{9}$	$\frac{F}{16}$

The magnitude of the force decreases by the square of the distance.

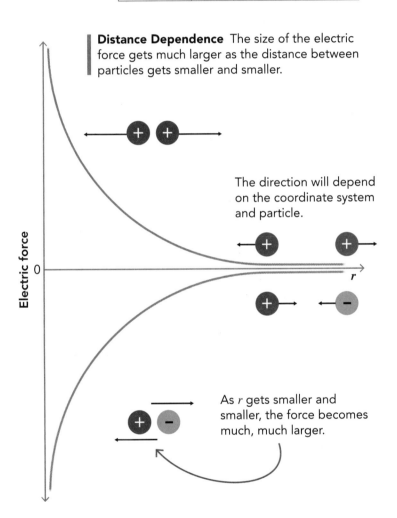

Distance Dependence The size of the electric force gets much larger as the distance between particles gets smaller and smaller.

The direction will depend on the coordinate system and particle.

As r gets smaller and smaller, the force becomes much, much larger.

Electroscope Charge on the comb induces charge on the electroscope leaves, which repel each other and move apart.

(6) **SEP Ask Questions** If opposite charges experience greater and greater attraction as they get closer, what questions can you ask about the attraction between a charged rubber balloon and a sweater?

(7) **SEP Use Mathematics** If the distance between two charges is increased by a factor of five, how much does the force between the charges increase or decrease?

Electric Force and Vectors

The superposition principle is used to model a system with more than two charged objects. For three charged objects, the force on each object can be determined by drawing a free-body diagram. Each free-body diagram has two forces. The net force on one object is the sum of the two forces acting on that object.

To stay organized, it is helpful to use the subscript system learned in a previous investigation. The force F_{12} represents the force exerted by particle 1 on particle 2, and the force F_{21} represents the force exerted by particle 2 on particle 1.

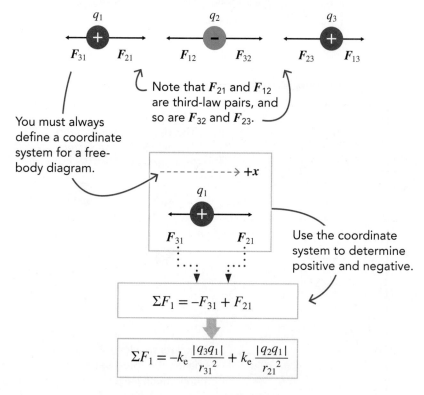

Superposition The principle of superposition is used to add all of the forces acting on q_1.

Note that F_{21} and F_{12} are third-law pairs, and so are F_{32} and F_{23}.

You must always define a coordinate system for a free-body diagram.

Use the coordinate system to determine positive and negative.

$$\Sigma F_1 = -F_{31} + F_{21}$$

$$\Sigma F_1 = -k_e \frac{|q_3 q_1|}{r_{31}^2} + k_e \frac{|q_2 q_1|}{r_{21}^2}$$

Which Way? The signs on the post are similar to vector representations. They show a direction and a magnitude.

8 **SEP Systems and System Models** You look at a classmate's notes and see the following equation: $\Sigma F_2 = F_{12} - F_{32} - F_{42}$. Sketch a free-body diagram for the charge the equation might represent. Also, sketch a possible model of the entire charge system. (Note that there are multiple configurations possible.)

9 **SEP Argue from Evidence** A positive charge $+q$ is released from rest at a distance r from a charge of $+Q$ and a distance $2r$ from a charge of $+2Q$, as shown. How does $+q$ move immediately after being released?

Electric Force Between Particles

Three point charges are arranged in a straight line. The charges are $q_1 = 10 \ \mu\text{C}$, $q_2 = -10 \ \mu\text{C}$, and $q_3 = 10 \ \mu\text{C}$. Charge q_1 is 10 cm from charge q_2, and charge q_3 is 10 cm from charge q_2. Determine the magnitude of the net electric force on charge q_1.

1. DRAW A PICTURE Sketch a picture of the situation.

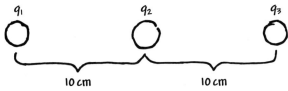

10 cm   10 cm

Free-body diagram

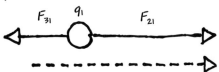

2. DEFINE THE PROBLEM List knowns and unknowns and assign values to variables.

$q_1 = 10 \times 10^{-6} \text{ C}$	$r_{31} = 0.200 \text{ m}$
$q_2 = -10 \times 10^{-6} \text{ C}$	$r_{21} = 0.100 \text{ m}$
$q_3 = 10 \times 10^{-6} \text{ C}$	$k_e = 8.99 \times 10^9 \text{ N·m}^2/\text{C}^2$

3. PLAN AND EXECUTE Use mathematical relationships, the picture, and your definitions to plan and execute a solution.

Use the free-body diagram to write the net force. Use the coordinate system to determine positive and negative.

$$\Sigma F_1 = F_{21} - F_{31}$$

Use Coulomb's law to determine the magnitude of the force between q_1 and q_2.

$$F_{21} = k_e \frac{|q_2 q_1|}{r_{21}^2} = 8.99 \times 10^9 \text{ N·m}^2/\text{C}^2 \frac{|(10 \times 10^{-6} \text{ C})(-10 \times 10^{-6} \text{ C})|}{(0.100 \text{ m})^2}$$
$$= 89.9 \text{ N}$$

Use Coulomb's law to determine the magnitude of the force between q_1 and q_3.

$$F_{31} = k_e \frac{|q_3 q_1|}{r_{31}^2} = 8.99 \times 10^9 \text{ N·m}^2/\text{C}^2 \frac{|(10 \times 10^{-6} \text{ C})(10 \times 10^{-6} \text{ C})|}{(0.200 \text{ m})^2}$$
$$= 22.5 \text{ N}$$

Determine the net force.

$$\Sigma F_1 = 89.9 \text{ N} - 22.5 \text{ N} = 67.4 \text{ N}$$

4. EVALUATE Reflect on your answer.
All of the units are appropriate for the given quantities. The result is positive, which is consistent with the free-body diagram.

 GO ONLINE for more **math support**.

📱 **Math Practice Problems**

---

(10) Three point charges are arranged in a straight line. The charges are $q_1 = 8 \ \mu\text{C}$, $q_2 = -8 \ \mu\text{C}$, and $q_3 = 8 \ \mu\text{C}$. Charge q_1 is 8.00 cm from charge q_2, and charge q_3 is 8.00 cm from charge q_2. Determine the magnitude of the net electric force on charge q_1.

📖 **NEED A HINT?** Go online to your **eText Sample Problem** for stepped out support.

Comparing Electric and Gravitational Forces

How **strong** are **electric forces** compared to **gravitational forces**?

Coulomb's Law

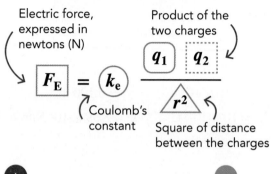

Electric force, expressed in newtons (N)

Product of the two charges

$$F_E = k_e \frac{q_1 \, q_2}{r^2}$$

Coulomb's constant

Square of distance between the charges

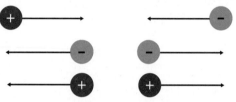

Two types of charge lead to **attractive and repulsive forces.**

Universal Law of Gravitation

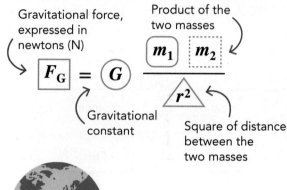

Gravitational force, expressed in newtons (N)

Product of the two masses

$$F_G = G \frac{m_1 \, m_2}{r^2}$$

Gravitational constant

Square of distance between the two masses

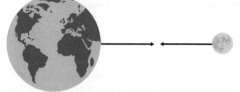

One type of mass means **only attractive forces.**

The Coulomb constant is **1.35 × 10²⁰ times larger** than the gravitational constant. That's about 100 quintillion times larger!

135,000,000,000,000,000,000x

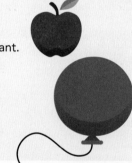

An apple weighs about 1 N. It takes a mass **the size of Earth** to generate that force.

A charged balloon only 1 cm from a sweater can experience a force of 1 N.

$$\frac{F_E}{F_G} = \frac{\left(k_e \frac{|q_1 \, q_2|}{r^2} \right)}{\left(G \frac{m_1 m_2}{r^2} \right)} = \frac{k_e \left(|q_1 \, q_2| \right)}{G \left(m_1 m_2 \right)}$$

The ratio of the electric force to the gravitational force doesn't depend on the distances between charges and masses. **The distances cancel each other out!** The **electric force will be stronger than the gravitational force** unless the masses are very large or the charges are very small. For an electron in a hydrogen atom, the ratio is 2.27 × 10³⁹.

---

(11) **SEP Use Mathematics** Show that the ratio of the electric force to the gravitational force for an electron in a hydrogen atom is 2.27 × 10³⁹.

(12) **SEP Use Mathematics** Assuming that a balloon and a sweater have opposite electric charges of equal magnitude, determine the magnitude of the charges if the force between them is 1 N when they are separated by 1.0 cm.

Charge by Contact

Macroscopic materials can become charged either by gaining or losing electrons. **Triboelectric charging** is a process in which an object becomes charged after coming in direct contact with another object and then separating from it. One of the objects loses some electrons, and it becomes positively charged. The other object gains those electrons, and it becomes negatively charged.

A **triboelectric series** is a list of materials ranked according to the tendency to gain or lose electrons. For example, a triboelectric series can be used to predict what will happen when a cotton sheet comes into contact with a polyester T-shirt in a clothes dryer. Since cotton is higher in the series, it more readily gives up electrons to the polyester, causing the cotton sheet to become positively charged.

Gecko Adhesion Scientists have only recently learned that geckos use triboelectric charging to stick to very smooth surfaces.

Triboelectric Series Materials are ranked by their tendency to either gain or lose electrons.

Nylon is lower than human hair in the series. When a nylon comb is run through hair, the hair loses electrons to the comb.

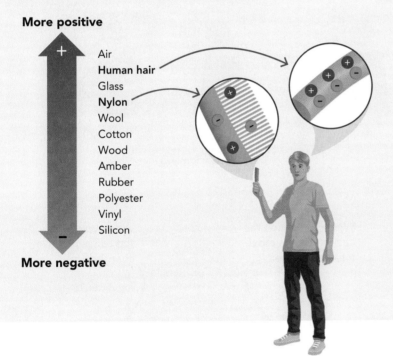

More positive

+
- Air
- **Human hair**
- Glass
- **Nylon**
- Wool
- Cotton
- Wood
- Amber
- Rubber
- Polyester
- Vinyl
- Silicon
-

More negative

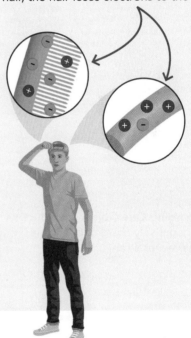

(13) **SEP Argue from Evidence** Use the triboelectric series to support the claim that a rubber balloon will become negatively charged when rubbed on a wool sweater.

(14) **SEP Plan an Investigation** Design an experiment using a rubber balloon, a piece of wool, and an unknown material to collect data that place the three objects in a triboelectric series.

Charge by Induction

Objects can also be charged without direct contact. **Electrostatic induction** is the redistribution of electric charge in an object by the influence of a nearby charge. When charged objects are brought close to each other and the electrons in the objects can move freely, the electric force redistributes the electrons without direct contact.

In materials where electrons can move freely, such as metals, charging by induction is very effective. A large separation of charge can result. In other materials, such as rubber, induced charge is confined to small regions, since electrons cannot easily leave their atoms.

Charging Two Objects by Induction A negatively charged balloon is brought near the metal cans. Electrons move away from the balloon.

When the two cans are separated, they have opposite charges.

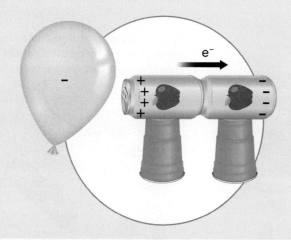

Charging One Object by Induction A negatively charged balloon is brought near a metal can.

When you touch the can, electrons move into your finger.

When you let go, the can is positively charged.

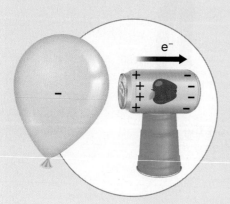
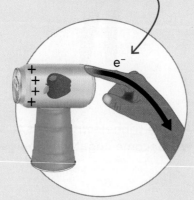
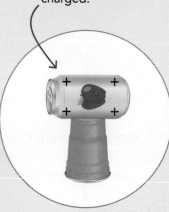

(15) **SEP Design Solutions** For an experiment, you need a positively charged metal can. Using a glass rod and a cotton shirt, design a solution.

Balloon on Wall A charged balloon will stick to a neutral wall.

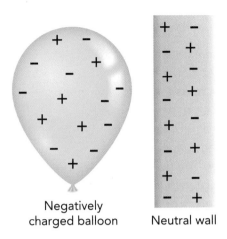

Negatively charged balloon
Neutral wall

Attraction

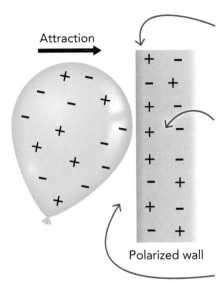

Polarized wall

A region of net positive charge is formed on the wall surface.

Electrons near the surface of the wall move away from the balloon. They cannot go far because they are bound to their atoms.

The negatively charged balloon is attracted to the positive charge near the surface and repelled by the negative charge farther away. The attractive force wins because the positive charge is closer.

Intermolecular Forces

Dispersion forces are distance-dependent interactions between nonbonding atoms and molecules that you may have learned about in chemistry. Electron motion results in a momentary uneven distribution of charges in one atom that induces redistribution in the other, causing an attractive electric force.

Dispersion Force Two neutral atoms can experience a net attractive force when close together, as a balloon is attracted to a wall.

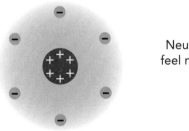

Neutral atoms far away feel no net electric force.

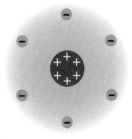

As they get closer, electrons redistribute themselves, resulting in an attractive force.

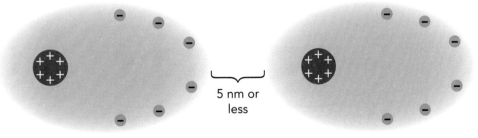

5 nm or less

(16) **SEP Ask Questions** Since opposite charges experience a greater and greater attraction as they get closer, why do the two atoms in the figure not crash into each other? For the balloon, what keeps the charges far enough away that the force can be overcome by simply pulling the balloon off the wall? What other questions might you ask?

Modeling Electric and Contact Forces

Atoms Getting Close Electrostatic induction explains the attraction between nonbonding atoms. However, if the atoms get closer, then they start to repel one another. What causes the repulsion? Electrons form clouds around the nuclei of atoms. Interactions with other atoms can redistribute the clouds, but the clouds typically cannot overlap due to rules established by quantum mechanics. This resistance to overlapping electron clouds results in a rapidly increasing repulsive force as atoms get closer. The point where the attractive electric force is balanced by the repulsive resistance to overlapping electron clouds is called the **contact distance.** When electron clouds do overlap, a chemical bond is formed.

Atoms in Contact There are both attractive and repulsive components between atoms as they get closer. The repulsive components dominate at very short distances.

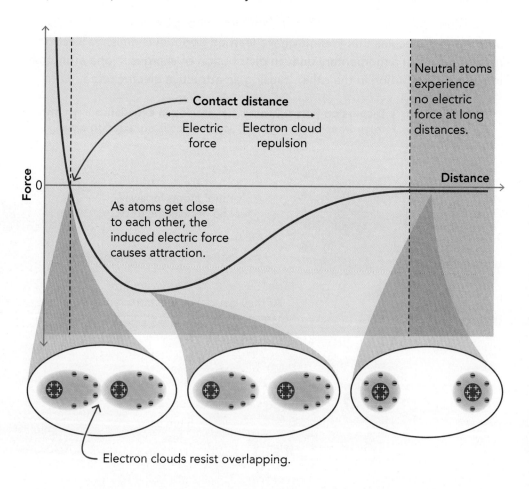

Contact distance

Electric force   Electron cloud repulsion

Neutral atoms experience no electric force at long distances.

Force

0

Distance

As atoms get close to each other, the induced electric force causes attraction.

Electron clouds resist overlapping.

(17) **SEP Use a Model** Based on the microscopic model for interactions between atoms, would the macroscopic force exerted by the floor on you be more accurately described as a result of the electric force or quantum mechanics?

Forces at the Surface Due to surface roughness, a large majority of the atoms at the surface of a macroscopic object do not get close enough to one another for dispersion forces to be significant. That is why an uncharged balloon does not stick to the ceiling and why you cannot climb walls like a superhero. However, you can model the electric and contact forces on a macroscopic scale.

Using a free-body diagram, you can model the electric and macroscopic contact forces acting on a charged balloon stuck to the ceiling. For the balloon, there are noncontact forces (the electric force and gravity) and one contact force (the force exerted by the ceiling on the balloon). If you graphed the sum of the attractive electric force and the repulsive contact force as a function of distance, the result would look like the force graph for atoms in contact.

Sticky Forces Many glues work by filling in the valleys on rough surfaces to increase the attractive electric dispersion forces between objects.

Modeling a Stuck Balloon You can think about the difference between contact forces and noncontact forces by modeling a balloon stuck to the ceiling by the electric force.

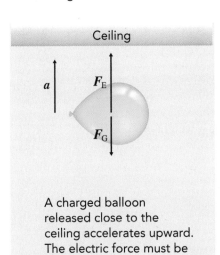

A charged balloon released close to the ceiling accelerates upward. The electric force must be greater than the weight.

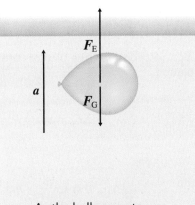

As the balloon gets closer to the ceiling, the electric force and the acceleration get larger.

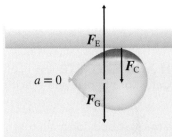

When in contact with the ceiling, the balloon's acceleration and velocity drop to zero. Stopping requires another, different force—the contact force the ceiling exerts on the balloon.

(18) **SEP Plan an Investigation** Plan an investigation to estimate the strength of the electric force on a charged balloon stuck to a ceiling by adding a series of small masses to the balloon.

(19) **SEP Develop a Model** Since most surfaces are rough at the microscopic scale, only a few atoms actually get close enough to experience attractive forces. Sketch a side-view microscopic model of two rough surfaces held together by glue.

Levitating Ball

A small polyester ball is given a negative charge, q. A piece of polyvinyl chloride (PVC) pipe is given the same charge, concentrated at a point near one end. The ball is then placed over the PVC pipe, where it is observed to remain at rest 50 cm from the pipe. The mass of the polyester ball is 1.0 gram. Determine the charge on the ball.

1. DRAW A PICTURE Sketch a picture of the situation.

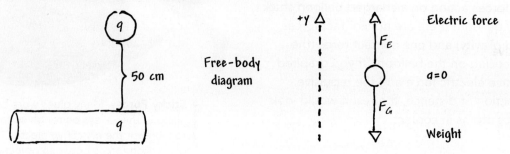

2. DEFINE THE PROBLEM List knowns and unknowns, and assign values to variables.

$m = 1.0 \times 10^{-3}$ kg $g = 9.8$ m/s^2 Convert quantities to similar units.

$r = 0.50$ m $a = 0$ m/s^2 1 g = 1 × 10^{-3} kg

$k_e = 8.99 \times 10^9$ Nm^2/C^2 $q = ?$ 50 cm = 0.50 m

3. PLAN AND EXECUTE Use mathematical relationships, the picture, and your definitions to plan and execute a solution.

Use the free-body diagram to write a force-acceleration equation for the charged ball.	$\Sigma F_b = ma = 0 = F_E - \text{weight} = F_E - F_G$
Use Coulomb's law to determine the electric force exerted by the pipe on the ball. The weight is the product of the mass and the acceleration due to gravity.	$0 = k_e \dfrac{|q|^2}{r^2} - mg$
Solve for the unknown charge.	$k_e \dfrac{q^2}{r^2} = mg \rightarrow q = r\sqrt{\dfrac{mg}{k_e}}$
Determine the charge.	$q = (0.5 \text{ m}) \sqrt{\dfrac{(1.0 \times 10^{-3} \text{ kg})(9.8 \text{ m/s}^2)}{(8.99 \times 10^9 \text{ Nm}^2/\text{C}^2)}} = \pm 5.2 \times 10^{-7}$ C $= -0.52 \ \mu\text{C}$ (as the charge is negative)

4. EVALUATE Reflect on your answer.

All of the units are appropriate for the given quantities. One μC would be about 6×10^{13} charges, which would be 10^{-10} mole of charges, and that means a small fraction of the atoms in the pipe and the ball are ionized. That seems reasonable.

 GO ONLINE for more math support.

▶ Math Tutorial Video

▣ Math Practice Problems

(20) A small polyester ball is given a negative charge, q. A piece of polyvinyl chloride (PVC) pipe is given the same charge, concentrated at a point near one end. The ball is then placed over the PVC pipe, where it is observed to remain at rest 35 cm from the pipe. The mass of the polyester ball is 0.80 grams. Determine the charge on the ball.

📖 **NEED A HINT?** Go online to your **eText Sample Problem** for stepped out support.

(21) A charged polyester ball is placed over a charged PVC pipe. The ball, which has a mass of 1.2 grams, rests 42 cm above the pipe. If the ball and pipe have the same negative charge, what is the charge on the ball?

(22) During an experiment, students placed a small polyester ball over a PVC pipe, where it is observed to remain at rest 55 cm from the pipe. The mass of the polyester ball is 0.75 grams. Determine the charge on the ball. Assume that the ball and the pipe have the same charge.

(23) Both a small polyester ball and a piece of PVC pipe are given a charge of 0.417 μC. The mass of the polyester ball is 1.0 grams. The ball is then placed over the PVC pipe. Determine how many centimeters from the pipe the ball will remain at rest.

(24) Both a small polyester ball and a piece of PVC pipe are given a charge of –0.639 μC. The ball is then placed over the PVC pipe, where it is observed to remain at rest 50.0 cm from the pipe. Determine the mass of the ball.

(25) A 0.70-gram ball is given a charge of –0.45 μC. A second ball with a mass of 0.75 grams is given a charge of –0.42 μC. Each ball is levitated over a PVC pipe given the same negative charge as the ball. Which ball will levitate higher? By how many centimeters more will it levitate above its pipe?

(26) You are making an electrostatic glider using a negatively charged piece of a plastic bag. The piece of plastic is 0.50 grams. You give the same charge to a balloon, which causes the plastic to levitate 45 cm above the balloon. Determine the charge on the plastic.

(27) You cut a 0.9-gram piece of plastic from a bag to make another glider. What charge would you need to give the plastic and the balloon in order for the glider to levitate 60 cm above the balloon?

INVESTIGATIVE PHENOMENON

 GO ONLINE to revisit your **Investigative Phenomenon CER** with the new information you have learned about Coulomb's Law.

These questions will help you apply what you learned in this experience to the Investigative Phenomenon.

28 **CCC Scale, Proportion, and Quantity** The value for the Coulomb constant is very large. What does that suggest about the value of two equal charges that have been placed close together and are experiencing a force of 1 N between them?

29 **SEP Develop a Model** Revisit your model of the balloon stuck to a wall that you constructed at the beginning of this investigation. What revisions do you think you need to make? Make those revisions by drawing a new free-body diagram for a balloon stuck to a wall by an electric force.

30 **SEP Plan an Investigation** Design an experiment to measure the size of the electric force on the balloon using a very sensitive scale.

31 **CCC Scale, Proportion, and Quantity** You experience contact forces every day on a macroscopic scale. On the microscopic scale, what do you think happens when one atom in your hand gets close to one atom in a wall?

 GO ONLINE for a **quiz** to evaluate what you learned about Coulomb's Law.

Electric Fields

GO ONLINE to do a **hands-on lab** to practice drawing electric field lines and interpreting their shapes.

What Is a Field?

A **field** is a region of space where a physical quantity is assigned to every point. A region of space with a value of temperature for each point is an example of a **scalar field,** which means a number represents the physical quantity at each point. A **vector field,** also called a tensor field, has vectors representing the physical quantities.

A meteorological wind map is an example of a vector field, where wind velocity is the physical quantity. Fields are real, physical entities that occupy space and contain energy. You can put a small sail in the wind to measure the velocity. However, the wind blows whether or not there is a sail to measure it.

Vector Field At each point in space, the map shows both the magnitude and direction of the wind velocity.

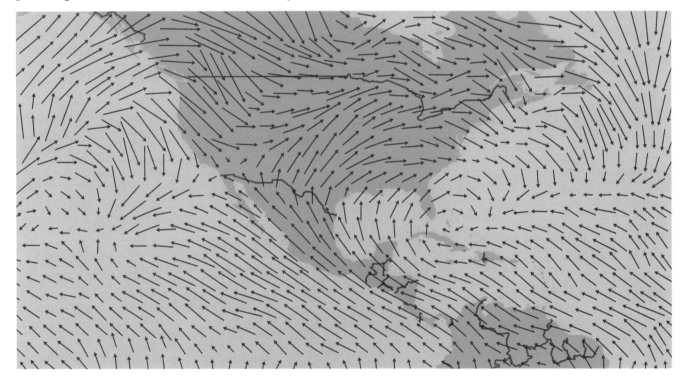

(32) **SEP Develop a Model** Sketch a large sail and a small sail in a wind field. Using your model, show that a large sail would affect the wind field, whereas a very small sail would not.

Electric Field

An **electric field** is a vector field in which the physical quantity is the electric force per unit charge. You use a small positive "test" charge to measure the force so that it does not affect the field. This is similar to how you use a small sail to measure wind speed.

Magnitude of the Electric Field for a Charged Particle
$$E = \frac{F}{q_{\text{test}}} = \frac{k_e \lvert qq_{\text{test}}\rvert}{r^2}\frac{1}{q_{\text{test}}} = \frac{k_e \lvert q\rvert}{r^2}$$

E = magnitude of electric field
$k_e = 8.99 \times 10^9$ N·m²/C²
q = object charge

q_{test} = test charge
r = distance between object and test charge

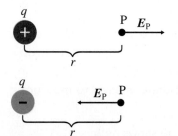

Field at a Point The electric field at a point (P) in space is represented as a vector.

You model a field at a point in much the same way you model a force: draw a free-body diagram for the point using field vectors instead of force vectors. The direction of the electric field vector is determined by the charges of the objects producing the field and by the coordinate system you define.

Superposition The principle of superposition is used to add all of the forces contributing to the field.

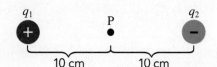

To determine directions, assume there is a tiny positive charge at the point.

$$\Sigma E_P = E_1 + E_2$$

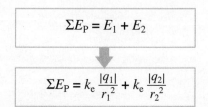

$$\Sigma E_P = k_e \frac{\lvert q_1\rvert}{r_1^2} + k_e \frac{\lvert q_2\rvert}{r_2^2}$$

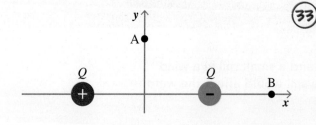

(33) **SEP Use Models** Two equal but opposite charges are placed on the x-axis as shown. The positive charge is placed to the left of the origin, and the negative charge is placed to the right. Copy the figure on a piece of paper. Sketch the direction of the net electric field at points A and B.

Electric Field Due to Two Charges

Two point charges are arranged in a line with point P. The point charges are $q_1 = 10 \times 10^{-6}$ C and $q_2 = -10 \times 10^{-6}$ C. Charge q_1 is 0.10 m to the left of charge q_2, and charge q_2 is 0.10 m to the left of point P. Determine the magnitude of the net electric field at point P.

1. DRAW A PICTURE Sketch a picture of the situation.

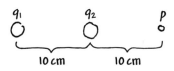

2. DEFINE THE PROBLEM List knowns and unknowns, and assign values to variables.

$q_1 = 10 \times 10^{-6}$ C	$r_1 = 0.2$ m
$q_2 = -10 \times 10^{-6}$ C	$r_2 = 0.1$ m
$k_e = 8.99 \times 10^9$ N·m²/C²	$E_P = ?$

3. PLAN AND EXECUTE Use mathematical relationships, the picture, and your definitions to plan and execute a solution.

Use the free-body diagram to write the net field. Use the coordinate system to determine positive and negative.	$\Sigma E_P = E_1 - E_2$
Use the electric field equation to determine the field at point P due to charge q_1.	$E_1 = k_e \dfrac{|q_1|}{r_1^2} = 8.99 \times 10^9 \ \text{N·m}^2/\text{C}^2 \dfrac{|(10 \times 10^{-6} \ \text{C})|}{(0.2 \ \text{m})^2}$ $= 2.25 \times 10^6$ N/C
Use the electric field equation to determine the field at point P due to charge q_2.	$E_2 = k_e \dfrac{|q_2|}{r_2^2} = 8.99 \times 10^9 \ \text{N·m}^2/\text{C}^2 \dfrac{|(-10 \times 10^{-6} \ \text{C})|}{(0.1 \ \text{m})^2}$ $= 8.99 \times 10^6$ N/C
Determine the net electric field.	$\Sigma E_P = (2.25 \times 10^6 \ \text{N/C}) - (8.99 \times 10^6 \ \text{N/C})$ $= -6.74 \times 10^6$ N/C

4. EVALUATE Reflect on your answer.
All of the units are appropriate for the given quantities. The result is negative, which is consistent with the free-body diagram. The field represents a force per coulomb that is very large, but a small test charge would experience a moderate force, so the answer is reasonable.

 GO ONLINE for more **math support**.

Math Practice Problems

---

34 Two point charges are arranged in a line with point P, which is on the right. The point charges are $q_1 = 7 \times 10^{-6}$ C and $q^2 = -7 \times 10^{-6}$ C. Charge q_1 is 0.12 m to the left of charge q_2 and charge q_2 is 0.12 m to the left of point P. Determine the magnitude of the net electric field at point P.

NEED A HINT? Go online to your **eText Sample Problem** for stepped out support.

35 Two point charges are arranged in a line with point P, which is on the right. The point charges are $q_1 = 9 \times 10^{-6}$ C, and $q_2 = -5 \times 10^{-6}$ C. The net electric field at point P is -2.2×10^5 N/C. The field at point P due to charge q_2 is 2.02×10^6 N/C. How far to the right is point P from charge q_1 and charge q_2?

Representing Electric Fields

How do you **represent electric fields** in space?

| **Modeling Fields** Electric fields in space around a charged object can be represented by using **vectors at points** or **field lines**.

Field vectors are represented by arrows. **The direction of the arrow indicates the direction of the electric field.**

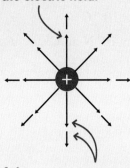

The length of the arrow represents the strength of the field at that point. The field gets weaker farther away from the charge.

Field lines replace vectors with continuous lines. **The direction of the line indicates the direction of the electric field.**

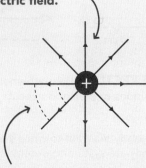

The distance between the lines represents the strength of the field. The field gets weaker farther away from the charge.

The **direction** of the field lines indicates the charge. Lines point away from positive charges and toward negative charges.

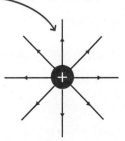
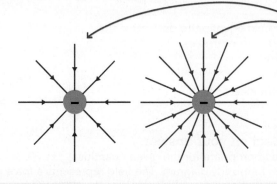

The **number** of field lines represents the amount of the charge. More lines indicate a larger charge.

Field Line Rules

1. Field lines must begin on positive charges and terminate on negative charges or at infinity.
2. The number of field lines leaving or entering a charge is proportional to the strength of the charge.
3. The strength of the field is proportional to the closeness of the field lines.
4. The direction of the electric field is tangent to the field line at any point in space.
5. Field lines can never cross.

㊱ **CCC Systems and System Models** A small section of an electric field is shown with points A, B, and C. Rank the magnitude of the electric field at those three points from largest to smallest.

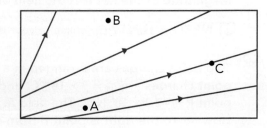

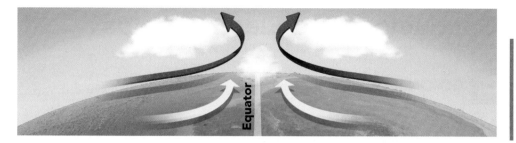

Doldrums Near the equator, trade winds from both the north and south converge, producing a band of reduced surface winds called the Intertropical Convergence Zone.

Field Lines for Multiple Charges

📄 **GO ONLINE** to do a PhET **simulation** that allows you to investigate charges and fields.

When wind blows from two sources at once, the wind velocity due to one source can cancel or add to the velocity from the other. For example, a piece of paper hanging between two similar fans will not move, since the wind from one fan cancels the wind from the other. If you move one fan next to the other, the paper will move, since the contributions from the two fans will add together. When modeling an electric field due to multiple sources, you similarly add together all the contributions.

Field Lines and Vectors For multiple charges, the resulting field becomes complex. The field at a point is calculated as the sum of the contributions from all of the charges.

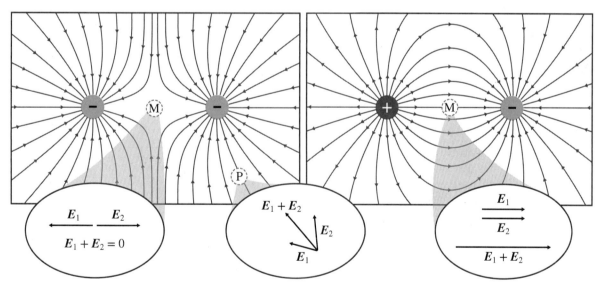

At the midpoint between two equal, like charges, the electric field is zero.

The direction and magnitude of the electric field at any point is determined by vector superposition.

At the midpoint between two equal, opposite charges, the electric field is double that of a single charge.

(37) **SEP Use Math** Using an equation, show that the electric field halfway between two like charges of equal magnitude is zero.

(38) **SEP Use a Model** The figure shows the electric field for three charges, A, B, and C. What is the sign of each charge? Rank the charges according to magnitude from largest to smallest.

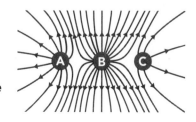

2 Electric Fields **175**

Conductors and Electric Fields

▶ **GO ONLINE** to watch a **video** about how to survive a lightning strike.

A **conductor** is a material, such as a metal, through which electric charges can easily move throughout. Since charges can easily move, any unbalanced charges on a conductor repel one another and spread out across the surface. At equilibrium, the electric field is perpendicular to the surface of the conductor. If the field had any component along the surface, charges would move to cancel that component.

The shape of a conductor affects the way that charges distribute themselves and therefore also affects the strength of the electric field. Excess charge becomes concentrated in regions of greatest curvature. That is because the repulsion of like charges is most effective on flat surfaces and least effective on highly curved surfaces.

VOCABULARY

The word **conductor** is derived from the Latin word *conducere*, meaning "to bring or lead together." In the same way a train conductor leads a series of train cars, an electrical conductor "leads," or transmits, electric charges.

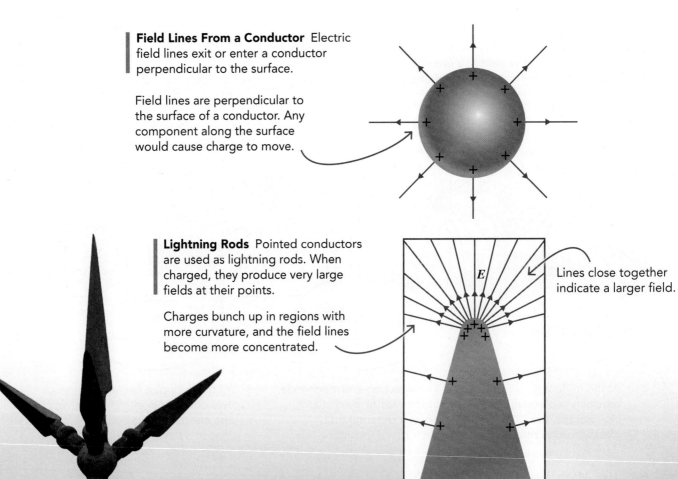

Field Lines From a Conductor Electric field lines exit or enter a conductor perpendicular to the surface.

Field lines are perpendicular to the surface of a conductor. Any component along the surface would cause charge to move.

Lightning Rods Pointed conductors are used as lightning rods. When charged, they produce very large fields at their points.

Charges bunch up in regions with more curvature, and the field lines become more concentrated.

E

Lines close together indicate a larger field.

(39) **SEP Construct an Explanation** Construct an explanation for why the charges in a lightning bolt are drawn to a lightning rod instead of a flat roof.

Uniform Electric Fields

Vector fields with evenly spaced field lines and a constant magnitude throughout space are called **uniform fields.** A uniform electric field can be generated by placing an excess charge on a large metal sheet. Since electric field lines are perpendicular to the surface of a conductor, the resulting field is uniform close to the surface of the sheet. In a uniform electric field, the force experienced by a charge does not depend on distance.

The gravitational field is a vector field in which the physical quantity at each point is the gravitational force per mass. Near the surface of Earth, there is a uniform gravitational field. That is why your weight appears constant.

Electric Force Near a Sheet of Charge
$F = qE$
E = electric field $\qquad q$ = charge

Uniform Fields Vector fields with evenly spaced field lines are called uniform and have a constant magnitude in space.

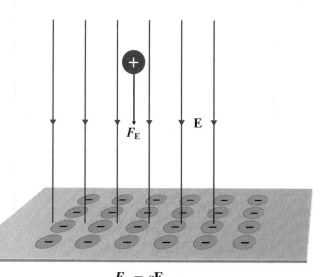

$$F_E = qE$$

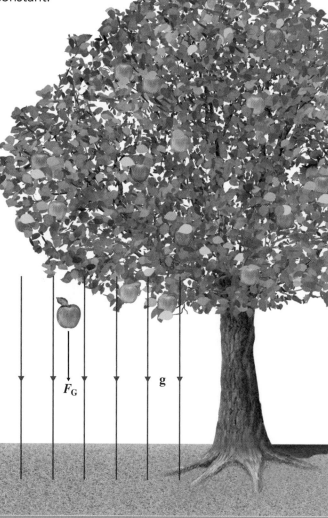

$$F_G = mg$$

Uniform electric and gravitational fields result in constant force.

(40) **SEP Argue from Evidence** Sketch a graph of acceleration and velocity as functions of time for the positive charge shown in the uniform electric field. How do your graphs compare to the acceleration and velocity graphs for an apple falling from the tree?

Parallel Plates

Capacitors A device that stores electrical energy in the electric field between two parallel sheets is a **capacitor.** Two metal sheets can be given opposite charges by connecting them to the terminals of a battery. When the sheets are placed parallel to each other with a small separation, a uniform electric field forms between them. Once the battery is removed, the charges remain due to their electrostatic attraction, and they store energy.

If an electron is placed between the sheets, the electron experiences a constant force directed toward the positively charged sheet. Due to superposition, that force is twice as large as the force the electron would experience near a single charged sheet.

> **Constant Acceleration** Connecting two parallel plates of metal to opposite terminals of a battery gives them opposite charges. The result is a constant field between the plates.

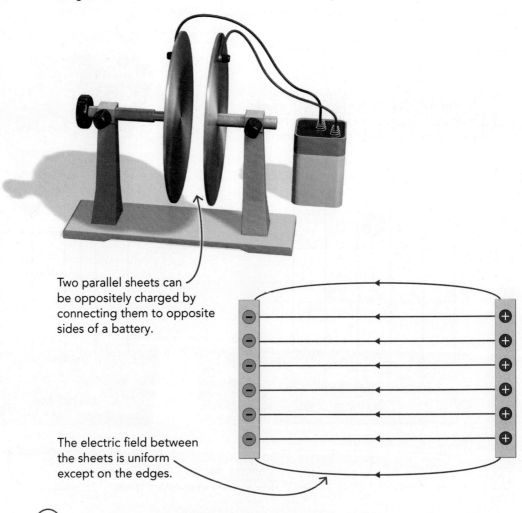

Two parallel sheets can be oppositely charged by connecting them to opposite sides of a battery.

The electric field between the sheets is uniform except on the edges.

(41) **SEP Develop and Use a Model** Sketch two oppositely charged sheets. Draw a free-body diagram for one charge in the center of each sheet. Use the model to construct an explanation of why the charge remains on each sheet when the battery is removed.

Ion Thrusters *BepiColombo*, a mission to Mercury launched in 2018 by the European Space Agency, uses an ion thruster much like this one for propulsion.

Changing Particle Velocity The constant force on a charged particle between two parallel charged sheets results in constant acceleration. You can use graphical methods and equations for constant accelerated motion to model changing velocity, similar to mass falling in a uniform gravitational field.

Electrons accelerated in a constant field were used in the cathode ray tubes of older television sets. More recently, space missions have begun using ion thrusters that operate in a similar manner for propulsion.

Accelerating Electrons A simple ion thruster accelerates charged particles using an electric field. The positive sheet is typically a grid material, so that the negatively charged particles can pass through and leave the spacecraft.

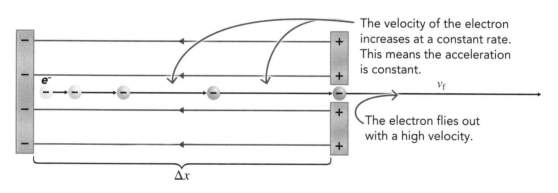

The velocity of the electron increases at a constant rate. This means the acceleration is constant.

The electron flies out with a high velocity.

v_f

Δx

Constant force means constant acceleration.

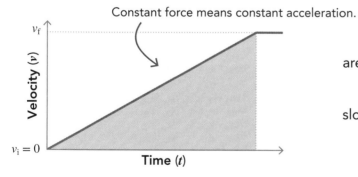

$$\text{area} = \Delta x = \frac{1}{2}at^2$$

$$\text{slope} = a = \frac{\Delta v}{\Delta t} = \frac{(v_f - v_i)}{\Delta t}$$

(42) SEP Use Mathematics Show the steps necessary to get the speed v_f, as a function of the plate separation, Δx, and the acceleration, a. You will need to solve the two equations shown for time, set them equal to each other, and then solve for v_f.

Ion Thruster

An electrostatic ion thruster accelerates positively charged xenon ions ($q = 1.60 \times 10^{-19}$ C) from rest using two oppositely charged plates separated by $\Delta x = 0.100$ m. A uniform electric field $E = 1.10 \times 10^4$ N/C is maintained between the plates. Each xenon ion has a mass of 2.18×10^{-25} kg. Determine the electric force on a xenon ion between the plates and the ion's final velocity as it leaves the ion thruster.

1. DRAW A PICTURE Sketch a picture of the situation.

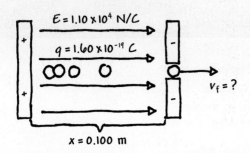

2. DEFINE THE PROBLEM List knowns and unknowns and assign values to variables.

$q = 1.60 \times 10^{-19}$ C	$m = 2.18 \times 10^{-25}$ kg
$x = 0.100$ m	$F_E = ?$
$E = 1.10 \times 10^4$ N/C	$v_f = ?$

3. PLAN AND EXECUTE Use mathematical relationships, the picture, and your definitions to plan and execute a solution.

Determine the electric force from the electric field.	$F_E = qE = (1.60 \times 10^{-19}$ C$)(1.10 \times 10^4$ N/C$)$ $F_E = 1.76 \times 10^{-15}$ N
Determine the acceleration from the electric force. The electric force is the net force.	$a = \dfrac{F_E}{m} = \dfrac{1.76 \times 10^{-15}\text{ N}}{2.18 \times 10^{-25}\text{ kg}} = 8.10 \times 10^9$ m/s^2
As in most problems involving constant acceleration, time links the equations. Determine the time that the ion is accelerated.	$x = \frac{1}{2}at^2 \rightarrow t = \sqrt{\dfrac{2x}{a}} = \sqrt{\dfrac{2(0.100\text{ m})}{8.10 \times 10^9 \text{ m/s}^2}}$ $= 4.97 \times 10^{-6}$ s
Determine the velocity of the ion.	$a = \dfrac{v_f}{t} \rightarrow v_f = at = (8.10 \times 10^9 \text{ m/s}^2)(4.97 \times 10^{-6}$ s$)$ $v_f = 4.03 \times 10^4$ m/s

4. EVALUATE The exit velocity is high, which makes sense for a device that needs to produce usable thrust.

 GO ONLINE for more **math support**.

▶ **Math Tutorial Video**

🖵 **Math Practice Problems**

(43) An electrostatic ion thruster accelerates positively charged xenon ions ($q = 1.60 \times 10^{-19}$ C) from rest using two oppositely charged plates separated by $\Delta x = 0.200$ m. A uniform electric field $E = 2.00 \times 10^4$ N/C is maintained between the plates. Each xenon ion has a mass of 2.18×10^{-25} kg. Determine the electric force on a xenon ion between the plates and the ion's final velocity as it leaves the ion thruster.

📖 **NEED A HINT?** Go online to your **eText Sample Problem** for stepped out support.

(44) An electrostatic ion thruster accelerates positively charged xenon ions ($q = 1.60 \times 10^{-19}$ C) from rest using two oppositely charged plates separated by $\Delta x = 0.15$ m. A uniform electric field $E = 1.5 \times 10^4$ N/C is maintained between the plates. Each xenon ion has a mass of 2.18×10^{-25} kg. Determine the electric force on a xenon ion between the plates and the ion's final velocity as it leaves the ion thruster.

(45) Xenon ions with a charge of 1.60×10^{-19} C are accelerated from rest by an electrostatic ion thruster using two oppositely charged plates separated by $\Delta x = 0.0900$ m. A uniform electric field $E = 1.30 \times 10^4$ N/C is maintained between the plates. Each xenon ion has a mass of 2.18×10^{-25} kg. Determine the electric force on a xenon ion between the plates and the ion's final velocity as it leaves the ion thruster.

(46) Xenon ions are given a charge of 1.60×10^{-19} C. They are accelerated using two oppositely charged plates that are 0.150 m apart. A uniform electric field $E = 1.20 \times 10^4$ N/C is maintained between the plates. Each xenon ion has a mass of 2.18×10^{-25} kg. Determine the electric force on a xenon ion between the plates and the ion's final velocity as it leaves the ion thruster.

(47) Xenon ions leave an ion thruster at a velocity of 4.50×10^4 m/s after they are accelerated by the thruster for 4.80×10^{-6} s. Each xenon ion has a mass of 2.18×10^{-25} kg. Determine the electric force on a single xenon ion in the thruster.

(48) Xenon ions leave an ion thruster at a velocity of 4.00×10^4 m/s. Each xenon ion has a mass of 2.18×10^{-25} kg and a charge of 3.20×10^{-19} C. If a uniform electric field $E = 1.25 \times 10^4$ N/C is maintained between the plates, then how long are the ions accelerated in the ion thruster?

(49) In an ion thruster, xenon ions are accelerated at 8.23×10^9 m/s² for 4.85×10^{-6} s. How far apart are the charged plates in the thruster? What is the velocity of a xenon ion as it leaves the thruster?

INVESTIGATIVE PHENOMENON

GO ONLINE to revisit your **Investigative Phenomenon CER** with the new information you have learned about Electric Fields.

These questions will help you apply what you learned in this experience to the Investigative Phenomenon.

50 **SEP Develop a Model** Sketch two pairs of particles, one pair with small electron cloud radii and another pair with large electron cloud radii, representing more electrons. When the particles in a pair are brought close to each other, the clouds redistribute to produce a dispersion force. Sketch a model of the electric field for the two interacting pairs of small particles and large particles.

51 **SEP Construct an Explanation** The elements fluorine, chlorine, bromine, and iodine belong to the same element family, or group, but have increasing size and number of electrons. Using your model from the previous item, explain why their boiling points increase with increasing atomic radius. (Hint: would particles with large electron clouds experience stonger or weaker dispersion forces?)

52 **SEP Argue from Evidence** Sketch two smooth, oppositely charged sheets of metal. Then sketch two jagged, oppositely charged metal surfaces. Construct an argument from evidence to explain why the smooth sheets experience a larger force of attraction than the jagged surfaces.

53 **CCC Structure and Function** You cannot walk through walls, but you can use glue to stick something to a wall. With your model of jagged surfaces, show how a fluid such as glue can be used to smooth out a surface.

GO ONLINE for a **quiz** to evaluate what you learned about Electric Fields.

EXPERIENCE 3

Electric Current

 GO ONLINE to do a **hands-on lab** to investigate the relationship between the size of a wire and its electrical resistance.

Conductors and Insulators

Materials can be classified by how easily electric charges move through them. A conductor is a material containing electrons or charged ions that can move easily through it. Metals and ionic solutions are examples of conductors. An **insulator** is a material in which electrons cannot move easily. Most materials that are not metals or ionic solutions, such as covalent and ionic solids, are insulators. In such insulators, the electrons are stuck in localized chemical bonds near a specific nucleus. Therefore, they cannot move very far.

Moving Electrons Copper is used in electrical power lines due to its availability and the ease with which electrons flow through it.

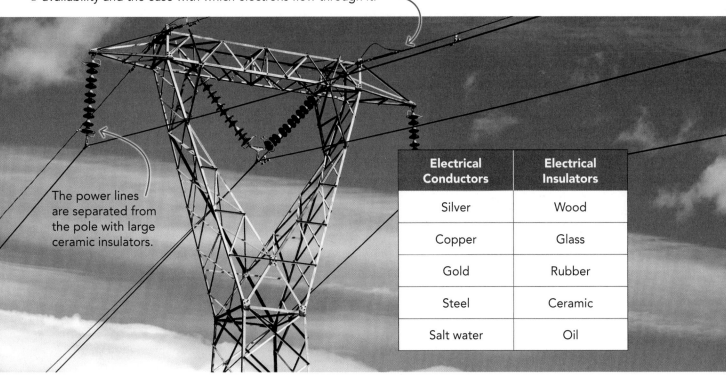

The power lines are separated from the pole with large ceramic insulators.

Electrical Conductors	Electrical Insulators
Silver	Wood
Copper	Glass
Gold	Rubber
Steel	Ceramic
Salt water	Oil

(54) **SEP Construct an Explanation** When salt is dissolved in water, it forms positively charged sodium ions and negatively charged chloride ions. Construct an explanation for why salt water is a conductor, but solid salt is an insulator.

Metals

Delocalized Charge Most atoms in a solid metal are tightly bound to their respective atoms. However, the outermost electrons, called valence electrons, are not tightly bound to a particular atom. **Delocalized electrons** are electrons that are not associated with a single atom or a covalent bond. Such free-roaming electrons give metals their interesting properties.

Delocalized Electrons in Metals

How are **delocalized electrons** responsible for the **properties of metals?**

Zinc A zinc atom has two **valence electrons.** The clouds represent the inner electron shells. Two zinc atoms by themselves do not form a chemical bond.

Metallic Solids When enough zinc atoms come together, the **valence electrons become delocalized.** The electrons can move freely from one atom to another. Cations and the inner electron shells remain.

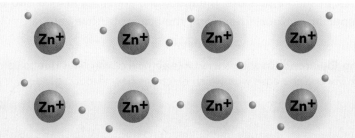

External force

Metal is deformed

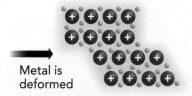

Malleability When metal is compressed, the cations can easily change positions. Therefore, the metal can be **deformed** without breaking.

Ductility A sea of delocalized electrons insulate metal cations from each other. When metal is forced through a die, the cations easily slide past one another, allowing the metal to be **stretched into wire.**

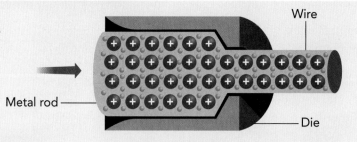

Wire

Metal rod

Die

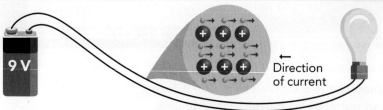

9 V

Direction of current

Electrical Conductivity Electric current is the movement of electrons. Delocalized electrons in metals can move easily, making metals **conductive.**

(55) **SEP Develop a Model** Does information spread faster in a gym, where all of the students can move around freely, or in a classroom, where students are confined to desks? Develop an analogy for the difference in conductivity between metals and ionic and covalent solids.

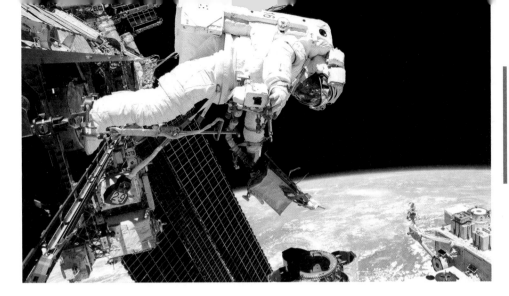

Problem in Space When two metals come in contact in the vacuum of space, they can chemically bond together. Such bonding caused an antenna on NASA's *Galileo* spacecraft to fail during its mission to Jupiter.

Cold Welding When two solids are brought close to each other, their respective atoms typically do not chemically bond. Instead, the repulsive component of intermolecular forces keeps them separated. However, the presence of delocalized electrons in metals can result in the formation of a bond. **Cold welding** is the process of joining two metals together without heat. When pieces of metal are placed in contact, the electrons at the surfaces do not know which sheet they belong to, so metallic bonds form. Cold welding does not happen in air due to the presence of oxide layers, dirt, and grease on the surfaces. Cold welding does happen in space and on the microscopic scale.

Ionic and Covalent Solids The electrons are stuck in their chemical bonds. When brought close to each other, the electron clouds cannot overlap, resulting in a repulsive contact force (unless enough energy is available for chemical bonding).

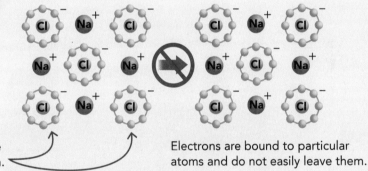

Electrons in an ionic solid are confined to a particular atom.

Electrons are bound to particular atoms and do not easily leave them.

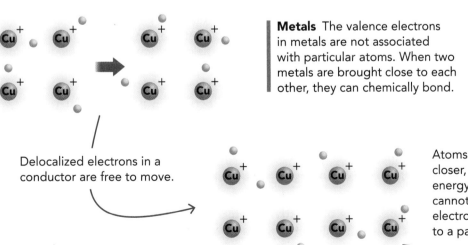

Metals The valence electrons in metals are not associated with particular atoms. When two metals are brought close to each other, they can chemically bond.

Delocalized electrons in a conductor are free to move.

Atoms cannot get any closer, since their lower-energy electron clouds cannot overlap. Those electron clouds are bound to a particular atom.

Electric Fields Along a Wire

GO ONLINE to do a PhET **simulation** that allows you to investigate how circuits are constructed.

If the terminals of a battery are connected to two parallel conducting sheets, a uniform electric field is produced between the sheets. If, instead, the terminals of the battery are connected together using a conductor, such as copper wire, a uniform field is generated in the conductor. The delocalized electrons in the wire experience a constant force due to the uniform field. As the electrons move, they collide with the inner electron clouds of the metal atoms, resulting in what you can think of as "electric friction." The friction cancels the force due to the field, and result is a constant average electron velocity called the **drift velocity.**

A Simple Circuit One end of a battery is connected to the other via wires, a switch, and a light bulb.

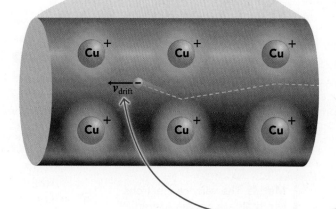

Drift Velocity A uniform field throughout the wire causes all the electrons to move in the same general direction. Their interaction with immobile nuclei and inner electron clouds limits their velocity.

$$\overset{F_E}{\longleftarrow} \bullet \overset{f}{\longrightarrow}$$
$$a = 0$$

The force from the electric friction cancels the force from the field. Increasing the field strength increases the drift velocity.

56 **CCC Patterns** How is the motion of electrons in a wire similar to the motion of a small ball reaching terminal velocity as it falls through the air?

57 **SEP Obtain Information** At ordinary temperatures, electrons in a conductor collide with vibrating metal ions. At low temperatures, the vibration of ions in a conductor is significantly reduced. The result is the disappearance of resistivity, which is known as superconductivity. Conduct research online to learn more about superconductors. Share your understanding of why resistance vanishes.

Flow of Water A gravitational field causes the particles of water in the river to flow from the mountains into the ocean. That flow is the current.

Current

The rate at which water passes through an area of a stream is called the current. Similarly, **electric current** is the rate at which charge passes through an area of wire. The unit for electric current is the ampere (A), which is one Coulomb per second (C/s).

Electric Current
$$I = \frac{\Delta Q}{\Delta t}$$
I = current ΔQ = change in charge Δt = change in time

Flow of Electrons A uniform electric field causes a flow of electrons.

Current is the number of charges that pass through this area each second.

The current direction is defined as the direction of the electric field. Note that the electrons go the opposite way!

Increasing the current requires increasing the rate at which the electrons move, which can be done by increasing the magnitude of the electric field.

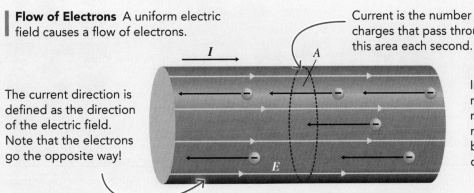

(58) **SEP Construct an Explanation** When you flip a switch to turn on a light, the average drift velocity of the electrons in the wire to the light bulb is only about 20 μm/s. That is slow! Use the image of marbles in a tube to construct an explanation for why the lights seem to turn on instantly.

Conductivity and Resistivity

VOCABULARY

Resistance is derived from the Latin word *resistere*, which means "make a stand against or oppose."

An **intensive property,** such as the density of electrons, is a property that does not change with scale. An **extensive property,** such as the length of a wire, is a property that does change with scale. **Resistivity,** which is intensive, is how much a unit amount of material opposes the flow of electric current. **Resistance,** which is extensive, is how much a particular object opposes the flow of current.

Electrical Resistance
$$R = \frac{\rho L}{A}$$

R = resistance L = length of a wire
ρ = resistivity A = area of cross section

Opposition The resistance depends on the length of a wire, its cross section, and the resistivity of the metal it is made of.

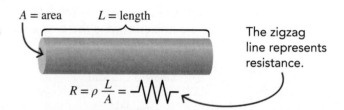

A = area L = length

The zigzag line represents resistance.

$$R = \rho \frac{L}{A} = -\text{/\/\/}-$$

A Model for Resistance Imagine everyone trying to get to the door after class. The speed with which students can exit depends on the layout of the classroom.

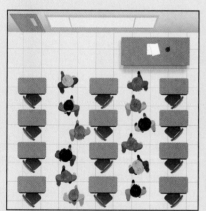

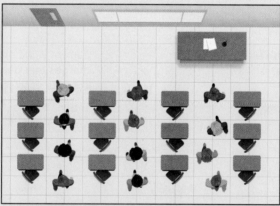

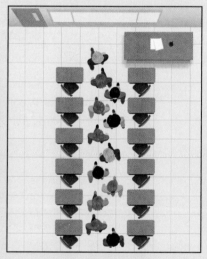

Students' progress is slowed by interactions with desks and chairs, which correspond to the ions of a metal.

A wider room with more aisles allows students to interact with fewer obstacles. It speeds up the movement. The arrangement is analogous to a wire with a large cross section.

A longer, narrower room forces each student to interact with more obstacles, which slows the students' movement. The arrangement is analogous to a long wire.

(59) **SEP Plan an Investigation** It is difficult to measure the resistivity of a material directly, but it is easy to measure the resistance and length of a wire. Plan an investigation that would allow you to determine the resistivity for a constant cross section from resistance data plotted as a function of length.

Current and Resistivity

Current density is the amount of current flow through an area, and it is a vector quantity. The current density in a wire is proportional to the electric field. Increase the electric field, and the current increases. On the other hand, a larger resistivity requires a larger field to produce the same current. The proportional relation of current and field is called **Ohm's law.** The figure shows the vector form of Ohm's law. There is also a scalar form of Ohm's law.

Ohm's Law (Vector Form)
$$\boldsymbol{E} = \rho \boldsymbol{J}$$
$\boldsymbol{E}$ = electric field ρ = resistivity $\boldsymbol{J} = \dfrac{I}{A}$ = current density

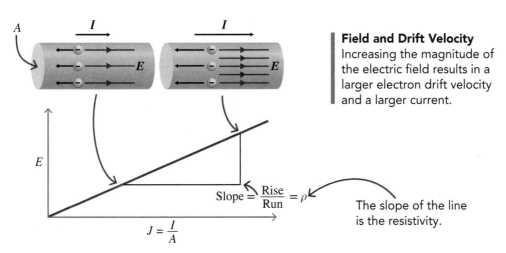

Field and Drift Velocity
Increasing the magnitude of the electric field results in a larger electron drift velocity and a larger current.

$$\text{Slope} = \frac{\text{Rise}}{\text{Run}} = \rho$$

The slope of the line is the resistivity.

$J = \dfrac{I}{A}$

Increasing the electric field linearly increases the current density.

60) SEP Analyze and Interpret Data
The graph shows the electric field as a function of the current density for copper and silver. From the data, determine the resistivity of each. If you wanted to use the metal with lower resistance, which would you choose? Why do you think the wiring in homes is copper and not silver?

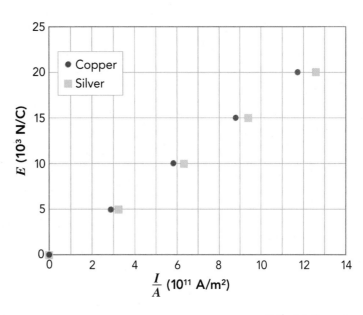

Series and Parallel Resistance

EXPERIENCE IT!

Gather a few friends and walk one behind the other in a circle around a desk. What happens when one friend starts to slow down?

Series Resistance A zigzag line represents an object that has resistance, which is called a **resistor.** When multiple resistors are connected one after another, the arrangement is a **series combination.** The total resistance of the combination is the **equivalent resistance,** and it can be calculated by adding the resistances.

Series Combination of Resistors
$$R_{equ} = R_1 + R_2 + R_3 + \ldots$$
R_{equ} = equivalent resistance R_2 = resistance of resistor 2
R_1 = resistance of resistor 1 R_3 = resistance of resistor 3

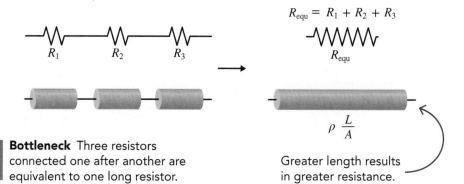

$$R_{equ} = R_1 + R_2 + R_3$$

$\rho \dfrac{L}{A}$

Bottleneck Three resistors connected one after another are equivalent to one long resistor.

Greater length results in greater resistance.

(61) **SEP Construct an Explanation** During construction on a highway, all of the traffic can be forced into one lane. Construct an explanation for why the restriction slows down traffic. How is it analogous to series resistance?

GO ONLINE to watch a **video** about series and parallel circuits.

Parallel Resistance When resistors are connected such that both ends of each resistor are connected together, the arrangement is called a **parallel combination.** The equivalent resistance of a parallel combination is lower than the lowest individual resistance. By connecting resistors in parallel, you are providing more paths for the current, which lowers the resistance. The inverse of the equivalent resistance is found by adding the inverses of the individual resistances.

Parallel Combination of Resistors
$$\frac{1}{R_{\text{equ}}} = \frac{1}{R_1} + \frac{1}{R_2} + \frac{1}{R_3} + \cdots$$
R_{equ} = equivalent resistance R_2 = resistance of resistor 2
R_1 = resistance of resistor 1 R_3 = resistance of resistor 3

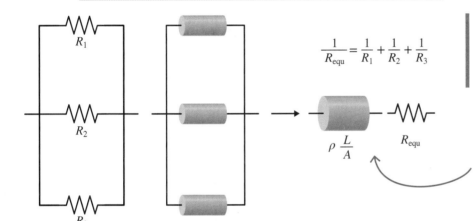

$$\frac{1}{R_{\text{equ}}} = \frac{1}{R_1} + \frac{1}{R_2} + \frac{1}{R_3}$$

$$\rho \frac{L}{A} \qquad R_{\text{equ}}$$

More Paths Three resistors connected in a parallel combination are equivalent to one resistor with a large area.

Greater area results in decreased resistance.

(62) **SEP Develop and Use a Model** Using the definition of *current*, make an analogy to the flow of traffic. Use your traffic flow model to predict what would happen if an extra lane were added to a highway. When does your traffic analogy stop working?

Combining Series and Parallel Resistors

Three resistors are connected in a combination of series and parallel. Resistor R_1 is in series with the combination of resistors R_2 and R_3 in parallel. The resistors have resistance $R_1 = 10\ \Omega$, $R_2 = 12\ \Omega$, and $R_3 = 15\ \Omega$. Determine the equivalent resistance of the combination of resistors.

1. DRAW A PICTURE Sketch a picture of the situation.

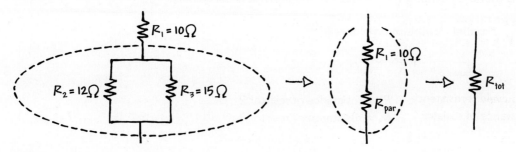

2. DEFINE THE PROBLEM List knowns and unknowns, and assign values to variables.

$$R_1 = 10\ \Omega \ \Big| \ R_2 = 12\ \Omega \ \Big| \ R_3 = 15\ \Omega$$

3. PLAN AND EXECUTE Use mathematical relationships, the picture, and your definitions to plan and execute a solution.

Determine the equivalent resistance of R_2 and R_3 in parallel.	$\dfrac{1}{R_{2\|3}} = \dfrac{1}{R_2} + \dfrac{1}{R_3} \rightarrow \dfrac{1}{R_{2\|3}} = \dfrac{1}{12\ \Omega} + \dfrac{1}{15\ \Omega} = 0.15\ 1/\Omega$ $R_{2\|3} = \dfrac{1}{0.15\ 1/\Omega} = 6.67\ \Omega$
Determine the equivalent resistance of R_1 in series with the parallel combination of R_2 and R_3.	$R_{1+2\|3} = R_1 + R_{2\|3} = 10\ \Omega + 6.67\ \Omega = 16.67\ \Omega$ $R_{\text{equ}} = 16.67\ \Omega$

4. EVALUATE Reflect on your answer.
All of the units are appropriate for the given quantities. The resistance is larger than $10\ \Omega$ but smaller than the sum of the resistances.

 GO ONLINE for more **math support**.

▶ **Math Tutorial Video**

🖥 **Math Practice Problems**

---

(63) Three resistors are connected in a combination of series and parallel. Resistor R_1 is in series with the combination of resistors R_2 and R_3 in parallel. The resistors have resistance $R_1 = 15\ \Omega$, $R_2 = 14\ \Omega$, and $R_3 = 14\ \Omega$. Determine the equivalent resistance of the combination of resistors.

📖 **NEED A HINT?** Go online to your **eText Sample Problem** for stepped out support.

64 Three resistors are connected in a combination of series and parallel. Resistor R_1 is in series with the combination of resistors R_2 and R_3 in parallel. The resistors have resistance $R_1 = 8\ \Omega$, $R_2 = 13\ \Omega$, and $R_3 = 8\ \Omega$. Determine the equivalent resistance of the combination of resistors.

65 Three resistors are connected in a combination of series and parallel. Resistor R_1 is in series with the combination of resistors R_2 and R_3 in parallel. The first two resistors have resistance $R_1 = 5\ \Omega$ and $R_2 = 8\ \Omega$. If the equivalent resistance of the combination of resistors is $9.44\ \Omega$, then determine the resistance R_3.

66 Three resistors are connected in a combination of series and parallel. Resistor R_1 is in series with the combination of resistors R_2 and R_3 in parallel. The two resistors in parallel have resistance $R_2 = 13\ \Omega$ and $R_3 = 10\ \Omega$. If the equivalent resistance of the combination of resistors is $19.65\ \Omega$, then determine the resistance R_1.

67 Three resistors are connected in a combination of series and parallel. Resistor R_3 is in series with the combination of resistors R_1 and R_2 in parallel. Two resistors have resistance $R_1 = 20\ \Omega$ and $R_3 = 20\ \Omega$. If the equivalent resistance of the combination of resistors is $25.71\ \Omega$, then determine the resistance R_2.

68 Four resistors are connected in a combination of series and parallel. Resistor R_1 is in parallel with resistor R_2. This pair of resistors is in series with the combination of resistors R_3 and R_4 in parallel. The resistors have resistance $R_1 = 10\ \Omega$, $R_2 = 15\ \Omega$, $R_3 = 12\ \Omega$, and $R_4 = 14\ \Omega$. Determine the equivalent resistance of the combination of resistors.

69 Four resistors are connected in a combination of series and parallel. Resistor R_1 is in series with the combination of resistors R_2, R_3, and R_4 in parallel. The resistors have resistance $R_1 = 5\ \Omega$, $R_2 = 10\ \Omega$, $R_3 = 15\ \Omega$, and $R_4 = 20\ \Omega$. Determine the equivalent resistance of the combination of resistors.

70 Three resistors are connected in a combination of series and parallel. The resistors have resistance $R_1 = 12\ \Omega$, $R_2 = 18\ \Omega$, and $R_3 = 10\ \Omega$. If the equivalent resistance is $17.14\ \Omega$, then explain how the three resistors are connected.

INVESTIGATIVE PHENOMENON

 GO ONLINE to revisit your **Investigative Phenomenon CER** with the new information you have learned about Electric Current.

These questions will help you apply what you learned in this experience to the Investigative Phenomenon.

71 **CCC Patterns** Cold welding is caused by the easy transfer of electrons from one surface to another. Interestingly, a charged balloon will stick to a wall but not to a piece of metal. How can the cause of cold welding also explain why the charged balloon does not stick to a piece of metal?

72 **SEP Develop a Model** There are two types of electric current: direct current (DC), in which the field always points in one direction, and alternating current (AC), in which the electric field switches directions. Sketch a model of the motion of an electron in a wire with an alternating electric field.

73 **SEP Construct an Explanation** Electricity can be transmitted effectively from its source for only about 450 kilometers. Construct an explanation for why there is a distance limit on the transmission of electricity.

74 **SEP Develop a Model** A surge protector is a device used to protect sensitive electronic devices from electric surges. A surge can occur when lightning strikes a power line. Most surge protectors use a variable resistor in parallel with the protected device. Under normal conditions, the resistance of the variable resistor is high, and current passes into the device. During a surge, the resistance drops, and current passes through the variable resistor. Sketch a model for a device protected by a surge protector for both normal and surge conditions, showing the pathway of current in both states.

  **GO ONLINE** for a **quiz** to evaluate what you learned about Electric Current.

These questions will help you apply what you learned in this investigation to the Anchoring Phenomenon.

(75) **SEP Develop and Use a Model** The ability of a material to dissolve in water is called solubility, and solubility is greater when the molecules of the material experience larger electric forces from molecules of water. Limestone is primarily calcium carbonate, which has a low solubility. However, when calcium carbonate reacts with carbon dioxide in the oceans, it forms calcium bicarbonate, which is much more soluble. Sketch a simple free-body diagram showing the difference in the electric force between a water molecule and a calcium carbonate molecule and also in the electric force between a water molecule and a calcium bicarbonate molecule. Why would increasing carbon dioxide levels in the ocean lead to greater coastal erosion of limestone rock formations?

(76) **CCC Patterns** Sketch the electric field for two positively charged particles, with one particle having a significantly greater charge. Earth and the moon produce a similar gravitational field. Sketch that gravitational field.

☑ INVESTIGATION ASSESSMENT

 GO ONLINE for activities that will give you an opportunity to **demonstrate what you have learned:**

☑ **Engineering Performance-Based Assessment** Build and use an electroscope to detect charges and demonstrate Coulomb's law.

📄 **Engineering Workbench** Design an electronic quiz board to convert electrical energy into signals.

🖥 **Career Connections** Learn about how a wind turbine engineer applies knowledge of physics.

☑ **Investigation Test** Take this test to evaluate your understanding of electric forces.

☑ **Virtual Lab Performance-Based Assessment** Determine the charge on one electron.

INVESTIGATIVE PHENOMENON

GO ONLINE to engage with real-world phenomena by watching a **phenomenon video** and completing a **CER worksheet**.

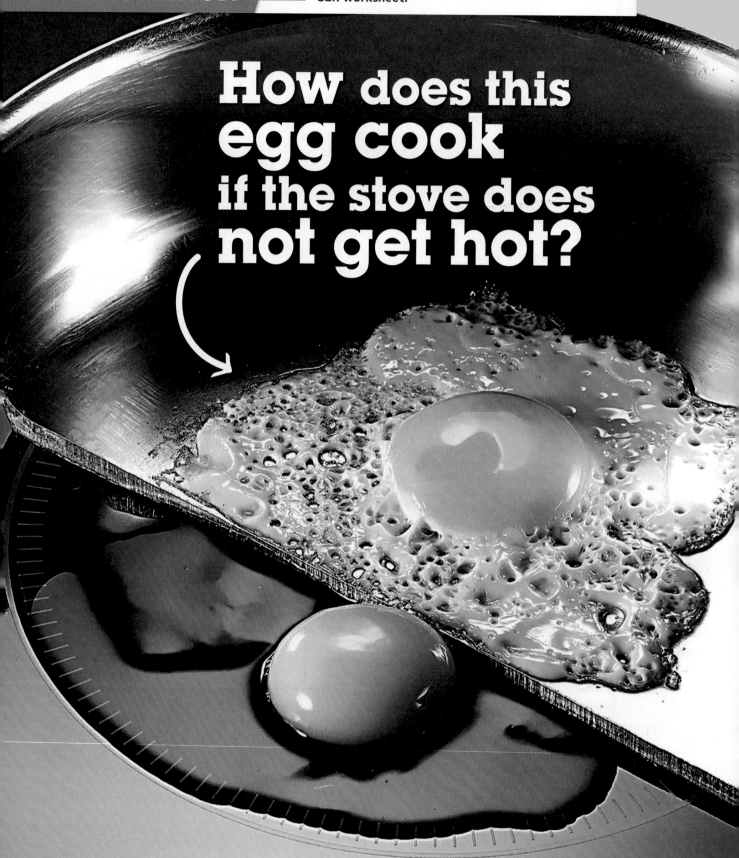

How does this egg cook if the stove does not get hot?

Magnetic Forces

On a traditional electric stove, a thick coil of wire (called a burner) with a high electrical resistance heats up when a large electric current passes through it. A pan placed on the burner gets hot through direct contact with the burner. The hot pan cooks food through a similar type of heat transfer. Using an electric stove to cook food is a very inefficient process, however, because it wastes energy heating materials that do not directly aid in cooking your food.

Induction stoves, like the one shown, also convert electric current into heat. However, unlike regular electric stoves, the burner itself does not get hot, and the current is much smaller. A sheet of glass separates the coil and the pan, so the process works without direct contact. Also, neither the coil nor the glass gets hot; only the pan does. This way of cooking is significantly more safe and efficient, allowing cooks to prepare food faster with less energy.

1. **SEP Develop a Model** On an induction stove, the glass forms a barrier between the coil and the pan. In your notebook, sketch a side-view model of the system shown in the image. Include the egg on the glass and the egg in the pan. Model where you think the energy comes from and where it goes in this system.

2. **SEP Construct an Explanation** Why do you think the egg in the pan cooks while the egg on the glass does not? How do you think the explanation might rely on the concept of magnetic force?

3. **CCC Energy and Matter** How do you think the electrical energy in the induction stove gets transferred to the pan to heat up and cook the egg?

Magnetic Forces and Fields

 GO ONLINE to do a **hands-on lab** to model how magnetic force varies with distance.

Magnetism

EXPERIENCE IT!

Play around with two magnets and describe the types of interactions that can occur. Now use one of the magnets to see how it interacts with everyday objects, such as paper clips, keys, and rubber bands.

Magnetic Interactions A **magnet** is a material that attracts iron and some other metals. When two magnets interact, they can either attract or repel each other depending on their orientation.

Magnets have two regions called **magnetic poles** where the attractive and/or repulsive interactions are the strongest. The two different poles of a magnet are called north and south, after the geographic designations. Scientists use these names to distinguish them from electric charges and because the first magnets were used in compasses that measured geographic orientation. Similar to electric charges, two opposite magnetic poles will attract, and two like magnetic poles will repel.

Magnetic Interactions Magnetic poles attract and repel each other similarly to electric charges, but they are different, which is why different names are used.

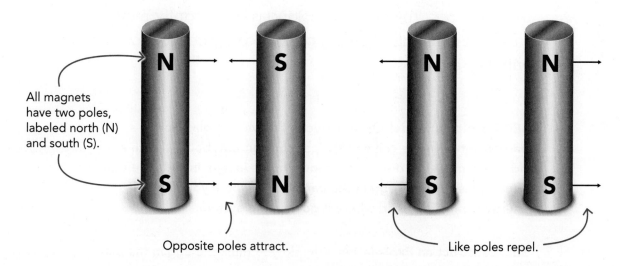

All magnets have two poles, labeled north (N) and south (S).

Opposite poles attract.

Like poles repel.

(4) **SEP Plan an Investigation** Using only a paper clip and a ruler, plan an investigation that would allow you to compare the strength of two magnets.

Magnetic Force If you cut a magnet into two pieces, then the result is two magnets. If you divide those magnets, you end up with four magnets. You cannot divide the north from the south pole, because even an individual electron can behave like a tiny magnet with a pair of poles.

An electron cannot be divided, so this means that magnetic poles always come in pairs. The pairing of poles is also why you cannot write a simple equation for the magnetic force between magnets as you can for the electric force between charges.

In fact, **magnetic force** is the noncontact force that arises between moving electric charges. In essence, electrons moving around the atom behave like tiny bar magnets. The attraction or repulsion that arises between two large bar magnets is the result of the combined motions of the trillions of electrons in the materials. The magnitude of the magnetic force is determined by the strength of the charge and speed of motion, while the direction of the magnetic force is determined by the relative direction of motion.

| **Paired Poles** Unlike electric charge, magnetic poles always come in pairs.

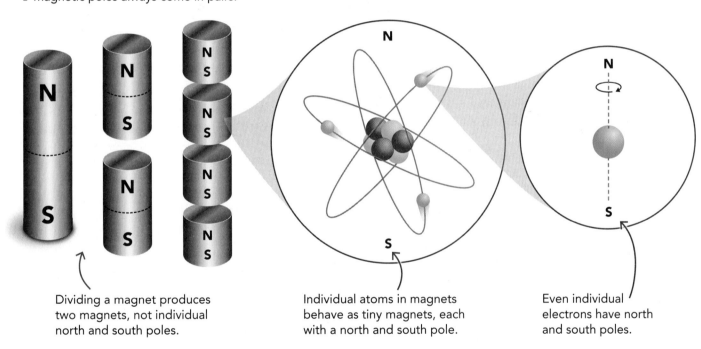

Dividing a magnet produces two magnets, not individual north and south poles.

Individual atoms in magnets behave as tiny magnets, each with a north and south pole.

Even individual electrons have north and south poles.

(5) **SEP Obtain, Evaluate, and Communicate Information** Several advanced theories in particle physics, such as string theory, do predict the existence of unpaired magnetic poles called *monopoles*. Go online and obtain information about magnetic monopoles. Have scientists found any evidence of the existence of monopoles? How can you confirm that the sources you are using are reliable?

What Makes Materials Magnetic?

Magnetic force results from the interaction of moving charges. In materials, the moving charges of interest are the electrons in each atom's outer shells.

An electron can be modeled as orbiting the atomic nucleus and spinning about its own axis. Each type of motion produces a **magnetic moment,** which is a vector that represents the strength and orientation of a magnet. The head of the vector represents the north pole, and the tail represents the south pole. The orbital magnetic moment combines with the spin magnetic moment to produce a resultant magnetic moment for the electron.

Magnetic Moment Some atoms in materials are magnetic due to the combined motions of their electrons. When all electrons are considered, an atom with a magnetic moment will behave like a small bar magnet.

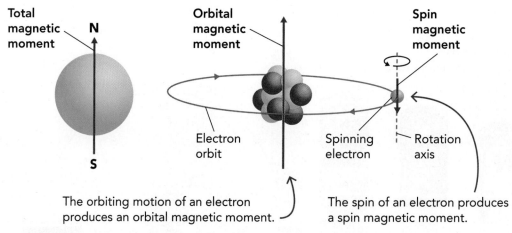

Total magnetic moment

Orbital magnetic moment

Electron orbit

The orbiting motion of an electron produces an orbital magnetic moment.

Spin magnetic moment

Spinning electron

Rotation axis

The spin of an electron produces a spin magnetic moment.

The direction of magnetic moments for electrons can be determined by curling the fingers of your left hand in the direction of electron motion. Your thumb points in the direction of the moment.

6. **SEP Construct an Explanation** In chemistry, an electron pair, or Lewis pair, consists of two electrons that occupy the same orbital but have opposite spin magnetic moments. The electron spins for the 1s orbital in helium are shown. Construct an explanation for why the electrons pair in the way shown.

$1s$

He $\boxed{1\!\downarrow}$

7. **SEP Analyze and Interpret Data** The spin magnetic moments of the electrons in the five 3d orbitals for iron and copper are shown. Which of the two elements is likely to exhibit greater magnetic properties and why?

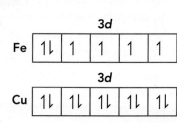

Magnetic Materials

Types of Materials A magnetic material whose atoms have permanently aligned magnetic moments is called a **permanent magnet.** Permanent magnets can be made from some ceramics, rare-earth metals, and iron alloys containing aluminum, nickel, and cobalt. Magnets made from iron alloys that contain aluminum, nickel, and cobalt are called AlNiCo magnets.

Ferromagnetic materials exhibit magnetic effects, but only in the presence of magnets. Their atoms exhibit magnetic moments, but in random orientations, requiring the influence of a magnet to align. Materials that exhibit very weak magnetic properties or none at all are called nonmagnetic.

VOCABULARY

Ferromagnetic comes from the Latin word *ferrum*, which means "iron," the most common ferromagnetic material. Iron's chemical symbol is Fe because of this Latin root.

Magnetic Magnets come in all shapes and sizes. Some have their poles marked, while others do not.

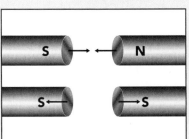

Magnets are both attracted and repelled by other magnets.

Ferromagnetic Materials containing iron, nickel, and/or cobalt are typically ferromagnetic.

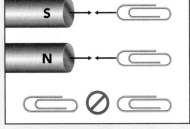

Ferromagnets are attracted to magnets, but they do not repel. They do not interact with each other.

Nonmagnetic Materials that do not interact with magnets are called nonmagnetic.

Nonmagnetic materials do not interact with magnets, ferromagnets, or each other.

(8) **SEP Analyze and Interpret Data** The three identical-looking cylinders shown are tested for various interactions. A student observes that end 1A attracts end 2A, end 1A attracts end 3A, and objects 2 and 3 do not interact. From these data, determine whether each object is magnetic, ferromagnetic, or nonmagnetic.

EXPERIENCE IT!

Touch a paper clip to a magnet for a short time. Remove the magnet and test if this paper clip attracts another paper clip. Now, throw the first paper clip hard against the table. Does it still attract other paper clips?

Magnetizing a Ferromagnet The process of aligning the magnetic moments in a ferromagnetic material is called **magnetization.** In ferromagnetic materials, large groupings of similarly aligned magnetic moments form naturally. These groupings are called **magnetic domains.** However, the domains typically exhibit random orientations, resulting in no net orientation for the material as a whole. This is why ferromagnets are not magnetic and do not interact with each other.

A ferromagnet can be magnetized by placing it between the opposite poles of two permanent magnets. Usually, a small amount of energy is required to "unstick" the domain orientations, either through heating or by hitting the material. Once unstuck, the domain magnetic moments align, producing a magnetic material. The material will maintain its magnetization even after the permanent magnets are removed, at least until some new energy is supplied to randomize the domain moments once again.

Magnetization An unmagnetized piece of iron is magnetized when placed between two permanent magnets and given energy.

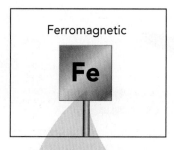
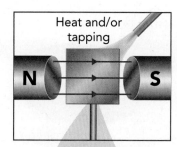
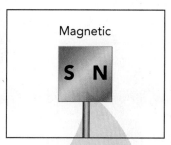

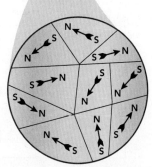
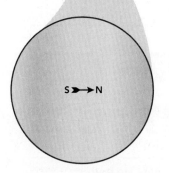

The moments of the magnetic domains are randomly oriented, resulting in no net magnetic moment.

Adding heat and an external magnet causes the domains to mostly align, with some domains merging.

When heat is removed, the orientations "stick," resulting in a permanent magnet.

(9) **SEP Ask Questions** Why do you think adding energy through heat or mechanically through tapping is usually necessary to reorient the magnetic domains?

(10) **SEP Develop and Use a Model** In your notebook, sketch a model for the magnetization of a circular object. Repeat for a diamond-shaped object. Clearly indicate the locations of the poles. Based on your model, is it possible for a bar magnet to have poles along the long sides instead of its ends?

Magnetic Fields

Field Lines Similar to gravitational and electric fields, a **magnetic field** is a vector field that describes a material's magnetic influence throughout space. Also, like gravitational and electric fields, magnetic fields can be represented using vectors at all points in space or by using field lines.

Representing Magnetic Fields

How do you **represent the magnetic field** around a magnet?

Test Magnet To probe an electric field, a small test charge that does not disrupt the field is used. Similarly, **a tiny magnet may be used to probe a magnetic field.**

A compass needle is a tiny magnet.

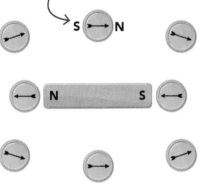

Field Lines The lines representing the magnetic field **point in the direction of the compass needle.** The field lines point **away from the magnet's north pole and toward its south pole.**

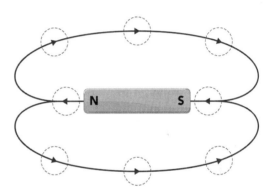

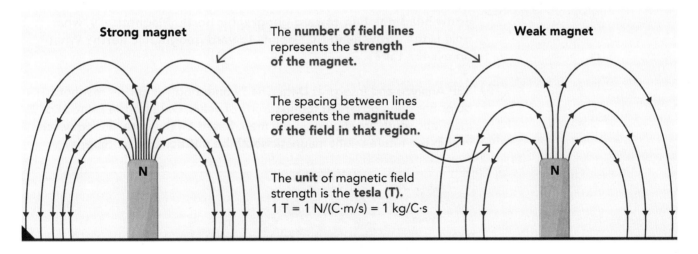

Strong magnet

The **number of field lines** represents the **strength of the magnet.**

The spacing between lines represents the **magnitude of the field in that region.**

The **unit** of magnetic field strength is the **tesla (T).**
$1\ T = 1\ N/(C \cdot m/s) = 1\ kg/C \cdot s$

Weak magnet

(11) **SEP Develop a Model** What does the magnetic field look like inside a magnet? To answer, imagine breaking the magnet in half between the poles and placing a compass in between the two halves. In which direction would the compass needle point? Sketch a model, and remember what happens when you break a magnet in two pieces.

GO ONLINE to watch a **video** about the location of the north pole and do a PhET **simulation** that allows you to describe magnetic fields.

Earth's Magnetic Field Earth behaves as a giant magnet, and as a result is surrounded by a magnetic field. Earth has two types of poles: **geographic poles,** which are at the points on the surface that are intersected by the axis of Earth's rotation, and magnetic poles. The axis of rotation and the magnetic poles do not align, and this difference changes over time. For any point on Earth's surface, the **magnetic declination** is the horizontal angle between true north (the direction to the geographic pole) and magnetic north (the direction a magnetic compass would point).

Earth's Magnetic Field The magnetic field lines produced by Earth's core come out of Earth's surface in the Southern Hemisphere and go back into the surface in the Northern Hemisphere.

The names of the poles are flipped. Geographic North corresponds to magnetic south.

The magnitude of Earth's magnetic field near the surface is approximately 5×10^{-5} T.

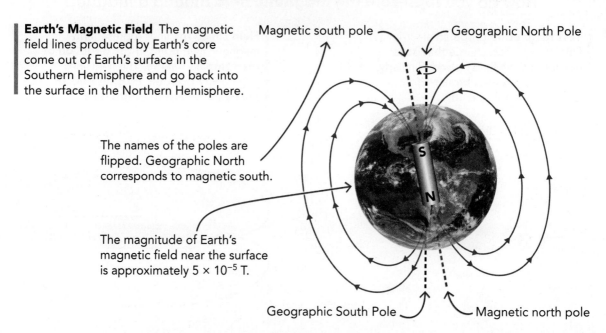

Magnetic south pole — Geographic North Pole

Geographic South Pole — Magnetic north pole

(12) **SEP Develop a Model** Sketch a model for a compass needle with the arrow head pointing toward geographic north. Magnetically, what pole is the arrow head that points toward geographic north? What pole is the tail?

(13) **SEP Analyze and Interpret Data** The "wandering" of Earth's magnetic poles has been observed for hundreds of years. Data for the location of magnetic south are shown on the map. Based on the data, during which year in the future might magnetic south be positioned over Siberia?

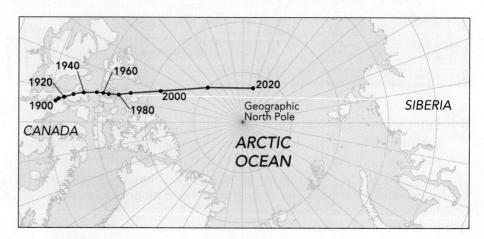

Modeling Multiple Magnets

To model the magnetic field due to multiple magnets, use the principle of superposition, similar to modeling an electric field due to multiple charges. However, the approach for magnetic fields will be qualitative, because the equations for magnetic fields are not as simple as for electric charges.

At each point in space, imagine a compass. Sketch the direction the compass would point due to the presence of one magnet. Then, sketch the direction it would point due to the other magnet. The compass will actually point somewhere in between those two directions, depending on the strength of the field from each magnet.

Superposition The magnetic field between the like poles of two equal-strength magnets is found using superposition.

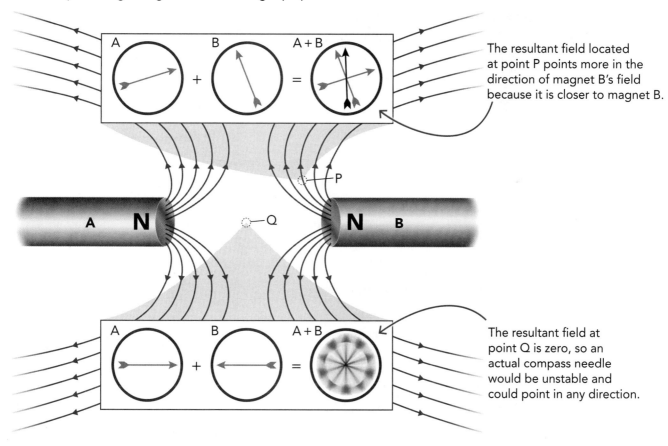

The resultant field located at point P points more in the direction of magnet B's field because it is closer to magnet B.

The resultant field at point Q is zero, so an actual compass needle would be unstable and could point in any direction.

(14) **SEP Develop a Model** Sketch a model of the magnetic field between the opposite poles of two equal-strength magnets.

(15) **SEP Argue from Evidence** A compass is placed the same distance away from two magnets, as shown. Make a claim about which magnet is stronger, and argue your claim from evidence.

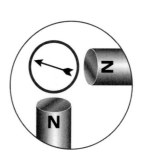

Magnetic Fields From Moving Charges

Magnetic force is the result of an interaction between moving charges. Because the field represents that potential force in space, moving charges also generate magnetic fields. The current through a wire is a stream of moving electrons and, therefore, should produce a magnetic field.

You can observe the magnetic field around a wire using a compass. The magnetic field around a wire forms circles around the outside of the wire. This is different than the field around a coil of wires, which is similar to the field around a bar magnet. You will learn more about how to quantitatively describe these fields in the next learning experience.

Magnetic Field From Electric Current A magnetic field is produced by any current-carrying wire, such as this straight wire and loop of wire.

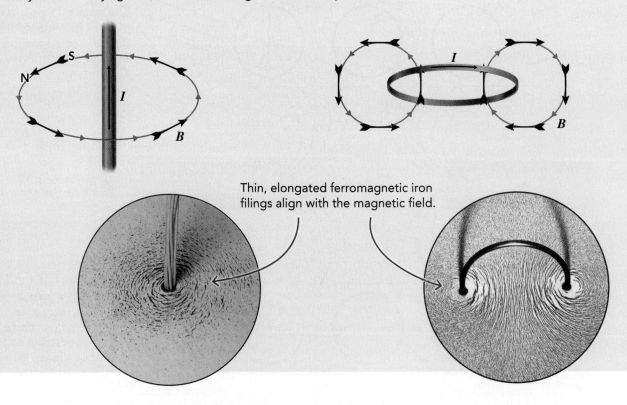

Thin, elongated ferromagnetic iron filings align with the magnetic field.

(16) **SEP Design a Solution** Using only some wire and a battery, design a solution for picking up a pile of paper clips without you, the wire, or the battery directly touching the pile of paper clips.

(17) **CCC Energy and Matter** Electrical energy confined to a wire is converted into a magnetic field, which propagates throughout space. How might this relate to induction cooking?

Force on a Moving Charge

The **Lorentz force equation** is the mathematical representation of the total force on a charged particle, including both the electric and magnetic force. The force is written in terms of the fields.

Lorentz Force
Magnetic force $$F = qE + (qv \times B)$$ Electric force
F = Lorentz force $\qquad$ v = velocity q = charge $\qquad\qquad$ B = magnetic field E = electric field

The equation shows that a charged particle must be moving to experience a magnetic force. The magnetic component of the Lorentz force uses a mathematical operation called the cross product (represented by the symbol "×"). The result is a force vector that points perpendicular to both the velocity vector and the magnetic field vector.

Magnitude of the Magnetic Component
$$F_M = qv_{\text{perp}}B$$
F_M = magnitude of magnetic force q = charge v_{perp} = velocity perpendicular to the magnetic field B = magnitude of magnetic field

The right-hand rule is used to determine the direction of the magnetic force on positive charges. The left-hand rule is used for negative charges. The magnitude of the magnetic components of the Lorentz force can also be determined from the equation above.

Right-Hand Rule The force on a charged particle due to an external magnetic field is perpendicular to both the field direction and the direction of charge motion. You use your right hand for positive charges and your left for negative.

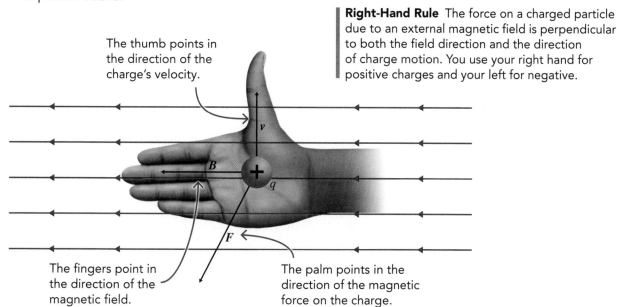

The thumb points in the direction of the charge's velocity.

The fingers point in the direction of the magnetic field.

The palm points in the direction of the magnetic force on the charge.

Force on a Charged Particle

You rub a small glass ball with a piece of silk, giving the ball a charge of 1.0×10^{-8} C. Determine the magnitude and direction of the force due to Earth's magnetic field if you throw the ball with a velocity of 8.0 m/s toward geographic west. (Hint: 1 T = 1 kg/C·s)

1. DRAW A PICTURE Sketch a picture of the situation.

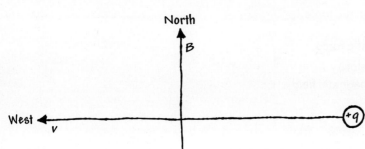

2. DEFINE THE PROBLEM List knowns and unknowns, and assign values to variables.

$$q = 1.0 \times 10^{-8} \text{ C} \qquad F_M = ?$$
$$v = 8.0 \text{ m/s}$$
$$B_{Earth} = 5.0 \times 10^{-5} \text{ T}$$

3. PLAN AND EXECUTE Use mathematical relationships, the picture, and your definitions to plan and execute a solution.

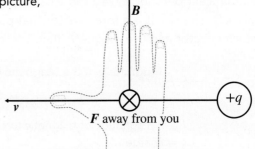

Determine the direction of the magnetic force on the positively charged ball using the right-hand rule.

Calculate the magnitude of the force on the ball using the magnetic component of the Lorentz force.

$$F_M = qv_{perp}B$$
$$= (1.0 \times 10^{-8} \text{ C})(8.0 \text{ m/s})(5.0 \times 10^{-5} \text{ T})$$
$$= (1.0 \times 10^{-8} \text{ C})(8.0 \text{ m/s})(5.0 \times 10^{-5} \text{ kg/C·s})$$
$$= 4.0 \times 10^{-12} \text{ N}$$

4. EVALUATE Reflect on your answer.
The result has the correct unit. The force is very small, indicating that the forces due to Earth's magnetic field are nearly imperceptible in day-to-day life.

 GO ONLINE for more **math support**.

▶ **Math Tutorial Video**

📱 **Math Practice Problems**

---

(18) You rub a small glass ball with a piece of silk, giving the ball a charge of 2.5×10^{-8} C. Determine the magnitude and direction of the force due to Earth's magnetic field if you throw the ball with a velocity of 10.0 m/s toward geographic east.

📖 **NEED A HINT?** Go online to your **eText Sample Problem** for stepped out support.

Charged Particles in Magnetic Fields

Circular Motion A charged particle in a uniform magnetic field will experience a centripetal force and move in a circular path. The magnetic force is always perpendicular to the velocity of the charge, so the magnitude of the velocity does not change. However, the direction of the velocity will change, resulting in circular motion. In this case, the magnetic force is the centripetal force causing the circular motion with a defined radius.

Circular Motion in a Magnetic Field
$$R = \frac{mv}{qB}$$
R = radius of motion $\qquad$ q = charge
m = mass of charged particle $\qquad$ B = magnitude of
v = velocity of charged particle $\qquad$ magnetic field

Circular Motion A charge moving through a uniform magnetic field experiences a centrifugal force and moves in a circular path.

An "X" indicates a magnetic field that points away from you, perpendicular to the plane of the diagram.

For a negative charge, you use your left hand to determine the direction of the force.

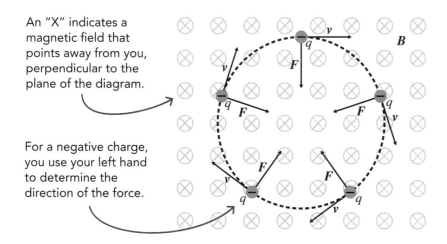

The magnetic force *is* the centripetal force.

$$F_M = ma_c \quad\Rightarrow\quad F_M = m\left(\frac{v^2}{R}\right) \quad\Rightarrow\quad qvB = m\left(\frac{v^2}{R}\right) \quad\Rightarrow\quad R = \frac{mv}{qB}$$

19 **SEP Apply Mathematical Concepts** Scientists use a bubble chamber to study subatomic particles. Charged particles leave behind a trail of tiny bubbles as they move through the liquid in the chamber, shown in the photo. A magnetic field is also applied, resulting in the particles' circular motions. How can you determine which particles have a positive charge and which particles have a negative charge?

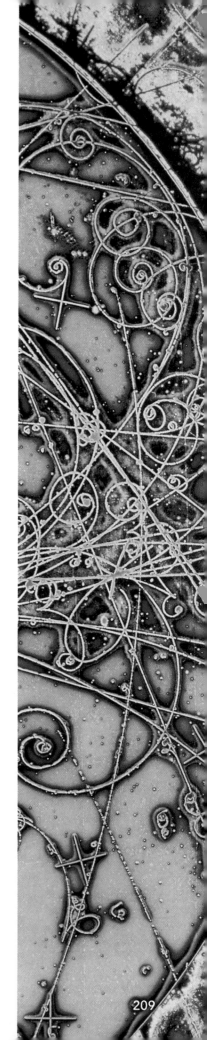

Cosmic Rays

Cosmic rays are charged particles that originate from the sun and other stars outside our solar system. A slow-moving cosmic ray proton with charge 1.6×10^{-19} C has a velocity of 8.0×10^4 m/s and travels perpendicular to Earth's magnetic field. If the field strength is 2.0×10^{-5} T at the altitude of the proton, then what is the radius of the circular motion?

1. DRAW A PICTURE Sketch a picture of the situation.

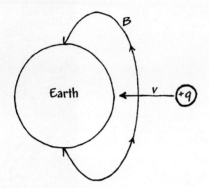

2. DEFINE THE PROBLEM List knowns and unknowns, and assign values to variables.

$q = 1.6 \times 10^{-19}$ C

$v = 8.0 \times 10^4$ m/s

$B = 2.0 \times 10^{-5}$ T

$m_{\mathrm{p}} = 1.7 \times 10^{-27}$ kg

$R = ?$

3. PLAN AND EXECUTE Use mathematical relationships, the picture, and your definitions to plan and execute a solution.

Write a force-acceleration equation for the force exerted by the magnetic field on the proton.	$F = ma_{\mathrm{c}}$
Substitute expressions for magnetic force and centripetal acceleration and solve for the radius.	$qvB = m\dfrac{v^2}{R} \rightarrow R = \dfrac{mv}{qB}$
Determine the radius using the known values.	$R = \dfrac{(1.7 \times 10^{-27}\,\text{kg})(8.0 \times 10^4\,\text{m/s})}{(1.6 \times 10^{-19}\,\text{C})(2.0 \times 10^{-5}\,\text{kg/C·s})} = 43$ m

4. EVALUATE Reflect on your answer.
The answer has the correct unit. The particle will move in a 43-meter circle as long as the magnetic field remains constant. The diameter of the circular path would be less than 10% of a kilometer, smaller than the expected altitude of the proton if the altitude was beyond Earth's atmosphere.

 GO ONLINE for more **math support**.

📱 **Math Practice Problems**

20) A cosmic ray electron with charge -1.6×10^{-19} C has a velocity of 5.0×10^6 m/s and travels perpendicular to Earth's magnetic field. If the field strength is 1.5×10^{-5} T, then what will be the radius of the circular motion?

📖 **NEED A HINT?** Go online to your **eText Sample Problem** for stepped out support.

21) A cosmic ray proton travels in a circle with a radius of 95 m perpendicular to Earth's magnetic field. If the proton's speed is 10^6 m/s, then what is the field strength at the proton's location?

Polar Lights Commonly referred to as northern lights or southern lights, auroras are light displays caused by the interaction of gas molecules in Earth's atmosphere with charged particles ejected from the sun that are funneled down Earth's magnetic field lines.

Nonperpendicular Motion A charged particle with a velocity that is at a nonperpendicular angle to a uniform magnetic field will move in a helical path along the direction of the field lines. The perpendicular components of the velocity cause a centripetal force, resulting in circular motion perpendicular to the field. The parallel component of the velocity causes no force, resulting in uniform motion parallel to the field.

Helical Motion A helical path is caused by the combination of components of the velocity both parallel and perpendicular to the magnetic field.

The perpendicular components of the velocity cause circular motion.

The parallel component of the velocity does not change because there is no force in this direction.

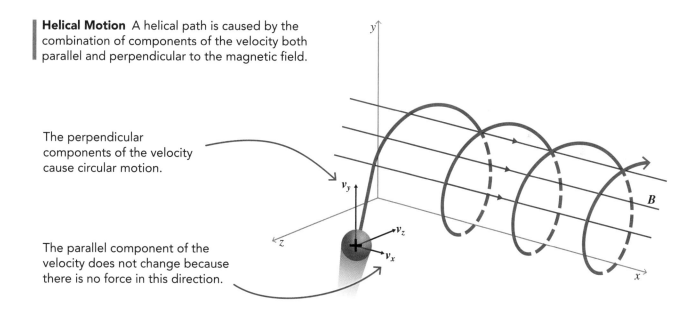

(22) **SEP Construct an Explanation** The figure shows charged solar particles and their trajectories as they encounter Earth's magnetic field. Construct an explanation for why auroras are observed in the sky near the Arctic and Antarctic regions.

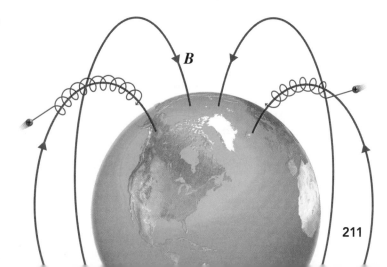

INVESTIGATIVE PHENOMENON

 GO ONLINE to revisit your **Investigative Phenomenon CER** with the new information you have learned about Magnetic Forces and Fields.

These questions will help you apply what you learned in this experience to the Investigative Phenomenon.

23) **SEP Develop a Model** An induction stove is an electrical device that generates a magnetic field to heat a pan. How do you think this magnetic field is generated? Sketch a model.

24) **SEP Design a Solution** Exciting the electrons in iron increases the energy in the iron atoms, which can cause heating. How might a magnetic field be used to excite electrons in atoms?

25) **SEP Argue from Evidence** Your friend claims that a copper pan will not work on an induction stove. Do you agree or disagree? Construct an argument from evidence.

26) **CCC Energy and Matter** How do you think the electrical energy in the induction stove is transferred to the egg in the pan? What medium is used to transfer the energy?

 GO ONLINE for a **quiz** to evaluate what you learned about Magnetic Forces and Fields.

Inducing Magnetism

 GO ONLINE to do a **hands-on lab** on the magnetic force that a current-carrying wire can generate.

Magnetic Force on a Wire

Force on Electrons in a Wire Charges moving through a magnetic field will experience a force. If those moving charges are trapped inside of a wire as a current, then the wire will also experience a force.

The force on the wire and its dependence on the current can be measured by placing the wire between the opposite poles of two magnets attached to a scale. The magnets generate an approximately uniform magnetic field. Remember, the direction of the current is the direction in which positive charges move, so use the right-hand rule to determine the direction of the force. The force is perpendicular to both the field and the scale, so the difference in the scale reading indicates the amount of force on the wire.

| **Force on Charges** The individual moving charges in a current-carrying wire all experience a force when placed in a magnetic field.

EXPERIENCE IT!

Bend a piece of wire into a U shape. Place the bottom of the U near the pole of a permanent magnet. Briefly attach the ends of a battery to the ends of the wire. What happens? Try switching the battery terminals.

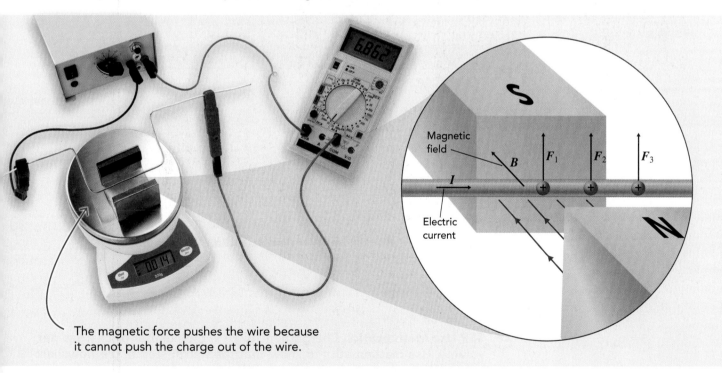

The magnetic force pushes the wire because it cannot push the charge out of the wire.

(27) **SEP Develop and Use a Model** The actual charges that move in a current-carrying wire are negatively charged electrons. Resketch the figure to show the motion of electrons. Does the force still point in the same direction?

2 Inducing Magnetism   **213**

▶ **GO ONLINE** to watch a **video** about an electric generator.

Modeling the Force on a Wire You can mathematically model the force on a current-carrying wire by adding up the individual forces exerted by the field on each electric charge in the current. The force is proportional to the current, the magnetic field, and the length of wire in the field. Only the length of the wire that is perpendicular to the field will contribute to the force, because only the component of the current direction perpendicular to the magnetic field produces a magnetic force.

Force on a current-carrying wire
$$F = IlB$$
F = magnitude of magnetic force exerted by the field on the wire I = current l = length of the wire within and perpendicular to the field B = magnitude of magnetic field

Force on a Wire The total force on the wire is the sum of all the forces exerted by the field on the individual charges.

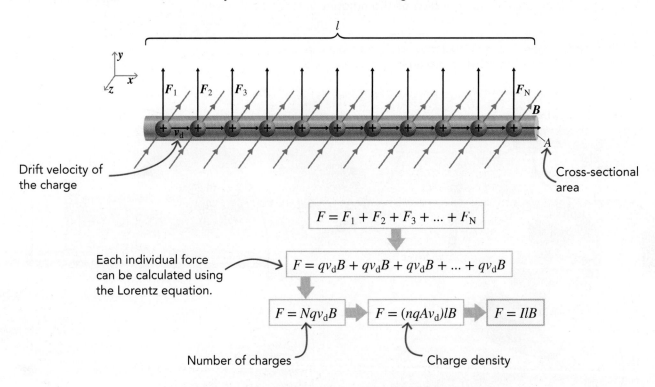

28) **SEP Use Mathematics** Charge density (n) is the number of charges per volume. Use mathematics to show that the fourth step in the flowchart is true. Write the current in terms of the charge density.

29) **SEP Plan an Investigation** Devise an experiment that would allow you to measure the magnitude of the magnetic field between two permanent magnets.

Calculating Force on a Wire

You are facing a 10-cm length of wire placed inside a uniform 2.0-T magnetic field directed up. A 10.0-A current is passed through the wire directed to the right, perpendicular to the magnetic field. Determine the direction and magnitude of the force on the wire.

1. DRAW A PICTURE Sketch a picture of the situation

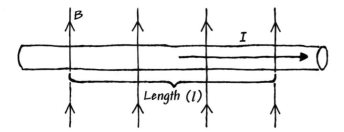

2. DEFINE THE PROBLEM List knowns and unknowns, and assign values to variables.

$l = 10$ cm $= 0.10$ m | $F = ?$

$B = 2.0$ T

$I = 10.0$ A

3. PLAN AND EXECUTE Use mathematical relationships, the picture, and your definitions to plan and execute a solution.

> Use the right-hand rule to determine the direction of the force.

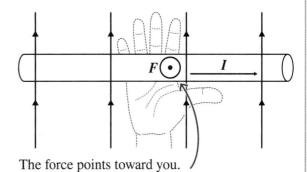

The force points toward you.

> Calculate the magnitude of the magnetic force exerted by the field on the wire.

$F = IlB$
$\quad = (10.0 \text{ A})(0.10 \text{ m})(2.0 \text{ T})$
$\quad = (10.0 \text{ C/s})(0.10 \text{ m}) (2.0 \text{ kg/C·s})$
$\quad = 2.0$ N

4. EVALUATE Reflect on your answer.
The calculation results in the correct unit for force. The magnetic force is nearly half of a pound, which would exceed the magnitude of the weight of the wire, causing the wire to rise.

 GO ONLINE for more **math support**.

▶ **Math Tutorial Video**

🖳 **Math Practice Problems**

---

(30) You are facing a 15-cm length of wire placed inside a uniform 4.0-T magnetic field directed down. A 5.0-A current is passed through the wire directed to the left, perpendicular to the magnetic field. Determine the direction and magnitude of the force on the wire.

📖 **NEED A HINT?** Go online to your **eText Sample Problem** for stepped out support.

(31) Using a scale, you measure the force on a 20.0-cm length of wire to be 0.800 N. The wire carries a current of 3.0 A. What is the magnitude of the magnetic field?

Torque on Loops

Torque Caused by Magnetic Fields Forces applied at different locations on an extended system can cause rotational motion. Think about a loop of wire in a uniform magnetic field. When a current travels through the loop, it moves in the opposite direction on either side of the loop. This results in forces acting on the opposite sides in opposite directions.

Because the points of application of the forces are separated on the wire loop, a lever arm is present. Remember that a lever arm is the distance from the axis of rotation to the point where the force is applied, and it is perpendicular to the axis of rotation. Therefore, a torque is produced on each side of the loop. Depending on the loop orientation, this results in a net torque that causes the loop to rotate.

Rotating Loop of Wire The magnetic force on opposite wire segments produces a net torque around an axis through the center of the loop. The other poles of these magnets are not shown for simplicity.

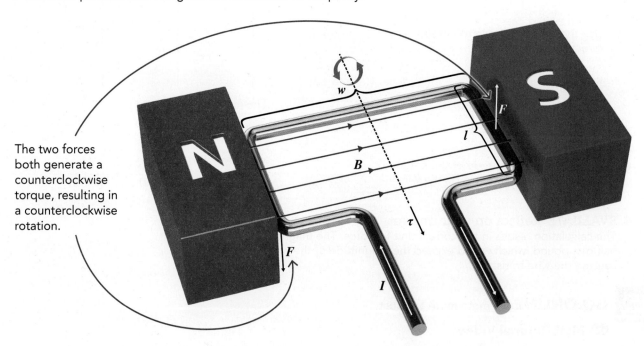

The two forces both generate a counterclockwise torque, resulting in a counterclockwise rotation.

(32) **SEP Develop and Use a Model** In your notebook, sketch the current loop shown in the figure, but orient the loop such that it is perpendicular to the magnetic field. Use your model to explain why these forces do not produce a net torque in this orientation.

(33) **SEP Argue from Evidence** You read a claim that a magnetic field always produces zero net force on a closed loop of wire. Argue for or against this claim using evidence from your model.

Modeling Rotations The torque on a current-carrying loop can be modeled by drawing an extended free-body diagram for the loop and analyzing the various torques that are produced. This can be done for multiple orientations of the loop as it rotates inside the magnetic field. When the lever arms are at their maximum, the torque is at its maximum. When the lever arms are zero, the torque is zero.

You can also write a mathematical model for the net torque about a symmetric loop of wire in terms of the lever arm and the force on each wire length.

Torque on a Current-Carrying Rectangular Loop

$$\tau = r_{\text{perp}}\, F_{\text{wire 1}} + r_{\text{perp}}\, F_{\text{wire 2}} = 2r_{\text{perp}}\, IlB$$

τ = torque
r_{perp} = lever arm, equal to half the loop width
l = length of the loop
I = current
B = magnitude of magnetic field

| **Magnitude of Torque** A top-view diagram of the loop in the magnetic field is shown at several points during a rotation.

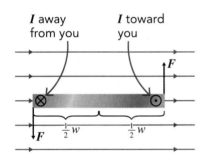

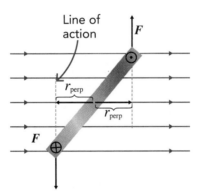

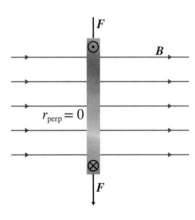

$$\tau = \tfrac{1}{2}wIlB + \tfrac{1}{2}wIlB$$

$$\tau = r_{\text{perp}}IlB + r_{\text{perp}}IlB$$

$$\tau = 0 + 0$$

$$\tau = wIlB = \tau_{\max}$$

$$\tau < wIlB$$

$$\tau = 0$$

The torque is maximum when the loop is parallel to the field.

The torque is zero when the loop is perpendicular to the field.

---

(34) **SEP Develop a Model** Sketch a model of the forces on a current-carrying triangular loop of wire placed in a uniform magnetic field. The top of the loop should be one side of the triangle. Label the direction of the force on each side.

Torque on a Loop

A square loop of wire with sides of length 20.0 cm and carrying a current of 10.0 A is placed inside a magnetic field with magnitude 5.0 T. What is the maximum magnitude of torque on the loop?

1. DRAW A PICTURE Sketch a picture of the situation.

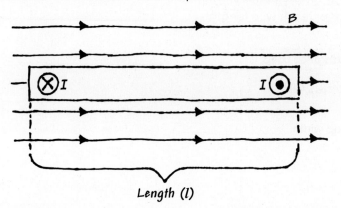

Length (*l*)

2. DEFINE THE PROBLEM List knowns and unknowns, and assign values to variables.

$l = 20.0 \text{ cm} = 0.200 \text{ m}$ $\tau = ?$

$I = 10.0 \text{ A}$

$B = 5.0 \text{ T}$

3. PLAN AND EXECUTE Use mathematical relationships, the picture, and your definitions to plan and execute a solution.

Determine the lever arm for the two forces when the maximum torque is reached.

$$r_{\text{perp}} = \frac{l}{2} = \frac{0.200 \text{ m}}{2} = 0.100 \text{ m}$$

Calculate the torque on the loop of wire.

$$\tau = 2r_{\text{perp}}IlB$$
$$= 2(0.100 \text{ m})(10.0 \text{ A})(0.200 \text{ m})(5.0 \text{ T})$$
$$= 2(0.100 \text{ m})(10.0 \text{ C/s})(0.200 \text{ m})(5.0 \text{ kg/C·s})$$
$$= 2.0 \text{ N·m}$$

4. EVALUATE Reflect on your answer.
The torque on the loop changes from 2 N·m to zero as it spins in the magnetic field. This is a small torque, which is expected because the lever arm is small and both the current and the magnetic field do not have a large magnitude.

    GO ONLINE for more **math support**.

   Math Practice Problems

---

(35) A square loop of wire with sides of length 15.0 cm and carrying a current of 12.0 A is placed inside a magnetic field with magnitude 8.0 T. What is the maximum magnitude of torque on the loop?

   NEED A HINT? Go online to your **eText Sample Problem** for stepped out support.

(36) What current would be required to produce a maximum 16 N·m torque on a square loop of wire with sides of length 16.0 cm placed inside a magnetic field with magnitude 4.0 T?

Modeling a Simple Motor

 GO ONLINE to do a PhET **simulation** that allows you to explore moving a magnet near a coil of electrically conducting wire.

Electric motors are the most common application of magnetically induced torque on wire loops. There are many different types of electric motor designs, but they all utilize magnetic fields and loops of wire to produce rotations.

One of the simplest designs is the **brushed direct current motor,** which uses a direct current power source, such as a battery, and alternates the direction of the current through a coil of wire using a set of electrically conductive brushes. The motor converts electrical energy into the kinetic energy of the spinning coil.

A Simple Motor This simple motor consists of a fixed set of magnetic poles of opposite polarity and a loop of wire on a rotatable shaft. The other poles of these magnets are not shown for simplicity.

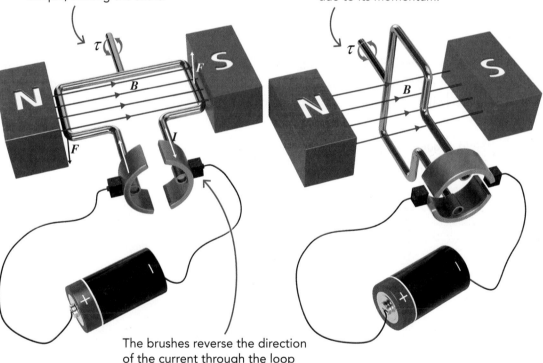

Current travels through the loop. The magnetic field produces a torque, turning the shaft.

In this orientation, the torque is zero. The shaft keeps rotating due to its momentum.

The brushes reverse the direction of the current through the loop to maintain the same direction of torque and rotation.

(37) **SEP Design a Solution** You can construct a simple motor as shown using a battery, a magnet, some paper clips, and some thin insulated wire. Design a solution that would allow the coil of wire to continually spin.

Current and Magnetic Fields

Current-Carrying Wires You have discovered that mass produces a gravitational field and charge produces an electric field. Similarly, moving charge, which is just current, produces a magnetic field.

In Newton's law of universal gravitation, the gravitational field is proportional to the mass. In Coulomb's law, the electric field is proportional to the charge. The **Biot-Savart law** states that the magnitude of the magnetic field is proportional to the current. For a current-carrying wire, a right-hand rule is used to determine the field direction.

Biot-Savart Law for a Straight Current-Carrying Wire

$$B = \frac{\mu_0 I}{2\pi r}$$

B = magnitude of the magnetic field
μ_0 = permeability of free space ($4\pi \times 10^{-7}$ T·m/A)
I = current
r = distance from the wire

The **permeability of free space** is a constant that represents the ability of a magnetic field to permeate, or fill, empty space. It is also connected to the amount of energy that can be stored in a magnetic field.

Field Around a Wire Compasses placed near a long, straight current-carrying wire show circular field lines around the wire.

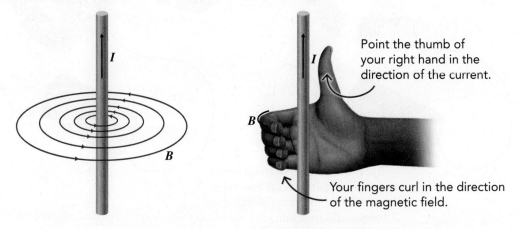

Point the thumb of your right hand in the direction of the current.

Your fingers curl in the direction of the magnetic field.

(38) SEP Develop and Use a Model Sketch a model of the magnetic field for two current-carrying wires side by side. Assume the current is going in the same direction through each wire. Use your model to explain why the wires would be attracted to each other.

(39) CCC Patterns Make a table of the various fields you have learned about, what property produces those fields, the equations that relate them to that property, and the names given to those equations.

Current-Carrying Loops The general Biot-Savart law is actually a complicated calculus expression, so you will not learn how to derive mathematical equations for more complicated wire shapes. However, even for more complicated wire shapes like a loop of wire, the magnetic field is still proportional to the current through the wire, and the same right-hand rule can be used to determine the field direction.

Biot-Savart Law for a Current-Carrying Circular Loop

$$B_{\text{center}} = \frac{\mu_0 I}{2R}$$

B_{center} = magnetic field at the center of the loop
μ_0 = permeability of free space ($4\pi \times 10^{-7}$ T·m/A)
I = current
R = radius of loop

This equation is similar to that for a straight wire. However, the equation for a loop is valid only at the center of the loop. The magnetic field strength gets smaller farther away from the loop.

Field Around a Loop The right-hand rule can be used to determine the direction of the magnetic field through a current-carrying loop.

The magnetic field around a loop looks similar to the magnetic field around a bar magnet.

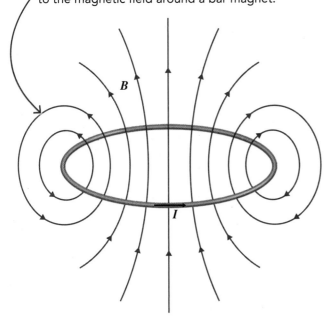

Your fingers curl in the direction of the magnetic field.

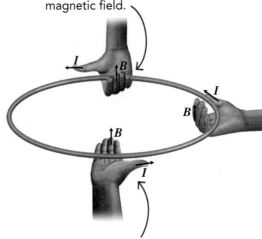

Your thumb points in the direction of the current.

(40) **SEP Use Mathematics** Imagine you have three identical loops of wire placed on top of each other, all carrying the same current moving in the same direction. Calculate the magnitude of the magnetic field in the middle of the loops. (Hint: Use superposition.)

Current-Carrying Solenoid A **solenoid** is a long current-carrying wire wound into a helical coil. Imagine wrapping a long piece of wire around a piece of pipe and attaching the wire ends to a battery. The result would be a solenoid.

You can think of a solenoid as multiple individual loops of wire placed on top of each other. Similar to the straight wire and the loop, you determine the field direction with the right-hand rule, and the magnitude of the field inside is proportional to the current. The field inside a solenoid is very uniform, like the electric field between the plates of a parallel-plate capacitor.

Biot-Savart Law for a Solenoid
$$B_{inside} = \frac{\mu_0 N I}{l}$$
B_{inside} = magnetic field inside a solenoid μ_0 = permeability of free space ($4\pi \times 10^{-7}$ T·m/A) I = current N = number of loops l = length of the solenoid

Solenoids are used to produce electromagnets. An **electromagnet** is a type of magnet in which a magnetic field is generated by an electric current. Electromagnets often consist of a wire wrapped around an iron core.

Field Around a Solenoid The magnetic field inside a solenoid is uniform. The field outside is much smaller.

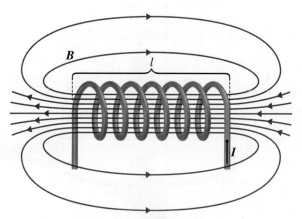

The right-hand rule can be used to determine the direction of the magnetic field through a current-carrying loop.

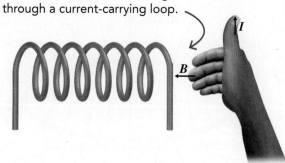

(41) **SEP Develop and Use a Model** Sketch a model of a solenoid with a cylinder of iron through the center. In your model, show why the iron cylinder will become magnetized. With the addition of the iron core, will the magnetic field produced by the solenoid increase, decrease, or stay the same? Use your model and the concept of superposition to explain your answer.

Field Inside a Solenoid

A 0.25-m-long solenoid made up of 2000 loops carries a 12.0-A current. What are the magnitude and direction of the magnetic field inside in the solenoid?

1. DRAW A PICTURE Sketch a picture of the situation.

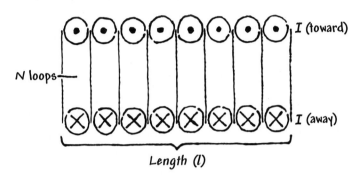

2. DEFINE THE PROBLEM List knowns and unknowns, and assign values to variables.

$l = 0.25$ m

$N = 2000$

$I = 12.0$ A

$B_{inside} = ?$

3. PLAN AND EXECUTE Use mathematical relationships, the picture, and your definitions to plan and execute a solution.

> Use the right-hand rule to determine the field direction inside the solenoid.

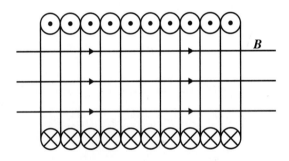

> Calculate the magnitude of the magnetic field.

$$B_{inside} = \frac{\mu_0 N I}{l}$$

$$= \frac{(4\pi \times 10^{-7}\,\text{T·m/A})(2000)(12.0\,\text{A})}{0.25\,\text{m}}$$

$$= 0.12\,\text{T}$$

4. EVALUATE Reflect on your answer.
The units are correct for the magnetic field. The magnetic field is oriented as shown in the diagram. The measured magnetic field far exceeds the magnitude of Earth's magnetic field on Earth's surface.

 GO ONLINE for more **math support**.

📖 **Math Practice Problems**

(42) A 0.5-m-long solenoid made up of 5000 loops carries an 8.0-A current. What are the magnitude and direction of the magnetic field inside the solenoid?

📖 **NEED A HINT?** Go online to your **eText Sample Problem** for stepped out support.

(43) You measure the magnetic field inside a solenoid to be 0.3 T. The current through the solenoid is 22.0 A, and the length is 0.3 m. How many individual loops make up the solenoid?

Modeling Earth's Magnetic Field

Dynamo Effect Now that you know that Earth behaves as a giant magnet with its own magnetic field and that magnetic fields are produced by moving charges, you can start to develop a model that explains why Earth is a magnet. The **geomagnetic field,** another name for Earth's magnetic field, extends from deep in Earth's core and out into space. The magnetic field is produced and sustained by electric currents swirling around in the fluid outer core, which make up a **geodynamo.**

There are three components to Earth's geodynamo. Convection in the outer core results from heat lost to the bottom of the mantle and the crystallization of iron onto the solid inner core. The convection of liquid metal also carries electric currents of mobile electrons within it. Last, these convection patterns are twisted up into cylinders by Earth's rotation, which also twist up the magnetic field lines. As a result, the magnetic field is both induced and continually maintained by the patterns of flow within Earth's outer core.

Geodynamo Swirling currents of liquid metal in Earth's outer core produce the geomagnetic field.

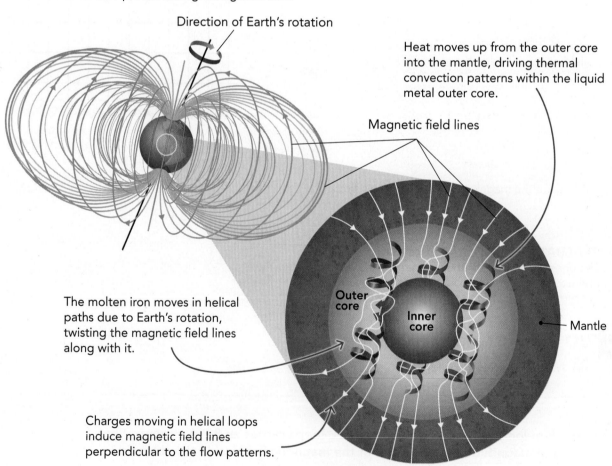

Direction of Earth's rotation

Heat moves up from the outer core into the mantle, driving thermal convection patterns within the liquid metal outer core.

Magnetic field lines

The molten iron moves in helical paths due to Earth's rotation, twisting the magnetic field lines along with it.

Outer core

Inner core

Mantle

Charges moving in helical loops induce magnetic field lines perpendicular to the flow patterns.

(44) **CCC Systems and System Models** Explain how the generation of Earth's magnetic field by the flow of metal in the outer core is both similar to and different from the magnetic field resulting from a solenoid.

Pole Reversals

How do you know that Earth's magnetic poles have reversed?

Seafloor Spreading Earth's surface is divided into tectonic plates that are slowly pulled apart as part of Earth's mantle convection. At mid-ocean ridges, where oceanic plates are pulled apart, hot magma rises to fill the gap. As it cools, it forms **new oceanic crust that gradually gets pulled apart** by the moving plates and dragged away from the ridge.

As **magma cools** and crystallizes, the **moments of magnetic domains** within metal-rich minerals **partially align with Earth's magnetic field.** Once the new rocks harden, the **induced magnetization** within these minerals **becomes permanent.**

In the 1960s, **alternating magnetic polarities of crustal rocks** were found across the entire ocean floor, parallel to mid-ocean ridges, suggesting **multiple past reversals of Earth's magnetic field direction.**

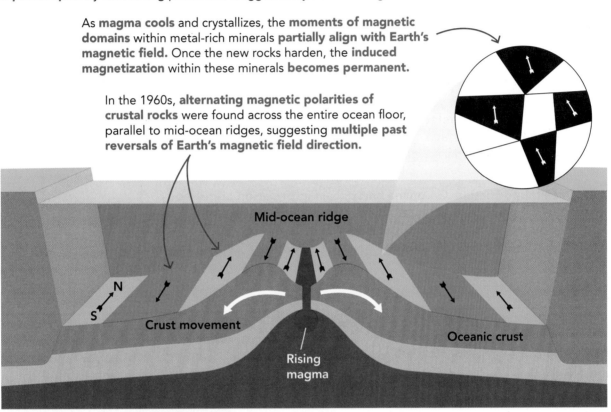

Dating Reversals Using radiometric dating and magnetometer measurements of seafloor minerals, **scientists can determine the periods** during which the **magnetic poles were reversed.** The timing of these reversals is random, and therefore unpredictable.

Normal magnetic polarity

Reversed magnetic polarity

Mid-ocean ridge

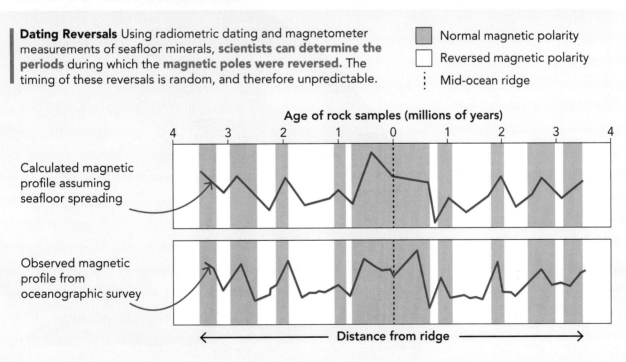

INVESTIGATIVE PHENOMENON

 GO ONLINE to revisit your **Investigative Phenomenon CER** with the new information you have learned about Inducing Magnetism.

These questions will help you apply what you learned in this experience to the Investigative Phenomenon.

45 **SEP Construct Explanations** Suppose that the ages of all past magnetic field reversals are known. Explain how this could be used to map the ages of Earth's ocean crust.

46 **SEP Develop a Model** In your notebook, sketch a model for the force on a moving electron in a metal pan when a uniform magnetic field is applied perpendicular to the surface. Your model should specifically describe the trajectory of the electron.

47 **SEP Obtain Information** Go online and obtain information about eddy currents. Compared to the model of electron motion you sketched for the previous question, what is similar and what is different?

 GO ONLINE for a **quiz** to evaluate what you learned about Inducing Magnetism.

Inducing Current

 GO ONLINE to do a **hands-on lab** to explore how to generate an electric current by moving a bar magnet through a coil of wire.

Magnetic Flux

Magnetic flux is a measure of the amount of magnetic field that is passing through a given area. The flux is proportional to the size of the area and the magnitude of the magnetic field that is perpendicular to the area.

You can use an analogy with light to think about magnetic flux. The amount of light from a lamp is analogous to the magnetic field. The surface area of your hand is analogous to the area. The size of the shadow cast by your hand represents the flux, which is the amount of light that would have passed through that area if your hand had not been in the way.

> **EXPERIENCE IT!**
>
> Hold out your hand directly under a light source with your palm facing down. Observe the shadow that your hand casts. Then, tilt your hand slightly so that your palm no longer faces directly down. Explain what happens to the shadow.

Magnetic Flux
$\Phi = B_{perp}A$

Φ = magnetic flux through an area
B_{perp} = magnetic field perpendicular to the area
A = area

Flux Magnetic flux is a measure of the magnetic field passing through an area. The flux depends on the magnitude of the field, the area, and the orientation of the area with respect to the field.

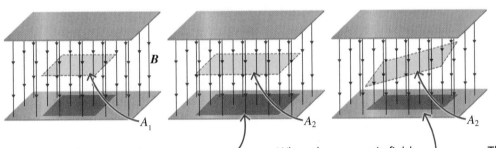

Increasing the area increases the number of field lines through the area. This is analogous to the size of the shadow cast by your hand.

When the magnetic field strikes the area at an angle, the flux is reduced. This is analogous to tilting your hand to cast smaller shadows.

The perpendicular component of the field points normal to the area.

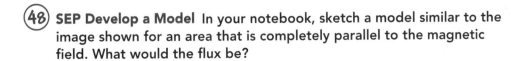

48 SEP Develop a Model In your notebook, sketch a model similar to the image shown for an area that is completely parallel to the magnetic field. What would the flux be?

Calculating Magnetic Flux

A square loop with sides of length 0.5 m is oriented parallel to the y- and z-axes. A uniform magnetic field passes through the loop. The field is $\boldsymbol{B} = (0.3\ \text{T})\hat{\boldsymbol{x}} + (0.2\ \text{T})\hat{\boldsymbol{y}}$. Determine the magnetic flux through the loop.

1. DRAW A PICTURE Sketch a picture of the situation.

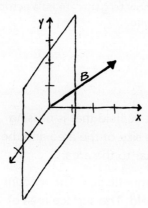

2. DEFINE THE PROBLEM List knowns and unknowns, and assign values to variables.

$l = 0.5$ m	$A = ?$
$B_x = 0.3$ T	$B_{\text{perp}} = ?$
$B_y = 0.2$ T	$\Phi = ?$

3. PLAN AND EXECUTE Use mathematical relationships, the picture, and your definitions to plan and execute a solution.

Calculate the area of the loop.

> The loop is a square with equal-length sides.
> $A = l^2 = (0.5\ \text{m})^2 = 0.25\ \text{m}^2$

Determine the magnitude of the magnetic field perpendicular to the area.

> From the image, you can see that the x component of the magnetic field is perpendicular to the area.
> $B_{\text{perp}} = 0.3$ T

Calculate the magnetic flux through the loop.

> $\Phi = B_{\text{perp}}A = (0.3\ \text{T})(0.25\ \text{m}^2) = 0.08\ \text{T·m}^2$

4. EVALUATE Reflect on your answer.

The answer is in terms of a unit for magnetic field strength times units of area, which is the correct units for magnetic flux. Because the magnitudes for the field strength and area are less than 1 T and 1 m² respectively, the answer would be expected to be less than 1 T·m².

 GO ONLINE for more **math support**.

▶ **Math Tutorial Video**

🖥 **Math Practice Problems**

---

49 A square loop with sides of length 0.80 m is oriented parallel to the x- and z-axes. A uniform magnetic field passes through the loop. The field is $\boldsymbol{B} = (0.50\ \text{T})\hat{\boldsymbol{x}} + (0.60\ \text{T})\hat{\boldsymbol{y}}$. Determine the magnetic flux through the loop.

📖 **NEED A HINT?** Go online to your **eText Sample Problem** for stepped out support.

50 A square loop with sides of length 0.60 m is oriented parallel to the y- and z-axes. A uniform magnetic field passes through the loop. The field is $\boldsymbol{B} = (0.10\ \text{T})\hat{\boldsymbol{x}} + (0.90\ \text{T})\hat{\boldsymbol{y}}$. Determine the magnetic flux through the loop.

Electromotive Force

Electromotive force, also written as EMF, is a measure of the energy gained per unit of charge when energy is converted from one form into electrical energy. For example, a battery converts chemical energy into electrical energy. This conversion results in an action, the EMF, that drives current around a circuit.

In many ways, a battery in an electric circuit is analogous to a pump that drives water around a closed loop. The pump converts mechanical energy into kinetic energy of the water, driving the water through the pipes.

The EMF is measured in units called volts (V), after Italian physicist Alessandro Volta. This unit may be familiar, since it is commonly used to describe batteries. For example, a car battery is called a 12-V battery. In an ideal battery, an electron passing through it will gain energy. The total EMF produced by the battery is the energy gained per electron. Similarly, the EMF equivalent for a water pump would be the energy gained by the water per volume, referred to as pressure. In effect, the EMF is "electrical pressure."

Water Pump A water pump produces a difference in energy per volume, or pressure. The water moves from the high-pressure side to the low-pressure side, circulating around the loop.

Electric "Pump" Electromotive force is a difference in electrical energy per charge. The charges in the wire move from high to low energy, circulating around the loop.

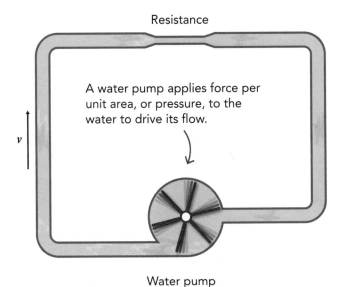

Resistance

A water pump applies force per unit area, or pressure, to the water to drive its flow.

v

Water pump

Resistance

A battery applies "electrical pressure" to drive the flow of current in a circuit.

I

EMF

(51) **CCC Cause and Effect** Imagine rolling a fixed number of marbles down a slide. If you want a continuous stream of marbles to roll down the slide, what action must you take? Develop an analogy between this situation and electromotive force.

Induction

 GO ONLINE to do a PhET **simulation** that allows you to investigate Faraday's law and electromagnetic induction.

Faraday's Law Just as a battery stores energy, a magnetic field stores energy. Therefore, magnetic fields can be used to produce an EMF when the field's energy is converted into electrical energy in a circuit. The most basic circuit is a simple loop of wire. **Induction** is the process of changing the amount of magnetic field going through a loop of wire (magnetic flux), which produces an EMF in the loop. The EMF drives current around the loop.

Faraday's Law
$$V_\varepsilon = -N\frac{\Delta\Phi}{\Delta t}$$
V_ε = induced electromotive force $\quad$ $\frac{\Delta\Phi}{\Delta t}$ = rate of change of
N = number of wire coils $\qquad\qquad\qquad$ magnetic flux

Faraday's law is a mathematical model used to predict how a magnetic field will produce an EMF in a loop of wire. Faraday's law tells you that in order to produce an EMF in a loop—and, therefore, a current—the magnetic flux must be varied. This can be done either by changing the strength of the magnetic field or by changing the area of the loop.

Inducing EMF Moving a magnet through a loop of wire generates an EMF in the loop, driving current around the loop.

A voltmeter measures the amount of EMF produced.

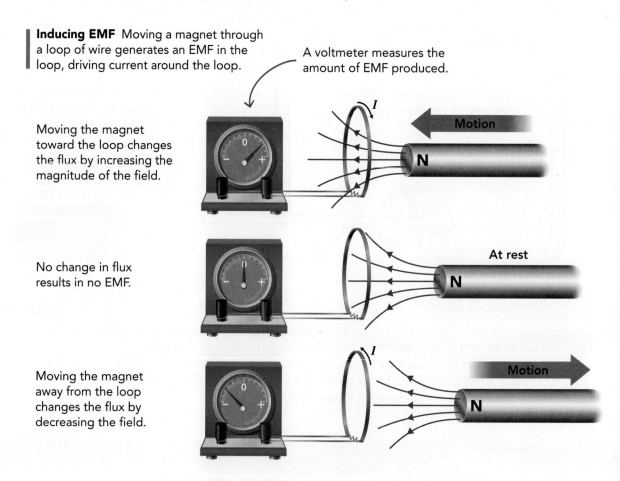

Moving the magnet toward the loop changes the flux by increasing the magnitude of the field.

No change in flux results in no EMF.

Moving the magnet away from the loop changes the flux by decreasing the field.

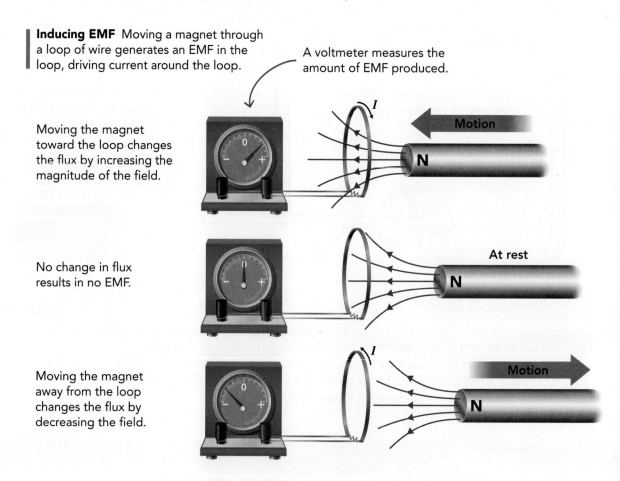 (labels in figure: *Motion*, *N*, *I*, *At rest*)

Lenz's Law Changing the flux through a loop generates an EMF and causes a current to flow around the loop. You learned previously, from the Biot-Savart law, that current produces its own magnetic field. Therefore, inducing a current in wire using a magnetic field involves two magnetic fields: the external field generated by the magnet and the induced field generated by the loop due to the induced current.

Known as **Lenz's law,** the negative sign in Faraday's law means that the induced current and induced magnetic field oppose the change in flux. When a magnet is pulled away from a loop, the external field gets smaller. The loop generates a magnetic field that opposes this change in flux by producing a current moving in the correct direction. Similar to how you used change in velocity vector diagrams to determine the directions of accelerations, you can use change in field vectors to determine the directions of induced fields.

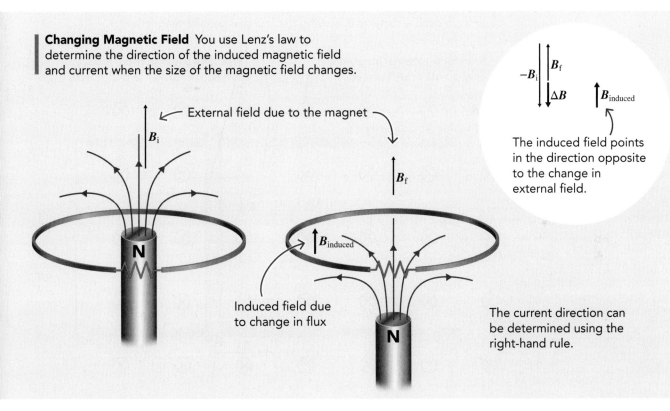

Changing Magnetic Field You use Lenz's law to determine the direction of the induced magnetic field and current when the size of the magnetic field changes.

External field due to the magnet

B_i

B_f

B_induced

Induced field due to change in flux

The induced field points in the direction opposite to the change in external field.

The current direction can be determined using the right-hand rule.

(52) **SEP Argue from Evidence** What would happen if you kept the magnet still but rotated the wire loop? Would an EMF be produced? Make a claim and argue from evidence.

(53) **SEP Construct an Explanation** If you drop a small rock down a vertical length of copper tube, it falls quickly out the other end. However, if you drop a magnet down the same tube, it takes significantly longer to fall. Construct an explanation for why a magnet would fall more slowly even though copper is nonmagnetic.

Motional EMF

Changing Area You can also change the magnetic flux by changing the area of the wire loop, either by rotating it or changing its size. The magnetic field strength remains constant, but the amount of field through the loop still changes.

A simple example of this is two metal rails connected via a fixed wire on one end and a metal bar that can move from side to side. This combination produces a rectangular wire loop, the size of which can be changed by moving the bar. The size of the induced EMF depends on the magnetic field strength, the distance between the rails, and the speed with which the bar is moved.

Simple Rail System Two metal rails are connected via a fixed wire and a movable metal rod. Moving the rod changes the magnetic flux.

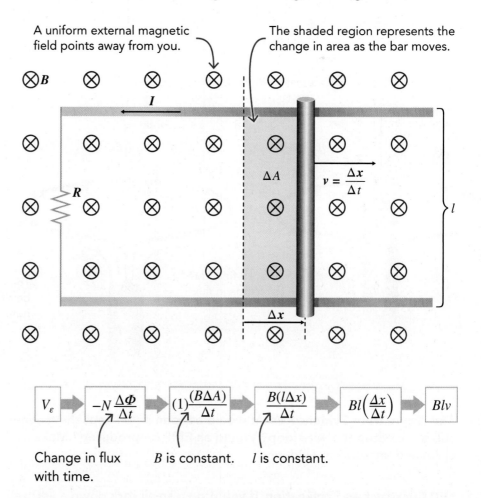

A uniform external magnetic field points away from you.

The shaded region represents the change in area as the bar moves.

$$V_\varepsilon \quad \rightarrow \quad -N\frac{\Delta\Phi}{\Delta t} \quad \rightarrow \quad (1)\frac{(B\Delta A)}{\Delta t} \quad \rightarrow \quad \frac{B(l\Delta x)}{\Delta t} \quad \rightarrow \quad Bl\left(\frac{\Delta x}{\Delta t}\right) \quad \rightarrow \quad Blv$$

Change in flux with time.   *B* is constant.   *l* is constant.

(54) **SEP Design a Solution** NASA has been investigating a system for launching payloads into space that is similar to a simple motional EMF rail system. Instead of moving the bar to produce current, current is used to launch the bar. Design a solution that could be used to launch the metal bar off the end of the rails.

Induced Field Use Lenz's law to determine the direction of both the induced magnetic field and the current. In this case, the external magnetic field vector stays constant, since the external field does not change. Instead, use the change in area to determine the directions of induced fields due to a flux change. An area can be represented using an **area vector.** The size of the arrow represents the magnitude of the area, and the direction of the arrow points perpendicular to the area. The induced field will oppose the change in area vector.

| **Changing Area Vector** The side view shows the direction of the change in area.

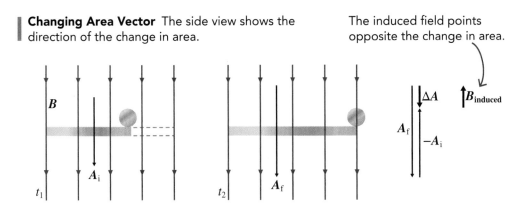

The top view shows the induced field and the direction of the current.

Use the right-hand rule to determine the direction of the current.

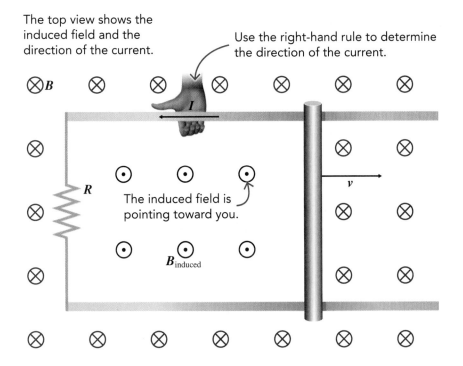

The induced field is pointing toward you.

55) **SEP Develop a Model** Sketch a model of a metal bar moving through a uniform magnetic field with no rails. Using what you know about the Lorentz force, show that negative charge in the bar would move in one direction and positive charge would accumulate at the opposite end of the bar. Assume that the bar, the field, and the direction of motion are mutually perpendicular.

56) **SEP Construct an Explanation** To produce an EMF across a metal bar, you do not need the rails. The equation works even without a loop. Construct an explanation for this fact.

Inducing Current by Decreasing Area

Two rails separated by a distance of 0.50 m are connected by a fixed wire on the left end and a movable metal rod on the right, forming a loop. A uniform magnetic field with magnitude 1.50 T points toward you through the loop. You move the rod to the left with a speed of 3.0 m/s. Calculate the induced EMF and determine the direction of the current.

1. DRAW A PICTURE Sketch a picture of the situation.

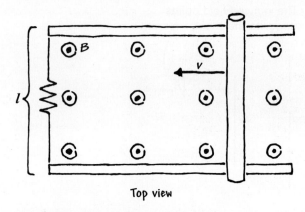

Top view

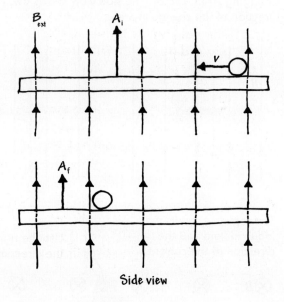

Side view

2. DEFINE THE PROBLEM List knowns and unknowns, and assign values to variables.

$l = 0.50$ m $\quad\Big|\quad V_\varepsilon = ?$

$B = 1.50$ T

$v = 3.0$ m/s

3. PLAN AND EXECUTE Use mathematical relationships, the picture, and your definitions to plan and execute a solution.

Use Lenz's law to determine the direction of the induced field.	$-A_i \Big\downarrow \quad \Big\uparrow{}^{A_f} \Big\downarrow{}_{\Delta A} \quad \Big\uparrow B_{\text{ind}}$
Use the right-hand rule to determine the direction of the current.	The current is counterclockwise around the loop.
Calculate the induced EMF.	$V_\varepsilon = Blv = (1.50 \text{ T})(0.50 \text{ m})(3.0 \text{ m/s}) = 2.3 \text{ V}$

4. EVALUATE Reflect on your answer.
Induced current opposes the change in flux of the external field. The loop shrinks, so the induced magnetic field inside the loop pointing in the same direction as the external field matches the expected result.

 GO ONLINE for more **math support**.

▶ **Math Tutorial Video**

☁ **Math Practice Problems**

(57) Two rails separated by a distance of 0.25 m are connected by a fixed wire on the left end and a movable metal rod on the right, forming a loop. A uniform magnetic field with magnitude 3.5 T points away from you through the loop. You move the rod to the left with speed 6.0 m/s. Calculate the induced EMF and determine the direction of the current.

📖 **NEED A HINT?** Go online to your **eText Sample Problem** for stepped out support.

(58) If you ran at 8.0 m/s in a direction that is perpendicular to Earth's magnetic field while holding a 1.0-m-long aluminum rod, what EMF would be generated across the rod due to Earth's magnetic field? Is this number large or small? (Assume that the orientation of the rod is also perpendicular to the field.)

(59) Airplanes are examples of long metal objects moving through Earth's magnetic field. Calculate the induced EMF across the entire 80.0-m wingspan of a jet airplane when it is flying at 320 m/s. Assume that the vertical component of Earth's magnetic field is 2.5×10^{-5} T.

(60) A television antenna consisting of a wire bent into a circular shape has a diameter of 0.12 m. The uniform magnetic field of a TV signal is perpendicular to the plane of the loop, and its magnitude is changing at the rate of 0.25 T/s. What EMF is induced in the antenna? Sketch the direction of the induced current.

(61) The graph shows data for the magnitude of a magnetic field as a function of time. The field is perpendicular to the plane of a square loop with sides having a length of 0.35 m. Determine the EMF induced in the field during the time period.

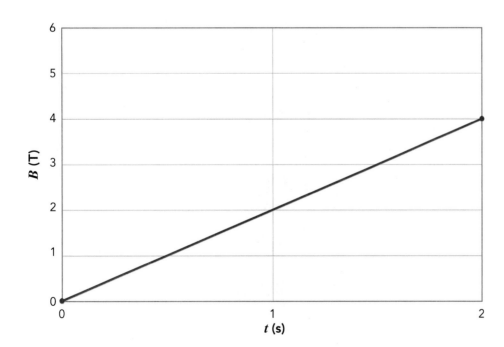

Wireless Induction

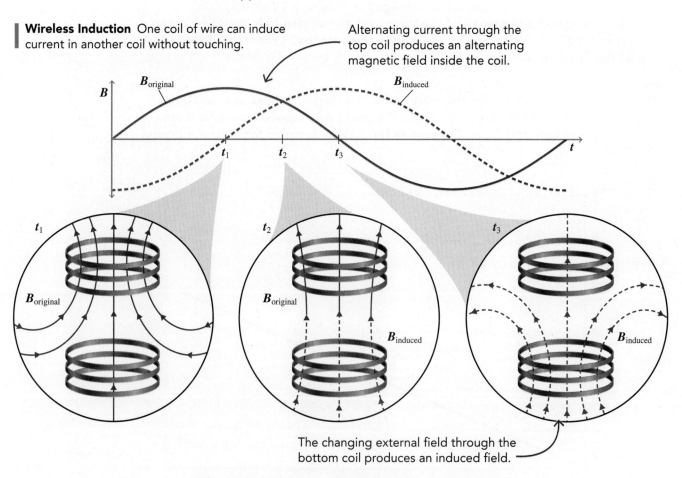

▶ **GO ONLINE** to watch a **video** about induction.

So far, you have explored inducing current by moving a magnet through a loop of wire or by changing the area of the loop. Instead of using a permanent magnet to generate the external field, a solenoid could be used. The magnitude of the external field produced by the solenoid could then be changed by varying the supplied current.

To continually change the magnetic field with time, the solenoid could be powered by **alternating current** (AC), which is an electric current that periodically reverses direction and changes its magnitude continuously with time. Because the magnetic field is proportional to the current, the field would also continuously change with time.

Wireless induction occurs when a constantly changing external magnetic field from a solenoid induces current in another solenoid. The solenoids do not have to be touching for wireless induction to occur; only one solenoid needs to be supplied with an electric current.

Wireless Induction One coil of wire can induce current in another coil without touching.

Alternating current through the top coil produces an alternating magnetic field inside the coil.

The changing external field through the bottom coil produces an induced field.

62 **SEP Construct an Explanation** Construct an explanation for why the current in the bottom coil increases while the current in the top coil decreases. To help with your explanation, sketch the change in field vector for the first two times shown.

Wireless Energy Transfer
How does **wireless charging work?**

How Wireless Charging Works Devices that can be charged wirelessly use a **metal coil in the device to pick up the changing magnetic field transmitted by another metal coil in a charger.** There are two main types of wireless charging—inductive and magnetic resonance.

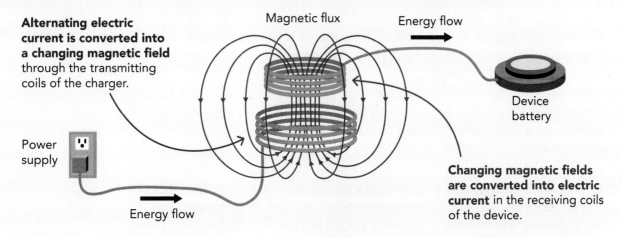

Alternating electric current is converted into a changing magnetic field through the transmitting coils of the charger.

Power supply

Energy flow

Magnetic flux

Energy flow

Device battery

Changing magnetic fields are converted into electric current in the receiving coils of the device.

Inductive Charging Devices using inductive charging must be placed directly on the charger's surface so their respective coils overlap.

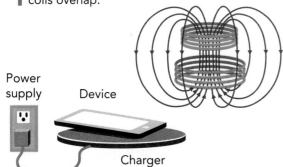

Power supply

Device

Charger

Magnetic Resonance Charging Using magnetic resonance, multiple devices can be charged at the same time without needing to be placed directly on the charger.

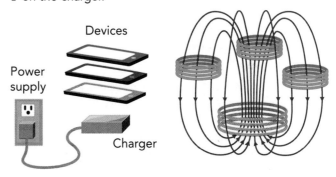

Devices

Power supply

Charger

Inducing Eddy Currents Induction produces an electromagnetic **eddy current** in a metal, causing the metal to heat.

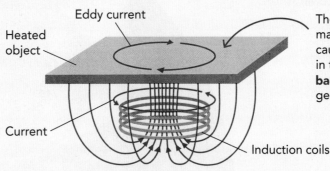

Eddy current

Heated object

Current

Induction coils

The changing magnetic field causes the **electrons** in the metal to **move back and forth,** generating **heat.**

63 **SEP Evaluate Information** How do you use wireless induction in your everyday life?

INVESTIGATIVE PHENOMENON

GO ONLINE to revisit your **Investigative Phenomenon CER** with the new information you have learned about Inducing Current.

These questions will help you apply what you learned in this experience to the Investigative Phenomenon.

64 **SEP Develop a Model** In your notebook, sketch a schematic model of an induction stove that you can use to explain how you can cook an egg without the stove itself getting hot.

65 **SEP Design a Solution** A wireless light bulb would be a neat engineering feat. Design a solution for lighting a small bulb using some wire and an induction stove.

66 **SEP Obtain, Evaluate, and Communicate Information** Magnetically induced eddy currents can be formed in any conductor, not just ferromagnets like iron. However, aluminum and copper pans do not work on induction stoves. Go online and obtain information about why this is the case. Communicate what you find to a classmate.

67 **SEP Use Mathematics** The maximum magnitude of the magnetic field generated by a single induction stove element is approximately 2×10^{-4} T. Calculate the maximum flux through a small and a large frying pan. Look up any information you might need.

68 **CCC Energy and Matter** To cook an egg on an induction stove, energy somehow gets from the electrical outlet to the egg. In your notebook, sketch a schematic diagram of the energy flow from the outlet to the egg. Note any conversions of energy from one form to another.

GO ONLINE for a **quiz** to evaluate what you learned about Inducing Current.

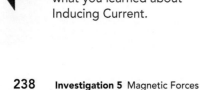

These questions will help you apply what you learned in this investigation to the Anchoring Phenomenon.

69 **CCC Cause and Effect** Variations in Earth's gravitational field caused by the influence of the sun and the moon are responsible for tides, which contribute to coastal erosion. How do the sun and the moon influence Earth's magnetic field? Does this influence lead to changes in Earth's surface landforms?

70 **SEP Construct an Explanation** Unlike Earth, the moon's interior is entirely solid. Discuss why this fact helps explain why the moon has no magnetic field.

☑ INVESTIGATION ASSESSMENT

 GO ONLINE for activities that will give you an opportunity to **demonstrate what you have learned:**

☑ **Engineering Performance-Based Assessment** Induce magnetic fields and electric currents.

📄 **Engineering Workbench** Design a flashlight that operates without batteries.

🖥 **Career Connections** Learn about how a highway engineer applies knowledge of physics.

☑ **Investigation Test** Take this test to evaluate your understanding of magnetic forces.

☑ **Virtual Lab Performance-Based Assessment** Optimize voltage in a generator.

What happens to this pole as it bends?

Forces in Materials

The world record for the high jump is 2.45 m (just over 8 feet), which is about 30% higher than the height of a typical male high jumper. The world record for the pole vault is 6.18 m, which is over three times the height of a typical pole vaulter.

During a vault, the vaulter uses speed and strength to apply force to a vaulting pole, which bends as a result. As the pole returns to its original shape, it propels the vaulter up in the air.

A typical vaulting pole is made of fiberglass or carbon fibers. These materials are flexible but durable, allowing the pole to bend without breaking. What accounts for these special properties in the materials? How do engineers determine which materials to use when designing and constructing objects and devices?

(1) **CCC Structure and Function** What properties of glass, bamboo, and iron make them unsuitable materials to use to make vaulting poles?

(2) **SEP Define the Problem** What forces are acting on the vaulting pole shown in the photo?

(3) **SEP Construct an Explanation** Do you think that flexibility or durability is the most important consideration when designing a vaulting pole? Explain your answer.

Atoms and Atomic Structure

GO ONLINE to do a **hands-on lab** to model how the structure of an atom was inferred.

The Atom

Atomic Theory The law of conservation of mass and the law of constant composition are important scientific ideas that developed in the 1700s. Building on these ideas in the early 1800s, John Dalton proposed that the observable behavior of gases is best understood if gases are composed of individual particles—atoms, which are the smallest indivisible piece of an elemental substance. Dalton's atomic theory states that all the atoms of a given element are identical to one another but different from atoms of other elements, especially in terms of mass.

Though this theory has undergone some modifications, it is still the basis of our modern understanding of the elements, and it is still the starting point for understanding chemistry. Every element consists of a fundamental particle known as an atom. Atoms of different elements are different from each other.

Dalton's Theory Dalton's atomic theory was derived from many observations of the behavior of gases. In this example, mass is conserved when 32 g of oxygen gas is combined with 28 g of nitrogen gas.

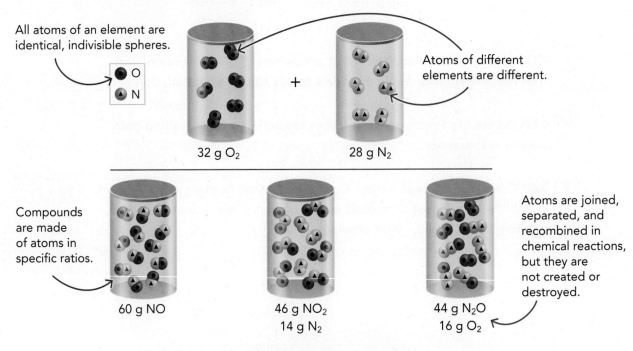

All atoms of an element are identical, indivisible spheres.

O
N

Atoms of different elements are different.

32 g O₂

28 g N₂

Compounds are made of atoms in specific ratios.

60 g NO

46 g NO₂
14 g N₂

44 g N₂O
16 g O₂

Atoms are joined, separated, and recombined in chemical reactions, but they are not created or destroyed.

(4) **SEP Construct an Explanation** The claims of Dalton's atomic theory have been revised over the past 200 years. Which claim or claims do you think have been proven incorrect based on new evidence?

Atoms as Building Blocks

▶ **GO ONLINE** to watch a **video** about a journey that explores the world at an atomic level.

Atoms can bond together to form molecules. Some molecules are compounds, meaning their constituent atoms are not all the same element. The elemental proportions of each compound molecule are given by chemical formulas. For example, every molecule of H_2O (water) is two atoms of hydrogen bonded with one atom of oxygen.

Some molecules are not compounds; instead, the molecule is made of multiple atoms of the same element. An example is hydrogen gas, H_2. The formula tells you that a hydrogen gas molecule is a bonded pair of hydrogen atoms, with no other types of atoms included.

The atoms of certain elements are able to bond in different combinations. For example, oxygen can form molecules of O_2, O_3, O_4, or O_8. Each of these molecules has different properties, making the term "pure oxygen" ambiguous—the chemical formula is needed to clarify which particular arrangement, or allotrope, is being referenced.

EXPERIENCE IT!

If possible, hold your arms out and make your hands into fists. Then, form arrangements with your classmates of two, three, four, and eight people so that everyone's fists are connected. How would the possible arrangements change if you had four arms instead of only two?

Phosphorus These are allotropes of pure phosphorus. These materials are the same atomically, but the ways in which the atoms bond yield differing properties.

White phosphorus is highly reactive in air, so it is stored in water.

Red phosphorus is more stable than white phosphorus and is typically found as a powder.

Black phosphorus has semiconductive properties.

⑤ **SEP Ask Questions** White phosphorus turns into red phosphorus after prolonged heating or exposure to sunlight. What questions would you ask to try to determine why this change occurs and what causes it at a molecular level?

Electrons

Dalton's theory viewed atoms as indivisible spheres. Almost a century later, J. J. Thomson's experiments with cathode rays resulted in the discovery of a particle having about 1/1800th the mass of the lightest known atom. Thomson had discovered a subatomic particle that is now called the electron.

Today, cathode rays are understood to be beams of electrons, and atoms are understood to consist of electrons and other subatomic particles, including protons and neutrons.

Further experimentation has shown no difference between electrons from atoms of different elements. Electrons in a hydrogen atom are physically identical to electrons in a uranium atom. Our current understanding is that electrons are indivisible particles, although their behavior is still the subject of a great deal of research.

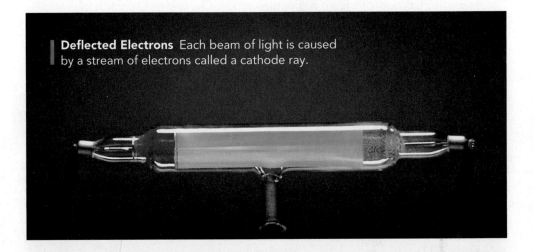

Deflected Electrons Each beam of light is caused by a stream of electrons called a cathode ray.

A magnet deflects the beam, so the beam must be made of charged particles.

(6) **SEP Design an Experiment** Design an experiment or experiments with a cathode ray tube to determine the factors that affect how much the beam of electrons is deflected by a magnet.

Speed of an Electron

A cathode ray is subjected to a magnetic field of strength 1.50 milliTeslas, which is directed perpendicular to the path of the ray. This interaction causes the path of the ray to bend in an arc of radius 24.3 cm. Using the known values of electron charge and mass, what is the speed of each electron in the beam? Note: 1 T = 1 kg/C·s

1. DRAW A PICTURE Sketch a picture of the situation.

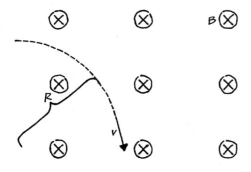

2. DEFINE THE PROBLEM List knowns and unknowns, and assign values to variables.

$B = 1.50 \times 10^{-3}$ T

$R = 24.3$ cm $= 0.243$ m

$q = 1.60 \times 10^{-19}$ C

$m = 9.11 \times 10^{-31}$ kg

$v = ?$

3. PLAN AND EXECUTE Use mathematical relationships, the picture, and your definitions to plan and execute a solution.

Write a force-acceleration equation for the force by the magnetic field on the electron.

$$F = ma_c$$

Substitute expressions for magnetic force and centripetal acceleration and solve for the velocity.

$$qvB = m\frac{v^2}{R} \rightarrow v = \frac{qBR}{m}$$

Determine the velocity using the known values.

$$v = \frac{(1.60 \times 10^{-19} \text{ C})(1.50 \times 10^{-3} \text{ kg/C·s})(0.243 \text{ m})}{9.11 \times 10^{-31} \text{ kg}}$$

$$= 6.40 \times 10^7 \text{ m/s } \hat{\theta} \leftarrow \hat{\theta} \text{ denotes the direction perpendicular to } \hat{r}.$$

4. EVALUATE Reflect on your answer.
The units are units of velocity. This speed is very fast, but it is still one order of magnitude slower than the speed of light, which is about 3×10^8 m/s.

 GO ONLINE for more **math support**.

▶ **Math Tutorial Video**

🖥 **Math Practice Problems**

---

⑦ A cathode ray is subjected to a magnetic field of strength 22.0 milliTeslas, which is directed perpendicular to the path of the ray. This interaction causes the path of the ray to bend in an arc of radius 5.75 cm. Using the known values of electron charge and mass, what is the speed of each electron in the beam?

📖 **NEED A HINT?** Go online to your **eText Sample Problem** for stepped out support.

The Nucleus

VOCABULARY

The original meaning of the Latin-derived term **nucleus** was the "kernel of a nut," which eventually came to refer to the essential center of a group of objects.

Discovery of the Nucleus Once the existence of subatomic particles was established, experiments were devised to determine their roles in the makeup of an atom. Initial theories suggested that electrons sit inside an atom rather than contribute to the inherent atomic structure.

The prevailing view changed dramatically when Ernest Rutherford and his team discovered that all of an atom's positive charge—along with more than 99% of the atom's mass—is concentrated in a small, dense area at the atom's center they termed the nucleus, after the nucleus of a cell. The nucleus contains the other two major subatomic particles: protons and neutrons. As with electrons, these subatomic particles are identical from element to element. The data showed that most of the atom—the building block of matter—is just empty space.

Bohr's Model of the Atom The model developed by Niels Bohr altered Rutherford's model in order to address why electrons do not simply get pulled into the nucleus by Coulomb attraction. In turn, Bohr's model was refined by others, and the concept of an electron as a particle orbiting the nucleus eventually changed into the modern view of the electron as a wave of probable positions that can take various shapes called orbitals.

Scale of an Atom An atom is mostly empty space with positive charge concentrated in the nucleus, surrounded by rapidly moving electrons.

The diameter of the nucleus is about 100,000 times smaller than the diameter of the entire atom.

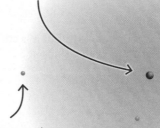

The electron is more than 1000 times smaller in diameter than the nucleus.

Diameter of atom (one ten-billionth of a meter)

8) **CCC Scale, Proportion, and Quantity** Use the information in the diagram to determine the approximate diameter of the nucleus of an atom and of an electron.

Periodic Physical Trends

Periodic Table Scientists have organized the elements into the periodic table, which groups different elements with similar properties into the same columns. The periodic table also reveals trends in the properties of elements relative to one another. These trends can be explained by the interaction in Coulomb forces within atoms of differing atomic number.

Major Trends on the Periodic Table

What are some of the patterns in the properties of elements?

Periodic Patterns The patterns in the properties of elements on the periodic table can be explained by the concept of nuclear charge. It increases as protons are added, exerting a stronger force on the outermost electrons. However, as electrons are added to an atom, the outermost electrons experience weaker attraction because they are farther from the nucleus.

Atomic radius is the distance from the nucleus to the outermost electrons. A stronger nuclear charge pulls outer electrons in closer and reduces the atomic radius, while adding electrons increases the radius.

Electronegativity refers to how easily an atom or molecule can attract electrons in a chemical bond. It is dependent on the attractive force exerted by the nucleus on the electrons in an atom.

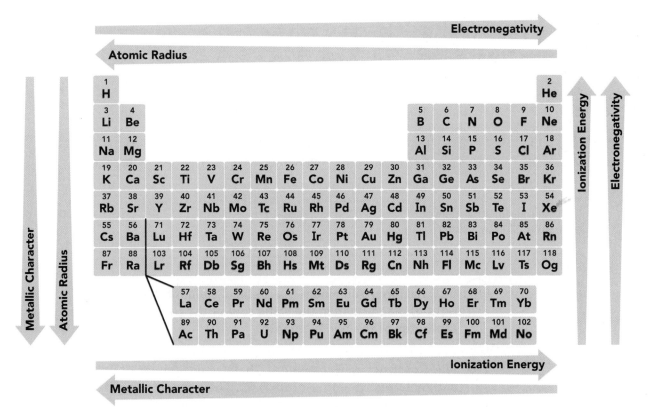

Metallic character refers to properties such as ductility and conductivity of heat and electricity. Elements with the greatest metallic character have outer electrons that are loosely held to the nucleus.

Ionization energy is the energy required to remove an electron from an atom. When protons are added, the stronger nuclear charge makes it harder to remove an electron.

Atomic Radius The mass of an atom is almost entirely due to the number of protons and neutrons in its nucleus. However, atoms of different elements not only have different weights, but they also have different sizes. Moving left to right across a period in the periodic table, elements have progressively heavier atoms due to more crowded nuclei. But as the nuclei increase in size, the atom's volume does not get larger; in fact, its volume gets smaller.

Adding more protons to the nucleus not only increases both the mass and the atomic number, but it also increases the amount of positive charge in the nucleus. The greater positive charge generates a stronger Coulomb attraction on each electron orbital, drawing them each into a smaller volume. However, each row of the periodic table only corresponds to a particular electron shell. Each new shell produced is farther from the nucleus. This means the atomic radius becomes larger as you move down the periodic table to include each new shell of electrons.

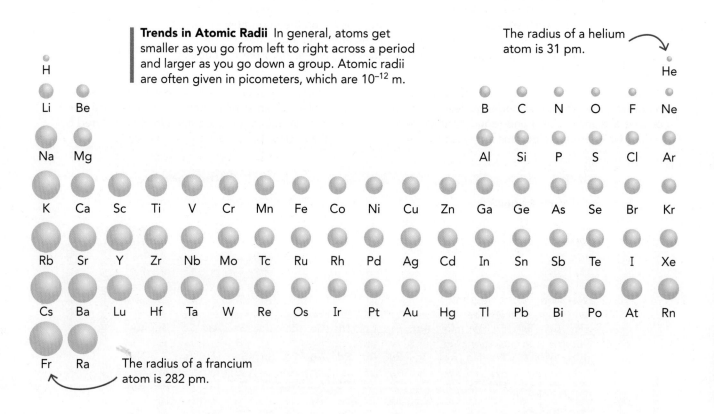

Trends in Atomic Radii In general, atoms get smaller as you go from left to right across a period and larger as you go down a group. Atomic radii are often given in picometers, which are 10^{-12} m.

The radius of a helium atom is 31 pm.

The radius of a francium atom is 282 pm.

9 **CCC Patterns** Aluminum is a metallic element that is located to the right of magnesium in the same row of the periodic table. Compare the attributes of the two elements.

10 **SEP Construct an Explanation** The atomic number of lithium is 3, and the atomic number of tin is 50. Their atomic weights are about 7 atomic mass units (amu) and 119 amu, respectively. However, despite the large difference in atomic number and weight, lithium and tin atoms are not too different, 145 pm in radius. Explain why this is the case.

Relative Sizes of Atoms

Every neutral lithium-7 atom has a mass of 7.02 amu and a radius of 145 pm. Fluorine-19 has a mass of 19.0 amu and a radius of 50 pm. As a percentage of lithium-7, what are the volume and mass of a neutral atom of fluorine-19?

1. DRAW A PICTURE Sketch a picture of the situation.

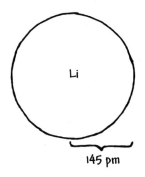 

Li

F

50 pm

145 pm

2. DEFINE THE PROBLEM List knowns and unknowns, and assign values to variables.

$m_{Li} = 7.02$ amu

$m_F = 19.0$ amu

$R_{Li} = 145$ pm
$= 1.45 \times 10^{-10}$ m

$R_F = 50$ pm
$= 5.0 \times 10^{-11}$ m

% by volume = ?

% by mass = ?

3. PLAN AND EXECUTE Use mathematical relationships, the picture, and your definitions to plan and execute a solution.

Find the volume of an atom of lithium-7.

$$V_{Li} = \frac{4}{3}\pi r^3 = \frac{4}{3}\pi(1.45 \times 10^{-10} \text{ m})^3 = 1.28 \times 10^{-29} \text{ m}^3$$

Find the volume of an atom of fluorine-19.

$$V_F = \frac{4}{3}\pi r^3 = \frac{4}{3}\pi(5.0 \times 10^{-11} \text{ m})^3 = 5.2 \times 10^{-31} \text{ m}^3$$

Calculate the percentages using the percent formula.

$$\% \text{ by volume} = \frac{V_F}{V_{Li}} = \frac{5.2 \times 10^{-31} \text{ m}^3}{1.28 \times 10^{-29} \text{ m}^3} \times 100 = 4.1\%$$

$$\% \text{ by mass} = \frac{m_F}{m_{Li}} = \frac{19.0 \text{ amu}}{7.02 \text{ amu}} \times 100 = 271\%$$

4. EVALUATE Reflect on your answer.
Fluorine-19 is much more massive than lithium-7 but just a tiny fraction of the volume. The answer agrees with the expected trend in the periodic table, because fluorine is to the right of lithium in the same period.

 GO ONLINE for more **math support**.

▶ **Math Tutorial Video**

🖥 **Math Practice Problems**

⑪ Every neutral sodium-23 atom has a mass of 23.0 amu and a radius of 186 pm. Argon-36 has a mass of 36.0 amu and a diameter of 97.0 pm. As a percentage of argon-36, what are the volume and mass of a neutral atom of sodium-23?

📖 **NEED A HINT?** Go online to your **eText Sample Problem** for stepped out support.

⑫ A certain cesium atom has a radius that is 520% that of a fluorine-19 atom and a mass that is 14.3% that of a fluorine atom. What are the cesium atom's atomic weight and radius?

INVESTIGATIVE PHENOMENON

GO ONLINE to revisit your **Investigative Phenomenon CER** with the new information you have learned about Atoms and Atomic Structure.

These questions will help you apply what you learned in this experience to the Investigative Phenomenon.

13 **CCC Matter and Energy** Three elements commonly found in fiberglass poles are shown in the table. Based on the positions of the elements in the periodic table, complete the table with the words "greater" and "lesser" to compare the properties of sodium and silicon with those of aluminum.

Element	Symbol	Atomic Number	Atomic Radius	Electro-negativity	First Ionization Energy
Sodium	Na	11			
Aluminum	Al	13	143 pm	1.6	578 kJ/mol
Silicon	Si	14			

14 **SEP Evaluate Claims** A fiberglass pole contains many different types of atoms. A friend claims that all of the atoms in the pole can be treated as inert spheres of different radii, depending on the type of atoms. What evidence suggests that your friend is incorrect?

15 **SEP Ask Questions** Over 99.9999999% of the atoms that make up fiberglass are empty space. What questions can you ask to help determine why objects that are mostly empty space can feel solid to the touch and do not allow your hand to pass through them?

GO ONLINE for a **quiz** to evaluate what you learned about Atoms and Atomic Structure.

Attractive and Repulsive Forces

 GO ONLINE to do a **hands-on lab** that explores the attractive forces that cause surface tension in liquids.

Coulomb Forces Between Atoms

An atom is only electrically neutral if the number of electrons in its orbitals equals the number of protons in the nucleus. When these quantities are not equal, the atom is known as an ion. An ion has a net charge that causes it to interact with other charged particles (including other ions) via the Coulomb force. The Coulomb attraction between cations (positively charged ions) and anions (negatively charged ions) forms the basis of ionic bonds.

Ions can form lattice patterns of alternately charged particles extending in three dimensions. This pattern occurs because an ion exerts a Coulomb force on all the other oppositely charged ions nearby, not just its closest neighbor, so a single ion can attract multiple ions of the opposite charge.

Ionic Crystals Ionic solids form crystalline patterns, meaning the ions in crystals such as this salt (sodium chloride) crystal line up in repeating geometric shapes. Note: The size ratio of Cl^- to Na^+ does not reflect the size ratio of the neutral atoms because the size of a neutral atom changes when it becomes an ion.

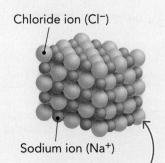

Chloride ion (Cl^-)

Sodium ion (Na^+)

Stress

Stress

Repulsion

Each cation attracts anions on all sides. Each anion attracts cations on all sides.

The pattern does not respond well to bending or sliding, so ionic solids cleave, or break along a surface, more easily than metals.

 (16) **SEP Construct an Explanation** Explain how the salt crystal shown in the photograph may have formed such smooth surfaces through only natural forces.

Covalent Bonds

VOCABULARY

Valence electrons are the electrons in an atom's outermost shell. When one of these electrons becomes shared between two atoms, it has joint valence with both atoms, or covalence, and thus has formed a **covalent bond.**

Forming Molecules In a **covalent bond,** at least one electron from the two atoms forming the bond no longer interacts only with one nucleus. Instead, it interacts with both nuclei. Once two or more atoms are bonded covalently, they have formed a molecule.

A molecule's bond length is defined by the distance between the two nuclei. The attraction of the bonding electrons to each nucleus pulls the nuclei closer together. At the same time, the nuclei also experience repulsion from one another due to their positive charges. At low-energy conditions, the two effects would balance the nuclei at a set distance from each other.

Outside agitation can cause the two nuclei to move too close together, at which point their mutual repulsion will drive them apart until the repulsion is weaker than the covalent bond that pulls them back together. Thus, the agitated atoms in the molecule experience internal harmonic motion, like blocks attached to the ends of a spring.

Covalent Bonding The graph shows the potential energy held by a covalent bond, but the steepness of the curve also describes the force between the two atoms. Where the curve is horizontal, the force is zero. Where the curve is steep, the force is strong. (A positive slope indicates attraction; a negative slope, repulsion.)

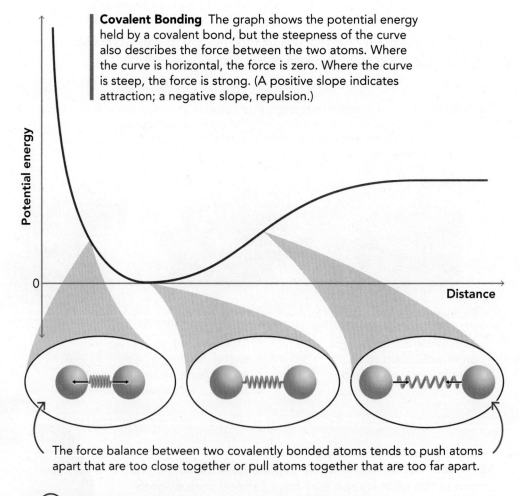

The force balance between two covalently bonded atoms tends to push atoms apart that are too close together or pull atoms together that are too far apart.

(17) **CCC Energy and Matter** Suppose two bonded atoms are moved too far apart for the restoring force to pull the atoms together again. What happens to the bond between the atoms?

Building Chains Some atoms can easily form multiple covalent bonds. Without this ability, no molecule of more than two atoms could ever form. For example, a single carbon atom can bond covalently with four hydrogen atoms to form methane (CH_4). The four hydrogen nuclei repel one another, so they will arrange themselves around the carbon in a tetrahedron, maximizing their distance from one another in the three dimensions of space.

Because carbon atoms can also covalently bond with each other, they are able to form molecules that are chains or rings. In these molecules, each carbon atom bonds with at least one other carbon and with other atoms along the side. The complex nature of these structures introduces an increased chance that two molecules with the same components will form different shapes. These different molecular shapes lead to different physical properties, even for molecules with the same chemical formula.

EXPERIENCE IT!

Place your hands flat on a table in front you. Then adjust one hand so that the thumbs of both hands are on the left side. Using only the appearance of your two hands, how can you explain to someone else which hand is your left hand and which hand is your right hand?

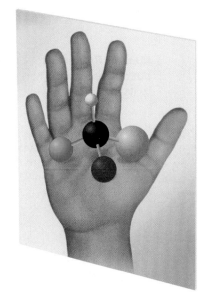

Chirality Chiral molecules have the same chemical formula but a different physical arrangement—a mirror image of one another.

Turning a left hand over does not make it a right hand. No amount of turning makes them the same.

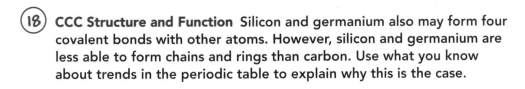

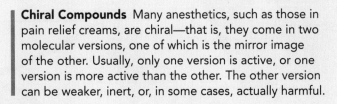

Chiral Compounds Many anesthetics, such as those in pain relief creams, are chiral—that is, they come in two molecular versions, one of which is the mirror image of the other. Usually, only one version is active, or one version is more active than the other. The other version can be weaker, inert, or, in some cases, actually harmful.

(18) **CCC Structure and Function** Silicon and germanium also may form four covalent bonds with other atoms. However, silicon and germanium are less able to form chains and rings than carbon. Use what you know about trends in the periodic table to explain why this is the case.

Metallic Bonds

A majority of elements on the periodic table are metals. One characteristic of metals is that the atoms bond by sharing electrons but in a way that is different from covalent bonding.

Metallic bonds are similar to covalent bonds in that valence electrons cease to interact with only one nucleus and instead interact with multiple nuclei. Unlike covalent bonds, however, each valence electron in a bulk metal sample is able to move relatively freely among all of the nuclei in the sample.

Metallic bonds do not form molecules and do not have a specific elemental ratio or formula; they are simply the collective sharing of all valence electrons among all the metal nuclei in the sample. The arrangement is often referred to as a "sea of electrons" existing throughout a collection of nuclei.

Metallic Properties Metal is strong, but it is also pliable and ductile due to its metallic bonding.

The attraction of the aluminum cores keeps the valence electrons within the material but allows them freedom of movement throughout the material.

Every aluminum atom contributes three electrons to the "sea of electrons."

Core of aluminum atom

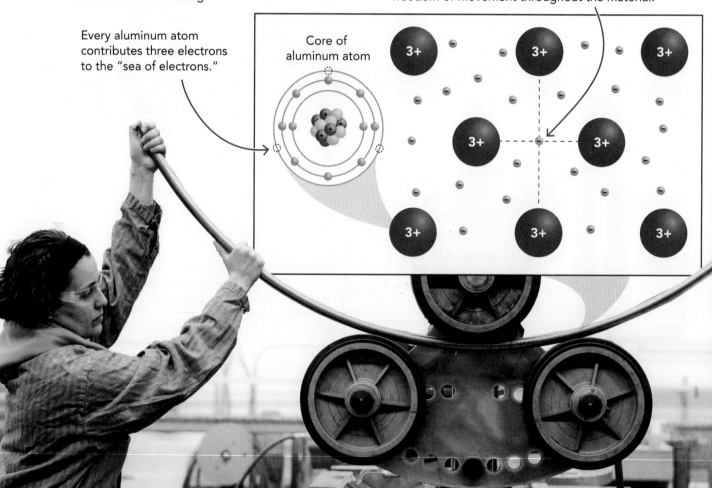

(19) **CCC Structure and Function** Write an explanation for how the "sea of electrons" model of metallic bonding explains the strength and pliability of metals.

Gas Particle Interactions The air above hot springs contains thick clouds of liquid steam droplets and gaseous water molecules, called water vapor. The water vapor gas particles interact through collisions but remain separate from each other.

Other Atomic and Molecular Interactions

 GO ONLINE to do a PhET **simulation** about the forces that act between molecules.

Coulomb forces can cause atoms in a material to interact in ways other than covalent, metallic, or ionic bonding. Coulomb forces also cause attractions between electrically neutral molecules in a material. These other interatomic and intermolecular forces are much weaker interactions compared to bonding, but they can still have important, observable effects. The formation of water drops, which is a result of these weak intermolecular interactions, is one example.

Another example is hydrogen bonding, which is the Coulombic attraction of a covalently bonded hydrogen atom to an atom it is not bonded to. This occurs when hydrogen bonds covalently with a strongly electronegative element, forming a dipole separation of charges within its molecule. This arrangement means the hydrogen is able to experience a weak Coulomb attraction to the negative end of a similar dipole in a nearby molecule.

Some interactions, especially between gas molecules, are best modeled as particle collisions, which is the basis for scientific models of the behavior of gases. The pattern of collisions and the intermolecular forces that a gaseous compound undergoes explain the macroscopic properties of the gas.

20 **CCC Cause and Effect** Steam from a pot of boiling water is extremely dangerous due to its ability to burn. Use the microscopic properties of the water vapor in steam to explain the source of this danger.

States of Matter

▶ **GO ONLINE** to watch a **video** about why the state of matter of glass is a solid.

The strength of the interatomic or intermolecular interactions in a material defines the state of the material. In the solid state, atoms or molecules are constantly experiencing close interactions with one another and are not energetic enough to rearrange their relative orientations. In the liquid state, particles are still in constant close interaction, but the particles are energetic enough to move past one another, interacting with other particles like people moving through a crowd. In a gaseous state, particles are so energetic that they have relatively large spaces between each other.

The stronger the attractive forces between atoms or molecules of a substance, the more energy it takes to separate those atoms or molecules from one another. This fact explains why ionic solids have higher melting points than covalent solids or metallic solids.

States of Matter Whether a material is a solid, liquid, or gas is explained by the strength of the forces between the particles and the energy of the particles.

Temporary attractions between particles

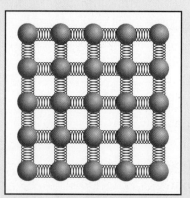

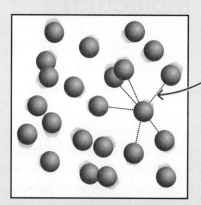

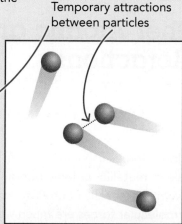

Ionic and metallic bonds between atoms in an ionic or metallic **solid** keep the atoms locked in place, only able to vibrate back and forth.

Particles in a **liquid** have more energy than particles in a solid. There are attractions between particles, but these attractions are not strong enough to keep them in place.

The particles in a **gas** have enough energy to break free from most, but not all, of the forces between particles. Generally, substances made of low-mass molecules are gases at most temperatures.

(21) **SEP Construct an Explanation** In general, covalently bonded substances have lower melting points than metallically bonded substances. Use the nature of covalent and metallic bonds to explain why this is the case.

(22) **SEP Use a Model** When enough heat is added to a solid, it becomes a liquid. Use the models of solids and liquids shown in the diagram to explain what happens to the forces within a material when it transitions from the solid to the liquid state.

Other States of Matter

What are some **other states of matter** beyond solids, liquids, and gases?

What's the Matter? With the development of new technologies and advances in scientific knowledge, our understanding of matter in the universe has changed significantly.

The **fundamental states** of solids, liquids, and gases, and other categories are not always as distinct as previously thought.

Solid

A **crystalline solid** has an ordered internal structure.

A **quasi-crystal** has an ordered internal structure, but it is not periodic like a crystalline solid.

A **plastic crystal** consists of weakly interacting particles, causing it to be easily deformed.

An **amorphous solid** lacks an ordered internal structure.

Liquid

A **liquid crystal** flows like a liquid but has an internal structure like a crystal.

A **non-Newtonian fluid** changes the way it flows when under stress, getting thicker and acting more like a solid.

Gas **Plasma**

When enough energy is added to a **gas,** electrons are stripped away from their atoms, forming **plasma,** an ionized gas of positively charged nuclei, or ions, and free roaming electrons. Lightning, aurorae, and the sun's core are examples of plasma, which can conduct electricity and be confined in magnetic fields. Scientists estimate that 99% of the observable matter in the universe is plasma. It is now considered a fundamental state.

Scientists have observed **other states** of matter that only exist in extreme conditions in the universe or those created in the lab, some of which are discussed here.

Quark-Gluon Plasma (QGP)
Scientists think that this state of matter existed just after the Big Bang. It consisted of a hot, thick soup of subatomic particles known as quarks and gluons moving at speeds close to the speed of light.

Degenerate Matter
Under extreme pressure, a condition found in white dwarfs, atoms are packed so tightly together that electrons leave their orbits. In the case of neutron stars, nuclei actually break down.

Bose-Einstein Condensate (BEC)
Named after the physicists who predicted the existence of this state of matter, BEC is a group of atoms cooled close to absolute zero. With little thermal energy, the barely moving atoms clump together as they fall to the same low energy state. They behave as if they were a single atom.

23 **SEP Obtain Scientific Information** Choose one of the alternate states of matter described in the diagram and obtain additional information about it. Write a paragraph about this state of matter and explain why it is not commonly encountered in everyday life.

Revisit

INVESTIGATIVE PHENOMENON

GO ONLINE to revisit your **Investigative Phenomenon CER** with the new information you have learned about Attractive and Repulsive Forces.

These questions will help you apply what you learned in this experience to the Investigative Phenomenon.

(24) **SEP Use Scientific Reasoning** Given the properties of a flexible fiberglass pole, what type of bonding would you expect to find in the structure of the pole: covalent, ionic, or metallic? Support your answer using the nature of the different types of bonds.

(25) **SEP Analyze Data** The melting points and boiling points of three solid substances you find at a track meet are given in the table. The three substances are aluminum (metallic bonding), fructose (covalent bonding), and magnesium oxide (ionic bonding). Use what you know about the nature of bonding to identify substances A, B, and C.

Compound	Melting Point	Boiling Point
Substance A	103°C	440°C
Substance B	2852°C	3600°C
Substance C	660°C	2470°C

(26) **CCC Structure and Function** An aluminum rod can be bent similar to the way that a pole vaulter's pole bends. Using the nature of metallic bonds, explain why an aluminum rod would not be suitable material for a vaulting pole.

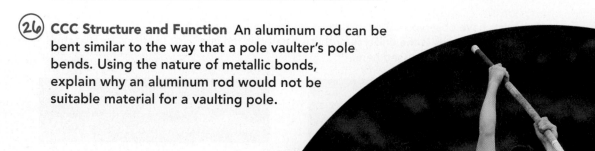

GO ONLINE for a **quiz** to evaluate what you learned about Attractive and Repulsive Forces.

EXPERIENCE 3

Material Properties

 GO ONLINE to do a **hands-on lab** to explore the macroscopic properties of materials.

Conductivity of Materials

Electrical conductivity is a measure of the ability of a material's charge carriers to move through the material—to become a current of moving charge. Gases have very low conductivity due to their lack of free electrons, unless they are subjected to an electric potential strong enough to ionize the gas molecules into the plasma state. Liquid conductivity varies greatly—liquid metal conducts very well, but pure water does not. Water's ability to conduct electricity is a function of the presence of ions dissolved in it.

In solid materials, the charge carriers are valence electrons, which means that a solid material's conductivity is related to how loosely bound its valence electrons are to a specific nucleus. A lattice of metallic bonds, with its corresponding "sea of electrons," makes charge flow easy, making most metals good electrical conductors.

Nonmetals, including many compounds, are poor conductors because of how tightly bound their valence electrons are to one or more atomic nuclei. For this reason, covalent compounds are usually good electrical insulators.

Electrical Conductivity Air is not a good conductor, which means a relatively high potential is needed across this spark gap before charge carriers will travel from one side to the other.

(27) **CCC Structure and Function** Explain why most metallic wiring used in household electric circuits is covered by plastic instead of being bare metal.

3 Material Properties 259

Stress and Strain

EXPERIENCE IT!

Have a friend hold a heavy textbook or other flat, heavy object in place on a table by pushing on it from one side. Stand on the other side and push on the book to try to move it, slowly increasing the strength of your push. What do you feel in your hands and arms as you push? How does the book respond to the pushes from both sides?

Solid objects have structural rigidity. In other words, solids have definite macroscopic shapes in a way that liquids and gases do not. However, some solid objects are much more rigid than others. For example, a brick and a sweater are both solid, but their physical properties are dramatically different. Both the shape and rigidity of a solid object are determined by the strength of the collective intermolecular forces within the object.

When any solid is subjected to an external force, its shape changes as its individual atoms or molecules react to that force and to their bonds with one another. Even something as rigid as a brick wall flexes at the atomic scale when you push it, although the effect may be imperceptible.

Stress The mechanical stress, or simply **stress,** an object experiences is an expression of that object's internal intermolecular forces per unit of cross-sectional area. Stress is a restorative reaction either to external forces or to internal changes in temperature or chemical structure. Stress can be tensile, compressive, etc. depending on its cause (tension, compression, etc.).

Stress Equation
$$\sigma = \frac{F}{A}$$
σ = stress $\qquad$ A = cross-sectional F = tension $\qquad\qquad$ area

Warped Shelves An object subject to constant external force, such as a bookshelf holding many heavy books, experiences tension on one side and compression on the other. Reactions on each side of the shelf manifest as stress.

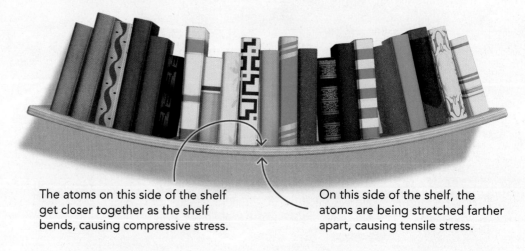

The atoms on this side of the shelf get closer together as the shelf bends, causing compressive stress.

On this side of the shelf, the atoms are being stretched farther apart, causing tensile stress.

28 **SEP Use Mathematics** A compressive force of 1850 N is applied to a section of a cylindrical rod with a diameter of 13.5 cm. What is the stress on the rod? Note that stress is measured in pascals (Pa), which are equivalent to N/m².

Tensile Strength Spider webs have greater tensile strength than equally sized strands of steel.

Each strand of spider silk is made of nanostrands—protein fibrils on the scale of 20 nm in diameter and 1 μm in length.

GO ONLINE to watch a **video** about the properties of spider silk.

Strain When a stressed object deforms, the fractional change in the object's length in each spatial dimension is called the **strain** on the material. Because strain is a fractional expression, it is unitless. The ratio of stress to strain is called **Young's modulus.** A material with a low Young's modulus is more pliable and ductile, while a material with a high modulus is more brittle.

Young's Modulus
$$E = \frac{\sigma}{\varepsilon}$$
E = Young's modulus $\quad \varepsilon$ = strain = $(\Delta L/L)$
σ = stress $\quad\quad\quad\quad\quad L$ = length

When Young's modulus is constant in a material, there is a direct relationship between stress and strain. Once a material is stressed too far, its intermolecular forces will begin to fail. At that point, the intermolecular forces cannot provide the restoring force needed to return the material to its original shape, even after the external distorting force is removed. Stress-induced deformation that is not temporary is called **plastic deformation.** If enough intermolecular forces are broken, the object in question will fracture.

(29) **SEP Use Mathematics** A wire with a length of 3.0 m and a cross-sectional area of 0.0020 m² is stretched 0.10 cm by a 98-kg hanging weight. Determine Young's modulus for the wire.

Bulk Modulus

Young's modulus is useful for understanding a material's response to an external force applied in a single direction, such as a spring stretching or a support column compressing. However, Young's modulus is not applicable to an object that is subjected to a three-dimensional compressive environment. Furthermore, it only applies to materials in the solid state.

The bulk modulus, or incompressibility, is the measure of a substance's resistance to compressive environments and applies to both solids and fluids.

Bulk Modulus
$$B = \frac{-V\Delta P}{\Delta V}$$

B = bulk modulus ΔP = change in pressure
V = volume ΔV = change in volume

In solid materials, it is possible for the bulk modulus value to be different along different axes if the molecular structure of the material is **anisotropic,** which means it looks different when viewed from different directions. An example of this is a block of wood, which behaves differently in the direction of the grain than it does across the grain of the wood.

Bulk Modulus In a compressive environment, an object experiences a pushing in from all sides. How much it resists this deformation depends on the bulk modulus of its material.

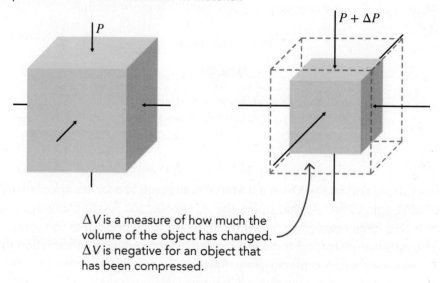

ΔV is a measure of how much the volume of the object has changed. ΔV is negative for an object that has been compressed.

(30) **SEP Apply Mathematical Concepts** Show that for a solid in a compressive environment where the change in pressure is negative, the volume must increase.

Bulk Modulus

The bulk modulus of diamond is 4.43×10^{11} Pa. Determine the change in volume experienced by a diamond that is taken from an environment of 83,481 Pa pressure to an environment at 101,325 Pa. The original volume of the diamond is 0.057 cm^3.

1. DRAW A PICTURE Sketch a picture of the situation.

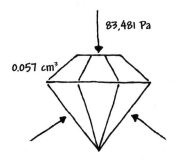
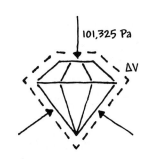

2. DEFINE THE PROBLEM List knowns and unknowns, and assign values to variables.

$B = 4.43 \times 10^{11}$ Pa

$V = 0.057$ cm^3

$P_f = 101{,}325$ Pa

$P_i = 83{,}481$ Pa

$\Delta V = ?$

3. PLAN AND EXECUTE Use mathematical relationships, the picture, and your definitions to plan and execute a solution.

Determine the change in pressure.

$\Delta P = P_f - P_i = 101{,}325 \text{ Pa} - 83{,}481 \text{ Pa}$
$= 17{,}844 \text{ Pa}$

Rewrite the equation for bulk modulus to isolate the unknown change in volume.

$B = \dfrac{-V\Delta P}{\Delta V} \rightarrow \Delta V = \dfrac{-V\Delta P}{B}$

Determine the change in volume using the known values.

$\Delta V = \dfrac{-(0.057 \text{ cm}^3)(17{,}844 \text{ Pa})}{4.43 \times 10^{11} \text{ Pa}}$

$\Delta V = -2.3 \times 10^{-9} \text{ cm}^3$

4. EVALUATE Reflect on your answer.
ΔV should be negative because pressure increased on the diamond. The fact that the answer is an extremely small value makes sense because diamond is not very compressible.

 GO ONLINE for more **math support**.

▶ **Math Tutorial Video**

🖥 **Math Practice Problems**

(31) The bulk modulus of steel is 1.60×10^{11} Pa. Determine the change in volume experienced by a steel beam that is taken from an environment of 24,500 Pa pressure to an environment at 15,800 Pa. The original volume of the steel is 3.70 m^3.

📖 **NEED A HINT?** Go online to your **eText Sample Problem** for stepped out support.

Metallic Properties in Alloys

Metallic bonds do not require a specific elemental ratio or formula. An **alloy** is a mixture of two or more metallic elements. Metallic bonds are able to form in alloys even though dissimilar atoms are scattered throughout. Alloys are stronger and harder than their constituent elements because the atomic crystalline pattern is less regular in an alloy. If the atoms of two or more metallic elements are nearly the same size, they form a **substitutional alloy.**

If the atoms of two or more metallic elements are significantly different sizes, then atoms of one element cannot fit into the crystal pattern of the other, forming an **interstitial alloy.** Instead, the new atoms reside in defects among the other element's crystal pattern. The interstitial element does not need to be metallic. For example, steel is an alloy of interstitial carbons in an iron lattice.

In both types of alloys, the alternating crystal pattern makes it more difficult for bond dislocations to occur, so the material is stronger. However, this same disruption also makes the alloy less conductive and less ductile than its constituent elements.

Interstitial Alloy These iron atoms form a crystalline structure that is interrupted by an interstitial carbon atom.

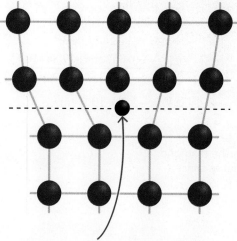

This carbon atom is trapped at a dislocation site in the iron lattice, preventing easy movement. This makes steel stronger than pure iron.

Substitutional Alloy These iron atoms form a crystalline structure with some atoms substituted with chromium atoms.

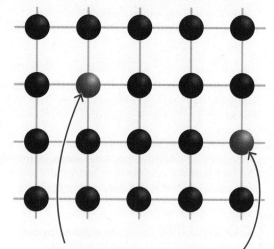

Chromium alloys are less reactive with oxygen, giving stainless steel its anticorrosive property.

 SEP Synthesize Information In the history of civilizations, many ancient cultures transitioned from a Stone Age to a Bronze Age. Describe the advantages and disadvantages craftspeople might have in working with bronze versus working with stone.

Determining Alloy Density

Students in an art class are pouring a homogeneous mixture of 85.0% copper and 15.0% tin for use in casting small statues. Given the known density of pure solid copper (8.96 g/cm³) and of pure solid tin (7.27 g/cm³), determine the density of the alloy (bronze) that is formed.

1. DRAW A PICTURE Sketch a picture of the situation.

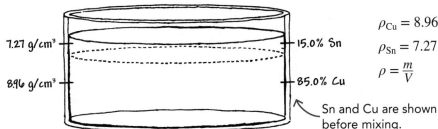

7.27 g/cm³ ← → 15.0% Sn

8.96 g/cm³ ← → 85.0% Cu

↖ Sn and Cu are shown before mixing.

2. DEFINE THE PROBLEM List knowns and unknowns, and assign values to variables.

$$\rho_{Cu} = 8.96 \text{ g/cm}^3 \qquad \rho_{bronze} = ?$$

$$\rho_{Sn} = 7.27 \text{ g/cm}^3$$

$$\rho = \frac{m}{V}$$

3. PLAN AND EXECUTE Use mathematical relationships, the picture, and your definitions to plan and execute a solution.

> Choose the masses of copper and tin that are being mixed to form bronze.

Assume you are mixing 850 g Cu and 150 g Sn to make 1000 g bronze.

> Find the volume of bronze formed.

$$V_{bronze} = V_{Cu} + V_{Sn} = \frac{m_{Cu}}{\rho_{Cu}} + \frac{m_{Sn}}{\rho_{Sn}}$$

$$= \frac{850 \text{ g}}{8.96 \text{ g/cm}^3} + \frac{150 \text{ g}}{7.27 \text{ g/cm}^3} = 115 \text{ cm}^3$$

> Determine the density of the bronze from the mass and volume.

$$\rho_{bronze} = \frac{m_{bronze}}{V_{bronze}} = \frac{1000 \text{ g}}{115 \text{ cm}^3} = 8.70 \text{ g/cm}^3$$

4. EVALUATE Reflect on your answer.
The units are appropriate for density. The answer is between the density of tin and that of copper, which makes sense.

 GO ONLINE for more **math support**.

▶ **Math Tutorial Video**

🖥 **Math Practice Problems**

(33) Students in an art class are pouring a homogeneous mixture of 68.0% copper and 32.0% zinc for use in casting small statues. Given the known density of pure solid copper (8.96 g/cm³) and of pure solid zinc (7.13 g/cm³), determine the density of the alloy (brass) that is formed.

📖 **NEED A HINT?** Go online to your **eText Sample Problem** for stepped out support.

(34) Nichrome is an alloy of nickel and chromium that is used in the heating elements of stoves and toaster ovens. If a certain alloy consists of 80% nickel and 20% chromium, and the density of nichrome is 8.47 g/cm³, what is the density of chromium? Use 8.91 g/cm³ as the density of nickel.

Glass A glassblower inflates a bubble of molten glass into a spherical shape that can be manipulated to make glass objects.

Ceramics and Glass

▶ **GO ONLINE** to watch a **video** about the properties of glass.

Artists, builders, and other people in creative professions need to understand the physical properties of the materials they work with. These properties determine what can and cannot be built from each material, and may include **thermal conductivity** (the ability to conduct heat), rigidity, elasticity, and many others.

Ceramics Ceramics are a broadly useful category of materials due to their resistance to deformation under stress, their ability to withstand high temperatures, and their low susceptibility to corrosion. They are also good thermal and electrical insulators.

Ceramics are made by heating clay or other fine-grain, nonmetallic mineral compounds. These compounds can be shaped when wet. Then, after a heating process, the material loses its pliability and becomes hard and brittle. Examples of ceramics include bricks, pottery, and orthopedic and orthodontic implants.

Glasses A subset of ceramic materials in which the molecular structure is amorphous is called **glass.** Amorphous materials have molecules that are randomly arranged relative to one another. This is in contrast to other ceramics, which are crystalline or semicrystalline.

Because glass is amorphous, heating it to a certain range (still below the melting point) causes the material to transition from a hard, brittle state to a viscous, flexible state. This transition is called vitrification. Ceramic glazes, which are actually a type of glass, are vitreous substances that are used to provide nonporous finishes to some products.

(35) **SEP Use Scientific Reasoning** Archaeologists have found pottery fragments from objects in China that are up to 20,000 years old. What properties of ceramic material allow pottery to survive for so long?

Fracturing When ionic solids fracture, they demonstrate a tendency to split, or cleave, along specific planes in the crystalline three-dimensional structure. This behavior is due to the Coulombic repulsion between each ion and those ions near it that have the same polarity charge. Ceramic materials, even those that have crystalline structures, have less orderly fracture patterns due to the lack of ions in their structures.

The study of brittle fracture in ceramics and other materials is complex, but the failure of ceramic material can usually be traced to concentrations of stress around imperfections in the crystalline pattern. Stress from applied forces or changes in temperature can cause chemical bonds to be broken at the site of the imperfection, transferring that stress to neighboring atoms. Cracks can travel throughout a structure in a very short time, shattering the ceramic object. If you have ever dropped a ceramic plate or glass cup on the floor, then you are probably familiar with this phenomenon.

Safety Glass The material used for car windshields and windows is a combination of glass and plastic designed to dissipate the energy from an impact by forming a large network of cracks that prevents shattering or only shatters in small pieces.

36 **CCC Structure and Function** Explain why the properties of safety glass make the material suitable for a car windshield. What are some other useful applications of this material?

Ceramics and Glass in Everyday Life

What are some **useful applications** of ceramics and glass?

Structure and Function The **properties** of ceramics and glass make them useful for a **variety of applications.** These properties can be tailored for specific purposes by changing the material's composition or altering the way it is processed.

 Ceramics and Glass

- electric insulator
- high elastic modulus
- high hardness

- high resistance to corrosion
- low ductility
- low thermal expansion

- low to medium tensile strength
- low to medium thermal conductivity

Transportation

Ceramics and glass are lightweight, resistant to high temperatures, and good electrical and thermal insulators. Ceramics are used in **engine and exhaust parts** in cars and planes and in **heat shields** in spacecraft. Glass is used in windows, as well as sensor and instrumentation protection.

Because ceramics are strong, have low thermal expansion, withstand high temperatures and corrosion, and are good electrical and thermal insulators, they are used to make **mortar, bricks and tiles, and sinks and toilets.** Glass is used for **windows and mirrors,** and glass fibers are used in **insulation.**

Construction

Electronics

Ceramics are found in most electronics in the form of **capacitors and resistors.** Glass, which has high transparency, is used as both rigid and flexible panels, such as **smartphone and computer screens.**

Both ceramics and glass are pliable in their initial states and then can be hardened when fired in ovens (ceramics) or cooled (glass). Artists use ceramics to make **pottery, sculptures, mosaic tiles, and jewelry.** Glass is used to make **stained glass windows, glassware, mosaics, and jewelry.**

Art

Medicine

Because they are resistant to high temperatures and corrosion and they are good electrical and thermal insulators, ceramics known as **bioceramics** are used in medicine. They include dental implants, pumps and valves, defibrillators, and pacemakers and other implants. Glass is commonly used in labware and as containers for medications.

 SEP Construct an Explanation Using the definition of glass and ceramics, explain why glass is a subset of ceramics.

INVESTIGATIVE PHENOMENON

GO ONLINE to revisit your **Investigative Phenomenon CER** with the new information you have learned about Material Properties.

These questions will help you apply what you learned in this experience to the Investigative Phenomenon.

(38) **CCC Structure and Function** Describe the stresses and strains that a fiberglass vaulting pole undergoes when it is used in a vaulting competition.

(39) **CCC Structure and Function** Explain, using the nature of each respective material, why ceramics and glass would not be suitable materials for use in a vaulting pole.

(40) **SEP Apply Scientific Reasoning** Write an explanation for whether a material with a low value or a high value of Young's modulus would be more suitable for a vaulting pole. Use the definition of strain in your answer. How would your answer change when considering the bulk modulus of a material?

(41) **SEP Design a Solution** Suppose you are an engineer testing a new material for a vaulting pole. What qualities would you look for in this new material that might make it superior to a standard fiberglass pole?

GO ONLINE for a **quiz** to evaluate what you learned about Material Properties.

Structure and Function

 GO ONLINE to do a **hands-on lab** that explores the properties of polymers.

Chain Molecules

Because carbon atoms can bond with each other, they are able to form carbon-based chains. Each carbon atom along the chain bonds with two other carbons, one on either side. Every one of these atoms is still able to form up to two additional bonds radiating out from the chain axis. In fact, entire side chains can branch off from the main chain.

Carbon is not the only element that forms chains. Boron, silicon, and sulfur all have this ability, though not to the same extent as carbon.

Carbon Chain Carbon is one of the few elements that can form enough bonds to be the "backbone" of a molecular chain.

Chemical reactions are largely determined by specific links that remain chemically reactive even though they are part of the chain. These are called functional groups.

Links in the chain must be capable of bonding to each other and to atoms or molecules that branch off.

Polymers The process of making chains does not occur one atom at a time. Entire molecules, known as monomers, bond together to form long chains called polymers. Some monomers are shorter-chain molecules that have curled into a ring shape, meaning that the resultant polymer can have rings as part of the length of its chain.

42 **SEP Make a Claim** Organic molecules are so named because they make up, and are produced by, organisms (living things). Explain why life on Earth is sometimes referred to as carbon-based life. Do you think silicon-based life might be possible on other worlds? Why or why not?

Natural and Synthetic Polymers Examples of naturally occurring polymers (and the monomers that are their building blocks) include proteins, which are made from amino acids; carbohydrates, which are made from monosaccharides (sugars); and the nucleic acids RNA and DNA, which are made of nucleotides.

Synthetic polymers include nylon, neoprene and other synthetic rubbers, and all plastics, which are organic but artificially made. Inorganic polymers can have very different properties from organic polymers, including electrical conductivity and resistance to flame.

Because of their long-chain structure, polymers are strong but flexible molecules; some are able to bend and coil into chaotic masses. Others can become entwined with each other. The complex shapes and varied patterns of polymers contribute to the variety of reactions and behaviors of the molecule.

EXPERIENCE IT!

If possible, form a ring of six people by holding hands. Move around the classroom trying to maintain this shape. Then break the ring and form a string of six people and repeat the exercise. What are the advantages and disadvantages of each of these structures?

Polymers Natural polymers perform many important functions in the body. Whole synthetic polymers often make the materials that protect our bodies.

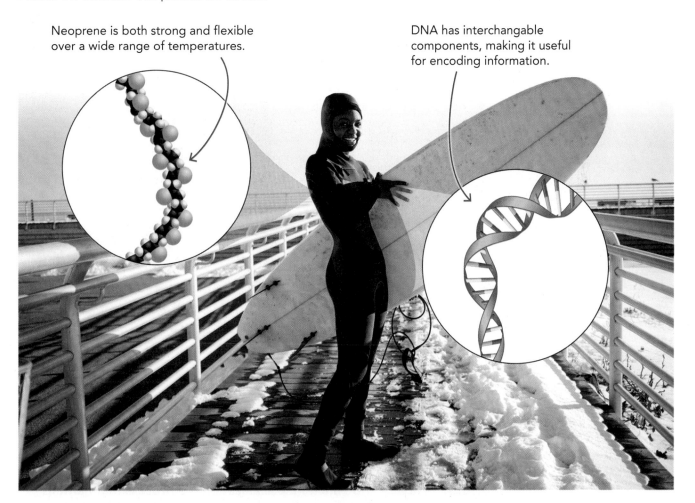

Neoprene is both strong and flexible over a wide range of temperatures.

DNA has interchangable components, making it useful for encoding information.

(43) **CCC Structure and Function** Plastics are synthetic polymers that can be molded into a solid form with varying degrees of elasticity, depending on composition and purpose. Think of some plastic objects in your household, and compare their properties and functions.

Elastomers

Certain polymer materials, known as **elastomers,** display elasticity at ambient temperatures and, as a result, have a wide range of uses. Natural and synthetic rubber are examples of elastomers.

Natural rubber is made from rubber tree extracts. Though natural rubber is a viscous polymer liquid when collected, it becomes an elastic solid through vulcanization, a process of heating with sulfur that loosely bonds the long-chain molecules together with cross-links. These cross-link bonds are much weaker than the bonds the long-chain polymer molecules are made of, which means that external forces exerted on the material will stress the cross-links long before the polymer bonds would break. Thus, the amorphous mass can flex and stretch under load.

Elastomers can transition to a hard, brittle state if cooled to a low enough temperature (similar to a glass transition but at a much colder temperature). Because elastomers are comparatively soft and flexible while still being strong, they are used in things like shoe soles, sports equipment, gaskets, o-rings, and other soft seals.

Elasticity Elastomers act much in the same way as this toy. They can be repeatedly distorted without breaking apart.

The hinges on this toy allow it to be stretched and compressed without falling apart.

(44) **CCC Structure and Function** Vulcanization is a process that hardens rubber while allowing it to keep its elastic properties. Vulcanization keeps rubber from softening when heated and cracking when cooled. Explain why vulcanized rubber is a suitable material for automobile tires.

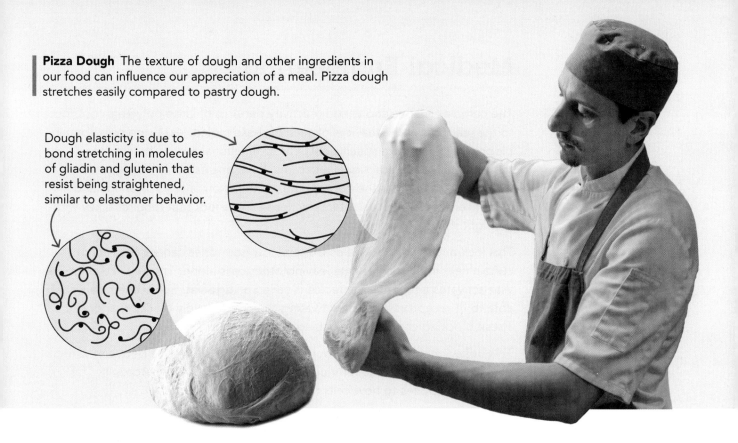

Pizza Dough The texture of dough and other ingredients in our food can influence our appreciation of a meal. Pizza dough stretches easily compared to pastry dough.

Dough elasticity is due to bond stretching in molecules of gliadin and glutenin that resist being straightened, similar to elastomer behavior.

Culinary Molecules

Proteins and carbohydrates are among the organic polymers that are vital to life. They are key components to the human diet. Another important biological material is a kind of lipid called triglycerides, usually referred to as fats and oils. Fats and oils comprise three fatty acid monomers that do not bond with one another but instead attach to a common glycerol. The presence of a carbon double bond in a fatty acid monomer prevents the material from being saturated with hydrogen atoms. Saturated fats (meat fats, dairy fats) are relatively solid and inflexible, while unsaturated fats (most plant oils) are liquid at room temperature.

In cooking, the ratio of flour to water to egg to triglycerides makes the difference between pasta, pie crust, and bread. Entire culinary careers are made from understanding the chemistry and physics that take place in our kitchens!

(45) **SEP Use a Model** Determine whether the triglyceride shown is a saturated or unsaturated fat.

(46) **CCC Structure and Function** Besides making dough elastic, sheets of gluten that form in stretched and kneaded dough tend to trap gas molecules that form inside the dough. Explain how this helps dough to rise.

Medical Engineering

The complex shapes and varied reactivity patterns of large polymers contribute to the reactions and behaviors of each of these molecules. Living cells contain biopolymers that have specific patterns of functional groups that make them useful as chemical signal receptors. Each one can only be triggered by a molecule that has the appropriate combination of physical shape and receptiveness to noncovalent interactions—like a lock that requires a key with the right shape.

This lock-and-key model helps explain how hormones can stir into action certain cells in the body while leaving other cells alone. The key-like chemical that activates a receptor molecule is called an **agonist.** Some chemicals are able to fit receptors without activating them, effectively blocking agonists. These blocking chemicals are called **antagonists.**

This behavior is how each of your cells knows the difference between various hormones, such as the difference between adrenaline and serotonin. This model also applies to how cells react to drugs in the body.

Some pharmaceuticals are designed specifically to act as artificial agonists or antagonists. An example is naloxone, which is an antagonist that fits opioid receptors, temporarily blocking or diminishing the effects of opioids.

Many protein receptors on the surface of your cells work via the lock-and-key process.

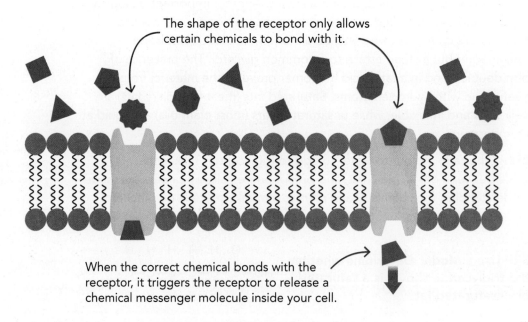

The shape of the receptor only allows certain chemicals to bond with it.

When the correct chemical bonds with the receptor, it triggers the receptor to release a chemical messenger molecule inside your cell.

(47) **SEP Construct an Explanation** When a protein bonds to a lock-and-key receptor, it forms hydrogen bonds or other intermolecular forces with the receptor to hold it in place. Why do you think these types of forces occur and not covalent bonds or ionic bonds?

Targeting Receptors to Treat Disease

How are **medications engineered** to treat diseases?

Adrenaline The adrenal glands are located on top of both kidneys, and they produce the hormone adrenaline (also known as epinephrine). **Adrenaline increases blood pressure and heart rate.**

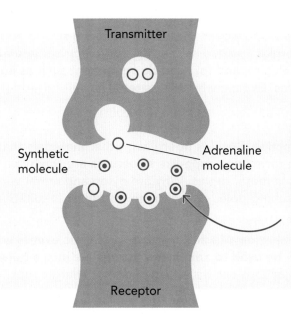

People who suffer from bradycardia have a **slow heart rate,** often due to an adrenaline deficiency.

Scientists have engineered a synthetic agonist molecule, called isoprenaline, whose structure and function mimic those of adrenaline.

The synthetic molecules are similar enough in structure to adrenaline that they are able to "bond" with the receptors, making up for the deficiency and increasing heart rate.

Transmitter

Synthetic molecule

Adrenaline molecule

Receptor

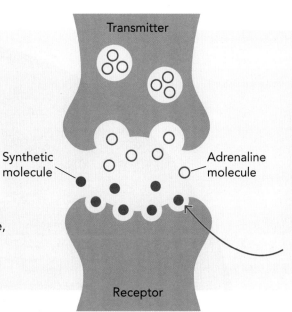

For people who suffer from **high blood pressure,** adrenaline can be dangerous.

Scientists have engineered a synthetic antagonist molecule, known as a beta blocker, whose structure mimics that of adrenaline.

The synthetic molecules are similar enough in structure to adrenaline that they "bond" with the adrenaline receptors. The synthetic molecules have no direct effect on blood pressure, and they prevent adrenaline molecules from reaching the receptor.

Transmitter

Synthetic molecule

Adrenaline molecule

Receptor

48 **CCC Structure and Function** Some viruses fool cells by bonding with the receptors to gain entry into the cell. The virus then uses the cell's own organelles to replicate. Why are lock-and-key receptors susceptible to viral invasion?

INVESTIGATIVE PHENOMENON

GO ONLINE to revisit your **Investigative Phenomenon CER** with the new information you have learned about Structure and Function.

These questions will help you apply what you learned in this experience to the Investigative Phenomenon.

49 **CCC Structure and Function** Fiberglass is composed of many long strands of glass fibers, or glass wool, woven together to make a strong and flexible structure. Fiberglass is used as thermal and electrical insulation, in boat hulls and other vehicles, and for athletic equipment such as hockey sticks and vaulting poles. Explain why this material is well suited for a vaulting pole.

50 **CCC Structure and Function** Besides fiberglass, other materials that make use of woven fibers to form long, rope-like structures are the nylon in nylon ropes and metal wires in metal cables. Why are nylon and metal wire not suitable for use in a vaulting pole, even though fiberglass is suitable?

51 **SEP Construct an Explanation** Medical trainers at athletic events usually have injectors that can be used to administer adrenaline into a person's bloodstream. Quick injections can be used to combat allergic reactions or asthma attacks. Look up more information on adrenaline's effect on the human body and describe how it helps treat allergic reactions.

GO ONLINE
for a **quiz** to evaluate what you learned about Structure and Function.

These questions will help you apply what you learned in this investigation to the Investigative Phenomenon.

(52) **SEP Develop a Model** One way that coastal erosion can occur is through the dissolution of coastal rock. For example, rocks made of limestone and chalk will slowly erode over time as seawater dissolves them. Dissolution separates the ions in the minerals of these rocks (such as calcium carbonate, $CaCO_3$). Construct a model that describes how a lattice of Ca^{2+} and $(CO_3)^{2-}$ ions would be dissolved by water.

(53) **CCC Cause and Effect** Describe how both gravitational and electromagnetic forces contribute to coastal erosion.

☑ INVESTIGATION ASSESSMENT

 GO ONLINE for activities that will give you an opportunity to **demonstrate what you have learned:**

☑ **Engineering Performance-Based Assessment** Change a polymer to attain a desired change in properties.

📄 **Engineering Workbench** Design and test an earthquake-resistant foundation.

💻 **Career Connections** Learn about how a materials scientist develops materials.

☑ **Investigation Test** Take this test to demonstrate your understanding of forces in materials.

☑ **Virtual Lab Performance-Based Assessment** Manipulate molecules to see how the macroscopic properties of a material change.

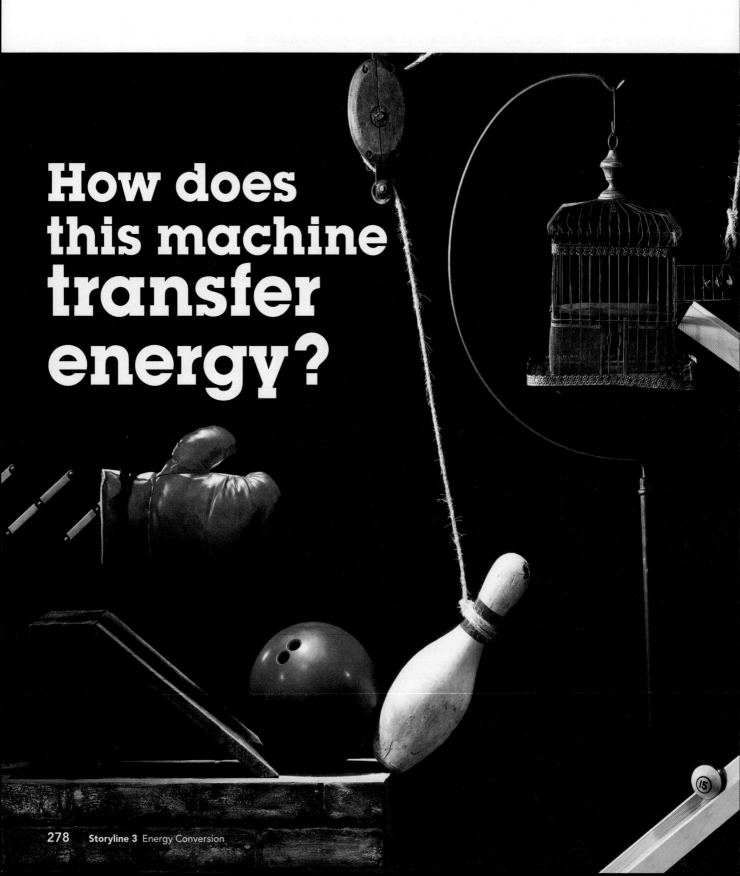

Energy Conversion

How does
this machine
transfer
energy?

Investigation 7
Energy

Investigation 8
Collisions

Investigation 9
Thermal Energy

Investigation 10
Electromagnetic Energy

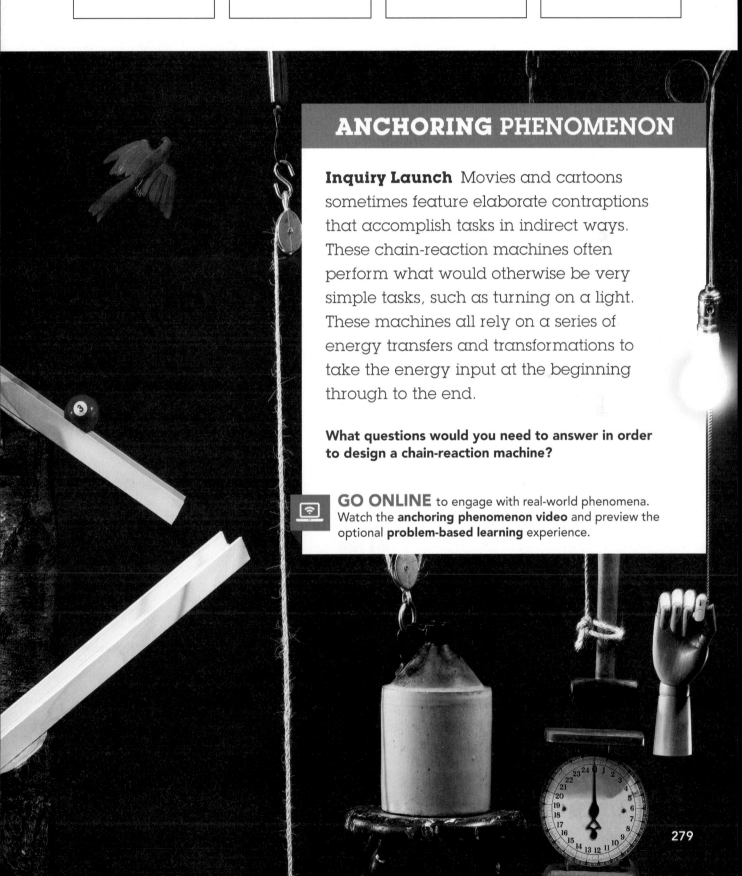

ANCHORING PHENOMENON

Inquiry Launch Movies and cartoons sometimes feature elaborate contraptions that accomplish tasks in indirect ways. These chain-reaction machines often perform what would otherwise be very simple tasks, such as turning on a light. These machines all rely on a series of energy transfers and transformations to take the energy input at the beginning through to the end.

What questions would you need to answer in order to design a chain-reaction machine?

GO ONLINE to engage with real-world phenomena. Watch the **anchoring phenomenon video** and preview the optional **problem-based learning** experience.

INVESTIGATIVE PHENOMENON

GO ONLINE to engage with real-world phenomena by watching a **phenomenon video** and completing a **CER worksheet**.

Why does a bungee jumper bounce up and down?

Energy

Bungee jumping is an extreme sport that many people enjoy. People can bungee jump at numerous locations, some of which involve heights greater than 200 meters. When bungee jumping, a person jumps or drops off a platform with only an elastic cord attached to their ankles or waist with harnesses.

While you may consider bungee jumping to be exciting, or perhaps crazy, the physics behind this sport is well understood. A bungee jumper starts from a very high position relative to the ground, and energy is associated with this position. After leaving the platform, the bungee jumper begins to move, and energy is associated with this motion. During the fall, the elastic cord connected to the jumper stretches, storing energy. To understand the motion of a bungee jumper during a jump, you must understand the different forms of energy and how energy is converted from one form to another.

1. **SEP Define a Problem** What characteristics could you use to define a bungee jump? In particular, what requirements would you use to differentiate a bungee jump from an ordinary jump, such as jumping off a swing at a playground? What characteristics make a bungee jump a special kind of jump?

2. **CCC Patterns** The velocity of a jumper changes throughout the jump. What patterns do you notice regarding the changes in velocity during the jump?

3. **SEP Ask Questions** List some physics-related questions you would need to answer to ensure the adequacy of safety measures for a commercial bungee-jumping operation.

Classifying Work and Energy

 GO ONLINE to do a **hands-on lab** to explore the kinetic energy of gas particles and their ability to perform work.

Positive, Negative, and Zero Work

Understanding Work The everyday meaning of *work* is different from its meaning in physics. For example, you might think of cleaning out a desk as physical work and solving homework problems as mental work. You may say that you go to the gym to "work out" or, when you are successful at something, that things "worked out." In physics, *work* has a very specific meaning. In physics, work is related to forces and displacement, physical quantities that you studied previously.

Work and Movement It can be hard work moving heavy objects. However, in physics, this doesn't necessarily mean that *work* is done.

(4) **SEP Ask Questions** People use machinery, such as cranes, to help them perform work. What questions could you ask to determine how a crane reduces the amount of work required to move a heavy object?

Defining Work in Physics **Work** is a change in state of a system caused by a force applied along a displacement. When an external force exerted by an external object on a system is in the direction of the system's displacement, then there is **work done on** the system. If the system exerts a force on an external object in the direction of the object's displacement, then there is **work done by** the system on the surroundings. Work is positive when the force and displacement are in the same direction. Work is negative when the force and displacement are in opposite directions. If the external force and the displacement are perpendicular to each other, no work is being done. In any situation, you can tell whether a force does positive or negative work on the system by whether a component of the force is in the same direction as the displacement.

Force and Displacement Sweeping, stopping a sliding basket, and carrying a box are examples of actions that do positive work, negative work, and no work. In each scenario, note the relative orientation of the displacement and the force by the person on the system, F_{PS}.

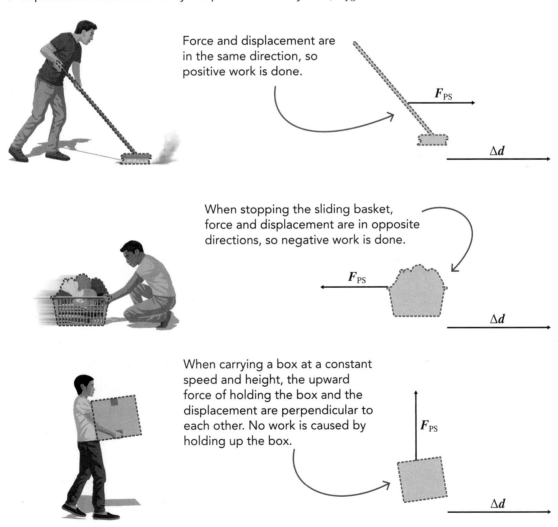

Force and displacement are in the same direction, so positive work is done.

F_{PS}

Δd

When stopping the sliding basket, force and displacement are in opposite directions, so negative work is done.

F_{PS}

Δd

When carrying a box at a constant speed and height, the upward force of holding the box and the displacement are perpendicular to each other. No work is caused by holding up the box.

F_{PS}

Δd

5. **SEP Analyze Data** For each of the following three actions, determine if positive, negative, or no work is done on the box: (1) a box is lifted off the ground, (2) a box is held in place above the ground, (3) a box is lowered to the ground.

Calculating Work

EXPERIENCE IT!

Perform several push ups. If your torso is the system, when is the work being done on your torso by your arms positive? When is it negative?

Sometimes the direction of a force exerted on a system and the displacement of the system are not aligned. When using a rope to pull a sled, some of the force exerted by the rope is in the direction of motion and some of it is perpendicular. Only the component of the force in the direction of motion causes work to be done on the system.

Work
$W = Fd\cos\theta$

W = work d = displacement
F = force θ = angle between force and displacement

The SI unit of measure for work is the joule, abbreviated J. One joule equals a newton times a meter, N•m. When determining the work done on a system, it is important to identify all the forces being exerted on the system. For the sled, work is done *on* the sled (the system) *by* the rope (an object applying a force on the system). Sometimes more than one force acting on the system results in work being done. To calculate the total work done on a system, add up all of the work, keeping track of positive and negative signs, because work can be both positive or negative.

Angled Force This sled is being pulled at an angle. The rope is exerting a force on the sled through tension.

The angle θ is the angle between the applied force and the displacement, d. $F\cos\theta$ represents the parallel component of the force with respect to the displacement.

F

θ

$F\cos\theta$

d

(6) **SEP Use Models** Compare a hockey puck sliding across ice, where friction is negligible, to a hockey puck being pushed across ice by a hockey stick. Is work being done on the hockey puck in either scenario? If so, is the work done on the hockey puck positive or negative?

(7) **SEP Develop a Model** Draw a simple force diagram to model a skier pulling directly up on the rope attached to the sled. Explain whether the scenario is an example of positive work, negative work, or no work.

Work Done by a Gas

Pressure and Force *Pressure* is another word that has many meanings in everyday language and a specific meaning in physics. In physics, **pressure** is the magnitude of the perpendicular component of a force per unit area.

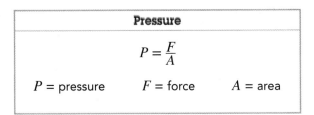

Pressure
$P = \dfrac{F}{A}$
P = pressure F = force A = area

Unlike force, pressure is a scalar quantity. You can use pressure to understand how work can be done by a gas. Gases are made of particles that are moving. When an individual particle collides with a wall of the container, it exerts a force on some small area of the container. Because there are many particles hitting the wall, the situation is modeled as a constant force exerted on the container walls. If the number of collisions with the container walls increases, the gas expands if the container is flexible. The expansion is a displacement of the system, and the gas is doing positive work on the container walls.

Work and Pressure If the gas particle collisions inside a container with a freely movable piston increase, the piston will move. This allows the pressure to remain constant while the volume increases.

The pressure from the gas supports the weight of the piston. *A* is the area of the piston head that is in contact with the gas.

The distance the piston moves is the displacement of the system. This displacement results in an increase in volume.

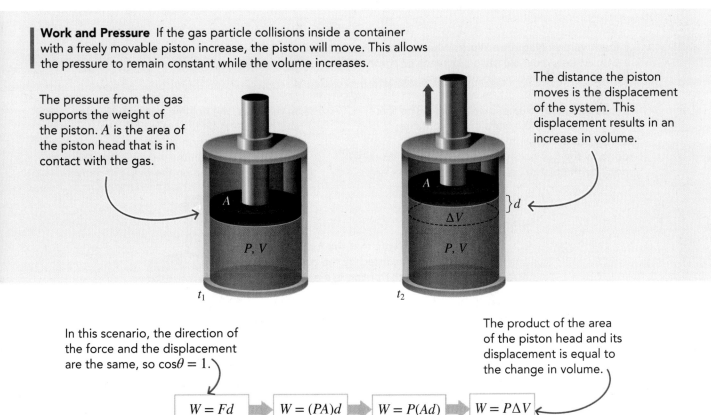

In this scenario, the direction of the force and the displacement are the same, so $\cos\theta = 1$.

The product of the area of the piston head and its displacement is equal to the change in volume.

$$W = Fd \quad\Rightarrow\quad W = (PA)d \quad\Rightarrow\quad W = P(Ad) \quad\Rightarrow\quad W = P\Delta V$$

8 **SEP Analyze Data** In the scenario of the gas in a container with a freely movable piston, the gas can also contract. If the gas contracts, in which direction will the piston move? What would be the sign of the work done on the piston by the gas in this scenario?

Pressure Performing Work When a gas inside a container with a freely moving wall (like a movable piston) expands or contracts at a constant pressure, the volume changes, causing work to be done on the gas. This situation is called an **isobaric process,** a thermodynamic process in which pressure remains constant. You can calculate the work being done in an isobaric process.

Work Done in an Isobaric Process
$$W = P\Delta V$$
W = work P = pressure exerted by the gas ΔV = change in volume of the gas

The sign on the work done depends on how the system is defined, which can be done in any way you wish. If a gas inside a container expands and causes the volume to increase, then the force the gas exerts is in the same direction as the displacement of the piston. Thus, the gas does positive work on the piston. In the same scenario, the gas expands and the volume increases, so the piston does negative work on the gas because it exerts a force on the gas that is in the opposite direction of the displacement.

Positive and Negative Work When a gas inside a container with a freely movable piston expands or contracts, the change in volume causes work to be done on the gas.

In this case, the volume is decreasing. The force the gas exerts on the walls of the container is in the opposite direction as displacement. So, work done by the gas on the piston is negative. Work done by the piston on the gas is positive.

In this case, the volume is increasing. The force the gas exerts on the walls of the container is in the same direction as displacement. So, work done by the gas on the piston is positive. Work done by the piston on the gas is negative.

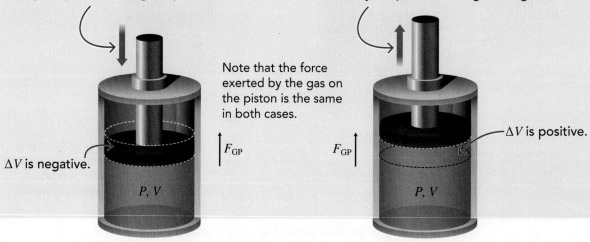

Note that the force exerted by the gas on the piston is the same in both cases.

ΔV is negative.

ΔV is positive.

F_{GP}

F_{GP}

P, V

P, V

9 **SEP Use Mathematics** A cylinder of gas has an initial volume of 0.30 m³. The gas expands, causing the volume to increase to 0.50 m³. If the pressure is constant at 100 N/m², what is the magnitude of the work done on the cylinder by the gas? Is the work done by the gas positive or negative?

Defining Energy of Motion

▶ **GO ONLINE** to watch a **video** about kinetic energy of objects.

Energy is a quantitative property of a system that is associated with the motion of particles and the relative positions of particles. The SI unit for energy is the joule, J, the same unit as for work. There are different types of energy. First, consider the types of energy that are associated with motion.

Kinetic energy is the energy associated with an object's motion. An object with velocity that is moving through space has **linear (translational) kinetic energy.** The faster an object is moving, the greater its linear kinetic energy. Kinetic energy is independent of the direction of motion.

VOCABULARY

The term *kinetic* comes from the Greek word *kinein*, meaning to move. In physics, **kinetic energy** is related to the energy of movement.

Linear Kinetic Energy of an Object
$KE = \frac{1}{2}mv^2$
KE = kinetic energy m = mass v = velocity

Kinetic Energy vs. Velocity The graph shows how an object's mass and velocity affect its kinetic energy.

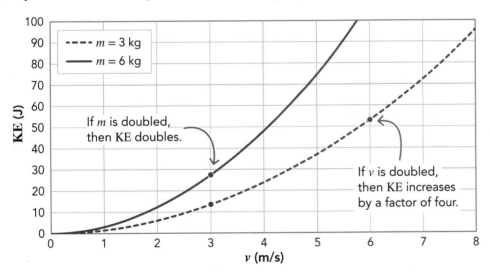

Kinetic energy associated with stationary objects rotating about an axis is known as **angular (rotational) kinetic energy.** The **total kinetic energy** of an object or system is the sum of any linear kinetic energy and any angular kinetic energy. The kinetic energy in the random motion of particles that make up an object is known as **thermal energy.** The total kinetic energy of a system refers to the energy of macroscopic objects in the system and the system itself, not the thermal energy of the system.

10. **SEP Use Mathematics** Kinetic energy can be considered as the work a moving object can do, described by $W = Fd$. Use Newton's second law of motion ($F = ma$) and the motion equation $v_f^2 + v_i^2 = 2ad$ to show that $KE = \frac{1}{2}mv^2$. (Assume that the initial velocity is 0.)

Kinetic Energy and the Work-Energy Theorem

When positive work is done on a system, energy external to the system is transferred into the system. Many different things can happen to the system as a result of that transfer of energy. However, when looking at the work done by the net force on a system, the system's kinetic energy changes as a result of that work. The **work-energy theorem** states that the total work done on a system is equal to the change in the system's kinetic energy.

Work-Energy Theorem
$$W_{\text{total}} = \Delta KE = KE_f - KE_i$$
W_{total} = total work done on a system ΔKE = change in kinetic energy of a system KE_i, KE_f = initial/final kinetic energy

Work and Energy You can derive the work-energy theorem by examining work over intervals when a net force is constant, or nearly constant, over a distance.

For a constant force over a distance, $F = ma$, where a is constant.

For a constant acceleration, an object's final velocity is given by the motion equation $v_f^2 = v_i^2 + 2ad$.

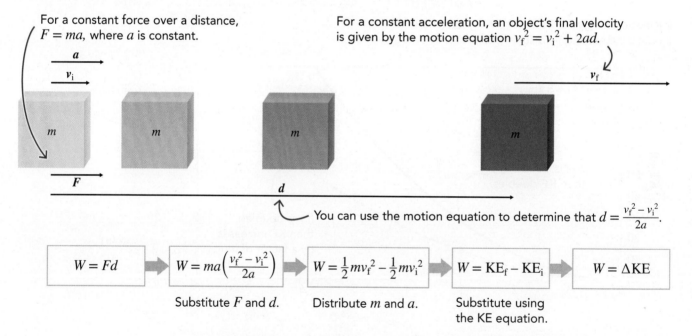

You can use the motion equation to determine that $d = \frac{v_f^2 - v_i^2}{2a}$.

$$W = Fd$$ → $$W = ma\left(\frac{v_f^2 - v_i^2}{2a}\right)$$ → $$W = \frac{1}{2}mv_f^2 - \frac{1}{2}mv_i^2$$ → $$W = KE_f - KE_i$$ → $$W = \Delta KE$$

Substitute F and d.   Distribute m and a.   Substitute using the KE equation.

When the total work done on a system is positive, the kinetic energy of the system increases. If the mass of the system remains constant, then the work causes an increase in the velocity of the system. If the total work done on a system is negative, then the kinetic energy of the system decreases. Thus, the velocity of the system decreases.

11 **SEP Use Mathematics** A shopping cart is pushed and released, and eventually it slows to a stop. If the velocity of the 28-kg cart after release is 3.5 m/s and it travels a distance of 6.0 meters before stopping, determine the magnitude of the friction on the cart.

Energy Bar Charts

 GO ONLINE to do a PhET **simulation** that allows you to explore energy forms and conversions for a spring–mass system.

The work-energy theorem shows how to mathematically keep track of changes in energy in a system. An energy bar chart is another tool that allows you to keep track of changes in a system. An **energy bar chart** is a visual representation, or model, of the changes in a system's energy.

Constructing an Energy Bar Chart

How can you **visually represent changes** in a **system's energy?**

Skidding to a Stop A car with mass m and moving at an initial velocity v_i skids to a complete stop in d meters. An energy bar chart represents the car's **energy in its initial and final states** by means of **vertical bars.** The sum of the heights of the bars for the initial state and any external work is **equal** to the sum of the heights of the bars for the final state.

Step 1 Draw and analyze the situation. Identify the system, as well as the forms of energy in the initial and final states. Include vectors for relevant physical quantities, such as force and velocity, even when the magnitudes are unknown.

Step 2 Analyze the forces acting on the system. As the car skids to a stop, work is done on the system by the pavement exerting external friction on the tires. The force acts in the opposite direction to the car's velocity.

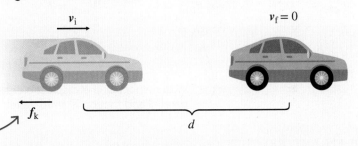

Step 3 Draw a bar to represent each form of energy for the initial and final states. The relative length of each bar is equivalent to the amount of energy. Draw a box around work to signify that it is external to the system.

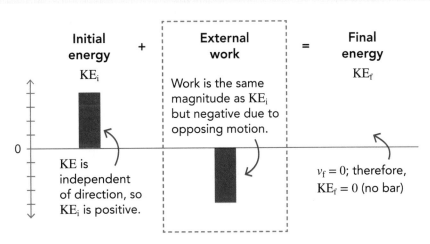

Step 4 Convert the energy bar chart to a mathematical expression using the work-energy theorem.

$$\text{KE}_i + W = \text{KE}_f \quad \blacktriangleright \quad \tfrac{1}{2}mv_i^2 + f_k d\cos\theta = \tfrac{1}{2}mv_f^2$$

Work Done on a Book

A 1.25-kg physics textbook is initially at rest on a steel table. The textbook is then pushed with a constant force of 3.0 N. Friction with a magnitude of 2.5 N is exerted on the moving book by the surface of the table. Determine the final velocity of the textbook after it has been pushed 0.60 meter across the table.

1. DRAW A PICTURE Sketch a picture of the situation.

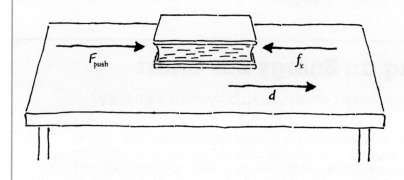 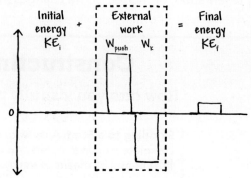

2. DEFINE THE PROBLEM List knowns and unknowns, and assign values to variables.

$m = 1.25$ kg	$KE_i = 0$ J	$KE_f = ?$
$F_{push} = 3.0$ N	$\cos \theta_{push} = 1$	$W_{push} = ?$
$f_k = 2.5$ N	$\cos \theta_k = -1$	$W_k = ?$
$d = 0.60$ m		$v_f = ?$

With respect to the displacement, the push is parallel and friction is antiparallel.

3. PLAN AND EXECUTE Use mathematical relationships, the picture, and your definitions to plan and execute a solution.

Use the work equation to determine the work done on the book as a result of the applied push and friction.

$$W = Fd\cos\theta$$
$$W_{push} = (3.0 \text{ N})(0.60 \text{ m})(1) = 1.8 \text{ J}$$
$$W_k = (2.5 \text{ N})(0.60 \text{ m})(-1) = -1.5 \text{ J}$$

Use the bar chart and associated mathematical representation to determine the final kinetic energy of the book.

$$W_{total} = \Delta KE \rightarrow W_{push} + W_k = KE_f - KE_i \rightarrow$$
$$KE_f = KE_i + W_{push} + W_k$$
$$= 0 \text{ J} + 1.8 \text{ J} - 1.5 \text{ J} = 0.3 \text{ J}$$

Use the linear kinetic energy equation to determine the final velocity of the book.

$$KE_f = \frac{1}{2}mv_f^2$$
$$v_f = \sqrt{\frac{2KE_f}{m}} = \sqrt{\frac{2(0.3 \text{ J})}{(1.25 \text{ kg})}} = 0.7 \text{ m/s}$$

4. EVALUATE Reflect on your answer.
The answer has the correct units. Pushing a book slightly harder than the friction resisting the movement will result in a fairly low velocity after less than a meter, so the answer makes sense. The answer is also verified by applying Newton's second law of motion to find the constant acceleration and applying the equations of motion.

 GO ONLINE for more **math support**.

▶ **Math Tutorial Video**

▣ **Math Practice Problems**

12 A 1.5-kg physics textbook is initially at rest on a steel table. The textbook is then pushed with a constant force of 5.0 N. Friction with a magnitude of 3.0 N is exerted on the moving book by the surface of the table. Determine the final velocity of the textbook after it has been pushed 0.50 meter across the table.

📖 **NEED A HINT?** Go online to your **eText Sample Problem** for stepped out support.

13 A 1.5-kg physics textbook is initially at rest on a steel table. The textbook is then pushed with a constant force of 3.0 N. Friction with a magnitude of 1.8 N is exerted on the moving book by the surface of the table. Determine the final velocity of the textbook after it has been pushed 1.0 meter across the table.

14 A 0.20-kg hockey puck initially traveling 5.0 m/s is pushed on ice by a hockey stick with a constant force of 7.0 N over a distance of 8.0 m. Friction is negligible. Determine the final velocity of the hockey puck.

15 A 0.095-kg dodge ball is traveling at 22 m/s along the concrete ground. Friction with a magnitude of 0.75 N is exerted on the moving ball by the surface of the concrete. Someone also uses their foot to slow the motion of the ball to a stop. If the ball travels 0.20 m before stopping, then determine the amount of force applied to the ball by the foot.

16 A box at rest on a belt of rollers is given a push by a constant force over the distance shown in the diagram. It is opposed by friction with a constant magnitude. What is the velocity of the box after the push is complete?

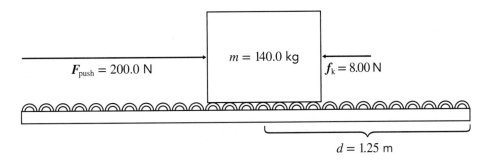

17 The box in the previous problem continues to coast down the belt of rollers after the push is complete. At what distance after the initial push is complete does the box come to a stop?

Power

It is sometimes helpful or important to consider the rate at which either energy is transmitted or work is done on a system. For example, a car starting from rest increases its speed to 3.2 m/s. Work is a change in kinetic energy, so whether the change in speed happens over 12 seconds or 40 seconds, the car's engine does the same amount of work. However, the rate at which the work is done is quite different. **Power** is the rate at which energy is transmitted in a system. When external forces are doing work, then power is defined as the rate at which work is done on the system.

Power and Work
$P = \dfrac{W}{\Delta t}$
P = power $\qquad \Delta t$ = change in W = work $\qquad\qquad$ time

The SI unit of power is the watt, abbreviated W.

Work, Time, and Power Suppose the jogger and the dog-walker are the same mass, 58 kg. It takes the dog-walker 22 seconds to reach a speed of 1.4 m/s starting from rest, while it takes the jogger half that time to reach the same speed. Both of them do the same amount of work, but their power requirements are different.

$$W = \tfrac{1}{2}mv_f^2 - \tfrac{1}{2}mv_i^2$$
$$= \tfrac{1}{2}(58 \text{ kg})(1.4 \text{ m/s})^2$$
$$- \tfrac{1}{2}(58 \text{ kg})(0 \text{ m/s})^2$$
$$= 57 \text{ J}$$

$$P = \frac{W}{\Delta t}$$
$$= \frac{57 \text{ J}}{11 \text{ s}}$$
$$= 5.2 \text{ W}$$

$$W = \tfrac{1}{2}mv_f^2 - \tfrac{1}{2}mv_i^2$$
$$= \tfrac{1}{2}(58 \text{ kg})(1.4 \text{ m/s})^2$$
$$- \tfrac{1}{2}(58 \text{ kg})(0 \text{ m/s})^2$$
$$= 57 \text{ J}$$

$$P = \frac{W}{\Delta t}$$
$$= \frac{57 \text{ J}}{22 \text{ s}}$$
$$= 2.6 \text{ W}$$

(18) **SEP Use Mathematics** Use the equation for power to determine how to express 1 watt in basic SI units.

INVESTIGATIVE PHENOMENON

GO ONLINE to revisit your **Investigative Phenomenon CER** with the new information you have learned about Classifying Work and Energy.

These questions will help you apply what you learned in this experience to the Investigative Phenomenon.

19 **SEP Use Mathematics** A 70.0-kg bungee jumper reaches a maximum velocity of 13 m/s during the course of a jump. Determine the maximum kinetic energy of the bungee jumper.

20 **SEP Use Mathematics** After dropping 75 meters, what is the magnitude of the work that the gravitational force has done on a 70.0-kg bungee jumper?

21 **SEP Argue from Evidence** Three friends of three different masses bungee jump, dropping from the same height. All three friends determine that they will have the same velocity at 30 meters prior to their bands stretching. Argue from evidence why this may be the case.

22 **CCC Cause and Effect** Consider a system that includes only a bungee jumper as she bounces during her jump. What external forces do work on the bungee jumper, and what are the signs of the work done?

GO ONLINE
for a **quiz** to evaluate what you learned about Classifying Work and Energy.

Mechanical Energy

 GO ONLINE to do a **hands-on lab** that explores the transformation of potential energy into kinetic energy.

Potential Energy

The kinetic energy of a system is a result of the motion of all of its components. When work is done on the system, its energy changes.

A system also has energy simply in the way it is organized. Objects in the system may have the tendency to come together or move apart depending on their arrangement. **Potential energy** is the energy associated with the position of an object or the arrangement of a system of objects that exert forces on one another. You can think of potential energy as an object's potential to have kinetic energy.

Different types of potential energy include gravitational potential energy, elastic potential energy, electrostatic potential energy, intermolecular potential energy, nuclear potential energy, and chemical potential energy. All these forms of energy are due to the relative positions of objects. In addition, you can consider these forms of energy to be stored in fields, such as gravitational fields or electric fields.

(23) **CCC Energy and Matter** Where in the photograph do you think the roller coaster car would have the most potential energy? Explain your reasoning.

Gravitational Potential Energy

The force of gravity is an attraction between every object in the universe to every other object. At Earth's surface, this force is an object's weight, given by $F_g = mg$, where m is the mass of the object and g is the acceleration due to gravity.

Gravitational potential energy is the energy an object has due to its position in a gravitational field. An object has more potential to fall to Earth's surface the farther away it is from the surface. Because the gravitational force is approximately constant for objects on Earth's surface when the height is small compared to the radius of Earth, the change in an object's potential to fall is proportional to its height. The change in gravitational potential energy is the work required to move an object a certain distance against the pull of gravity.

Gravitational Potential Energy
$$\Delta PE_g = mg(\Delta h)$$
ΔPE_g = change in gravitational potential energy m = mass g = acceleration due to gravity = 9.8 m/s^2 Δh = change in height

To use gravitational potential energy in calculations, a location ($h = 0$) should be defined where PE$_g$ is zero. Often, it is convenient to define an object as having zero gravitational potential energy at Earth's surface, so that the potential energy of an object at height h is given simply by PE$_g = mgh$.

Energy from Gravity When a basketball and Earth are considered part of a system, the system has gravitational potential energy.

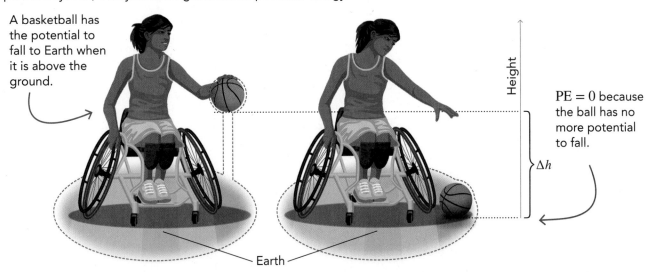

A basketball has the potential to fall to Earth when it is above the ground.

Height

PE = 0 because the ball has no more potential to fall.

Δh

Earth

(24) **SEP Analyze Data** Rank the rock climbers in order from greatest to least amount of gravitational potential energy: a 55-kg climber 24 m high, a 58-kg climber 22 m high, a 49-kg climber 30 m high, a 54-kg climber 25 m high, and a 60-kg climber 24 m high.

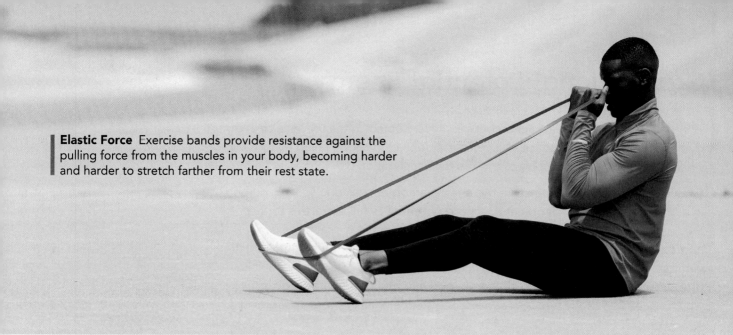

Elastic Force Exercise bands provide resistance against the pulling force from the muscles in your body, becoming harder and harder to stretch farther from their rest state.

Elastic Potential Energy

Deriving Elastic Potential Energy The material that makes up an object can also affect the energy of a system. Elastic objects can be stretched or compressed and then return to their original shape. Examples of elastic objects include springs, rubber bands, and bungee cords. A system with elastic objects may contain **elastic potential energy,** which is the ability of an object to do work as a result of being deformed from its original shape.

Using Hooke's Law The amount of potential energy in a spring can be derived from Hooke's law.

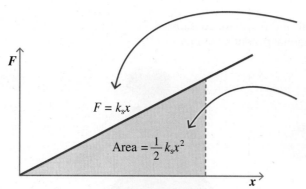

$F = k_s x$

Area $= \frac{1}{2} k_s x^2$

According to Hooke's law, the force a spring exerts on an object is proportional to its displacement.

Work is force times displacement, so this area is the amount of energy needed to displace the spring a distance x.

Unlike gravitational force, the force a spring exerts on an object is not constant. The force is proportional to the spring's displacement. But as the graph shows, you can use the formula for the area of a triangle to determine the energy needed to compress or stretch a spring a distance x from its equilibrium position.

$$\text{Area} = \tfrac{1}{2}\text{base} \times \text{height} = \tfrac{1}{2}(x) \times (k_s x) = \tfrac{1}{2}k_s x^2$$

The spring now has the potential to release this energy when it returns to its equilibrium position, so it has potential energy.

Calculating Elastic Potential Energy The elastic potential energy is proportional to the square of the displacement of the spring from its equilibrium position. This relationship is due to the fact that a spring gets harder and harder to compress (or stretch) the more it is moved from equillibrium. And the more energy used to compress the spring, the more energy is stored in the spring.

Elastic Potential Energy
$$PE_s = \frac{1}{2}k_s x^2$$
PE_s = elastic potential energy
k_s = spring constant
x = displacement from equilibrium position

EXPERIENCE IT!

Hold a rubber band between two of your fingers. Can you stretch the rubber band so that it has a positive displacement? Can you hold it between your two fingers so that it is in the equilibrium position? Can you figure out how to give it a negative displacement?

You already know that the force of gravity decreases with distance above Earth's surface, but too slowly for you to notice. Because you can treat gravity as a constant in your daily interactions, you experience gravitational potential energy differently from elastic potential energy: only proportional to the first power of displacement. In other words, an object does not seem seem to get easier to lift as you move it farther from Earth's surface.

Comparing Elasticity and Gravity Elastic potential energy is proportional to the square of an object's displacement (x), while gravitational potential energy is proportional to an object's displacement (h).

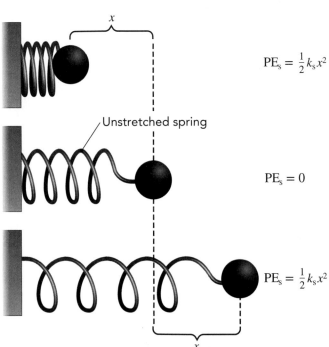

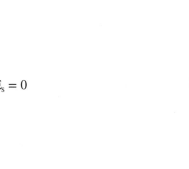

$$PE_s = \frac{1}{2}k_s x^2 \qquad PE_g = mgh$$

$$PE_s = 0$$

$$PE_s = \frac{1}{2}k_s x^2 \qquad PE_g = 0$$

Unstretched spring

(25) **CCC Cause and Effect** Suppose a ball attached to a spring, such as in the diagram, is pulled so that the spring is stretched by a distance x. Assuming no friction, what will happen when the ball is let go?

Cart on a Spring

You attach a cart with a mass of 1.8 kg to a spring and compress the cart-spring system so that the cart is located 12 cm behind the spring's equilibrium position. The spring constant for the spring is 55 N/m. When the spring is released, what is the cart's velocity as it passes the equilibrium position?

1. DRAW A PICTURE Sketch a picture of the situation.

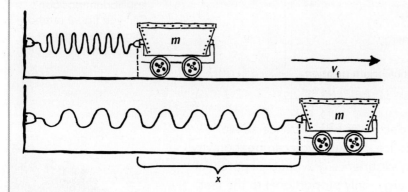
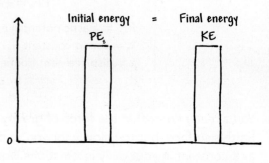

2. DEFINE THE PROBLEM List knowns and unknowns, and assign values to variables.

$m = 1.8$ kg $\qquad$ $v_f = ?$

$x = 12$ cm $= 0.12$ m

$k_s = 55$ N/m

$KE_i = 0$

3. PLAN AND EXECUTE Use mathematical relationships, the picture, and your definitions to plan and execute a solution.

Find the elastic potential energy stored in the spring.

$$PE_s = \tfrac{1}{2}k_s x^2$$
$$= \tfrac{1}{2}(55 \text{ N/m})(0.12 \text{ m})^2$$
$$= 0.40 \text{ J}$$

Use the potential energy to find the work and the final kinetic energy using the work-energy theorem.

$$PE_s = W = \Delta KE = KE_f - KE_i = KE_f - 0 = KE_f$$
$$= 0.40 \text{ J}$$

Use the kinetic energy equation to find the final velocity of the cart.

$$KE_f = \tfrac{1}{2}mv_f^2 \rightarrow v_f = \sqrt{\tfrac{2KE_f}{m}}$$
$$v_f = \sqrt{\frac{2(0.40 \text{ J})}{1.8 \text{ kg}}} = 0.67 \text{ m/s}$$

4. EVALUATE Reflect on your answer.

Less than 0.5 J was added to the system. Therefore, a cart with a mass of about 2 kg should have a final speed of about 0.7 m/s, because $\frac{1}{2}$(2 kg) (0.7 m/s)^2 = 0.5 J. The answer makes sense.

GO ONLINE for more **math support**.

▶ **Math Tutorial Video**

🖥 **Math Practice Problems**

26. You attach a cart with a mass of 700 g to a spring and compress the cart-spring system so that the cart is located 15 cm behind the spring's equilibrium position. The spring constant for the spring is 120 N/m. When the spring is released, what is the cart's velocity as it passes the equilibrium position?

📖 **NEED A HINT?** Go online to your **eText Sample Problem** for stepped out support.

27. You attach a cart with a mass of 1500 g to a spring and compress the cart-spring system so that the cart is located 40 cm behind the spring's equilibrium position. The spring constant for the spring is 65 N/m. When the spring is released, what is the cart's velocity as it passes the equilibrium position?

28. You attach a cart with a mass of 2.6 kg to a spring and compress the cart-spring system so that the cart is located 8.0 cm behind the spring's equilibrium position. If the cart is released and has a velocity of 2.0 m/s when it reaches the equilibrium position, what is the spring constant?

29. You attach a cart with a mass of 0.92 kg to a spring and compress the cart-spring system. The spring constant for the spring is 130 N/m. Your objective is to propel the cart with a velocity of 1.4 m/s along a frictionless surface. How far do you need to compress the spring in order to meet your target velocity?

30. A man drops a 2.7-kg bag out a window 11 meters above ground to his friend, 1.7 meters above ground. Determine the velocity of the bag just before it reaches his friend's hands.

31. A 0.10-kg ball is ejected from a spring-loaded launcher straight into the air. The top of the launcher is 5.0 m high. The launcher's spring has a spring constant of 84 N/m and was compressed 22 cm. How high does the ball travel? What velocity does the ball have when it strikes the ground?

32. A 0.12-kg ball is ejected from a spring-loaded launcher straight into the air. The top of the launcher is 1.9 m high. The launcher's spring has a spring constant of 280 N/m and was compressed 19 cm. What speed is the ball traveling when the ball reaches a height of 2.0 m?

Electromagnetic Potential Energy

Another fundamental force, the electromagnetic force, acts only on charged particles, but this force can either attract or repel. The potential of a charged particle to move toward or away from another charged particle within a system is a form of energy.

Electrostatic Potential Energy You can think of potential energy as the work a field would do on an object to move it to a location that has zero potential energy. For electric fields, infinity is set to zero potential energy. The **electrostatic potential energy** of a charged particle is the work required to move it infinitely far away from another charged particle. This work is positive if the two particles are opposite in charge, but it is negative if two particles have the same charge because the electrostatic force would be repulsive.

Electrostatic Potential Energy of a Particle
$$PE_e = k_e \frac{q_1 q_2}{r} \quad \text{and} \quad \Delta PE_e = k_e q_1 q_2 \left(\frac{1}{r_f} - \frac{1}{r_i} \right)$$
$PE_e, \Delta PE_e$ = electrostatic potential energy, change in electrostatic potential energy
k_e = Coulomb's constant = 8.99×10^9 N·m²/C²
q_1, q_2 = charge of particles 1 and 2
r, r_i, r_f = distance between particles, initial/final distance

As with gravitational force, electrostatic force follows an inverse square law. Therefore, both types of potential energy are inversely proportional to distance. It is more difficult to move two attractive particles apart when they are close together than it is when they are far away.

Comparing Universal Gravitation and Electrostatic Energy Just as the equations for gravitational force and electric force are similar, so too are the equations for potential energy related to these forces. While both forces are proportional to $\frac{1}{r^2}$, both energy equations are proportional to $\frac{1}{r}$.

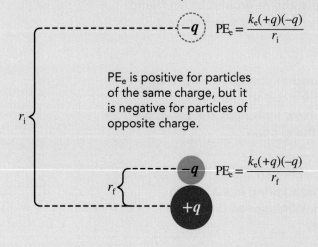

$$PE_e = \frac{k_e(+q)(-q)}{r_i}$$

PE_e is positive for particles of the same charge, but it is negative for particles of opposite charge.

$$PE_e = \frac{k_e(+q)(-q)}{r_f}$$

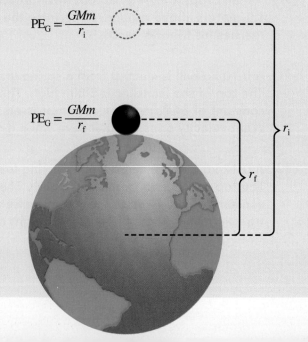

$$PE_G = \frac{GMm}{r_i}$$

$$PE_G = \frac{GMm}{r_f}$$

Maglev Train Powerful magnetic fields provide the potential energy for maglev trains to move on a track. One set of magnets repels the train to keep it hovering within the track, while another set repels the train to push it forward.

Magnetic Potential Energy The electromagnetic force is expressed in magnetic fields as well as electric fields. The ability of an object to do work due to its position and orientation in a magnetic field is called **magnetic potential energy,** or electrodynamic potential energy.

Magnetized objects will move in a way that reduces their magnetic potential energy. This motion is similar to objects with gravitational potential energy moving in a gravitational field. For gravity, objects fall toward Earth and lower their gravitational potential energy.

A magnet generates a magnetic field, but a free magnet will adjust its position and align itself with other, stronger magnetic fields. In this way, the magnet reaches the state of lowest magnetic potential energy because it no longer has the potential to move. The needle of a compass is a magnet that behaves in this manner. If you move the compass, then the needle will spin until it lines up with Earth's magnetic field.

33 **SEP Use Mathematics** Particle A has a charge of +8.0 μC, while particle B has a charge of −5.0 μC. The two particles are 20 cm apart. What is the change in the electrostatic potential energy of particle A if it is moved 5.0 cm further away from particle B?

34 **CCC Energy and Matter** A bar magnet with its center fixed in place is allowed to come to equilibrium in a strong magnetic field. How would you reorient the magnet in order to give it the maximum amount of magnetic potential energy?

Mechanical Energy and Work

 GO ONLINE to do a PhET **simulation** that explores mechanical energy conversions in a skate park and to watch a **video** about different types of energy.

As you have seen, objects in systems have kinetic energy due to their motion, and they have potential energy due to their position, orientation, or elasticity. The **mechanical energy** of a system is the sum of all the kinetic energy and potential energy in the system.

Conservative and Nonconservative Forces Mechanical energy is conserved when no work is done to a system of objects and only conservative forces act within the system. A **conservative force** is a force for which the work done depends on the initial and final positions and not the path taken. The mechanical energy of individual objects may change, such as through collisions, but the total mechanical energy of the system does not change.

Mechanical energy can be converted to thermal energy by nonconservative forces, such as friction. A **nonconservative force** is a force that takes energy away from a system and is path dependent. In this case, mechanical energy is not conserved, but the total energy of the system is still conserved.

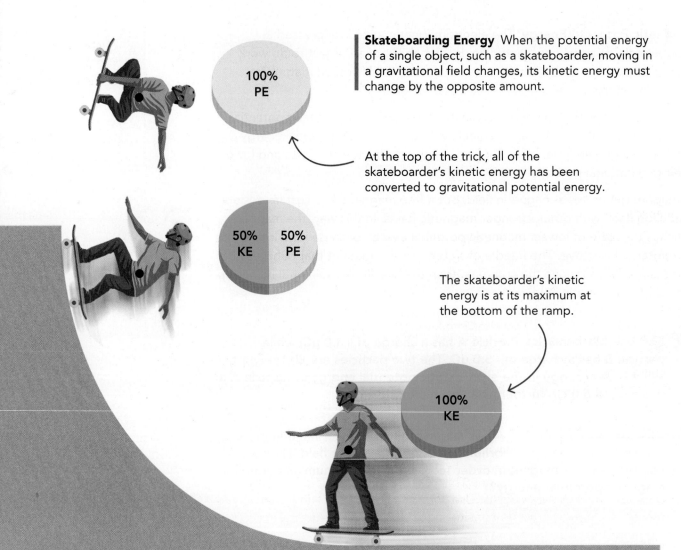

Skateboarding Energy When the potential energy of a single object, such as a skateboarder, moving in a gravitational field changes, its kinetic energy must change by the opposite amount.

100% PE

At the top of the trick, all of the skateboarder's kinetic energy has been converted to gravitational potential energy.

50% KE   50% PE

The skateboarder's kinetic energy is at its maximum at the bottom of the ramp.

100% KE

Work as a Change in Mechanical Energy To change the mechanical energy of a system, work must be done on the system. Moving objects, reorienting objects, or adding and subtracting heat are examples of how to change the mechanical energy of a system.

Mechanical Energy Bar Charts

How can you **represent changes** in the **mechanical energy** of a system?

No Change, No External Work An acrobat drops onto the trampoline and lands back on the platform.

The trampoline is not stretched in its initial and final states, so $PE_s = 0$.

Energy is in the form of PE_g due to the acrobat's position. The trampoline has no PE_g since its height is 0. No external work is applied.

Some Change, No External Work Two particles with the same negative charge are next to one another and then repel each other.

The particles only have PE_e in the initial state.

As the particles repel each other, some PE_e is converted into KE.

External Work A rollercoaster car rushes downhill and then comes to a complete stop after the brakes are applied.

PE_g is converted into KE as the car travels down the hill.

The brakes apply an external force opposing the motion of the car, bringing it to a stop.

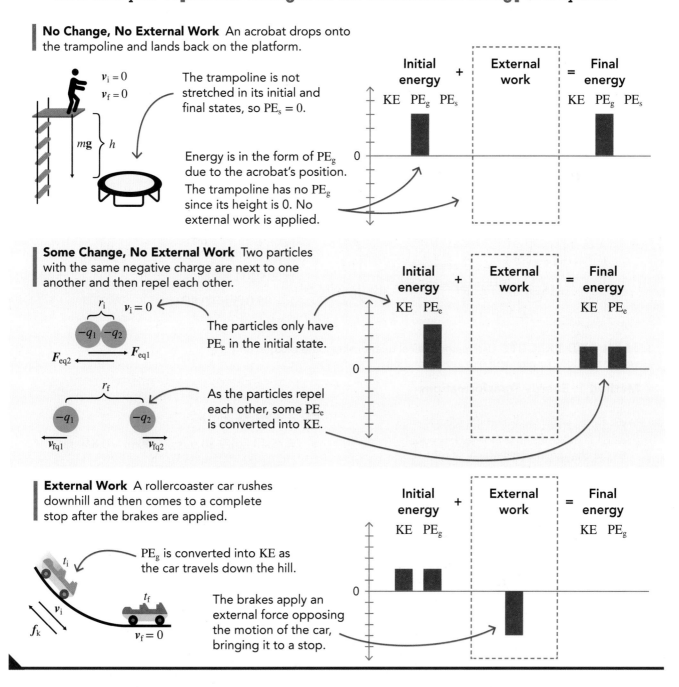

35 **SEP Construct an Explanation** Think about a bowling ball moving down a lane toward the pins. Use this situation to explain why mechanical energy can be considered as the ability to do work.

Bowling Ball Bounce

For a physics experiment, a friend stands in a treehouse 6.00 m off the ground. He drops a bowling ball of mass 5.40 kg onto a highly elastic trampoline 85.0 cm above the ground. The bowling ball lands on the trampoline, which stretches downward until the ball stops, just barely before touching the ground. What is the elastic spring constant of the trampoline fabric?

1. DRAW A PICTURE Sketch a picture of the situation.

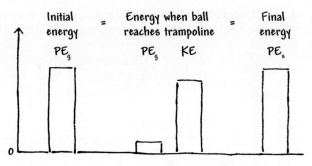

2. DEFINE THE PROBLEM List knowns and unknowns, and assign values to variables.

$h = 6.00$ m

$m = 5.40$ kg

$x = 85.0$ cm $= 0.850$ m

$k_s = ?$

3. PLAN AND EXECUTE Use mathematical relationships, the picture, and your definitions to plan and execute a solution.

Method 1: Energy Transformations

Find the kinetic energy of the bowling ball when it strikes the trampoline. It is equal to the change in gravitational potential energy of the bowling ball from its fall.

$$KE = \Delta PE_g = mg\Delta h$$
$$= (5.40 \text{ kg})(9.80 \text{ m/s}^2)(6.00 \text{ m} - 0.850 \text{ m})$$
$$= 273 \text{ J}$$

Find the elastic potential energy of the trampoline when the ball reaches the ground. This comes from all the mechanical energy in the ball converting into elastic potential energy.

$$PE_s = PE_g + KE \rightarrow$$
$$PE_s = mg\Delta h + KE$$
$$= (5.40 \text{ kg})(9.80 \text{ m/s}^2)(0.850 \text{ m}) + 273 \text{ J} = 318 \text{ J}$$

Use the equation for elastic potential energy to find the spring constant.

$$PE_s = \tfrac{1}{2}k_s x^2 \rightarrow$$
$$k_s = \frac{2PE_s}{x^2} = \frac{2(318 \text{ J})}{(0.850 \text{ m})^2}$$
$$= 880 \text{ N/m}$$

Method 2: Conservation of Mechanical Energy

Define the mechanical energy of the system.

$$ME = PE_g + PE_s + KE$$

Find the initial mechanical energy of the system.

$$ME_i = mgh + 0 + 0 = mgh$$

Find the final mechanical energy of the system.

$$ME_f = 0 + \frac{1}{2}k_s x^2 + 0 = \frac{1}{2}k_s x^2$$

Use the concept of conservation of mechanical energy to determine the spring constant.

$$ME_i = ME_f \rightarrow mgh = \frac{1}{2}k_s x^2 \rightarrow k_s = \frac{2mgh}{x^2}$$

$$k_s = \frac{2(5.40 \text{ kg})(9.80 \text{ m/s}^2)(6.00 \text{ m})}{(0.850 \text{ m})^2} = 879 \text{ N/m}$$

4. EVALUATE Reflect upon your answer.

Both methods yield the same answer, within the limits of round-off error. The second method is quicker because determining the energy at the intermediate step of the bowling ball first striking the trampoline is not necessary.

 GO ONLINE for more **math support**.

▶ **Math Tutorial Video**

💻 **Math Practice Problems**

---

36 Another friend is in a treehouse 4.00 m off the ground. She drops a bowling ball of mass 7.30 kg onto a highly elastic trampoline with cloth 60.0 cm above the ground. The bowling ball lands on the trampoline, which stretches downward until the ball stops, 10.0 cm above the ground. What is the elastic spring constant of the trampoline fabric?

📖 **NEED A HINT?** Go online to your **eText Sample Problem** for stepped out support.

37 You stand in a treehouse 8.00 m off the ground. You drop a bowling ball of mass 6.30 kg onto a highly elastic trampoline with cloth 75.0 cm above the ground. The bowling ball lands on the trampoline, which stretches downward for 60.0 cm, when the ball stops. What is the elastic spring constant of the trampoline fabric?

38 A friend drops a bowling ball with mass 6.8 kg onto a trampoline from a height of 5.50 m. The trampoline has a spring constant of 1120 N/m. The bowling ball lands on the trampoline, which stretches downward until the ball stops, 5.0 cm above the ground. How high is the trampoline fabric off of the ground before the bowling ball strikes it?

Friction as a Change in Energy

Mechanical energy is a summary of the macroscopic state of a system. A system's **internal energy** is the energy on a microscopic scale associated with the random motion of molecules. It includes thermal energy, and the chemical and nuclear potential energy stored in the atoms and molecules that are in the system.

When considering the conservation of energy in a system, the system's total internal energy must be taken into consideration. For example, when an object in a system is slowed by friction, it loses mechanical energy. But that energy is not lost. It is converted into thermal energy. Through heating, thermal energy, which is directly proportional to temperature, increases.

At a macroscopic level, the thermal energy of a system can be considered part of the system's internal potential, or stored, energy. This internal energy has the potential to do work on other objects in the system, such as by transferring energy to them through heating.

Change in Energy Due to Friction
$$\Delta U_{\text{int}} = |fd|$$
ΔU_{int} = change in system's internal energy f = friction component of the surface force d = distance over which friction acts

Friction and Tires When a driver slams on a car's brakes, the brakes lock the tires so that they don't rotate, and the tires skid along the ground. The skid marks are evidence of the friction between the tires and the ground.

As this infrared image shows, the outside surface of the tire heats up due to the friction between the tire and road.

(39) **CCC Matter and Energy** Use the concepts of conservation of mechanical energy and work to explain why friction can never subtract from the internal energy of a system.

Car Skidding to a Stop

A car traveling at 30.0 m/s skids to a stop on a dry road. If the coefficient of kinetic friction between the tire and the road is 0.48, what distance does the car skid before it stops?

1. DRAW A PICTURE Sketch a picture of the situation.

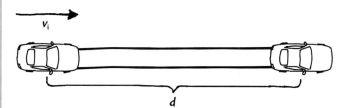

2. DEFINE THE PROBLEM List knowns and unknowns, and assign values to variables.

$v_i = 30.0$ m/s | $m = ?$

$\mu_k = 0.48$ | $d = ?$

3. PLAN AND EXECUTE Use mathematical relationships, the picture, and your definitions to plan and execute a solution.

Write an equation for the change in internal energy in the system. Include both the car and pavement in the system.

$$\Delta U_{int} = |fd|$$

The system's change in internal energy is the kinetic energy of the car transformed into thermal energy.

Examine the energy transfer. Express the equation in terms of known and unknown values.

$$\Delta U_{int} = -\Delta KE = KE_i - KE_f = KE_i - 0 = KE_i$$
$$\tfrac{1}{2}mv_i^2 = (\mu_k mg)d \rightarrow \tfrac{1}{2}v_i^2 = \mu_k gd$$

Solve for the unknown distance, d.

$$d = \frac{v_i^2}{2\mu_k g} = \frac{(30.0 \text{ m/s})^2}{2(0.48)(9.8 \text{ m/s}^2)} = 96 \text{ m}$$

4. EVALUATE Reflect on your answer.

The answer does not depend on the mass of the car. For a car traveling this fast, it makes sense that it would take a long distance (almost 100 m) to skid to a stop.

 GO ONLINE for more **math support**.

Math Practice Problems

---

40 A car traveling at 25.0 m/s skids to a stop on a wet road. If the coefficient of kinetic friction between the tire and the road is 0.310, what distance does the car skid before it stops?

📖 **NEED A HINT?** Go online to your **eText Sample Problem** for stepped out support.

41 A motorcycle skids to a stop on a dry road over 70.0 m. If the coefficient of kinetic friction between the tire and the road is 0.52, how fast was the motorcycle moving before it started to skid?

Revisit

INVESTIGATIVE PHENOMENON

GO ONLINE to revisit your **Investigative Phenomenon CER** with the new information you have learned about Mechanical Energy.

These questions will help you apply what you learned in this experience to the Investigative Phenomenon.

42 **CCC Energy and Matter** Describe the energy transformations that occur from the time a bungee jumper jumps off the platform and the time the bungee cord is stretched to its maximum displacement during the jump.

43 **SEP Construct an Explanation** If no energy is lost to heat, friction, or drag during the bungee jumper's fall, the bungee jumper could oscillate up and down forever. How do you think the jumper is brought to a complete stop in order to end the bouncing?

44 **SEP Use Mathematical Thinking** Explain how you can determine the spring constant for the bungee cord using the total height of the jump, the mass of the jumper, and the length of the bungee cord when unstretched.

45 **SEP Construct an Explanation** Every bungee jump site is engineered so that the jumps are safe for people of many different sizes and weights. Explain why choosing a bungee cord with the correct elastic spring constant is important. Use the concepts of elastic and gravitational potential energy in your explanation.

 GO ONLINE for a **quiz** to evaluate what you learned about Mechanical Energy.

Conservation of Energy

 GO ONLINE to do a **hands-on lab** to investigate how conservation of energy applies to a pendulum.

Energy—A Conserved Quantity

The **law of conservation of energy** states that energy is neither created nor destroyed. It is one of the most fundamental concepts in science.

In physics, energy is a measure of the state of the internal structure of a system, but at its most basic level, it is the ability to do work. When energy is used to do work, it is changed to a different form, either stored as potential energy or used to increase kinetic energy. So, any change in the internal energy in a system indicates that work was done on the system.

VOCABULARY

In everyday conservation, **energy conservation** usually refers to the preservation of energy resources, such as minimizing the use of electricity. In physics, conservation refers to a quantifiable characteristic of a system that remains constant, such as energy.

> **Conservation of Energy**
>
> $$E_i + W = E_f$$
>
> E_i = initial energy of the system
> W = net work done on the system
> E_f = final energy of the system

46 **SEP Construct an Explanation** Consider the system of a weightlifter, a barbell, and Earth. When the weightlifter raises the barbell over her head, she increases the gravitational potential energy of the barbell, but the overall energy in the system does not change because the work was performed within the system, not on the system. Further explain how the energy of the system is conserved.

Defining Systems

In order to solve problems in physics, the situation must be defined. This often means choosing coordinates, defining the system, defining variables, and choosing references. You have the freedom to choose these definitions because the answers to the problem are independent of these definitions. For example, how you choose to define a system affects whether the flow of mass and energy is within the system or between the system and its surroundings.

Open Systems Systems are characterized by their boundaries. Whether or not energy and/or mass escapes the system depends on what the boundaries of the system are. An **open system** is a system that allows energy or matter to be transferred between the system and the surroundings.

Closed Systems A **closed system** is a system that allows energy in the form of heat or work, but not mass, to be transferred between the system and its surroundings. An **isolated system** is a special type of a closed system that does not allow energy or matter to be transferred between the system and its surroundings.

> **Hot Soup Systems** Mass and energy flow in different ways in open, closed, and isolated systems.

Soup particles and thermal energy can escape from this cup to the surroundings, making it an open system.

Soup particles cannot escape from the cup to the surroundings, but thermal energy can, making it a closed system.

Neither soup particles nor thermal energy can escape the insulated container, making it an isolated system.

Total Energy of a System The **total energy** of a system is given by the sum of all energy within the system. In an isolated system, the total energy of the system is constant. In contrast, in open and closed systems, the total energy changes when work is done on the system.

Total Energy of a System
$$E_{total} = KE + PE_g + PE_s + U_{int}$$
E_{total} = total energy of system
KE = kinetic energy of system
PE_g = gravitational potential energy of system
PE_s = elastic potential energy of system
U_{int} = internal energy of system

> **Rocket Systems** Mass exits the rocket system, but it remains within the rocket-Earth system. Similarly, Earth applies work external to the rocket system but internal to the rocket-Earth system.

Modeling Systems

How can you use **energy bar charts** to compare energy changes in **open, closed, and isolated** systems?

Skidding to a Stop Suppose a motorcycle with mass m and moving at an initial velocity v_i skids to a complete stop. The scenario can be modeled with energy bar charts to represent **how energy is lost, gained, or conserved** in open, closed, and isolated systems.

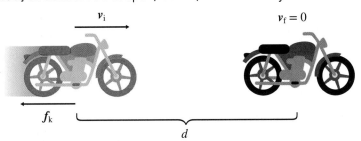

System 1: Motorcycle In **open and closed systems,** forces external to the system perform work so that the system can **gain or lose energy** from the initial state to the final state.

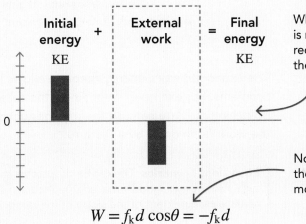

When f_k is external, W is negative, therefore reducing the energy in the final state.

Note that f_k is always in the opposite direction of motion and displacement.

$$W = f_k d \cos\theta = -f_k d$$

System 2: Motorcycle and Pavement In an **isolated system,** the total energy of the system is **conserved** from the initial to the final state. The change in the internal energy of the system is represented by ΔU_{int}.

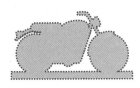

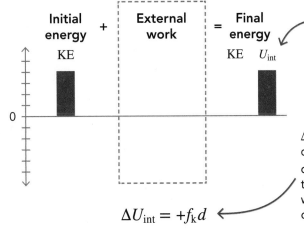

ΔU_{int} is always in the final state. It has the opposite sign as ΔME.

ΔU_{int} takes into account changes in the system due to f_k, such as the tires and pavement warming up and changing shape.

$$\Delta U_{int} = +f_k d$$

---

(47) **SEP Use Math** Calculate the total energy of a system consisting of Earth and a passenger airplane with a mass of 125,000 kg that is flying at a speed of 220 m/s, 8.0 km above Earth's surface. Define the gravitational potential energy of the airplane as zero at Earth's surface, and ignore the difference in the acceleration of gravity at the two heights.

Expanded Work-Energy Theorem

 GO ONLINE to watch a **video** about the mathematical representation of conservation of energy.

For an isolated system, you can use the conservation of energy to equate the total energy of a system at two different points in time. For an open or closed system, on which work may be done, you can expand the work-energy theorem using the conservation of energy and focus on the energies that are changing within a system.

Expanded Work-Energy Theorem
$$KE_i + PE_{gi} + PE_{si} + W = KE_f + PE_{gf} + PE_{sf}$$

KE_i, KE_f = initial/final kinetic energy
PE_{gi}, PE_{gf} = initial/final gravitational potential energy
PE_{si}, PE_{sf} = initial/final elastic potential energy
W = net work done on the system

The expanded work-energy theorem allows you solve a wide variety of problems. For example, if you know the total energy of a system at two points in time, you can use the expanded work-energy theorem to calculate the work done on or by a system.

Equivalent Scenarios The car-Earth systems shown are isolated systems. The expanded work-energy theorem shows that the result is independent of the slope of the ramp.

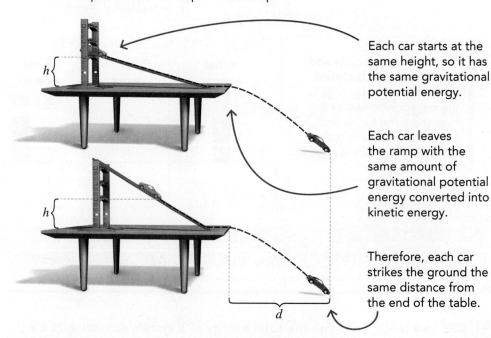

Each car starts at the same height, so it has the same gravitational potential energy.

Each car leaves the ramp with the same amount of gravitational potential energy converted into kinetic energy.

Therefore, each car strikes the ground the same distance from the end of the table.

(48) SEP Develop a Model Construct an energy bar chart for the car-Earth system shown in the top row of the figure. How would this energy bar chart change for the bottom row?

Energy Transformed Within a System

 GO ONLINE to do a PhET **simulation** that allows you to explore energy transformations within a machine.

For complex scenarios involving many different types of energy, it is often convenient to define the system so that no work is done on the system. In these cases, the expanded work-energy theorem simplifies to a statement of conservation of energy. The total energy at the initial point in time is equal to the total energy at the final point in time.

The conservation of energy implies that change in a system is due only to energy transformations within the system. Any change in a specific type of energy, such as elastic potential energy, requires an equivalent change in other forms of energy, such as gravitational potential energy, kinetic energy, or thermal energy.

EXPERIENCE IT!

Make a pendulum using a piece of tape to attach a small weight or marble to a length of string. Hold up the pendulum, pull back the weight from its resting position, and then let go. How is energy transformed within this pendulum system?

Energy Transformations The puck-spring-Earth system shown is a closed system, so the puck's kinetic energy comes only from potential energy stored within the system.

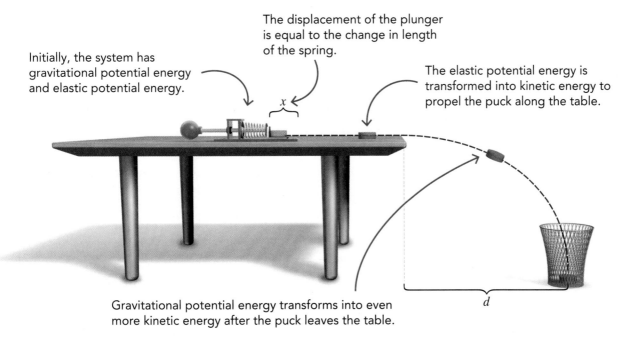

The displacement of the plunger is equal to the change in length of the spring.

Initially, the system has gravitational potential energy and elastic potential energy.

The elastic potential energy is transformed into kinetic energy to propel the puck along the table.

Gravitational potential energy transforms into even more kinetic energy after the puck leaves the table.

49) **SEP Develop a Model** Construct an energy bar chart for the puck-spring-Earth system shown in the diagram. How would the bar chart change if you define the system so that it includes only the puck?

50) **SEP Use Mathematics** Suppose a person with a mass of 58 kg jumps on a trampoline and compresses the fabric a distance of 40 cm. How high will the person then bounce above the rim of the trampoline if the spring constant of the trampoline is 1250 N/m?

Roller Coaster Energy

A 750-kg roller coaster car drops from rest at a height of 90.0 m along a frictionless track. What is the velocity of the roller coaster at the top of a second hill that is 60.0 m high? What average force is required to bring the car to a stop along a 120-m stretch of horizontal track at ground level at the end of the ride?

1. DRAW A PICTURE Sketch a picture of the situation.

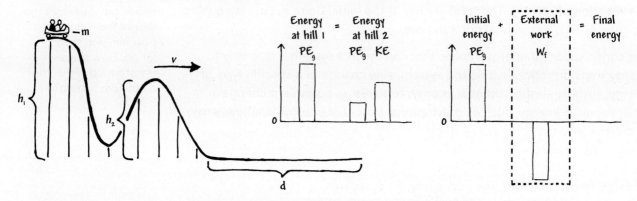

2. DEFINE THE PROBLEM List knowns and unknowns, and assign values to variables.

$m = 750$ kg	$d = 120$ m	$v_2 = ?$
$h_1 = 90.0$ m	$KE_1, KE_3 = 0$	$F = ?$
$h_2 = 60.0$ m		
$h_3 = 0.0$ m		

The subscript 3 refers to the position at the end of the track.

3. PLAN AND EXECUTE Use mathematical relationships, the picture, and your definitions to plan and execute a solution.

Use the work-energy theorem to equate the energies at the top of the first and second hills.

$$KE_1 + PE_{g1} + W = KE_2 + PE_{g2}$$
$$0 + mgh_1 + 0 = \frac{1}{2}mv_2^2 + mgh_2$$

Solve for the unknown velocity, v_2.

$$mgh_1 = \frac{1}{2}mv_2^2 + mgh_2 \rightarrow v_2 = \sqrt{2g(h_1 - h_2)}$$
$$v_2 = \sqrt{2(9.8 \text{ m/s}^2)(90.0 \text{ m} - 60.0 \text{ m})}$$
$$v_2 = 24 \text{ m/s}$$

Use the work-energy theorem to equate the energies at the top of the first hill and the end of the ride.

$$KE_1 + PE_{g1} + W = KE_3 + PE_{g3}$$
$$0 + mgh_1 + Fd\cos\theta = 0 + mgh_3$$

Solve for the unknown force, F.

$$mgh_1 + Fd\cos\theta = mgh_3 \rightarrow F = \frac{mg(h_3 - h_1)}{d\cos\theta}$$
$$F = \frac{(750 \text{ kg})(9.8 \text{ m/s}^2)(0.0 \text{ m} - 90.0 \text{ m})}{(120 \text{ m})(-1)}$$
$$F = 5500 \text{ N}$$

4. EVALUATE Reflect on your answer.
The units of the answer are correct because a newton is a kilogram-meter per second squared. The answer makes sense because a large force is necessary to stop a 750-kg object that is moving rapidly.

 GO ONLINE for more **math support**.

▶ **Math Tutorial Video**

🖥 **Math Practice Problems**

---

51. An 850-kg roller coaster car drops from rest at a height of 110 m along a frictionless track. What is the velocity of the roller coaster at the top of a second hill that is 75 m high? What average force is required to bring the car to a stop along a 150-m stretch of horizontal track at ground level at the end of the ride?

   📖 **NEED A HINT?** Go online to your **eText Sample Problem** for stepped out support.

52. A 920-kg roller coaster car drops from rest at a height of 80.0 m along a frictionless track. What is the velocity of the roller coaster at the top of a second hill that is 65.0 m high? What average force is required to bring the car to a stop along a 170-m stretch of horizontal track at ground level at the end of the ride?

53. A 750-kg roller coaster car drops from rest at a height of 90.0 m along a frictionless track. How high should the second hill be in order for the car to have a velocity of 30.0 m/s at the top of the second hill?

54. A 750-kg roller coaster car drops from rest at a height of 90.0 m along a frictionless track. If the coefficient of kinetic friction due to braking along a horizontal track at the end of the ride is 0.720, over what distance does the car need to brake to come to a complete stop?

55. An engineer is designing a roller coaster with the profile shown in the diagram. How fast does the roller coaster car have to be traveling at the top of the first hill for the roller coaster to stop at the top of the second hill?

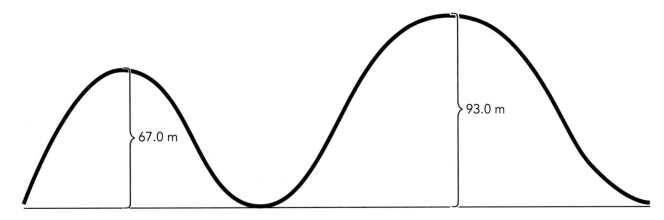

67.0 m

93.0 m

Power—The Rate of Energy Transfer

Recall that power is the amount of work done over a given amount of time. If the same amount of work is done over a shorter time, then more power is applied. Using the expanded work-energy theorem, you can consider power as the rate at which energy is transferred into or out of a system.

Power and Change in Energy
$$P = \frac{\Delta E}{t}$$
P = power ΔE = change in energy t = time

Power and Work Many roller coasters have two instances where work is done on, and therefore power is applied to, the system of the roller coaster cars and Earth. First, the roller coaster cars are often towed up the first hill in order to maximize the gravitational potential energy in the system. Second, the brakes are applied at the end of the ride to dissipate any remaining kinetic energy so that the ride comes to a complete stop before people disembark.

In terms of the work alone, any amount of force could potentially achieve the desired result of lifting or stopping the roller coaster car. However, in order to make the ride exciting and give more people a chance to ride, enough power needs to be applied to lift the car up the first hill quickly. Furthermore, the power applied to stop the car at the end of the ride needs to be great enough to stop the car before the end of the track, but not so great that the car stops too suddenly to be safe.

 SEP Construct an Explanation When your hands are cold, you may rub them together. It seems the faster you rub them together, the warmer they become. Use the concept of power to construct an explanation for this observation.

Elevator Power Power is used to tow an elevator up or down an elevator shaft. To do this work, a motor applies tension to the cable that moves the elevator over time.

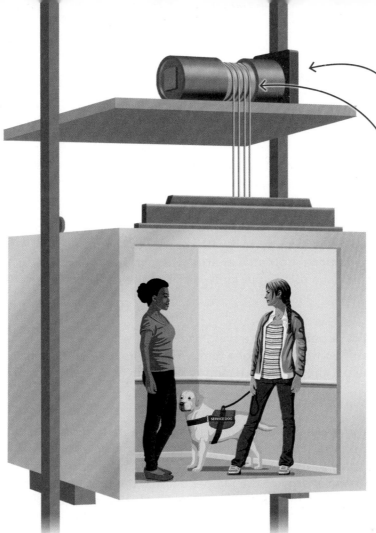

Tension generated by the motor exerts power on the elevator to raise the car.

Friction between the cables and the spinning motor resists the upward movement of the elevator.

Power and Friction Engineers must design mechanical systems to overcome the energy lost by the system due to friction. For example, consider the system of an elevator motor and the cables that tow the elevator up and down the elevator shaft. As the elevator moves up the elevator shaft, the motor must transfer electricity into tension that exerts power on the elevator. This power is used to offset both the energy that is being converted to gravitational potential energy as the elevator rises as well as the energy that is being converted into thermal energy by the friction between the cable and the pulley. If this power is not great enough, then the elevator will not be able to maintain its speed.

(51) SEP Analyze Data Rank the four people from greatest power expended to least power expended while skating in a 500-m speed skating race. Assume all the skaters started from rest.

Person	Mass (kg)	Final Velocity (m/s)	Time (s)
A	69.0	15.1	34.2
B	77.0	13.8	37.7
C	73.0	14.2	39.1
D	84.0	14.9	40.5

INVESTIGATIVE PHENOMENON

GO ONLINE to revisit your **Investigative Phenomenon CER** with the new information you have learned about Conservation of Energy.

These questions will help you apply what you learned in this experience to the Investigative Phenomenon.

58 **SEP Evaluate Information** A friend claims that at the bottom of a bungee jump, when the jumper has come to rest with respect to the ground, all of the change in gravitational potential energy was lost due to friction. Support or refute this claim using your knowledge of the conservation of energy.

59 **SEP Use Mathematics** A person with a weight of 52 kg walks up a flight of stairs to the takeoff point of a bungee jump. The stairs are 3.1 m high. How much time would it take for the person to climb the stairs with exactly 250 W of power?

60 **SEP Use Mathematics** Make an energy bar chart for the system of the bungee jumper, the bungee cord, and Earth that shows the relative amounts of gravitational potential energy, elastic potential energy in the bungee cord, and kinetic energy of the jumper. Sketch the graphs for three situations: before takeoff, at the point of maximum velocity, and at the bottom of the jump.

61 **CCC Energy and Matter** When the bungee jumper has come to a complete stop after the jump, what has happened to her initial gravitational potential energy?

GO ONLINE
for a **quiz** to evaluate what you learned about Conservation of Energy.

These questions will help you apply what you learned in this investigation to the Anchoring Phenomenon.

62 **CCC Systems and System Models** How can you define the system in the chain-reaction machine shown in the image so that the system is closed? What are the different types of energy transfers that are shown in the image?

63 **SEP Construct an Explanation** Between each occurrence of a chain-reaction machine performing its task, the components of the machine must be reset to their initial positions. How is this "resetting" akin to performing work on the system that comprises the chain-reaction machine?

☑ INVESTIGATION ASSESSMENT

 GO ONLINE for activities that will give you an opportunity to **demonstrate what you have learned:**

- ☑ **Engineering Performance-Based Assessment** Use a magnetic field to induce an electric current.

- 📄 **Engineering Workbench** Design your own roller coaster.

- 💻 **Career Connections** Learn about how a roller coaster engineer uses an understanding of energy.

- ☑ **Investigation Test** Take this test to demonstrate your understanding of energy and energy transformations.

- ☑ **Virtual Lab Performance-Based Assessment** Determine the amount of energy needed for a rocket to escape Earth's gravity and fly into space.

GO ONLINE to engage with real-world phenomena by watching a **phenomenon video** and completing a **CER worksheet.**

How does the collision affect the motion?

Collisions

A collision is an interaction between two objects, when at least one of the objects is in motion. Collisions can occur at different scales. For example, subatomic particles collide at high speeds at the microscopic scale, unseen by human eyes. At a larger, more familiar scale, you may have seen collisions like the one between the two hockey players in the photo. Collisions can also occur at the even larger astronomic scale, such as when stars or galaxies collide with each other.

The length of time that two objects interact during a collision is determined by their motion and the materials that make up the objects. Very hard objects collide for a very short amount of time. For example, a collision between two billiard balls usually lasts only 250 to 300 millionths of a second. A collision of a soft snowball with a wall might last 6 thousandths of a second. However, a collision between Earth's continents can last for tens of millions of years. How do the laws of physics govern colliding objects and help you determine how an object's motion is affected by a collision?

1. **CCC Cause and Effect** When two hockey players moving toward each other collide, there are many possible outcomes. Qualitatively describe what would happen to each player after the collision for at least three different scenarios.

2. **CCC Patterns** You have seen many collisions occur at the macroscopic level. Make a list of collisions you have observed. Then, explain how you might classify the different collisions.

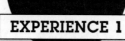
Momentum and Impulse

 GO ONLINE to do a **hands-on lab** to investigate measuring momentum and impulse.

Introduction to Linear Momentum

EXPERIENCE IT!

Drop a heavy object with one hand and catch it with the other. Repeat the experiment with a lighter object. Compare what happens to your hand after you catch the heavy object with what happens after you catch the lighter object.

Linear momentum, often referred to simply as momentum, is the product of the mass and the velocity of a body in linear motion. Momentum is a vector; it has both magnitude and direction. The direction of an object's momentum is the same as the direction of the object's velocity. Because momentum depends on velocity, which is defined for a particular frame of reference, momentum is also defined for a particular frame of reference.

Momentum depends on mass as well as velocity, so bodies with the same momentum may have very different speeds. For instance, for a golf ball to have the same momentum as a bowling ball traveling at 1 m/s, the golf ball would require a much greater velocity.

Linear Momentum
$p = mv$
p = linear momentum m = mass v = velocity

Momentum is the product of mass, which has units of kg, and velocity, which has units of m/s. Therefore, momentum has units of kg·m/s. Remember that momentum depends on mass, not on weight.

Colliding Cars Each toy car has a momentum determined by its mass and velocity. What happens to the cars after the collision is largely determined by each car's momentum prior to the collision.

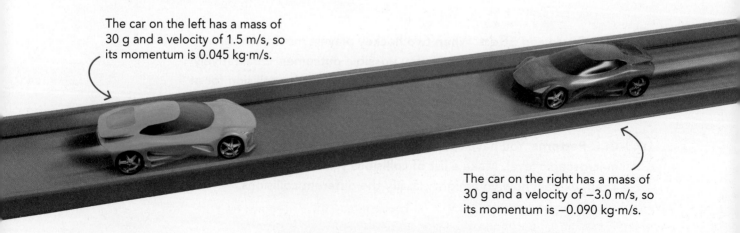

The car on the left has a mass of 30 g and a velocity of 1.5 m/s, so its momentum is 0.045 kg·m/s.

The car on the right has a mass of 30 g and a velocity of −3.0 m/s, so its momentum is −0.090 kg·m/s.

Momentum—a Vector Quantity

As with any vector quantity, momentum can be represented using a coordinate system. A two-dimensional system has an x-axis and a y-axis, and a three-dimensional system has an x-axis, a y-axis, and a z-axis.

In some cases, the velocity of an object is not entirely along one axis. The same, therefore, is true of momentum. You can find the resultant momentum of an object from its mass and velocity by using the momentum equation. You can use trigonometry to break the momentum equation into its components. Then, you can determine the momenta (plural of *momentum*) separately for the x-, y-, and z-directions. As with velocity, the x-, y-, and z-components of momentum are independent of one another.

Vector Nature of Momentum The momentum for the crop duster airplane in the figure is toward the north and east. The plane has a mass of 6500 kg. The legs of the triangle give the relative proportions of the x- and y-components.

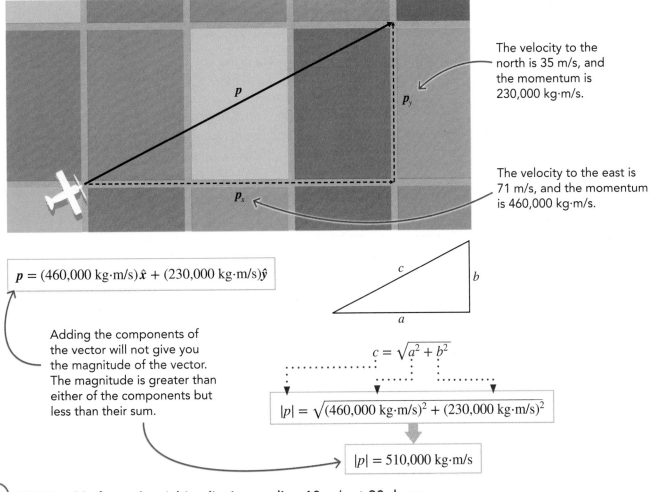

The velocity to the north is 35 m/s, and the momentum is 230,000 kg·m/s.

The velocity to the east is 71 m/s, and the momentum is 460,000 kg·m/s.

$$p = (460{,}000 \text{ kg·m/s})\hat{x} + (230{,}000 \text{ kg·m/s})\hat{y}$$

Adding the components of the vector will not give you the magnitude of the vector. The magnitude is greater than either of the components but less than their sum.

$$c = \sqrt{a^2 + b^2}$$

$$|p| = \sqrt{(460{,}000 \text{ kg·m/s})^2 + (230{,}000 \text{ kg·m/s})^2}$$

$$|p| = 510{,}000 \text{ kg·m/s}$$

(3) **SEP Use Mathematics** A bicyclist is traveling 10 m/s at 30 degrees south of east. The cyclist and bicycle have a combined mass of 70 kg. First, determine the momentum of the cyclist and bicycle using the momentum equation directly. Then solve for momentum by separating velocity into x- and y-components, using the momentum equation for each component, and finding the resultant momentum. How do your answers compare?

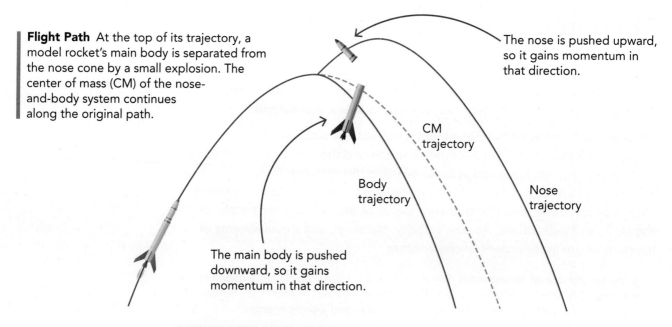

Flight Path At the top of its trajectory, a model rocket's main body is separated from the nose cone by a small explosion. The center of mass (CM) of the nose-and-body system continues along the original path.

The nose is pushed upward, so it gains momentum in that direction.

CM trajectory

Body trajectory

Nose trajectory

The main body is pushed downward, so it gains momentum in that direction.

Net Momentum

The **total momentum** of a system is the vector sum of the momenta of all of the individual objects in the system. For a system with more than one object or part, such as the model rocket example, it is useful to break the momenta of the individual parts or objects in the system into horizontal and vertical components. Then you can add the momenta together to determine the total momentum.

Each numbered subscript represents a different object or mass within the system.

Total Momentum	Component Momentum
$\boldsymbol{p}_{\text{net}} = \boldsymbol{p}_1 + \boldsymbol{p}_2 + \ldots + \boldsymbol{p}_n$ $\boldsymbol{p}_{\text{net}}$ = total momentum $\boldsymbol{p}_{1, 2, n}$ = momenta of objects 1, 2, and n	$p_{\text{net}, x} = p_{1x} + p_{2x} + \ldots + p_{nx}$ $p_{\text{net}, y} = p_{1y} + p_{2y} + \ldots + p_{ny}$ $p_{\text{net}, x}$ = total horizontal momentum $p_{\text{net}, y}$ = total vertical momentum

When calculating total momentum, you must use a consistent reference frame. For example, suppose that for a two-car system, an observer on the ground sees one car traveling 16 m/s toward the west and a second car traveling 23 m/s toward the west. Then, a passenger traveling in the first car must see the first car traveling 0 m/s and the second car traveling 7 m/s to the west. If the momentum for the two cars is determined by different observers, then adding the two momenta gives an incorrect value for the total momentum of the system.

(4) **SEP Use Mathematics** A 1300-kg car is traveling north at 15 m/s. A 1250-kg car is traveling east at 17 m/s. A third car with a mass of 1350 kg is traveling in a direction 45 degrees north of east at 25 m/s. All speeds are determined from the same frame of reference. Determine the total momentum of the three-car system using the same frame of reference.

The Moment of Inertia

The relations between mass, velocity, and momentum in linear motion have parallels to the motions of spinning objects and systems. Mass is a measure of inertia, which is the tendency of an object to resist any changes to its linear motion. The **moment of inertia** is the tendency of an object to resist any change to its rotational motion. An object rotates around a line called the **axis of rotation.** An object's moment of inertia depends on the mass of the object and how the mass is distributed around its axis of rotation. For a system of point masses, the moment of inertia is a sum:

Moment of Inertia
$$I = m_1 r_1^2 + m_2 r_2^2 + \ldots + m_n r_n^2$$
I = moment of inertia $m_{1,2,n}$ = mass of point 1, 2, and n $r_{1,2,n}$ = distance from axis for point 1, 2, and n

Understanding Rotational Inertia

How does the **mass** of a spinning object affect its ability to **change rotation?**

Rotational Inertia It can be very difficult to move, stop, or speed up a spinning object with a lot of mass. A spinning object's resistance to a change in the rate of rotation around an axis is called **rotational inertia** and is measured as the object's **moment of inertia in kg•m^2.**

Two properties control the strength of this resistance: **the object's mass and how that mass is distributed with respect to the axis of the object's rotation.**

A spinning top stays upright because its mass is concentrated in an area that is relatively far from its axis of rotation.

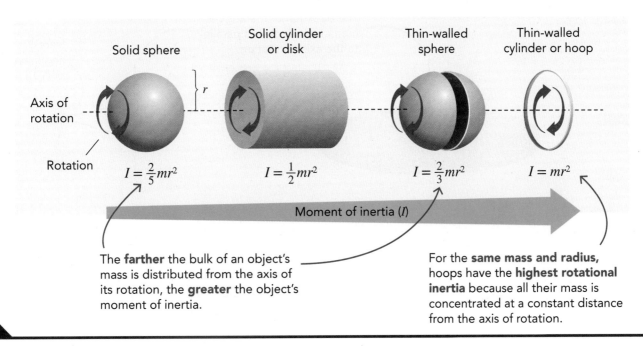

Solid sphere $I = \frac{2}{5} mr^2$

Solid cylinder or disk $I = \frac{1}{2} mr^2$

Thin-walled sphere $I = \frac{2}{3} mr^2$

Thin-walled cylinder or hoop $I = mr^2$

Axis of rotation

Rotation

Moment of inertia (*I*)

The **farther** the bulk of an object's mass is distributed from the axis of its rotation, the **greater** the object's moment of inertia.

For the **same mass and radius,** hoops have the **highest rotational inertia** because all their mass is concentrated at a constant distance from the axis of rotation.

Angular Momentum

Linear motion is a physical quantity associated with linear motion. Angular momentum is a physical quantity associated with angular motion. **Angular momentum** is the product of the object's moment of inertia and the object's angular velocity. The units of angular momentum are kg·m²/s.

Angular Momentum
$$L = I\omega$$
L = angular momentum I = moment of inertia ω = angular velocity

You can use the equation to model the angular momentum of an object revolving around an axis, such as a spinning top or a planet revolving around the sun. When the diameter of the mass is much smaller than the distance to the axis of rotation, you can model the mass as if it were a point particle. Therefore, the angular momentum for the mass is $mr^2\omega$, and $r\omega$ is the linear velocity perpendicular to the radius vector, r. If the orbit is perfectly circular, the angular momentum is rmv, or the radius times the linear momentum.

Angular Momentum (for a Particle Orbiting an Axis)
$$L = |r||p|\sin(\theta)$$
L = angular momentum p = linear momentum r = radius θ = the angle between r and p

Rotational Motions Angular momentum is a vector that has both a magnitude and a direction that is perpendicular to the radius and the linear momentum. To determine the direction of this vector, use your right hand to curl your fingers in the direction of angular motion. Your thumb will point in the vector's direction. This is known as the right-hand rule.

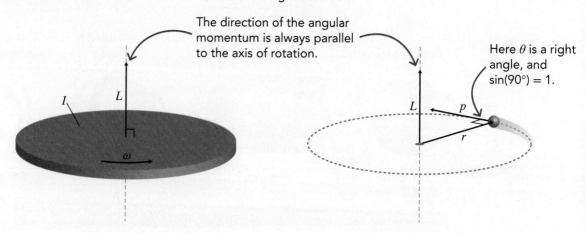

The direction of the angular momentum is always parallel to the axis of rotation.

Here θ is a right angle, and $sin(90°) = 1$.

(5) **SEP Develop a Model** Using your understanding of vector addition and angular momentum, describe how you can determine the angular momentum of a spherical planet, such as Earth, that is rotating along one axis while revolving around another axis. Would the combined angular momentum point along either axis? Explain.

Impulse

 GO ONLINE to do a PhET **simulation** to explore the relationships among force, time, mass, velocity, impulse, and momentum and to watch a **video**.

Impulse During a collision, the momentum of each colliding object changes. You can often treat the interaction as occurring over a finite amount of time, Δt. The magnitude of the force during a collision often changes quickly during the time that the objects are in contact. Therefore, it is useful to work with a quantity called **impulse,** which is the average collision force multiplied by the time the objects are in contact. Impulse is a vector quantity, and the direction of the impulse is the same as the direction of the collision force. A collision force is also known as an impulse force or an impulsive force.

Impulse
$J = F_{avg}\Delta t$
J = impulse F_{avg} = average force Δt = duration of applied force

The units of impulse are newton·seconds (N·s). That makes sense because the impulse is the product of the average impulsive force, with units of newtons, and the time interval, with units of seconds. The units of impulse can also be written as kg·m/s. That way of writing the units makes clear that the units of impulse are the same as the units of momentum. This fits with our understanding of force. Recall that Newton's second law for momentum states that a force is equal to the change in momentum per change in time. This implies that the impulse from a net force is equal to the change in momentum, which is why it has units of momentum.

Tennis Ball When a tennis ball strikes a wall, the force produces a large change in the velocity of the ball. The change in the wall's momentum is too small to notice.

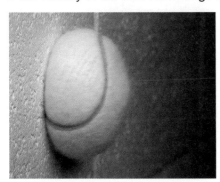

When a tennis ball collides with a wall, the wall exerts an impulsive force on the ball. The ball deforms, or changes shape, drastically.

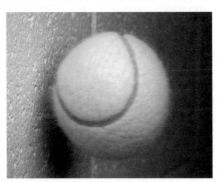

During the short time interval of the collision, the tennis ball is compressed and then expands back to its original shape.

 SEP Use Mathematics Suppose a 75-kg crash dummy is in contact with an airbag for 0.075 seconds during a crash, and the impulse delivered is 1900 N·s. Calculate the average force exerted by the airbag on the dummy and compare that force with the gravitational force on the crash dummy.

Angular Impulse

In the same way that momentum and impulse are related for motions in a straight line, angular momentum and angular impulse are related for rotational motions.

Angular Impulse
$\Delta L = \tau \Delta t$

ΔL = angular impulse $\quad$ Δt = duration of
τ = average torque $\qquad\qquad$ applied torque

You can think of the relationship as Newton's second law of motion as it applies to rotational motion. If a rotating object is in motion, then its angular momentum will remain constant unless a net torque is applied to it. Therefore, angular impulse can be measured as the change in angular momentum, or ΔL.

Round and Round Pushing a revolving door in the same direction it is rotating will make it move faster, due to the angular impulse. Angular impulse depends on the torque and the duration of time it is applied.

Torque takes into account the magnitudes of the force, F; the distance from the axis of rotation, r; and the angle between F and r. When F is perpendicular to r, $\tau = rF$.

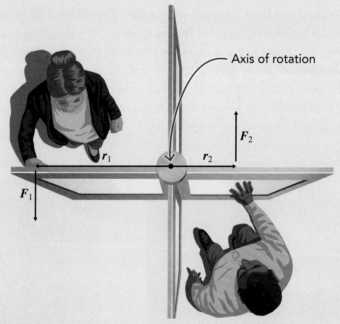

Axis of rotation

Suppose both people apply the same force for the same amount of time. The angular impulse on the right side is less than that on the left side because the person on the right is applying the force closer to the axis of rotation.

(7) **SEP Construct an Explanation** As part of the volcanic eruption of Mount St. Helens in 1980, there was a large horizontal blast and accompanying landslide that had a horizontal force of about 3.4×10^{21} N that lasted for about 2.5 minutes. Calculate the angular impulse this generated if Earth's radius is 6371 km. Explain why this did not have a measurable effect on Earth's angular momentum ($L = 5.9 \times 10^{33}$ kg·m^2/s).

INVESTIGATIVE PHENOMENON

GO ONLINE to revisit your **Investigative Phenomenon CER** with the new information you have learned about Momentum and Impulse.

These questions will help you apply what you learned in this experience to the Investigative Phenomenon.

8 **SEP Construct an Explanation** Explain how a collision between two hockey players is governed by Newton's laws of motion.

9 **SEP Use Mathematics** Two hockey players, each with a mass of 60.0 kg, are traveling toward each other at a speed of 8.0 m/s and stop after they collide. Determine the magnitude and direction of the change in momentum resulting from the collision for each player. Determine the change in momentum for a system consisting of both hockey players.

10 **SEP Use Mathematics** Two hockey players are traveling toward each other and collide with an average force of 3000 N and an impulse of 900 N·s. Determine the time interval of the force each hockey player exerts on the other player during the collision.

11 **SEP Use Mathematics** A hockey player in motion collides with another player who is standing still. The first hockey player applies an average force of 2000 N to the second player for a time of 0.4 seconds. Determine the impulse experienced by the second hockey player.

GO ONLINE
for a **quiz** to evaluate what you learned about Momentum and Impulse.

Conservation of Momentum

 GO ONLINE to do a **hands-on lab** to investigate elastic and inelastic collisions.

Conserving Mass

A conserved quantity is a quantity that remains constant, or keeps the same value, in an isolated system. If a system is not isolated and an external object interacts with the system, then the quantity may change. Therefore, it is no longer conserved.

Mass is a quantity that is conserved. The mass of a system is constant unless the system interacts with something external, causing a transfer of matter. In such a case, the system can be redefined by including the external object as part of the system. Then, the mass of the entire system remains conserved.

Open Systems When a system exchanges matter with the surrounding environment, the mass of the system may change.

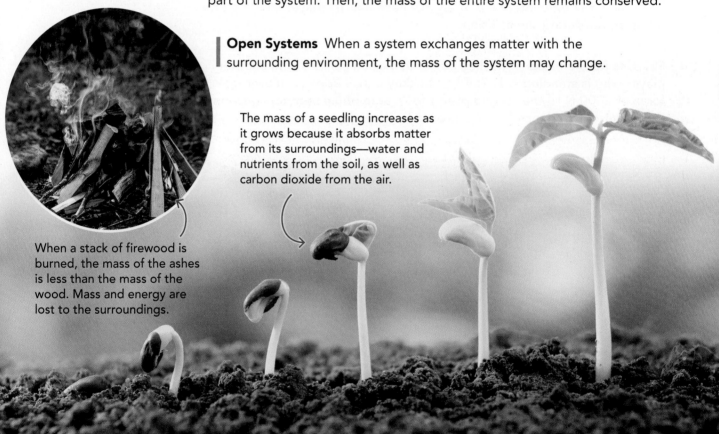

The mass of a seedling increases as it grows because it absorbs matter from its surroundings—water and nutrients from the soil, as well as carbon dioxide from the air.

When a stack of firewood is burned, the mass of the ashes is less than the mass of the wood. Mass and energy are lost to the surroundings.

(12) **SEP Develop Models** When the wick of a wax candle burns, some of the wax melts. Develop a model explaining why the mass of the melted wax and the remaining wick is less than the mass of the original candle. Define a system in which mass is conserved as the candle burns.

Conserving Momentum

 GO ONLINE to do a PhET **simulation** that allows you to model conservation of momentum when two objects interact.

Linear momentum is another example of a physical quantity that is conserved. The **law of conservation of linear momentum** states that if no external force acts on a system of particles, then the total linear momentum of the system does not change. The law is an extension of Newton's second and third laws of motion. Newton's second law states that a net force applied for a duration of time causes a change in momentum. Newton's third law states that all forces come with another force of equal magnitude but opposite in direction. Whenever one object exerts a force that changes the momentum of a second object, a third-law pair force from the second object acts on the first object, causing the first object's momentum to change in the opposite direction. When the two objects are in the same system, the total momentum of the system is constant.

Conservation of Linear Momentum
$$\boldsymbol{p}_i = \boldsymbol{p}_f$$
$\boldsymbol{p}_i$ = initial linear momentum $\boldsymbol{p}_f$ = final linear momentum

For a system made up of multiple objects or particles, interactions among the objects or particles do not change the total momentum of the system. In collisions, the total momentum of the system before the collision always equals the total momentum of the system after the collision, regardless of any forces that the objects or particles exert on each other.

> **Ice Skaters in a System** In a system of two ice skaters, the total momentum of the skaters remains constant unless they interact with something external to the system.

(13) **SEP Argue from Evidence** The impulse exerted on a system is 0 N·s. Determine whether the system is open, closed, or isolated. Justify your answer using the law of conservation of linear momentum.

Conserving Momentum in Space

An 80-kg astronaut in space is holding a 15-kg toolbox in her hands. She pushes the toolbox to the right, giving it a velocity of 1.6 m/s. Determine the final velocity of the astronaut.

1. DRAW A PICTURE Sketch a picture of the situation.

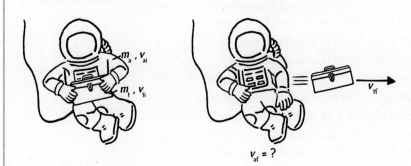

2. DEFINE THE PROBLEM List knowns and unknowns, and assign values to variables.

$$m_a = 80 \text{ kg}$$
$$m_t = 15 \text{ kg}$$
$$v_{ai} = 0 \text{ m/s}$$
$$v_{ti} = 0 \text{ m/s}$$
$$v_{tf} = 1.6 \text{ m/s}$$

$$v_{af} = \, ?$$

3. PLAN AND EXECUTE Use mathematical relationships, the picture, and your definitions to plan and execute a solution.

Write the conservation of linear momentum equation and rearrange to solve for v_{af}.

$$p_i = p_f$$
$$(m_{ai}v_{ai} + m_{ti}v_{ti}) = (m_{af}v_{af} + m_{tf}v_{tf}) \rightarrow$$
$$v_{af} = \frac{(m_{ai}v_{ai} + m_{ti}v_{ti}) - (m_{tf}v_{tf})}{m_{af}}$$

Calculate the final velocity of the astronaut.

$$v_{af} = \frac{(80 \text{ kg} \cdot 0 \text{ m/s} + 15 \text{ kg} \cdot 0 \text{ m/s}) - (15 \text{ kg} \cdot 1.6 \text{ m/s})}{80 \text{ kg}}$$
$$= -0.3 \text{ m/s}$$

4. EVALUATE Reflect on your answer.
The total momentum is conserved. The momentum of the astronaut-and-toolbox system is 0 kg·m/s in the initial state: 80 kg(0 m/s) + 15 kg(0 m/s) = 0 kg·m/s. The momentum of the system is 0 kg·m/s in the final state: 80 kg(−0.3 m/s) + 15 kg(1.6 m/s) = −24 kg·m/s + 24 kg·m/s = 0 kg·m/s. The velocity of the astronaut is negative because she will move to the left.

 GO ONLINE for more **math support**.

📖 **Math Practice Problems**

---

(14) A 68-kg astronaut in space is holding a 12-kg toolbox in her hands. She pushes the toolbox to the right, giving it a velocity of 1.8 m/s. Determine the final velocity of the astronaut.

📖 **NEED A HINT?** Go online to your **eText Sample Problem** for stepped-out support.

(15) A 72-kg astronaut in space is holding a toolbox. He pushes the toolbox to the right, giving it a velocity of 2.1 m/s. If the final velocity of the astronaut is −0.40 m/s, then determine the mass of the toolbox.

Conserving Angular Momentum

Similar to linear momentum, angular momentum is a conserved quantity. The **law of conservation of angular momentum** states that if a system is isolated, then the angular momentum of the system remains constant.

Conservation of Angular Momentum
$$L_i = L_f$$
L_i = initial angular momentum
L_f = final angular momentum

Remember that an object's angular momentum is the product of its moment of inertia and its angular velocity. If the distribution of mass changes in an isolated system, then the moment of inertia changes. Therefore, the angular velocity will change because angular momentum must remain constant.

Spinning Speed The angular velocity of the woman in the chair increases when she pulls her arms in, due to the conservation of angular momentum.

The woman begins to spin with her arms extended.

When she pulls in her arms, the distance of the books from the axis of rotation decreases. Her moment of inertia also decreases, so her angular velocity increases, and she spins faster.

$$I_i \omega_i \qquad = \qquad I_f \omega_f$$

(16) **SEP Use Models** Draw a model of the woman in the chair obeying the law of conservation of angular momentum. Use the model to explain how the woman can affect her angular velocity as she pulls her arms in.

A Rotating Disk and a Hoop Interact

A solid disk of mass 6.5 kg and radius 0.30 m is rotating clockwise about its axis of rotation at 21 radians per second. A cylindrical hoop of mass 2.0 kg with radius 0.10 m is rotating counterclockwise about its axis of rotation at 26 radians per second. The two axes are the same, and the cylindrical hoop is dropped so that it is centered on the rotating disk. Determine the angular velocity of the system of the hoop and disk together.

1. DRAW A PICTURE Sketch a picture of the situation.

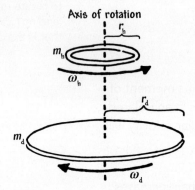

2. DEFINE THE PROBLEM List knowns and unknowns, and assign values to variables.

$m_d = 6.5$ kg	$I_d = ?$
$r_d = 0.30$ m	$I_h = ?$
$\omega_d = -21$ rad/s	$\omega_f = ?$
$m_h = 2.0$ kg	
$r_h = 0.10$ m	
$\omega_h = 26$ rad/s	

3. PLAN AND EXECUTE Use mathematical relationships, the picture, and your definitions to plan and execute a solution.

Use the appropriate equation from Experience 1 to determine the moment of inertia of the solid disk.	$I_d = \frac{1}{2}m_d r_d^2 = \frac{1}{2}(6.5 \text{ kg})(0.30 \text{ m})^2 = 0.29 \text{ kg·m}^2$
Use the appropriate equation from Experience 1 to determine the moment of inertia for the cylindrical hoop.	$I_h = m_h r_h^2 = (2.0 \text{ kg})(0.10 \text{ m})^2 = 0.020 \text{ kg·m}^2$
Calculate the initial angular momentum for the solid disk using the equation for angular momentum.	$L_d = I_d \omega_d$ $= (0.29 \text{ kg·m}^2)(-21 \text{ rad/s}) = -6.1 \text{ kg·m}^2/\text{s}$
Calculate the initial angular momentum for the cylindrical hoop.	$L_h = I_h \omega_h$ $= (0.020 \text{ kg·m}^2)(26 \text{ rad/s}) = 0.52 \text{ kg·m}^2/\text{s}$
Calculate the initial angular momentum for the hoop-disk system.	$L_i = L_d + L_h = -6.1 \text{ kg·m}^2/\text{s} + 0.52 \text{ kg·m}^2/\text{s}$ $= -5.6 \text{ kg·m}^2/\text{s}$
Write the law of conservation of angular momentum equation for this scenario and rearrange to solve for the final angular velocity.	$L_i = L_f = (I_d + I_h)\omega_f \rightarrow \omega_f = \dfrac{L_f}{I_d + I_h}$
Calculate the final angular velocity of the hoop-disk system.	$\omega_f = \dfrac{-5.6 \text{ kg·m}^2/\text{s}}{0.29 \text{ kg·m}^2 + 0.020 \text{ kg·m}^2}$ $\omega_f = -18 \text{ rad/s}$

4. EVALUATE Reflect on your answer.

The hoop and the disk were rotating in opposite directions. It makes sense that the angular velocity of the hoop-disk system has a lesser magnitude than either of the initial angular velocities. It also makes sense that the object with the greater moment of inertia would dictate the direction of the system's angular velocity, given that the two objects had initial angular velocities of similar magnitudes.

 GO ONLINE for more **math support**.

▶ **Math Tutorial Video**

🛜 **Math Practice Problems**

⑰ A solid disk of mass 9.2 kg and radius 0.55 m is rotating clockwise about its axis of rotation at 19 radians per second. A cylindrical hoop of mass 5.1 kg with radius 0.35 m is rotating counterclockwise about its axis of rotation at 21 radians per second. The two axes are the same, and the cylindrical hoop is dropped so that it is centered on the rotating disk. Determine the angular velocity of the system of the hoop and disk together.

📖 **NEED A HINT?** Go online to your **eText Sample Problem** for stepped-out support.

⑱ A solid disk of mass 10.1 kg and radius 0.62 m is rotating clockwise about its axis of rotation at 27 radians per second. A cylindrical hoop of mass 4.4 kg with radius 0.28 m is rotating counterclockwise about its axis of rotation at 23 radians per second. The two axes are the same, and the cylindrical hoop is dropped so that it is centered on the rotating disk. Determine the angular velocity of the system of the hoop and disk together.

⑲ A 7.5-kg solid disk with radius 0.52 m is rotating clockwise about its axis of rotation at 22 radians per second. A 6.1-kg cylindrical hoop with radius 0.20 m is rotating counterclockwise about that same axis of rotation. The hoop is dropped so that it is centered on the rotating disk, and the angular velocity of the hoop-disk system is 17 radians per second. What is the initial angular velocity of the hoop before it is dropped onto the disk?

⑳ Three solid disks of equal mass are rotating counterclockwise around their axes of rotation. Order the angular momenta of the three disks from greatest to least.

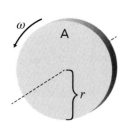

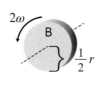

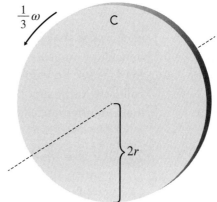

Impulse-Momentum Theorem

Impulse as a Change in Momentum Acceleration is defined in terms of velocity, and Newton's second law explains how it is related to force.

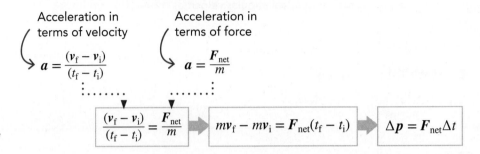

Acceleration in terms of velocity

$$a = \frac{(v_f - v_i)}{(t_f - t_i)}$$

Acceleration in terms of force

$$a = \frac{F_{net}}{m}$$

$$\frac{(v_f - v_i)}{(t_f - t_i)} = \frac{F_{net}}{m} \quad\Rightarrow\quad mv_f - mv_i = F_{net}(t_f - t_i) \quad\Rightarrow\quad \Delta p = F_{net}\Delta t$$

Newton introduced his second law in terms of changing momentum, and that form shows that force and the time interval both affect momentum. A large force exerted over a short period of time—as in a collision of a rubber bouncing ball against the ground—changes an object's momentum markedly, but a small force exerted over a long period of time can have the same effect.

Force vs. Time Graph The area under a force vs. time graph is the impulse.

The average force (F_{avg}) over the time period is represented by this line.

The area under the the actual force curve, which represents the impulse, is equal to the rectangular area under the average force line. Thus, impulse can be thought of as a product of the average force and the time interval.

The magnitude of the actual force (F_{actual}) changes over time.

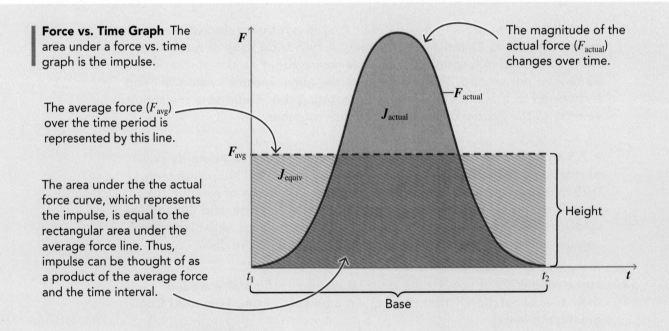

In collisions that take place during a very short amount of time, it is often difficult to measure the impulsive forces acting on the objects. It is easier to measure the velocity of the objects involved prior to and after the collision. Representing impulse as caused by a constant force may also make mathematical analysis of the collision easier.

(21) **SEP Use Mathematics** Since impulse is a change in momentum, impulse and momentum must have the same units. Prove that the units N·s are the same as kg·m/s.

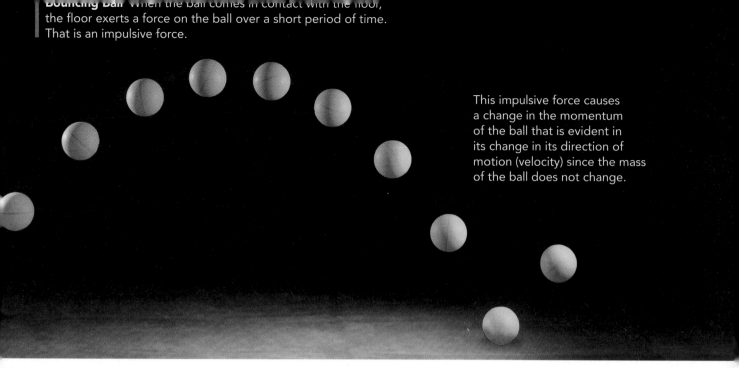

Bouncing Ball When the ball comes in contact with the floor, the floor exerts a force on the ball over a short period of time. That is an impulsive force.

This impulsive force causes a change in the momentum of the ball that is evident in its change in its direction of motion (velocity) since the mass of the ball does not change.

Net External Impulse Impulse produces a change in momentum for an object, but an impulse internal to the system will not change the momentum of that system. The **impulse-momentum theorem** states that the change in momentum of a system is equal to the net external impulse acting on it.

Impulse-Momentum Theorem

$$\boldsymbol{p}_{\text{net, i}} + \boldsymbol{J} = \boldsymbol{p}_{\text{net, f}} \quad \text{—vector form}$$

$$(p_{\text{net, i}x} + J_x)\hat{\boldsymbol{x}} + (p_{\text{net, i}y} + J_y)\hat{\boldsymbol{y}} = (p_{\text{net, f}x})\hat{\boldsymbol{x}} + (p_{\text{net, f}y})\hat{\boldsymbol{y}} \quad \begin{array}{l}\text{component}\\\text{form}\end{array}$$

$\boldsymbol{p}_{\text{net, i}}$ = total initial momentum $\boldsymbol{J}$ = impulse
$\boldsymbol{p}_{\text{net, f}}$ = total final momentum

When you use the equation, remember that you must first define the system. Defining the system is important because you need to be sure the impulse is from an external force. In some cases, it is convenient to include all the interacting objects in a system. Then the external force is zero. In other cases, it is more convenient to include only one object in the system.

A net external angular impulse causes a change in angular momentum, just as an impulse causes a change in linear momentum. For linear momentum, $\boldsymbol{p}_i + \boldsymbol{F}_{\text{avg}}\Delta t = \boldsymbol{p}_f$. For angular momentum, $\boldsymbol{L}_i + \boldsymbol{\tau}\Delta t = \boldsymbol{L}_f$.

(22) **SEP Develop a Model** A 76-kg astronaut in space is holding a 12-kg toolbox in her hands. She pushes the toolbox to the right at a velocity of 1.4 m/s. Use the impulse-momentum theorem to determine the average force that the astronaut exerts on the toolbox if she pushes on it for 0.020 s.

Analyzing a Car Crash Whether the forces acting on two cars in a collision are internal or external depends on how the system is defined.

Impulse and Momentum in Collisions

Suppose two cars collide with each other. You can analyze the collision by including both cars in the system or by including only one car in the system.

Two Cars If both cars are in the system, then they have initial and final momenta proportional to their masses and their initial and final velocities. There is no impulse, because there is no external object exerting a force on the two cars in the horizontal direction. The two-car system tells you about the motion before and after the collision. To analyze the forces exerted on each car during the collision, it is often easier to examine the one-car system.

One Car If you include only one car in the system, then the second car is an external object that exerts a force on the system. An external force produces an impulse and, therefore, a change in momentum. Knowing the change in momentum and the time the cars are each experiencing a net force, or acceleration, allows you to determine the average force that the external car exerts on the system car.

(23) **SEP Argue from Evidence** Two balls of equal mass, one made of plastic and one made of rubber, are traveling at 16 m/s to the right toward a wall. After colliding with the wall, the plastic ball stops. The rubber ball bounces off the wall after the collision and begins traveling toward the left at 12 m/s. In which case did the wall exert a greater impulsive force on the ball? Use mathematics to support your answer.

Comparing Momenta in Systems

How can you **analyze collisions** between cars?

A 2-Car System In a system where **all the forces are internal, the total momentum** of the system **before the collision** equals the total momentum of the system **after the collision.**

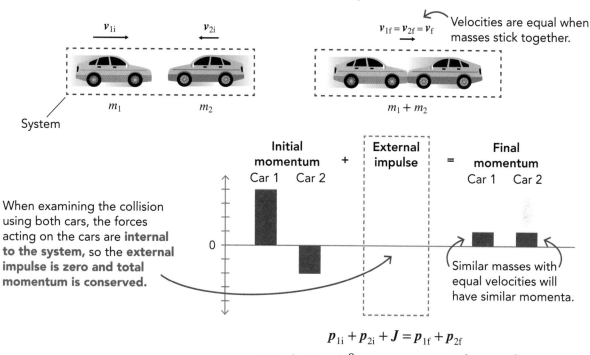

When examining the collision using both cars, the forces acting on the cars are **internal to the system,** so the **external impulse is zero and total momentum is conserved.**

$$p_{1i} + p_{2i} + J = p_{1f} + p_{2f}$$
$$m_1 v_{1i} + m_2 v_{2i} + 0 = m_1 v_{1f} + m_2 v_{2f} = (m_1 + m_2) v_f$$

A 1-Car System If the system includes only the first car, then the **force exerted by the second car** in the collision is **external to the system.**

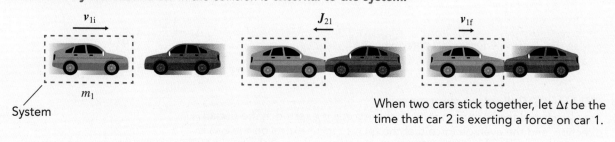

When two cars stick together, let Δt be the time that car 2 is exerting a force on car 1.

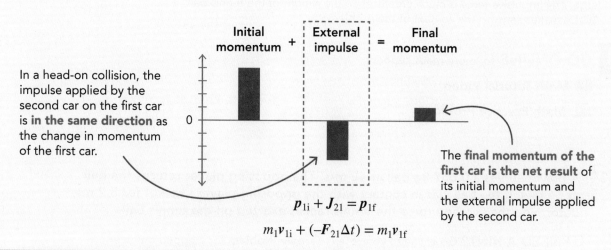

In a head-on collision, the impulse applied by the second car on the first car is **in the same direction** as the change in momentum of the first car.

The **final momentum of the first car is the net result** of its initial momentum and the external impulse applied by the second car.

$$p_{1i} + J_{21} = p_{1f}$$
$$m_1 v_{1i} + (-F_{21} \Delta t) = m_1 v_{1f}$$

What a Racket

A tennis player serves a 0.060-kg ball at 57 m/s. The opposing player returns the ball to the server at 63 m/s. If the ball was in contact with the opposing player's racket for 6.0 ms, determine the average force the tennis racket exerted on the tennis ball.

1. DRAW A PICTURE Sketch a picture of the situation.

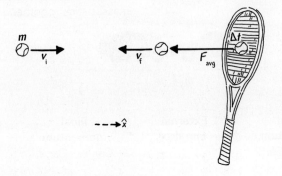

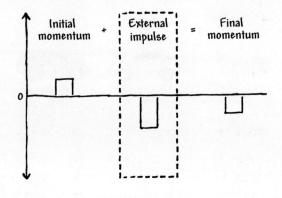

2. DEFINE THE PROBLEM List knowns and unknowns, and assign values to variables.

$v_i = 57$ m/s	$\Delta t = 6.0$ ms $= 0.0060$ s	$J = ?$
$v_f = -63$ m/s	$m = 0.060$ kg	$F_{avg} = ?$

3. PLAN AND EXECUTE Use mathematical relationships, the picture, and your definitions to plan and execute a solution.

Determine the initial and final momentum values. Then, use the impulse-momentum theorem to calculate the impulse.

$$p_i = mv_i = (0.060 \text{ kg})(57 \text{ m/s}) = 3.4 \text{ kg·m/s}$$
$$p_f = mv_f = (0.060 \text{ kg})(-63 \text{ m/s}) = -3.8 \text{ kg·m/s}$$
$$p_i + J = p_f \rightarrow J = p_f - p_i$$
$$J = (-3.8 \text{ kg·m/s}) - (3.4 \text{ kg·m/s}) = -7.2 \text{ kg·m/s}$$

Use the impulse equation to determine the average force the racket exerts on the ball.

$$J = F_{avg} \Delta t \rightarrow F_{avg} = \frac{J}{\Delta t}$$
$$F_{avg} = \frac{-7.2 \text{ kg·m/s}}{0.0060 \text{ s}} = -1200 \text{ N}$$

4. EVALUATE Reflect on your answer.
The sketch and the bar graph show that the force is exerted in the negative direction, and the average force that the tennis racket exerts on the ball is large. The impulsive force is much greater than the weight of the tennis ball. All this makes sense in the context of the problem.

 GO ONLINE for more **math support**.

▶ **Math Tutorial Video**

🖥 **Math Practice Problems**

---

(24) A player serves a 0.057-kg ball at 42 m/s. The opposing player returns the ball at 66 m/s. If the ball was in contact with the opposing player's racket for 5.2 ms, determine the average force the tennis racket exerted on the tennis ball.

📖 **NEED A HINT?** Go online to your **eText Sample Problem** for stepped-out support.

High-Speed Collision

A 1500-kg truck traveling west at 23 m/s collides with a 1100-kg car traveling north at 15 m/s. After the collision, the vehicles do not separate. Determine the x- and y-components of the velocity of the combined vehicles immediately after the collision.

1. DRAW A PICTURE Sketch a picture of the situation.

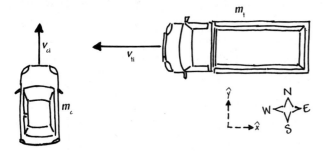

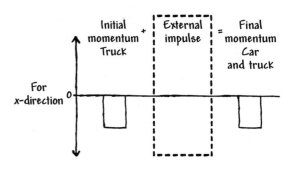

2. DEFINE THE PROBLEM List knowns and unknowns, and assign values to variables.

$m_t = 1500$ kg	$v_{ti} = 23$ m/s west	$v_f = ?$
$m_c = 1100$ kg	$v_{ci} = 15$ m/s north	

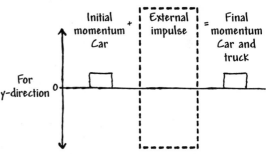

3. PLAN AND EXECUTE Use mathematical relationships, the picture, and your definitions to plan and execute a solution.

> Write and rearrange the impulse-momentum theorem to solve for the final velocity of the combined vehicles.

$$p_i + J = p_f \rightarrow m_i v_i + J = m_f v_f = (m_c + m_t)v_f \rightarrow$$
$$v_f = \frac{m_i v_i + J}{m_c + m_t}$$

> Use the known values and associated bar chart to determine the final velocity of the combined vehicles in the x-direction.

$$v_{xf} = \frac{(1500 \text{ kg} \cdot -23 \text{ m/s} + 1100 \text{ kg} \cdot 0 \text{ m/s}) + 0 \text{ kg} \cdot \text{m/s}}{1100 \text{ kg} + 1500 \text{ kg}}$$
$$v_{xf} = -13 \text{ m/s, or } 13 \text{ m/s west}$$

> Use the known values and associated bar chart to determine the final velocity of the combined vehicles in the y-direction.

$$v_{yf} = \frac{(1500 \text{ kg} \cdot 0 \text{ m/s} + 1100 \text{ kg} \cdot 15 \text{ m/s}) + 0 \text{ kg} \cdot \text{m/s}}{1100 \text{ kg} + 1500 \text{ kg}}$$
$$v_{yf} = 6.3 \text{ m/s, or } 6.3 \text{ m/s north}$$

4. EVALUATE Reflect on your answer.
The direction of the final velocity is neither completely north nor completely west, which makes sense given that the momentum of the truck-and-car system must be conserved.

GO ONLINE for more **math support**.

Math Practice Problems

---

(25) A 1350-kg truck traveling west at 25 m/s collides with a 1050-kg car traveling north at 14 m/s. After the collision, the vehicles do not separate. Determine the x- and y-components of the velocity of the combined vehicles immediately after the collision.

📖 **NEED A HINT?** Go online to your **eText Sample Problem** for stepped-out support.

Types of Collisions

▶ **GO ONLINE** to watch a **video** about elastic and inelastic collisions.

In a collision, two objects interact, and at least one of those objects must be moving prior to the collision. That means that there is kinetic energy as well as linear momentum prior to the collision. The linear momentum of the system is constant in all collisions unless there is an external impulsive force on the system, in keeping with the law of conservation of momentum. The kinetic energies of the objects involved in the collision can change. Collisions can be categorized based on what happens to the kinetic energy of the system during the collision.

Elastic Collisions If the kinetic energy of the system is constant, meaning that the total kinetic energy does not change during the collision, then the collision is an **elastic collision.** In an elastic collision, the objects in the system are not changed or distorted, and the internal energy of the system remains constant. No energy is lost as heat or sound.

In nature, there are no perfectly elastic collisions, but there are some that are very close. They are generally collisions that involve rigid objects, such as billiard balls. Some collisions among subatomic particles can be very close to perfectly elastic, because, for many colliding particles, the total kinetic energy of the system prior to the collision is very nearly the same as the total kinetic energy after the collision.

Elastic Collisions When one ball collides with another on a pool table, momentum is transferred. The total momentum of the system of billiard balls remains constant, and the total kinetic energy of the system changes very little.

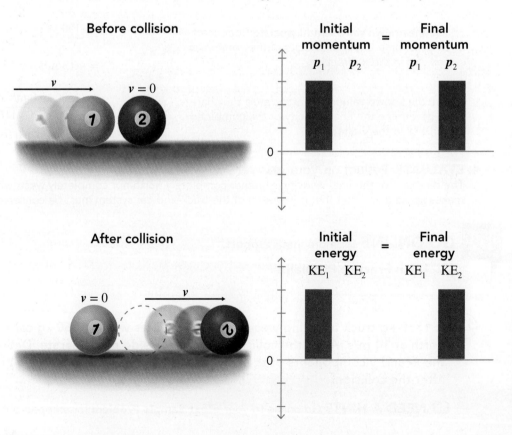

Totally Inelastic Collision If the player catches the ball, then she and the ball stay together after the collision. The collision is totally inelastic.

Inelastic Collisions A collision in which there is a loss of kinetic energy in a system is an **inelastic collision.** The lost kinetic energy may be transformed to sound energy or thermal energy, and the objects in the collision are usually distorted or damaged. As an example, think of a ball dropped from some height above the ground. It bounces back up to a height that is less than the original height. Its potential energy has decreased, which means that it lost kinetic energy during the bounce. The more times the ball bounces, the smaller the height to which it rebounds, demonstrating that kinetic energy decreases with each collision. A golf ball dropped to a hard surface may rebound to approximately 60 percent of its initial height—a good example of an inelastic collision.

Totally Inelastic Collisions An inelastic collision is a collision in which the colliding objects move apart after the collision. A **totally inelastic collision** is a collision in which the colliding objects stick together, and the maximum amount of kinetic energy is lost.

26) **SEP Argue from Evidence** Think about two situations, one in which a player catches a ball and another in which the ball bounces off her arm. Which collision is perfectly inelastic? Explain why more kinetic energy is lost in one case than in the other case.

27) **SEP Use Mathematics** A 1.00-kg metal pendulum swings toward the right with a speed of 7.50 m/s to hit a 4.00-kg stationary wooden block. After the collision, the block is dented and moves with a constant speed of 2.25 m/s toward the right. The pendulum bounces back to the left with a speed of 1.50 m/s. Classify the collision.

A Ballistic Pendulum

In a ballistic pendulum, a pellet with a mass of 0.030 kg is fired with an initial speed of 23 m/s at a pendulum block that is at rest. The block has a mass of 2.2 kg. After the pellet collides with the block, they both stick together and swing upward. Determine the maximum height reached by the pellet-block system.

1. DRAW A PICTURE Sketch a picture of the situation.

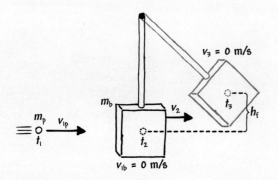
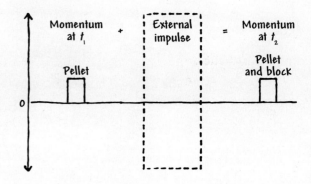

2. DEFINE THE PROBLEM List knowns and unknowns, and assign values to variables.

$m_p = 0.030$ kg	$v_{1b} = 0$ m/s	$v_2 = ?$
$m_b = 2.2$ kg	$v_3 = 0$ m/s	$h_f = h_{max} = ?$
$v_{1p} = 23$ m/s	$h_i = 0$ m	

3. PLAN AND EXECUTE Use mathematical relationships, the picture, and your definitions to plan and execute a solution.

Use the impulse-momentum bar chart to write and rearrange the impulse-momentum equation to determine the velocity of the pellet and block immediately after the collision.	$(m_p v_{1p} + m_b v_{1b}) + J = (m_p + m_b)v_2 \rightarrow$ $v_2 = \dfrac{(m_p v_{1p} + m_b v_{1b}) + J}{m_p + m_b}$
Substitute the known values and calculate v_2.	$v_2 = \dfrac{[(0.030 \text{ kg})(23 \text{ m/s}) + (2.2 \text{ kg})(0 \text{ m/s})] + 0}{(0.030 \text{ kg} + 2.2 \text{ kg})} = 0.31 \text{ m/s}$
Apply the conservation of mechanical energy to determine how the initial KE relates to the final PE of the system.	$KE_2 + PE_2 = KE_3 + PE_3 \rightarrow KE_2 + 0 = 0 + PE_3 \rightarrow$ $KE_2 = PE_3$
Use the associated equation for KE to determine the initial KE of the system after the collision.	$KE_2 = \frac{1}{2}(m_p + m_b)v_2^2$ $= \frac{1}{2}(0.030 \text{ kg} + 2.2 \text{ kg})(0.31 \text{ m/s})^2 = 0.11 \text{ J}$
Write and rearrange the associated equation for the final PE to determine the maximum height reached by the pellet-block system.	$PE_3 = (m_p + m_b)gh_f \rightarrow h_f = \dfrac{PE_3}{(m_p + m_b)g}$ $h_f = \dfrac{0.11 \text{ J}}{(0.030 \text{ kg} + 2.2 \text{ kg})\ 9.8 \text{ m/s}^2} = 0.0050 \text{ m}$

4. EVALUATE Reflect on your answer.
The mass of the pellet is quite small, so it makes sense that the pendulum does not reach a great height.

GO ONLINE for more **math support**.

▶ **Math Tutorial Video**

🖳 **Math Practice Problems**

---

(28) In a ballistic pendulum, a pellet with a mass of 0.025 kg is fired with an initial speed of 24 m/s at a pendulum block that is at rest. The block has a mass of 3.0 kg. After the pellet collides with the block, they both stick together and swing upward. Determine the maximum height reached by the pellet-block system.

📖 **NEED A HINT?** Go online to your **eText Sample Problem** for stepped-out support.

(29) In a ballistic pendulum, a pellet with a mass of 0.10 kg is fired with an initial speed of 28 m/s at a pendulum block that is at rest. The block has a mass of 5.5 kg. After the pellet collides with the block, they both stick together and swing upward. Determine the maximum height reached by the pellet-block system.

(30) In a ballistic pendulum, a pellet with a mass of 0.035 kg is fired with an initial speed of 27 m/s at a pendulum block that is at rest. After the pellet collides with the block, they both stick together and swing upward to a maximum height of 0.090 m. Determine the mass of the block.

(31) For one part of a chain-reaction machine that she is designing, a classmate will roll a ball with a mass of 1.2 kg down a ramp. At the bottom of the ramp, the ball will collide with a 1.8-kg pendulum block. Only the pendulum block will swing upward after the collision, and it must reach a maximum height of 0.075 m in order to continue the chain reaction. Determine the velocity of the ball just before it collides with the block in order for this part of the chain reaction machine to work.

(32) You are performing an experiment with a ball and pendulum. You roll the ball toward the pendulum and record the maximum height that the pendulum reaches in each trial. The results are recorded in the table. Based on the data, in which trial would you expect the speed of pendulum after the collision to be the greatest? Explain.

Trial	1	2	3	4	5
Max height (m)	0.120	0.126	0.118	0.122	0.120

Inelastic Collision

An object with a mass of 0.75 kg is moving with an initial speed of 30.0 m/s in the positive x-direction and strikes and sticks to a 0.48-kg object moving 45.0 m/s in the positive y-direction. Determine the amount of kinetic energy lost in the collision.

1. DRAW A PICTURE Sketch a picture of the situation.

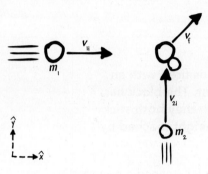

2. DEFINE THE PROBLEM List knowns and unknowns, and assign values to variables.

$m_1 = 0.75$ kg

$m_2 = 0.48$ kg

$v_{1i} = +(30.0$ m/s$)\hat{x}$

$v_{2i} = +(45.0$ m/s$)\hat{y}$

$v_f = ?$

$\Delta KE = ?$

3. PLAN AND EXECUTE Use mathematical relationships, the picture, and your definitions to plan and execute a solution.

Use conservation of momentum to determine the final velocity of the two objects in the x-direction.	$(0.75$ kg$)(30.0$ m/s$) + 0$ kg·m/s $= (0.75$ kg $+ 0.48$ kg$)v_{xf}$ $v_{xf} = 18.3$ m/s
Use conservation of momentum to determine the final velocity of the two objects in the y-direction.	$(0.48$ kg$)(45.0$ m/s$) + 0$ kg·m/s $= (0.75$ kg $+ 0.48$ kg$)v_{yf}$ $v_{yf} = 17.6$ m/s
Determine the magnitude of the final velocity of the two objects after the collision.	$v_f = \sqrt{v_{xf}^2 + v_{yf}^2} = \sqrt{18.3^2 + 17.6^2} = 25.4$ m/s
Determine the kinetic energy of the two-object system before and after the collision.	$KE_i = \frac{1}{2}(0.75$ kg$)(30.0$ m/s$)^2 + \frac{1}{2}(0.48$ kg$)(45.0$ m/s$)^2$ $= 824$ J $KE_f = \frac{1}{2}(0.75$ kg $+ 0.48$ kg$)(25.4$ m/s$)^2 = 397$ J
Determine the change in kinetic energy.	$\Delta KE = 397$ J $- 824$ J $= -430$ J

4. EVALUATE Reflect on your answer.
Since the two objects stick together, there will be a large loss of kinetic energy, which is what the calculation shows.

 GO ONLINE for more **math support**.

 Math Practice Problems

33 A 0.50-kg object moving with a speed of 40.0 m/s in the positive x-direction strikes and sticks to a 0.24-kg object moving 55.0 m/s in the negative y-direction. Determine the amount of kinetic energy lost in the collision.

 NEED A HINT? Go online to your **eText Sample Problem** for stepped-out support.

INVESTIGATIVE PHENOMENON

GO ONLINE to revisit your **Investigative Phenomenon CER** with the new information you have learned about Conservation of Momentum.

These questions will help you apply what you learned in this experience to the Investigative Phenomenon.

34 **SEP Argue from Evidence** Two hockey players collide. Their pads are tangled, so they do not move apart after the collision. What is the best classification for this collision?

35 **SEP Construct an Explanation** During a collision between two hockey players, each player exerts a large impulsive force on the other player. Supposing that the total impulse exerted on the players cannot be changed, what solution can you design to reduce the magnitude of the impulsive force?

36 **SEP Use Mathematics** Prior to colliding, one hockey player with mass 60 kg is traveling 8 m/s directly toward a second hockey player. The second player has a mass of 60 kg and is traveling 13 m/s toward the first hockey player. After the collision, the first hockey player travels 6 m/s in a direction opposite to his initial motion. What is the velocity of the second hockey player after the collision? Determine the magnitude of any change in kinetic energy of the two-player system. Classify the collision.

37 **SEP Construct an Explanation** Imagine that you are trying to spin two balls. The two balls have the same mass, but one is solid and the other is hollow. Determine which ball is the easiest to spin. Explain your reasoning.

GO ONLINE
for a **quiz** to evaluate what you learned about Conservation of Momentum.

Collisions in Earth's Crust

 GO ONLINE to do a **hands-on lab** to investigate plate interactions.

Crustal Deformation

Imagine a collision in slow motion—so slow that the objects move at the rate your fingernails grow. That is the speed of collisions in Earth's crust. Continental crust is made up of blocks of rock that retain the scratches, dents, and other deformations from billions of years of collisions with other parts of Earth's crust. Rock is pushed up when plates collide and drops down when they pull apart. Unlike the collisions you've studied so far, momentum has no role in the collisions of continents—the velocities are far too slow. Instead, the collisions are driven by forces deep within Earth.

Geologic Topography A map of the topography of the continental United States shows that much of the middle of the country is relatively flat. The eastern edge and most of the West have greater relief.

The various topographic ridges, rifts, and mountains that extend from the Pacific coast to the Rocky Mountains are the result of many different plate collisions over the past 200 million years, some of them still going on.

The line of mountains that stretches from Alabama to Maine, including the Appalachian Mountains, is a result of collisions hundreds of millions of years ago with Eurasia, Africa, and South America.

Cascade Range

Coast Range

Sierra Nevada Range

Rocky Mountains

Appalachian Mountains

KEY
Elevation in meters

4000
3000
2000
1000
0

0   400 mi
0   400 km

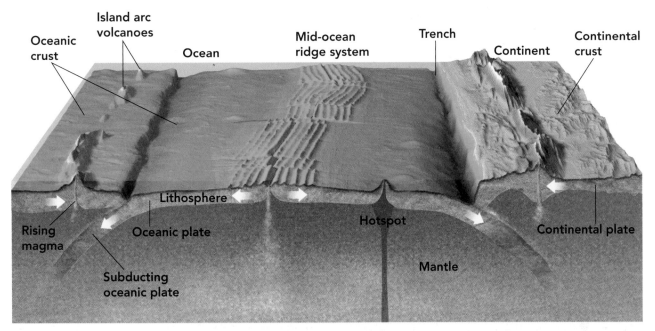

Island arc volcanoes

Oceanic crust

Ocean

Mid-ocean ridge system

Trench

Continent

Continental crust

Lithosphere

Hotspot

Rising magma

Oceanic plate

Continental plate

Subducting oceanic plate

Mantle

Plate Tectonics This simplified diagram of plate tectonics shows how the ocean lithosphere forms at mid-ocean ridges and eventually sinks back into the mantle at subduction zones. Ocean plates move independently of continental plates, which remain at Earth's surface.

Plate Tectonics

Earth's surface layer, which is called the **lithosphere,** is broken into about a dozen large pieces and another dozen smaller pieces called **tectonic plates.** Those plates move about Earth's surface at speeds of 0 to 10 cm/yr. Their interactions—colliding, separating, or sliding past each other—have produced the rock features you see on Earth's surface. The system of plate motions on Earth's surface is called **plate tectonics.**

The lithosphere has two layers: the crust at the top and the uppermost part of the mantle at the bottom. There are two different kinds of lithospheric plates. Ocean plates are thin, 80–100 km, with a very thin crust of 2–12 km. Continental plates are generally much thicker, 120–160 km, with a thicker crust of about 40 km.

Ocean plates form at mid-ocean ridges from the rock of the deeper mantle. They slowly move horizontally away from the ridges for as long as 200 million years. Finally, the plates sink back into the mantle at places called **subduction zones.** Continental crust is too buoyant to sink into the mantle, so it can last at the surface for billions of years.

(38) **SEP Use Mathematics** Find the momentum of the continental crust of the 48 contiguous states in the figure. Compare it to the momentum of a loaded train stretching from New York to Los Angeles and traveling 80 km/h. For the 48 states, assume mass = 1.4×10^{21} kg and velocity = 2.0 cm/year. For the train, assume mass = 2.4×10^{10} kg and velocity = 80 km/h = 22 m/s.

Current Plate Motions

Scientists measure tectonic plate motion using different methods. The most common method uses the network of GPS satellites in much the way smart phones do. Such measurements are accurate to within a millimeter per year. Because scientists are not sure exactly how the lithosphere moves in relation to Earth's deeper layers, plate velocities are measured with respect to the average velocity of all the plates. The reference frame of the average plate velocity is called the **no-net-rotation reference frame**.

The Rigid-Plate Model About 85 percent of Earth's surface moves as parts of plates that are, to a rough approximation, internally rigid. Deformation of the crust occurs mostly at the edges of the plates. You can think of pieces of egg shell moving about the surface of a hard-boiled egg.

Tectonic Plate Velocities The velocity vectors on the map show the direction and magnitude of velocity for the tectonic plates. The boundaries of large plates and microplates are also shown. The vectors are measured with respect to the no-net-rotation reference frame.

KEY
Length and direction of arrows show speed and direction of the motion for each plate:
⟶ 10 cm/year
— Plate boundary

The fact that the vectors are very similar within a plate shows that Earth's plates behave much like rigid shells.

Motion vectors for some plates, such as North America, show a considerable amount of rotation.

Data from Blewitt, G., W. C. Hammond, and C. Kreemer (2018), Harnessing the GPS data explosion for interdisciplinary science, Eos, 99, https://doi.org/10.1029/2018EO10462, created using GMT software courtesy of

39 **SEP Analyze Data** Using the vectors for Antarctica, explain how Antarctica's motion is similar to that of a figure skater doing a spin. [Hint: Remember that Earth is round and that the left and right sides of the map are connected. Look at the region where the two sides connect.]

Plate Boundaries Tectonic plates are not really perfectly rigid. Large areas of them are deforming internally, primarily through the continuous folding and stretching of the crust. Most intraplate deformation occurs at plate boundaries. You can think of plate boundaries not as lines but as zones that are hundreds or even thousands of kilometers wide. Plate boundaries are of three types. **Divergent boundaries** are boundaries where plates are moving apart. **Convergent boundaries** are boundaries where plates are moving together. **Transform boundaries** are boundaries where plates are sliding past each other.

Intraplate Deformation About 15 percent of Earth's crust is deforming internally.

Boundaries of colliding plates often have the largest areas of intraplate deformation.

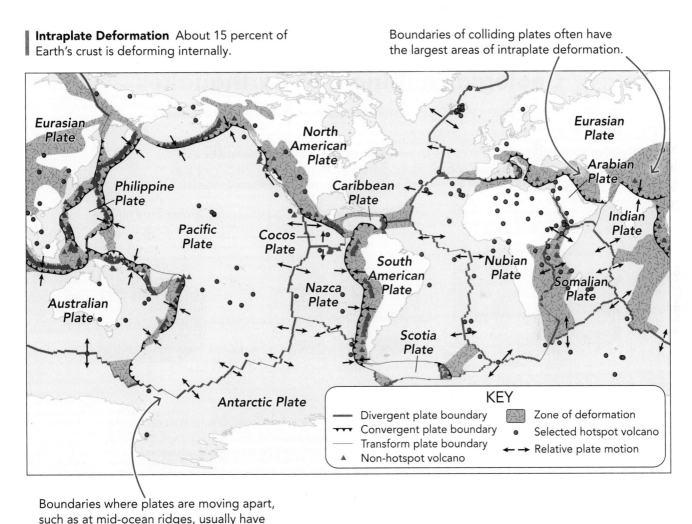

Boundaries where plates are moving apart, such as at mid-ocean ridges, usually have very narrow zones of intraplate deformation.

KEY
— Divergent plate boundary
⊤⊤⊤ Convergent plate boundary
— Transform plate boundary
▲ Non-hotspot volcano
▨ Zone of deformation
• Selected hotspot volcano
←→ Relative plate motion

40. **CCC Patterns** Examine the patterns of the velocity vectors across the plate velocities map. Explain what general statement you can make about the speed of the Pacific Plate, which does not contain any continental area, in comparison to plates that do contain continents.

41. **SEP Construct an Explanation** In light of the information about intraplate deformation, explain what it would mean if the amount of new ocean crust formed each year at spreading boundaries was more than the amount of ocean crust sinking at subduction zones.

Force, Stress, and Earthquakes

▶ **GO ONLINE** to watch a **video** about earthquakes.

Earth's crust experiences forces from gravity and the convection of Earth's mantle as it transfers heat from Earth's interior to the surface. The crust's responses to those stress forces are strains that may take the form of the slow flowing and folding of layers of rock, often seen within mountains. Strain can also appear in the form of elastic compression, extension, or bending of rock. To relieve the stress, rock can break and snap back in an earthquake.

Geologic Faulting and Earthquakes

How are geologic **faults and earthquakes related?**

Types of Faulting Geologic faults are **large fractures or sudden discontinuities in Earth's surface** caused by non-uniform mass movement of rock. The direction of the movement is dependent on the **net forces** acting on all sides of the rocks at the fault.

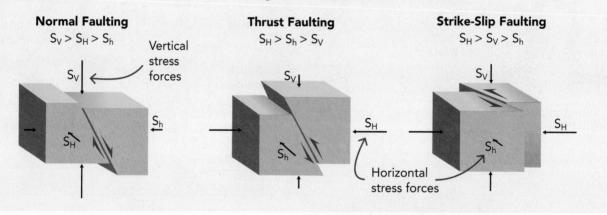

Normal Faulting
$S_V > S_H > S_h$

Vertical stress forces

Thrust Faulting
$S_H > S_h > S_V$

Horizontal stress forces

Strike-Slip Faulting
$S_H > S_V > S_h$

Elastic Rebound A road built over a strike-slip fault will **deform over time** as the underlying rock moves in different directions. When the rock's internal rigidity is overcome, it releases energy as an earthquake. The road breaks and its parts **"snap back" to their original forms.**

At a subduction zone, elastic rebound can result in the displacement of a large volume of water called a **tsunami.**

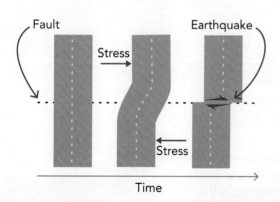

Fault

Earthquake

Stress

Stress

Time

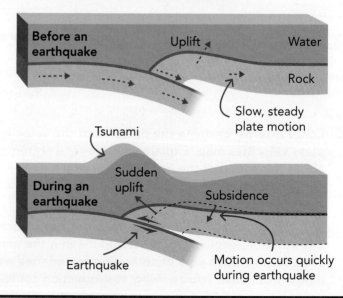

Before an earthquake

Uplift

Water

Rock

Slow, steady plate motion

Tsunami

During an earthquake

Sudden uplift

Subsidence

Earthquake

Motion occurs quickly during earthquake

San Andreas Fault System One of the best-known transform plate boundaries in the world is the San Andreas Fault, which separates the Pacific Plate from the North American Plate.

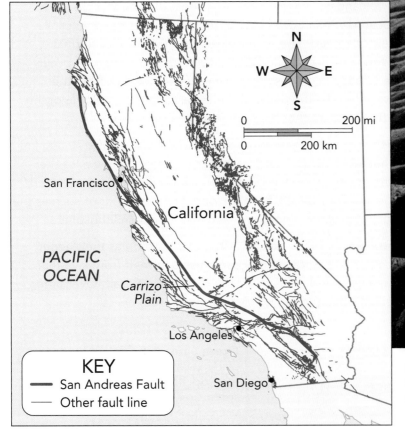

KEY
— San Andreas Fault
— Other fault line

In places such as the Carrizo Plain shown here, the San Andreas Fault can be seen at the surface, a result of many strike-slip earthquakes.

The San Andreas Fault system is a plate boundary that is actually hundreds of kilometers wide, with earthquakes occurring on many different faults, not just the San Andreas Fault.

Transform Plate Boundaries

The least common sort of plate boundary on continents is the transform boundary, where two plates move parallel to the boundary that separates them. Motion along the boundary can happen continuously. It can also happen intermittently, through the occurrence of multiple strike-slip earthquakes. Over time, such earthquakes can move rock great distances. For example, at current rates of motion across the San Andreas Fault system, Los Angeles will be next door to San Francisco in about 13 million years.

The situation is different for plate boundaries within ocean crust. In ocean crust, plate boundaries usually consist of large numbers of alternating spreading ridges and transform faults that zigzag across the ocean floor. Each of the small transform fault segments is a site of strike-slip earthquakes.

(42) **SEP Construct an Explanation** Think about all the different ways that two adjacent plates can move relative to each other. Then, explain why transform plate boundaries are so uncommon.

Divergent Plate Boundaries

EXPERIENCE IT!

Demonstrate the three kinds of earthquakes with a block of clay. What happens if there is a bend in the fault? Can you find any places on Earth where such a fault has formed?

Divergent Plate Boundaries Divergent boundaries are the sites of many earthquakes and volcanoes. However, because most divergent plate boundaries are located within ocean basins, the earthquakes and volcanic eruptions are rarely observed. The earthquakes take the form of normal faulting because the crust is stretched and extended. The volcanoes occur through **pressure release,** a process that occurs when hot rock from the mantle flows upward to take the place of the separating plates. Some of the rock melts when the pressure that has kept it solid is removed.

Mid-Ocean Ridges Most divergent plate boundaries are part of a 70,000-km chain of interconnected divergent and transform segments that circles the globe. Because the rising hot rock is buoyant, such boundaries are elevated above the average sea floor depth, forming long connected ridges such as the Mid-Atlantic Ridge. Mid-ocean ridges are factories for ocean lithosphere.

Most ocean lithosphere, or plate, has the same composition as the deeper mantle, but it is colder and stiffer. The ocean crust is formed from lava that rises toward the sea floor and cools to form a rock called basalt. Over time, the basalt is covered with a thickening layer of ocean sediments.

Ocean Spreading Centers As ocean plates separate due to tectonic forces, new rock flows up from below to fill the space. Some of the rock melts to form ocean floor basaltic lava.

Strike-slip earthquakes occur along the transform segments; normal-fault earthquakes occur along the divergent boundaries.

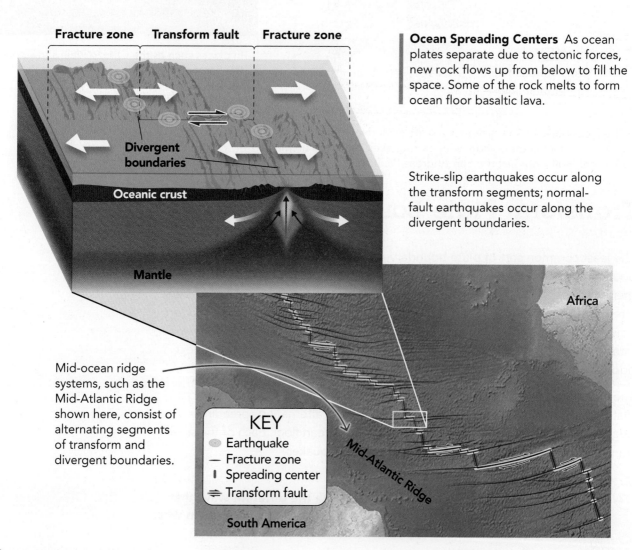

Fracture zone   Transform fault   Fracture zone

Divergent boundaries

Oceanic crust

Mantle

Mid-ocean ridge systems, such as the Mid-Atlantic Ridge shown here, consist of alternating segments of transform and divergent boundaries.

Africa

KEY
- Earthquake
- Fracture zone
- Spreading center
- Transform fault

Mid-Atlantic Ridge

South America

GO ONLINE to do a PhET **simulation** that allows you to explore the role of fluid pressure on plate motions.

Continental Rifting Another form of divergent plate boundary is a **continental rift**, where a continent breaks into two or more small plates. Continental rifting is common when supercontinents break apart, such as during the breakup of Pangaea. That breakup is still going on, with the splitting of the African Plate. As rifting continues, the continental rift eventually becomes an ocean, with basaltic ocean crust forming underwater. Continental rifting between the east coast of North America and the west coast of Africa began about 200 million years ago. Spreading has continued ever since, forming the ever-widening Atlantic Ocean.

Wherever continental rifting occurs, volcanoes can form, such as Kilimanjaro in Kenya and Erta Ale in Ethiopia, shown here.

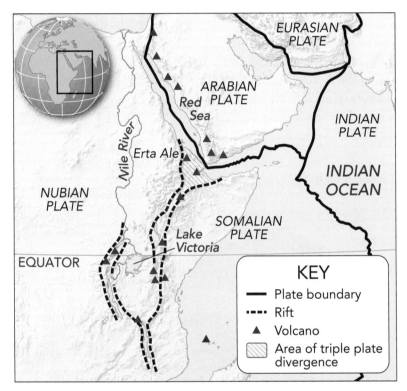

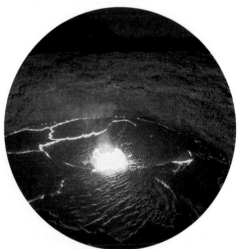

Erta Ale is one of the few volcanoes in the world to have a continuously bubbling lava lake in its crater.

African Continental Rifting The African Plate is in the process of separating into three smaller plates. Continental rifting between the African Plate and the Arabian Plate began 30 million years ago, forming the Red Sea. Now, the rest of the African Plate is separating into the smaller Nubian and Somalian plates, and deep rift valleys extend far down the continent.

(43) **SEP Construct an Explanation** Earthquakes are common along ocean transform segments but not along the fracture zones that they are connected with. Explain why that is the case.

(44) **CCC Cause and Effect** It is common for rivers to flow down the centers of ancient rift valleys. In New Mexico, the Rio Grande River flows down the Rio Grande Rift, and in the central United States, the Mississippi River flows down through the ancient Reelfoot Rift. Explain why such river courses are common.

Ocean-Continent Collision

Most of the world's visible volcanoes, such as Mount St. Helens, Mt. Fuji, and Mt. Vesuvius, occur where ocean lithosphere sinks back into the mantle beneath the edge of a continent. Ocean-continent collision zones are also the sites of the world's largest earthquakes, such as in Chile, Alaska, Sumatra, and Japan. Ocean-continent collisions are important for the growth of continents, adding rock to the edges of continents and building up tall mountain ranges such as the Andes in South America and the Sierra Nevada in North America.

Subduction Zone Dynamics Ocean crust is made of denser rock that is richer in iron and magnesium than continental crust. Thus, when the two collide, the ocean crust sinks beneath the continent. However, the process is not gentle. The ocean crust is a 100-km-thick sheet of solid rock, so bending and then unbending it causes large numbers of earthquakes. All of the world's magnitude-9 earthquakes occur along the frictional boundary between two colliding plates. The subduction zone is compressed, so it can push up giant mountain ranges like the Andes. At the same time, continents can grow outward by the continual accumulation of ocean sediments and slivers of ocean crust that are scraped off the sinking plate.

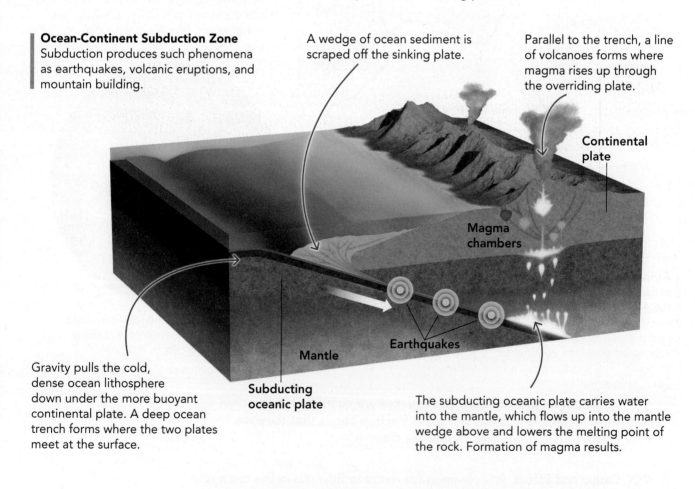

Ocean-Continent Subduction Zone Subduction produces such phenomena as earthquakes, volcanic eruptions, and mountain building.

A wedge of ocean sediment is scraped off the sinking plate.

Parallel to the trench, a line of volcanoes forms where magma rises up through the overriding plate.

Continental plate

Magma chambers

Earthquakes

Mantle

Subducting oceanic plate

Gravity pulls the cold, dense ocean lithosphere down under the more buoyant continental plate. A deep ocean trench forms where the two plates meet at the surface.

The subducting oceanic plate carries water into the mantle, which flows up into the mantle wedge above and lowers the melting point of the rock. Formation of magma results.

(45) **CCC Cause and Effect** Explain why the largest earthquakes occur where the two kinds of lithosphere are in contact and not deeper in the subduction zone.

Pacific Northwest Volcanoes More than 15 active volcanoes exist as part of the Cascade Range, from California to British Columbia.

Such volcanoes result from the subduction of a small piece of the Pacific Ocean lithosphere, the Juan de Fuca Plate, beneath North America.

The most recent eruption occurred at Mount St. Helens in 2005. An earlier eruption there, in 1980, blew away the whole north face of the mountain.

Subduction Zone Volcanoes Large volcanoes are found along the edges of continents wherever subduction occurs, including a good portion of the rim of the Pacific Ocean known as the Ring of Fire. Explosive volcanoes occur at subduction zones because of the large amounts of water that enter such zones and generate magma. The water rapidly expands into steam during eruptions, which can then blast thousands of cubic kilometers of rock and ash into the atmosphere. Volcanoes are therefore part of a giant deep-Earth water cycle. Subduction zone volcanoes usually form from alternating layers of falling volcanic ash and flowing lava.

46 SEP Use Models North America is moving westward and will eventually entirely override the Juan de Fuca Plate. Using the shapes of the Juan de Fuca and Gorda Plates on the map, explain which volcanoes will be the first to stop erupting, and why. [Hint: Which plate will disappear first?]

Ocean-Ocean Collision

Although not as common as ocean-continent collision zones, there are still many places where two oceanic plates collide. Ocean lithosphere cools and sinks deeper as it moves away from a hot mid-ocean ridge, so older ocean crust is not only denser than younger crust but also deeper. As a result, older ocean plate usually sinks beneath newer ocean plate. Earthquakes are common at ocean-ocean collision zones, but they are never extremely large because the contact area between the two pieces of lithosphere is small. Ocean-ocean collision zones also have many volcanoes, and the composition of the lava is similar to that of the ocean crust basalt.

Ocean-Ocean Subduction Zone The subduction resulting from the collision of two oceanic plates has many similarities to ocean-continent subduction. The older, colder, denser ocean plate is usually subducted into the mantle.

Ocean-ocean subduction trenches, such as the Mariana Trench between the Pacific and Philippine plates, are the deepest places in the ocean.

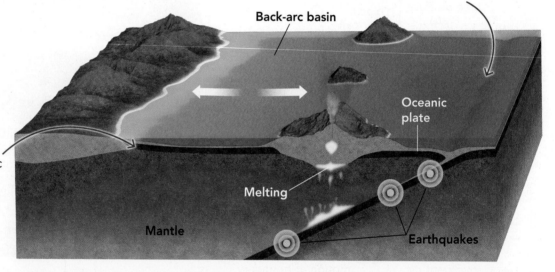

Back-arc basin

The sinking of the ocean lithosphere can pull the volcanic island arc toward the trench, opening up a spreading region behind it.

Oceanic plate

Melting

Mantle

Earthquakes

(47) **SEP Develop a Model** A line of volcanic islands usually takes the shape of an arc. The shape results from the ocean plate being a curved shell and not a flat layer. Explain the process using the analogy of a knife cutting through an orange peel at a slanted angle.

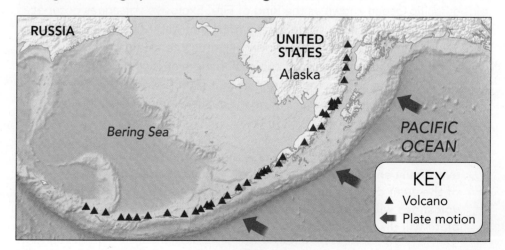

RUSSIA

UNITED STATES
Alaska

Bering Sea

PACIFIC OCEAN

KEY
▲ Volcano
← Plate motion

Continent-Continent Collision

Ocean crust sinks back into the mantle at collision zones, but continental crust is not dense enough to sink. It adjusts to the collision by deforming through folding and faulting. The faults are mostly thrust faults, which result in a shortening of the crust. Layers of rock such as limestone, sandstone, and shale can be folded dramatically. Continent-continent collisions generate long mountain chains called **orogens,** or orogenic belts, because the compressed rock on the surface is forced to move upward. At the same time, deeper rock is pushed down into the mantle, forming roots to mountains that are much deeper than the mountains are high. The Appalachian Mountains in the eastern United States resulted from several different continent-continent collisions during the formation of the supercontinent Pangaea. The Appalachians used to be much taller than they are today, but erosion has decreased their height by about 10 kilometers.

VOCABULARY

The word **orogen** is derived from the ancient Greek words *oros*, meaning "mountain," and *genesis*, meaning "creation." The process of orogeny is one by which mountains are created.

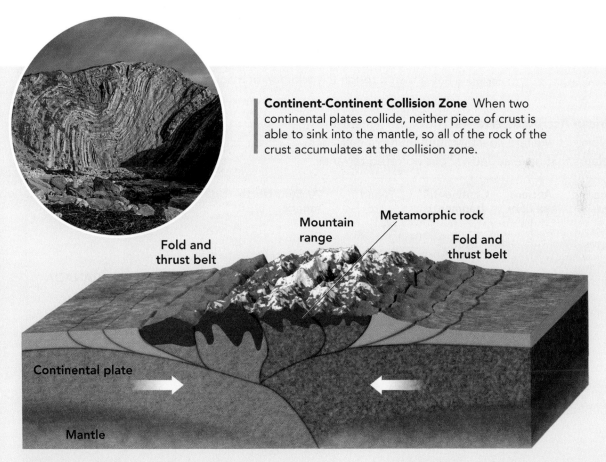

Continent-Continent Collision Zone When two continental plates collide, neither piece of crust is able to sink into the mantle, so all of the rock of the crust accumulates at the collision zone.

Fold and thrust belt

Mountain range

Metamorphic rock

Fold and thrust belt

Continental plate

Mantle

During the collision, some rock is thrust upward, forming mountains, and some is pushed downward into the mantle, forming mountain roots. The crust thickens through a combination of folding and earthquake faulting that forms broad fold and thrust belts.

Rock layers that are pushed down deep are subject to high temperatures and pressure. They are transformed into new types of rock through a process called metamorphism.

 SEP Analyze Data The Eurasian continent contains a long north-south orogenic belt called the Ural Mountains. What can you conclude from that feature about the history of Europe and Asia?

The Wilson Cycle of Multiple Collisions

Through chemical and physical analysis of the properties of ancient rocks, geologists have pieced together the histories of the locations of continents going back billions of years. That history involves a complex dance of continental fragments that move all about Earth's surface. They bang into and slide past each other, coming together to form supercontinents and then breaking apart again. The most recent supercontinent was Pangaea, which existed from 350 to 200 million years ago. However, there were many other supercontinents before Pangaea, each with a different arrangement of continents, that date back to at least 3.6 billion years ago.

Accreted Terranes An important result of tectonic plate collisions is that many continents have grown in size through the addition of multiple accreted terranes. An **accreted terrane** is a piece of new crust that has been added to the side of a continent through plate collisions. Accreted terranes can be slivers of crust from other continents or the deformed remnants of island arc volcanoes, ocean crust, or sediments scraped off subducting ocean plates. The western coast of North America has grown through the addition of many such accreted terranes.

North American Accreted Terranes The North American Plate has grown along its western coast through multiple collisions with other plates that have added various accreted terranes.

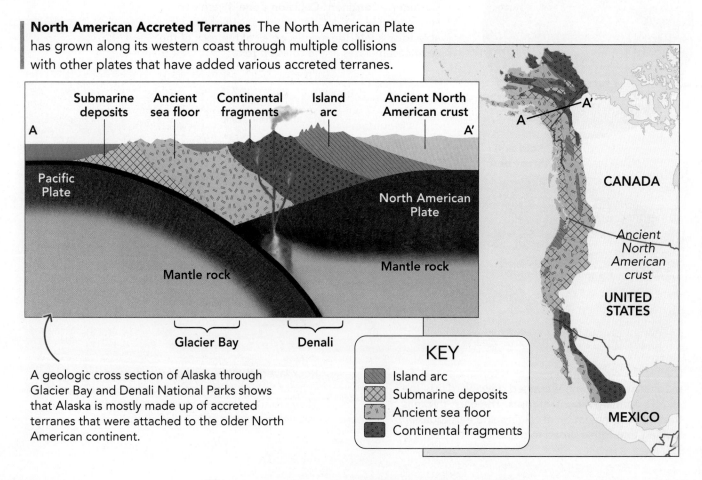

A geologic cross section of Alaska through Glacier Bay and Denali National Parks shows that Alaska is mostly made up of accreted terranes that were attached to the older North American continent.

KEY

- Island arc
- Submarine deposits
- Ancient sea floor
- Continental fragments

(49) **SEP Construct an Explanation** Using the geologic cross section through Alaska, explain whether the rock of Glacier Bay National Park or the rock of Denali National Park is the older part of North America.

Wilson Cycle The Wilson cycle describes how ocean basins repeatedly open and close as continents move back and forth across Earth's surface. The cycle begins with continental rifting within a large landmass. Soon, a new ocean is born, and it grows in size until subduction zones form. A mature ocean basin such as the Pacific can maintain both ocean spreading and subduction for a long time. Once there is no more spreading, the ocean basin shrinks until continents collide, again forming a large landmass.

Stages of the Wilson Cycle The Wilson cycle of the opening and closing of ocean basins consists of several different stages totaling at least 500 million years. Support for the idea comes from the fact that current examples for each of the stages can be found on Earth's surface.

Stage	Motion	
Embryonic	Uplift (rifting)	East African rift valleys
Juvenile	Divergence (subsidence)	Red Sea
Mature	Divergence (spreading)	Atlantic and Arctic Oceans
Complex	Divergence and convergence (spreading and subduction)	Pacific Ocean
Terminal	Convergence (collision and uplift)	Mediterranean Sea
Suturing	Convergence (horizontal shrinkage)	Himalaya Mountains

50. **SEP Use Models** The Indian Ocean basin contains three different mid-ocean ridge spreading centers and one subduction zone, beneath Southeast Asia. Using the table, explain which stage of the Wilson cycle the Indian Ocean is in.

INVESTIGATIVE PHENOMENON

 GO ONLINE to revisit your **Investigative Phenomenon CER** with the new information you have learned about Collisions in Earth's Crust.

These questions will help you apply what you learned in this experience to the Investigative Phenomenon.

51 **SEP Construct an Explanation** Suppose that a group of skaters huddled together on the ice push away from each other, sliding out in different directions. Explain what the sum of their velocity vectors is before and after pushing apart. How is the situation similar to the no-net-rotation reference frame of tectonic plate velocities?

52 **SEP Use Mathematics** The explosivity of volcanic eruptions is measured on a logarithmic scale known as the volcanic explosivity index. Use the logarithmic pattern of values to complete the table.

Volcanic explosivity index	Volume of ejected tephra	Approximate interval	Example
3	> 0.01 km^3	1 month	Etna, Italy: 2013, 0.02 km^3
4			Eyjafjallajökull, Iceland: 2010, 0.27 km^3
5	> 1 km^3	10 years	Mount St. Helens, United States: 1980, 1 km^3
6			Krakatau, Indonesia: 1883, 18 km^3
7	> 100 km^3		Tambora, Indonesia: 1815, 100 km^3
8		10,000 years	Toba, Indonesia: 74,000 years ago, 2800 km^3

53 **CCC Stability and Change** Some of the largest volcanic eruptions have ejected many cubic kilometers of ash and sulfuric acid droplets, which stay in the atmosphere for years, reducing the amount of incoming sunlight. Some large eruptions—for instance, Mt. Tambora in 1815, and the following 'year without a summer'—have altered the course of human history. Construct an explanation for why eruptions may have such great effects.

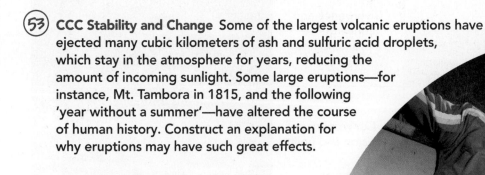

 GO ONLINE for a **quiz** to evaluate Collisions in Earth's Crust.

These questions will help you apply what you learned in this investigation to the Anchoring Phenomenon.

(54) **CCC Energy and Matter** Some of the processes involved in collisions in Earth's crust are similar to a chain-reaction machine. For example, the largest landslide ever witnessed occurred down the north face of Mount St. Helens just seconds before the giant eruption of 1980 and moments after two magnitude-5 earthquakes just beneath it. The weight of the rock that slid had been applying enough pressure to keep the eruption from occurring. Describe how the flow of energy during the earthquakes, landslide, and eruption is like a chain-reaction machine.

(55) **SEP Construct an Explanation** Choose one of the collisions depicted in the image of the chain-reaction machine, such as the bowling ball and pin or the hammer and scale. Classify the collision. Then, identify the forces acting on the objects, describe what happens to each object's momentum during the collision, and explain the energy changes that occur in that part of the system.

☑ INVESTIGATION ASSESSMENT

 GO ONLINE for activities that will give you an opportunity to **demonstrate what you have learned**:

☑ **Engineering Performance-Based Assessment** Analyze data to refine a device that minimizes the force on an object during a collision.

📄 **Engineering Workbench** Design a parachute to help minimize the force on an egg when dropped.

🖥 **Career Connections** Learn about how an aerospace engineer applies knowledge of physics.

☑ **Investigation Test** Take this test to evaluate your understanding of collisions.

☑ **Virtual Lab Performance-Based Assessment** Use experimental evidence to identify car design choices that will minimize passenger injuries in a collision.

GO ONLINE to engage with real-world phenomena by watching a **phenomenon video** and completing a **CER worksheet**.

Why does **sand** warm faster than **water** on a sunny day?

Thermal Energy

Many people look forward to cooling themselves off at the beach on a summer day. Sometimes, however, the sand is too hot to walk on. For example, sand on some beaches can reach a temperature of 60°C (140°F)! Nearby, the water may feel refreshingly cool. What causes this stark difference in temperature?

The two areas—the sand and water—are right next to one another. The sun is shining on both areas. Yet the sand may feel much warmer. This phenomenon has led many people to seek a scientific explanation.

What is thermal energy, and how is it transferred between objects? What factors affect the ways that thermal energy is transferred? Answering these questions helps explain why sand warms faster than water on a sunny day.

1. **CCC Patterns** Write about an experience you have had in which two different objects, subjected to the same heating conditions for the same amount of time, felt different to the touch.

2. **CCC Matter and Energy** What factors do you think may cause the difference you wrote about in the previous question and the difference in the sand/water example?

3. **SEP Plan an Investigation** A friend tells you that different kinds of sand take different amounts of time to warm up to the same temperature in sunlight. Describe an experiment you could perform to investigate your friend's claim.

Temperature

 GO ONLINE to do a **hands-on lab** to investigate and model the molecular-level changes that occur with changes in temperature.

States of Matter

Matter is made of particles, small pieces of matter, in the form of atoms, molecules, or subatomic particles. Matter is characterized by different arrangements of those particles, called **states of matter.** Familiar states of matter include solids, liquids, and gases. Gases and liquids share several characteristics and are sometimes referred to as fluids. Particles in fluids move randomly and in all directions. The particles have empty space between them, so all the particles of the fluid can mix freely. In solids, the particles are very close together and do not freely move past one another.

Comparing States of Matter Water exists in solid, liquid, and gaseous forms on Earth. These three states of matter differ fundamentally in shape and volume.

Ice, a solid, has a fixed shape and volume.

The shape and volume of a gas, for example, water vapor, depend on the container's shape and volume.

Seawater, a liquid, has a fixed volume but not a fixed shape.

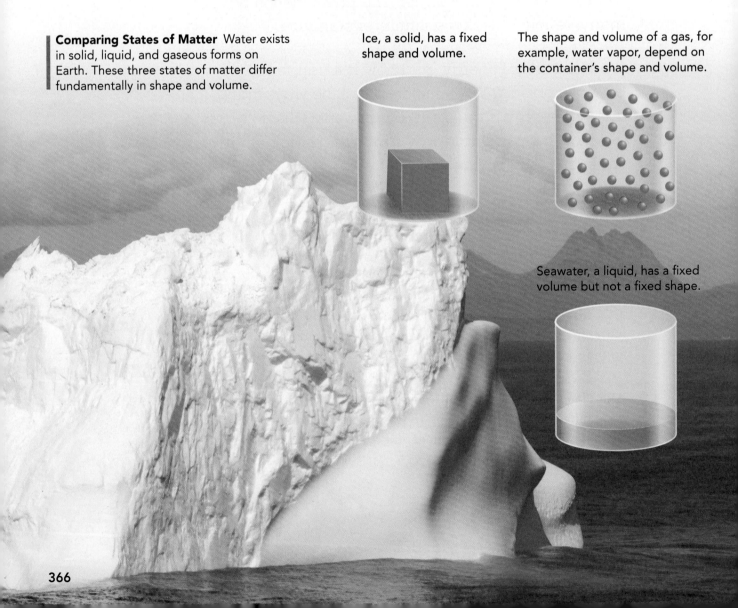

Structure of Matter

Particle Interaction and Potential Energy Potential energy is associated with the position and arrangement of particles in a system, which are held together mostly by electric forces. In liquids and solids, the particles are close together, which increases the attractive forces. In gases, the particles are spread out, reducing the attractive forces. You can model gas particles as exerting no attractive forces on each other.

Particle Movement and Kinetic Energy Particles are always in motion, and so they always have kinetic energy—the energy associated with motion. However, the way they move is determined by their state. In solids, particles are close together and vibrate about fixed points. In liquids, the particles are farther apart and have greater freedom of movement. In gases, the particles are very far apart and move quite freely.

Comparing Structures The familiar macroscopic differences among solids, liquids, and gases arise from differences at the microscopic scale.

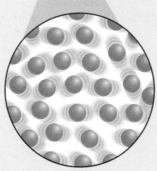
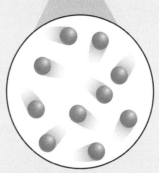

Solid	Liquid	Gas
In solids, the particles are arranged in regular, repeating patterns. The particles are held in place by attractive forces, but they always vibrate.	In liquids, the particles flow easily around each other. They have greater freedom of movement than in solids, but attractive forces keep them within the liquid.	In gases, the particles have so much space between them that the attractive forces are insignificant. Thus, the particles that make up a gas can fly away from other particles.

(4) **SEP Plan an Investigation** Plan an investigation to determine the state of matter for peanut butter at room temperature.

Ideal Gases: A Microscopic Approach

VOCABULARY

The word *ideal* comes from the Latin word *idealis*, meaning "existing in idea."
An **ideal gas** exists only as a model that approximates real gases' behavior at specific ranges of pressure and temperature.

An **ideal gas** is a hypothetical gas made up of randomly moving particles that have negligible volume and no attractive forces between the particles. Although an ideal gas does not exist, it serves as a useful model because many real gases behave very much like an ideal gas at high temperatures and low pressures.

In an ideal gas, the potential energy of particles is insignificant in comparison to the particles' kinetic energy. A microscopic approach to an ideal gas looks at interactions among particles within a container as they exchange kinetic energy. For example, when a gas with a fixed volume is in a container, increasing the kinetic energy of each particle increases the magnitude of the force a particle exerts on the wall during a collision, as well as the frequency of collisions between gas particles and the walls of the container. This results in an increase in pressure.

Pressure and Volume A piston can be used to force a gas in a cylinder into a smaller volume. When the volume decreases, the pressure the gas exerts increases.

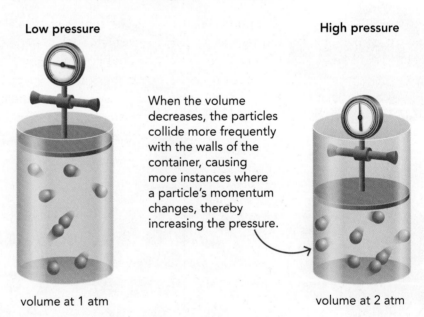

Low pressure

High pressure

When the volume decreases, the particles collide more frequently with the walls of the container, causing more instances where a particle's momentum changes, thereby increasing the pressure.

volume at 1 atm

volume at 2 atm

For a gas in a container with walls that can move freely, an increase in the frequency of particle collisions results in the walls moving—there is an increase in volume. If the temperature of the gas is held constant while the volume is decreased, the gas particles will collide with the walls of the container more often, causing an increase in pressure.

(5) **CCC Cause and Effect** An ideal gas is inside a container with a fixed, rigid top. The kinetic energy of each particle is increased through an interaction between the gas and an external source of energy. Use the ideal gas model to explain how the increase in the kinetic energy of the gas particles affects the pressure of the gas.

Average Kinetic Energy of Gas Particles

 GO ONLINE to do a PhET **simulation** that allows you to explore the relationship between particle motion and temperature.

Increasing the energy of the particles of a gas in a container increases the force they exert on the walls. To treat the behavior of an ideal gas quantitatively, scientists use the **average kinetic energy,** which is the average translational energy of a particle in the gas. As with objects on the macroscopic level, the kinetic energy of a microscopic particle depends on the square of its velocity.

Average Kinetic Energy

$$\overline{KE} = \frac{1}{2}m\bar{v}^2$$

$\overline{KE}$ = average kinetic energy of particle
m = mass of particle
$\bar{v}$ = average speed of particle

The average kinetic energy of the particles in an object or substance is related to how warm or cool it is. In fact, **temperature** is a measure of the average kinetic energy of particles in matter. Since an ideal gas has no potential energy, the internal energy of the gas depends only on the average kinetic energy of the particles and the number of particles in the sample. The energy associated with the kinetic energy of the particles in a sample or an object, measured as temperature, is known as **thermal energy.**

Characteristics of Gases The rapid, constant motion of particles in a gas causes them to collide with one another and with the walls of their container. As a result, the gas particles spread out to fill the available space in the container.

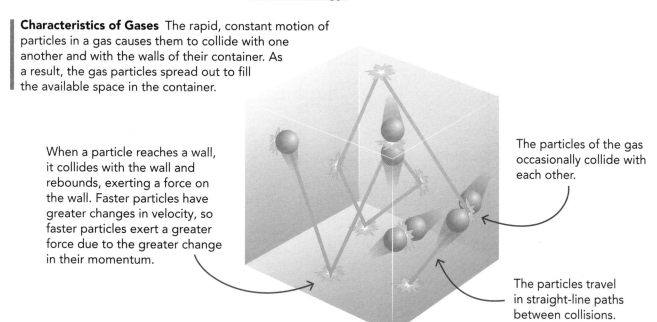

When a particle reaches a wall, it collides with the wall and rebounds, exerting a force on the wall. Faster particles have greater changes in velocity, so faster particles exert a greater force due to the greater change in their momentum.

The particles of the gas occasionally collide with each other.

The particles travel in straight-line paths between collisions.

6 **SEP Use Mathematics** Determine the average kinetic energy of an oxygen molecule with a mass of 5.31×10^{-26} kg and an average speed of 482 m/s.

Understanding Temperature

▶ **GO ONLINE** to watch a **video** about the history of temperature measurement.

Measuring Temperature A liquid thermometer is a slender tube attached to a bulb filled with liquid. When the thermometer gains thermal energy from its surroundings, the liquid expands. The resulting column height of liquid inside the tube can be compared to markings on the thermometer to "read" the temperature.

Different thermometers use different temperature scales. The Celsius scale and the Fahrenheit scale are based on the freezing and boiling points of water. The **Kelvin scale** is a temperature scale that assigns 0 K to the lowest possible temperature and 273.15 K to the freezing point of water. Temperature on the Kelvin scale is also known as **absolute temperature.** Since all temperatures are greater than the lowest possible temperature, absolute temperatures are always greater than zero. You can convert temperatures from one scale to another.

Fahrenheit and Celsius	Kelvin
$T_F = \dfrac{9}{5} T_C + 32 \qquad T_C = \dfrac{5}{9}(T_F - 32)$	$T_K = T_C + 273.15$
T_F = Fahrenheit temperature T_C = Celsius temperature	T_K = Kelvin temperature T_C = Celsius temperature

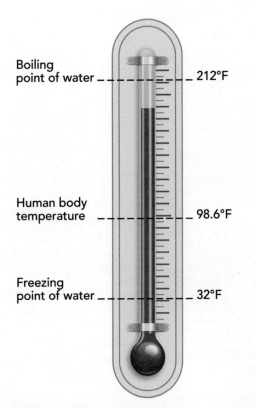

Boiling point of water — 212°F

Human body temperature — 98.6°F

Freezing point of water — 32°F

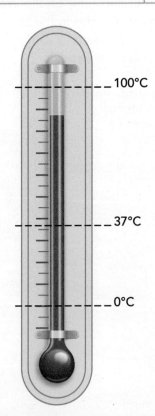

— 100°C

— 37°C

— 0°C

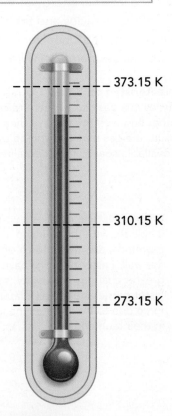

— 373.15 K

— 310.15 K

— 273.15 K

Fahrenheit (°F) On the Fahrenheit scale, the freezing point of water is 32°F, and the boiling point is 212°F.

Celsius (°C) On the Celsius scale, the freezing point of water is 0°C, and the boiling point is 100°C.

Kelvin (K) On the Kelvin scale, water's freezing point is 273.15 K, and the boiling point is 373.15 K.

Temperature and Energy The microscopic approach to ideal gases reveals that the average kinetic energy of gases is related to the pressure and volume of gases. Therefore, temperature is also related to pressure and volume. The ratio of pressure, P, and volume, V, to the number of particles, N, is the same for all gases at a given temperature, T, measured in the Kelvin scale. The relationship can be expressed as follows, where k_B is Boltzmann's constant, which is approximately 1.38×10^{-23} J/K.

$$\frac{PV}{N} = k_B T$$

For an ideal gas, temperature is proportional to the average kinetic energy of the gas particles. However, the total internal energy for a gas is the average kinetic energy per particle multiplied by the total number of particles. The subscript th is used because thermal energy is another name for internal energy.

Average Kinetic Energy and Temperature	Thermal Energy
$$\overline{KE} = \frac{3}{2} k_B T$$	$$U_{th} = \frac{3}{2} k_B N T$$
$\overline{KE}$ = average kinetic energy k_B = Boltzmann's constant = 1.38×10^{-23} J/K T = temperature (expressed in Kelvins)	U_{th} = thermal energy N = number of particles T = temperature (expressed in Kelvins)

Energy and Numbers Thermal energy depends on the number of particles in a sample. There are twelve particles in each half of the box. Therefore, the total energy of both halves of the box is twice the energy of either half.

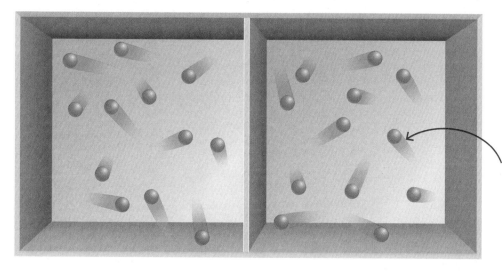

By comparing the indicated motions of the particles, you can see the average kinetic energy is the same in both halves of the box. Therefore, the temperature is also the same.

(7) **SEP Use Mathematics** Suppose the temperature of a cup of coffee is 85°C. Determine the average temperature of the coffee in Fahrenheit and Kelvin.

(8) **CCC Energy and Matter** Two containers, one smaller container and one larger container, hold identical gases. The average kinetic energy per particle is the same for both gases. How would the temperatures of the gases in the two containers compare? How would the thermal energies compare?

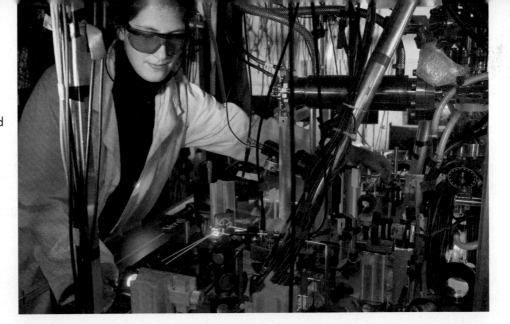

How Cold? Laser cooling, shown here, is a process used by physicists to cool down samples of atoms and molecules to near absolute zero. Light particles from the laser are absorbed and re-emitted by the particles, which lowers their kinetic energies and, therefore, their temperature.

Absolute Zero The theoretical temperature at which the individual particles of matter that make up a substance have zero kinetic energy is called **absolute zero.** Scientists predict that there would be no particle motion at absolute zero. It is the lowest possible temperature, the zero point on the Kelvin scale. Physicists have constructed devices to cool samples to 50 microKelvins. That's only 0.000050 K above absolute zero!

A liquid thermometer measures temperature by means of the volume of a liquid. Temperature can also be measured by means of a substance that does not expand, using a constant-volume gas thermometer. It is a rigid sphere filled with gas. Since the sphere does not expand with temperature, the pressure of the gas in the sphere increases in direct proportion with temperature. A gas thermometer is calibrated by taking pressure readings at two temperatures, usually the boiling point and freezing point of water. After calibration, the sphere is brought into contact with a system at an unknown temperature. The pressure of the gas is proportional to the temperature of that system.

Pressure vs. Temperature For any gas, as temperature decreases, pressure decreases in a straight line back to absolute zero. On the graph, the number of particles of each gas is given in moles. One mole is 6.02×10^{23} particles.

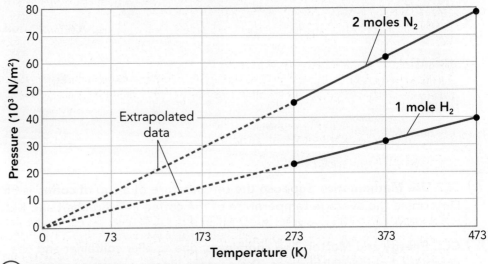

(9) **SEP Use Models** Using both the microscopic approach and the macroscopic approach, explain why a temperature of absolute zero corresponds to a pressure of 0.

Ideal Gases: A Macroscopic Approach

Recall that in the microscopic approach, the average kinetic energy of particles is related to the collisions with the walls of the container. The macroscopic approach focuses on the connection between temperature and the volume and pressure of a gas. The relationship among the quantities is referred to as the ideal gas law. It can be written in two ways.

Ideal Gas Law	
$PV = Nk_BT$	$PV = nRT$
P = pressure V = volume N = number of particles k_B = Boltzmann's constant = 1.38×10^{-23} J/K T = temperature (in Kelvins)	P = pressure V = volume n = number of moles R = ideal gas constant = 8.31 J/(K·mol) T = temperature (in Kelvins)

The ideal gas law states that when the volume is held constant and the temperature increases, the pressure increases. This is the same conclusion drawn from the microscopic approach; raising the temperature means the kinetic energy of the gas particles increases, so the pressure increases.

Ice water (0°C)   **Boiling water (100°C)**

Gas and Temperature Temperature, like average kinetic energy, is directly proportional to the pressure and volume of an ideal gas. The ratio $\frac{PV}{N}$ is the same for all gases at a given temperature.

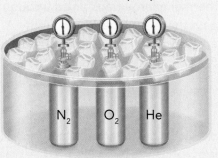
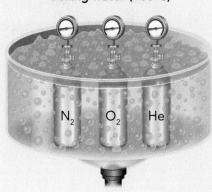

$V_1 = 0.02$ m³
$P_1 = 50$ kPa

$V_2 = 0.01$ m³
$P_2 = 100$ kPa

Constant Temperature According to the ideal gas law, keeping temperature constant while decreasing volume from V_1 to V_2 will cause the pressure to increase from P_1 to P_2.

10 **SEP Use Mathematics** Determine the Kelvin temperature of 3.00 moles of gas at a pressure of 120 N/m² and a volume of 40.0 m³.

Transferring Energy Through Heating

Energy Flow When two objects at different temperatures come into contact, the thermal energy transferred between objects is called **heat.** The amount of thermal energy the cooler object gains is equal to the amount of thermal energy the warmer object loses, which is expressed by the equation $Q_{HC} + Q_{CH} = 0$. In that equation, Q_{HC}, heat flow from the hotter object to the colder object, is heat lost, so it has a negative value. The energy-flow equation is true only when the two objects are part of an isolated system where thermal energy is conserved.

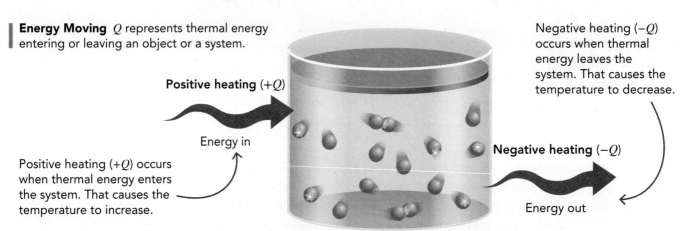

Energy Moving Q represents thermal energy entering or leaving an object or a system.

Positive heating (+Q)

Energy in

Positive heating (+Q) occurs when thermal energy enters the system. That causes the temperature to increase.

Negative heating ($-Q$) occurs when thermal energy leaves the system. That causes the temperature to decrease.

Negative heating (−Q)

Energy out

Temperature Change Energy that raises the temperature of a substance can be the result of thermal energy transferred through heating, Q, or through work being done on the substance. The quantity ΔU represents the amount of both sorts of energy added to increase temperature.

Change in Thermal Energy
$$\Delta U_{th} = mc\Delta T$$
ΔU_{th} = change in thermal energy c = specific heat of substance m = mass of substance ΔT = change in temperature

The amount of energy needed to increase the temperature of 1 kg of a substance by 1°C is the substance's **specific heat,** c. Specific heat is a property of the substance. The table gives the specific heats for a few common substances.

Substance	Specific Heat [J/(kg·°C)]	Substance	Specific Heat [J/(kg·°C)]
Ice	2090	Lead	130
Water	4180	Copper	390
Sand	800	Aluminum	900

Phase Energy Transferring energy through heating can also cause matter to change its state. A change in the state of matter is also called a **phase change.** When a transfer of energy changes the phase of matter, the temperature remains the same. The energy needed to melt or freeze 1 kg of a substance, a phase change between solid and liquid, is referred to as the phase energy of fusion, or **heat of fusion.** The energy needed to vaporize or condense 1 kg of a substance, a phase change between liquid and gas, is the phase energy of vaporization, or **heat of vaporization.**

Heat of Fusion	Heat of Vaporization
$$\Delta U_{int} = \pm mL_f$$	$$\Delta U_{int} = \pm mL_v$$
ΔU_{int} = change in internal energy m = mass of substance L_f = heat of fusion	ΔU_{int} = change in internal energy m = mass of substance L_v = heat of vaporization

It is important to keep track of the sign for phase energy. When energy is added to a substance, in melting or vaporizing, then ΔU_{int} is positive ($+mL$). When energy is taken out of a substance, in freezing or condensing, ΔU_{int} is negative ($-mL$).

Temperature and Phase Change Energy is required to change a substance's temperature and its phase. The temperature and the phase do not change at the same time. The graph shows the energy requirements for the heating and phase changes of water.

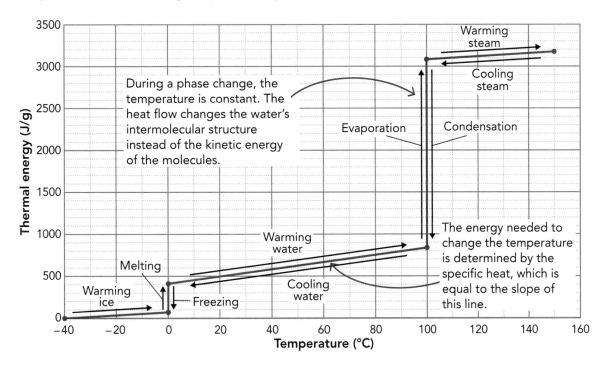

(11) **SEP Analyze Data** How much energy is required to raise the temperature of 75 kg of water from 60°C to 75°C? How much energy is required to raise the temperature of 50 kg of water from 80°C through a phase change and then to steam at 120°C?

The First Law of Thermodynamics

Changing Internal Energy As well as energy transferred through heating, an object can gain energy by having work done on it. Work and heat energy can be combined to express the first law of thermodynamics. The **first law of thermodynamics** states that the change in a system's internal energy is equal to the amount of work done on the system plus the amount of energy transferred into the system through heating.

First Law of Thermodynamics
$$W + Q = \Delta U_{int}$$
W = work done on the system
Q = energy transferred by heating
ΔU_{int} = change in internal energy

Some thermodynamic processes result in changes in the internal energy of a system. Other thermodynamic processes result in no change in the internal energy of the system. However, energy is always conserved in each system.

Staying Cool Refrigerators obey the first law of thermodynamics. Positive work is done on a system so that the thermal energy is moved from a cooler region (inside the refrigerator) to a warmer region (outside the refrigerator) in a cyclic fashion. The change in internal energy for each cycle is zero.

12. **SEP Use Mathematics** Suppose 450 J of work is done on a system and 200 J of thermal energy is transferred out of the system through heating. Determine the change in the internal energy of the system.

Thermodynamic Processes

How do you model the ways that **thermal energy moves** within a system or between systems?

System Changes In a thermodynamic process, thermal energy moves through a system and causes changes in the system's state. There are several types of these processes, resulting from energy transfer or changes in pressure, volume, or temperature. In the cases that follow, the contained gas is the system.

In an **isobaric process,** the **pressure remains constant.** Energy transfer through heating does work and changes the internal energy of the system.

 Energy is transferred into the system through heating, and the expansion of the gas (or increase in volume) causes negative work to be done on the gas. Both of these result in a change in the system's internal energy.

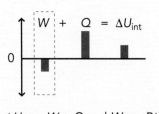

$$\Delta U_{int} = W + Q \text{ and } W = -P\Delta V$$

In an **adiabatic process, no energy enters or leaves** the system through the process of heating. Any energy transferred to the surroundings, such as the piston, is done as work.

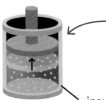 The piston in an insulated cylinder containing a hot, compressed gas is released. V increases, while P and T decrease.

insulation

$$Q = 0, \text{ so } \Delta U_{int} = W$$

In an **isochoric (isovolumetric) process,** the pressure or temperature changes, but the **volume remains constant.**

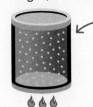 Gas is heated in a sealed, rigid container, so the volume remains constant.

$$\Delta V = 0, \text{ so } W = 0 \text{ and } \Delta U_{int} = Q$$

In an **isothermal process,** the **temperature remains constant,** usually through energy exchange with the system and surroundings.

 When the piston is raised, the gas expands. The gas is maintained at a constant temperature by a water bath.

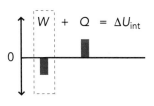

$$\Delta T = 0, \text{ so } \Delta U_{int} = 0 \text{ and } W = -Q$$

13) **CCC Patterns** In the infographic, you may notice that the name of each process relates to holding some physical quantity constant. For each thermodynamic process, qualitatively describe the relationship between the process and the quantity that is constant. Then, describe what distinguishes an adiabatic process from the other processes.

Expansion of an Ideal Gas

A volume of an ideal gas is enclosed in a container with a movable piston. During an isothermal process, 5.00 moles of the gas expands from 0.0200 m^3 to 0.0500 m^3. At the same time, the pressure decreases from 1411 kPa to 564 kPa. Determine the temperatures of the gas during the process.

1. DRAW A PICTURE Sketch a picture of the situation.

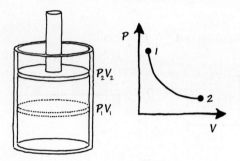

2. DEFINE THE PROBLEM List knowns and unknowns, and assign values to variables.

$n = 5.00$ mol	$T_1 = ?$
$V_1 = 0.0200$ m^3	$T_2 = ?$
$V_2 = 0.0500$ m^3	
$R = 8.31$ J/(K·mol)	
$P_1 = 1411$ kPa $= 1.411 \times 10^6$ Pa	
$P_2 = 564$ kPa $= 5.64 \times 10^5$ Pa	

3. PLAN AND EXECUTE Use mathematical relationships, the picture, and your definitions to plan and execute a solution.

Use the ideal gas law. Rearrange the equation to solve for T.	$P_1 V_1 = nRT_1$ $T_1 = \dfrac{P_1 V_1}{nR}$
Determine the temperature for State 1.	$T_1 = \dfrac{(1.411 \times 10^6 \text{ Pa})(0.0200 \text{ m}^3)}{5.00 \text{ mol}[8.31 \text{ J/(K·mol)}]}$ $= 679$ K
Determine the temperature for State 2.	$T_2 = \dfrac{(5.64 \times 10^5 \text{ Pa})(0.0500 \text{ m}^3)}{5.00 \text{ mol}[8.31 \text{ J/(K·mol)}]}$ $= 679$ K

4. EVALUATE Reflect on your answer.
The answer is appropriate because the initial temperature and the final temperature are the same. The initial and final temperatures should be the same in an isothermal process.

 GO ONLINE for more **math support**.

▶ **Math Tutorial Video**

🖥 **Math Practice Problems**

(14) A volume of an ideal gas is enclosed in a container with a movable piston. During an isothermal process, 3.00 moles of the gas expands from 0.0100 m^3 to 0.0405 m^3. At the same time, the pressure decreases from 850 kPa to 210 kPa. Determine the temperature of the gas during the process.

📖 **NEED A HINT?** Go online to your **eText Sample Problem** for stepped-out support.

(15) A volume of an ideal gas is enclosed in a container with a movable piston. During an isothermal process, 3.00 moles of the gas expands from 0.0200 m^3 to 0.0640 m^3. At the same time, the pressure decreases from 540 kPa to 167 kPa. Determine the temperature of the gas during the process.

(16) A volume of an ideal gas is enclosed in a container with a movable piston. During an isothermal process, 2.00 moles of the gas expands from 0.0300 m^3 to 0.0500 m^3. At the same time, the pressure decreases from 250.0 kPa to 150.0 kPa. Determine the temperature of the gas during the process.

(17) A volume of an ideal gas undergoes an isochoric process as it gains 300 J of energy through heating. Determine the change in internal energy for the gas.

(18) During an isobaric process, a volume of an ideal gas does 220 J of work on the surroundings as it gains 250 J of energy through heating. Determine the change in internal energy for the gas.

(19) During an adiabatic process, the change in internal energy for a volume of an ideal gas is −265 J. Determine the amount of work done by the gas.

(20) During an isothermal process, $W = nRT \ln\left(\frac{V_2}{V_1}\right)$. A group of students compresses 4 moles of an ideal gas in an isothermal process from 2.00 m^3 to 1.00 m^3 at 300.0 K. Determine the amount of thermal energy that must be transferred out of the system when the gas is compressed.

(21) During an isothermal process, $W = nRT \ln\left(\frac{V_2}{V_1}\right)$. A group of students is investigating different piston systems. In each system, a certain amount of an ideal gas is allowed to expand isothermically to do work on a piston. Their data are recorded in the table. In which of the following systems does the gas do the greatest amount of work on the piston?

System	Moles of Gas (mol)	Initial Volume (m³)	Final Volume (m³)	Temperature (K)
1	8	0.15	0.20	273
2	5	0.12	0.24	300
3	10	0.10	0.30	280
4	6	0.10	0.40	320

GO ONLINE to revisit your **Investigative Phenomenon CER** with the new information you have learned about Temperature.

These questions will help you apply what you learned in this experience to the Investigative Phenomenon.

(22) **SEP Use Mathematics** The specific heat of dry sand is approximately 800 J/(kg·°C). Determine the amount of energy required to raise the temperature of 300 kg of sand from 10°C to 32°C.

(23) **SEP Use Mathematics** The specific heat of water is approximately 4180 J/(kg·°C). Determine the amount of energy required to raise the temperature of 300 kg of water from 10°C to 32°C.

(24) **CCC Energy and Matter** Using your understanding of specific heat, explain why the sand on a beach might warm faster than the water.

(25) **SEP Construct an Explanation** Suppose you are swimming in the ocean at the beach. Would you expect the temperature of the water to be warmer or cooler as you get closer to the shore? Explain your answer.

(26) **CCC Systems and System Models** Another way of stating the first law of thermodynamics is that energy is always conserved in a system. Suppose you step barefoot on some hot sand at the beach, and you burn the soles of your feet. Explain how energy is transferred as heat in the system of the sun, the sand, and your feet, and how energy is conserved in the system.

GO ONLINE for a **quiz** to evaluate what you learned about Temperature.

Thermal Equilibrium and Heat Flow

 GO ONLINE to do a **hands-on lab** to investigate heat transfer between different metals and water.

Thermal Equilibrium

When a hot object and a cold object are in contact, energy moves from the hot object to the cold object until their temperatures are equal. You can think about the process using a microscopic approach. As the particles of a warm tabletop and cold ice cream collide, the average kinetic energies of all the particles eventually become the same, so the temperatures become the same. The ice cream melts, and the tabletop grows cooler. The state of equal average kinetic energies and equal temperatures for objects is called **thermal equilibrium.**

A Model for Thermal Equilibrium When the two boxes come in contact, energy from the warmer gas is transferred to the cooler gas until they both reach the same temperature.

High temperature

Low temperature

The gases in each box are at two different temperatures. The gas in the left box is at a higher temperature than the gas in the box on the right. No energy flows between the boxes because they are not in contact.

 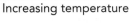
Decreasing temperature   Increasing temperature

When the boxes come into contact, energy from the gas in the box on the left is transferred to the gas in the box on the right because the gas in the box on the left is at a higher temperature.

Equilibrium

After some time, both gases reach the same temperature. Thermal equilibrium is reached when there is no net flow of energy between the boxes.

 SEP Construct an Explanation Explain what happens when a cold object and a hot object are in contact. Explain using both macroscopic and microscopic approaches.

Energy Transfer Through Heating

When thermal energy is transferred from one object to another, the process is known as heating. There are three different mechanisms by which energy is transferred through heating: radiation, conduction, and convection.

Radiation The process by which an object transfers heat to another object through electromagnetic waves is called **radiation.** All objects transfer energy to and from their surroundings through radiation. The hotter the object, the greater the rate of radiation is. When an object is in thermal equilibrium with its surroundings, it radiates energy and absorbs energy at the same rate, so its temperature remains constant.

Conduction When a solid object is placed in contact with a heat source, atoms and electrons in the object absorb the energy. Atoms near the surface heat first, and they then transfer their energy of vibration throughout the material. The mechanism that transfers energy through direct physical contact is called **conduction.** A material that resists changes in temperature is called a **thermal insulator.** In insulators, molecules are bonded tightly, and the energy of vibration propagates only through the bonds. When electrons in a material can move freely, they collide more often, increasing the rate of temperature change. A material that does not resist changes in temperature is called a **thermal conductor.**

28 **SEP Construct an Explanation** Suppose you lock your car on a sunny day with a chocolate bar inside it. No objects enter or leave the car, yet an hour later, the chocolate bar has melted. Explain why it melted.

Convection The mechanism by which heat is transferred through fluid flow is **convection.** When a fluid, which can be a liquid or a gas, comes in contact with an object that is at a higher temperature, the temperature increases in the part of the fluid that is in direct contact with the warmer object.

Natural convection is a process in which fluids rise or sink because their density decreases as their temperature increases. The increase in temperature in that part of the fluid causes it to expand, making it less dense. The less dense fluid rises up. The denser, cooler fluid surrounding it flows in to take its place. The convection currents of solid rock inside Earth are examples of natural convection. **Forced convection** is a process in which fluids at different temperatures are made to flow past each other so that the thermal energy of the warmer fluid is transferred to the cooler fluid. Air conditioners are examples of systems that use forced convection.

Energy Transfer During a process, energy can be transferred through more than one heating mechanism. As a saucepan heats up, energy is being transferred through all three mechanisms for heating.

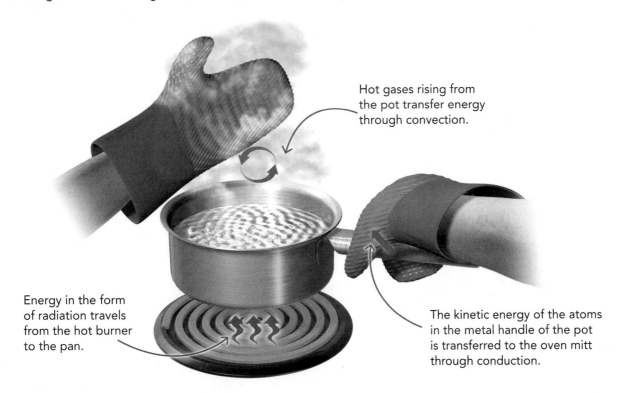

Hot gases rising from the pot transfer energy through convection.

Energy in the form of radiation travels from the hot burner to the pan.

The kinetic energy of the atoms in the metal handle of the pot is transferred to the oven mitt through conduction.

29. **CCC Energy and Matter** Even if you do not exercise on a hot day, you may get warm if you stand in direct sunlight. Which mechanism(s) of heating transfer(s) energy to your body? Explain your reasoning.

30. **SEP Argue from Evidence** If there is no physical contact between a hot object and a cold object, then which mechanism(s) of energy transfer cannot operate? Use your understanding of heating mechanisms to support your answer.

The Second Law of Thermodynamics

Entropy Systems naturally become more disordered over time. They do not naturally become more ordered. The amount of disorder in a system is called **entropy**, represented with the letter S. Different states of matter have different levels of order, with solids having the most order. A system's level of disorder is inversely proportional to its temperature, T, as order tends to zero as temperature increases. Heat, Q, can cause a phase transition, which results in less order in the system. The change in entropy for a system can be described by the equation $\Delta S = \frac{\Delta Q}{T}$ for a constant T.

Order and Disorder A drop of ink in water starts off ordered; all of the ink is in one location. As the ink particles move in all directions, the system becomes more disordered. The ink will not naturally go back to being more ordered.

The first law of thermodynamics states that energy is conserved within a system. The **second law of thermodynamics** states that the net change in entropy of a system and its surroundings must always be greater than or equal to zero. In other words, $\Delta S \geq 0$ for an isolated system.

Entropy and Probability There is a certain probability for each arrangement of coins. The more disordered the arrangement, the greater the probability it will occur and the greater the entropy it has.

| High probability
High entropy | Moderate probability
Lower entropy | Low probability
Low entropy |

(H, H, T, T)
(H, T, H, T)
(H, T, T, H)
(T, H, H, T)
(T, H, T, H)
(T, T, H, H)

(H, H, H, T)
(H, H, T, H)
(H, T, H, H)
(T, H, H, H)

There are six ways to get two heads (H) and two tails (T). Thus, 2H 2T has a high probability of occurring and high entropy.

There are four ways to get three heads and one tail, so 3H 1T has a lower entropy than 2H 2T.

There is only one way to get four heads. Thus, 4H is the most ordered. It has the least probability of occurring and the lowest entropy.

 SEP Construct an Explanation Two dice are rolled at the same time. Which arrangement has greater entropy, rolling a sum of 7 or 12? Support your answer with your understanding of entropy.

GO ONLINE to do a PhET **simulation** to explore heat flow and to watch a **video** about heat flow and conduction.

Heat Flow The second law of thermodynamics governs how heat flows. In an isolated system, thermal energy always flows from a warmer region to a cooler region. When the temperature of a system is lower than that of its surroundings, energy is transferred from the surroundings to the system. When the temperature of a system is higher than that of its surroundings, thermal energy is transferred from the system to the surroundings.

If a warm object is placed in contact with an object at a lower temperature, then the warm object transfers energy to the cool object until the two objects reach thermal equilibrium. That is another way of stating the second law of thermodynamics.

| **Heat Flow and Entropy** Heat is transferred from the warmer region to the cooler region. Energy is conserved, but there is a net increase in entropy.

EXPERIENCE IT!

Put one cup of hot water and one cup of cold water on a table. Label each cup and do not place the cups next to each other. After 10 minutes, dip a finger in each cup and record your observations about the water temperature. What explains the change in temperature of the water in each cup?

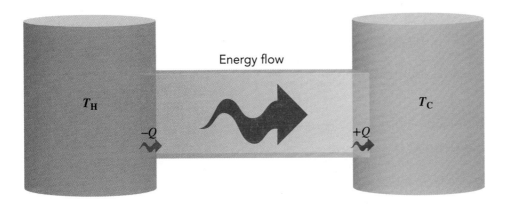
Energy flow

T_H $-Q$ $+Q$ T_C

Suppose that heat flows from a hot reservoir at 350 K to a cold reservoir at 250 K. By the first law of thermodynamics, the energy lost by the hot reservoir is equal to the energy gained by the cold reservoir: $|-Q| = |+Q|$. However, the changes in entropy are not equal. Assuming both regions maintain a constant temperature, then $\Delta S_H = \frac{-Q}{350 \text{ K}}$ and $\Delta S_C = \frac{+Q}{250 \text{ K}}$. The positive change in entropy for the cold reservoir is a fraction with a smaller denominator, so it has a greater magnitude than the negative change in entropy of the hot reservoir. The natural flow of heat therefore increases overall entropy. This confirms the second law of thermodynamics that states $\Delta S \geq 0$ for an isolated system.

(32) **SEP Develop a Model** Using a system of ice cubes in a glass, develop a model that explains what is happening in the system at the particle level. Write an explanation of why the entropy is higher when the ice is melted and the water is in liquid form.

(33) **CCC Energy and Matter** Two objects are placed in contact with each other. Object A has a temperature of 273 K, and Object B has a temperature of 298 K. The two objects remain in contact until they have reached thermal equilibrium. Use your understanding of the second law of thermodynamics to explain how energy is transferred between the two objects.

Thermodynamic Heat Engines

A thermodynamic heat engine, or simply a **heat engine,** is an engine that uses thermal energy to do mechanical work. Many heat engines operate by means of an expanding fluid, such as a gas. When the gas is warmed, it expands and does work on the surroundings, often by pushing a piston. After the gas has expanded and done work on the surroundings, the gas must be brought back to a lower temperature so that it can be warmed again. Then, the cycle repeats itself.

Understanding Heat Engines
How does a **heat engine function?**

Energy and Heat Flow A heat engine uses energy transfer in the form of **heat to do work.** The first and second laws of thermodynamics describe the **conservation of energy** and the **direction of heat flow** in the system.

As described by the second law of thermodynamics, a hot source, T_H, heats a substance, usually a gas, that then **flows through the engine.**

The heated substance in the engine **does work** on the surroundings.

The heat engine **loses some thermal energy** to the surroundings as heat flows from inside the engine to a cold source, T_C.

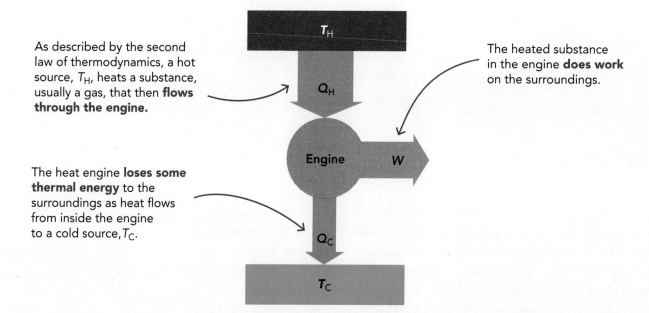

According to the first law of thermodynamics, **energy must be conserved in the engine.** Therefore, the energy used to do work and the thermal energy lost to the surroundings **must equal** the thermal energy added to the engine by the hot reservoir, $|W + Q_C| = Q_H$.

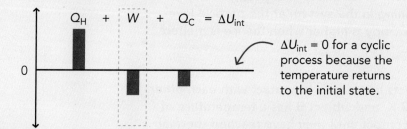

$$Q_H + W + Q_C = \Delta U_{int}$$

$\Delta U_{int} = 0$ for a cyclic process because the temperature returns to the initial state.

In a gas-powered vehicle, fuel is placed inside the engine and ignited. The burning fuel is the hot source, and the surroundings are the cold source.

Carnot's Principle Heat engines need fuel. However, the fuel itself cannot directly do work. The fuel is used to warm the fluid in the engine, and the fluid does work on a piston.

When fuel transfers thermal energy to the fluid, only a fraction of that energy is used to do work. Some of the energy is exhausted into a cold reservoir. There is a theoretical limit on how much of the thermal energy can be converted to work, which is Carnot's principle. In the real world, engines never reach that theoretical limit.

Carnot's principle is another way of understanding the second law of thermodynamics. Not all of the thermal energy that flows through a heat engine can be used to do work. As a system increases in entropy, the amount of work it can do on the surroundings or other systems decreases.

How Steam Engines Work A steam engine is a type of heat engine that uses steam to do work. Hot steam supplied by a boiler expands within the engine and does work on a piston.

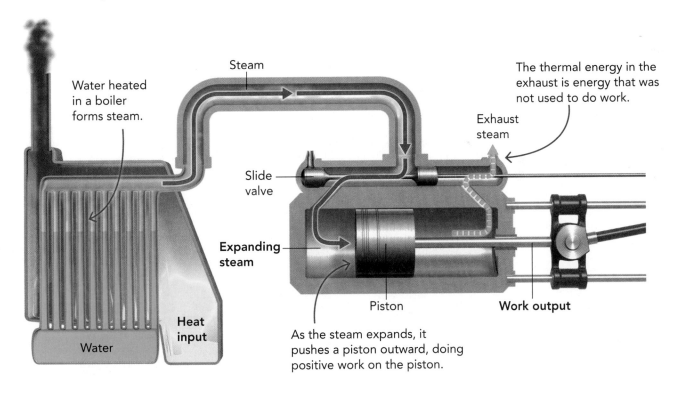

Steam

Water heated in a boiler forms steam.

The thermal energy in the exhaust is energy that was not used to do work.

Exhaust steam

Slide valve

Expanding steam

Piston

Work output

Heat input

Water

As the steam expands, it pushes a piston outward, doing positive work on the piston.

(34) **SEP Use Mathematics** A heat engine uses 300 J of thermal energy to do work. Determine if it is possible to do 250 J of work and exhaust 50 J of thermal energy to a cold reservoir. Support your answer with your understanding of heat engines.

(35) **SEP Construct an Explanation** The net change in internal energy for a heat engine is always equal to zero. Use your understanding of heat engines, temperature, and internal energy to explain why that is true.

Thermodynamic Cycles

Carnot Cycle A **Carnot cycle** is a theoretical or idealized model of a heat engine cycle, consisting of four thermodynamic processes: two isothermal processes and two adiabatic processes. The first part of the cycle is isothermal expansion, during which the gas expands, while the temperature is held constant and heat is absorbed by the system. The heat is used to do work on the surroundings. Because the temperature is constant, there is no change in internal energy. Thus, the magnitude of the heat absorbed is equal to the amount of work done on the surroundings.

The second part of the cycle is adiabatic expansion. There is no heat added to or entering the system because the system is insulated. The gas continues to expand, doing work on the surroundings. Positive work is done by the system, and negative work is done on the system. The negative work done on the system is equal to the change in internal energy of the system. During the adiabatic expansion, the temperature of the gas decreases.

Following isothermal and adiabatic expansion, the third part of the cycle is isothermal compression, during which the gas transfers energy to a cold reservoir. The fourth part of the cycle is adiabatic compression, which returns the gas to its original volume, pressure, and temperature.

A Carnot Engine In a Carnot engine, an ideal gas is enclosed in a cylinder with a piston.

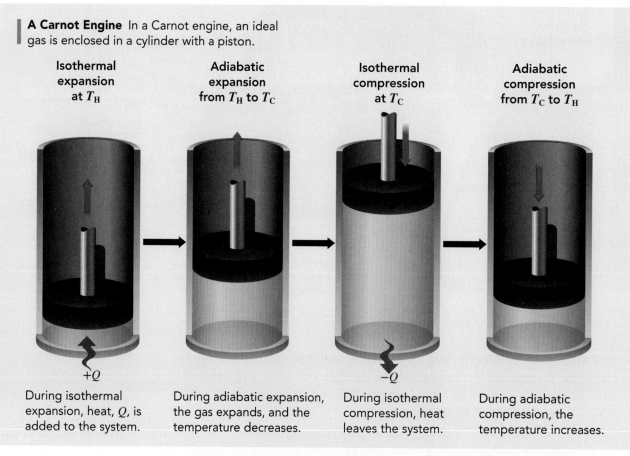

| Isothermal expansion at T_H | Adiabatic expansion from T_H to T_C | Isothermal compression at T_C | Adiabatic compression from T_C to T_H |

$+Q$ $-Q$

During isothermal expansion, heat, Q, is added to the system.

During adiabatic expansion, the gas expands, and the temperature decreases.

During isothermal compression, heat leaves the system.

During adiabatic compression, the temperature increases.

36 **SEP Develop Models** Construct an energy bar chart for each of the four thermodynamic processes in a Carnot cycle. Consider the relative amount and direction of flow for any heat entering or leaving the system, work being done on the system, and the change in internal energy of the system.

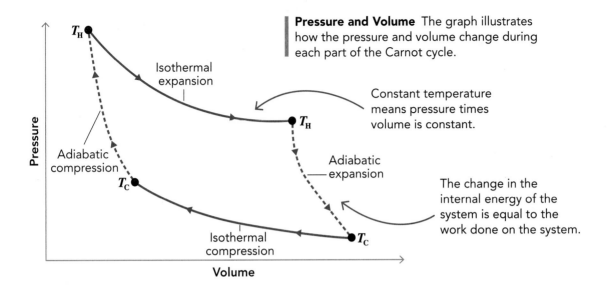

Pressure and Volume The graph illustrates how the pressure and volume change during each part of the Carnot cycle.

Constant temperature means pressure times volume is constant.

The change in the internal energy of the system is equal to the work done on the system.

Calculating Efficiency The goal of a heat engine is to use thermal energy to do work. Thus, the efficiency of the heat engine is determined by how much work the engine can do with a given amount of thermal energy absorbed. The first law of thermodynamics dictates that the efficiency cannot be greater than 1. Efficiency is often expressed as a percentage, which involves multiplying the ratio by 100.

Heat Engine Efficiency
$$e = \left| \frac{W}{Q_H} \right|$$

e = efficiency of engine Q_H = thermal energy
W = work done by system   absorbed by system

Increasing Efficiency Heat engines have many important applications, including propelling cars and generating electricity, so it is important that they be as efficient as possible. From the second law of thermodynamics, the change in entropy of the hot and cold sources can be expressed as $S = \frac{Q_H}{T_H} + \frac{Q_C}{T_C} \geq 0$. In other words, $Q_C \geq \frac{T_H}{T_C} Q_H$. Because a heat engine is a cyclical process, $Q_H + W + Q_C = 0$. Putting that all together in the heat engine efficiency equation, the maximum possible efficiency depends on the ratio $(T_H - T_C) : T_H$. Therefore, one way to increase the efficiency is to raise the temperature of the hot reservoir. That can be done by using a fuel that burns at a higher temperature. For example, diesel fuel burns hotter than gasoline, so diesel engines are more efficient. A second method is to make the cold reservoir colder. That can be done by improving the cooling system.

(37) SEP Use Mathematics Determine the efficiency of a heat engine that absorbs 250 J of energy and exhausts 75 J of energy.

(38) CCC Systems and System Models Using your understanding of the first law of thermodynamics, explain why the efficiency of a heat engine cannot be greater than 1.

Heat Pumps

A **heat pump** is a device that moves heat from a cooler region to a warmer region. It is the reverse of a thermodynamic heat engine. A familiar example is an air conditioner. Instead of the system absorbing thermal energy to do work, positive work is done on the system to move thermal energy. The substance that flows through the system of the heat pump is called the **refrigerant.** Work is done on the refrigerant, and it is the refrigerant that transfers the thermal energy from the cooler region to the warmer region.

Energy Flow You know from the second law of thermodynamics that thermal energy does not naturally flow from cooler regions to warmer regions. Therefore, work has to be done on the system by a motor outside of the system. Because heat pumps, like heat engines, are cyclic, the change in internal energy for a full cycle of the system is 0. Heat pumps can be used to warm houses as well as to cool them. In that case, thermal energy from the cool outdoors is pumped into the warmer house. The result is that the house becomes warmer.

Energy Flow for a Heat Pump
$$Q_C + W = Q_H$$
Q_C = thermal energy removed from cold reservoir W = work done on the system Q_H = thermal energy added to hot reservoir

Heat Engines vs. Heat Pumps Both heat engines and heat pumps go through thermodynamic cycles that include thermal energy being transferred and work being done.

In a heat engine, thermal energy flows from a warm reservoir to a cold reservoir, and some of the energy is used to do work.

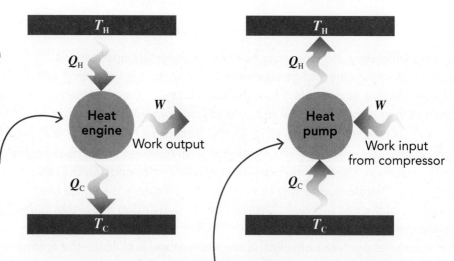

In a heat pump, thermal energy is taken away from a cool region and moved to a warmer region, allowing the cooler region to remain cool. Thus, a refrigerator can remain cool and an air conditioner can keep the air cool.

(39) **CCC Energy and Matter** Suppose a refrigerator removes 3050 J of thermal energy from inside the refrigerator to the refrigerant and then carries 4020 J of thermal energy outside of the refrigerator. Determine the amount of work done on the refrigerant.

Efficiency The goal of a heat pump is to transfer thermal energy to a warmer region. That process is possible because work is being done on the system. You can measure the efficiency of a thermodynamic heat pump by determining how much thermal energy is transferred to the hot reservoir when a given amount of work is done on the system.

Performance Coefficient

$$K = \left| \frac{Q_H}{W} \right|$$

K = thermal performance coefficient
Q_H = thermal energy added to hot reservoir
W = work done on the system

The performance coefficient is always greater than 1. There is a theoretical limit to how much thermal energy can be transferred to the hot reservoir given the amount of work done on the system. Note that the performance coefficient for a heat pump is the inverse of the equation for heat engine efficiency.

Maximum Performance Coefficient

$$K_{max} = \frac{T_H}{(T_H - T_C)}$$

K_{max} = maximum performance coefficient
T_H = temperature of hot reservoir
T_C = temperature of cold reservoir

How Efficiently Heat Pumps Perform The performance coefficient is a measure of how efficiently a heat pump performs. The amount of thermal energy being transferred to the warmer region should be greater than the amount of work being done on the system.

Thermal energy is removed from a cooler region and added to a working substance, the refrigerant. Thus, Q_C is positive.

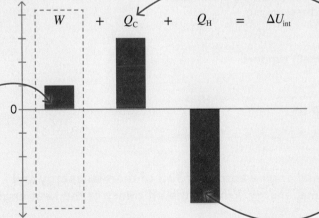

Work must be done on the system in order to transfer thermal energy from a cooler region to a warmer region. Positive work done on the system is always positive on a bar chart.

The thermal energy is then transferred to a warmer region and is denoted by Q_H. Because it is leaving the system, it is negative on the bar chart.

40 **SEP Use Mathematics** A heat pump is used to warm a house. 10,700 J of thermal energy from outside of the house is pumped into the house, and 1550 J of work is done on a substance in a compressor to make that possible. What is the performance coefficient for the heat pump?

Heat Engine Efficiency

During one cycle, the diesel engine of a lawn tractor absorbs 310 J of thermal energy and exhausts 220 J of thermal energy. What is the efficiency of the heat engine?

1. DRAW A PICTURE Sketch a picture of the situation.

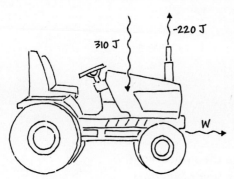

310 J   -220 J   W

2. DEFINE THE PROBLEM List knowns and unknowns, and assign values to variables.

$$Q_H = 310\text{ J} \qquad W = ?$$
$$Q_C = -220\text{ J} \qquad e = ?$$

3. PLAN AND EXECUTE Use mathematical relationships, the picture, and your definitions to plan and execute a solution.

Use the equation for energy flow in a heat engine to determine the amount of work that is done by the engine.	$\Delta U_{int} = Q_H + W + Q_C = 0$ $W = -Q_H - Q_C$ $W = -310\text{ J} - (-220\text{ J})$ $W = -90\text{ J}$
Use the equation for the efficiency of a heat engine to calculate the efficiency.	$e = \left\| \dfrac{W}{Q_H} \right\| = \left\| \dfrac{-90\text{ J}}{310\text{ J}} \right\| = 0.29$
Express the efficiency as a percentage by multiplying by one hundred.	$e = 0.29 \times 100 = 29\%$

4. EVALUATE Reflect on your answer.
The value for the efficiency is 29%, which is a reasonable answer for the efficiency of a diesel engine.

 GO ONLINE for more **math support**.

▶ **Math Tutorial Video**

🖥 **Math Practice Problems**

---

41 During one cycle, a diesel engine absorbs 730 J of thermal energy and exhausts 480 J of thermal energy. What is the efficiency of the heat engine?

📖 **NEED A HINT?** Go online to your **eText Sample Problem** for stepped-out support.

42 During one cycle, a diesel engine exhausts 460 J of thermal energy. The engine has an efficiency of 40%. How much thermal energy is absorbed during one cycle?

INVESTIGATIVE PHENOMENON

GO ONLINE to revisit your **Investigative Phenomenon CER** with the new information you have learned about Thermal Equilibrium and Heat Flow.

These questions will help you apply what you learned in this experience to the Investigative Phenomenon.

(43) **SEP Construct an Explanation** Suppose you place a cup of ice water in the hot sand at the beach. Explain why there is a net increase in entropy when heat is transferred from the hot sand to the ice water.

(44) **CCC Energy and Matter** Explain the mechanism by which energy is transferred through heating in each of the following situations: (1) the sand gets hot on a sunny day at the beach and (2) cooler air moving over the ocean water rises up as it reaches the warmer land on the shore.

(45) **SEP Design a Solution** Apply what you have learned about heat flow and thermal equilibrium to design a possible solution for cooling the sand during a hot day at the beach.

(46) **SEP Construct an Explanation** Apply the second law of thermodynamics and what you have learned about entropy to explain why wet sand at the shoreline is cooler than the dry sand on the beach farther away from the shore.

GO ONLINE for a **quiz** to evaluate what you learned about Thermal Equilibrium and Heat Flow.

EXPERIENCE 3

Heat Flow Within Earth

GO ONLINE to do a **hands-on lab** to investigate the roles of convection, conduction, and radiation at Earth's surface and interior.

Heat Flow at Earth's Surface

Global Heat Flow Early in its history, Earth was mostly or entirely molten. Over time, Earth's temperature has dropped, and the rock of the crust and mantle has mostly solidified. Earth continues to cool, with heat escaping into space at a rate of 47 TW (terawatts, or trillions of joules per second). That may seem like a tremendous amount, as it is more than twice the power that humans use (20 TW). However, it is only a fraction of the power in the sunlight that reaches Earth's surface (125,000 TW). The energy in sunlight is much greater, but it affects only Earth's surface geologic processes. It is the 47 TW of internal heat flow that drives the dynamics of Earth's interior. Earth's interior geologic processes include mantle convection, plate tectonics, earthquakes, volcanoes, and the generation of Earth's magnetic field.

Regional Variations in Heat Loss A map of the rate of outward heat flow at Earth's surface shows large variations that reflect Earth's regional geology. Earth's average heat flow is very low—less than 0.1 W/m².

Heat flow is highest where there are many volcanoes, both at mid-ocean ridges and at subduction zones.

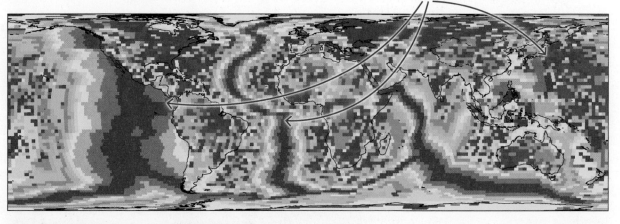

Heat flow (mW/m²) (Area-weighted mean)

| 3–51 | 52–60 | 61–62 | 63–65 | 66–68 | 69–72 | 73–77 | 78–94 | 95–131 | 132–1,237 |

Source: Davies, J. H. (2013)

(47) **SEP Use Mathematics** Using Earth's radius of 6371 km and the total outward heat flow of 47 TW, show that the average heat flow per area at Earth's surface is 0.092 W/m².

Volcanoes and Plate Boundaries Most above-ground volcanoes are found at subduction zones, a result of water carried down within the ocean seafloor. More volcanism, however, occurs underwater along the interconnected mid-ocean spreading ridges.

Volcanoes not located at plate boundaries, such as at Hawaii, are usually found above hotspot mantle plumes, where hot rock rises toward the surface from very deep in the mantle.

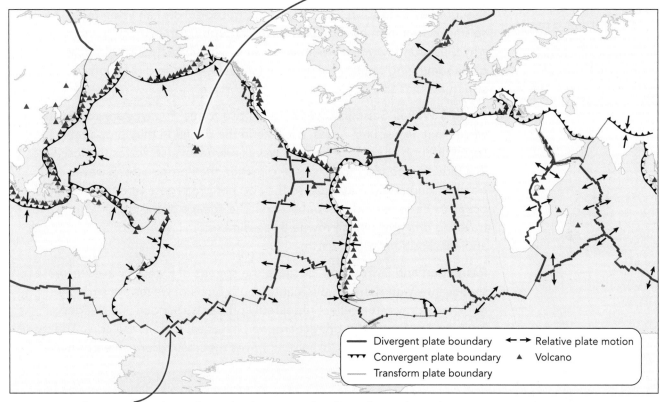

Divergent plate boundary — ← → Relative plate motion
Convergent plate boundary — ▲ Volcano
Transform plate boundary

Mid-ocean spreading ridges, the divergent plate boundaries shown here, consist of 70,000 km of nearly continuous connected volcanism. Hot rock is constantly rising toward the surface to fill the gaps made by the spreading plates.

Heat Flow and Plate Tectonics Heat flow is greatest at mid-ocean ridges because that is where hot rock rises within the mantle to take the place of spreading ocean lithosphere. The ocean plates cool as they move away from the ridge in both directions, and the cooling can be seen in the gradually decreasing heat flow rates. Heat flow is least in the oldest and therefore coldest regions of the ocean sea floor. Old ocean floor is often found adjacent to continents, such as on either side of the Atlantic Ocean. When the ocean floor eventually sinks into the mantle at subduction zones, large volcanoes erupt, bringing magma to the surface. As a result, heat flow rates at subduction zones are great as well.

Surprisingly, continental rock has greater heat flow rates than old ocean crust, even though it is usually older by billions of years. That is because continental crust contains higher amounts than the ocean crust does of the long-lived radioactive isotopes potassium-40, thorium-232, uranium-235, and uranium-238, so it generates more of its own heat.

48 **SEP Use Models** Study the bands of high rates of heat flow in the eastern part of the Pacific Ocean, which parallel the East Pacific Rise. Note that they are wider than the bands of high rates of heat flow along the Mid-Atlantic Ridge. Explain what that pattern suggests about the relative spreading rates in the East Pacific and Mid-Atlantic Ocean Basins.

Probing Earth's Interior

EXPERIENCE IT!

Tie one end of a spring toy to a chair. Stand back to stretch the spring. How can you move the toy to make P waves? How can you move it to make S waves?

Understanding how and why Earth's heat flows to the surface requires looking into the planet, but of course, light doesn't go through rock. However, even though they cannot see into the planet, geoscientists can listen to it. The seismic waves from earthquakes travel through Earth in much the same way that sound waves travel through air or water. Analyzing seismic waves gives something similar to a medical CT scan—a three-dimensional image of structures that cannot be seen from the surface.

P and S Waves Seismic waves come in two forms. P waves are compression waves that, like sound waves, oscillate in the direction they propagate. They travel through all parts of Earth. S waves are transverse waves that oscillate in a direction perpendicular to the direction they propagate. S waves only travel through rigid materials, so they do not propagate through the liquid ocean or Earth's liquid iron outer core. The speeds and amplitudes of waves traveling different paths provide three-dimensional profiles of temperatures and compositions within Earth.

Refraction and Diffraction Because the speeds of P and S waves increase significantly with depth in the mantle, both types of waves are strongly refracted. They often reflect repeatedly off Earth's surface and deeper boundaries. Waves also diffract around obstacles, such as the core. The result is a very complex pattern of seismic waves that result from an earthquake.

Seismic Wave Propagation The locations of seismic P and S waves within Earth are modeled for three time points following the occurrence of a deep earthquake. The speed, amplitude, and patterns of refraction of the seismic waves are used to determine three-dimensional variations in Earth's temperature and composition.

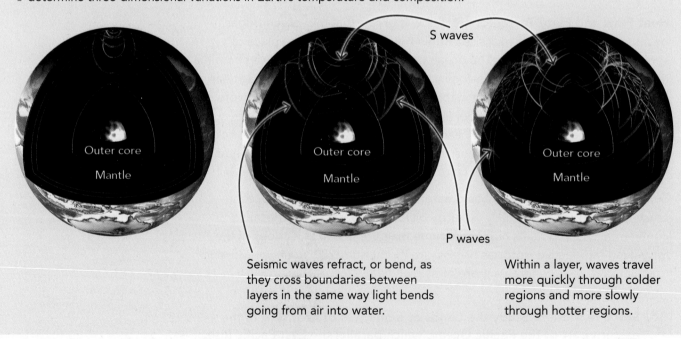

Seismic waves refract, or bend, as they cross boundaries between layers in the same way light bends going from air into water.

Within a layer, waves travel more quickly through colder regions and more slowly through hotter regions.

(49) **SEP Use Models** Are P waves faster or slower in the core than in the lower mantle? Use evidence from the images to explain your answer.

Earth's Composition

Seismic waves are not the only source of information about the temperature and composition of Earth's interior. Geoscientists also study surface maps of Earth's gravitational and magnetic fields. In laboratories, they heat and squeeze small samples of rock to replicate conditions deep within Earth.

About 95 percent of the variation in Earth's composition depends on depth below the surface. That is because gravity pulls the heaviest materials, metals, to the center of the planet. If you shook a jar of iron filings, sand, and water and let it settle, then you would end up with three layers. Iron would be at the bottom, and water at the top. Those three layers are a simple model of Earth.

The remaining 5 percent of the variation in Earth's composition depends on horizontal changes in the composition of the mantle and crust. Those slight variations are the product of mantle convection and the resulting plate tectonics. The variations show scientists where dense rock is sinking and hot rock is rising—both mostly the result of large variations in temperature.

Density vs. Depth in Earth's Interior Nearly all of Earth's variation in chemical composition depends on depth, determined by the effects of gravity on different densities. At greater depths, higher pressures cause the atoms of minerals to rearrange into more densely packed structures.

The thin crust overlies a mantle with four layers that vary both in composition and in mineral phase.

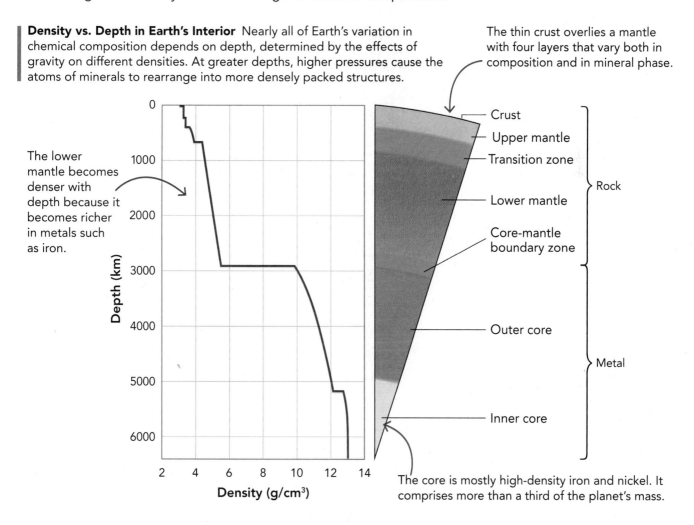

The lower mantle becomes denser with depth because it becomes richer in metals such as iron.

The core is mostly high-density iron and nickel. It comprises more than a third of the planet's mass.

(50) **SEP Analyze and Interpret Data** The difference in density at the boundary between bedrock and air is about 2.8 g/cm³. Describe how the density difference at the boundary between Earth's core and mantle compares to the surface difference of 2.8 g/cm³.

Earth's Temperature and Heat

Heat Flow Another layered profile is found in Earth's temperature variations. Temperature affects viscosity, the resistance to flow, and therefore affects material behavior. Earth's rocky part forms four layers, based on how stiff they are. The cold outer **lithosphere** is mostly rigid, and it forms the tectonic plates that move about Earth's surface. The lithosphere overlies the **asthenosphere,** a weaker layer of rock that is close to its melting temperature and allows the lithosphere to slide over it. The deeper **mesosphere** is a layer that is hotter still, but high pressure makes it stiffer than the lithosphere. The **core-mantle boundary zone,** the layer of rock that comprises the bottom of Earth's mantle, is heated by the core and is weaker and more fluid than the mesosphere.

Earth's core was entirely molten for most of its history. Starting about one billion years ago, a small solid inner core began to grow as Earth's overall temperature decreased. About 15 percent of the core is a mixture of lighter elements. Those elements remain liquid as the iron and nickel continue to freeze out to grow the solid inner core, adding to the density difference between the inner core and outer core.

Understanding Earth's Thermal Structure

How are Earth's **heat and structure related?**

Heat Inside Earth As with chemical composition and density, **Earth's temperature depends mostly on depth.** The large difference between the center temperature of about 5000°C and the surface temperature of about 15°C means that **a large amount of heat flows outward.**

Heat flows by **conduction** into and out of the mantle. Within the mantle, heat flows primarily by **convection.**

Because of the high thermal conductivity of iron, heat flows within the core primarily by **conduction.** The liquid outer core also undergoes **convection.**

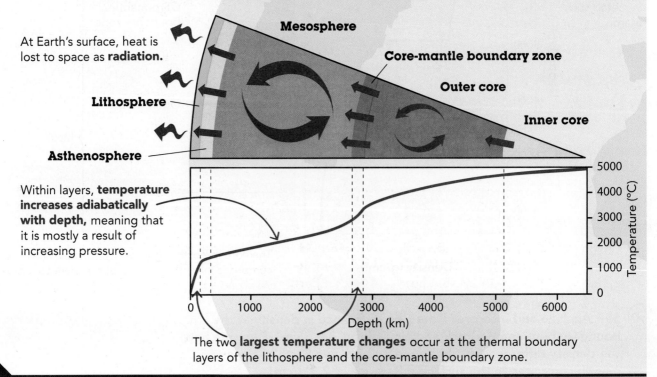

At Earth's surface, heat is lost to space as **radiation.**

Mesosphere

Core-mantle boundary zone

Outer core

Lithosphere

Inner core

Asthenosphere

Within layers, **temperature increases adiabatically with depth,** meaning that it is mostly a result of increasing pressure.

The two **largest temperature changes** occur at the thermal boundary layers of the lithosphere and the core-mantle boundary zone.

GO ONLINE to watch a **video** about heat flow through Earth.

Sources of Energy At about 5300 K, the temperature at Earth's core is almost the same as the temperature of the surface of the sun. Roughly half of the thermal energy producing that temperature is a result of adiabatic compression. As you just saw, when you compress matter, its temperature goes up. If you could somehow instantaneously release the pressure on a bit of Earth's solid core, it would expand, and its temperature would drop by about half.

The other half of Earth's thermal energy is a product of the planet's formation. From many sorts of evidence, geoscientists have concluded that Earth formed through the accretion of many colliding planetary objects. All of the kinetic energy of those impacts ended up as thermal energy. Some of the atoms that formed Earth were highly radioactive, and they provided another source of heat for Earth early in its history. Since then, Earth has cooled, but it is still heated internally by the slow radioactive decay of long-lived isotopes.

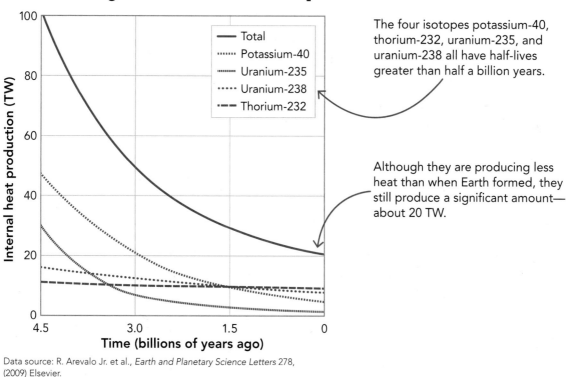

Heating Earth with Radioactivity

Internal heat production (TW) vs. Time (billions of years ago)

Legend:
— Total
⋯⋯ Potassium-40
▬▬ Uranium-235
⋯⋯ Uranium-238
▪–▪ Thorium-232

The four isotopes potassium-40, thorium-232, uranium-235, and uranium-238 all have half-lives greater than half a billion years.

Although they are producing less heat than when Earth formed, they still produce a significant amount—about 20 TW.

Data source: R. Arevalo Jr. et al., *Earth and Planetary Science Letters 278,* (2009) Elsevier.

(51) **CCC Energy and Matter** As the graph shows, only 20 TW of Earth's heat loss can be explained by radiogenic heat produced today. How can it be that much more than 20 TW of Earth's current heat loss comes from radioactivity? (Remember that heat flow within Earth is very slow.)

(52) **SEP Interpret Data** Identify which isotope provided the most heat 4.5 billion years ago and which provides the most heat today. Explain which one has the slower rate of radioactive decay.

Heat Conduction and Melting

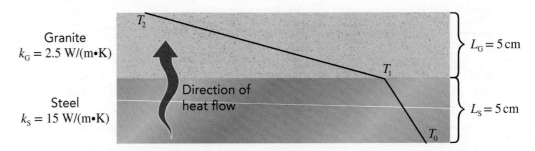

GO ONLINE to do a PhET **simulation** that allows you to explore the heat flow through different materials.

Within most of Earth (the mantle and outer core), heat moves mostly through convection because that is the most efficient way. However, for heat flowing from the core into the mantle, heat flows by conduction. Rocks have low thermal conductivities, and the result is a bottleneck for heat flow. The temperature changes rapidly with depth, so thermal gradients become very steep. The regions of rapid temperature change, called **thermal boundary layers,** occur at the boundaries at the top and bottom of Earth's mantle. At the bottom, heat conducts in from the core. At the top, heat conducts out across the lithosphere. Across the lithosphere, the surface thermal boundary layer, temperature increases rapidly with depth. In places where the ground is unusually hot, such as near volcanoes, this steep temperature gradient makes it possible to harness geothermal energy. Water pumped deep into the ground absorbs enough heat to be used to generate electricity. The steeper the temperature gradient, the greater rate of thermal energy transfer.

Heat Flux The rate of thermal energy transfer via conduction in a given area is called **heat flux** and has units of W/m². The greater the difference in temperature between two cross-sectional areas, the greater the heat flux due to conduction between those two areas.

Rate of Heat Conduction

$$\phi = \frac{Q}{A} = -k\frac{\Delta T}{L}$$

ϕ = heat flux
Q = energy transferred by heating
A = cross-sectional area

k = thermal conductivity constant
ΔT = difference in temperature
L = thickness of material

Heat Conduction Through Stone and Metal In this example, the amount of heat flowing out of the metal and into the granite must be the same. Because the layer thicknesses are the same, the change in temperature must be inversely proportional to the conductivity. This shows why the temperature difference is so great across layers of low conductivity, such as the base of Earth's mantle.

Granite
$k_G = 2.5$ W/(m•K)

T_2

Direction of heat flow

T_1

$L_G = 5$ cm

Steel
$k_S = 15$ W/(m•K)

T_0

$L_S = 5$ cm

(53) **SEP Use Mathematics** If the ΔT across the steel is 2.0°C, what is the ΔT across the granite? Explain, using conservation of energy, why the diagram is a good model for heat flow across the core-mantle boundary.

Geotherm and Solidus The variation with depth of Earth's temperature is called the **geotherm.** The variation with depth of the minimum temperature at which rock melts is called the **solidus.** If at any depth the geotherm temperature equals or exceeds the solidus temperature, the rock will begin to melt there. At most places on Earth, the mantle geotherm temperature is less than the solidus temperature, which means no melting occurs, and no volcanoes form. However, in three types of locations, mid-ocean ridges, hotspots, and subduction zones, melting occurs and volcanoes form.

> **The Causes of Melting, Magma, and Volcanoes** Magma, liquid rock, forms wherever Earth's temperature is greater than the melting point of rock, which means the geotherm is greater than the solidus. Because magma is less dense than solid rock, it moves toward the surface as soon as it forms, producing volcanoes.

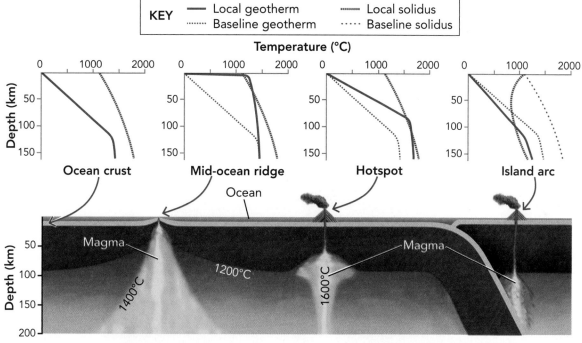

Graphs by Woudloper/Woodwalker, licensed under CC BY 4.0 International Public License. Savvas Learning Company modified the material.

As the figure shows, rock at mid-ocean ridges moves upward to fill the space left by separating tectonic plates. As the hot rock rises into the cooler lithosphere, pressure drops and the solid rock melts. The corresponding graph shows that the curve representing the geotherm is raised and intersects the solidus.

Melting at hotspots occurs because the rock is hotter than the surrounding mantle. The hot rock of the rising plume begins to melt when it reaches the asthenosphere. The graph shows that the geotherm is raised.

The figure shows that at subduction zones, water brought into the mantle by the sinking ocean floor lowers the melting temperature of the rock and forms magma. The corresponding graph shows that melting occurs there because the melting point is lowered (not because the temperature is raised).

54 **SEP Use Models** For the subduction zone, notice that the geotherm is actually colder than elsewhere. Explain why that is so.

Mantle Convection

For fluid materials, convection is often the fastest and therefore dominant way that heat flows. On Earth, convection is the dominant means of heat flow for gases in the atmosphere, liquids in the ocean and outer core, and even solids in the mantle. Although the mantle is almost entirely solid rock, it still undergoes convection. The speed of the movements is slow, just centimeters per year, but convection is still more efficient at moving heat than conduction.

Viscosity The resistance to flow is called **viscosity,** and it is measured in units of pascal-seconds, or kg/m·s. Water has a viscosity of 0.001, honey 10, and tar 30,000 kg/m·s. Solid mantle rock has a viscosity of roughly 10^{20} kg/m·s, which is very high, but still low enough to flow under the right conditions.

Computer Simulation of Mantle Convection From a model of Earth's layers and the pattern of plate tectonics, geoscientists can calculate what the pattern of Earth's mantle convection should be.

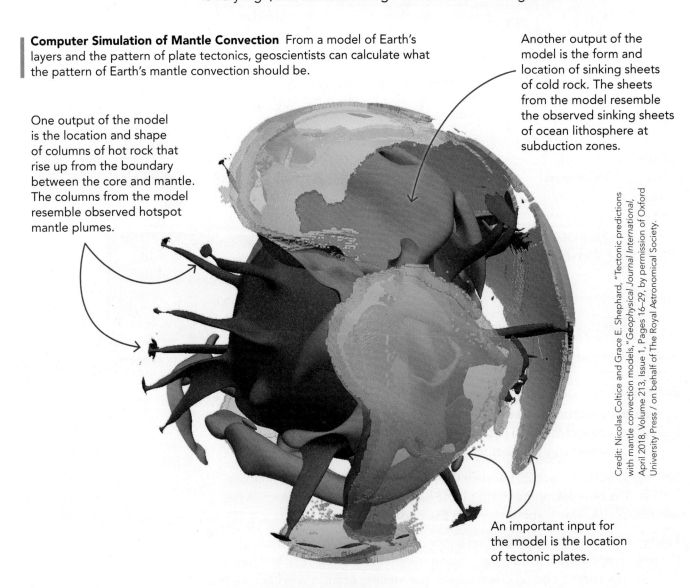

One output of the model is the location and shape of columns of hot rock that rise up from the boundary between the core and mantle. The columns from the model resemble observed hotspot mantle plumes.

Another output of the model is the form and location of sinking sheets of cold rock. The sheets from the model resemble the observed sinking sheets of ocean lithosphere at subduction zones.

An important input for the model is the location of tectonic plates.

Credit: Nicolas Coltice and Grace E. Shephard, "Tectonic predictions with mantle convection models," *Geophysical Journal International*, April 2018, Volume 213, Issue 1, Pages 16–29, by permission of Oxford University Press / on behalf of The Royal Astronomical Society.

(55) **CCC Energy and Matter** The viscosity of rock becomes significantly higher when it is colder and significantly lower when it is hotter. Describe how that might affect the shapes of the sinking sheets of ocean lithosphere and rising mantle plumes. Think about how this moving rock would interact with the surrounding rock.

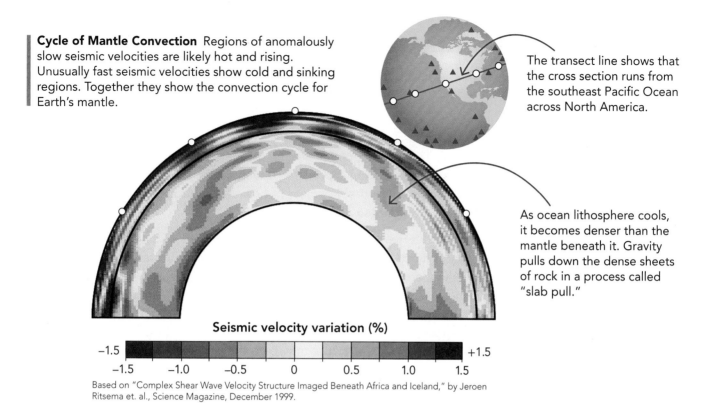

Cycle of Mantle Convection Regions of anomalously slow seismic velocities are likely hot and rising. Unusually fast seismic velocities show cold and sinking regions. Together they show the convection cycle for Earth's mantle.

The transect line shows that the cross section runs from the southeast Pacific Ocean across North America.

As ocean lithosphere cools, it becomes denser than the mantle beneath it. Gravity pulls down the dense sheets of rock in a process called "slab pull."

Seismic velocity variation (%)

| −1.5 | | | | | | | | | +1.5 |

−1.5   −1.0   −0.5   0   0.5   1.0   1.5

Based on "Complex Shear Wave Velocity Structure Imaged Beneath Africa and Iceland," by Jeroen Ritsema et. al., Science Magazine, December 1999.

Seismic Tomography Computer models reveal what the patterns of convection should look like for a planet such as Earth, but geoscientists need to compare the models to Earth's actual behavior. To do so, they collect large amounts of earthquake data. The travel times and amplitudes of millions of seismic waves from thousands of earthquakes are combined in a modeling process called **seismic tomography.**

Seismic waves travel slightly more slowly and have damped amplitudes when they travel through hot regions of Earth's interior. The slowing reveals regions of hot rock. Examples are the columns of hot mantle plumes upwelling, or rising, from the core-mantle boundary to the lithosphere, forming hotspots such as those in Hawaii, Yellowstone, and Iceland. Slowing seismic waves also reveal the melting rock of mid-ocean ridges, but those extend only 100 or 200 km deep.

Seismic waves travel slightly more quickly and have greater amplitudes when they travel through cold regions. The speeding up reveals the locations of ancient sheets of subducted, or downwelling, ocean lithosphere. In most cases, lithosphere can be seen sinking all the way to the bottom of the mantle. Global seismic tomography shows that Earth's deep mantle structure is dominated by the sinking of cold, dense, ocean lithosphere around the rim of the Pacific Ocean. On the surface, that region is recognized as the Ring of Fire. The arrival at the core-mantle boundary of the subducted ocean lithosphere pushes material at the base of the mantle into immense piles of hot rock.

56 **SEP Construct an Explanation** Medical CT scans make three-dimensional images of the interior of a human body by putting a person in a cylindrical chamber and moving sensors around to gather images from X-rays at uniform intervals and from all angles. Explain why such even coverage is not possible with seismic tomography.

Mantle Convection and Plate Tectonics

It is clear from the images of seismic tomography and computer convection modeling that tectonic plates are not separate from the pattern of mantle convection. The tectonic plates are the top part of the mantle convection cells. Earth's mantle convection is primarily driven by the sinking of old, cold, dense ocean plates. In a way that is similar to how a big spoon stirs a bowl of cake batter, the sinking ocean plates stir the mantle.

Some of Earth's mantle convection is also driven by the rising of hot rock. Such rock is mostly heated by the radioactive decay of potassium, thorium, and uranium, and it slowly rises up across most of the mantle to take the place of sinking ocean plates. A small amount of heat enters the mantle from the core, forming the narrow columnar mantle plumes that rise to the surface. The overall pattern of Earth's mantle convection, however, is determined by the cold sinking ocean plates rather than by hot rising mantle rock.

Forces that Drive Mantle Convection This computer simulation of mantle convection shows the connection between plate tectonics and patterns of mantle convection.

The pattern in a cell of mantle convection is determined by the location of a subduction zone. Subduction is the dominant force driving the convection cycle.

A broad upward flow of rock replaces the sinking ocean slabs, and small regions of upwelling rock appear in the form of hot mantle plumes.

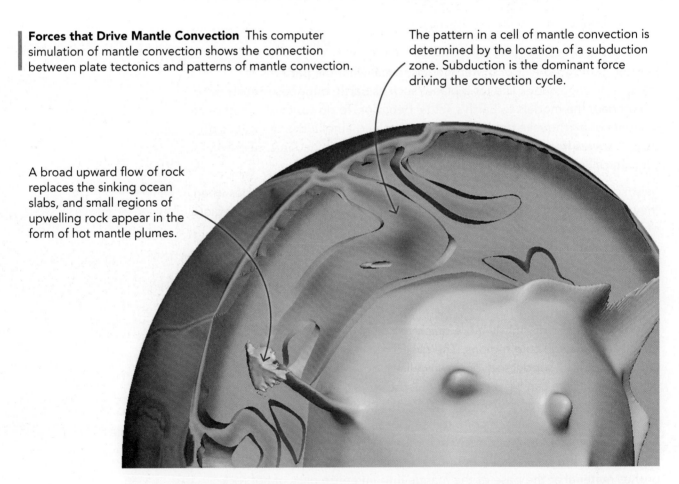

(51) **CCC Systems and System Models** Suppose surface oceanic plates, subducting ocean lithosphere, rising mantle plumes, and horizontal flow at the base of the mantle all move about 5 cm per year. Estimate how long it takes to complete one full cycle of mantle convection.

Core Convection and Magnetism

In the liquid iron of the outer core, convection takes place vigorously, although the exact patterns of convection are not known. This convection produces Earth's magnetic field. Geoscientists have been able to learn about the core's convection through computer modeling of the direction, amplitude, and time variations of Earth's magnetic field. Earth's field is always shifting, including movement of the magnetic north and south poles. The direction in which a compass points can change more than 10° over a person's lifetime. In fact, the magnetic south pole has recently moved so far north that it is located within the Indian Ocean basin. Small perturbations in the magnetic field tend to drift westward over time, and the magnetic field is also capable of entirely reversing direction. Taken together, such observations have allowed for a model of convection that explains the existence of Earth's magnetic field.

Earth's External and Internal Magnetic Field Earth's magnetic field is primarily dipolar, meaning that it is dominated by a north pole and a south pole, with magnetic field lines connecting the two. Earth's magnetic field fluctuates over time, but it is usually roughly aligned with Earth's axis of rotation.

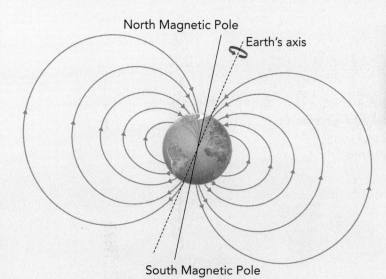

Field lines of the magnetic dipolar field, the field that you know about, extend out of and return into Earth's core.

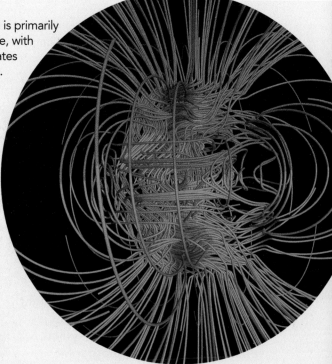

A computer model shows the magnetic field that is generated by convection within Earth's outer core. The field lines are trapped within the liquid iron, and as the convection goes on, they get wrapped up and twisted.

(58) **SEP Use Models** Imagine one compass at Earth's equator and another far out in space, directly above the equator. Based on the magnetic field lines shown in the diagram, describe how the direction and magnitude of the magnetic field would differ at the two locations.

INVESTIGATIVE PHENOMENON

 GO ONLINE to revisit your **Investigative Phenomenon CER** with the new information you have learned about Heat Flow Within Earth.

These questions will help you apply what you learned in this experience to the Investigative Phenomenon.

59 **CCC Energy and Matter** Heat flow at Earth's surface, such as at a beach, is different than heat flow in the rest of the planet. On a separate sheet of paper, complete the table about heat flow through Earth's different regions.

Location within Earth	Primary means of heat flow	Relative rate of vertical temperature change
Surface		
Lithosphere		fast
Mid-mantle	convection	
Lowermost mantle		
Outer core		slow
Inner core	conduction	

60 **CCC Scale, Proportion, and Quantity** Use the comparison between the rates of conductive heat flow through steel and granite to determine whether heat would be conducted more quickly through dry quartz sand [$k = 0.4$ W/(m·K)] or wet sand [$k = 2.5$ W/(m·K)].

61 **Apply Concepts** Energy from sunlight usually determines whether sand is hot or cool. However, identify and describe one kind of geographic area where heat flow from inside Earth would be more significant.

 GO ONLINE for a **quiz** to evaluate what you learned about Heat Flow Within Earth.

These questions will help you apply what you learned in this investigation to the Anchoring Phenomenon.

62 **SEP Develop and Use a Model** Draw a model of a chain-reaction machine that relies on a few thermal energy transfers to complete a simple task. Write captions for your model that explain how energy is transferred in each step and how that energy is used to do work.

63 **CCC Energy and Matter** Refer to your model of the chain-reaction machine. Explain how energy is conserved in the system and describe the net change in the system's entropy.

☑ INVESTIGATION ASSESSMENT

GO ONLINE for activities that will give you an opportunity to **demonstrate what you have learned:**

☑ **Science Performance-Based Assessment** Determine the transfer of energy by analyzing a heating curve.

📄 **Engineering Workbench** Design a travel mug that slows heat loss.

📲 **Career Connections** Learn about how an HVAC technician applies knowledge of physics.

☑ **Investigation Test** Take this test to demonstrate your understanding of thermal energy.

☑ **Virtual Lab Performance-Based Assessment** Use microscopic-level properties of materials to explain macroscopic observations of heat flow.

GO ONLINE to engage with real-world phenomena by watching a **phenomenon video** and completing a **modeling worksheet**.

How can we sustainably generate electrical energy?

Electromagnetic Energy

Your morning alarm pierces the quiet, waking you up from a deep sleep. You reach for the light next to the alarm clock and turn it on. You head to the kitchen, where you put some bread in the toaster and check your email on your phone, and then you get ready for school.

Your daily life depends on electricity. By the most recent estimates, the United States currently uses 15 quintillion joules of electricity annually. That's about 45 billion joules per person each year! The consumption of electrical energy has profound implications for the future of the planet. Nonrenewable fossil fuels, such as coal and natural gas, represent the majority of the energy sources used to generate electricity. One of the consequences of increasing energy demand is the release of greenhouse gases into the atmosphere. However, there are sustainable technologies that can help meet our energy needs while minimizing the impact on planet Earth.

Determining how to generate electricity sustainably requires understanding how electric current is produced, the factors that affect the flow of current, the features of electric circuits, and how electric power is generated.

(1) **CCC Cause and Effect** Think about how your school uses electricity during a typical day. What are some concrete steps that students and staff might take to reduce energy usage at your school?

(2) **SEP Design a Solution** What do you think are some of the most important considerations that engineers must take into account when modifying existing technologies or developing new technologies to meet demand for electrical energy?

EXPERIENCE 1

Electric Potential

📄 **GO ONLINE** to do a **hands-on lab** to investigate batteries, which convert chemical potential energy to electrical energy.

Electrostatic Potential Energy

In studying electric fields, you learned that electric force is a vector field that depends on the magnitude of the charges interacting. Increasing the charges increases the force. By Newton's third law of motion, the attractive or repulsive force that one particle exerts on another is equal and opposite to the force exerted on it by the other particle. Since electric charges attract or repel one another, there is electric potential energy, also called electrostatic potential energy when the charges are not in motion, in a system of interacting charges. Like the universal gravitational force between two masses, the electric force between charged particles decreases with distance. At great distances, the force between two particles and their potential energy approach zero.

> **Attractive Force** Two oppositely charged bodies attract each other. The force of attraction drops off as the inverse square of the distance.

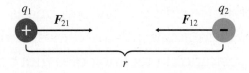

The electrostatic force between the pair of charges is four times smaller if the distance between them is two times larger.

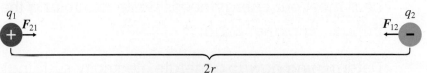

3 **CCC Patterns** The girl gains a charge from touching the metal sphere. What do you think explains what is happening to her hair?

410

Energy Transformation

 GO ONLINE to do a PhET **simulation** that allows you to explore capacitors.

Transformation of Electrostatic Potential Energy Like any other object, a charged object has zero kinetic energy when it is at rest. As a charged object is accelerated by an electric field, its electrostatic potential energy is converted to kinetic energy, and the amount of electrostatic potential energy in the system decreases.

To calculate the energy gained by a charge moving through a uniform electric field, such as between the plates of a capacitor, you multiply the force times the distance. In general, however, the force on a charge decreases with distance to another charge. Since the force is not constant, you must use more advanced math (such as calculus) to find the gain in energy.

Picking Up Speed When the negatively charged toy bowling ball is released, it accelerates toward the positive ball. Gaining speed means gaining kinetic energy. When the ball reaches the pins, it has enough kinetic energy to knock them down.

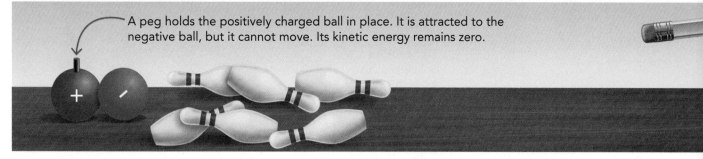

A peg holds the positively charged ball in place. It is attracted to the negative ball, but it cannot move. Its kinetic energy remains zero.

④ **SEP Develop a Model** A ball rolls along a level surface, down a short slope, and then onto another level surface, as in the figure. Draw an energy bar chart for the process.

⑤ **CCC Matter and Energy** How would the behavior of the negatively charged toy bowling ball in the figure differ if the ball was released from a greater distance? A shorter distance? Draw an energy bar chart for each case.

⑥ **SEP Use Models** How do the energy bar charts for the ball rolling down the slope and the charged bowling ball in the figure rolling toward the oppositely charged ball compare?

Expanded Bar Charts Bar charts graphically represent that the initial energy and the external work combine to result in the total final energy of a system. You can expand the initial and final energy of a system to include each component. You have seen work take on positive and negative values, increasing or decreasing the system's total energy, respectively. When it comes to charged particles, the potential energy can be positive or negative, depending on the charges of the particles relative to each other. A system of two like charges has positive potential energy, and a system of two opposite charges has negative potential energy. Whether the energy or work is positive or negative, the initial energy plus the external work must equal the final energy of the system.

Energy Changes in Systems with Electric Charges

How can you track **energy changes** in a **system of charged objects?**

Charged Changes You can use force diagrams and energy bar charts to help you understand the **changes in electrostatic potential energy (PE$_e$)** and the **total energy of a system** involving charged objects.

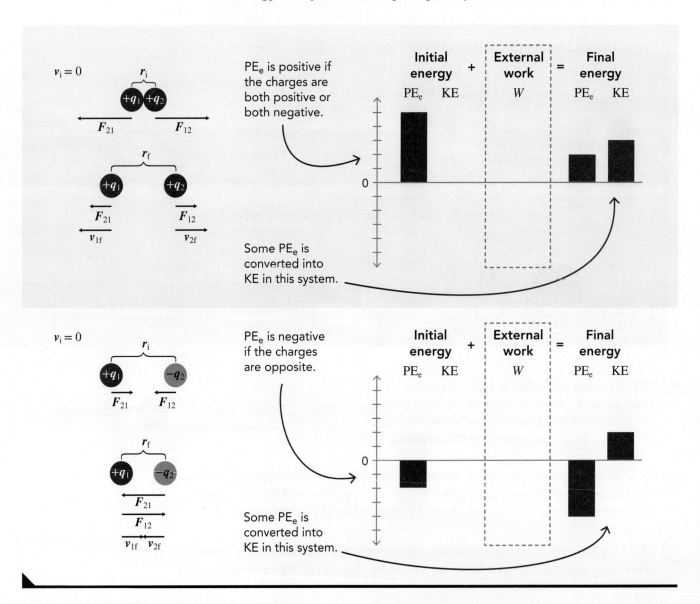

Speed of an Alpha Particle

During a transformation, a uranium-238 nucleus gives off an alpha particle and becomes a thorium-234 nucleus. The positive thorium nucleus repels the positive alpha particle, giving it an initial electrostatic potential energy of 6.84×10^{-13} J. How fast is the alpha particle moving when it is far away from the thorium nucleus? The alpha particle has a mass of 6.64×10^{-27} kg.

1. DRAW A PICTURE Sketch a picture of the situation.

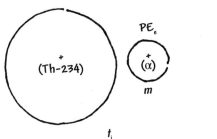 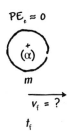 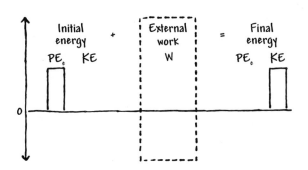

2. DEFINE THE PROBLEM List knowns and unknowns, and assign values to variables.

$m = 6.64 \times 10^{-27}$ kg $\quad\bigg|\quad v_f = ?$

$PE_e = 6.84 \times 10^{-13}$ J

3. PLAN AND EXECUTE Use mathematical relationships, the picture, and your definitions to plan and execute a solution.

The initial potential energy of the alpha particle is equal to its final kinetic energy. Write and rearrange the energy equation to determine the final velocity of the particle.

$E_i + W = E_f$

$PE_e + 0 = KE_f$

$PE_e = \frac{1}{2}mv_f^2 \rightarrow v_f = \sqrt{\frac{2PE_e}{m}}$

Substitute values of the known quantities and solve for the final velocity.

$v_f = \sqrt{\dfrac{2(6.84 \times 10^{-13}\,\text{J})}{6.64 \times 10^{-27}\,\text{kg}}}$

$v_f = \sqrt{2.06 \times 10^{14}\,\text{J/kg}} = 1.43 \times 10^7$ m/s

4. EVALUATE Reflect on your answer.

The velocity is high, which is reasonable; an online search shows that alpha particles carry a large amount of energy. However, it is less than the speed of light, 3.0×10^8 m/s, which must be the case for any object.

 GO ONLINE for more **math support**.

💻 **Math Practice Problems**

---

⑦ During a transformation, a thorium-228 nucleus gives off an alpha particle and becomes a radium-224 nucleus. The positive radium nucleus repels the positive alpha particle, giving it an energy of 8.67×10^{-13} J. How fast is the alpha particle moving when it is far away from the radium nucleus? The alpha particle has a mass of 6.64×10^{-27} kg.

📖 **NEED A HINT?** Go online to your **eText Sample Problem** for stepped-out support.

Electric Potential Field

VOCABULARY

The word *scalar* is derived from the Latin root *scandere*, meaning "to climb." A **scalar field** can be measured but has only a single dimension.

In many situations, it is easier to deal directly with the energy of a system of charges instead of dealing with the electric forces. Recall that the electric force on a charge is proportional to the magnitude of the charge. The same is true of the electrical potential energy. Suppose you want to know the potential energy, PE_e, of a charge at a particular point; you can place a small test charge, q, in a field to measure its PE_e. Then you can define an **electric potential field,** which is the potential energy of a particle in an electric field divided by its charge. Electric potential is independent of the test charge.

Electric Potential Field
$$V = \frac{PE_e}{q}$$

V = electric potential

PE_e = electrostatic potential energy for a test charge

q = test charge

The electric potential is a scalar, not a vector. Therefore, electric potential is a **scalar field,** which is a field that has a magnitude at every point but no direction associated with it. Electric potential has units of joules per coulomb (J/C), also known as volts (V). At a given distance, equivalent charges have potentials proportional to the source charge, the charge producing the potential field. A greater source charge produces a greater field.

Energy of a Test Charge At equal distances from the source charge, the magnitude of the force exerted on equal test charges is directly proportional to the charge of the source charge.

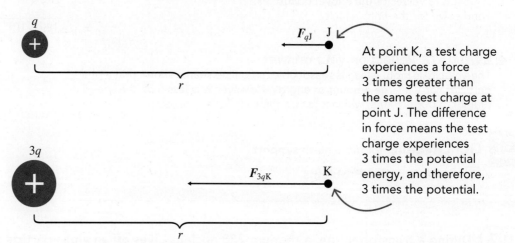

At point K, a test charge experiences a force 3 times greater than the same test charge at point J. The difference in force means the test charge experiences 3 times the potential energy, and therefore, 3 times the potential.

8. **CCC Scale, Proportion, and Quantity** In the figure, points J and K are the same distance away from charges q and 3q, respectively. Suppose a test charge at point J has the same electrical potential energy as another test charge at point K. Compare the charges of the two test charges.

Point Charges

It is useful to think of an ideal charge as being just a single point charge. Electric potential due to a point charge depends on the amount of the source charge. As with electrical potential energy, the magnitude of the potential field of a charged particle drops off with distance, although as the inverse of the distance instead of the inverse square.

Electric Potential Field of a Point Charge
$$V = k_e \frac{q}{r}$$
V = electric potential $\qquad\qquad$ q = source charge k_e = Coulomb's constant = 8.99×10^9 N·m²/C² $\quad$ r = distance

Like work, a potential field may be positive or negative. For a positive charge in a positive field, potential energy decreases with increasing distance; moving a positive charge closer to the source of the field means doing work. For a negative charge, the potential increases with distance, meaning it becomes less negative. For both, it is convenient to define zero potential energy as the energy at an infinite distance. At that distance, the field does not exert a force on the charge.

Charge and Distance Both electric force and electric potential have greater magnitude closer to the source charge.

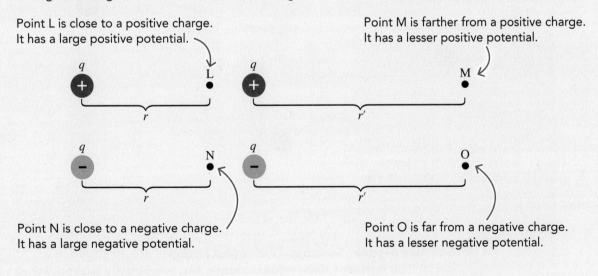

Point L is close to a positive charge. It has a large positive potential.

Point M is farther from a positive charge. It has a lesser positive potential.

Point N is close to a negative charge. It has a large negative potential.

Point O is far from a negative charge. It has a lesser negative potential.

9 **SEP Use Mathematics** Calculate the electric potential at points F and G due to the +9 μC charge.

Superposition

Both electric fields and electric potential fields are produced by the superposition of multiple charges. However, for an electric potential field, it is the simple addition of the scalar fields for all the particles. A single charge has a field that varies inversely with distance, and the field produced by two particles is simply the sum of the two fields at every point in space. The result is that you can write a single equation to represent a superposition of any number of fields.

Superposition of Fields
$$V_{total} = V_1 + V_2 + \ldots + V_n = k_e\frac{q_1}{r_1} + k_e\frac{q_2}{r_2} + \ldots + k_e\frac{q_n}{r_n}$$

V_{total} = total electric potential of test charge
k_e = Coulomb's constant
$q_1, q_2, \ldots, q_n$ = source charges
$r_1, r_2, \ldots, r_n$ = distances from source charges

The field at any point depends on the charges and the distances for all of the particles. Sometimes, calculating r_1, r_2, and r_3 can take some work, and you also have to keep track of the signs of the particles. Positive charges add to a potential, and negative charges subtract.

Multiple Charges A single quantity represents the electric potential at any point.

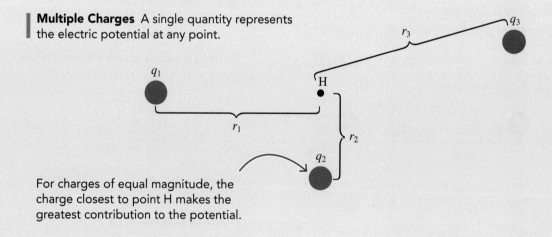

For charges of equal magnitude, the charge closest to point H makes the greatest contribution to the potential.

(10) **SEP Use Models** Suppose 12 charged particles are arranged in a circle. The particles have equal charges and are equally spaced. What is the potential at the center of the ring? What is the magnitude of the electric field? (Hint: You can use the symmetry of the situation to simplify the calculation.)

(11) **SEP Use Models** Suppose 16 charged particles are arranged in a circle. The particles have equal magnitudes and are equally spaced, but they are alternately positive and negative. What is the potential at the center of the ring? What is the magnitude of the electric field?

Potential Due to Point Charges

A negative charge of –5.0 μC, q_1, and a positive charge of +5.0 μC, q_2, are 10 cm apart. Find the electric potential at point P that is at a distance of 15 cm from the negative charge on a line that makes a 90° angle with the line segment connecting the two charges.

1. DRAW A PICTURE Sketch a picture of the situation.

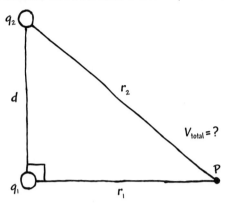

2. DEFINE THE PROBLEM List knowns and unknowns, and assign values to variables.

$q_1 = -5\ \mu C = -5.0 \times 10^{-6}\ C$ $r_2 = ?$

$q_2 = 5\ \mu C = 5.0 \times 10^{-6}\ C$ $V_{total} = ?$

$d = 10\ cm = 0.10\ m$

$r_1 = 15\ cm = 0.15\ m$

3. PLAN AND EXECUTE Use mathematical relationships, the picture, and your definitions to plan and execute a solution.

Apply the Pythagorean theorem to find r_2, the distance from the positive charge to point P.

$$r_2 = \sqrt{d^2 + r_1^2} = \sqrt{(0.10\ m)^2 + (0.15\ m)^2} = \sqrt{0.033\ m}$$
$$= 0.18\ m$$

Calculate the electrical potential from each source.

$$V_1 = k_e \frac{q_1}{r_1} = \left(8.99 \times 10^9\ \frac{N \cdot m^2}{C^2}\right)\left(\frac{-5.0 \times 10^{-6}\ C}{0.15\ m}\right)$$
$$= -3.0 \times 10^5\ V$$

$$V_2 = k_e \frac{q_2}{r_2} = \left(8.99 \times 10^9\ \frac{N \cdot m^2}{C^2}\right)\left(\frac{5.0 \times 10^{-6}\ C}{0.18\ m}\right)$$
$$= 2.5 \times 10^5\ V$$

Write a superposition equation and sum the potentials to find the total.

$$V_{total} = V_1 + V_2 = -3.0 \times 10^5\ V + 2.5 \times 10^5\ V$$
$$= -0.5 \times 10^5 = -5 \times 10^4\ V$$

4. EVALUATE Reflect on your answer.
A negative potential makes sense because, although both charges are the same magnitude, point P is closer to the negative charge than it is to the positive charge.

 GO ONLINE for more **math support**.

▶ **Math Tutorial Video**

📶 **Math Practice Problems**

(12) A negative charge of –4 μC, q_1, and a positive charge of +4 μC, q_2, are 9.0 cm apart. Find the electric potential at point P that is a distance 12 cm from the negative charge, on a line that makes a 90° angle with the line segment connecting the two charges.

📖 **NEED A HINT?** Go online to your **eText Sample Problem** for stepped-out support.

Equipotential Surfaces

EXPERIENCE IT!

Walk on different floors of a building and take stairs to travel between them. What surfaces have equal gravitational potential energy? When are you doing work?

Although you can't see them, field lines are very useful in studying forces. In a similar way, equipotentials are very useful in studying the electric potential field. An **equipotential surface** is a surface that has the same electric potential everywhere. For example, the electric field between two charged plates in a capacitor is constant, so the potential depends only on the distance from the plates. Therefore, every point on a plane parallel to the plates has the same electric potential.

Since there is no difference in potential between points on an equipotential, there is no electric force acting along an equipotential surface. You can think of an equipotential as a line of constant elevation on a contour map. In areas where the equipotentials are close together, the potential changes rapidly. A steep slope in the potential is a strong electric field.

Contours If you walk along any of the contour lines on a topographic map, you will remain at the same altitude.

Work and Electric Potential As the 2D and 3D models demonstrate, the surface of a sphere is a constant distance from a point at the center, so a point charge has spherical equipotentials. You can model how the potential energy of a system changes as a charged particle changes position.

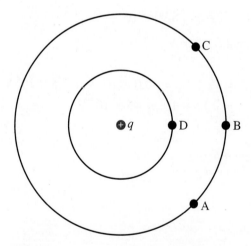

Points A, B, and C are on the same equipotential, so there is no energy difference between them. That means no work is required to move a charge from A to B or C.

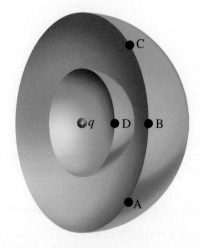

Point D is on a different equipotential, since it is closer to the test charge. Moving a negative charge from point A, B, or C to point D will require doing negative work on the system.

13) **SEP Use a Model** Points A, B, and C are at the same potential, so there is no electric force tangent to the surface. What is the geometrical relation between electric field lines of force and an equipotential surface? Sketch the field lines for a point charge to guide your thinking.

Charging The batteries in an electric car can store a large amount of potential energy. You can charge an electric car at home, at 110 volts. Fast chargers may use potentials as high as 600 volts.

Potential Difference

▶ **GO ONLINE** to watch a **video** about how batteries work.

A charged particle between two surfaces at different potentials experiences an electric force. The force is proportional to the difference in potential and inversely proportional to the distance between the surfaces.

Potential Difference
$$\Delta V = V_f - V_e$$
ΔV = potential difference
V_f = potential of surface f
V_e = potential of surface e

A positive charge tends to move from higher to lower potential, and a negative charge tends to move from lower to higher potential. If two points at different potentials are connected with an electrical conductor, the difference in potential energy means that there is an electric force, and charges move through the conductor. You know such a setup as an electric circuit. Anything electrical depends on differences in potential to do work, and the difference is measured in volts (V).

(14) **SEP Use Mathematics** Two metal plates are at potentials of +5 V and –12 V. What is the potential difference between them?

GO ONLINE to revisit your **Investigative Phenomenon modeling activity** with the new information you have learned about Electric Potential.

These questions will help you apply what you learned in this experience to the Investigative Phenomenon.

15. **SEP Develop a Model** All technologies used to generate electric power involve electric potential and electric fields. Suppose you have a metal sphere with positive charge on the outside. Using what you know about conductors, electric potential, and electric fields, explain why the charge must be uniformly distributed over the surface.

16. **SEP Develop a Model** Suppose you have a metal sphere with positive charge on the outside. Using what you know about conductors, electric potential, and electric fields, explain why the potential inside the sphere is constant, and explain what the electric field inside the sphere is.

17. **CCC Patterns** An important aspect of electric power management is energy storage. Using what you know about electric potential and electric fields, explain why the energy stored in a capacitor is proportional to the square of the charge on either plate.

 GO ONLINE for a **quiz** to evaluate what you learned about Electric Potential.

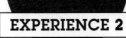

EXPERIENCE 2

Energy in Electric Circuits

 GO ONLINE to do a **hands-on lab** to investigate the laws that explain how electric circuits work.

What Causes Current?

In atoms, positive charges are bound in atomic nuclei, whereas negatively charged electrons are not. It is electrons that move from location to location, producing a flow of charge is called current. However, physicists discovered the equations for relating electric forces and current before they discovered that electrons have a negative charge. So the convention is that current is the movement of positive charge.

A potential difference is sometimes modeled as an imbalance in electric charges between two locations where positive charges move freely. The potential difference causes an electric field that exerts force on charges, pushing positive charges toward the negatively charged location. If you connect the two locations with a conducting material, such as a copper wire, then positive charge can flow from the positive location to the negative location, forming an electric current.

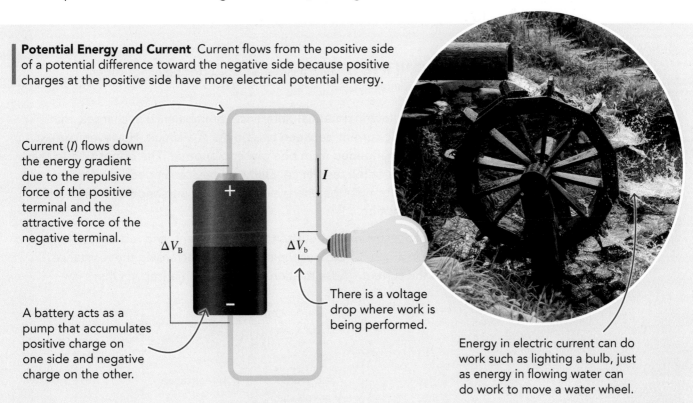

Potential Energy and Current Current flows from the positive side of a potential difference toward the negative side because positive charges at the positive side have more electrical potential energy.

Current (*I*) flows down the energy gradient due to the repulsive force of the positive terminal and the attractive force of the negative terminal.

ΔV_B

ΔV_b

I

A battery acts as a pump that accumulates positive charge on one side and negative charge on the other.

There is a voltage drop where work is being performed.

Energy in electric current can do work such as lighting a bulb, just as energy in flowing water can do work to move a water wheel.

(18) **CCC Patterns** An electrical outlet maintains a current by causing a potential difference. What are some examples of other such devices?

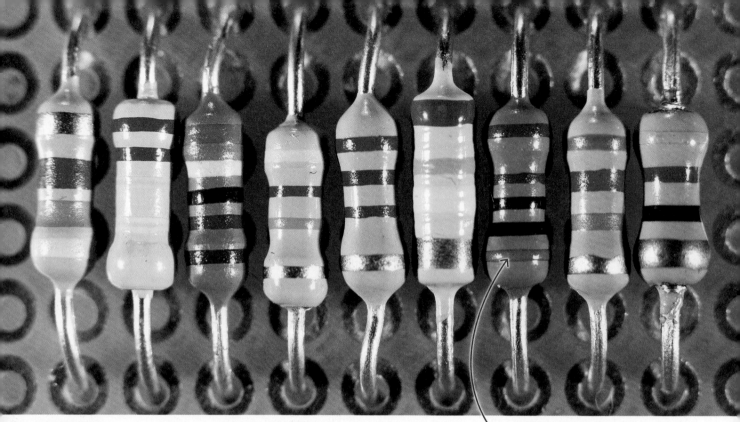

Resistors A typical resistor is a tightly wound, thin wire surrounded by a ceramic shell with painted stripes. Forcing the current to travel a great distance through a thin wire impedes the current and, therefore, increases the resistance.

The colored stripes are a code that tells an electrical engineer the amount of resistance the resistor adds to a circuit.

Ohm's Law

 GO ONLINE to watch a **video** about electric potential, current, and resistance.

Voltage is the electric potential difference, or imbalance in charges, that produces electric current between two points in a circuit. However, current does not flow unimpeded from one place to another. The opposition to the flow of current is called resistance. Electrical devices impede the flow of current by transforming the energy in the current into another form, such as heat, light, or motion.

A simple relationship exists between voltage, current, and resistance. Increasing the voltage in a circuit increases the current, and increasing the resistance decreases the current. Those relationships are summarized in Ohm's law.

Ohm's Law
$$I = \frac{V}{R}$$
I = current $\qquad R$ = resistance V = voltage

(19) **SEP Use Mathematics** A 180-ohm resistor is connected across the terminals of a 9-V battery. Determine the current through the resistor.

Ohmic Materials

Ohm's law is a general statement that relates voltage, current, and resistance. However, Ohm's law only applies in situations with a material having a constant resistance. The resistance of an object is dependent on several factors, including temperature, length, cross section, and the material from which the object is made.

An **ohmic material** is a material that follows Ohm's law. It has a constant resistance and, therefore, a linear relationship between voltage and current. A metal wire is ohmic because it is made of homogeneous material with a uniform cross section, so the resistance is constant throughout the wire.

Most materials are nonohmic, because their resistances are not constant. One example of a nonohmic material is the tungsten filament in an incandescent light bulb. The wire is very thin, and its small cross section impedes current, which causes it to get so hot that it glows. The rise in temperature increases the resistance, so a greater current produces a greater resistance in the wire. Because of the large variations in resistance, the filament is nonohmic.

VOCABULARY

The word **ohmic** comes from Georg Ohm, who discovered the relation of current and voltage in the 1820s. Other electrical terms taken from the names of early researchers are the ampere, the coulomb, and the volt.

Voltage-Current Relationship From Ohm's law, $\frac{I}{V} = \frac{1}{R}$, the slope of a current-versus-voltage graph is the multiplicative inverse of the resistance of an object. Nonohmic materials have curved graphs.

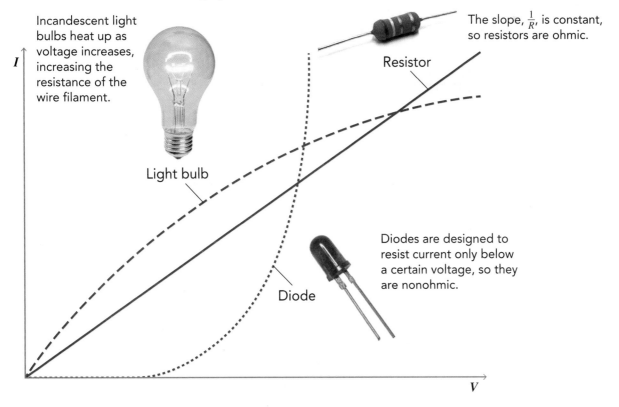

Incandescent light bulbs heat up as voltage increases, increasing the resistance of the wire filament.

Light bulb

The slope, $\frac{1}{R}$, is constant, so resistors are ohmic.

Resistor

Diodes are designed to resist current only below a certain voltage, so they are nonohmic.

Diode

(20) **SEP Plan an Investigation** Design an experiment to determine whether a material is ohmic or nonohmic.

Circuit Boards A circuit board is nonconductive material with thin layers of conductive material printed on top, connecting different circuit elements attached to the board.

Each dark line is a conducting path between two elements of the circuit.

Circuit Elements and Diagrams

Simple Circuits A circuit is a closed path that allows electric charges, or current, to flow from one location to another. The simplest circuits contain three elements: a voltage source, a conductive wire, and an electrical device.

The potential difference of a voltage source provides the potential energy needed to produce an electrical current. The conductive wire provides a path for the current to flow between the terminals of the voltage source. The electrical device provides resistance so that the current does not all flow immediately down the potential gradient, leading to a hazardous release of energy.

The purpose of a circuit is to provide energy to the electrical device, which performs a useful task, such as illuminating a light bulb, powering a motor, or generating heat. Additional elements can be added to circuits. Switches can be opened and closed either to allow or to prevent current flow. A capacitor can store electrical energy to be released at a later time. Diodes regulate the flow of current, often with the purpose of preventing the current from reversing direction.

(21) **SEP Develop Models** Draw as many configurations as possible of a simple circuit given two wires, a light bulb, and a battery.

Modeling Circuits A circuit can be represented with circuit diagrams that use icons to represent the elements in the circuit. Even for circuits with complicated wiring, the setup can be represented with symbols for circuit elements, connected by a grid of horizontal and vertical lines representing wires. These models allow engineers to check whether a circuit will perform as intended. Electricians can check whether the possibility of a short circuit, a circuit that allows current to travel along unintended paths with low resistance, exists. Electricians calculate important quantities such as voltage and current to ensure that the safety parameters of the circuit are not exceeded.

Circuit Diagram The table contains commonly used symbols, each of which is a compact representation of a circuit element. An example of a circuit diagram shows a simple circuit that is activated by closing a switch.

The battery provides energy to the circuit by producing a voltage differential.

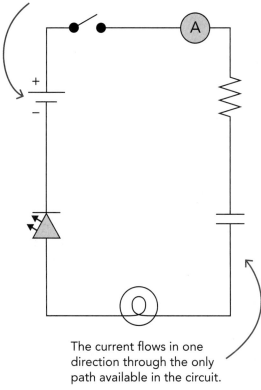

The current flows in one direction through the only path available in the circuit.

Circuit element	Symbol
Battery	
Wire	
Light bulb	
Resistor	
Open switch	
Closed switch	
Ammeter	
Voltmeter	
LED	
Capacitor	

22. **SEP Develop Models** Draw a circuit that provides two paths for current to flow from one terminal of a battery to the other. Explain how to determine the current in each of the two branches of the circuit.

23. **SEP Communicate Technical Information** Write a paragraph describing how each element operates in the circuit you drew.

Measurements for Circuits

You can use different devices to measure different characteristics of a circuit. A **voltmeter** is a device used to measure the voltage between two points in a circuit and is connected in parallel with the circuit. The current either runs through the voltmeter or through the circuit between the points, but not both. Voltmeters have a high resistance so that very little current runs through them, altering the circuit very little.

An **ammeter** is a device that measures current in a circuit. It must be connected in series with the circuit, so that all of the current in the circuit flows through it. An ammeter has very little resistance, similar to a small piece of conducting wire. As a result, the ammeter changes the current very little. Care must be taken with ammeters, because connecting one to a circuit in parallel with a resistor can cause a short circuit that damages the ammeter.

Measuring Circuits A circuit diagram shows the different ways an ammeter and a voltmeter must be connected to a circuit in order to safely make accurate measurements of the circuit.

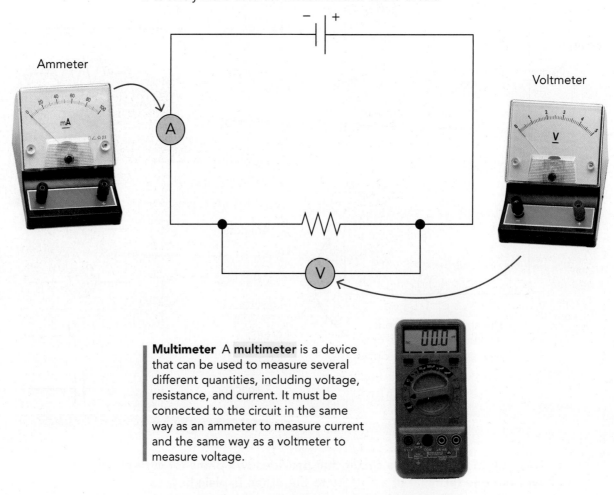

Multimeter A **multimeter** is a device that can be used to measure several different quantities, including voltage, resistance, and current. It must be connected to the circuit in the same way as an ammeter to measure current and the same way as a voltmeter to measure voltage.

(24) **SEP Plan an Investigation** Draw a circuit that includes three resistors wired in parallel with a battery. Design it so that the current passes through only one resistor in every possible path through the circuit. Explain how to use an ammeter to measure the current through each branch of the circuit.

Joule's Law

The energy used by a device in a circuit is given by Joule's law, which can be expressed with the equation $\Delta E = I^2 R \Delta t$. Because power is defined as the change in energy (ΔE) in a given time (Δt), it can be expressed as follows.

Joule's Law (Power)
$$P = I^2 R = IV = \frac{V^2}{R}$$
P = power R = resistance
I = current V = voltage

Joule's law is derived from Ohm's law ($V = IR$), and both can be combined to derive other forms of the equation for calculating power. For example, you can substitute IR for V in Joule's law to get $I^2 R$, which allows you to calculate power when the current and resistance are known but not the voltage. Power is expressed in watts, and electrical devices are rated by the power they require to operate. For example, a 15-W light bulb requires 15 watts of power when it is turned on.

Powering a Toaster A toaster passes electricity through nichrome wires, which have a relatively high resistance to electric current. The amount of heat they produce can be calculated with Joule's law.

A toaster like this one, operating on 120 volts, draws 7.5 amperes of current—900 watts of power.

The wire is wrapped around an insulating sheet to increase its length and thus its resistance. The coils glow when heated, emitting radiation that toasts food.

(25) **SEP Use Mathematics** Suppose heating a jug of water to the boiling point takes 150,000 J of energy. Calculate how long it will take to boil a jug of water with a 120-V power supply and a heating coil that has a resistance of 35 ohms.

Kirchhoff's Loop Rule

While an ammeter measures current at a single point, a voltmeter measures the voltage difference between two points in a circuit. A single point cannot have a voltage difference, because an electric potential has only a single value at one point. Therefore, a charge that travels around a loop and returns to the same point must have the same electric potential that it had to start. **Kirchhoff's loop rule** states that in a complete circuit, all of the decreases in potential from resistance and all of the increases in potential from electromotive force must sum to zero.

Kirchhoff's Loop Rule
$$\Delta V_{\text{loop}} = \Delta V_1 + \Delta V_2 + \ldots + \Delta V_n = 0$$ $\Delta V_{\text{loop}} =$ potential difference in a loop $\Delta V_i =$ individual voltage drop

Kirchhoff's loop rule can be applied to any closed loop in a circuit, whether it consists of the entire circuit or two parallel paths that split the current. When you apply the rule, choose a direction to travel around the loop and consider each element of the circuit in turn.

Circuit Loops The current in the circuit experiences a voltage gain and three voltage drops, which sum to zero. The circular arrow denotes the positive direction for current, similar to arrows used to define the positive direction of a coordinate system.

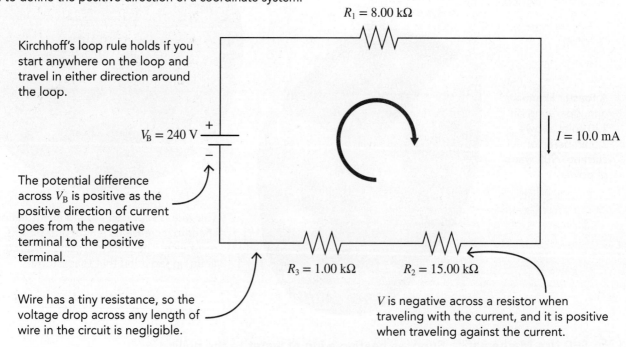

Kirchhoff's loop rule holds if you start anywhere on the loop and travel in either direction around the loop.

$V_B = 240$ V

The potential difference across V_B is positive as the positive direction of current goes from the negative terminal to the positive terminal.

Wire has a tiny resistance, so the voltage drop across any length of wire in the circuit is negligible.

$R_1 = 8.00$ kΩ

$I = 10.0$ mA

$R_3 = 1.00$ kΩ $R_2 = 15.00$ kΩ

V is negative across a resistor when traveling with the current, and it is positive when traveling against the current.

26) **SEP Construct an Explanation** Show that Kirchhoff's loop rule holds for the circuit in the figure when traveling clockwise around the loop and when traveling counterclockwise around the loop.

Applying Kirchhoff's Loop Rule

For the circuit shown in the diagram, $V_1 = 3$ V, $V_2 = 5$ V, $V_3 = 8$ V, $R_1 = 4$ Ω, and $R_2 = 4$ Ω. Determine the direction and magnitude of the current through both resistors.

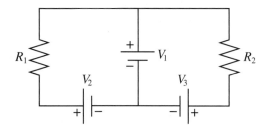

1. EXAMINE THE PICTURE Sketch a picture of the situation.

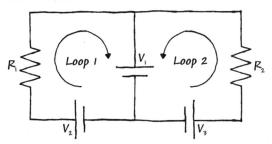

2. DEFINE THE PROBLEM List knowns and unknowns, and assign values to variables.

$V_1 = 3$ V	$I_1 = ?$
$V_2 = 5$ V	$I_2 = ?$
$V_3 = 8$ V	
$R_1 = R_2 = 4$ Ω	

3. PLAN AND EXECUTE Use mathematical relationships, the picture, and your definitions to plan and execute a solution.

Use Kirchhoff's loop rule to solve for the current in loop 1, based on your sketch. For loop 1, current traveling in the clockwise direction is positive.

$$V_2 - I_1R_1 - V_1 = 0 \ \rightarrow \ I_1 = \frac{V_2 - V_1}{R_1}$$

$$I_1 = \frac{5 \text{ V} - 3 \text{ V}}{4 \text{ Ω}} = 0.5 \text{ A}$$

I_1 is 0.5 A clockwise because the value is positive.

Use Kirchhoff's loop rule to solve for the current in loop 2, based on your sketch. For loop 2, current traveling in the counterclockwise direction is positive.

$$V_3 - I_2R_2 - V_1 = 0 \ \rightarrow \ I_2 = \frac{V_3 - V_1}{R_2}$$

$$I_2 = \frac{8 \text{ V} - 3 \text{ V}}{4 \text{ Ω}} = 1.25 \text{ A}$$

I_2 is 1.25 A counterclockwise because the value is positive.

4. EVALUATE Reflect on your answer.
The current in loop 1 is clockwise, and the current in loop 2 is counterclockwise. That makes sense, since $V_2 > V_1$ and $V_3 > V_1$. If the value for current was negative, then the current actually flowed in the opposite direction that was drawn in the sketch.

 GO ONLINE for more **math support**.

Math Practice Problems

27 For the circuit shown in the Sample Problem, suppose $V_1 = 6$ V, $V_2 = 2$ V, $V_3 = 10$ V, $R_1 = 5$ Ω, and $R_2 = 2$ Ω. Determine the direction and magnitude of the current through both resistors.

NEED A HINT? Go online to your **eText Sample Problem** for stepped-out support.

Kirchhoff's Junction Rule

 GO ONLINE to do a PhET **simulation** that allows you to explore different types of electric circuits.

Look at the diagram of a simple circuit with two resistors in parallel. The circuit has two junctions. A **junction** is a point in a circuit where three or more conductors come together. At a junction, either a current splits into a number of smaller currents, or smaller currents combine into a single larger current.

The same amount of current that flows into a point flows out of it, even at a junction where current splits or combines. The concept is summarized by **Kirchhoff's junction rule,** which states that the sum of the currents entering a junction is equal to the sum of the currents leaving the junction.

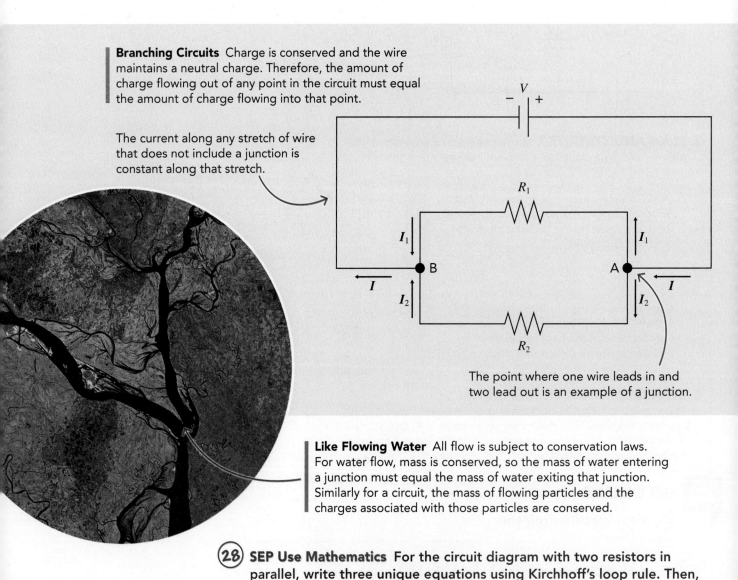

Branching Circuits Charge is conserved and the wire maintains a neutral charge. Therefore, the amount of charge flowing out of any point in the circuit must equal the amount of charge flowing into that point.

The current along any stretch of wire that does not include a junction is constant along that stretch.

The point where one wire leads in and two lead out is an example of a junction.

Like Flowing Water All flow is subject to conservation laws. For water flow, mass is conserved, so the mass of water entering a junction must equal the mass of water exiting that junction. Similarly for a circuit, the mass of flowing particles and the charges associated with those particles are conserved.

(28) **SEP Use Mathematics** For the circuit diagram with two resistors in parallel, write three unique equations using Kirchhoff's loop rule. Then, explain why you can only write one unique equation using Kirchhoff's junction rule even though the circuit contains two junctions.

Analyzing a Circuit

Circuits can be analyzed using a combination of Ohm's law and Kirchhoff's rules. Such an analysis tells you whether there is enough current to power a device in the circuit, whether the current is dangerously high at any point in the circuit, or whether you might reduce the voltage of the power supply to save energy.

How to Analyze a Circuit
How can you **analyze circuits** using circuit diagrams?

Circuit Sense Suppose you know some of the resistances and voltages on this circuit. You can use your knowledge of circuits to **determine the readings on the ammeter and voltmeter.**

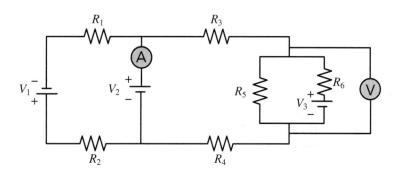

Step 1 Determine the loops and the direction of positive current flow.

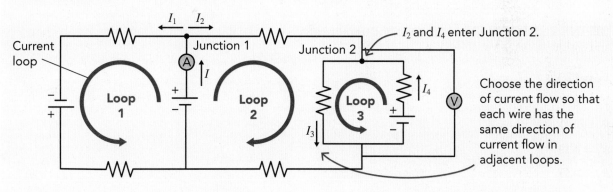

I_2 and I_4 enter Junction 2.

Choose the direction of current flow so that each wire has the same direction of current flow in adjacent loops.

Step 2 Write equations for the loops and junctions. Ensure you have as many equations as variables.

Loop 1 $V_1 - I_1R_2 + V_2 - I_1R_1 = 0$ **Loop 3** $V_3 - I_4R_6 - I_3R_5 = 0$

Loop 2 $V_2 - I_2R_3 \overbrace{- I_3R_5}^{} - I_2R_4 = 0$

$$V_2 - I_2R_3 + \boxed{V} - I_2R_4 = 0$$

Voltmeter reading

Junction 1 $I = I_1 + I_2$ Ammeter reading

Junction 2 $I_3 = I_2 + I_4$

Step 3 Substitute any known values in the equations you've written to form a system of equations that isolate the unknown values. Solve them to determine the readings on the ammeter and voltmeter.

Applying Kirchhoff's Rules

For the circuit shown in the diagram, $V_1 = 12$ V, $V_2 = 8$ V, $R_1 = 4\ \Omega$, $R_2 = 6\ \Omega$, and $R_3 = 4\ \Omega$. Determine the direction and magnitude of the current through all three resistors.

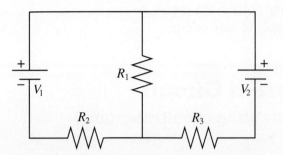

1. DRAW A PICTURE Sketch a picture of the situation.

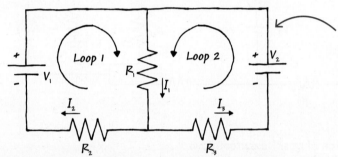

First, choose the direction to follow the loop in each circuit. Use a clockwise direction for the left loop and a counterclockwise direction for the right loop.

2. DEFINE THE PROBLEM List knowns and unknowns, and assign values to variables.

$V_1 = 12$ V	$I_1 = ?$
$V_2 = 8$ V	$I_2 = ?$
$R_1 = 4\ \Omega$	$I_3 = ?$
$R_2 = 6\ \Omega$	
$R_3 = 4\ \Omega$	

3. PLAN AND EXECUTE Use mathematical relationships, the picture, and your definitions to plan and execute a solution.

Write three equations using Kirchhoff's loop rule and Kirchhoff's junction rule.

Loop 1: $V_1 - I_1 R_1 - I_2 R_2 = 0$

Loop 2: $V_2 - I_1 R_1 - I_3 R_3 = 0$

Junction: $I_1 = I_2 + I_3$

Substitute known values to form a system of three equations with three unknowns.

Loop 1: $(12\ \text{V}) - (4\ \Omega)I_1 - (6\ \Omega)I_2 = 0 \rightarrow$
$(4\ \Omega)I_1 + (6\ \Omega)I_2 = 12$ V

Loop 2: $(8\ \text{V}) - (4\ \Omega)I_1 - (4\ \Omega)I_3 = 0 \rightarrow$
$(4\ \Omega)I_1 + (4\ \Omega)I_3 = 8$ V

Junction: $I_1 = I_2 + I_3$

$$(4\ \Omega)I_1 + (6\ \Omega)I_2 = 12\ \text{V} \rightarrow$$
$$(4\ \Omega)(I_2 + I_3) + (6\ \Omega)I_2 = 12\ \text{V} \rightarrow$$
$$(10\ \Omega)I_2 + (4\ \Omega)I_3 = 12\ \text{V}$$

Substitute the expression for I_1 into the first two equations.

$$(4\ \Omega)I_1 + (4\ \Omega)I_3 = 8\ \text{V} \rightarrow$$
$$(4\ \Omega)(I_2 + I_3) + (4\ \Omega)I_3 = 8\ \text{V} \rightarrow$$
$$(4\ \Omega)I_2 + (8\ \Omega)I_3 = 8\ \text{V}$$

Solve the system of equations.

$$(4\ \Omega)I_2 + (8\ \Omega)I_3 = 8\ \text{V} \rightarrow I_2 = 2\ \text{A} - 2I_3$$
$$(10\ \Omega)I_2 + (4\ \Omega)I_3 = 12\ \text{V} \rightarrow$$
$$(10\ \Omega)(2\ \text{A} - 2I_3) + (4\ \Omega)I_3 = 12\ \text{V} \rightarrow$$
$$20\ \text{V} - (20\ \Omega)I_3 + (4\ \Omega)I_3 = 12\ \text{V} \rightarrow$$
$$8\ \text{V} = (16\ \Omega)I_3 \rightarrow I_3 = 0.5\ \text{A}$$

Solve for I_2 in the second equation from the previous step and substitute into the first equation to solve for I_3. Then use the solution to find I_1.

$$I_2 = 2\ \text{A} - 2I_3 = 2\ \text{A} - 2(0.5\ \text{A}) = 1\ \text{A}$$
$$I_1 = I_2 + I_3 = 1\ \text{A} + 0.5\ \text{A} = 1.5\ \text{A}$$

I_1 is 1.5 A downward, I_2 is 1 A clockwise, and I_3 is 0.5 A counterclockwise.

4. EVALUATE Reflect on your answer.

Current is greatest through I_1, which is part of both loops. Current is least through I_3, in the loop with the lower-voltage battery. Both make sense.

 GO ONLINE for more **math support**.

▶ **Math Tutorial Video**

🖥 **Math Practice Problems**

---

(29) For the circuit shown in the Sample Problem, suppose $V_1 = 8\ \text{V}$, $V_2 = 12\ \text{V}$, $R_1 = 2\ \Omega$, $R_2 = 6\ \Omega$, and $R_3 = 6\ \Omega$. Determine the direction and magnitude of the current across all three resistors.

📖 **NEED A HINT?** Go online to your **eText Sample Problem** for stepped-out support.

(30) For the circuit shown in the Sample Problem, suppose $V_1 = 15\ \text{V}$, $V_2 = 12\ \text{V}$, $R_1 = 10\ \Omega$, $R_2 = 4\ \Omega$, and $R_3 = 10\ \Omega$. Determine the direction and magnitude of the current across all three resistors.

(31) For the circuit shown in the Sample Problem, suppose you keep all the values the same but increase V_2 to 12 V. Without performing any calculations, explain what effect the increased voltage will have on I_1, I_2, and I_3. Support your answer using Kirchhoff's rules.

INVESTIGATIVE PHENOMENON

GO ONLINE to revisit your **Investigative Phenomenon modeling activity** with the new information you have learned about Energy in Electric Circuits.

These questions will help you apply what you learned in this experience to the Investigative Phenomenon.

32 **CCC Energy and Matter** Electricity is dependent on conductors. All metals are good conductors of electricity, yet some are ohmic materials, such as the copper wires in a circuit, and some are nonohmic materials, such as the tungsten filament in an incandescent light bulb. Explain how different materials in a circuit may affect the behavior of the current.

33 **SEP Design a Solution** As scientists and engineers search for sustainable ways to meet a growing demand for energy, electronics engineers are looking for ways to reduce the power consumed by electronic devices, such as smartphones, TVs, and computers. Based on your knowledge of circuits, what are some ways that you think the power requirements of a smartphone could be reduced?

34 **SEP Construct an Explanation** Explain what happens to electrical energy in a current when it crosses a resistor in a circuit. In what ways do resistors result in lost or wasted energy?

 GO ONLINE for a **quiz** to evaluate what you learned about Energy in Electric Circuits.

Power Generation

 GO ONLINE to do a **hands-on lab** to investigate how to build a motor.

Electric Generators

The electricity you use at home and at school likely comes from an electric generator. An **electric generator** is a device that converts mechanical energy into electrical energy. The mechanical energy can come from simple sources, such as a hand crank on a flashlight, a flowing river, wind, and steam. A generator uses that mechanical energy to power anything that runs on electricity from small devices to entire cities.

Just as there are different forms of electric current, there are different types of electric generators. Alternating current generators produce alternating current (AC) and direct current generators produce direct current (DC).

Turbines A turbine is a machine consisting of a set of blades arranged in a circle around a central shaft. A moving fluid, such as wind, water, or steam, exerts a force on the blades, causing them to move and rotate the shaft, which drives a generator.

VOCABULARY

The word *generator* comes from the Latin word *generare*, which means "to bring forth or produce." Michael Faraday built the first **electric generator** in 1831 during his experiments with electromagnetism.

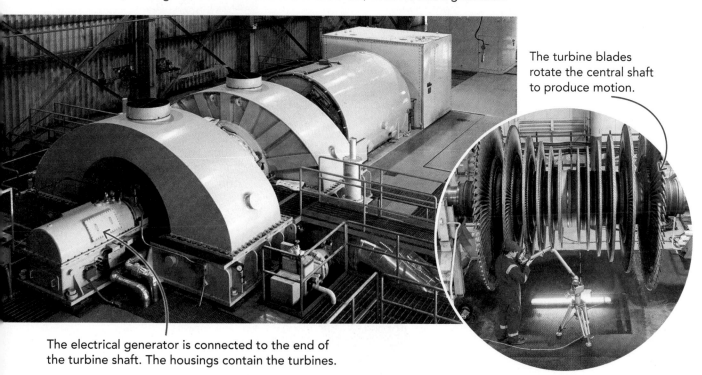

The turbine blades rotate the central shaft to produce motion.

The electrical generator is connected to the end of the turbine shaft. The housings contain the turbines.

(35) **CCC Cause and Effect** Suppose you are using a flashlight with a hand crank while camping. When you turn the crank faster, do you expect the light to become brighter or dimmer? Explain your answer.

Alternating Current Generators

▶ **GO ONLINE** to watch a **video** about electromotive force, alternating current generators, and transformers.

Generators operate according to Faraday's law. A wire coil rotates through a magnetic field, which induces an electromotive force (EMF) along with a current in the wire.

A simple AC generator consists of a wire coil attached to a pair of slip rings, which rotate along with the coil. Brushes are small conducting components connected to an external electrical circuit, and the brushes slide along as the rings spin under them. As one side of the wire coil moves up and the other side moves down through the magnetic field, a potential difference is induced in the wire in one direction, and current flows through the wire. As the coil rotates, the voltage and the current reverse direction. The current reverses direction twice as the coil rotates through 360°. The voltage generated is proportional to the speed of the coil's rotation, as well as to the number of loops of wire in the coil. AC generators are used in automobile electrical systems in cars, to power small motors in household electrical appliances, and in commercial electric power plants.

EXPERIENCE IT!

Use tape to mark the outline of a simple loop of wire on the floor. Model an electron in the wire loop by standing on a spot on the tape and then moving along the wire to represent the alternating flow of current generated by an AC generator.

AC Generator As the coil rotates, the magnetic flux through the coil changes, which produces a potential difference between the ends of the wire. An alternating current is induced through the wire as the coil rotates through the field. The other poles of these magnets are not shown for simplicity.

The current flows through the brushes to the slip rings, which provide a continuous connection to the external circuit.

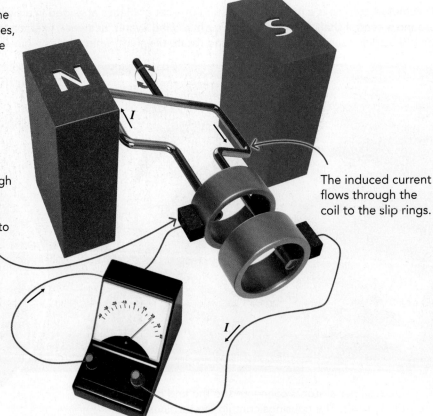

The induced current flows through the coil to the slip rings.

36 **SEP Construct an Explanation** In order to generate large currents, a generator must use stronger magnets, more coil loops, or rotate faster. It then becomes more efficient to rotate the magnetic field inside a fixed coil, so that the field cuts the coil to induce a current, rather than the coil cutting the field. Explain why that is the case.

Direct Current Generators

A direct current (DC) generator is similar to an AC generator in that a coil rotates in a magnetic field to induce a current in a wire. However, a DC generator produces direct current rather than an alternating current. Such a generator employs a split-ring commutator instead of the slip rings used in AC generators. Every half turn, just as the induced current is about to change direction, the split ring reverses the coil connections. As a result, the current constantly flows in one direction only. Unfortunately, rubbing against the breaks in the commutator rings causes the brushes to wear away.

DC generators generally are used to power large electric motors, and most devices with sensitive electronic circuits require the steady, unidirectional current provided by DC generators. However, AC generators are more reliable and practical than DC generators. AC generators can also operate at higher speeds than DC generators, as well as produce more power at lower speeds.

Remember that you can determine the electromotive force (EMF) induced in a wire passing through a magnetic field by applying Faraday's law.

$$V_\varepsilon = -N\frac{\Delta\Phi}{\Delta t}$$

DC Generator As in an AC generator, the magnetic flux through the coil changes as the wire rotates, which produces a potential difference between the ends of the wire. The other poles of these magnets are not shown for simplicity.

By switching the connections every half turn, a split-ring commutator allows the current to flow in one direction through the external circuit.

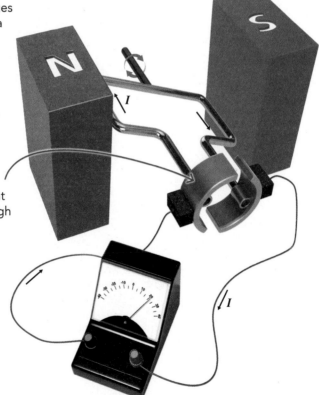

(37) **SEP Develop a Model** Draw a diagram to explain how both matter and energy flow within the system of an AC or DC generator. On your diagram, be sure to show how mechanical energy, electrical energy, and matter move within the system.

EMF Induced in a Generator

A generator coil is rotated one quarter of a full revolution, from $\theta = 0°$ to $\theta = 90°$, in 14 ms. The coil has 250 loops, and it is a square 8.0 cm on a side. If the coil is in a uniform magnetic field of 0.85 T, what is the maximum electromotive force induced in the coil by the generator?

1. DRAW A PICTURE Sketch a picture of the situation.

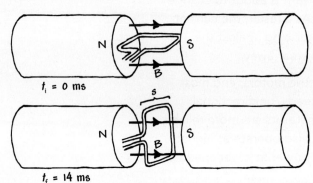

t_i = 0 ms

t_f = 14 ms

2. DEFINE THE PROBLEM List knowns and unknowns, and assign values to variables.

$N = 250$	$A = ?$
$\Delta t = 14$ ms	$V_\varepsilon = ?$
s = 8.0 cm	
$B = 0.85$ T	

3. PLAN AND EXECUTE Use mathematical relationships, the picture, and your definitions to plan and execute a solution.

Write the equation for Faraday's law to determine the electromotive force induced.

$$V_\varepsilon = -N\frac{\Delta\Phi}{\Delta t}$$

Remember that the change in magnetic flux is the product of the strength of the magnetic field and the area of the loop. Substitute those values in the equation for Faraday's law.

$$\Delta\Phi = -BA$$
$$V_\varepsilon = N\frac{BA}{\Delta t}$$

Calculate the area of the squared-shaped coil, first converting the length to meters.

$$A = s^2 = (0.080 \text{ m})^2 = 0.0064 \text{ m}^2$$

Determine the maximum electromotive force.

$$V_\varepsilon = N\frac{BA}{\Delta t}$$
$$= 250\frac{(0.85 \text{ T})(0.0064 \text{ m}^2)}{0.014 \text{ s}} = 97 \text{ V}$$

4. EVALUATE Reflect on your answer.
House current is generally 110–120 V. A maximum electromotive force of 97 V through one quarter of a revolution seems reasonable.

 GO ONLINE for more **math support**.

💻 **Math Practice Problems**

---

(38) A generator coil is rotated one half of a full revolution, from $\theta = 0°$ to $\theta = 90°$, in 25 ms. The coil has 400 loops, and it is a square 9.0 cm on a side. If the coil is in a uniform magnetic field of 0.75 T, then what is the maximum electromotive force induced in the coil by the generator?

📖 **NEED A HINT?** Go online to your **eText Sample Problem** for stepped-out support.

Motors

 GO ONLINE to do a PhET **simulation** that allows you to explore energy transformations in electric motors and generators.

An **electric motor** is a device that converts electrical energy into mechanical energy. A motor operates according to the same principle as a generator but in reverse.

In a simple motor, electric current flows through a coil of wire in a magnetic field. The field exerts opposite forces on the current in the opposite sides of the coil. The combination of forces causes the coil to rotate.

As with generators, some motors run on alternating current, and other motors run on direct current. In general, AC motors are more efficient and are found in devices that require a large amount of power. DC motors, however, operate over a wider range of current and speed. DC motors are commonly found in smaller devices.

The spinning coil in a motor also acts as a generator. As the coil rotates, the magnetic field induces what is known as **back EMF,** which is a potential that acts against the voltage driving the motor. As a result, a motor requires more current and, hence, more power to begin spinning than it does to run at operating speed. To determine how much power a motor needs at operating speed, subtract the back EMF from the applied voltage.

Commutator and Coils
To be efficient, a real motor needs a commutator and coils arranged at several different angles.

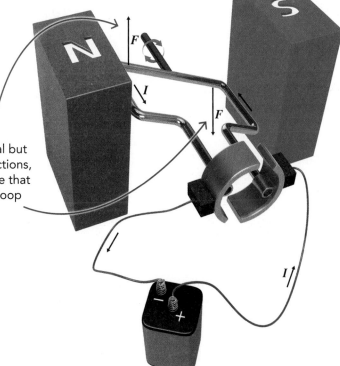

Electric Motor An energy source (a battery) supplies electrical energy to a wire loop in a magnetic field, causing the loop to move. The other poles of these magnets are not shown for simplicity.

Two forces, equal but in opposite directions, produce a torque that causes the wire loop to rotate.

39) **SEP Use Models** Examine the diagrams of AC and DC generators, and compare them to the diagram of the motor. Explain how the flow of energy through a generator system is both similar to and different from the flow of energy through a motor system.

Starting a Motor

The coils in a motor have a resistance of 0.050 Ω and are driven by an EMF of 50 V. The back EMF induced in the motor is 40 V. Determine the current drawn when the motor starts operating and the current drawn when the motor reaches operating speed. Then, calculate the difference in power required by the motor at startup and at operating speed.

1. DRAW A PICTURE Sketch a picture of the situation.

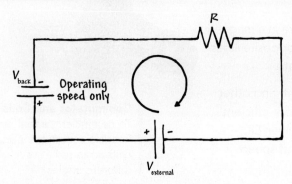

2. DEFINE THE PROBLEM List knowns and unknowns, and assign values to variables.

$R = 0.050 \ \Omega$	$I_{start} = ?$
$V_{external} = 50 \ \text{V}$	$I_{operating} = ?$
$V_{back} = 40 \ \text{V}$	$\Delta P = ?$

3. PLAN AND EXECUTE Use mathematical relationships, the picture, and your definitions to plan and execute a solution.

Use Kirchhoff's loop rule to find the effective current through the motor at startup.

$$V_{external} - I_{start} R = 0$$
$$I_{start} = \frac{V_{external}}{R} = \frac{50 \ \text{V}}{0.050 \ \Omega} = 1000 \ \text{A}$$

Use Kirchhoff's loop rule to find the effective voltage of the motor while it is operating.

$$V_{external} - V_{back} - I_{operating} R = 0$$
$$I_{operating} R = 50 \ \text{V} - 40 \ \text{V} = 10 \ \text{V}$$

Then, determine the operating current.

$$I_{operating} = \frac{V}{R} = \frac{10 \ \text{V}}{0.050 \ \Omega} = 200 \ \text{A}$$

Calculate the power required by the motor at startup and at operating speed.

$$P = IV$$
$$P_{start} = (1000 \ \text{A})(50 \ \text{V}) = 50,000 \ \text{W} = 50 \ \text{kW}$$
$$P_{operating} = (200 \ \text{A})(50 \ \text{V}) = 10,000 \ \text{W} = 10 \ \text{kW}$$

Subtract to find the difference in the power required at startup and at operating speed.

$$50 \ \text{kW} - 10 \ \text{kW} = 40 \ \text{kW}$$

4. EVALUATE Reflect on your answer.
The current drawn and power requirement for a motor should be greater at startup than at operating speed, so the answers are reasonable.

GO ONLINE for more **math support**.

▶ **Math Tutorial Video**

▣ **Math Practice Problems**

(40) The coils in a motor have a resistance of 0.040 Ω and are driven by an EMF of 40.0 V. The back EMF induced in the motor is 36.0 V. Determine the current drawn when the motor starts operating and the current drawn when the motor reaches operating speed. Then, calculate the difference in power required by the motor at startup and at operating speed.

   📖 **NEED A HINT?** Go online to your **eText Sample Problem** for stepped-out support.

(41) The coils in a motor have a resistance of 0.075 Ω and are driven by an EMF of 65 V. The back EMF induced in the motor is 25 V. Determine the current drawn when the motor starts operating and the current drawn when the motor reaches operating speed. Then, calculate the difference in power required by the motor at startup and at operating speed.

(42) The coils in a motor have a resistance of 0.060 Ω. The current drawn when the motor reaches operating speed is 300.0 A. The back EMF induced in the motor is 25 V. Calculate the voltage required by the motor at startup.

(43) The coils in a motor have a resistance of 0.022 Ω. The voltage that drives a motor is 45 V, and the current drawn by the motor at operating speed is 900.0 A. What is the back EMF induced in the motor?

(44) A student calculates the difference between current drawn at startup and the current at running speed for an electric motor. She knows that the resistance of the coil in the motor is 0.040 Ω, the EMF is 60.0 V, and the back EMF is 56.0 V. The student calculates that the current drawn when the motor starts up is 15 A and at operating speed is 14 A. Is her answer correct? If not, explain what she did wrong, and determine the correct answer.

(45) Portable household generators are usually rated with starting and running watts because motors require more power when starting up than at operating speed. Suppose you're helping a relative purchase a generator to power a few devices during power outages. Refer to the table for the devices that need to be powered. Which generator would you recommend, one with 3500 starting watts and 2000 running watts, or one with 3000 starting watts and 1800 running watts? Explain your answer.

Device	Starting current (A)	Running current (A)	Input voltage (V)
Small refrigerator	5.0	1.1	115
Fan	5.0	2.0	110
Laptop	—	4.0	22
Lamp	—	8.3	12
Air conditioner	17.3	6.1	115

Induction Devices

Electromagnetic induction is a phenomenon that occurs when an electrical conductor is in a changing magnetic field. The change can be either a conductor in motion relative to a magnetic field or a varying field produced by a changing electric current.

Transformers A **transformer** is an electrical device that increases or decreases voltage by means of sets of wire coils wrapped around a shared iron core. Current through a primary coil magnetically induces a current in a secondary coil close to it. A step-up transformer has more secondary coils than primary coils, and its output is at a higher voltage than its input. A step-down transformer has fewer secondary coils than primary coils, and its output is at a lower voltage. A transformer's output voltage depends on the input voltage and the ratio of the number of primary coils to secondary coils.

Transformer A transformer is an electromagnetic device that works through Faraday's law of induction, converting electrical energy from one potential to another.

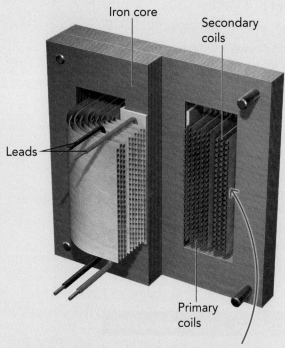

Iron core

Secondary coils

Leads

Primary coils

Voltage can be increased or decreased by correspondingly increasing or decreasing the number of turns in the secondary coils.

Transformers can be built in many sizes. There is a small one in your phone charger.

(46) **CCC Cause and Effect** According to the law of conservation of energy, energy cannot be created or destroyed. A transformer only increases or decreases voltage, not power. For that to be true, what must happen to the current when the voltage is increased or decreaed by a transformer? Explain your answer.

Metal Detectors and Their Applications

How do **metal detectors work?**

Detecting Metal Objects The steps show how metal detectors locate metallic objects by **generating an electromagnetic (EM) field** and alert the user when an **induced external EM field** produces a counter-current in the detector.

Step 1 The detector **produces a current that generates an EM field** strong enough to penetrate the top layers of the ground.

Step 4 A sound or change in tone is produced when an **induced current is detected.**

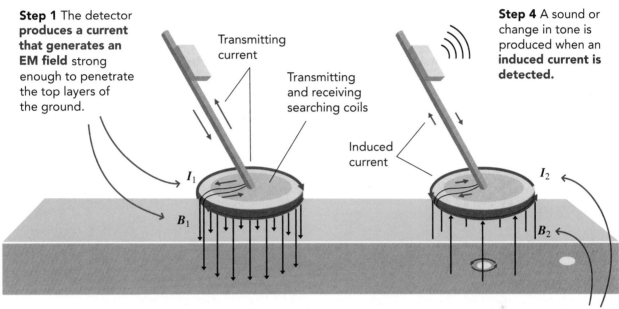

Transmitting current

Transmitting and receiving searching coils

Induced current

I_1

B_1

I_2

B_2

Step 2 When the transmitted EM field passes over a metallic object, such as a coin, **the object is energized and produces an eddy current.**

Step 3 The **eddy current in the object produces its own EM field** that induces a current in the detector's receiving coils.

Other Applications **Metal detectors have applications** beyond finding lost treasure. They are also used in different situations to scan for metal weapons and to help ensure food is free of dangerous metallic contaminants.

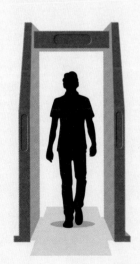

Metal detectors are commonly used near the entrances of public places, like airports and government buildings, to **alert security of the possible presence of metal weapons.**

Specialized metal detectors are used in the food industry to **alert food and health inspectors of the presence of metallic contaminants or particles** that can be harmful to consumers' health.

INVESTIGATIVE PHENOMENON

GO ONLINE to revisit your **Investigative Phenomenon modeling activity** with the new information you have learned about Power Generation.

These questions will help you apply what you learned in this experience to the Investigative Phenomenon.

47 **SEP Develop and Use a Model** The fundamental principles of electric power are the same at the large scale and the small scale. Suppose you are designing a DC generator that uses a hand crank to charge batteries. Draw a model of the generator, and then label your model to identify three ways you can increase the amperage of the current in the circuit.

48 **CCC Energy and Matter** A wind turbine relies on wind energy to turn blades in a generator, which tranforms mechanical energy into electrical energy. Apply what you have learned about power generation to evaluate wind energy as a sustainable source of power. What are some of the benefits of generating electrical energy from wind energy? What are some drawbacks?

49 **SEP Use Mathematics** The power grid depends on step-up and step-down transformers for efficient power transmission. For either kind of transformer, the ratio of the input voltage to the output voltage is equal to the ratio of the number of loops in the primary coil to the number of loops in the secondary coil. That relation can be written as what is known as the transformer equation: $\frac{V_P}{V_S} = \frac{N_P}{N_S}$. Suppose the primary coil in a transformer contains 90 loops, the input voltage is 415 V, and the secondary coil contains 380 loops. What is the output voltage? Suppose you want to increase the output voltage to 2490 V. How many additional loops do you need to add to the secondary coil?

GO ONLINE for a **quiz** to evaluate what you learned about Power Generation.

Energy Resources and Conservation

 GO ONLINE to do a **hands-on lab** to investigate and compare the sustainability of different energy-generation methods.

Human Use of Energy

Global Energy For hundreds of thousands of years, most human energy needs were supplied directly or indirectly by the sun. All work was done with human or animal muscles. Then, a few thousand years ago, humans began to tap into the power of wind with sailboats and windmills. They built watermills to harness the power of flowing water. In the past two centuries, coal and petroleum have driven worldwide industrialization, accompanied by an expansion in energy consumption.

In recent decades, petroleum has become more expensive, and its environmental effects are no longer acceptable. The world now faces the challenge of replacing coal and oil with renewable energy sources.

Human Energy Consumption The graph shows the different energy sources humans have relied on in the past and the capacity of these different energy sources over time.

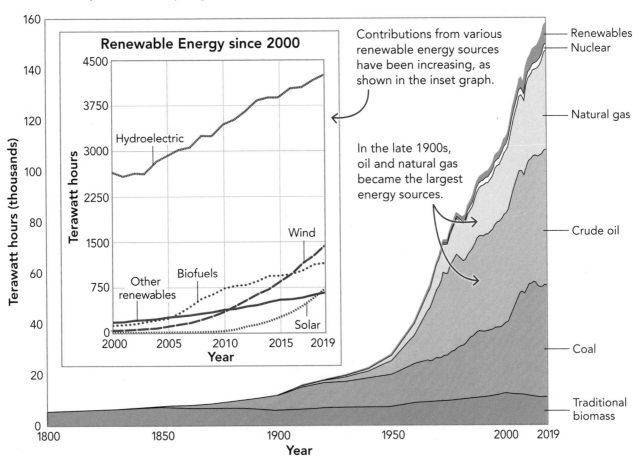

Data from: Vaclav Smil, *Energy Transitions: Global and National Perspectives* (2017), BP Statistical Review of World Energy & Our World in Data

Energy Use, Population, and Impact For most people during most of history, life was hard. Death rates were high and populations were small. Harnessing energy brought a higher standard of living, but that led to rapidly increasing populations, which required still more food and other resources. As the global population grows and each person uses more and more energy, there are greater and greater effects on Earth's biosphere. One way to quantify those effects is through the Ehrlich equation.

Ehrlich Equation
$I = PAT$
I = impact $\qquad\qquad$ A = affluence per person
P = human population $\qquad$ T = technological inefficiency

There are also other ways to use this equation. One way is to replace the impact per person, which is AT (the product of affluence and technological inefficiency), with the global gross domestic product (GDP) per person. Another way is to replace AT with the energy consumed per person, so that the total impact is proportional to the total energy consumed. However, neither GDP nor energy use is a direct measure of environmental impact.

Human Population Growth and Production Assisted by easy access to energy resources, the human population has risen rapidly over the past century. The amount of goods humans consume, represented here by the annual GDP per person, has also increased.

World population took hundreds of thousands of years to reach 3 billion in 1960. It then took nearly 60 years to reach 7.7 billion.

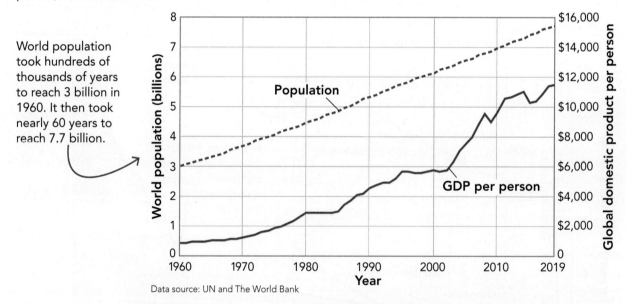

Data source: UN and The World Bank

(50) **SEP Use Mathematics** Assume that the graph of GDP per person is a measure of the impact per person (*AT*). Compute the total impact for 1960 and the total for 2019. Then find the ratio of the two. Repeat the calculation, with the assumption that the previous graph of total energy consumption is a measure of total impact.

(51) **SEP Analyze Data** Suppose that the human population eventually stops increasing and levels off. What are the requirements on *A* and *T* for human impact to decrease over time?

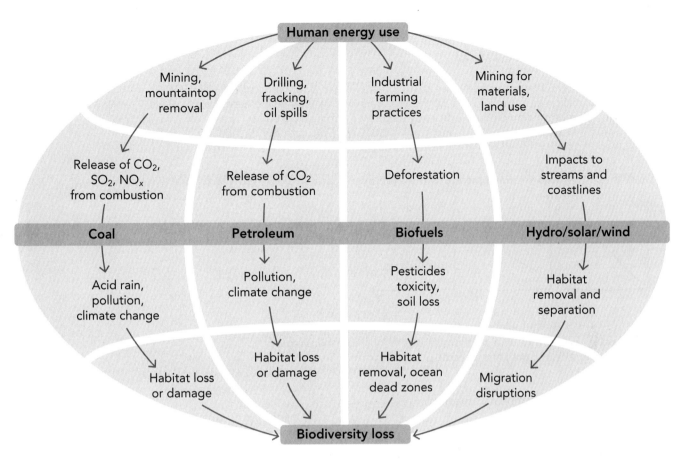

How Energy Use Impacts Biodiversity The upper part of the figure shows some of the activities related to developing energy sources. The bottom part shows the impacts of those activities on the biosphere.

Impacts on the Biosphere

 GO ONLINE to do a PhET **simulation** that allows you to explore the environmental impacts of energy-related activities.

Energy use by humans has significant impacts on Earth systems, particularly on the biosphere. Habitats for organisms require space as well as clean soil, air, and water. Many energy-related activities damage or destroy habitats. **Nonrenewable energy resources** are sources of energy that are limited and take very long periods of time to replenish, such as fossil fuels. The large amount of pollution associated with nonrenewables has damaging effects on organisms. **Renewable energy resources** are sources of energy that are readily available or replenished on a relatively short time scale, such as solar or hydroelectric power. Renewables do not cause the level of pollution that fossil fuels do, but they nonetheless can have harmful impacts on the biosphere. Humans get oxygen, food, shelter, and many medicines from the biosphere, and damaging its health also harms our health and well-being.

52 **CCC Cause and Effect** A 2020 United Nations report noted that as many as a million species are at risk of extinction. Pick a type of energy and explain how using it could drive a species to extinction.

Impact Reduction

Suppose that, for a number of years t after 2020, Earth's human population of 7.7 billion increases by 82 million each year. Also suppose that each year, affluence increases by 0.01, and an increase in technological efficiency decreases impact by $0.0002t$. That means $P = 7.7 + 0.082t$, $A = 1 + 0.01t$, and $T = 1 - 0.0002t^2$. Calculate the decade at which human impact on the environment stops increasing.

1. DRAW A PICTURE Sketch a picture of the situation.

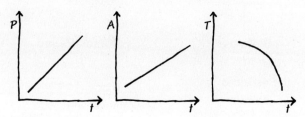

2. DEFINE THE PROBLEM List knowns and unknowns, and assign values to variables.

$$P = 7.7 + 0.082t \qquad I = ?$$
$$A = 1 + 0.01t$$
$$T = 1 - 0.0002t^2$$

3. PLAN AND EXECUTE Use mathematical relationships, the picture, and your definitions to plan and execute a solution.

Write the Ehrlich equation and substitute the terms provided.	$I = PAT$ $I = (7.7 + 0.082t)(1 + 0.01t)(1 - 0.0002t^2)$
Beginning with $t = 0$, calculate I for each successive decade ($t = 10, 20$, and so on).	$I = (7.7 + 0.082t)(1 + 0.01t)(1 - 0.0002t^2)$ $= (7.7 + 0)(1 + 0)(1 - 0) = 7.7$
Continue calculating I for successive decades, comparing the values until you observe a decrease.	$t = 0; I = 7.7$ $t = 10; I = 9.2$ $t = 20; I = 10.3$ $t = 30; I = 10.8$ $t = 40; I = 10.5 \leftarrow$

I begins to decrease after 40 years, which is 2060.

4. EVALUATE Reflect on your answer.
The answer is appropriate because the population and affluence are both increasing in proportion to time, but T (technological inefficiency) is decreasing as the square of the time. At some point, the impact stops increasing.

 GO ONLINE for more **math support**.

▶ **Math Tutorial Video**

🖥 **Math Practice Problems**

---

(53) Suppose that for a number of years t after 2020, Earth's human population of 7.7 billion increases by 82 million. Also suppose that affluence increases each year by 0.01, and that efficiency decreases impact by $0.0003t$. That means $P = 7.7 + 0.082t$, $A = 1 + 0.01t$, and $T = 1 - 0.0003t^2$. Calculate the decade at which human impact on the environment stops increasing.

📖 **NEED A HINT?** Go online to your **eText Sample Problem** for stepped-out support.

Human Power Needs

Energy Forms and Sectors Energy uses can be divided into four sectors: residential, commercial, industrial, and transportation. Their relative sizes vary by country and over time. For example, U.S. industrial energy needs have been decreasing over time, while transportation needs have been increasing.

Most of the energy used comes directly from fuels, such as burning gasoline to power a car or burning natural gas to heat a house. However, an increasing share of energy comes from electricity because of its flexibility, its ease of transport through power lines, and its ability to be generated by renewable sources, nuclear sources, or fossil fuels.

No thermodynamic process can ever be 100% efficient. Power plants fueled by combustion or nuclear reactors have efficiencies of about 30%–40%. Wind, solar, and hydroelectric power capture only about 20%–40% of the available power, a quantity called the *capacity factor*. The largest category of energy use is wasted energy, particularly heat from generating electricity.

EXPERIENCE IT!

Think about how often you use electronic devices throughout the day. Then, think about when you take in chemical potential energy from food and when you expend the most energy during the day. How do the two energy budgets compare?

U.S. Energy Sources and Uses The United States used 106 exajoules (1.06×10^{20} J) of energy in all forms in 2019; part was from direct use of energy sources and part was from electricity generation.

Two thirds of all energy consumed went to wasted energy, largely in the form of heating the environment.

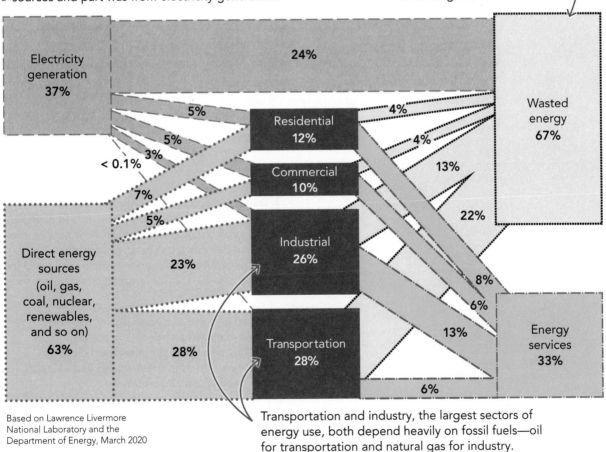

Based on Lawrence Livermore National Laboratory and the Department of Energy, March 2020

Transportation and industry, the largest sectors of energy use, both depend heavily on fossil fuels—oil for transportation and natural gas for industry.

54 **SEP Analyze Data** Using the diagram, calculate the efficiency of the most efficient of the four sectors and compare it to the efficiency of electric power generation.

Annual Load Management Both energy sources and energy consumption in the residential and commercial sectors vary with the seasons. **Load management** is a process that tracks and balances energy supply and demand in power generation networks.

Annual Supply and Demand Variations Energy demand varies throughout the year, but it does not match the variability of supplies of renewables.

Electricity for a sample home in Missouri varies annually with two peaks for summer cooling and winter heating. Natural gas use has a single peak for winter heating.

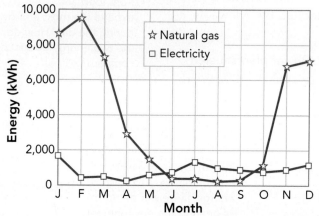

Wind and solar output vary over the course of a year, shown here as the capacity factor for the sums of U.S. wind and solar electricity farms during 2018–2019.

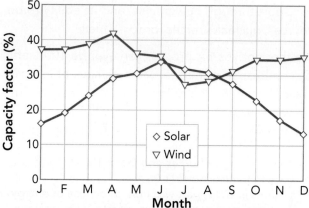

Daily Load Management Daily energy needs also vary tremendously, and they may be difficult to match with sources of energy. If you have a constant supply available from coal, nuclear, or hydroelectric generating plants, you can store energy during low-demand periods and retrieve it during high-demand periods. When your supply is variable, as is often the case for wind and solar power, you may need a large storage capacity. If your storage capacity is small, you may need another source you can turn on quickly to supply the demand.

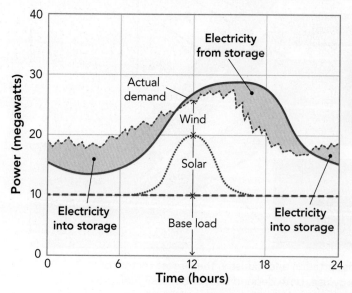

Daily Variations in Supply and Demand In a hypothetical scenario for a power grid over a day, the areas between the curves show how multiple sources and energy storage combine to satisfy the demand. The combination reduces the need for a more reliable, but more expensive, constant supply.

Together, wind and solar power provide more energy than needed in the morning but not enough in the afternoon. Surplus energy is stored in the morning and retrieved in the afternoon.

(55) **SEP Construct an Explanation** For the example home in Missouri, the average outdoor temperature was 25°C (77°F) in the summer and 3°C (37°F) in the winter. Use these data to explain the differences between the magnitudes of the natural gas and electricity curves.

Energy Storage Technologies

The use of wind and solar power has been increasing, but these resources aren't always available: the wind doesn't always blow, and the sun doesn't shine at night. As a result, there is an increasing need to store huge amounts of energy. Currently, nearly all energy storage is done through large hydroelectric dams, where water is pumped uphill into a reservoir when there is extra energy available and flows downhill when electricity is needed. Lithium-ion batteries are the most abundant form of large battery storage, but many new battery technologies are being explored. Energy stored by producing hydrogen through chemical processes can be retrieved using hydrogen fuel cells. Excess thermal energy can be stored and used at a later time.

Energy can be stored by pumping air into underground caverns. The compressed air later flows back out and spins turbines to retrieve the energy. Flywheels can store rotational kinetic energy.

Energy storage is a rapidly changing field, and there are many important factors to be considered, such as how fast energy can be retrieved, how many times a device can be charged and discharged, and the efficiency of the energy conversion. Of course, cost is always a factor. Lower storage costs will make power from fluctuating renewable sources more useful.

Storing Energy This high mountain reservoir at the Mooserboden Stausee dam in Austria stores water that can be used to generate electricity at a later time.

Storage technology	Capacity*	Cost ($/kWh)	Efficiency
Pumped hydroelectric	181 GW (94.8%)	165	70–85%
Battery	4.2 GW (2.2%)	469–928	60–95%
Thermal	3.2 GW (1.7%)	30	50–90%
Flywheel	1.0 GW (0.5%)	11,520	70–95%

*Total global storage capacity as of 2020 (% of total)

(56) **SEP Use Mathematics** There are currently about 1.5 billion cars and trucks on roads throughout the world. Suppose that a few decades in the future, each one could be an electric vehicle with a 50-kWh battery pack. Compare the total energy storage in such a global fleet to the amount of electrical energy humans use in a day, assuming a rate of 3 TW. (*Hint:* 1 kWh is equal to 3.6 million joules.)

Costs and Benefits

All energy sources come with benefits and costs, otherwise known as advantages and disadvantages. Costs and benefits take three forms: financial, environmental, and social. Financial costs and benefits include profits, jobs, taxes, and market values. Environmental costs include pollution, habitat damage, biodiversity loss, soil removal, resource damage, and climate change. There are no benefits. Social costs and benefits include human physical and mental health, loss of life, missed work days, and social injustice. Science can provide information about the costs and benefits, but the choices to be made are social and political.

Benefits of Fossil Fuels For fossil fuel sources, the main benefits are high energy densities, portability, and flexibility. Petroleum, natural gas, and coal are highly concentrated hydrocarbons that have high energy densities, meaning they release a great deal of energy when burned. Oil and gas can also be transported through pipelines.

Costs of Fossil Fuels The main costs of fossil fuels involve exploration, protection, mining, transportation, processing, refining, combustion, pollution, waste cleanup, and environmental remediation associated with the tremendous volumes of fuels consumed.

Fossil fuels must be transported great distances, which takes energy. Spills from train and ship accidents as well as leaks from drilling, pipelines, tankers, and storage tanks contaminate water.

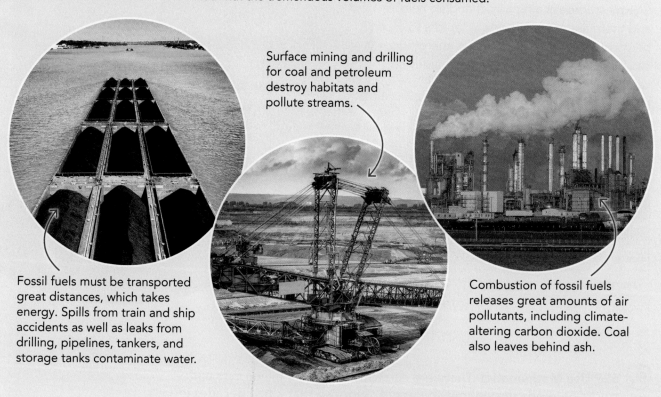

Surface mining and drilling for coal and petroleum destroy habitats and pollute streams.

Combustion of fossil fuels releases great amounts of air pollutants, including climate-altering carbon dioxide. Coal also leaves behind ash.

(57) **SEP Use Mathematics The solar panels needed to provide 1 megawatt (MW) of electricity have a mass of about 1.1 thousand metric tons and can operate for more than 25 years. If the energy density of coal is 25,000 MJ/metric ton, calculate the mass of coal needed to be mined and burned to provide 1 MW for 25 years if the efficiency is 35%.**

Costs and Benefits of Renewable Energy

What are some **costs** and **benefits** of using **renewable energy?**

The Good and the Bad Hydroelectric, solar, and wind power account for about 90% of the renewable energy sources used to generate electricity in the U.S. They each have costs and benefits to consider when making **decisions about sustainable energy use.**

Hydroelectric

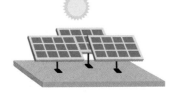

Solar

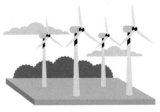

Wind

Benefits

Hydroelectric
- Clean energy source that produces almost no greenhouse gases
- More **reliable and affordable source** of energy than fossil fuels
- Can scale power generation up and down quickly

Solar
- Clean energy source that produces almost no greenhouse gases
- **Abundant energy source** (Earth receives more energy in a bit more than an hour than all humans use in a year)
- Less expensive than fossil fuels

Wind
- Clean energy source that produces almost no greenhouse gases
- Ability to generate energy in remote locations
- Often co-located within farms, using very little extra land
- **Least-expensive source** of electricity

Costs

Hydroelectric
- Requires proximity to source of moving water
- Construction of dams alters cycles of natural processes and changes river chemistry
- Changes to river habitats **can negatively impact fish** and other aquatic organisms

Solar
- Large-scale generation requires a large space for solar panel arrays and other equipment
- Solar **output is not constant,** varies by location, and is dependent on weather conditions
- Manufacturing solar panels requires mining for raw materials

Wind
- **Not a constant source** of reliable energy because wind strength cannot be controlled
- Can negatively impact surrounding wildlife
- Manufacturing turbines requires mining for raw materials, which damages the environment

Renewable Energy Sources The inexhaustible supplies of sunlight, wind, and rain, as well as the freedom from pollution, make renewable energy sources appealing. The biggest cost for renewables is large amounts of land. There are ingenious ways to intersperse solar panels and wind turbines within croplands and grazing lands, but the demands on land area are still large. Extending the power grid to support dispersed supplies also requires time and money.

 CCC Cause and Effect Croplands can be used to grow crops for liquid biofuels, such as gasoline-enhancing ethanol. However, vast areas of land are needed. Explain why many people eating more meat would affect the feasibility of using croplands for biofuels.

Costs and Benefits: Oil, Gas, and Coal

Fossil fuels continue to power most human activities because they release a great deal of energy when burned. However, the economic costs of electricity from fossil fuels are now greater than for wind and solar power—and much greater when health and environmental costs are added. Easily obtained fossil fuels are now gone, so developing new resources requires drilling in more challenging and costly conditions. Production has increased from low-grade sources, such as tar sands and oil shales, but those resources are also dwindling.

Changes in U.S. Electricity Generating Capacity Since 2009 More than 170 gigawatts of generating capacity were added between 2009 and 2019, but changes in capacity differ greatly from source to source.

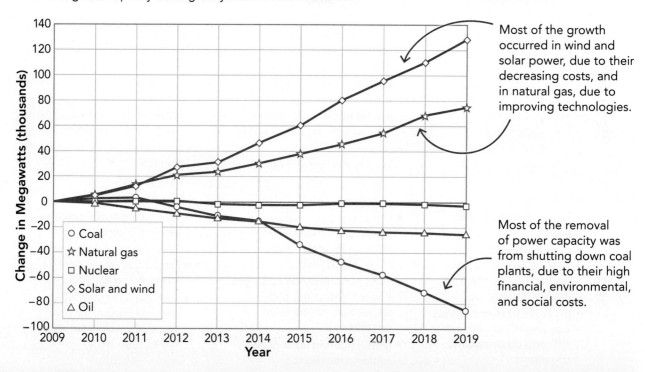

Most of the growth occurred in wind and solar power, due to their decreasing costs, and in natural gas, due to improving technologies.

Most of the removal of power capacity was from shutting down coal plants, due to their high financial, environmental, and social costs.

Energy source	Electricity cost ($/kWh)	Energy density (MJ/kg)	Greenhouse gases (kg CO_2eq/MWh)	Human deaths* (total per year)	Biosphere impacts
Oil	67	42	715	1.10 million	Pollution, climate change, habitat damage, smog, oil spills
Natural gas	56	54	490	120,000	Air pollution, climate change
Coal	109	10–35	820	1.16 million	Pollution, climate change, habitat damage and destruction, increasing water acidity

*Deaths are calculated from construction, mining, production, and resulting air pollution.

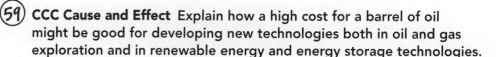

(59) **CCC Cause and Effect** Explain how a high cost for a barrel of oil might be good for developing new technologies both in oil and gas exploration and in renewable energy and energy storage technologies.

Costs and Benefits: Wind, Solar, and Biomass

The rapid growth in wind and solar power has occurred because they are now cheaper than fossil fuels. They are intermittent sources, so as their use grows, they will require increased energy storage capacity. Power from concentrated solar energy is an exception—sunlight heats a material, such as molten salt, that can continuously power a steam turbine overnight. Biomass energy, from wood or any crop used as fuel, is problematic because it requires large areas of land and competes with food crops.

Levelized Cost of Energy Sources Over a nine-year period, wind and solar went from being the most expensive to the least expensive, and they are still getting cheaper due to advances in related technologies.

Costs shown are inflation-adjusted to 2017 values and include construction, fuel, operations, and maintenance costs.

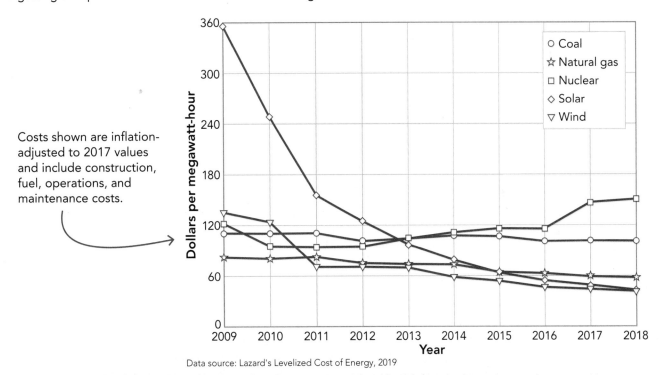

Data source: Lazard's Levelized Cost of Energy, 2019

Energy source	Electricity cost ($/kWh)	Power density (W/m²)	Greenhouse gases (kg CO₂eq/MWh)	Human deaths* (total per year)	Biosphere impacts
Wind turbines	41	3.5	4	70	Habitat disruption, danger to bats and birds
Solar panels	40	5.7	5	18	Habitat removal
Biomass	95	0.1–0.5	78–230	56,000	Air pollution, soil loss, ocean dead zones, habitat damage and destruction

*Deaths are calculated from construction, mining, production, and resulting air pollution.

60 **SEP Argue from Evidence** Of the three energy sources in the table, choose the one that you would most want for your town or city. Use the data to defend your argument.

Run-of-River Hydroelectric Power The photo shows an example of a run-of-river hydroelectric plant (in the foreground). Unlike a dammed hydroelectric plant, where a river is totally blocked, flooding a valley with a wide area of water, run-of-river plants channel off part of the flow for electricity without widening the river.

Costs and Benefits: Hydroelectric, Geothermal, Tides, and Waves

Hydroelectric power, which is electrical energy generated by moving water, provides 16 percent of the world's electricity, and it has been a major source for nearly a century. Most hydroelectric power comes from large dams, but there are almost 100,000 small hydroelectric plants around the world. Large power plants require both a high flow of water and a large vertical drop to be efficient, but there are few such sites, and most already have dams. Large dams are also environmentally disruptive, so there are incentives to use smaller, less disruptive dams. Ocean waves and tides carry tremendous quantities of power, but technologies to capture their power are in the early stages and have limited geographic applications. Geothermal power is limited by the slow rate that Earth cools off, which is only 47 TW. As a result, it is only practical in places where underground magma is close to the surface. Where it is available, however, geothermal power is fairly inexpensive and involves pumping cold water into the ground and pumping hot water out to run turbines.

Energy source	Electricity cost ($/kWh)	Power density (W/m^2)	Greenhouse gases (kg CO_2eq/MWh)	Human deaths* (total per year)	Biosphere impacts
Hydroelectric	53	0.8	34	105	Land habitat removal, river habitat damage, disrupted fish migration

*Deaths are calculated from construction, mining, production, and resulting air pollution.

61 **SEP Construct an Explanation** The power per area for hydroelectric power can vary greatly from the typical 0.8 W/m^2, depending on the geography and type of plant. Provide an example of each extreme.

62 **SEP Construct an Explanation** Along the Atlantic coast of North America, waves typically carry about 40 kW of power per meter of coastline. Explain why it would be difficult to capture a significant portion of that energy.

Costs and Benefits: Nuclear Power

Nuclear fission energy is a nonrenewable source; there is a fixed global supply of uranium and thorium, and once these atoms are split, they cannot provide more energy. At the same time, ample amounts of fuel can be filtered from seawater, so nuclear fission could potentially continue to produce power for thousands of years. Currently, most uranium is mined and processed using acidic or carbonate solutions, which have harmful environmental effects. Unlike burning coal and gas, nuclear fission produces almost no greenhouse gases. Even though new reactor designs have improved safety and efficiency, three factors have kept the industry from growing: its high cost, fears of a nuclear accident, and the long lifetime of radioactive waste.

Research has been underway for decades to develop nuclear fusion as a power source. Possible fuels are the hydrogen isotopes deuterium, which is abundant in seawater, and tritium, which is produced during fusion reactions. Due to the enormous engineering challenge of reproducing conditions within the cores of stars, where fusion occurs naturally, fusion reactors had not been built by 2020.

Nuclear Reactor Construction Through 2015 In 2020 there were 443 active commercial nuclear reactors in the world. They produced nearly 400 GW of power, which was about 10 percent of global electric power production.

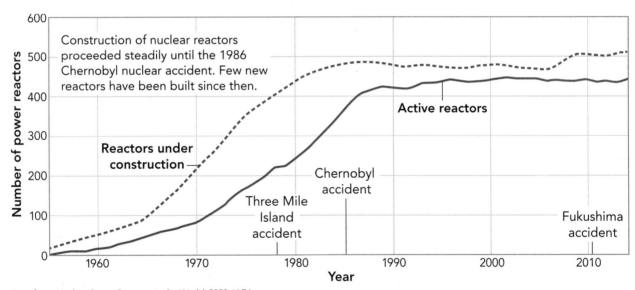

Data from: Nuclear Power Reactors in the World, 2020, IAEA

Energy source	Electricity cost ($/kWh)	Energy density (MJ/kg)	Waste	Human deaths* (total per year)	Biosphere impacts
Nuclear fission	155	80.6 million	Small volume, radioactive	245	Pollution and groundwater acidity (from mining)

*Deaths are calculated from construction, mining, production, and resulting air pollution.

 SEP Use Mathematics Suppose that the world's power consumption (20 TW) was entirely generated by nuclear fission. Assume 4% of the nuclear fuel becomes high-level nuclear waste. Use the data from the table to calculate how much waste (in metric tons) would be produced in a year.

Sustainable Energy Future

Over the past few hundred years, humans have found effective ways of harnessing energy. The population has boomed, and standards of living have risen. Today's world human population of 7.7 billion uses Earth's resources at a rate more than 50 percent greater than is sustainable. **Sustainability** refers to policies and practices that attempt to maintain ecological balance by not harming the environment or depleting natural resources. Finding sustainable ways of living will require restructuring how we get and use energy.

Factors for Sustainability Sustainable futures must be economically viable, environmentally supportable, and socially just. Energy industries will not be able to achieve those goals on their own. Since the 1970s, government actions have improved air and water quality in the United States. Similar action might produce a sustainable energy future, but it would require much broader legislation and more government oversight. Action would be needed by governments in the rest of the world as well.

> **The Success of 1970's U.S. Environmental Regulations** Since 1970, the number of U.S. vehicle miles traveled, energy consumption, and the U.S. economy as a whole have all grown. At the same time, the release of pollutants has steadily decreased, and climate-changing emissions are starting to drop as well.

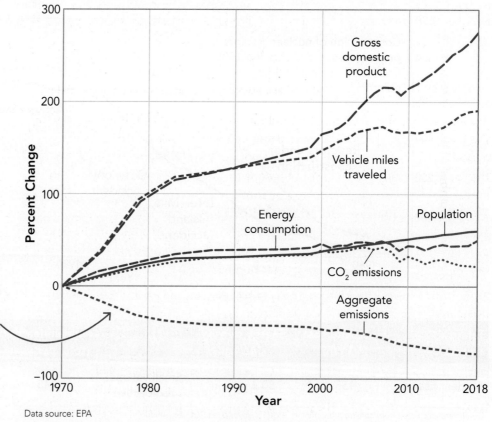

Aggregate emissions consist of carbon monoxide, ground-level ozone, lead, nitrous and sulfur oxides, and tiny particles (such as soot).

Data source: EPA

(64) **CCC Stability and Change** A study by the NAACP and Clear-Air Task Force found that African-Americans are 75 percent more likely than other Americans to live in so-called fence-line communities, defined as areas situated near facilities that produce hazardous waste. Explain why you think this has happened. Does this make for a sustainable future?

Energy in the Earth System Although humans use an extremely large amount of energy, this energy is still dwarfed by geologic events at Earth's surface, such as earthquakes. The largest earthquakes release as much energy as all humans use in a year (about 0.5 zettajoules). Capturing that energy is not currently feasible.

A massive volcanic eruption could bring as much as 5 zettajoules of heat to the surface, although it would produce a global climate catastrophe. Humans might one day be able to tap into the thermal energy of magma.

A hurricane can release 600 TW of power. Capturing the power would be difficult because turbines designed to operate in such high winds would generate no power the rest of the time.

Surface currents move massive amounts of energy across ocean basins. The warm Gulf Stream pumps about 4000 TW of power into the North Atlantic. Again, there is no known way to capture that energy.

▶ **GO ONLINE** to watch a **video** about energy sources and sustainability.

Sustainable Energy Sources Fossil fuels were essential in building the industrial society of the twenty-first century. However, their limited availability and harmful environmental impacts make them unsuitable in the long term. It is possible that humans may replace fossil fuels with the immense power of nuclear fusion or some other large energy source. At 20 TW, human energy use is only 0.016 percent of the 125,000 TW of sunlight that reaches Earth's surface. Just 80 minutes of sunlight provides as much energy as all humans use in a year. Scientists predict sunlight will eventually provide all the energy that humans use.

Transition to the Future Eventually is not tomorrow, and in the near term, many energy challenges exist. Building an energy infrastructure based around renewable energy sources will take time and resources. The electric power grid will need to be able to rapidly switch among sources. As resources dwindle, humans will need to be much better about recycling metals. Nuclear fission may have a role in the transition from fossil fuels to renewables, however long that takes. Throughout the process, scientific innovation, creative engineering, and effective government oversight will all be required.

(65) **SEP Construct an Argument** Suppose you are in charge of developing an energy plan for a city over the next century. Explain your reasons for why you would or would not include nuclear fission in your plan.

Revisit

INVESTIGATIVE PHENOMENON

GO ONLINE to revisit your **Investigative Phenomenon modeling activity** with the new information you have learned about Energy Resources and Conservation.

These questions will help you apply what you learned in this experience to the Investigative Phenomenon.

66 **CCC Scale, Proportion, and Quantity** A metric ton of TNT releases 4.2 gigajoules when it explodes. Calculate the number of tons of TNT that are equivalent to the 6.3×10^{20} J of energy humans consume each year.

67 **SEP Argue from Evidence** Coal power generation plants are typically 30%–40% efficient, and commercial solar panels are about 20% efficient. Explain why the lower efficiency of a solar panel does not mean it is more harmful to the environment than a coal plant.

68 **SEP Construct an Explanation** Pollution from petroleum industries in the United States grew for more than a century before action by the Environmental Protection Agency reversed the trend. Construct an explanation for why industries were unable to do so by themselves but often supported the regulations once they were enacted.

69 **SEP Use Mathematics** At Earth's orbit, 150 million km from the sun, the power available from sunlight is 1361 W/m². Suppose that a sphere could surround the sun and capture all of its sunlight. How much power could it theoretically capture? Would the size of the sphere matter in how much energy was captured?

GO ONLINE
for a **quiz** to evaluate what you learned about Energy Resources and Conservation.

These questions will help you apply what you learned in this investigation to the Anchoring Phenomenon.

(70) **CCC Matter and Energy** Imagine that you are listening to music from a portable speaker in your home that is plugged into an electrical outlet, and imagine that a coal-powered plant supplies your electricity. Describe the many energy transformations that occurred for you to be able to listen to the music.

(71) **SEP Communicate Information** Choose a renewable energy resource that you learned about in this investigation and evaluate its potential for sustainably meeting future energy needs in terms of land use, environmental impacts, and economic cost.

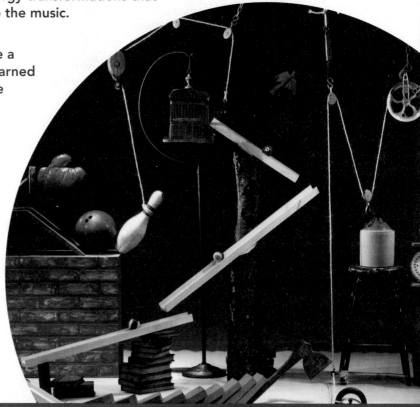

☑ INVESTIGATION ASSESSMENT

 GO ONLINE for activities that will give you an opportunity to **demonstrate what you have learned**:

☑ **Engineering Performance-Based Assessment** Build a device that generates electrical energy from another form of energy.

🗎 **Engineering Workbench** Evaluate the costs and benefits associated with the adoption of sustainable energy sources.

🖳 **Career Connections** Learn about how a geologist applies knowledge of physics.

☑ **Investigation Test** Take this test to evaluate your understanding of electromagnetic energy.

☑ **Virtual Lab Performance-Based Assessment** Design an electromagnet that maximizes performance and minimizes costs.

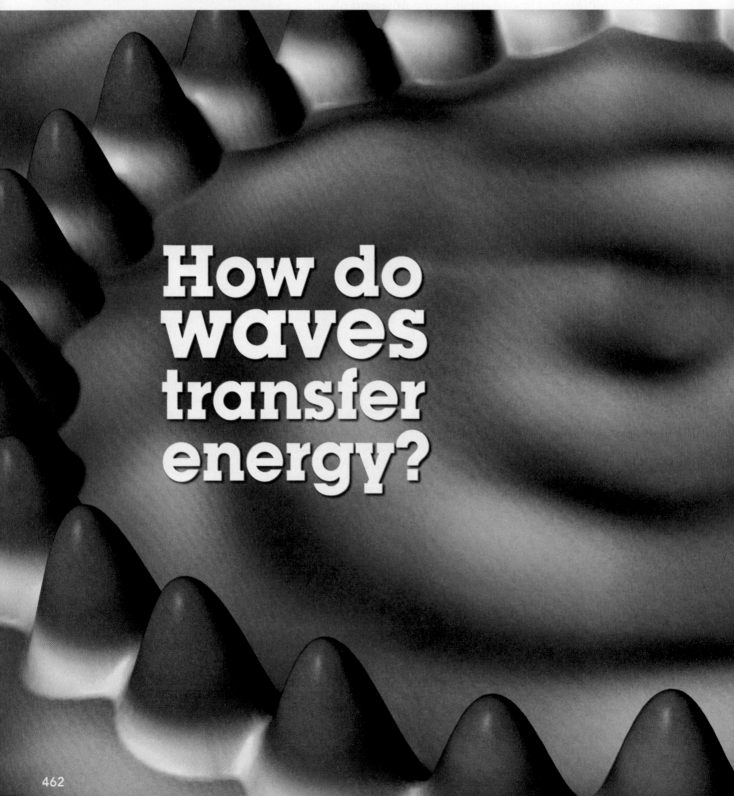

Waves and Electromagnetic Radiation

How do waves transfer energy?

Investigation 11
Waves

Investigation 12
Electromagnetic
Radiation

Investigation 13
Information and
Instrumentation

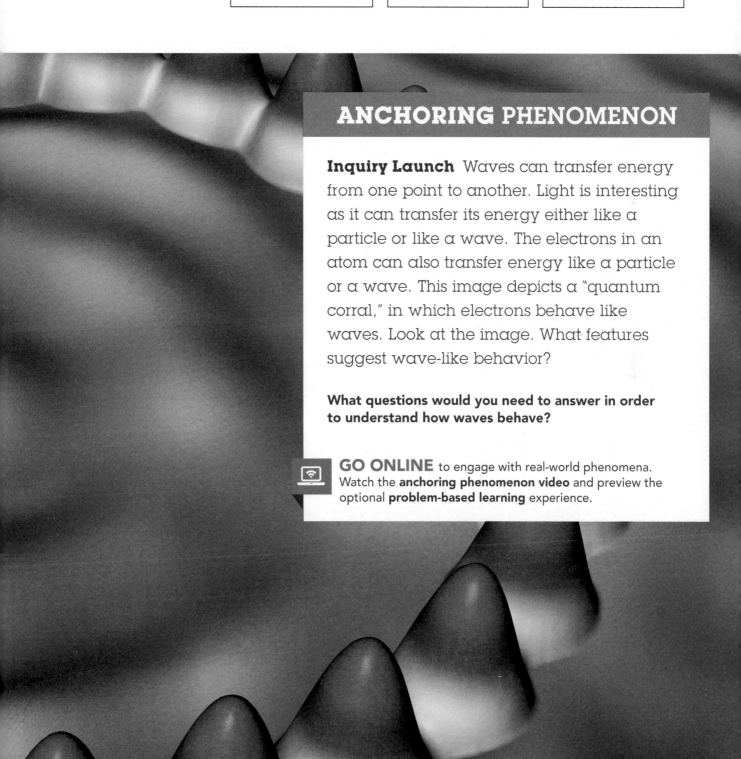

ANCHORING PHENOMENON

Inquiry Launch Waves can transfer energy from one point to another. Light is interesting as it can transfer its energy either like a particle or like a wave. The electrons in an atom can also transfer energy like a particle or a wave. This image depicts a "quantum corral," in which electrons behave like waves. Look at the image. What features suggest wave-like behavior?

What questions would you need to answer in order to understand how waves behave?

GO ONLINE to engage with real-world phenomena. Watch the **anchoring phenomenon video** and preview the optional **problem-based learning** experience.

463

GO ONLINE to engage with real-world phenomena by watching a **phenomenon video** and completing a **CER worksheet**.

How do waves change the coastline?

Waves

Waves transport energy through oscillations. Far out in the ocean, water is pushed up and down and side to side by the wind. This jostling causes nearby water to also oscillate, and the propagation of a wave begins. The wave can transport the initial energy for thousands of miles before finally crashing to shore.

As ocean waves come up to the shore, the local geology and decreasing water depth can cause the waves to bend and reflect. The energy carried by these waves shapes the shoreline through the processes of erosion and deposition.

Beach erosion occurs when waves remove sand, narrowing the beach and often putting homes and other oceanfront structures in danger. Unwanted deposition can also cause problems as the sand blocks entry into channels. Controlling beach erosion and deposition is a massive engineering challenge that requires an understanding of the physics of waves.

(1) **CCC Patterns** The distance between the peaks of water waves seems to depend on how close they are to the shore, as shown in the image. Qualitatively describe the pattern that you observe.

(2) **SEP Communicate Scientific Information** What properties could you use to define an ocean wave? Specifically, if you had to describe waves coming on shore at the beach to your friend, what features would you focus on?

Wave Properties

 GO ONLINE to do a **hands-on lab** to investigate and model transverse and longitudinal waves using a spring toy and a wave motion rope.

Mechanical Waves

A **mechanical wave** is any wave that results from the oscillation of matter. Mechanical waves transport energy from one point to another without transporting the matter from point to point. The type of matter through which the wave's energy propagates is called the **medium.**

Waves on a Rope When the athlete moves the ends of the ropes up and down, the energy transmitted through the ropes are visible in the up-down motion throughout the ropes. However, the ends of the ropes never leave the athlete's hands. Only energy is transmitted through the ropes.

 SEP Develop a Model Move a pencil up and down in a line on a sheet of paper. Have a classmate slowly pull the paper in a direction perpendicular to your up-down motion. Sketch the resulting shape.

Properties of Waves

There are two ways to graphically represent a wave: 1) the entire wave at one moment in time (distance graph), or 2) one section of the wave as it moves through time (time graph). These two types of representations reveal the distance and time properties of the wave.

The **wave speed,** v, is a combination of distance and time properties and represents the speed at which the wave propagates:

Speed of a Wave
$v = \frac{\lambda}{T}$ or $v = f\lambda$
v = speed of the wave T = period λ = wavelength f = frequency

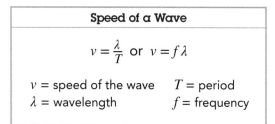

Wavelength, λ

Amplitude, A

Distance Graphs show a "snapshot" of the wave at one instant in time. The **amplitude,** A, is the maximum distance a particle moves from its starting point. The **wavelength,** λ, is the distance between successive similar points, such as crests, of a wave.

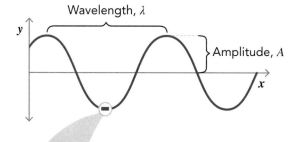

Period, T

Time Graphs show the up-down motion of one part of the medium. The **period,** T, is the time it takes for a particle to move through one full cycle of oscillation. The **frequency,** f, is the inverse of the period: $f = \frac{1}{T}$, and represents the number of wave cycles to pass a given point per unit of time.

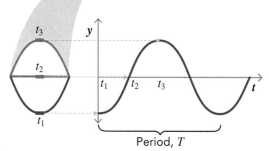

$t = 0$

$t = T$

λ

Wave Speed is how far the wave moves in a unit of time. One distance-cycle of the wave is the wavelength. One time-cycle of the wave is the period. The ratio of wavelength to period is the wave speed, $v = \frac{\lambda}{T}$.

(4) SEP Analyze Data Frequency is often given in units of hertz or Hz, which is equal to 1/s. Looking at the graphs, what units could you use for A, λ, and T?

(5) SEP Use Mathematics Use mathematics to show that $v = f\lambda$ for the speed of a wave and that it results in the correct SI units for speed.

Transverse Waves

EXPERIENCE IT!

As a class, do "the wave" like you would in a sports stadium. Discuss your individual motion compared to the motion of the wave.

Motion in Transverse Waves In a **transverse mechanical wave,** the motion of the oscillating particles in the medium is perpendicular to the direction of the wave. Think about waves on ropes. The particles that make up the rope move up and down, while the wave actually propagates from one end of the rope to the other. The particle motions and the wave propagation are perpendicular. Another example of transverse waves is shear waves during earthquakes, where the ground heaves side to side or up and down as the wave passes through the ground.

S Waves Shear waves, or S waves, are a type of seismic wave produced during an earthquake. S waves result from the shearing of rock, forcing the ground to move perpendicular to the wave direction.

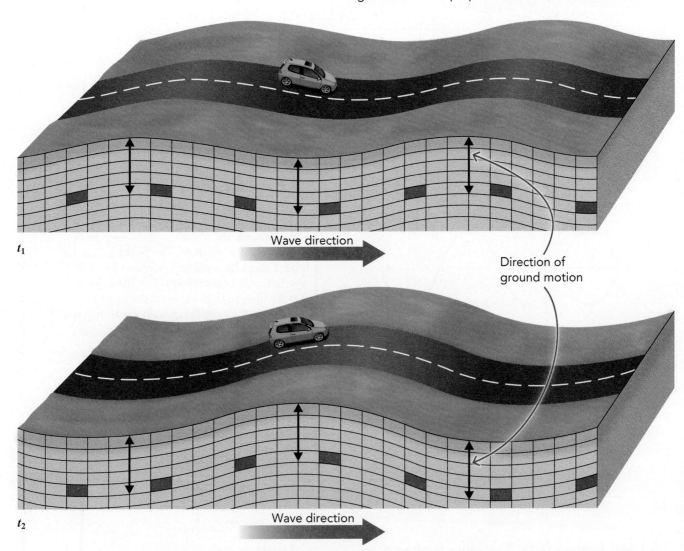

t_1

Wave direction

Direction of ground motion

t_2

Wave direction

6 **SEP Develop a Model** Think about the motions you and your classmate made for Question 3. What property does your motion represent? What property does your classmate's motion represent?

GO ONLINE to do a PhET **simulation** that allows you to explore wave properties on a string.

(7) **SEP Analyze and Interpret Data** The data show the densities for two different ropes and the wavelength, frequency, and speed of a wave traveling on each rope. Based on the data, which of the three other properties appears to cause a change in the speed?

Rope	Density (kg/m)	Wavelength (m)	Frequency (Hz)	Speed (m/s)
1	0.25	3.16	2.00	6.32
	0.25	1.58	4.00	6.32
2	0.15	4.08	2.00	8.16
	0.15	2.04	4.00	8.16

Speed of Waves on Ropes The time properties of a wave, such as frequency and period, are determined by the cause of the wave. For example, when you wiggle a rope up and down, you directly control the frequency. However, the speed at which a wave propagates through the rope is controlled by the properties of the rope. It doesn't matter how fast you wiggle the rope!

In general, wave speed through a medium is determined by the stiffness and density of the medium.

Speed of a Wave in a Rope

$$v = \sqrt{\frac{F_T}{\mu}}$$

v = speed of the wave
F_T = tension in the rope
μ = mass per unit length of the rope

Speed and Medium The speed at which a wave propagates depends on the properties of the medium—in this case, a rope.

Tension, F_T, is a force exerted along the length of a medium, such as a rope or cable.

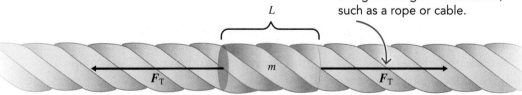

L

m

F_T

F_T

$$\mu = \frac{m}{L}$$

Linear density, μ, is a measure of the amount of mass in a given unit of length.

Wave on a Rope

A student holds a 5.0-m rope with a mass of 0.50 kg. The other end is connected to one side of a spring scale, which is attached to a wall. The scale reads 10.0 N. The student moves her hand up, down, and back to equilibrium all within 0.25 second, generating a wave that moves down the rope. Determine the speed, frequency, and wavelength of the wave.

1. DRAW A PICTURE Sketch a picture of the situation.

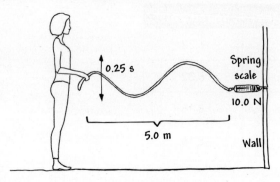

2. DEFINE THE PROBLEM List knowns and unknowns, and assign values to variables. (The length of the rope is 5 m, but that doesn't mean the wavelength is 5 m.)

$F_T = 10.0$ N	$v = ?$
$m = 0.50$ kg	$f = ?$
$T = 0.25$ s	$\lambda = ?$
$L = 5.0$ m	

3. PLAN AND EXECUTE Use mathematical relationships, the picture, and your definitions to plan and execute a solution.

Determine the wave speed from the tension and density of the rope.

$$v = \sqrt{\frac{F_T}{(m/L)}} = \sqrt{\frac{10.0 \text{ N}}{(0.50 \text{ kg}/5.0 \text{ m})}} = 10.0 \text{ m/s}$$

Determine the frequency from the period of the wave.

$$f = \frac{1}{T} = \frac{1}{0.25 \text{ s}} = 4.0 \text{ 1/s}$$

Use the wave speed and frequency to determine the wavelength.

$$v = \lambda f \rightarrow \lambda = \frac{v}{f} = \frac{10.0 \text{ m/s}}{4.0 \text{ 1/s}} = 2.5 \text{ m}$$

4. EVALUATE Reflect on your answer.
All of the units are appropriate for the given quantities. The wave speed is reasonable, and the wavelength is half the length of the rope.

 GO ONLINE for more **math support**.

📶 **Math Practice Problems**

---

⑧ A student holds one end of a 4.5-m rope with a mass of 1.0 kg. The other end is connected to one side of a spring scale, which is attached to a wall. The scale reads 15.0 N. The student moves her hand up, down, and back to equilibrium all within 1.0 second, generating a wave that moves down the rope. Determine the speed, frequency, and wavelength of the wave.

📖 **NEED A HINT?** Go online to your **eText Sample Problem** for stepped out support.

⑨ A 3.0-m long cable is shaken up, down, and back to equilibrium for 0.50 s with a force of 5.0 N. This sends a wave along the cable. If the cable's mass is 0.10 kg, find the speed, frequency, and wavelength of the wave.

Wave Speed at an Interface

The speed of water waves in relatively shallow water depends approximately on the depth of the water and the acceleration due to gravity, as follows:

Speed of a Wave in Water
$v \approx \sqrt{gd}$
v = speed of the wave
g = acceleration due to gravity
d = depth of water

EXPERIENCE IT!

With a partner, model two wave crests by moving at a constant speed with one person behind the other. At a predefined point, the first person slows down. The second person slows down when they get to the same point. Discuss what happened to the distance between you.

Depth is a property of the medium, so once again the speed is determined by the medium. When a wave moves from deeper to shallower water, such as when waves come ashore at the beach, the speed of the wave changes. This can be simulated in a ripple tank, which consists of an oscillator in a tank of water. As the wave slows down due to the decrease in depth, the crests begin to "bunch up," reducing the wavelength.

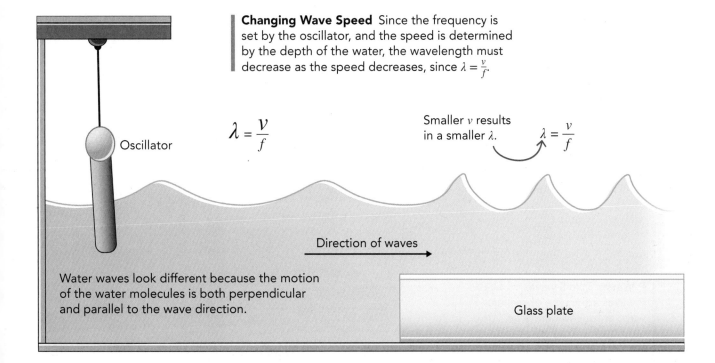

Changing Wave Speed Since the frequency is set by the oscillator, and the speed is determined by the depth of the water, the wavelength must decrease as the speed decreases, since $\lambda = \frac{v}{f}$.

$\lambda = \frac{v}{f}$

Oscillator

Smaller v results in a smaller λ.

$\lambda = \frac{v}{f}$

Direction of waves

Water waves look different because the motion of the water molecules is both perpendicular and parallel to the wave direction.

Glass plate

10) **SEP Develop a Model** A wave pulse moves through a rope into a more dense rope, as shown. Sketch the wave pulse before and after it moves into the more dense rope.

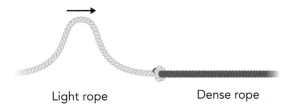

Light rope

Dense rope

Longitudinal Waves

<table>
</table>

VOCABULARY

Longitudinal means "running lengthwise rather than across." It is derived from the Latin root *longus*, meaning "long." It can refer to either a long time, such as a longitudinal study, or, in the case of a wave, along the "long" axis of distance.

Motion in Longitudinal Waves In a **longitudinal mechanical wave,** the motion of the oscillating particles in the medium is parallel to the direction of the wave. An example is a sound wave, where the particles of air get pushed back and forth by the speaker cone, while the wave propagates from one side of the room to the other.

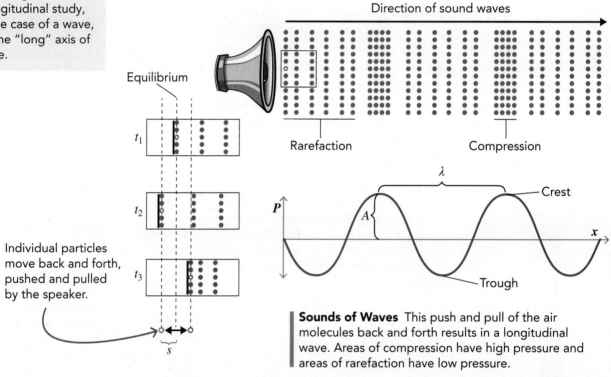

Equilibrium

t_1

t_2

Individual particles move back and forth, pushed and pulled by the speaker.

t_3

s

Direction of sound waves

Rarefaction

Compression

λ

Crest

P

A

x

Trough

Sounds of Waves This push and pull of the air molecules back and forth results in a longitudinal wave. Areas of compression have high pressure and areas of rarefaction have low pressure.

P Waves Like S waves, P waves are a type of seismic wave produced during an earthquake. They result from the back-and-forth motion of the ground as the wave passes.

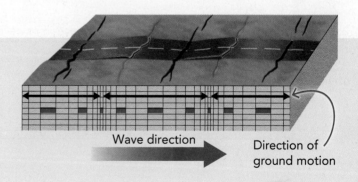

Wave direction

Direction of ground motion

(11) **SEP Plan an Investigation** Plan an investigation to determine the speed of a longitudinal wave pulse transmitted through a stretched spring.

▶ **GO ONLINE** to watch a **video** about wave propagation.

Speed of Sound Like transverse waves, the time properties of a longitudinal wave, such as frequency and period, are determined by the cause of the wave. The frequency of the sounds emitted by a speaker depends on what is played through the speaker. The speed with which the sound wave propagates is controlled by the properties of the material, for example, whether the material is air, water, or a solid and even the temperature of that material. The speed of sound in air is 343 m/s when the air temperature is 20°C. The speed of sound in colder air is slower.

Speed of a Sound Wave in a Fluid Medium

$$v_{sound} = \sqrt{\frac{B}{\rho}}$$

v_{sound} = speed of the sound wave
B = bulk modulus of the medium
ρ = density of material

How Sonar Works
How can the **speed of sound** be used to determine distances under the ocean's surface?

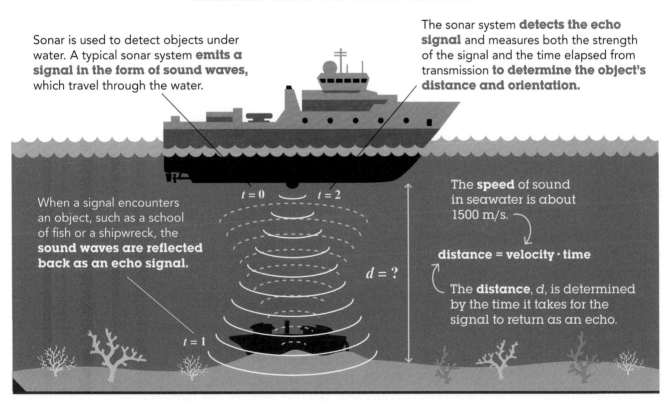

Sonar is used to detect objects under water. A typical sonar system **emits a signal in the form of sound waves,** which travel through the water.

The sonar system **detects the echo signal** and measures both the strength of the signal and the time elapsed from transmission **to determine the object's distance and orientation.**

When a signal encounters an object, such as a school of fish or a shipwreck, the **sound waves are reflected back as an echo signal.**

The **speed** of sound in seawater is about 1500 m/s.

distance = velocity · time

The **distance**, d, is determined by the time it takes for the signal to return as an echo.

$t = 0$ $t = 2$

$d = ?$

$t = 1$

---

(12) **CCC Cause and Effect** What causes a change in wave speed? What causes a change in frequency? Can you change the frequency of a wave to cause a change in the speed? How can you affect the wavelength of a wave?

Properties of Sound Waves

You are using sonar over a spot in the ocean known to be 60.0 m deep. The system emits a 50.0-kHz sound pulse into the water. It takes 78.4 ms for the sound to travel to the ocean floor and back to the sonar system. Determine the speed of sound in the ocean and the wavelength of the sonar pulse.

1. DRAW A PICTURE Sketch a picture of the situation.

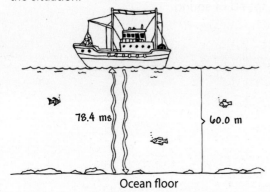

Ocean floor

2. DEFINE THE PROBLEM List knowns and unknowns, and assign values to variables.

$d = 60.0$ m	$v = ?$
$f = 50.0$ kHz	$\lambda = ?$
$t = 78.4$ ms	

3. PLAN AND EXECUTE Use mathematical relationships, the picture, and your definitions to plan and execute a solution. The picture shows that the wave must travel twice the depth.

Determine the wave speed from the distance and time. In 78.4 ms, the wave travels 120.0 m.

$$v = \frac{d}{t} = \frac{2d}{t} = \frac{120.0 \text{ m}}{78.4 \times 10^{-3} \text{ s}} = 1530 \text{ m/s}$$

Determine the wavelength from the frequency and wave speed.

$$v = \lambda f \rightarrow \lambda = \frac{v}{f} = \frac{1530 \text{ m/s}}{50{,}000 \text{ 1/s}} = 0.03 \text{ m}$$

4. EVALUATE Reflect on your answer.
All of the units are appropriate for the given quantities. The wave speed is approximately the expected wave speed for ocean water.

 GO ONLINE for more **math support**.

🖳 **Math Practice Problems**

---

⑬ You are using sonar over a spot in the ocean known to be 91.8 m deep. The system emits a 50.0-kHz pulse into the water. It takes 120.0 ms for the sound to travel to the ocean floor and back to the sonar system. Determine the speed of sound in the ocean and the wavelength of the sonar pulse.

📖 **NEED A HINT?** Go online to your **eText Sample Problem** for stepped out support.

⑭ A coach shouts "Go!" from the finish line of a 100.0-m track to the runners. It takes 292 ms for the 171-Hz sound wave to reach them. Calculate the speed of sound in air and the wavelength of her voice.

Modeling Waves

Wave motion can be modeled using distance and time graphs showing the oscillatory motion of the particles in the medium. This motion can also be described mathematically using the sine trigonometric function.

Wave Graph Equations
$y(x) = A \sin\left(\frac{2\pi}{\lambda} x\right)$ and $y(t) = A \sin(2\pi f t)$

Oscilloscope An oscilloscope is a tool used to measure the time variation of electronic signals. Frequency and wavelength can be calculated by converting the graphed data to an equation.

Math to Graph The figure shows how to convert the mathematical representations for one example wave into graphical representations.

Distance Representations

$y(x) = (2\ \text{m}) \sin[(3.15\ \text{m}^{-1})\, x]$

$$3.15\ \text{m}^{-1} = \frac{2\pi}{\lambda} \Rightarrow \lambda = \frac{2\pi}{3.15\ \text{m}^{-1}}$$

$$\lambda = 2.0\ \text{m}$$

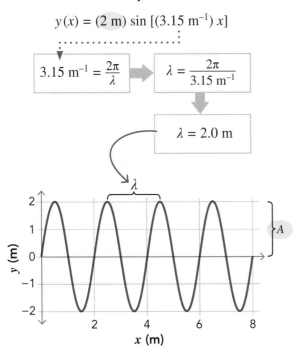

Time Representations

$y(t) = (2\ \text{m}) \sin[(1068\ \text{s}^{-1})\, t]$

$$1068\ \text{s}^{-1} = 2\pi f \Rightarrow f = \frac{1068\ \text{s}^{-1}}{2\pi} = 170\ \text{s}^{-1}$$

$$T = \frac{1}{f} = 5.9\ \text{ms}$$

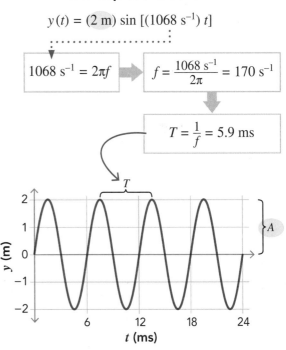

(15) **SEP Use Mathematics** Now try going the other way! Given the two graphs shown, determine the wave properties and write distance and time mathematical representations for the wave. What is the speed of this wave?

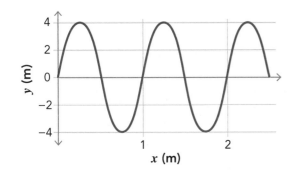

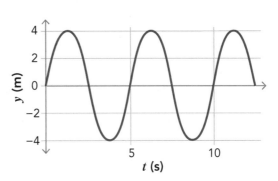

Modeling a Sound Wave

A speaker produces a tone at a frequency of 440 Hz. The speaker cone has a maximum displacement of 0.5 cm when turned on. Assume the speed of sound in air is 343 m/s. Construct mathematical and graphical representations of the wave.

1. DRAW A PICTURE Draw a picture of the scenario.

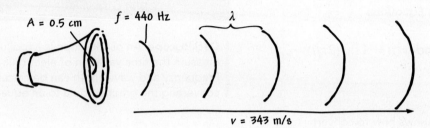

2. DEFINE THE PROBLEM List knowns and unknowns, and assign values to variables.

$f = 440\ 1/s$	$\lambda = ?$
$A = 0.5$ cm	$T = ?$
$v = 343$ m/s	

$$y(x) = A \sin\left(\frac{2\pi}{\lambda} x\right) \quad y(t) = A \sin(2\pi f t)$$

To construct graphical representations, you need to find A, T, and λ. To construct mathematical representations, you need A, f, and λ.

3. PLAN AND EXECUTE Use mathematical relationships, the picture, and your definitions to plan and execute a solution.

Determine the wavelength from the frequency and wave speed.

$$v = \lambda f \rightarrow \lambda = \frac{v}{f} = \frac{343 \text{ m/s}}{440 \text{ 1/s}} = 0.78 \text{ m}$$

Determine the period from the frequency.

$$f = \frac{1}{T} \rightarrow T = \frac{1}{f} = \frac{1}{440 \text{ 1/s}} = 2.3 \times 10^{-3} \text{ s} = 2.3 \text{ ms}$$

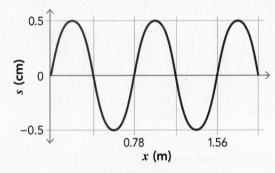

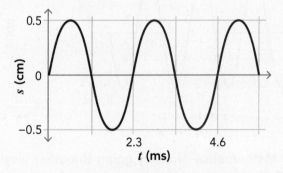

$$y(x) = (0.5 \text{ cm}) \sin\left(\frac{2\pi}{0.78 \text{ m}} x\right)$$

$$y(t) = (0.5 \text{ cm}) \sin[2\pi(440 \text{ 1/s})t]$$

4. EVALUATE Reflect on your answer.

All of the units are appropriate for the given quantities.

 GO ONLINE for more **math support**.

▶ **Math Tutorial Video**

🖥 **Math Practice Problems**

16 A speaker produces a tone at a frequency of 500 Hz. The speaker cone has a maximum displacement of 0.7 cm when turned on. Assume the speed of sound in air is 343 m/s. Construct mathematical and graphical representations of the resulting wave.

📖 **NEED A HINT?** Go online to your **eText Sample Problem** for stepped out support.

17 A speaker produces a tone at a frequency of 660 Hz. The speaker cone has a maximum displacement of 0.3 cm when turned on. Assume the speed of sound in air is 343 m/s. Construct mathematical and graphical representations of the resulting wave.

18 One end of a rope is shaken to create a wave with a frequency of 0.20 Hz. The rope is displaced with a maximum distance of 0.10 m away from its starting point. The speed of the wave through the rope is 10.0 m/s. A student graphs the wave. Complete the graphs by labeling the axes and write mathematical representations for the wave.

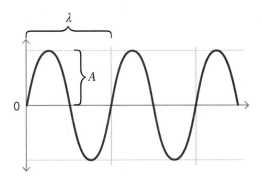 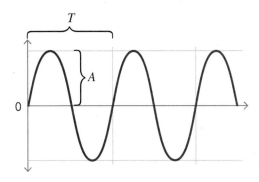

19 An engineer is designing a wave pool that will have 0.25-m-high waves crash down once every second at the deep end. The deep end is 40.0 m long and 1.0 m deep. Construct mathematical and graphical representations of the waves that would result from the engineer's design.

20 You are testing a sonar machine underwater by sending out sound waves to measure distances. Using the graphical representations shown for the wave, find the amplitude, frequency, wavelength, and speed of the wave, and write a mathematical representation of the wave.

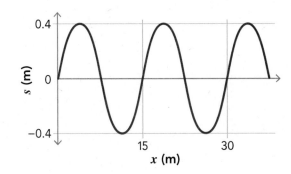 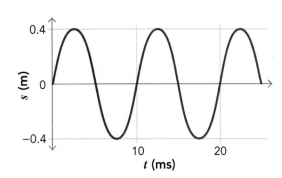

INVESTIGATIVE PHENOMENON

GO ONLINE to revisit your **Investigative Phenomenon CER** with the new information you have learned about Wave Properties.

These questions will help you apply what you learned in this experience to the Investigative Phenomenon.

21 **SEP Use Mathematics** At the beach, you time wave crests hitting the shore and determine there are 20 seconds between crests. Determine the frequency of the wave. Would you expect this frequency to change if you made your measurements further out from the shore?

22 **SEP Analyze and Interpret Data** After determining the frequency of the waves in the previous problem, you then use a handheld sonar system to determine the ocean depth at 10.0-m increments from the shore. The data are shown in the table. Complete the table and construct a graph of the wave speed as a function of the depth.

Distance (m)	Depth (m)	Speed (m/s)	Wavelength (m)
10.0	1.4		
20.0	2.8		
30.0	4.2		
40.0	5.6		

23 **SEP Develop a Model** For the waves in the previous two problems, construct both a distance graph and a time graph of the ocean wave. Assume a reasonable value for the wave amplitude. Also, draw a picture of what you think the wave crests would look like as they come closer to the shore.

GO ONLINE for a **quiz** to evaluate what you learned about Wave Properties.

Wave Behavior and Energy

 GO ONLINE to do a **hands-on lab** to investigate wave interference.

Wave Interactions

What happens when the source of a wave, such as the siren on a fire truck, moves? What happens when one wave passes through another? How is energy transferred from a wave to the particles that make up the wave? When an ocean wave breaks at the shore, how much energy goes into moving the sand or a surfer? To answer each of those questions, you must understand the interactions between waves and matter, and how waves behave.

(24) **CCC Energy and Matter** When a large stone is dropped into a pond, a circular wave forms and moves across the pond. The wave can cause a small rubber duck on the other side of the pond to move up and down. Sketch a model of the situation and show the flow of energy into and out of the various parts of the system.

EXPERIENCE IT!

Carry out two conversations between four friends, talking across each other in pairs. Does the sound of one conversation have an impact on the other? What does this suggest about how waves interact with each other?

Ripples in Water Circular waves are generated when stones are dropped into a pond. Each wave can interact with objects in the pond, and although the resulting waves do not interact with each other, they can superimpose to generate complex patterns.

Moving Wave Source

As a fire truck passes, the frequency of the siren's sound seems to change. Called the **Doppler effect,** the apparent change in frequency is the result of relative motion between the source of the waves and the observer, from either the source or the observer, or both. This relative motion causes the observed wavelength and frequency of the periodic wave to change. The Doppler effect occurs for any type of wave, including sound waves, water waves, and even light waves.

> ### Observed Frequency for a Moving Source of Sound
>
> $$f_\text{o} = f_\text{s} \left(\frac{v_\text{w}}{v_\text{w} \pm v_\text{s}} \right)$$
>
> f_o = observed frequency
> f_s = source frequency
> v_w = speed of the wave
> v_s = speed of the source in reference to the observer

For the frequency of an approaching source, use a minus sign in the denominator of the equation. For a receding source, use a plus sign.

Stationary Source Sound spreads out in spherical compressional waves from the point at which they originate. Because the vehicle and the observers are stationary, the wavelength and frequency are the same in all directions and to all observers.

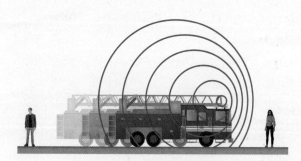

Moving Source When the source moves, the air compressions become closer together on one side and farther apart on the other. One observer hears the approaching siren at a higher frequency. The other observer hears the receding siren at a lower frequency.

(25) **SEP Construct an Explanation** Glowing hydrogen gas from stars, such as the sun, emits specific frequencies of light. However, the frequencies of the light observed from stars in distant galaxies are lower than expected. Construct an explanation for this phenomenon.

A Passing Ambulance

While you are standing still on the sidewalk, an ambulance traveling at 32.0 m/s passes you. The ambulance's siren produces a tone at a frequency of 701 Hz. Assume the speed of sound in air is 343 m/s. What frequency do you hear as the ambulance approaches you? What frequency do you hear as the ambulance moves away from you?

1. DRAW A PICTURE Sketch a picture of the situation.

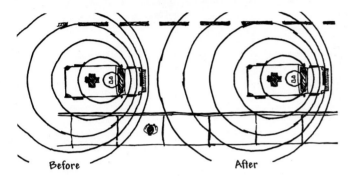

Before   After

2. DEFINE THE PROBLEM List knowns and unknowns, and assign values to variables.

$v_w = 343$ m/s	Approaching $f_o = ?$
$v_s = 32.0$ m/s	Moving away $f_o = ?$
$f_s = 701$ Hz	

3. PLAN AND EXECUTE Use mathematical relationships, the picture, and your definitions to plan and execute a solution.

Write the equation for the Doppler effect.

$$f_o = f_s \left(\frac{v_w}{v_w \pm v_s} \right)$$

Determine the observed frequency during the approach. Use a minus sign in the denominator.

$$f_o = 701 \text{ Hz} \left(\frac{343 \text{ m/s}}{343 \text{ m/s} - 32.0 \text{ m/s}} \right) = 773 \text{ Hz}$$

Determine the observed frequency as the ambulance moves away. Use a plus sign in the denominator.

$$f_o = 701 \text{ Hz} \left(\frac{343 \text{ m/s}}{343 \text{ m/s} + 32.0 \text{ m/s}} \right) = 641 \text{ Hz}$$

4. EVALUATE Reflect on your answer.
The units are appropriate for the calculated quantities. The siren has a higher frequency during the approach and a lower frequency when moving away, as would be expected.

 GO ONLINE for more **math support**.

▶ **Math Tutorial Video**

🖥 **Math Practice Problems**

---

26 While you are standing still on the sidewalk, an ambulance traveling at 30.0 m/s passes you. The ambulance's siren produces a tone at a frequency of 802 Hz. Assume the speed of sound in air is 343 m/s. What frequency do you hear as the ambulance approaches you? What frequency do you hear as the ambulance moves away from you?

📖 **NEED A HINT?** Go online to your **eText Sample Problem** for stepped out support.

27 A train's horn produces a 148-Hz sound while moving at 32.0 m/s. What frequencies are heard by a person standing still beside the tracks as the train approaches and after it passes?

Loud and Quiet Two people walking around at an outdoor concert notice that the music is very loud in some places and very quiet in others. What could make the wave amplitude vary so much?

Modeling Wave Interactions

VOCABULARY

Super is a Latin word meaning "above," and *position* means "to put in place." So **superposition** means to put one thing on top of another.

Wave interference is the phenomenon that occurs when two waves superimpose as they meet while traveling in the same medium. To model this interference, you add the positions of the colliding waves at each point in time to determine the resultant wave, a process called **wave superposition.**

Constructive Interference The **phase** of a wave describes how much the wave is shifted in time, typically with respect to another wave. Two waves that have the same frequency and perfectly aligned crests are said to be in phase. **Constructive interference** is the superposition of in-phase waves that produce a resultant wave with larger amplitude.

Constructive Interference Time graphs and wave equations for two waves in phase are shown. Add the positions at each point in time to get the resulting wave positions.

$y_1 = A \sin(2\pi ft)$

Wave 1

$y_2 = A \sin(2\pi ft)$

Wave 2

This combination results in a wave with twice the amplitude of each wave.

$y_1 + y_2 = 2A \sin(2\pi ft)$

Resultant wave

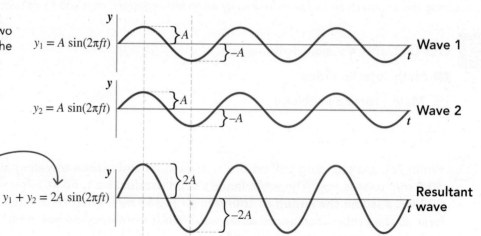

28 **SEP Develop a Model** Waves that are in phase do not need to have the same amplitude for constructive interference to occur. Sketch time graphs of two waves in phase with different amplitudes: wave 1's amplitude is 4 cm, and wave 2's amplitude is 2 cm. Then, sketch the resulting wave when the two waves meet.

Noise Canceling Headphones Some headphones can block out ambient noise by producing sound waves that are out of phase with the ambient noise by half of a wave period. Music can be enjoyed without the surrounding sounds when headphones produce both the music and additional sound to interfere with the ambient noise.

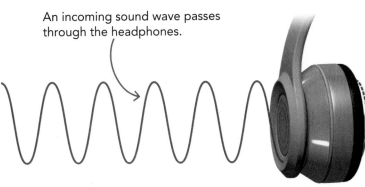

An incoming sound wave passes through the headphones.

The sound produced by the headphones is inverted to the incoming sound wave when it completely cancels out the noise.

The incoming sound wave and the inverted sound wave destructively interfere, resulting in no sound.

 GO ONLINE to do a PhET **simulation** that allows you to explore wave interference.

Destructive Interference In the equation representing a wave, scientists use the phase angle to represent the phase of one wave with respect to another. **Phase angle** is a measure of the waveform's shift in time relative to a reference, with a shift of one full period represented by the angle 2π. A wave with the same frequency as another wave but behind or ahead of it by half a period is considered to be completely out of phase, and it has a phase angle of π. The crest of one wave lines up with the trough of the other. Superposition of two waves that are completely out of phase with each other produces **destructive interference,** in which two waves combine to produce a smaller wave or cancel each other out entirely.

Destructive Interference Time graphs and wave equations for two waves completely out of phase are shown. Adding the positions at each point in time results in a wave with zero amplitude.

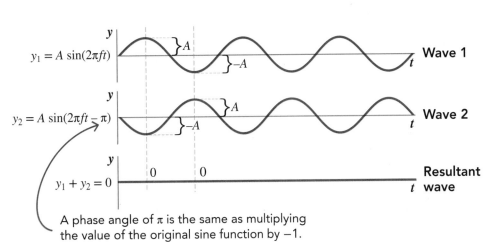

$y_1 = A \sin(2\pi ft)$

$y_2 = A \sin(2\pi ft - \pi)$

$y_1 + y_2 = 0$

Wave 1

Wave 2

Resultant wave

A phase angle of π is the same as multiplying the value of the original sine function by -1.

(29) **SEP Develop a Model** Waves out of phase do not need to have the same amplitude to produce partial destructive interference. Sketch time graphs of two waves with different amplitudes that are out of phase: wave 1's amplitude is 4 cm, and wave 2's amplitude is 2 cm. Then, sketch the resulting wave for the two waves interfering.

Beats

EXPERIENCE IT!

Strike two tuning forks with slightly different frequencies. Listen to the steadily repeating beats.

The principle of superposition works even when two waves have different frequencies. When two sound waves with different frequencies interact, you hear a pulsating sound called **beats.** Beats are produced when alternating constructive and destructive interference produce a sound that alternates between soft and loud. The frequency of the pulsations is referred to as the *beat frequency* and is equal to the absolute value of the difference in frequencies of the two waves.

Beat Frequency
$$f_{\text{beat}} = |f_2 - f_1|$$

f_{beat} = beat frequency
f_1 = frequency of wave 1
f_2 = frequency of wave 2

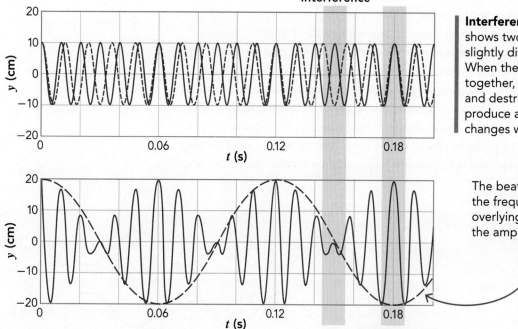

Destructive interference

Constructive interference

Interference The time graph shows two sound waves with slightly different frequencies. When the waves combine together, alternating constructive and destructive interference produce an amplitude that changes with time.

The beat frequency is the frequency of the overlying pulsation in the amplitude.

(30) **SEP Use Mathematics** A guitar player uses a tuning fork to tune his guitar. The fork produces a frequency of 330 Hz. The guitar string is out of tune and produces a frequency of 318 Hz. Determine the frequency of the beats he would hear when the string and fork sound together.

Standing Waves

When you pluck a string on a violin, the wave that is generated does not seem to move, so it is called a **standing wave.** You can think of two identical waves interacting as they move in opposite directions. They alternate between constructive and destructive interference as they pass each other, and the resulting wave appears to oscillate in place. All string and wind instruments produce consistent, uniform sounds by means of standing waves.

Wave Reflection A wave on the rope, shown as a solid line, travels toward the wall. It reflects and interferes with the back of the same wave. The reflected wave is shown as a dashed line. Distance graphs, showing the interference at different times, are pictured.

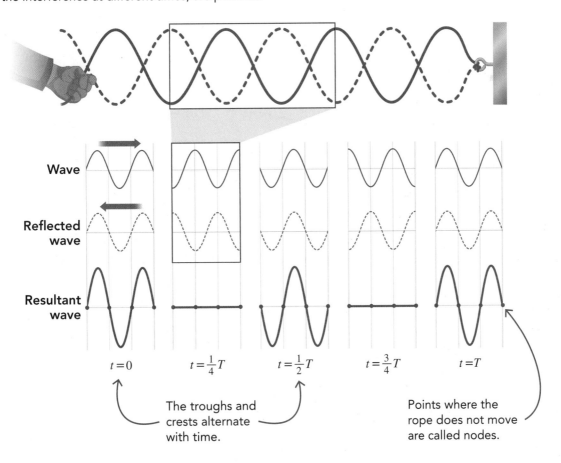

Wave

Reflected wave

Resultant wave

$t = 0$ $t = \frac{1}{4}T$ $t = \frac{1}{2}T$ $t = \frac{3}{4}T$ $t = T$

The troughs and crests alternate with time.

Points where the rope does not move are called nodes.

(31) **SEP Plan an Investigation** Incorporating a ruler, a frequency generator hooked to a speaker, and a gas-filled Rubens' tube, plan an investigation that would determine the speed of sound in the gas.

Waves on a String

The reflections of confined waves produce standing waves. For example, a string fixed at both ends results in standing waves that have a specific set of frequencies.

The wavelength depends on the number of half standing waves in the string. The wave speed is determined using the equation for wave speed on a rope from the previous experience. You can use the relationship between frequency, wavelength, and wave speed to determine the possible frequencies of standing waves in a string of a given length.

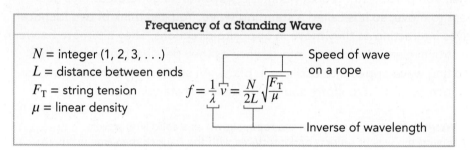

Frequency of a Standing Wave

N = integer (1, 2, 3, . . .)
L = distance between ends
F_T = string tension
μ = linear density

Speed of wave on a rope

$$f = \frac{1}{\lambda} v = \frac{N}{2L} \sqrt{\frac{F_T}{\mu}}$$

Inverse of wavelength

Fitting Nodes Because the fixed ends of the string do not move, the nodes must form at the fixed ends. This constrains what wavelengths can "fit." All other wavelengths result in destructive interference.

The longest wavelength produces what is called the fundamental frequency.

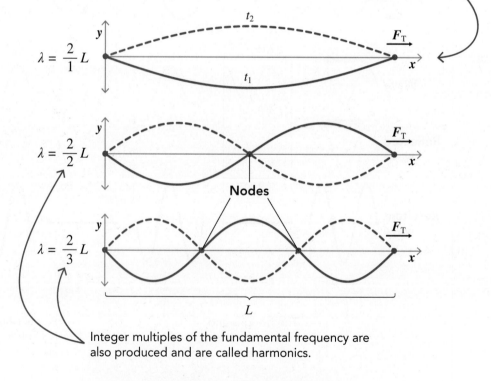

$$\lambda = \frac{2}{1} L$$

$$\lambda = \frac{2}{2} L$$

Nodes

$$\lambda = \frac{2}{3} L$$

L

Integer multiples of the fundamental frequency are also produced and are called harmonics.

(32) **SEP Construct an Explanation** The strings on a violin have different thicknesses. Construct an explanation for why the thinner strings produce sounds with higher frequencies.

Standing Waves on a Rope

A string attached to a frequency generator passes over a pulley of negligible mass 1.00 m away. A 5.00-kg hanging mass is attached to the other end of the string, which has a linear density of $\mu = 0.00500$ kg/m. Determine the speed of a wave on the string. List the three lowest possible frequencies that the frequency generator must be tuned to in order to produce standing waves.

1. DRAW A PICTURE Sketch a picture of the situation.

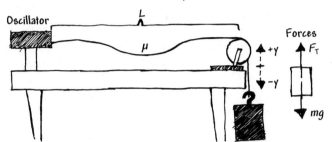

2. DEFINE THE PROBLEM List knowns and unknowns, and assign values to variables.

$L = 1.00$ m	$F_T = ?$
$m = 5.00$ kg	$v = ?$
$\mu = 0.00500$ kg/m	$f_{1, 2, 3} = ?$
$N = 1, 2, 3$	

3. PLAN AND EXECUTE Use mathematical relationships, the picture, and your definitions to plan and execute a solution.

Determine the tension in the string from Newton's second law and the free-body diagram.

$$\Sigma F = 0 = F_T - mg$$
$$F_T = mg = (5.00 \text{ kg}) 9.8 \text{ m/s}^2 = 49.0 \text{ N}$$

Determine the wave speed.

$$v = \sqrt{\frac{F_T}{\mu}} = \sqrt{\frac{49.0 \text{ N}}{(0.00500 \text{ kg/m})}} = 99.0 \text{ m/s}$$

Determine the fundamental frequency.

$$f = \frac{1}{\lambda}v = \frac{N}{2L}v$$
$$f_1 = \frac{1}{2L}v = \frac{1}{2(1.00 \text{ m})}(99.0 \text{ m/s}) = 49.5 \text{ Hz}$$

Determine the second and third harmonics.

$$f_2 = \frac{2}{2L}v = \frac{2}{2(1.00 \text{ m})}(99.0 \text{ m/s}) = 99.0 \text{ Hz}$$
$$f_3 = \frac{3}{2L}v = \frac{3}{2(1.00 \text{ m})}(99.0 \text{ m/s}) = 149 \text{ Hz}$$

4. EVALUATE Reflect on your answer.
   All units are appropriate, and the calculated frequencies are realistic values.

 GO ONLINE for more **math support**.

   🖥 **Math Practice Problems**

---

33 A string attached to a frequency generator passes over a pulley of negligible mass 2.50 m away. A 12.0-kg hanging mass is attached to the other end of the string, which has a linear mass density of $\mu = 0.00800$ kg/m. Determine the speed of a wave on the string. List the three lowest possible frequencies that the frequency generator must be tuned to in order to produce standing waves.

   📖 **NEED A HINT?** Go online to your **eText Sample Problem** for stepped out support.

Transfer of Wave Energy

EXPERIENCE IT!

Move your hand back and forth on a table. Does it take more or less energy to make larger amplitudes? Does it take more or less energy to move your hand back and forth faster?

Converting Wave Energy into Mechanical Energy Waves, such as water waves, carry energy. At the coast, their energy erodes rock where waves are strong and causes deposition where weaker, changing the shape of shorelines. In a water wave, the molecules of water that make up the wave move up and down. In the same way, a rubber duck floating on the surface of a pond moves up and down as a water wave passes, changing the duck's kinetic energy and potential energy. According to the work-energy theorem, the average work the wave does on the duck is proportional to the average square of the vertical speed of the duck ($W \propto$ average of v^2). Note that the duck and the wave can be moving at different speeds and in different directions!

Wave Energy Transfer

How is **wave energy converted into the mechanical energy** of an object?

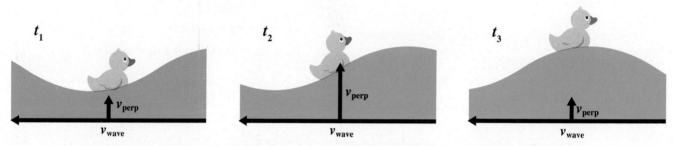

t_1 t_2 t_3

v_{perp} v_{wave}

As a duck rises from a trough to a crest, its **perpendicular velocity, v_{perp}, changes.**

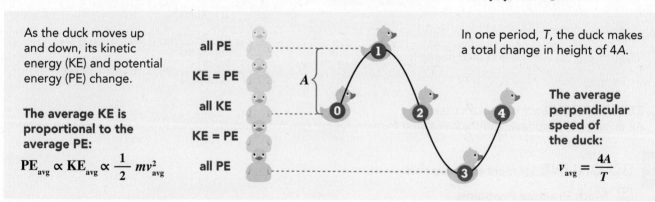

As the duck moves up and down, its kinetic energy (KE) and potential energy (PE) change.

The average KE is proportional to the average PE:

$$PE_{avg} \propto KE_{avg} \propto \frac{1}{2} mv^2_{avg}$$

all PE
KE = PE
all KE
KE = PE
all PE

A

In one period, T, the duck makes a total change in height of $4A$.

The average perpendicular speed of the duck:

$$v_{avg} = \frac{4A}{T}$$

$$\boxed{E_{duck} \propto v^2_{avg}} \rightarrow \boxed{v_{avg} = \frac{4A}{T}} \rightarrow \boxed{f = \frac{1}{T}} \rightarrow \boxed{v_{avg} = 4Af}$$

These expressions can be used to determine the energy transferred to the duck. The energy is proportional to the squares of the wave amplitude and frequency.

$$E_{duck} \propto A^2 f^2$$

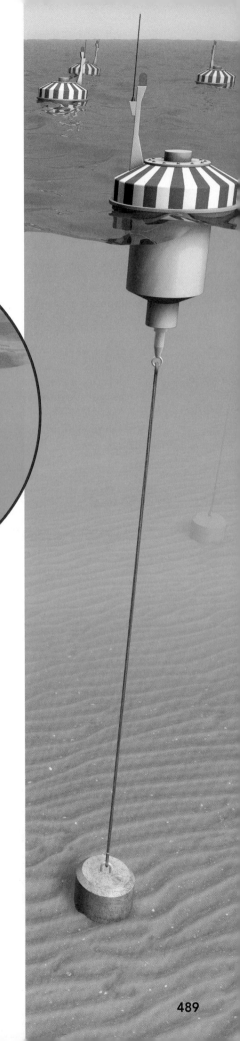

▶ **GO ONLINE** to watch a **video** about harnessing ocean wave energy.

Converting Wave Energy into Electrical Energy The up-and-down mechanical motion of a wave can be converted into electrical energy through various means. For example, a linear point absorber harvests wave energy. The motion of a wave in the ocean moves a buoy up and down, just as it moves a rubber duck. The motion is converted into electrical energy through electromagnetic induction—a changing magnetic field moving inside a coil of wire.

> **Wave Energy to Electricity** As the buoy moves up and down with a passing wave, a fixed magnet moves up and down through a coil of wire. The changing magnetic field within the coil induces a current.

The coil is attached to the moving buoy.

The magnet is anchored to the sea floor.

(34) **SEP Analyze and Interpret Data**
A power company is trying to determine where to install an array of devices that will generate electricity from ocean waves. The company measured the average amplitude of the waves at three locations. Complete the table.

Location	Wave Amplitude (m)	Energy Transferred (kJ)
A	2	500
B	3	
C	4	

(35) **SEP Argue from Evidence** You are evaluating a claim that wave energy harvesters should be placed at locations with high-frequency waves to generate the greatest voltages. Combine Faraday's law of induction and your understanding of wave energy to argue from evidence either for or against the claim.

489

Energy in Waves

Energy, Amplitude, Frequency, and Speed The rubber duck model demonstrates the average mechanical energy transferred to a single object interacting with a wave. However, to determine the energy of a wave over one wavelength, add up the transfer of energy for a wavelength of rubber ducks. When you evaluate the motion of a wavelength of rubber ducks, you find that the average energy is also proportional to the wavelength of the wave.

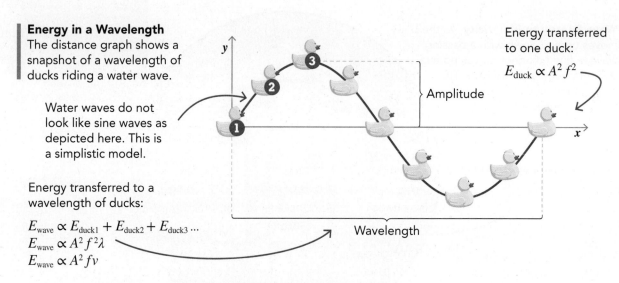

Energy in a Wavelength
The distance graph shows a snapshot of a wavelength of ducks riding a water wave.

Water waves do not look like sine waves as depicted here. This is a simplistic model.

Energy transferred to a wavelength of ducks:

$E_{wave} \propto E_{duck1} + E_{duck2} + E_{duck3} \dots$
$E_{wave} \propto A^2 f^2 \lambda$
$E_{wave} \propto A^2 f v$

Amplitude

Wavelength

Energy transferred to one duck:

$E_{duck} \propto A^2 f^2$

A tremendous amount of energy can be carried by waves. For example, typical ocean waves along one meter of shoreline carry enough energy to provide electricity for a few houses.

36 **SEP Use Mathematics** Show why the expression for energy can be written as proportional to either $A^2 f^2 \lambda$ or $A^2 f v$.

37 **SEP Use a Model** One crest of a wave 2 km in length with $\lambda = 28$ m and $A = 2$ m carries as much energy as a car needs to travel about 60 km. Expand the "rubber duck" model into three dimensions by modeling ducks a length parallel to the shore. Use your model to explain why wave energy would also depend on this length.

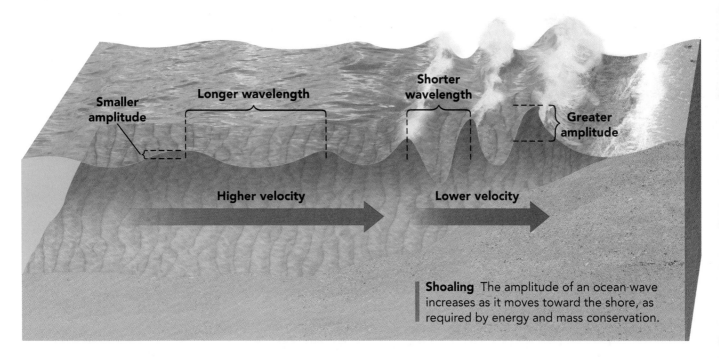

Shoaling The amplitude of an ocean-wave increases as it moves toward the shore, as required by energy and mass conservation.

Energy at an Interface Energy is conserved at an interface. When a wave passes from one medium to another, or the properties of the medium change, then the amplitude of the wave also changes. An example is wave shoaling, which is the change in height of water waves as they enter shallow water.

Frequency is determined by the source of the wave, so it does not change at an interface. The speed of the wave is determined by the depth of the water near shore. As the ocean wave moves toward the shore, its speed decreases. Since the total energy must stay the same, the amplitude must increase.

Energy Is Conserved Frequency and energy do not change at an interface. Decreasing wave speed or wavelength produces increasing amplitude.

$E \propto A^2 fv$	$A_B^2 f v_B = A_A^2 f v_A$	$A_B^2 v_B = A_A^2 v_A$	$A_B^2 v_B = A_A^2 v_A$
	The energy and frequency before are the same as after.	Cancel the f on both sides.	A decrease in v results in an increase in A.

(38) **SEP Construct an Explanation** Sketch a flowchart similar to the one shown that explains why an ocean wave's wavelength decreases during shoaling.

(39) **SEP Use a Model** A wave pulse moves through a rope as shown. Later, the pulse is seen continuing into the more dense rope on the right, and a reflected pulse is seen moving in the less dense rope on the left. Construct an energy bar chart for this situation. Why does the amplitude decrease, even though the speed decreased?

Light rope

Dense rope

INVESTIGATIVE PHENOMENON

GO ONLINE to revisit your **Investigative Phenomenon CER** with the new information you have learned about Wave Behavior and Energy.

These questions will help you apply what you learned in this experience to the Investigative Phenomenon.

40 **SEP Develop a Model** In this experience, you developed a mathematical model for the frequency of a standing wave on a string. A standing wave can also form in shallow water, though a mathematical model is more complicated in this situation. What would you need to generate a standing water wave? Sketch a model of a standing wave in shallow water and describe what features would affect the wave properties.

41 **SEP Construct an Explanation** A seiche is a standing wave formed in an enclosed body of water, such as a pond or lake. Lake Erie is known for wind-caused seiches with up to 5 meter amplitudes. Lake Tahoe is susceptible to seiches due to seismic activity. Construct an explanation for the formation of seiches. What would determine the wavelength for a seiche forming in Lake Erie and Lake Tahoe?

42 **SEP Construct an Explanation** Beach erosion is the loss of beach sand. Sand is lifted off the beach and transferred to deeper water or to another coastal area. During storms, wave amplitude increases and wave period decreases. Construct an explanation for why beach erosion can significantly increase during storms.

43 **SEP Design a Solution** Rocks are often stacked on beaches to form seawalls, designed to protect the coastline behind the wall from erosion. If you were designing a seawall, would you use large boulders or small rocks? Defend your choice.

GO ONLINE for a **quiz** to evaluate what you learned about Wave Behavior and Energy.

Wave Optics

 GO ONLINE to do a **hands-on lab** to investigate reflection and refraction.

Ray Model

So far, you have represented waves mathematically using both time and distance graphs, and using the sine function. You have also used the **wave front model,** a model of waves in which you draw only the moving crests of a wave. Another way to represent waves is with a ray model. A **ray model** is a model of waves that uses an arrow called a ray to represent the direction the wave is traveling. Rays are always drawn perpendicular to the wave fronts. Ray models look similar to electric fields and magnetic fields.

Ray Model of Waves Overhead photos of ripple tanks show the crests of parallel wave fronts and of circular waves. The motion of the waves can be modeled using rays drawn perpendicular to the wave fronts.

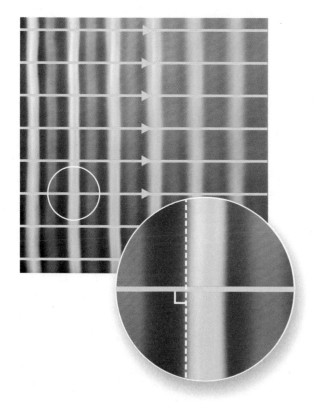

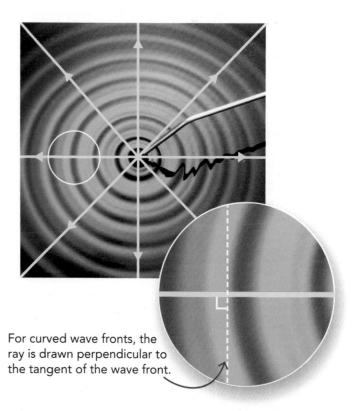

For curved wave fronts, the ray is drawn perpendicular to the tangent of the wave front.

(44) **SEP Use a Model** Describe what information can be gathered from the ray models in the two ripple tanks. When may the ray model be more useful than the wave front model?

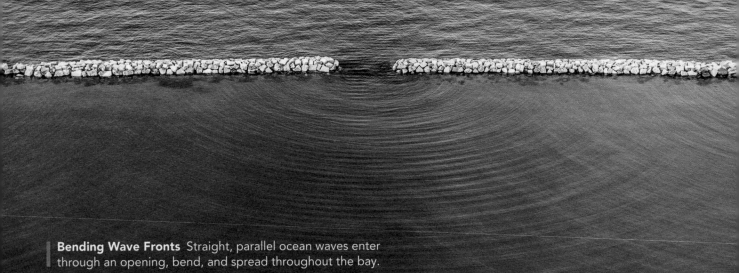

Bending Wave Fronts Straight, parallel ocean waves enter through an opening, bend, and spread throughout the bay.

Diffraction

The spreading and bending of ocean waves is an example of a phenomenon called diffraction. **Diffraction** is the bending of a wave around the edges of an opening or an obstacle. Wave front and ray models represent waves clearly, but they do not help you explain diffraction.

Huygens' Principle Dutch scientist Christiaan Huygens proposed an idea that could explain diffraction. **Huygens' wave model** is a model that represents every point on a wave front as a source of semicircular wavelets that spread out in the forward direction at the speed of the wave. A new wave front is tangent to all of the wavelets. You can use Huygens' wave model to understand diffraction and other wave phenomena.

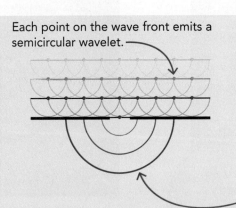

Each point on the wave front emits a semicircular wavelet.

Small Opening When the wave front encounters a small opening, only one small section of the wave front produces a semicircular wavelet, which then spreads out.

You can think of the small opening as approximately a single source of wavelets.

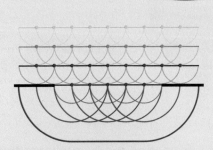

Larger Opening A larger opening has more sources for wavelets, represented as the dots in the opening. The resulting wave front is straight in the middle but bends around the corners of the opening.

Why Can You Hear, but Not See, Around Corners? You can hear someone calling your name from around a corner. You know that the sound waves must bend around the corner to get to your ears. Just as ocean waves diffract through an opening, sound waves diffract around corners or through doorways.

As you will discover later, light also behaves like a wave. However, you cannot see around corners. If water, sound, and light all behave like waves, then why do you not see light diffract in everyday life? The answer has to do with the tiny wavelength of light.

Sound Bends Around Corners If someone is playing music in another room, you can hear the music even if you are not standing at the doorway.

The sound wave bends toward you, so you can hear it.

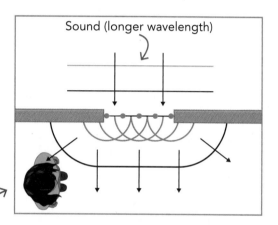
Sound (longer wavelength)

Light Does Not Bend Around Corners For light, large obstructions cast sharp shadows. The light waves do not bend around the corner as sound waves do.

In this case, the light does not diffract observably. If the wavelength were similar in size to the opening, the wave would noticeably diffract around the corners.

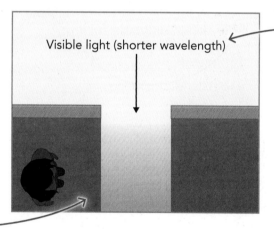
Visible light (shorter wavelength)

The wavelength of light is very small compared to the door—less than a millionth the size!

45 **CCC Scale, Proportion, and Quantity** Similar to sound and water waves, light waves diffract when the opening size is similar to the wavelength of light. The photo shows the diffraction pattern for a laser beam passed through a very narrow slit. Look up the average wavelength of visible light and estimate the width of the slit.

Reflection

When you dribble a ball, it bounces back to you. Similarly, a wave encountering an obstacle also bounces back. **Reflection** is a phenomenon that occurs when a wave or object bounces off an interface or another object.

Models for Reflection Huygens' wave model, a ray model, or a simple particle model can be used to show the reflection of waves, such as sound waves, water waves, seismic waves, and light waves. The **particle model** is a representation of light as simple spheres, like balls on a pool table or a basketball. All the models of waves make the same prediction; however, one model often provides a clearer explanation than the others.

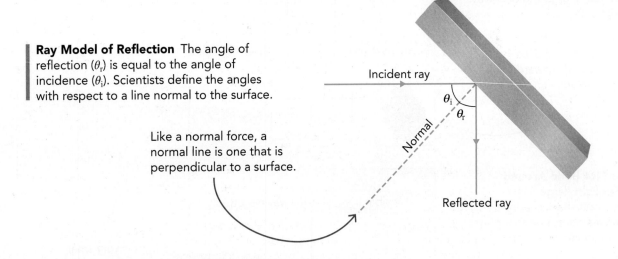

Ray Model of Reflection The angle of reflection (θ_r) is equal to the angle of incidence (θ_i). Scientists define the angles with respect to a line normal to the surface.

Like a normal force, a normal line is one that is perpendicular to a surface.

Incident ray

θ_i

θ_r

Normal

Reflected ray

Wave Model of Reflection Huygens' wave model produces the same relationship between incident and reflected angles.

The first wavelet is produced at the mirror surface.

A short time later, another wavelet is produced at the mirror surface.

All of the wavelets have joined together to form a new wave front.

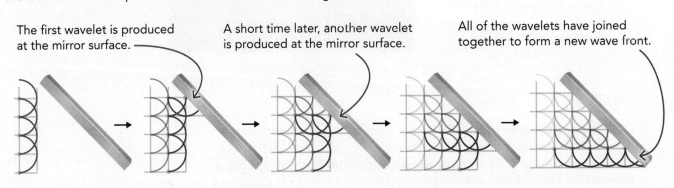

(46) SEP Evaluate and Communicate Information Reflection can be described with a wave, ray, or particle model. For some situations, one model is more useful than another. Compare diffraction and reflection, and describe which model gives the clearest explanation for each phenomenon.

Images Reflections produce images. You can see an image of a seal in the water. But is anything really there?

Forming a Mirror Image The wave model is helpful for understanding why reflection occurs as it does. However, for more complicated systems, the simpler ray model is typically used. The ray model allows you to make predictions about how and where an image will be formed due to reflection.

For reflection of light off a flat mirror or other shiny, flat surfaces, the image formed is called a virtual image. A **virtual image** is an image formed by light rays that appear to originate from a point. A **real image** is an image formed by light rays that actually do originate from a point. Reflections from a flat surface produce virtual images located a distance behind the surface that is equal to the object's distance in front of the surface.

Image Formation in a Mirror Rays representing light waves from your toes and your head are shown reflected into your eyes. The change in direction makes it appear that the reflected rays are coming from behind the mirror. It is like looking at a twin who is the same distance away and is the same size as the virtual image in the mirror.

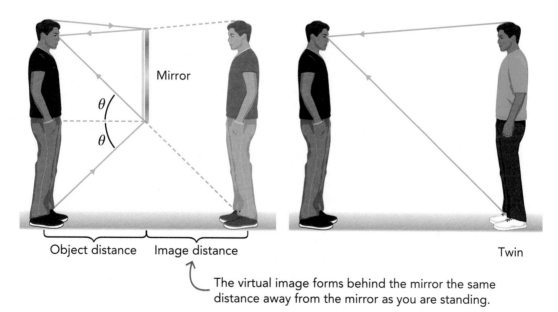

The virtual image forms behind the mirror the same distance away from the mirror as you are standing.

(47) **SEP Design a Solution** As you have learned, light does not noticeably bend around corners on its own. However, you can use reflection to overcome that limitation. Sketch a design for a system that would allow you to see around a corner.

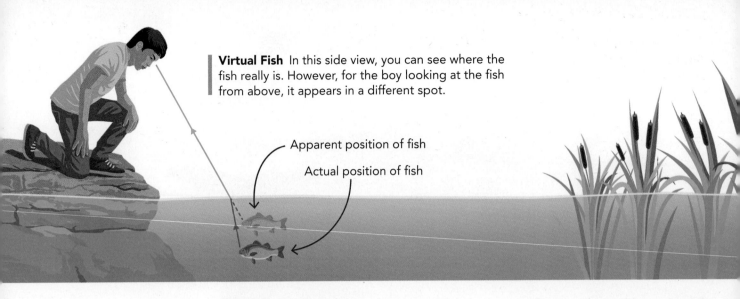

Virtual Fish In this side view, you can see where the fish really is. However, for the boy looking at the fish from above, it appears in a different spot.

Apparent position of fish

Actual position of fish

Refraction

GO ONLINE to do a PhET **simulation** that allows you to explore how light behaves at an interface and to see a **video** that explains refraction of light in animals.

Waves at an Interface The speed of a wave depends on properties of the medium. At an interface where properties of the medium change, wave speed and wavelength also change in response, with a resulting change in direction. **Refraction** is the change in direction of a wave as a result of a change in wave speed at different points along the wave front. Refraction happens for all types of waves, and as with reflection, the refraction of light waves can also result in the formation of images.

EXPERIENCE IT!

Find three friends and form a line of four people, side by side, holding hands. Walk straight ahead, all at the same speed. What happens if one person at the end of the line slows down as everyone continues to walk forward?

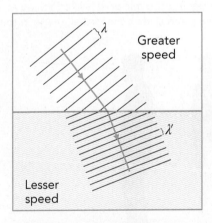

Wave Front Model When the wave speed is reduced in the new medium, the wavelength must also be reduced. The crests must line up at the interface, and the result is a change in wave direction.

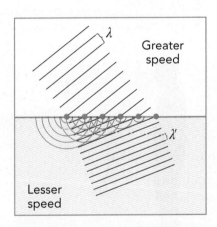

Huygens' Wave Model Points on the wave front at the interface serve as sources for wavelets. The wavelets propagate at a slower speed in the new medium, resulting in a change in direction for the wave front.

48 **SEP Develop a Model** Use a ruler to draw four parallel lines perpendicular to the edge of a sheet of paper and spaced 1 cm apart. Repeat on another sheet of paper but space the lines 0.5 cm apart. Bring the two pieces of paper together and try to connect the sets of lines. How must you orient the pieces of paper?

Snell's Law How much a wave bends depends on the ratio of the wave speed in the two mediums. The Dutch mathematician Willebrord Snell developed a mathematical model of refraction called **Snell's law,** which is the relation between velocities and directions of light passing from one medium to another.

For light refraction, scientists replace the ratio of wave speeds with a quantity called the index of refraction. The **index of refraction** of a material is the ratio of the speed of light in a vacuum to the speed of light in that material. With the index of refraction, you can write Snell's law in another way.

Snell's Law (Wave Speed)	Snell's Law (Index of Refraction)
$$\frac{\sin\theta_1}{v_1} = \frac{\sin\theta_2}{v_2}$$ θ_1 = angle of incidence v_1 = wave speed in medium 1 θ_2 = angle of refraction v_2 = wave speed in medium 2	$$n_1\sin\theta_1 = n_2\sin\theta_2$$ n_1 = index of refraction for medium 1 n_2 = index of refraction for medium 2

Slowing Down Suppose you push a lawnmower from a sidewalk onto grass. When the first wheel hits the grass, it slows down. The wheel on the other side keeps moving at its faster speed. The lawnmower turns toward the normal.

Speeding Up Pushing the lawnmower from the grass, where it moves slower, onto the sidewalk, where it moves faster, results in the lawnmower turning away from the normal.

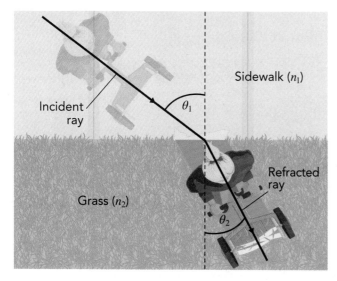

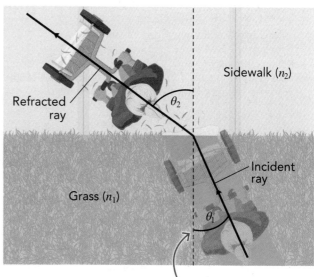

As in reflection, the angles are defined with respect to the line normal to the interface.

49 **SEP Use Mathematics** Show that the two mathematical versions of Snell's law are the same by writing the index of refraction in terms of the wave speed in a vacuum and the wave speed in a material.

Determining the Index of Refraction

A ray of light moving through air strikes the surface of an unknown transparent liquid at an angle of 30.0° with respect to the normal. The ray is observed to refract at an angle of 21.6°. Determine the index of refraction for and the speed of light in the unknown liquid. The index of refraction for air is 1.00 and the speed of light in a vacuum is 3.00×10^8 m/s.

1. DRAW A PICTURE Sketch a picture of the situation.

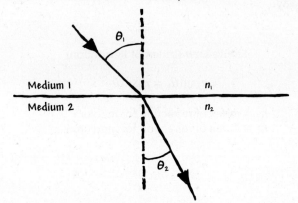

2. DEFINE THE PROBLEM List knowns and unknowns, and assign values to variables.

$\theta_1 = 30.0°$ $n_2 = ?$

$\theta_2 = 21.6°$ $v_2 = ?$

$n_1 = 1.00$

$c = 3.00 \times 10^8$ m/s

3. PLAN AND EXECUTE Use mathematical relationships, the picture, and your definitions to plan and execute a solution.

Write Snell's law in terms of the indices of refraction.	$n_1 \sin\theta_1 = n_2 \sin\theta_2$
Solve for the unknown index of refraction.	$n_2 = n_1 \dfrac{\sin\theta_1}{\sin\theta_2} = 1.00 \dfrac{\sin 30.0°}{\sin 21.6°} = 1.36$
Determine the speed of light in the unknown material from the definition of the index of refraction.	$n_2 = \dfrac{c}{v_2} \rightarrow v_2 = \dfrac{c}{n_2} = \dfrac{3.00 \times 10^8 \text{ m/s}}{1.36}$ $= 2.21 \times 10^8$ m/s

4. EVALUATE Reflect on your answer.
All of the units (or lack of units) are appropriate for the given quantities. Consulting a table of values tells you that the index of refraction found is the same as ethanol's index of refraction. The speed of light in ethanol is less than in a vacuum, which makes sense.

 GO ONLINE for more **math support**.

🖥 **Math Practice Problems**

(50) A ray of light moving through air strikes the surface of an unknown transparent liquid at an angle of 40.0° with respect to the normal. The ray is observed to refract at an angle of 26.1°. Determine the index of refraction for and the speed of light in the unknown liquid.

📖 **NEED A HINT?** Go online to your **eText Sample Problem** for stepped out support.

(51) Sunlight strikes the surface of a lake. The light strikes at an angle of 38.0° with respect to the normal and refracts at an angle of 27.7°. Determine the index of refraction for and the speed of light in water.

Lenses

A **lens** is a piece of glass or other transparent substance with curved sides that is used for concentrating or dispersing light rays. Lenses bend light by refraction. A **converging lens** (also known as a convex lens) is a lens shaped so that all rays entering parallel to the optical axis converge at a single point on the opposite side of the lens. A **diverging lens** (also known as a concave lens) is a lens shaped so that all parallel rays appear to diverge away from a single point on the same side of the lens. The point at which the rays converge or appear to diverge is called the **focal point,** F. The distance from the focal point to the lens is the **focal length,** which is determined by the index of refraction and the shape of the lens.

VOCABULARY

The word **lens** comes from the Latin word *lens,* which means "lentil." A converging lens looks like a lentil.

| **Lenses** Rays of light entering lenses parallel to the optical axis converge at a focal point. The **optical axis** is an imaginary line that goes through the center of the lens and is perpendicular to the lens plane.

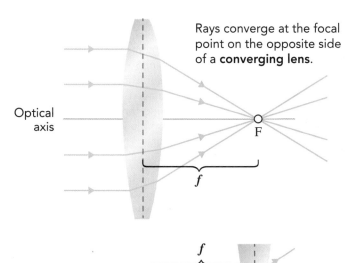

Rays converge at the focal point on the opposite side of a **converging lens.**

Optical axis

F

f

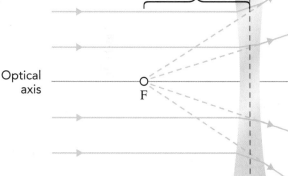

f

Optical axis

F

Rays appear to diverge from the focal point on the same side of a **diverging lens.**

Gravitational Lens Einstein's general theory of relativity demonstrates that a large mass bends space. Bent space bends light. The photo shows light from a galaxy that has bent around both sides of a large mass. The resulting double image forms a smiley face.

 SEP Plan an Investigation Plan an investigation that would allow you to determine the focal length of several different converging lenses.

Formation of Images

Real and Virtual Images So far, you have seen reflection and refraction producing only virtual images. However, lenses can produce real images as well as virtual images. For review, a virtual image is any image formed by light rays that appear to originate from a point. A real image is an image formed by light rays that actually do originate from a point.

A process called *ray tracing* is used to determine where and what type of images will form. When you follow the path that a light ray takes as it goes from an object, through a lens, and out through the other side, you are using the **ray tracing process.**

Ray Tracing

How do you **determine how light will behave** when going through a lens?

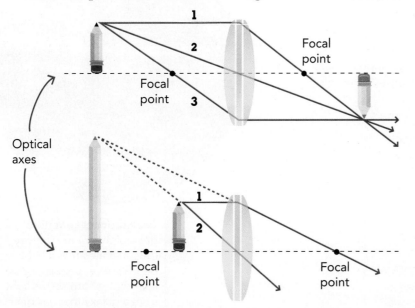

For converging lenses, draw **three principal rays:**

1. Rays parallel to the optical axis going in come out through the focal point.
2. Rays going through the center keep going straight.
3. Rays going through the focal point come out parallel to the optical axis.

If the object is between the focal point and the lens, then you can still use two of the principal rays. The rays diverge! You have to **extrapolate backward to determine location of the image.**

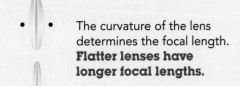

The curvature of the lens determines the focal length. **Flatter lenses have longer focal lengths.**

Real images form on the opposite side of the lens, compared to the object's position. **Virtual images form on the same side** of the lens.

(53) **SEP Argue from Evidence** A piece of black tape is placed over the upper half of a converging lens. Make a claim about whether an image would form and argue for your claim by sketching a model that includes principal rays.

(54) **SEP Develop a Model** Based on your experience with ray tracing for a converging lens, develop a process for ray tracing a set of principal rays for a diverging lens.

Magnification The process of making an object appear larger is called **magnification.** For images of objects formed by lenses, you can calculate the magnification as the ratio of the image height to the object height.

Magnification Equation
$$m = \frac{h_i}{h_o} = -\frac{d_i}{d_o}$$
m = magnification h_i = image height h_o = object height d_i = image distance d_o = object distance

A magnification with absolute value greater than 1 indicates an increase in size, whereas a magnification with absolute value less than 1 indicates a decrease in size. A positive magnification indicates an image that is upright with respect to the object, and a negative magnification indicates an image that is inverted.

Magnifying Glass A magnifying glass is a converging lens that is used to produce a larger virtual image of an object.

Magnification When the image height is larger than the object height, then the image has a magnification greater than 1.

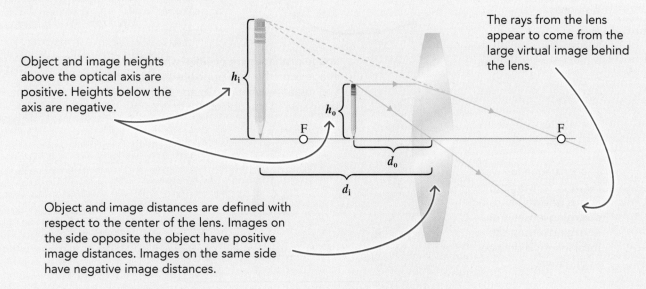

Object and image heights above the optical axis are positive. Heights below the axis are negative.

The rays from the lens appear to come from the large virtual image behind the lens.

Object and image distances are defined with respect to the center of the lens. Images on the side opposite the object have positive image distances. Images on the same side have negative image distances.

(55) **SEP Use a Model** Sketch a situation in which the magnification of the image is negative. Is the image real or virtual?

The Lens Equation

Ray tracing allows you to qualitatively estimate the location and size of an image formed by a lens. The **lens equation** is a mathematical model you can use to calculate image locations.

Lens Equation
$$\frac{1}{d_o} + \frac{1}{d_i} = \frac{1}{f}$$
d_o = object distance d_i = image distance f = focal length

With values for the object and image distances, you can use the magnification equation to find the size of the image.

Quantitative Lens Model The lens equation works for all lenses considered thin, which means the thickness is small compared to the radius of curvature.

Object distances are always assumed to be positive. If when solving the lens equation the object distance comes out as negative, the sign convention is reversed for the object and image distances.

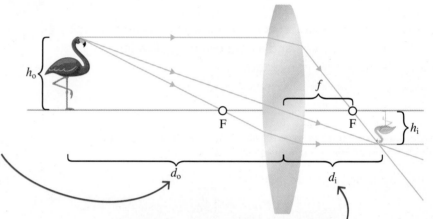

Image distances are positive when the image is on the side opposite the object and negative when the image is on the same side as the object.

The lens equation works for both converging lenses (shown here) and diverging lenses. For diverging lenses, the focal length is defined as negative.

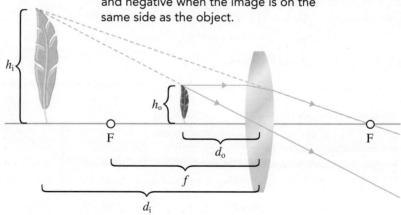

56 **SEP Use Computational Thinking** Values for object and image distances and heights can be positive or negative. Based on the lens equation and the magnification equation, write two short *If/then* statements that tell whether an image is real or virtual and upright or inverted.

Image of a Rubber Duck

A rubber duck is placed 0.60 m from a converging lens that has a 0.40-m focal length. Sketch a ray tracing model to get an approximate location for the image. Use the lens equation to calculate the location of the image and the magnification. Determine whether the image is real or virtual and upright or inverted.

1. DRAW A PICTURE Sketch a picture of the situation.

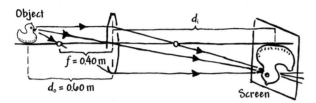

2. DEFINE THE PROBLEM List knowns and unknowns, and assign values to variables.

$d_o = 0.60$ m	$d_i = ?$
$f = 0.40$ m	$m = ?$

3. PLAN AND EXECUTE Use mathematical relationships, the picture, and your definitions to plan and execute a solution.

Write the lens equation and then solve for the image distance.

$$\frac{1}{d_o} + \frac{1}{d_i} = \frac{1}{f} \rightarrow \frac{1}{d_i} = \frac{1}{f} - \frac{1}{d_o}$$

$$d_i = \left(\frac{1}{f} - \frac{1}{d_o}\right)^{-1}$$

Calculate the image distance. If the image distance is positive, then the image is real. If it is negative, then the image is virtual.

$$d_i = \left(\frac{1}{0.40 \text{ m}} - \frac{1}{0.60 \text{ m}}\right)^{-1} = \left(\frac{3.00 - 2.00}{1.20 \text{ m}}\right)^{-1}$$

$$= 1.2 \text{ m} \quad \text{The image is real.}$$

Calculate the magnification. If the magnification is positive, then the image is upright. If it is negative, then the image is inverted.

$$m = -\frac{d_i}{d_o} = -\frac{1.2 \text{ m}}{0.60 \text{ m}}$$

$$= -2.0 \quad \text{The image is inverted.}$$

4. EVALUATE Reflect on your answer.
The units are appropriate for the calculated quantities. The calculated quantities are consistent with the model from ray tracing.

 GO ONLINE for more **math support.**

🖥 **Math Practice Problems**

---

57 A rubber duck is placed 0.50 m from a converging lens that has a 0.30-m focal length. Sketch a ray tracing model to get an approximate location for the image. Use the lens equation to calculate the location of the image and the magnification. Determine whether the image is real or virtual and upright or inverted.

📖 **NEED A HINT?** Go online to your **eText Sample Problem** for stepped out support.

58 Silvio puts a candle 0.30 m away from a converging lens. If the lens has a focal length of 0.60 m, what is the location of the image and its magnification? Identify if the image is real or virtual, as well as if the image is upright or inverted.

Reading with a Magnifying Glass

The letters in a book you are reading are 0.3 cm tall. To read the text more easily, you use a magnifying glass with a focal length of 15.0 cm. When the magnifying glass is held 10.0 cm from the book, how tall will the letters appear to be? Sketch a ray tracing model and use the lens equation to determine whether the image is real or virtual and upright or inverted.

1. DRAW A PICTURE Sketch a picture of the situation.

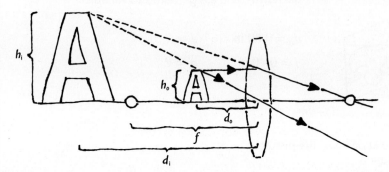

2. DEFINE THE PROBLEM List knowns and unknowns, and assign values to variables.

$h_o = 0.3$ cm	$d_i = ?$
$f = 15.0$ cm	$m = ?$
$d_o = 10.0$ cm	$h_i = ?$

3. PLAN AND EXECUTE Use mathematical relationships, the picture, and your definitions to plan and execute a solution.

Write the lens equation and then solve for the image distance.

$$\frac{1}{d_o} + \frac{1}{d_i} = \frac{1}{f} \rightarrow \frac{1}{d_i} = \frac{1}{f} - \frac{1}{d_o}$$

$$d_i = \left(\frac{1}{f} - \frac{1}{d_o}\right)^{-1}$$

Calculate the image distance. If the image distance is positive, then the image is real. If it is negative, then the image is virtual.

$$d_i = \left(\frac{1}{15.0 \text{ cm}} - \frac{1}{10.0 \text{ cm}}\right)^{-1}$$

$$= -30.0 \text{ cm} \quad \text{The image is virtual.}$$

Calculate the magnification. If the magnification is positive, then the image is upright. If it is negative, then the image is inverted.

$$m = -\frac{d_i}{d_o} = -\frac{-30.0 \text{ cm}}{10.0 \text{ cm}}$$

$$= 3.00 \quad \text{The image is upright.}$$

Using the magnification, calculate the image height.

$$m = \frac{h_i}{h_o} \rightarrow h_i = mh_o = 3.00 \times 0.3 \text{ cm} = 0.9 \text{ cm}$$

4. EVALUATE Reflect on your answer.
The units are appropriate for the given quantities, and the calculated quantities are consistent with the ray tracing model.

 GO ONLINE for more **math support**.

▶ **Math Tutorial Video**

🖥 **Math Practice Problems**

(59) The letters in a book you are reading are 0.4 cm tall. To read the text more easily, you use a magnifying glass with a focal length of 12.0 cm. When the magnifying glass is held 8.0 cm from the book, how tall will the letters appear to be? Sketch a ray tracing model and use the lens equation to determine whether the image is real or virtual and upright or inverted.

📖 **NEED A HINT?** Go online to your **eText Sample Problem** for stepped out support.

(60) The letters in a book you are reading are 0.5 cm tall. To read the text more easily, you use a magnifying glass with a focal length of 10.0 cm. When the magnifying glass is held 14 cm from the book, how tall will the letters appear to be? Sketch a ray tracing model and use the lens equation to determine whether the image is real or virtual and upright or inverted.

(61) A friend is using a converging lens to better view the image of a bird on an old postage stamp. The bird is 0.6 cm tall, and the lens has a focal length of 14.0 cm. If your friend holds the lens 9.0 cm from the stamp, how tall will the bird appear to be? Sketch a ray tracing model and use the lens equation to determine whether the image is real or virtual and upright or inverted.

(62) A jeweler wears magnifying glasses to help her see as she engraves a name in a ring. The focal length of the glasses is 20.0 cm. The letters are 0.4 cm tall, and she is holding the ring 10.0 cm away. How tall will the letters appear to be to her? Use the lens equation to determine whether the image is real or virtual and if the image is upright or inverted.

(63) Using a diverging lens, you look at a 7.0-mm-long insect hanging upside down. The lens has a focal length of –9.0 cm. How long will the insect appear to be if you hold the lens 2.25 cm from the insect? Use the lens equation to determine whether the image is real or virtual and if the image is upright or inverted.

(64) In a physics lab, a group of students observes how an object's image changes as they move the object closer to a diverging lens with a focal length of –1.0 m. Using the data recorded by the students, sketch a diagram that illustrates the data in the table. Consider how the image size changes for each data point, and whether the image is real or virtual and upright or inverted. Use the diagram to describe how image distance and size change as the object approaches the lens.

Object distance (m)	Image distance (m)
1.5	0.60
1.4	0.58
1.3	0.56
1.2	0.54
1.1	0.52
1.0	0.50

INVESTIGATIVE PHENOMENON

GO ONLINE to revisit your **Investigative Phenomenon CER** with the new information you have learned about Wave Optics.

These questions will help you apply what you learned in this experience to the Investigative Phenomenon.

65. **SEP Develop a Model** Coastal bays often have a semicircular shape. Describe how a scientist might model a coastal bay in a wave tank. Then, using the concept of diffraction, sketch how water waves might appear to change as they move from the larger part of the wave tank into the bay model.

66. **SEP Construct an Explanation** Examine the photo on this page. Using the concepts of wave refraction and wave energy, construct an explanation for why the sand and sediment in the area that juts out near the top of the image might be carried to the shoreline below it.

67. **SEP Argue from Evidence** At the beach, it appears that the waves are mostly parallel to the shore. If those waves are generated over a wide area far out at sea, why are all the waves heading in the same direction as they reach the shore? Make a claim and argue for your claim using evidence.

GO ONLINE for a **quiz** to evaluate what you learned about Wave Optics.

ANCHORING PHENOMENON

These questions will help you apply what you learned in this investigation to the Anchoring Phenomenon.

68 **SEP Analyze and Interpret Data** The quantum corral image shown looks like the circular standing waves that can form in an enclosed body of shallow water. The image shows 48 iron atoms on a sheet of copper. The circle is 14.26 nm (1.426×10^{-10} m) in diameter. Use this diameter to estimate the properties of the apparent standing electron wave.

69 **SEP Engage in Argument from Evidence** The electron wave patterns in the quantum corral were observed on a copper surface. Would you expect to observe exactly the same wave pattern on the surface of a different material? How might a different material affect the wave patterns observed? Explain and use evidence based on your understanding of forces in materials to support your response.

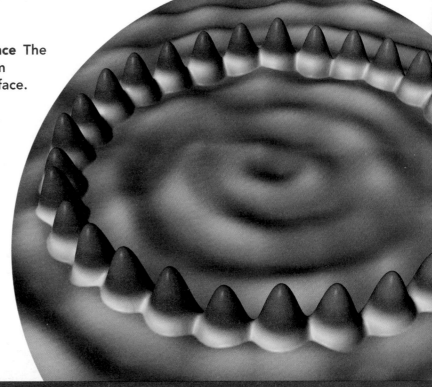

☑INVESTIGATION ASSESSMENT

GO ONLINE for activities that will give you an opportunity to **demonstrate what you have learned:**

☑ **Science Performance-Based Assessment** Find the speed of sound using a tuning fork and tube.

📄 **Engineering Workbench** Design a breakwater to reduce the erosion caused by water waves.

💻 **Career Connections** Learn about how a civil engineer applies knowledge of physics.

☑ **Investigation Test** Take this test to evaluate your understanding of waves.

☑ **Virtual Lab Performance-Based Assessment** Design a pool that deflects waves.

GO ONLINE to engage with real-world phenomena by watching a **video** and completing a **CER worksheet.**

How does this lens remove the glare?

Electromagnetic Radiation

When light interacts with a reflective surface, it can cause a glare. This effect can make it uncomfortable to look directly at the bright surface. It can also ruin a photograph by distorting parts of the image with a bright reflection.

Some sunglasses are simply tinted glass or plastic that blocks a portion of the light reaching your eyes. Other sunglasses, called polarized sunglasses, have polarizing films made of long, narrow polymer molecules. These polarizing films specifically filter out glare. Polarizing films are also used as filters on camera lenses to reduce glare in photographs.

How does a polarizing film do more than block some of the light? How can it specifically filter out glare? Answering these questions requires an understanding of the electromagnetic nature and wave behavior of visible light.

1. **SEP Construct an Explanation** How does the reflection of a wave cause a glare on a photograph? How does the reflection of a wave cause a glare on a television screen?

2. **SEP Construct an Explanation** Why do you think polarized sunglasses would be more effective at eliminating glare than regular tinted sunglasses?

3. **CCC Systems and System Models** What happens to the energy of the light waves from the glare as it reaches a polarizing filter? Would there be a change in temperature as the polarizer is exposed to light? Explain.

Electromagnetic Waves and Their Properties

 GO ONLINE to do a **hands-on lab** to investigate interference and diffraction patterns for electromagnetic waves using laser light sources.

Electromagnetic Waves

A wave is generated by a disturbance that causes matter to move back and forth around a fixed point. An **electromagnetic wave** (EM wave) is a wave generated by a disturbance in electric and magnetic fields. Just as a mechanical wave results from the movement of matter, EM waves result from the movement of electric charges. To generate an EM wave, the motion must be periodic. If it is not periodic, then the moving charge is simply a short-lived change in the electric and magnetic fields.

Transporting Energy EM waves impart energy, proportional to the square of the amplitude, to objects they interact with. An EM wave transports energy, or propagates, which means the disturbance caused by one oscillating charge can be passed on to other charges. The speed at which these disturbances pass from one location to another is called the wave speed. All EM waves travel at the same speed in a vacuum, called the speed of light, or c (3.00×10^8 m/s).

Wave Propagation The up-and-down motion of individual blocks of wood generates a wave that moves right to left across the device.

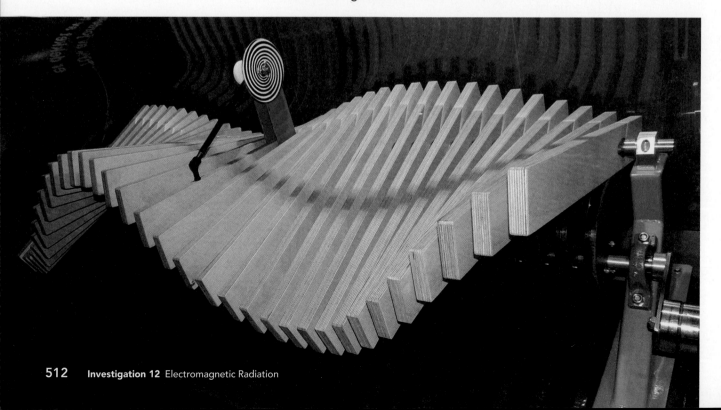

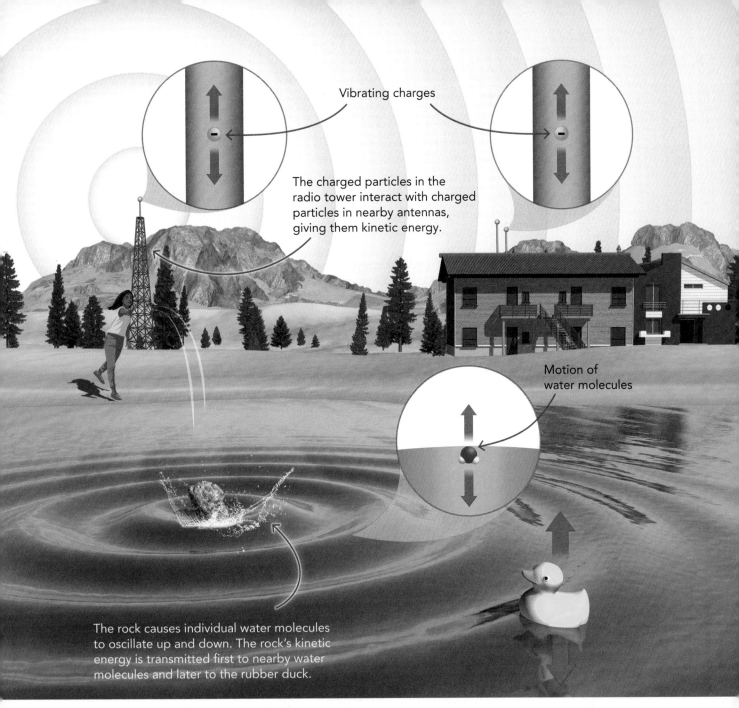

Vibrating charges

The charged particles in the radio tower interact with charged particles in nearby antennas, giving them kinetic energy.

Motion of water molecules

The rock causes individual water molecules to oscillate up and down. The rock's kinetic energy is transmitted first to nearby water molecules and later to the rubber duck.

EM Waves vs. Mechanical Waves Both types of waves transport energy from one place to another, but EM waves can pass disturbances between charged particles that are located far away from each other.

Comparing Waves Like mechanical waves, electromagnetic waves transport energy from one point to another without transporting matter. Also like mechanical waves, the speed of an EM wave depends on the medium through which it travels. Unlike a mechanical wave, however, an EM wave does not need a material medium in order to propagate. Electromagnetic waves are able to travel through the vacuum of empty space.

4 **SEP Argue from Evidence** A driver parks his car during a snowstorm and forgets to turn off the headlights. In the morning, the car's battery is dead, and there is a snow-free patch in front of each headlight. How would you use this as evidence that EM waves carry energy?

Properties of EM Waves

The Nature of Light The fact that EM waves move at the speed of light is a clue to the nature of light. The physiology of human eyes allows us to see only certain wavelengths of EM waves, but our inability to see other wavelengths does not mean they are a different phenomenon. In fact, experiments show they behave according to the same theories and equations as visible light. All EM waves can be modeled as transverse wave oscillations in electric and magnetic fields with specific wavelengths, frequencies, and amplitudes.

A Model for EM Radiation An EM wave is a pair of conjoined waves in the electric field and magnetic field, each perpendicular to the other, and both perpendicular to the direction of wave propagation.

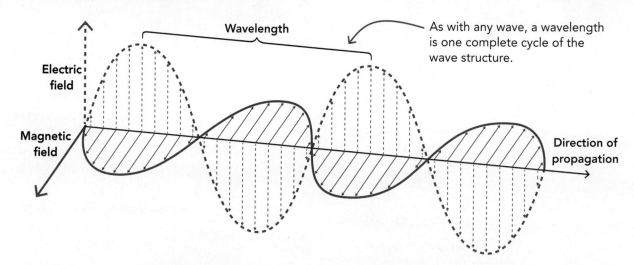

Wavelength

As with any wave, a wavelength is one complete cycle of the wave structure.

Electric field

Magnetic field

Direction of propagation

Visible Light EM waves of wavelengths between about 380 nm and 740 nm can be detected by your eyes. White light is the combination of all these wavelengths of visible light. White light can easily be separated into its constituent parts, or **dispersed,** by refracting it through a prism. The colors disperse because the prism has a slightly different index of refraction for each wavelength of light, which travels through the medium at a different speed.

Separating White Light The colors of light each refract at a slightly different angle. As a result, they are dispersed by the prism.

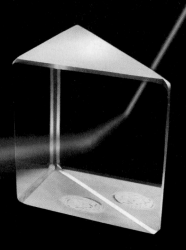

Other Wavelengths of Light The wide range of EM wavelengths is collectively known as the **electromagnetic spectrum.** EM waves of different wavelengths are called by different names to categorize their behaviors and energies. For example, most animals can see some light that is ultraviolet, a little beyond the spectrum that human eyes can see. Experiments with prisms led to the discovery of infrared light, which is not visible but can be detected by the thermal energy it imparts to objects that absorb it.

Waves of the Electromagnetic Spectrum

What are some of the **differences between electromagnetic waves** at different wavelengths?

Comparing EM Waves The EM spectrum is made up of EM waves. In order of **increasing frequency,** these are radio waves, microwaves, infrared rays, visible light, ultraviolet (UV) rays, X-rays, and gamma rays.

The **shorter the wavelength,** the **higher the frequency** and the **greater the energy** of the wave.

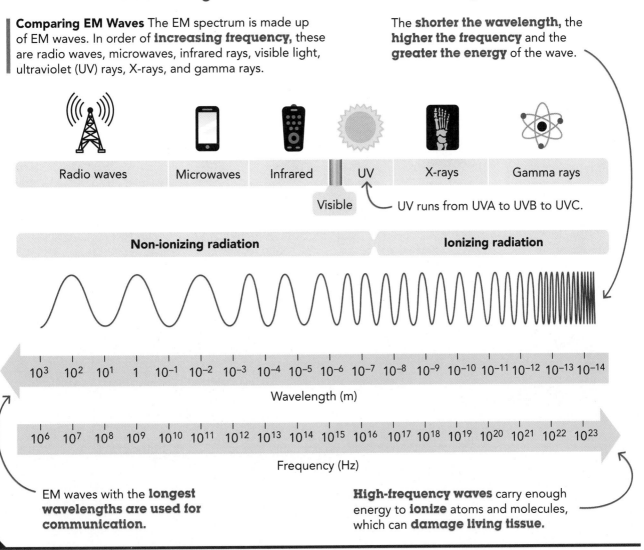

UV runs from UVA to UVB to UVC.

EM waves with the **longest wavelengths are used for communication.**

High-frequency waves carry enough energy to **ionize** atoms and molecules, which can **damage living tissue.**

(5) **SEP Argue from Evidence** There are many kinds of electromagnetic waves. Do you think purely electric or purely magnetic waves could exist? Use evidence to support your claim.

Wave Behavior of EM Radiation

 GO ONLINE to do a PhET **simulation** that allows you to investigate wave interference and to watch a **video** about double-slit interference.

When light, or any other form of EM radiation, passes through openings that are narrow compared to its wavelength, it produces diffraction patterns. These patterns, which support the theory that light takes the form of waves, can be difficult to observe in white light due to dispersion because the patterns made by the colors it contains do not line up exactly. They are easier to observe by passing **monochromatic light,** or light of a single color or wavelength, through closely spaced openings.

There are other behaviors of electromagnetic radiation that also support the theory that light takes the form of waves. For example, light exhibits the Doppler effect in the same way that sound does.

Double-Slit Interference When passing light waves through two openings whose widths are similar in magnitude to the incident wavelength, the light diffracts. The diffraction pattern includes dark fringes within the light fringes due to interference of light passing through two openings.

(6) **SEP Construct an Argument** Look at the pattern formed on the screen by a monochromatic laser passing through two slits. Use evidence to make a claim about what the pattern of bright and dark lines tells you about the nature of the light. How can two beams of light be combined to make those dark lines without an object there to cast a shadow on the screen?

Polarization

The fact that light can be polarized is also evidence that it is a wave. When electromagnetic waves travel, the direction of oscillation of the electric field is always perpendicular to the direction of propagation, but otherwise there is no preferred orientation from one wave to the next. Their electric fields are not oriented in the same direction and, in fact, change over time.

Electromagnetic waves can become polarized by reflection or by transmission through certain materials, such as polarizing films or certain natural crystals. To be **polarized** means that the electric field of the wave oscillates in a fixed direction. Polarizing light also reduces its **intensity,** which is a measure of the power per unit area. A polarizing filter reduces the intensity of unpolarized light by 50 percent and of polarized light according to this equation:

Intensity of Polarized Light
$$I = I_0 \cos^2(\theta)$$

I = intensity of light leaving the polarizer
I_0 = intensity of light incident on the polarizer
θ = angle between axes of polarizer and incident light

The films that can polarize light are made of long, thin molecules aligned with one another in a plastic. They allow light to pass through only if its electric field is aligned with the rows of the polarizing molecules. For example, many computers and phones use liquid-crystal display (LCD) screens. These screens use polarization to generate sharp, high-quality images.

EXPERIENCE IT!

While facing a partner, have one person hold both arms straight out, one over the other, with space in between to model a polarizer. The second person should wiggle their arm. Can the wiggling arm fit as easily when wiggling vertically as it can when wiggling horizontally?

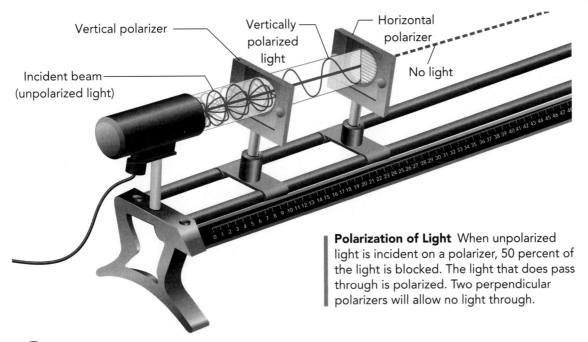

Polarization of Light When unpolarized light is incident on a polarizer, 50 percent of the light is blocked. The light that does pass through is polarized. Two perpendicular polarizers will allow no light through.

(7) **SEP Plan an Investigation** Make a plan for an investigation to use polarizing film to investigate LCD screens. Are the screens all polarized in the same direction with respect to the vertical? Why or why not?

Intensity of Polarized Light

A photodetector has three polarizing films between it and a source of unpolarized light. Each film is arranged so its polarizing orientation, θ_1, θ_2, or θ_3, differs from the others. θ_1 is oriented vertically, θ_2 is oriented 45° clockwise from θ_1, and θ_3 is oriented 45° clockwise from θ_2. What percentage of the original light intensity passes through all filters and reaches the detector?

1. DRAW A PICTURE Sketch a picture of the situation.

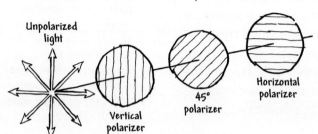

Unpolarized light

Vertical polarizer

45° polarizer

Horizontal polarizer

2. DEFINE THE PROBLEM List knowns and unknowns, and assign values to variables.

θ_1 = vertical $I_2 = ?$

$\theta_{2,1} = 45°$ $I_3 = ?$

$\theta_{3,2} = 45°$

$I_1 = 0.5 I_0$

Recall that 50% of unpolarized light gets filtered.

3. PLAN AND EXECUTE Use mathematical relationships, the picture, and your definitions to plan and execute a solution.

| Determine the proportion of the original intensity that passes through the second filter. | Use the equation $I = I_0 \cos^2(\theta)$. |

Use the equation $I = I_0 \cos^2(\theta)$.

$I_2 = I_1 \cos^2(\theta_{2,1}) = (0.5 I_0)\cos^2(45°) = 0.25 I_0$

Determine the proportion of the original intensity that passes through the third filter.

$I_3 = I_2 \cos^2(\theta_{3,2}) = (0.25 I_0)\cos^2(45°) = 0.125 I_0$

Determine the amount of light that reaches the detector as a percentage of I_0.

Express I_3 as a percentage of I_0.

Percentage $= \dfrac{I_3}{I_0} \times 100 = \dfrac{0.125 I_0}{I_0} \times 100 = 12.5\%$

4. EVALUATE Reflect on your answer.
The relationships between the intensities of light are realistic. The light intensity decreases as it passes through each filter.

 GO ONLINE for more **math support**.

▶ **Math Tutorial Video**

🖥 **Math Practice Problems**

---

(8) A photodetector has three polarizing films between it and a source of unpolarized light. Each film is arranged so its polarizing orientation, θ_1, θ_2, or θ_3, differs from the others. θ_1 is oriented horizontally, θ_2 is oriented 37° clockwise from θ_1, and θ_3 is oriented 53° clockwise from θ_2. What percentage of the original light intensity passes through all three filters and reaches the detector?

📖 **NEED A HINT?** Go online to your **eText Sample Problem** for stepped out support.

(9) A photodetector has three polarizing films between it and a source of unpolarized light. The first film is oriented vertically. At what angle should the second polarizing film be oriented so that 37.5 percent of the original light intensity reaches the detector?

Revisit

INVESTIGATIVE PHENOMENON

GO ONLINE to revisit your **Investigative Phenomenon CER** with the new information you have learned about Electromagnetic Waves and Their Properties.

These questions will help you apply what you learned in this experience to the Investigative Phenomenon.

(10) **SEP Develop a Model** In this experience, you learned that electromagnetic waves cause charged particles such as electrons to move. Develop a model to explain why polarizers need long polymer molecules that are parallel in order to block certain light waves.

(11) **SEP Construct an Explanation** Polarized sunglasses are vertically polarized and reduce the glare from horizontal surfaces, such as lakes. Construct an explanation for why polarized sunglasses reduce glare from such surfaces.

(12) **SEP Use Mathematics** For light passing through polarizers, light intensity depends on the square of the cosine of the angle between the axes of the filters. Give at least one reason why the cosine must be squared in order to find the light intensity passing through the second filter.

(13) **CCC Energy and Matter** Besides being polarized, sunglasses are often made to block out all incoming ultraviolet radiation. Use what you know about the electromagnetic spectrum to explain why it might be more important to block ultraviolet light than infrared light.

 GO ONLINE for a **quiz** to evaluate what you learned about Electromagnetic Waves and Their Properties.

Particle-Wave Duality

 GO ONLINE to do a **hands-on lab** to investigate the particle and wave natures of light.

Shortcomings of the Wave Theory

Despite a great deal of evidence for the wave behavior of electromagnetic radiation, some observations suggest that electromagnetic radiation is not a wave. Trying to fit these observations into the theory that light is a wave was a growing focus of the scientific community throughout the 19th century.

Finding the Medium One issue was the question of what medium light travels in. If a wave is defined as a propagation of a disturbance through a medium, what is an electromagnetic wave's medium? In other words, what is "doing the waving," or propagating the disturbance? All attempts to detect a physical medium for light failed, making scientists struggle to understand the source of its wavelike behaviors.

Comparing Sound and Light The sound of the alarm on a clock can wake a person from sleep. Once awake, they can see the clock to read the time. Suppose the clock was in a vacuum jar, with all air removed. The sound of the alarm would not be heard, but the person could still see the time when they woke up.

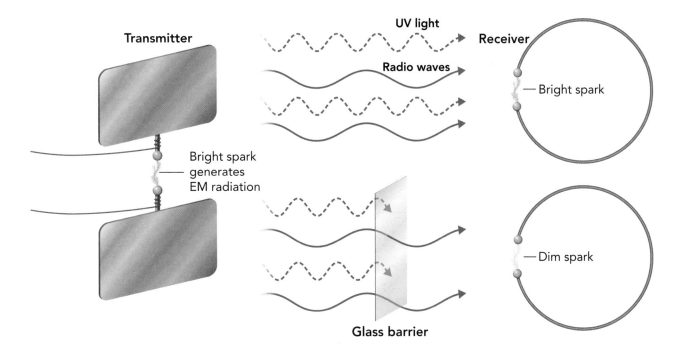

Transmitter

UV light

Radio waves

Receiver

Bright spark

Bright spark generates EM radiation

Dim spark

Glass barrier

Hertz's Spark-Gap Experiment A large voltage connected to the transmitter repeatedly sparks at regular intervals, generating a series of electromagnetic pulses that are received by a conducting loop. With no barrier, the receiver generates a bright spark. With a glass barrier blocking UV light, the receiver generates a dim spark.

Incorrect Predictions Another problem with the wave theory of light was suggested by an observation first made in 1887 by Heinrich Hertz. When light is incident upon a metal surface, electrons are ejected. Wave theory explains this as energy in the waves being transferred to the electrons at the surface of the metal. However, when varying the metals that were tested, and when varying the color and intensity of the light, experimenters found some unexpected results.

According to wave theory, the energy in a wave is proportional to the square of the wave amplitude. Therefore, a more intense light source should deliver more energy to the electrons that are ejected. However, that is not what is observed. Instead, a greater intensity of light causes more electrons to be ejected, not electrons of higher energy.

While a more intense light source does not cause each electron to be ejected with more energy, a higher frequency light source does cause this, which is not predicted by a wave theory of light. Hertz's experiment shows that blocking only the UV frequencies from a spark-gap transmitter significantly reduced the total energy of the received radiation.

EXPERIENCE IT!

Find a U-shaped ramp and roll a ball down it at different heights. Increase the height until the ball "ejects." You may need to drop the ball onto the ramp. Now, roll multiple balls at the same time. What determines if a ball will eject from the ramp?

(14) **SEP Evaluate Claims** Evaluate the claim that "light is a wave." Use evidence to both support and refute that claim.

(15) **SEP Develop a Model** Draw a picture to explain why increasing the intensity of light hitting a surface increases the number of electrons ejected but does not increase the kinetic energy of the electrons.

Photoelectric Effect

The **photoelectric effect** is the phenomenon in which electrons are emitted from a metal surface when visible and UV light are directed onto it. The wave theory of light predicts that a greater intensity of light causes greater energy in ejected electrons. However, experiments show that low frequencies of EM radiation do not eject electrons, even after an extended time. The energy of ejected electrons is correlated to increasingly higher frequencies, not greater intensity of light.

Understanding the Photoelectric Effect

Why are **electrons ejected when light strikes** the surface of a metal?

When light strikes a metal surface, **the energy from the incident light excites electrons in the metal.** If there is enough light energy, then these excited electrons are ejected from the surface of the metal. Solar cells are one practical application of **converting light energy into electrical energy.**

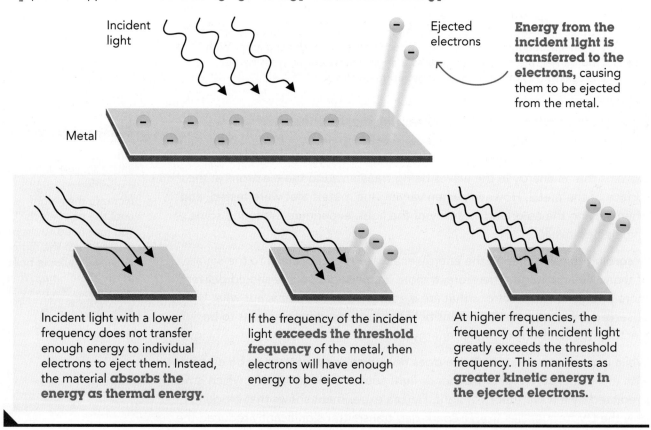

Incident light

Ejected electrons

Energy from the incident light is transferred to the electrons, causing them to be ejected from the metal.

Metal

Incident light with a lower frequency does not transfer enough energy to individual electrons to eject them. Instead, the material **absorbs the energy as thermal energy.**

If the frequency of the incident light **exceeds the threshold frequency** of the metal, then electrons will have enough energy to be ejected.

At higher frequencies, the frequency of the incident light greatly exceeds the threshold frequency. This manifests as **greater kinetic energy in the ejected electrons.**

(16) **SEP Use a Model** Use your knowledge of waves to explain why, for the photoelectric effect, a greater wave intensity of incident light would be expected to, although it does not in actuality, eject electrons with greater kinetic energy.

Particles of Light

A solution for the surprising results regarding the photoelectric effect was found in an alternate theory for the nature of light. The hypothesis was put forth that light exists in discrete packets with energy proportional to their frequency. Each particle of EM radiation, or quantum of light, is called a **photon.**

Energy of a Photon
$$E_{photon} = hf$$

E_{photon} = energy of a photon
h = Planck's constant = 6.626×10^{-34} J·s
f = frequency

Modeling EM radiation as particles does explain the photoelectric effect. Any photon that is incident to the metal surface either has enough energy to eject an electron or it does not. The amount of energy in the photon is a function of its frequency, so a photon below the threshold frequency will not generate the photoelectric effect. And, because each photon can transfer its energy to only one electron, a larger number of ejected electrons must be due to a more intense source of light, meaning one that contains more photons.

Ejected Electrons The graph shows whether photons of different frequencies have enough energy to eject electrons from four different metals.

A photon with a frequency greater than red light ejects an electron from cesium and gives it kinetic energy.

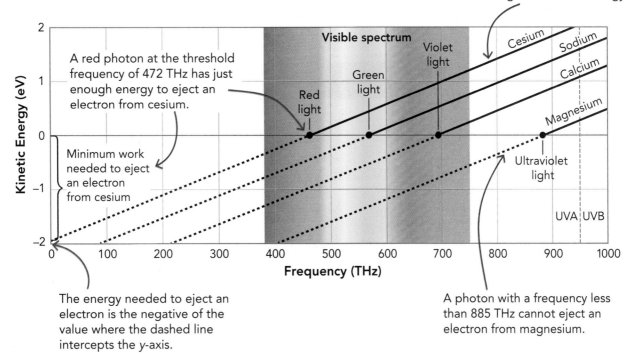

A red photon at the threshold frequency of 472 THz has just enough energy to eject an electron from cesium.

Minimum work needed to eject an electron from cesium

The energy needed to eject an electron is the negative of the value where the dashed line intercepts the *y*-axis.

A photon with a frequency less than 885 THz cannot eject an electron from magnesium.

⑰ **SEP Argue from Evidence** Use your knowledge of waves to argue that the results of the photoelectric effect experiment do not support the idea that light is a wave and, in fact, refute the theory that light is a wave.

The Dual Nature of Light

 GO ONLINE to do a PhET **simulation** that allows you to investigate the relationship between photons and sight and to watch a **video** about particle-wave duality.

The particle theory of light is necessary to explain the photoelectric effect. It also solves the problem of the lack of a medium because the energy propagates in the form of moving photons. However, the particle theory of light does not explain all of the observed wave behaviors of light.

Interference Patterns Despite the elegance of the particle theory of light, scientists still rely on light's wavelike nature to observe and measure its properties. For example, the wavelength of monochromatic light can be determined by passing it through a double-slit diffraction barrier.

Double-Slit Interference Patterns

For $d << L$
$$d\sin(\theta) = m\lambda \quad \text{and} \quad x = \frac{m\lambda L}{d}$$

d = distance between the slits
θ = angle between L and the maximum
m = an integer representing a maximum
λ = wavelength of incident light
x = distance on the screen, left or right from the center
L = distance between the screen and the slits

---

m is an integer value representing a maximum's position relative to the central maximum, which is designated $m = 0$.

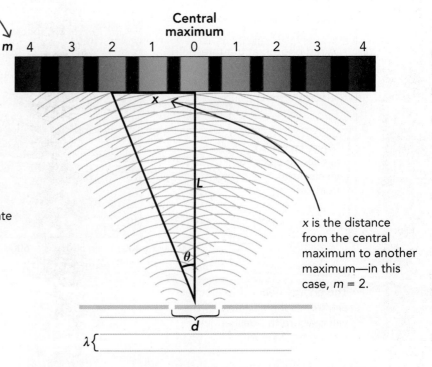

Interference Pattern When a plane wave strikes the barrier, it is blocked except at two small slits. On the other side of the barrier, those slits are sources of coherent waves. The resultant waves generate an interference pattern.

x is the distance from the central maximum to another maximum—in this case, $m = 2$.

---

(18) **SEP Use Mathematics** Why is $\sin(\theta)$ used in the equation for the double-slit interference pattern? What triangle is being referenced by the inclusion of $\sin(\theta)$?

Particle-Wave Duality This sequence of video frames shows an interference pattern being built up gradually by the detection of individual photons (dots).

  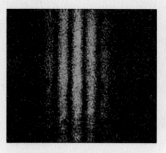 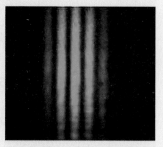

Each individual photon strikes the detector screen at one point.

Over time, more and more photons are detected at different points.

Particle theory does not explain why particles take different paths through the apparatus.

However, the composite pattern is a wave diffraction pattern.

Duality The fact that light behaves as a wave indicates that it must be a wave. The fact that light behaves as a quantized particle indicates that it must be a particle. And so, scientists understand that electromagnetic radiation is sometimes best understood as waves and sometimes best understood as very small particles. This combination of two competing concepts is known as particle-wave duality.

Because particle-wave duality was shown to be a useful predictive model for light, it was reasoned that it might apply to other phenomena as well. In 1927, wave behavior was observed in electrons, as predicted by Louis de Broglie three years earlier.

Dual Nature of Light Neither the wave theory nor the particle theory can explain all of the observed behaviors of electromagnetic radiation. Accepting both theories simultaneously is part of the unusual nature of quantum mechanics.

Phenomenon	Can it be explained in terms of waves?	Can it be explained in terms of particles?
Reflection	✓	✓
Refraction	✓	✓
Interference	✓	
Diffraction	✓	
Polarization	✓	
Photoelectric effect		✓

(19) **CCC Patterns** Look at the pattern formed over time in the photographs of the double-slit apparatus. Make a claim about what the pattern of bright and dark lines tells you about the nature of the particles called photons.

Double-Slit Interference Patterns

A laser beam with a wavelength of 450 nm is directed through two slits that are 2.40 m from a screen. The distance between the two slits is 0.150 mm. For an angle of 6.00°, what is the distance on the screen between the L-line (central maximum) and the farthest maximum within the 6.00°?

1. DRAW A PICTURE Sketch a picture of the situation.

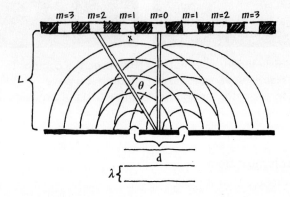

2. DEFINE THE PROBLEM List knowns and unknowns, and assign values to variables.

$d = 0.150$ mm	$m = ?$
$\theta = 6.00°$	$x = ?$
$\lambda = 450$ nm	
$L = 2.40$ m	

3. PLAN AND EXECUTE Use mathematical relationships, the picture, and your definitions to plan and execute a solution.

Convert all distances to meters.

$$d = 0.150 \text{ mm} \left(\frac{1 \text{ m}}{1000 \text{ mm}}\right) = 1.50 \times 10^{-4} \text{ m}$$

$$\lambda = 450 \text{ nm} \left(\frac{1 \text{ m}}{10^9 \text{ nm}}\right) = 4.50 \times 10^{-7} \text{ m}$$

Determine the number of maxima by using the double-slit interference pattern equation for d.

$$d\sin(\theta) = m\lambda \rightarrow m = \frac{d\sin(\theta)}{\lambda}$$

$$m = \frac{(1.50 \times 10^{-4} \text{ m})(\sin 6.00°)}{(4.50 \times 10^{-7} \text{ m})} = 34.8$$

Determine the distance on the screen by using the value of m rounded down to the nearest integer and the double-slit interference pattern equation for x.

$$x = \frac{m\lambda L}{d} = \frac{(34)(4.50 \times 10^{-7} \text{ m})(2.40 \text{ m})}{(1.50 \times 10^{-4} \text{ m})} = 0.245 \text{ m}$$

4. EVALUATE Reflect on your answer.

All units are appropriate for the given quantities. Because sin (6°) is about 0.1, the distance to the farthest maximum should be about one tenth of the distance to the screen.

GO ONLINE for more **math support**.

▶ **Math Tutorial Video**

🖥 **Math Practice Problems**

(20) A green laser beam with a wavelength of 525 nm is directed through two slits that are 3.60 m from a screen. The distance between the two slits is 200 μm. For an angle of 2.50°, what is the distance on the screen between the L-line (central maximum) and the farthest maximum within the 2.50°?

📖 **NEED A HINT?** Go online to your **eText sample problem** for stepped out support.

(21) An orange laser beam with a wavelength of 640 nm is directed through two slits that are 2.40 m from a screen. The distance between the two slits is 0.070 mm. For an angle of 1.00°, what is the distance on the screen between the L-line (central maximum) and the farthest maximum within the 1.00°?

(22) A laser beam with a wavelength of 450 nm is directed through two slits that are 1.00 m from a screen. The distance between the two slits is 0.150 mm. How many maxima appear within 2.40° of the central maximum?

(23) If a 450-nm light is directed through two slits that are 0.500 mm apart, and the interference pattern has its 5th maximum exactly 8.10 mm away from the central maximum, then what is the distance from the slits to the screen on which the pattern is projected?

(24) A laser is projected through a double slit in a barrier that is 3.00 m in front of a projection screen. The slits are 150 μm apart from each other. If the 12th maximum is 9.10 cm from the central maximum, what is the wavelength of the laser's light?

(25) A violet laser beam with a wavelength of 400 nm is directed through two slits that are 180 cm from a screen. If there are 21 total maxima on the screen within 15.0 cm of the central maximum (including the central maximum), how far apart are the two slits?

(26) A group of students is experimenting with double-slit interference patterns. They are comparing the patterns produced by five different laser colors. The students run the experiment for the violet laser, and find that the distance between adjacent maximums is 8.10 mm. Their partial data table is shown here. Using the data the students gathered for the violet laser, complete the data table on a separate sheet of paper.

Color	Wavelength (nm)	Distance between Maximums (mm)
violet	405	8.10
blue	440	
green	532	
yellow	593	
red	650	

Revisit

INVESTIGATIVE PHENOMENON

GO ONLINE to revisit your **Investigative Phenomenon CER** with the new information you have learned about Particle-Wave Duality.

These questions will help you apply what you learned in this experience to the Investigative Phenomenon.

27. **SEP Develop a Model** When polarized light goes through a polarizing lens, only a fraction of the light will pass through. Develop a model using photons to represent this phenomenon. What happens when the incident photons are polarized at a 45° angle to the filter?

28. **SEP Identify Criteria** You want to design an antiglare window that can be used as a solar panel using the photoelectric effect. Identify the criteria that would make such a window a success and describe how the window would operate.

29. **SEP Design a Solution** You shine a light on an unknown material right at the material's threshold frequency. Your goal is to maximize the current with as little energy input as possible, because glare makes the material less efficient at higher energies. Would you increase the frequency or the intensity of the light? Explain.

30. **SEP Use Evidence** Make a claim about whether the effectiveness of polarizing sunglasses supports the wave nature of light or the particle nature of light.

GO ONLINE
for a **quiz** to evaluate what you learned about Particle-Wave Duality.

Electromagnetic Radiation and Matter

 GO ONLINE to do a **hands-on lab** to investigate how light interacts with matter and the implications that has for interactions between light and living tissue.

Photon-Electron Interactions

When a photon encounters matter, it may impart its energy to a bound electron, exciting that electron to a higher energy state within the atom. If the photon has enough energy, it can even ionize the atom by causing an electron to leave the atom entirely, giving the atom a positive charge.

When a free electron is captured by an atom, the electron loses some of its energy in the form of a photon. This energy, called binding energy, will be described later. This also happens when an electron in an excited state descends to a lower energy state in an atom. The photon that is emitted has a frequency that is determined by the change in energy (ΔE) of the electron.

> **Gas Discharge Tubes** Some advertising lights use noble gases to give off their characteristic glow. In fact, each noble gas yields a different color that is defined by the energy level changes of electrons in the atoms of the gas.

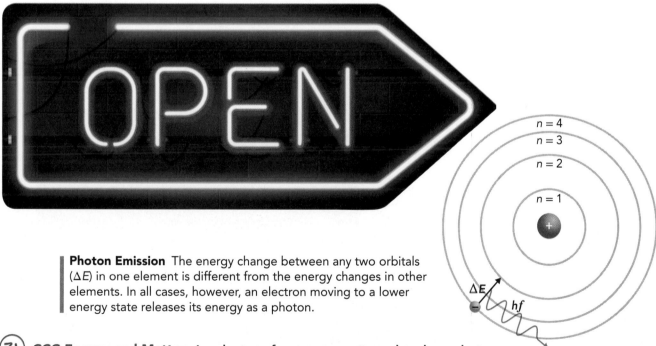

> **Photon Emission** The energy change between any two orbitals (ΔE) in one element is different from the energy changes in other elements. In all cases, however, an electron moving to a lower energy state releases its energy as a photon.

(31) **CCC Energy and Matter** An electron from a neon atom absorbs a photon with a wavelength of 640 nm and moves to an orbital at a higher energy level. The electron then returns to its initial state. What color of light will the emitted photon be? Justify your reasoning.

Photon Energy Absorption by Matter

The frequency of a photon determines how it will interact with the matter it encounters. For example, if a photon is released from an atom due to an electron going from an $n = 4$ orbital to an $n = 2$ orbital, then that photon is able to excite an electron in another atom of the same element from $n = 2$ to $n = 4$.

Characteristic Photons Atoms and molecules preferentially absorb certain photons—those with energies equal to the electron excitation changes that are possible in that substance. Thus, after radiation passes through a substance, those particular photon energies will be missing from its spectrum, leaving gaps that appear as dark lines. This pattern of dark lines is the absorption spectrum of the substance and is unique to it.

A substance can later re-emit photons with the same energy values that it previously absorbed. The emitted photons produce an emission spectrum—a pattern of bright lines corresponding to the energy given off by the substance.

Spectra for Hydrogen The photon energies a hydrogen atom can absorb are the same as those it can later release. The same is true for all substances.

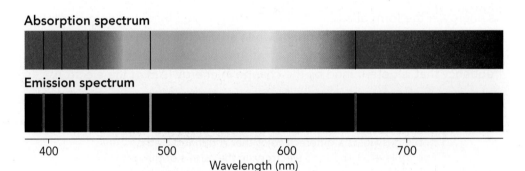

Absorption spectrum

Emission spectrum

400   500   600   700

Wavelength (nm)

Aurora Borealis The brilliant colors of an aurora are due to electrons in the solar wind being absorbed in the atmosphere, resulting in photon emission.

The green color in an aurora is often a mixture of blue light emitted from nitrogen and green light emitted from oxygen.

Nitrogen

Oxygen

GO ONLINE to do a PhET **simulation** that allows you to see how EM radiation affects matter and watch a **video** that explains interactions between light and matter.

Heat and Ionization Visible light and longer wavelengths are generally converted into thermal energy—a familiar experience for anyone who has sought shade on a sunny day.

In contrast, EM radiation of shorter wavelengths, such as ultraviolet light, X-rays, and gamma rays, has enough energy to eject electrons from atoms entirely. These ejected electrons can impart enough energy to break apart molecules. EM radiation of wavelengths shorter than visible light that has enough energy to ionize matter and break chemical bonds between atoms in molecules and other substances is called **ionizing radiation.**

Opacity and Transparency Matter that absorbs or reflects all incoming radiation in a particular frequency range is said to be opaque to that radiation. For example, many windows are made of glass that is opaque to ultraviolet light. Other materials permit radiation in a frequency range to transmit through, so these materials are transparent to the radiation. Stained glass is transparent to one wavelength of visible light while opaque to others.

VOCABULARY

The term **ionizing radiation** can be broken up into parts to determine its meaning; it is radiation that causes ionization. Recall that to *ionize* means to "form ions."

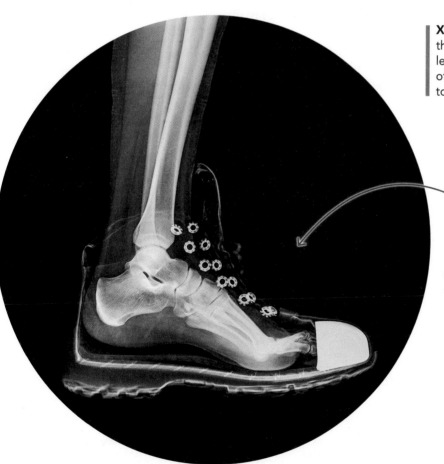

X-Ray Image In order to see the bones in the foot, the boot leather and the skin and tissue of the foot must be transparent to X-ray radiation.

Bones and the metal grommets and steel toe insert within this boot are opaque to X-ray radiation.

(32) **SEP Construct an Explanation** Most stars emit photons of all frequencies. The outer layers of most stars are gases that are less dense than the star cores. Construct an explanation for how astronomers would use absorption spectra to study stars.

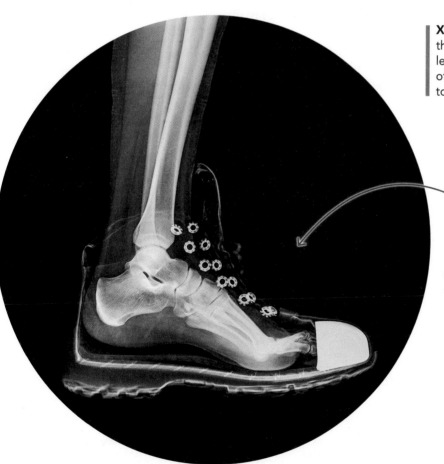

Blackbody Radiation

All physical objects in the universe emit electromagnetic radiation, and this radiation is a function of temperature. As an object gets hotter, the power of the radiation increases, meaning it gets brighter, and the wavelengths of the radiation decrease. A convenient way to understand this is through the blackbody radiation approximation. A **blackbody** is a theoretical object that absorbs all radiation that strikes it. The electromagnetic waves emitted by a blackbody are called **blackbody radiation.** Blackbody radiation occurs for a hypothetical opaque, nonreflecting object that is everywhere a single temperature; the object will emit a spectrum of radiation with a single-peaked curve.

Radiation Power and Temperature The energy radiated by an object changes along with the fourth power of the temperature measured in Kelvins.

Stefan-Boltzmann Law
$$j = \sigma T^4$$
j = radiosity (amount of emitted energy per area per time) T = temperature (in Kelvins) σ = Stefan-Boltzmann constant = 5.67×10^{-8} W/(m^2·K^4)

The result is that an object radiates much more heat for even small increases in temperature. One application of this phenomenon is an infrared thermometer, which can take your temperature without touching you by measuring the amount of radiation from your skin.

Blackbody Curves for Typical Terrestrial Temperatures For an object that is opaque, nonreflecting, and a single temperature, the spectrum of energy radiated follows a particular curve.

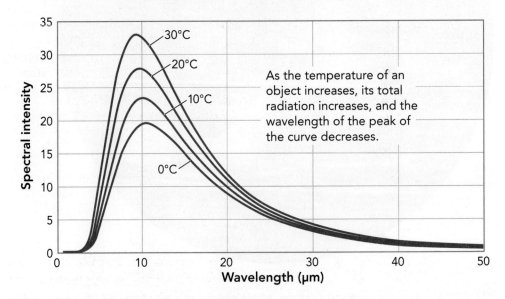

As the temperature of an object increases, its total radiation increases, and the wavelength of the peak of the curve decreases.

(33) **SEP Use Mathematics** Calculate the percent increase in heat an asphalt parking lot radiates on a hot sunny day when it is 35°C compared to a cold winter day when it is –20°C.

Radiation Wavelength and Temperature Although every object emits radiation across a wide spectrum of wavelengths, the peak of that spectrum is a direct result of temperature according to Wien's displacement law.

Wien's Displacement Law
$$\lambda_{peak} = \frac{b}{T}$$
λ_{peak} = wavelength of the blackbody spectrum peak T = temperature (in Kelvins) b = Wien's displacement constant = 2.90×10^{-3} m·K

Animal life on Earth has evolved to see a segment of the radiation spectrum known as visible light because that is where the peak of the sun's radiation is. The surface of the sun is about 5780 K, so the peak of its radiation curve is at about 2.90×10^{-3} m·K ÷ 5780 K = 502 nm, within the visible spectrum.

There are many applications of the change in radiation wavelength as a function of temperature. For example, temperatures at Earth's surface cause radiation to peak in the infrared spectrum, so infrared cameras can be used to see where heat leaks from a home, indicating where additional insulation is needed. Also, floating icebergs, which are dangerous for ships, are colder than the surrounding ocean water. The U.S. Navy can thus track icebergs by looking for their longer-wavelength radiation signals.

Radiation at Earth's Surface The figure shows theoretical blackbody radiation curves for two temperatures that approximate the temperatures and radiation spectra of the sun and Earth. However, the actual radiation spectra differ because the gases in Earth's atmosphere absorb radiation.

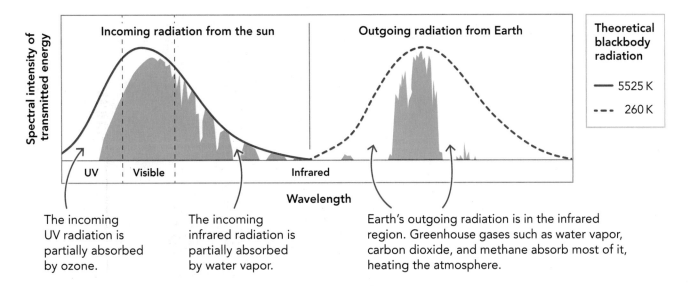

34 **SEP Use Mathematics** Suppose that you have a fever and the temperature of your forehead is 103.0°F. What would an infrared thermometer record as the wavelength of your forehead's radiation, and how different is this from when it is 98.6°F?

Damage to Living Cells

When ionizing radiation interacts with living tissue, it can damage the molecules in the tissue. Cell membranes, organelles, and other parts of the cell may be affected. Damage to individual cells can be repaired, but that takes time. The damage from repeated exposure to ionizing radiation can add up. The damage can accumulate from many photons in a high-intensity dose or from repeated doses over a period of time. If the damage is not repaired, or if the rate of damage to cells exceeds the rate of repair for a long enough period of time, cancer may develop.

Effects of UV Exposure

Why do you need protection from UV radiation?

The Sun's Damaging Rays UV radiation occurs in three bands: UVA (315–400 nm), UVB (280–315 nm) and UVC (100–280 nm). **Only UVA and UVB radiation reach Earth's surface** and interact with human tissue; UVC is thankfully absorbed by ozone in Earth's atmosphere. The energy in UVA and UVB is less than in UVC, but lower-energy UVA and UVB rays can still **damage skin and eye cells.** UV radiation can penetrate clouds, so you can still be exposed to UV radiation on overcast days.

UVA rays penetrate the epidermis and disperse in the dermis. Damage to the dermis contributes to **wrinkles and sagging skin.** UVA rays also can lead to **eye cataracts.**

Some sunscreens contain **chemicals that absorb the energy** from UV radiation and prevent it from penetrating the skin.

Some sunscreens contain **minerals that reflect harmful UV rays.**

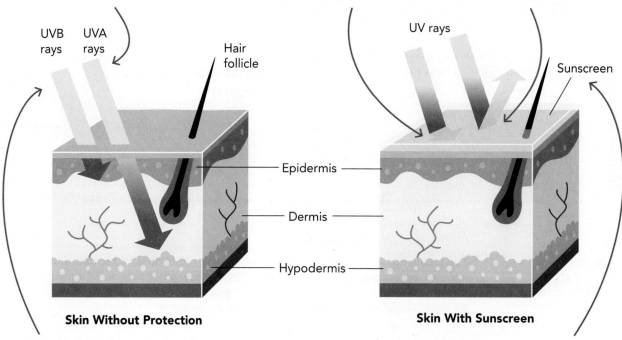

Skin Without Protection

Skin With Sunscreen

UVB rays penetrate the epidermis and cause **redness and sunburn.** UVB radiation can also **damage DNA,** which increases the risk of **skin cancer.**

Broad-spectrum sunscreen protects skin from the damaging energy of both UVA and UVB rays. (Sunglasses offer protection for eyes from these harmful rays.)

Damage From UV Light Because of the decrease in atmospheric ozone, more ultraviolet radiation reaches Earth's surface now than it did 40 years ago. Prolonged exposure to UV radiation is particularly dangerous to people's skin.

Damage From High-Energy Radiation The danger from all ionizing radiation is dose dependent, and it can be minimized by controlling the cumulative amount of time the exposure lasts and with the appropriate use of distance and shielding. Brief flashes of radiation at a relatively low intensity are safe for most healthy people to experience on occasion, but technicians often stand behind a metal wall during radiography to minimize their long-term exposure to the rays.

Some parts of the body are more susceptible to radiation. Cells in your stomach and your reproductive organs are constantly dividing and thus have a greater risk of damaged DNA from radiation exposure. For this reason, these organs are often shielded with lead when the body is scanned with high-energy radiation.

Protecting Layer The Earth's atmosphere protects life by absorbing much of the ionizing radiation coming from the sun. Space travel must include ways to protect against gamma rays, X-rays, and higher-energy UV radiation.

DNA Damage From X-rays An incoming X-ray photon can damage DNA. If the damaged DNA is not repaired, it can lead to death of the cell (for example, a skin cell) that contains the DNA, alterations to the DNA sequence (mutations), and even disease.

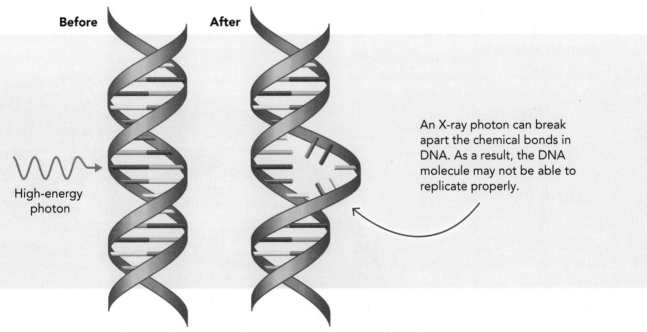

Before   **After**

High-energy photon

An X-ray photon can break apart the chemical bonds in DNA. As a result, the DNA molecule may not be able to replicate properly.

(35) **SEP Evaluate Claims** An article claims that higher-energy UVC radiation is more strongly absorbed by the body than lower-energy UVA and UVB rays and that UVB rays are the type most strongly linked to skin damage, including skin cancer. Evaluate these claims.

(36) **CCC Energy and Matter** Some hospitals use electromagnetic radiation to kill bacteria and viruses on surfaces and in the air. What difficulties does this technique pose?

GO ONLINE to revisit your **Investigative Phenomenon CER** with the new information you have learned about Electromagnetic Radiation and Matter.

These questions will help you apply what you learned in this experience to the Investigative Phenomenon.

(37) **CCC Energy and Matter** A polarizing lens will absorb some photons and transmit other photons. What happens to the energy in the photons that the lens absorbs?

(38) **SEP Argue from Evidence** Sunscreen is an important supply to have when boating on a sunny day due to glare. Use evidence from the photograph to explain why there is a greater danger of getting sunburn when boating on a lake than hiking on a mountain.

(39) **CCC Energy and Matter** When shopping for polarizing sunglasses, you compare two particular models. One pair of sunglasses blocks incoming UVA and UVB rays, but not UVC rays. The other pair blocks UVB and UVC rays, but not UVA rays. Which pair would you consider purchasing, and why?

(40) **SEP Evaluate Claims** Your friend claims that he can look safely at the sun through his polarizing sunglasses because they block all UV light and 50 percent of other wavelengths of light. Use evidence to argue that your friend is incorrect.

GO ONLINE
for a **quiz** to evaluate what you learned about Electromagnetic Radiation and Matter.

These questions will help you apply what you learned in this investigation to the Anchoring Phenomenon.

41 **SEP Form a Hypothesis** The quantum corral consists of a ring of iron atoms on a copper surface with a stream of electrons being fired at it. If, instead, scientists used a light source capable of emitting unpolarized light in a range of frequencies at the iron ring, what results would they find? Explain your reasoning. Assume they have access to a polarizer, a spectroscope, and a multimeter.

42 **SEP Argue from Evidence** The patterns in the quantum corral are formed by electrons. Explain how this pattern is evidence of the dual nature of matter as both waves and particles.

☑ INVESTIGATION ASSESSMENT

GO ONLINE for activities that will give you an opportunity to **demonstrate what you have learned:**

☑ **Science Performance-Based Assessment** Find materials that will best protect you from the harmful effects of sunlight.

📄 **Engineering Workbench** Design an aesthetically pleasing solar array to generate electricity that does not rely on fossil fuel consumption.

💻 **Career Connections** Learn about how a materials scientist applies knowledge of electromagnetic radiation.

☑ **Investigation Test** Take this test to demonstrate your understanding of electromagnetic waves.

☑ **Virtual Lab Performance-Based Assessment** Use observations from the double-slit experiment to explain the particle-wave duality of light.

INVESTIGATIVE PHENOMENON

GO ONLINE to engage with real-world phenomena by watching a **phenomenon video** and completing a **CER worksheet**.

What happens when information is transmitted from a mobile device?

Information and Instrumentation

In the past, computers communicated with each other by sending information as an electrical signal through a physical connection, such as a cable. Today, most computers and other electronic devices send and receive signals without any physical connections. Entire networks function wirelessly, allowing instantaneous communication over great distances. Have you ever considered exactly how this communication is possible?

Cellular networks and AM/FM radio are examples of wireless communication from one point to another across space. How do the signals transmitted by these devices become images on your screen or a voice you converse with? The answers to these questions require an understanding of the physics and engineering behind these devices and the numerous ways that technology can be used to capture, transmit, and store both energy and information.

(1) **CCC Cause and Effect** What does it mean when a wireless network is out of range? What does it mean when a cellular network is out of range?

(2) **CCC Systems and System Models** Do you think a smartphone is capable of sending a signal in a particular direction to reach a network? Why would this capability be helpful when making a call or sending a text?

Digital Information

 GO ONLINE to do a **hands-on lab** to investigate, represent, and process information using codes.

Analog Information

The world is full of information to observe and experience. That information must be encoded in some way in order to reproduce, store, or transmit it. **Encoding** is the process of converting data from one form to another. Encoding occurs when a person writes a sentence, performs a calculation, or draws a picture. Whether the encoded information is in pictures, letters, or numbers, it represents ideas that can be understood by a different person.

Before computers, information was usually stored in an analog manner. **Analog information** is information represented by a continuously variable quantity, such as the exact time or an exact amount of light or sound.

Timepieces The hands on a clock are calibrated to make a complete rotation in a specific period of time. Most analog timepieces encode time by having an hour hand complete a rotation twice in a day and a minute hand complete a rotation once per hour. The length of a day is not arbitrarily chosen. Instead, it is dictated by the rotation of our planet on its axis. We do not make time—we only represent and communicate it with these devices.

Encoding Time The position of the hands on an analog timepiece represents our understanding of what part of the day we are experiencing.

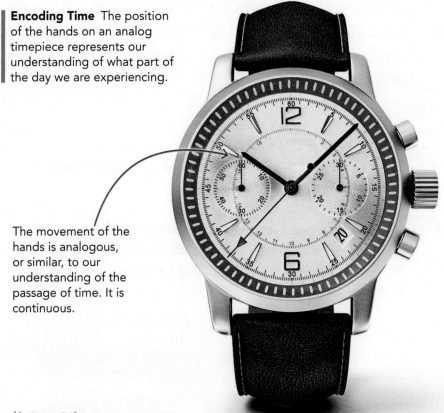

The movement of the hands is analogous, or similar, to our understanding of the passage of time. It is continuous.

Film-Based Photography Photography is the encoding of light patterns to represent a visual image of a moment in time. Before digital cameras, the process of exposing a thin film of photosensitive chemicals to light caused patterns of bright and dark to form, analogous to the patterns that someone's eyes would see in that moment.

Sound Recordings The groove on a vinyl record is a physical representation of sound waves. Recall that sound waves are vibrations in the air that cause fluctuations in air pressure. The shape of a record groove is an analog of a continuous graph of air pressure over time. The groove represents sound, but it is not actually a pressure wave. In order to hear a reproduction of the sound, a player device must be used.

back of camera   film

Encoding Images An image captured on film is called a *negative*, because it is a negative analog of the light intensity to which it was exposed.

The needle traces both the width and depth of the groove, which are each about 20 μm in length.

Encoding Sound A record player uses a needle to read the spinning record. The needle vibrates due to tracing the shape of the groove, producing sound.

③ **CCC Structure and Function** What kind of information is encoded in the growth rings of a tree? In an item's barcode at the supermarket? In the symbols on a page of sheet music?

④ **SEP Design Solutions** From most directions, sound waves will reach one of your ears a fraction of a second before they reach the other ear. Your brain can tell from that small discrepancy which direction the sound is coming from. This is called "stereo" sound. Suggest a way to record sound so that you can hear it "in stereo" when it is played back through headphones.

Representing Information Digitally

GO ONLINE to do a PhET simulation that allows you to investigate the construction of circuits.

VOCABULARY

The phrase *little bit* is helpful as a reminder that the **bit** is a small unit of information. However, it is actually a contraction of *binary digit*.

While information can be represented by analog objects, such as clock hands or record grooves, information can also be represented discretely. For example, symbols and images can be reproduced as a series of spaces that are each either dark or light. "Dark or light" is an example of a bit of information. A **bit** is a unit equivalent to the amount of information needed to specify a choice between binary alternatives, such as off or on, yes or no, or 0 or 1. One bit has $2^1 = 2$ possible values, 0 or 1, while 3 bits have $2^3 = 8$ different possible values, such as 101. **Digital information** is information represented by a discrete variable quantity, usually encoded in bits.

Much as a collection of letters can form words with meanings, a collection of bits can also be used to create a larger piece of information. A **byte** is an array of 8 bits that are read together to give more information than a single bit. A byte can have 2^8 different possible values and one byte is more than enough information to store a 7-bit liquid crystal display (LCD) digit.

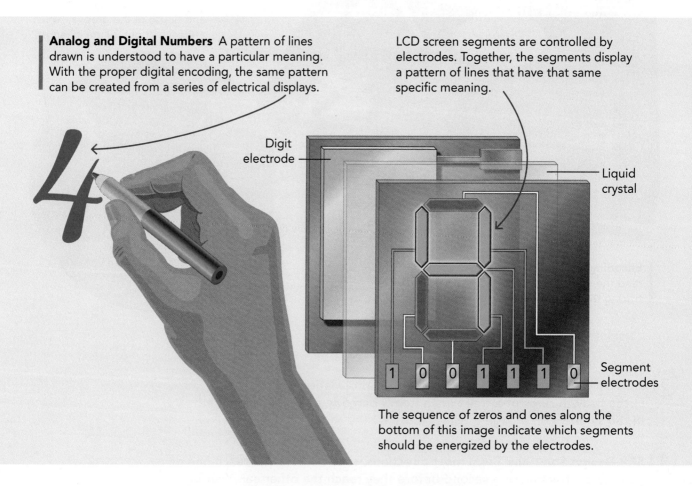

Analog and Digital Numbers A pattern of lines drawn is understood to have a particular meaning. With the proper digital encoding, the same pattern can be created from a series of electrical displays.

LCD screen segments are controlled by electrodes. Together, the segments display a pattern of lines that have that same specific meaning.

Digit electrode

Liquid crystal

Segment electrodes

1 0 0 1 1 1 0

The sequence of zeros and ones along the bottom of this image indicate which segments should be energized by the electrodes.

(5) **CCC Patterns** Copy the LCD on a sheet of paper and use it to represent the number 5. Write the corresponding 7-digit sequence of 0s and 1s that would be used to encode the digit 5 digitally.

Storing Pictures in Digital Code

To be encoded, a complex image needs to be broken into many individual parts. Each part is known as a pixel. For a black-and-white image, each pixel is either dark or light, but when many pixels are observed in aggregate, they form a recognizable image.

You can also add variations to each pixel by making it some gradation of gray. Instead of one bit of code to determine whether a pixel is "dark or light," you could use three bits together to encode how dark the square should be on a scale of 1 through 8.

To add color to a pixel-based image, each pixel must carry information about gradations of the three primary colors—red, blue, and green. Having 8 bits for red, gives $2^8 = 256$ different intensities for red. Using 8 bits for red, 8 bits for blue, and 8 bits for green allows for millions of possible color combinations for each pixel.

EXPERIENCE IT!

Cut 64 small squares from construction paper using a few different colors. Use the squares in an 8 × 8 grid to create an image that depicts an everyday object. See if classmates can identify the object in your pixelated image.

From Dots to Pictures By itself, a single pixel is not very interesting to observe. In this picture, the collective pattern forms a face, making the individual pixels less obvious.

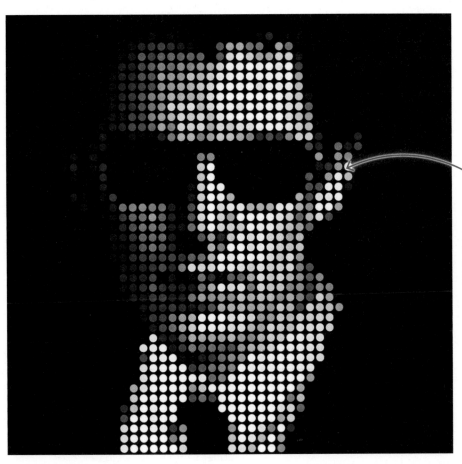

The word *pixel* comes from the term "picture element." Each pixel is one of the building blocks of the image.

🜶 **CCC Scale, Proportion, and Quantity** Plot the number of pixels that are in a square array as a function of how many pixels are in one side of the array, up to a length of 50 pixels. How would you describe the relationship between resolution (clarity of image) and information density (number of pixels)?

Storing Sounds in Digital Code

Analog sound recording devices convert the physical phenomenon of sound waves into proportionally strong voltage signals. To digitize this information requires approximating the signal as a discrete step function.

The act of capturing an amplitude value is called *sampling*. A sample is a digital representation of the value of the original analog waveform at a precise point in time. The number of samples taken per second is called the *sample rate*. To ensure that every crest and trough of a wave are recorded at least once, the sample rate needs to be a minimum of two times the wave frequency. The highest frequencies heard by humans are about 20 kHz. At that frequency, a sample rate of at least 40 kHz is needed to adequately record the sounds. The fidelity, or accuracy, of an audio recording depends upon the sampling rate.

Sampling a Waveform Beginning with a sound wave that is a continuous function, the process of digitizing will change how the sound can be transmitted and stored.

The frequency and amplitude of the analog signal are proportional to the frequency and amplitude of the recorded sound wave.

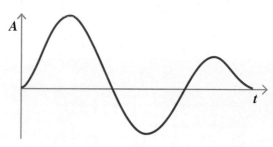

Individual points along the waveform can each be sampled, meaning each discrete point is recorded as an ordered pair of graph values.

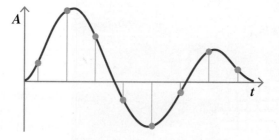
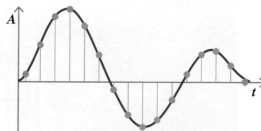

Playback of each sampled point yields a shape that approximates the original waveform.

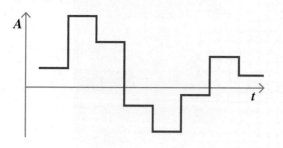
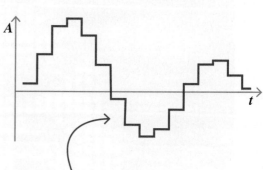

A higher sample rate yields a closer approximation of the original sound wave.

(7) **CCC Patterns** The word *smooth* can be used to describe things as different as cake batter, bike paths, and curves on a graph. What do smooth examples of these objects have in common?

Computer Memory

 GO ONLINE to analyze a set of data on computer memory and watch an Explain **video** about hard drives of the future.

When you are working on a computer or other electronic device and you "save" your work, where is it saved? Computers store information in binary format. On a computer chip, electric charge determines whether a 0 or a 1 is stored at a given location. On a computer hard drive, regions are magnetized or demagnetized to store the same information. If you save information to a remote drive or "the cloud," it is still being physically stored on a hard drive—just one that is remote to you.

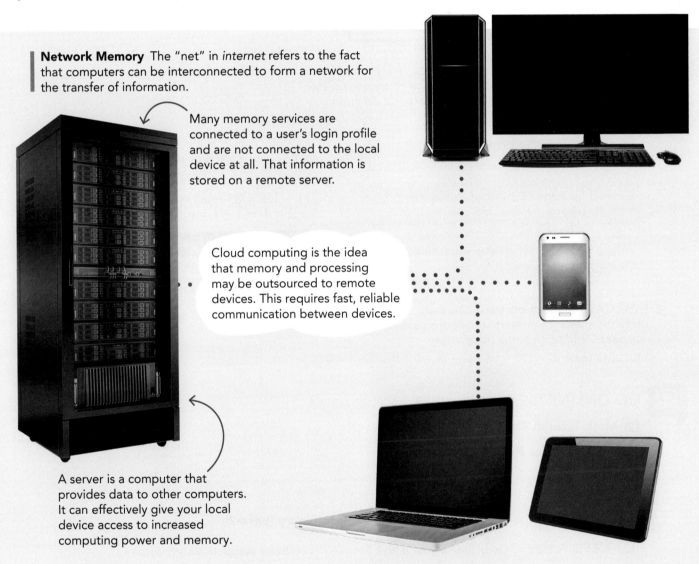

Network Memory The "net" in *internet* refers to the fact that computers can be interconnected to form a network for the transfer of information.

Many memory services are connected to a user's login profile and are not connected to the local device at all. That information is stored on a remote server.

Cloud computing is the idea that memory and processing may be outsourced to remote devices. This requires fast, reliable communication between devices.

A server is a computer that provides data to other computers. It can effectively give your local device access to increased computing power and memory.

⑧ Influence of Engineering on Society An architect has taken digital photos of a building and needs to edit the pictures, send them to a client by the end of the day, and add them to her portfolio. Her laptop does not have the necessary software to process the pictures, but a colleague at her office can help. Suggest appropriate technologies that she could use to store and transmit information so that everything gets done on time.

Converting Decimal Numbers to Binary

Convert the number 211 from decimal (base 10) to binary (base 2).

1. DRAW A PICTURE Sketch a picture of the situation.

Decimal Place Value		
10^2 (Hundreds)	10^1 (Tens)	10^0 (Ones)
2	1	1

2. DEFINE THE PROBLEM List knowns and unknowns, and assign values to variables.

$2^0 = 1$	$2^5 = 32$
$2^1 = 2$	$2^6 = 64$
$2^2 = 4$	$2^7 = 128$
$2^3 = 8$	$2^8 = 256$
$2^4 = 16$	

3. PLAN AND EXECUTE Use mathematical relationships, the picture, and your definitions to plan and execute a solution.

Determine the number of digits it will take to express 211 in binary.

211 is less than $2^8 = 256$, but greater than $2^7 = 128$, so the number will require 8 digits (2^0 to 2^7).

Subtract the largest powers of 2 possible from the original number until you get to 0.

$211 - 128 = 83 \rightarrow 83 - 64 = 19 \rightarrow 19 - 16 = 3 \rightarrow$
$3 - 2 = 1 \rightarrow 1 - 1 = 0$

Write a 1 for each place value you subtracted. Write a 0 for each other place value.

Binary Place Value							
2^7	2^6	2^5	2^4	2^3	2^2	2^1	2^0
1	1	0	1	0	0	1	1

$211 = 11010011$ (base 2)

4. EVALUATE Reflect on your answer.
Verify the answer by converting it back to a decimal number by adding all of the place values.

11010011 (base 2) = $128 + 64 + 0 + 16 + 0 + 0 + 2 + 1 = 211$

 GO ONLINE for more **math support**.

▶ **Math Tutorial Video**

📶 **Math Practice Problems**

9 Convert the number 74 from decimal (base 10) to binary (base 2).

📖 **NEED A HINT?** Go online to your **eText Sample Problem** for stepped out support.

10 A friend converts the number 514 to binary and records the result as 100000001. Is she correct? If not, what is the correct answer?

Advantages and Disadvantages of Digital Information

Digitizing an analog signal is comparable to recording a sequence of ordered pairs to represent a mathematical function. Along any curve, a number of value pairs can be recorded—typically as (x, y). Having just a few of these values will not capture the information adequately. However, having a lot of these values requires much more space to store the data.

Digital Data

What are some of the **benefits** and **drawbacks** of **digital information**?

The Good and the Bad Using **digital technology** is a **reliable** and **efficient** way to **record, store, and transmit information.** However, there are also downsides to it.

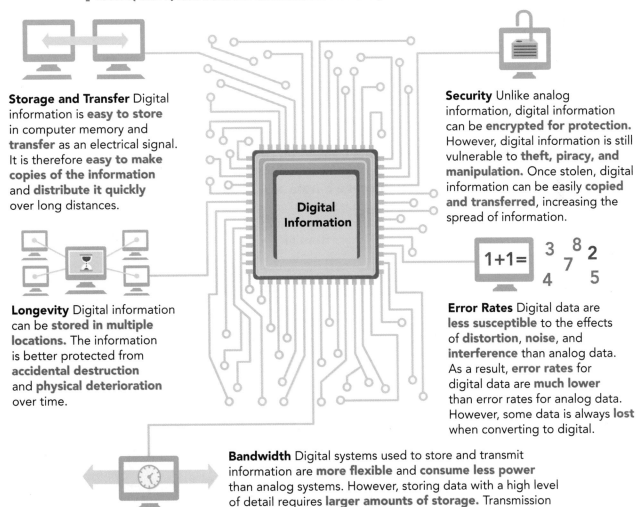

Storage and Transfer Digital information is **easy to store** in computer memory and **transfer** as an electrical signal. It is therefore **easy to make copies of the information** and **distribute it quickly** over long distances.

Longevity Digital information can be **stored in multiple locations.** The information is better protected from **accidental destruction** and **physical deterioration** over time.

Digital Information

Security Unlike analog information, digital information can be **encrypted for protection.** However, digital information is still vulnerable to **theft, piracy, and manipulation.** Once stolen, digital information can be easily **copied and transferred**, increasing the spread of information.

Error Rates Digital data are **less susceptible** to the effects of **distortion**, **noise**, and **interference** than analog data. As a result, **error rates** for digital data are **much lower** than error rates for analog data. However, some data is always **lost** when converting to digital.

Bandwidth Digital systems used to store and transmit information are **more flexible** and **consume less power** than analog systems. However, storing data with a high level of detail requires **larger amounts of storage.** Transmission of large files requires **more bandwidth** or **more time.**

11 **SEP Ask Questions** Someone has decided to move permanently to a new lunar colony. She has many boxes of videos, photos, music, scrapbooks, letters, medical records, and other personal items. What questions should she ask about available space and data storage on the lunar colony?

INVESTIGATIVE PHENOMENON

GO ONLINE to revisit your **Investigative Phenomenon CER** with the new information you have learned about Digital Information.

These questions will help you apply what you learned in this experience to the Investigative Phenomenon.

12 **CCC Scale, Proportion, and Quantity** You are on a remote mountain hike, and you would like to take and store scenic photographs on your smartphone. Find the missing values in the table that summarize the available options. Which resolution allows you to save the most pictures? Which resolution allows you to save the most detailed images?

Type	Length (pixels)	Height (pixels)	Number of pixels per image
Small size	400	300	120,000
Medium size	800		480,000
Large size	1200	900	
Panorama		500	1,000,000

13 **SEP Calculate** Bitrate is the number of bits transferred per second in a digital transmission. Suppose you are texting from a remote location over a network that transfers information at a bitrate of 40 Mbit/s. (An Mbit is a megabit, or 1,000,000 bits.) If each character in your text requires a byte of information to encode, about how long would it take to transmit a text with 100 characters of information?

14 **SEP Argue from Evidence** If you were planning a trip to a remote location where you intended to take a lot of photographs and videos, would you want to bring analog or digital recording equipment? Make an argument to support your decision.

GO ONLINE for a **quiz** to evaluate what you learned about Digital Information.

Capturing and Transmitting Information

 GO ONLINE to do a **hands-on lab** to investigate how speakers work.

Audio Information

Sound waves are longitudinal compression waves in air. They can be converted into analog electrical sounds using a microphone.

There are different types of microphones, but they all operate using the same physical principle. Sound waves cause relative motion between a magnet and a coil of wire inside the microphone, which induces an electrical signal in the wire. The frequency of the vibrations in the air is therefore the frequency of the changes in the electrical signal. A sound wave with greater amplitude will cause a greater back-and-forth motion of the microphone's coil. This results in an electrical signal with a larger induced voltage.

Converting Signals The construction of a speaker is essentially the same as that of a microphone. They are both devices that transduce between electrical energy and the wave energy of sound.

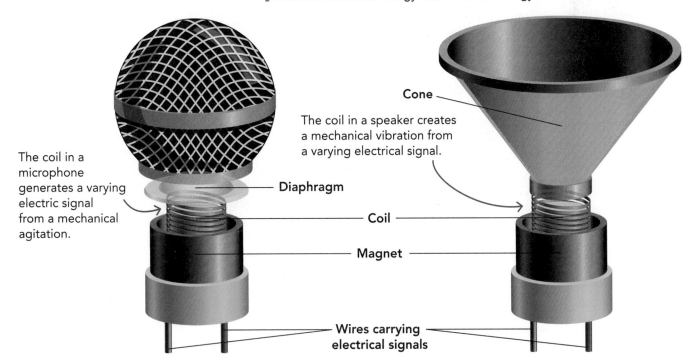

Cone

The coil in a speaker creates a mechanical vibration from a varying electrical signal.

The coil in a microphone generates a varying electric signal from a mechanical agitation.

Diaphragm

Coil

Magnet

Wires carrying electrical signals

(15) **CCC Energy and Matter** Most speakers work like microphones in reverse even though they look very different. Normally, people do not use speakers as microphones or vice versa. Based on their function, how do you think the magnet and the coil in a speaker differ from those in a microphone?

Visual Information

VOCABULARY

The words *scan* and **scanner** come from the Latin *scandere*, which means "to climb." To *scan* a poem historically meant to mark the rhythm of the poem by raising and lowering your foot, just like climbing. Eventually, the term also came to mean "examine."

Digital Photography Digital cameras operate similarly to film cameras to create images from light. The difference is that the focused light waves interact with an array of semiconductor photodetectors that generate electrical signals. The array may include cells that use filters to capture only red, green, or blue light for individual pixels. The greater the intensity of the light wave striking a detector, the greater the signal that detector produces for its pixel.

Scanners A **scanner** is a device that converts visual information in a physical format into a digital file. A print scanner operates on the same principle as a digital camera, essentially photographing a document and storing the information as a series of pixels. If information is captured for three dimensions, then a 3-D representation can be made and stored on a computer.

3-D Scans for 3-D Objects Scanners capture EM waves that are sent out to an object, like taking a photograph using a flash. However, the EM waves may or may not be a visible wavelength.

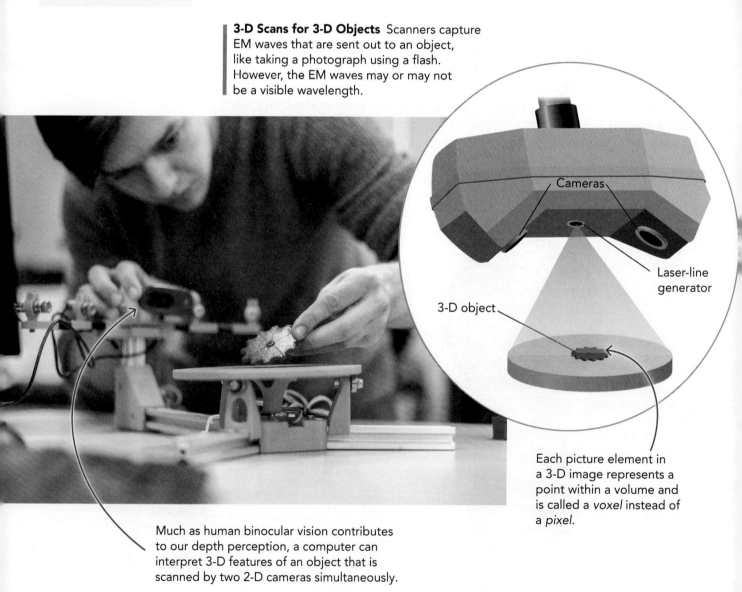

Cameras

Laser-line generator

3-D object

Each picture element in a 3-D image represents a point within a volume and is called a *voxel* instead of a *pixel*.

Much as human binocular vision contributes to our depth perception, a computer can interpret 3-D features of an object that is scanned by two 2-D cameras simultaneously.

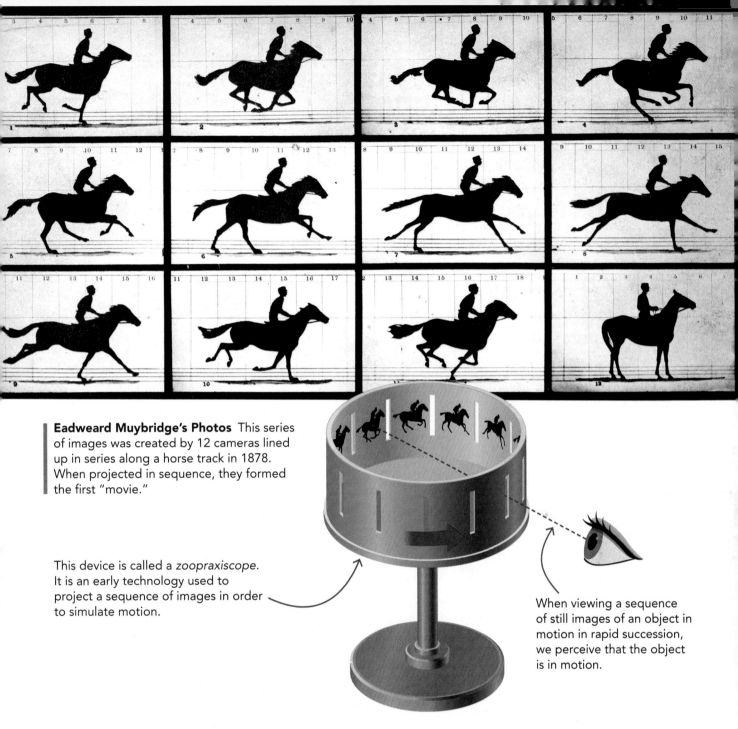

Eadweard Muybridge's Photos This series of images was created by 12 cameras lined up in series along a horse track in 1878. When projected in sequence, they formed the first "movie."

This device is called a *zoopraxiscope*. It is an early technology used to project a sequence of images in order to simulate motion.

When viewing a sequence of still images of an object in motion in rapid succession, we perceive that the object is in motion.

Video Many digital cameras and smartphones have the ability to record video. Video files are basically a sequence of images taken in rapid succession.

Once a series of images is created, the series may also be viewed in rapid succession. Much as a sequence of sounds can make music or language, our brains interpret a series of similar images as an object in motion. A film strip is an analog series of pictures that can be projected onto a screen. Digital movies operate in the same manner, projecting a series of digital images on a screen.

16) **SEP Design Solutions** Many parts of the ocean floor are mapped using sonar, which is a technology that uses sound waves to generate an image. How can a visible image, such as a map, be produced by scanning with waves that are not electromagnetic?

Medical Imaging

Photography and scanning are useful for obtaining images of an object's exterior. However, these technologies can also be used to take images of an object's interior without opening the object. These technologies capture and interpret information other than visible light waves. X-rays, for example, are able to penetrate human tissue to produce images of our bones and internal organs.

Ultrasound Ultrasound technology is a form of sonar that uses sound frequencies greater than those humans can hear. At these high frequencies, the mechanical waves are used to image internal organs without exposing those organs to the dangerous energy levels of ionizing radiation such as X-rays. The higher the frequency of the ultrasound waves, the greater the image resolution that can be attained. However, higher frequencies do not penetrate very deep into the body.

Ultrasound Imaging Because ultrasound waves do not pose a health risk even after several minutes of exposure, they are the preferred imaging method for observing a fetus during pregnancy.

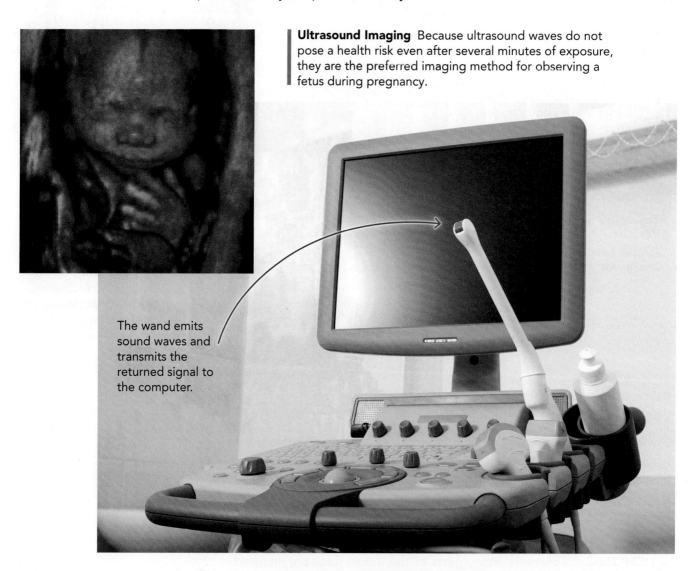

The wand emits sound waves and transmits the returned signal to the computer.

(17) **SEP Construct Explanations** How is a 3-D ultrasound image generated using a device that emits and detects high-frequency sound waves?

CT Scans A computerized tomography scan (CT scan, also known as a CAT scan) is a sequence of X-ray images that are stacked by a computer to form a composite 3-D image with much greater detail than a single X-ray. Because the images are taken from multiple directions, the composite image allows medical professionals to see cross sections of the interior of the body.

Magnetic Resonance Imaging Medical images of the interior of the body are also obtained through magnetic resonance imaging (MRI). Hydrogen atoms in a patient's body align with the very powerful magnetic field of the machine. The patient then receives a brief burst of radio waves that changes that alignment temporarily. As the protons in the hydrogen realign with the magnetic field, they emit small amounts of electromagnetic radiation that are detected by the MRI machine.

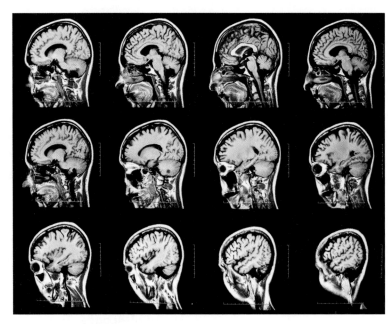

3-D X-rays This sequence of X-ray images can be stacked into a 3-D model by a computer to provide detailed imagery of the organs of the body.

Magnetic Imaging An MRI uses EM waves that are below ionizing frequencies. Therefore, there is no health risk from exposure to these waves.

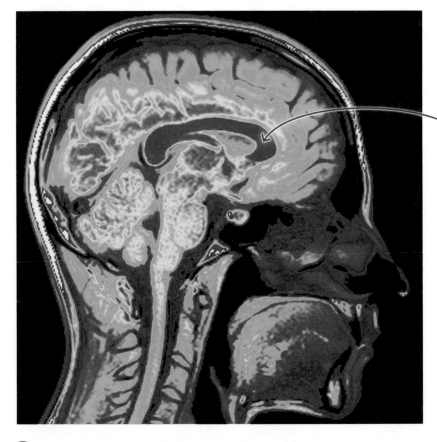

An MRI yields enhanced detail of soft tissue compared to X-rays and CT scans. MRIs are useful for examining the spine, blood vessels, tendons, and ligaments.

18 **CCC Energy and Matter** Thermal infrared cameras are also useful in medical imaging. Unlike other imaging technologies, thermal imaging does not require exposing the patient to EM radiation or sound. Explain why.

Antennas

 GO ONLINE to watch a **video** about radio telescopes and to do a PhET **simulation** to investigate transmitting and receiving EM waves.

EXPERIENCE IT!

Use your hands like a directional antenna dish while a partner speaks at a normal volume. First, place your hands behind your ears cupping forward, and then place them in front of your ears, cupping backward. Note the differences in sound quality.

Broadcast and Reception An **antenna** is a rod or wire used to transmit and receive electromagnetic waves. Antennas allow signals to be transmitted over long distances through air or a vacuum. However, these signals can be blocked or interfered with.

The oscillation of electrical charges in a broadcast antenna generates an EM wave that radiates outward at the speed of light. When the wave reaches another antenna, it induces the same oscillation of electrical charges as in the broadcast antenna.

Radio Telescopes The size of an antenna determines the size of the wave that will be transmitted or received. Radio telescopes are actually antennas with a parabolic dish that can be tens of meters across. These devices are used to observe very faint or weak radio waves from distant astronomical objects.

The parabolic dish helps focus a received signal. The curved surface of the dish reflects the incoming waves toward a focal point to help concentrate their energy, which aids in stronger signal reception. The dish does not look like a traditional mirror for visible light because a smooth metallic surface is not needed to reflect long wavelengths.

Radio Waves from Space The dish of this radio telescope at the Green Bank Observatory in West Virginia is 100 meters in diameter.

Wireless Wonders
How does an antenna **transmit** and **receive information?**

Transmitting Information Antennas work on the principle that when an **electric current is changed,** the **electric and magnetic fields** produced by the current **also change.** Examine the diagrams to explore how a simple antenna connected to an alternating current generator **produces EM waves.**

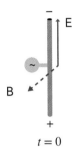

$t = 0$

A signal is sent to an antenna as an **electric potential** that causes a **charge separation** between the two ends of the antenna. The separated charges on the antenna generate an **electric field.** Their movement while separating generates a **magnetic field.**

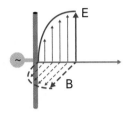

$t = \frac{1}{4}T$

As the signal potential **decreases,** the separation of charges **decreases,** so both fields also **decrease.**

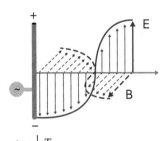

$t = \frac{1}{2}T$

When the potential **alternates,** the separation of charges switches from the earlier orientation, building both fields.

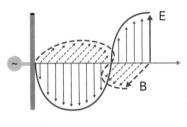

$t = \frac{3}{4}T$

As the signal potential **decreases a second time,** the separation of charges **decreases again,** so both fields also **decrease again.**

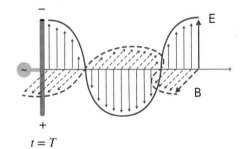

$t = T$

The signal potential has **completed a full cycle,** and the charge separation has **alternated twice** along the length of the antenna.

Receiving Information When an antenna receives a signal in the form of an electromagnetic wave, the entire process works in reverse. The electric and magnetic fields in the wave **induce a current** in the antenna wires. As the fields alternate, the current in the antenna alternates and the **original signal is generated.**

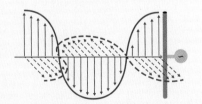

(19) **SEP Obtain Information** Use the library or reliable internet sources to find information about Earth's ionosphere. Present one positive effect and one negative effect of the ionosphere on information transmission.

INVESTIGATIVE PHENOMENON

GO ONLINE to revisit your **Investigative Phenomenon CER** with the new information you have learned about Capturing and Transmitting Information.

These questions will help you apply what you learned in this experience to the Investigative Phenomenon.

20. **SEP Reason Quantitatively** When you make a cellular call from a remote location, the signal is most likely routed to its destination by sending it to one or more communications satellites in orbit around Earth. Use the speed of light (3×10^8 m/s) to determine the time it takes your signal to reach its destination if it is routed through a satellite orbiting 36,000 km above Earth's surface.

21. **SEP Construct Explanations** You want to document a journey to a remote location using a digital camera. Explain why you can store more digital photographs than digital videos on the camera.

22. **CCC Energy and Matter** Suppose you call a friend while on a remote mountain hike. Describe the energy transformations and different forms the signal takes as it travels from your voice box to the ear of your friend on the other end.

23. **SEP Construct Explanations** While hiking on a very high mountain, you come across an observatory with a telescope. Explain why the telescope is most likely one that detects visible light instead of radio signals.

GO ONLINE
for a **quiz** to evaluate what you learned about Capturing and Transmitting Information.

Capturing and Transmitting Energy

 GO ONLINE to do a **hands-on lab** to investigate how solar energy is converted into electricity by building a solar powered car.

Capturing an EM Wave's Energy

Recall that waves transmit energy. You can model the sun as a point source of electromagnetic waves that radiate outward in every direction. These waves carry energy away from the sun.

Imagine a flat disc of photons emitted from the sun's surface at a particular instant. In a billionth of a second, that disc has expanded 30 cm away from the surface, and each photon is slightly farther away from its neighbors. As the light continues to expand outward in every direction, the surface area of the disc of photons increases, and the intensity of the light decreases. After 500 seconds, the disc is 150 million kilometers from the sun. A small portion of that light energy, at a much-decreased intensity than when it was emitted, strikes Earth.

Power Supply The sun is a source of electromagnetic wave energy across a spectrum of frequencies, emitting 3.828×10^{26} watts of power.

About 1,361 W/m²·of solar energy reaches Earth's surface when the sun is directly overhead.

As the emitted waves travel outward in every direction at the speed of light, they become spread out.

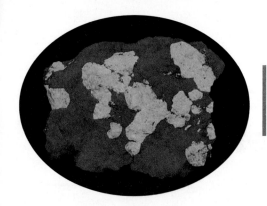

Fluorescence Willemite is a mineral that glows bright green under UV light. Some materials absorb UV light and re-emit the energy as light of a longer wavelength and lower energy. This phenomenon is called *fluorescence*.

VOCABULARY

The prefix *photo-* means "light." The root *voltaic* refers to the production of electricity, and it is a reference to the pioneering physicist Alessandro Volta. A **photovoltaic cell** uses light to produce electricity.

Energy From the Sun Electromagnetic energy may pass through an object (transmission) or bounce back (reflection). The energy can also be absorbed by the object, increasing its thermal energy. In some cases, the absorbed energy is re-emitted, often at a different wavelength.

When EM radiation from the sun reaches our planet, 30% of the energy is reflected back into space by Earth's surface and atmosphere. Some of the remaining energy is absorbed by the atmosphere. Approximately half of the solar radiation that reaches Earth actually makes it to the planet's surface.

Energy from the sun can be captured with photovoltaic cells for use in electronic devices. A **photovoltaic cell** is a device that converts energy from electromagnetic radiation into electrical energy. The efficiency of a photovoltaic cell is a measure of its ability to convert sunlight into useful electrical energy.

Efficiency of Energy Transformation

$$Eff = \frac{E_{out}}{E_{in}} \times 100\%$$

Eff = efficiency, expressed as a percentage
E_{out} = useful energy output
E_{in} = total energy input

Solar Cells Electricity can be generated from solar energy anyplace on Earth with a photovoltaic cell, even far from the electric power grid. Solar energy is a popular alternative to fossil fuels. However, without a battery backup, solar cells can be used only when it is sunny.

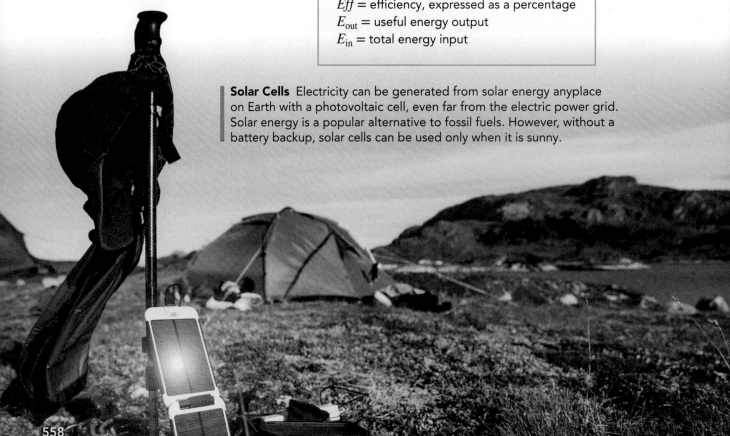

GO ONLINE do a PhET **simulation** that allows you to investigate the transformation of electromagnetic energy into different forms.

Solar Panels A solar panel is a structure composed of linked photovoltaic cells. Solar panels are designed to absorb as much solar energy as possible and turn it into electricity. Scientists continue to look for ways to improve the efficiency of solar panels. One method involves programming the panels to follow the path of the sun in the sky so that they receive the most direct sunlight possible.

Solar Cells

How does a **solar cell** convert **solar energy** into **electrical energy**?

Capturing the Sun's Energy Solar energy is the **most abundant source of energy** on Earth. Solar panels are designed to capture **energy from the sun** and convert it into **electricity.**

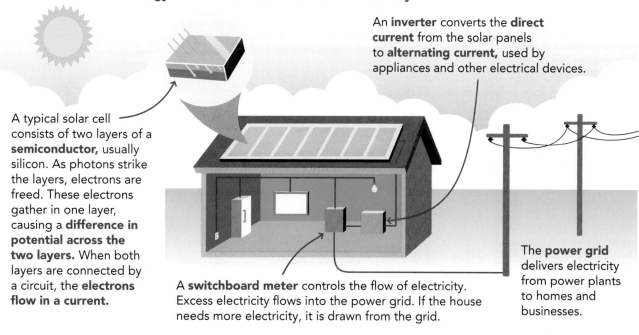

An **inverter** converts the **direct current** from the solar panels to **alternating current,** used by appliances and other electrical devices.

A typical solar cell consists of two layers of a **semiconductor,** usually silicon. As photons strike the layers, electrons are freed. These electrons gather in one layer, causing a **difference in potential across the two layers.** When both layers are connected by a circuit, the **electrons flow in a current.**

A **switchboard meter** controls the flow of electricity. Excess electricity flows into the power grid. If the house needs more electricity, it is drawn from the grid.

The **power grid** delivers electricity from power plants to homes and businesses.

Earth's surface receives **125,000 terawatts** of solar energy, which is 6250 times more than the rate that all humans consume energy.

Humans use energy in all forms at a total rate of about **20 terawatts**.

(24) SEP Construct Explanations Why does direct sunlight feel warmer at noon than shortly after sunrise or shortly before sunset?

(25) SEP Construct Explanations How do you think the angle of solar panels must be adjusted as you travel north from the equator to the North Pole? Explain your answer.

Efficiency of Solar Power

Suppose a set of solar panels has a 21.0% efficiency rating. A typical home uses about 30 kilowatt-hours of energy per day from electricity. Usable solar energy is often measured in peak sun hours, which are units of 1000 W/m². In New Orleans, LA, solar panels collect an average of 5 peak sun hours per day. Calculate the area of an array of solar panels needed to meet the power needs of a typical home in New Orleans, LA during peak sun hours. Ignore loss of power due to the solar panel tilt.

1. DRAW A PICTURE Sketch a picture of the situation.

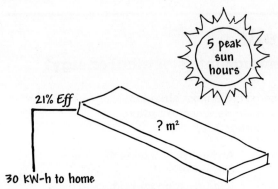

2. DEFINE THE PROBLEM List knowns and unknowns, and assign values to variables.

$Eff = 21.0\%$

E_{in} (per m²) $= 1{,}000$ W/m² $= 1.00$ kW/m²

Energy used per day $= 30$ kW·h

Number of peak sun hours per day $= 5.0$

E_{out} (per m²) $= ?$ kW/m²

Area of solar panels $= ?$ m²

3. PLAN AND EXECUTE Use mathematical relationships, the picture, and your definitions to plan and execute a solution.

Use the Efficiency of Energy Transformation equation to find the E_{out} per square meter of solar panel.	$Eff = \dfrac{E_{out}}{E_{in}} \times 100\% \rightarrow$ $E_{out} = \dfrac{E_{in} \times Eff}{100\%} = \dfrac{(1.00 \text{ kW/m}^2)(21.0\%)}{100\%} = 0.210 \text{ kW/m}^2$
Determine the power that needs to be generated in each hour of useful daylight.	$\dfrac{29.9 \text{ kW·h}}{8.00 \text{ h}} = 6.0 \text{ kW}$
Find the area of the solar panels by using E_{out} and the needed power.	$\text{Area} = \dfrac{6.0 \text{ kW}}{0.210 \text{ kW/m}^2} = 29 \text{ m}^2$

4. EVALUATE Reflect on your answer.
This answer is reasonable based on solar panels that are typically found on the roofs of homes and buildings. It is equivalent to a rectangular area that is about 4 m by 7 m.

 GO ONLINE for more **math support**.

Math Practice Problems

26 A certain solar panel has a 14% efficiency rating. A home uses about 65.5 kilowatt-hours of energy per day. Assume the home, on average, gets 6 peak sun hours of useful energy collection in a day, at 1000 W/m² per peak sun hour. Find the area of solar panels needed to power the home during peak sun hours. Ignore loss of power due to the solar panel tilt.

📖 **NEED A HINT?** Go online to your **eText Sample Problem** for stepped out support.

27 A store uses 41.7 kilowatt-hours of energy per day. Its solar panels are 16.5% efficient. Assume 4.0 peak sun hours of daily energy collection. How much area should the solar panels cover to power the store? Ignore loss of power due to the solar panel tilt.

Wireless Charging

Many devices in our homes and workplaces are powered by rechargeable batteries. Most of these devices can be charged by plugging them into a standard wall outlet using a cable. Many devices, such as phones and toothbrushes, can instead be charged wirelessly.

Wireless charging relies on the physics of electromagnetic induction. In other words, these chargers operate in the same manner that transformers do. The alternating current in the charger's wire coil induces a current in the secondary coil, which is inside the phone or other device.

One disadvantage of wireless charging is that it is much less efficient than using charging cables. But the technology is still appealing to many consumers for its ease of use.

Inductive Charging Rather than plugging a phone into an outlet, the charger is plugged into the outlet and the phone is simply placed on top of the charging pad.

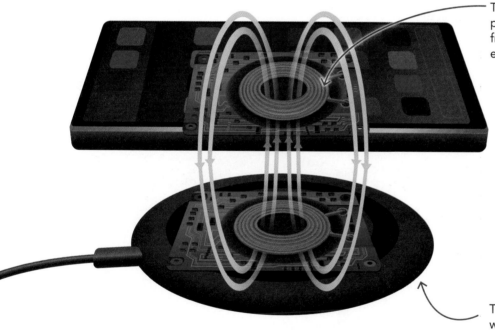

The secondary coil in the phone captures energy from the EM waves emitted by the charger.

The charger transmits EM waves over short distances.

28) **SEP Obtain Information** Aside from convenience, what other advantages does wireless charging offer?

29) **SEP Construct an Argument** For wireless charging technology, the device does not need to make contact with the charger, but the device does need to be very close to the charger in order to charge effectively. Using what you already know about the properties of magnetic and electric fields, explain why this is the case.

Cooking

GO ONLINE to watch an Explain **video** about microwaves and their alleged relationship to cancer.

EXPERIENCE IT!

Put some marbles in a plastic container to model the effect of microwaves on water molecules in food. Shake the container and observe the marbles. If you shake the container faster, what can you predict about the kinetic energy and temperature of the marbles?

Gas-powered ovens and stoves transfer energy to food by convection and conduction; convection of the hot air and conduction from the air and hot surfaces in contact with the food. Electric stoves heat only by conduction of the cooking surface heating the food due to direct contact. Microwave ovens don't use hot air or surfaces to cook things. Instead, they transmit electromagnetic energy to heat up food.

Microwave ovens use EM waves with a wavelength of about 12 cm that interact with the water molecules in food. The polarity of the water molecules allows them to act as tiny antennas that get stimulated by the incoming EM radiation. The EM energy is transformed into kinetic energy in the water molecules, which then undergo collisions with the molecules around them, distributing energy throughout the food. Most plastic, ceramic, and glass objects do not absorb microwave energy, so these items are not heated by the microwave oven—though they may become heated by the hot food they contain.

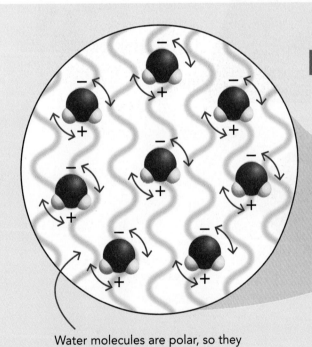

Water molecules are polar, so they follow the electric field when exposed to certain frequencies of EM radiation.

Microwave Oven The interior surfaces of a microwave oven do not conduct heat to the food.

It is still important to use caution, as the cooked items may be very hot inside.

(30) **SEP Construct Explanations** Microwave ovens cook food quickly by "zapping" it with radiation. What makes it difficult or impossible to use radiation to make a fast refrigerator?

Radiotherapy

Radiotherapy is the medical use of electromagnetic radiation to treat illnesses such as cancer. Ionizing radiation, including X-rays and gamma rays, can be targeted carefully to cause damage to the DNA of cancer cells. In some treatments, healthy cells may be damaged by the ionizing energy as well, but they are more likely to repair themselves than cancer cells are.

Stereotactic radiosurgery is a noninvasive procedure, meaning that no incision is made in the patient. Internal organs, such as the brain or spinal cord, are subjected to precise beams of radiation from multiple directions. These beams deliver greater energy at the point of intersection and cause little damage to the surrounding tissue.

Surgery Without Scalpels Radiotherapy techniques can precisely target locations deep within sensitive areas to treat small brain tumors and other causes of illness.

Up to 200 beams of EM rays can be concentrated at a single point inside the patient's skull.

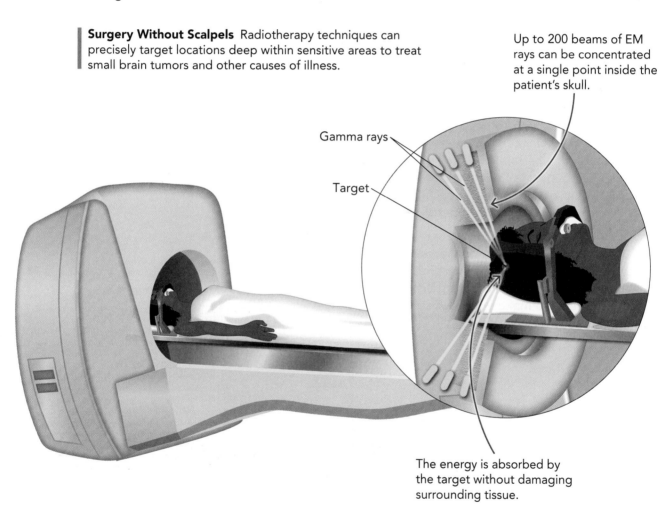

Gamma rays

Target

The energy is absorbed by the target without damaging surrounding tissue.

(31) SEP Construct Explanations Only a fraction of the energy carried by the beams of a stereotactic surgery machine is absorbed by living tissue. What do you think happens to the rest of the energy?

INVESTIGATIVE PHENOMENON

GO ONLINE to revisit your **Investigative Phenomenon CER** with the new information you have learned about Capturing and Transmitting Energy.

These questions will help you apply what you learned in this experience to the Investigative Phenomenon.

32 **CCC Matter and Energy** To make a phone call from a remote location, you use a portable antenna to help boost your reception. The antenna consists of copper wire encased in plastic to support the wire and prevent the copper from corroding. Why doesn't the plastic coating on the antenna interfere with reception?

33 **SEP Argue from Evidence** You are planning a hiking trip where there is no available electricity, but you want to be able to use your smartphone. Which would be more useful on your trip, a wireless charger or a solar cell? Explain your answer.

34 **SEP Use Mathematics** You charge your smartphone on a hiking trip using a solar cell. If the solar cell has an area of 200 cm² and you charge the phone for 10 hours on a certain day, how much electricity, in kilowatt-hours, does the solar cell generate? Assume that the solar cell has an efficiency of 20%, that 800 W/m² of solar energy reaches Earth's surface at that location, and that the solar cells are kept perpendicular to the incoming sun rays.

35 **SEP Design Solutions** Solar cookers can be used to cook meals on hikes in place of using a campfire. Solar cookers focus solar energy and use it to heat the food inside. What materials would you need to make your own solar cooker? Give reasons for your choices.

GO ONLINE for a **quiz** to evaluate what you learned about Capturing and Transmitting Energy.

These questions will help you apply what you learned in this investigation to the Anchoring Phenomenon.

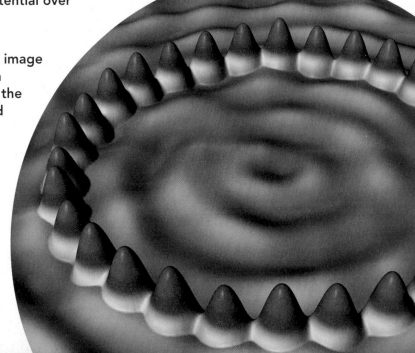

36 **CCC Energy and Matter** In today's computers, bits are stored as electric charges or in magnetic domains. Computer engineers hope to one day be able to use "quantum corrals" to construct quantum computers, in which bits would be stored in the quantum states of subatomic particles. Explain the advantages quantum computers would have in computing potential over today's computer technology.

37 **SEP Apply Mathematical Concepts** This image of a "quantum corral" was taken using a very sensitive scanner that can measure the induced current between the device and the surface that is being imaged. The scanner can also infer the distance to the surface based on the strength of the current. If a pixel in this image is about 0.1 nm across, about what size is each ripple in the image? Does this answer make sense based on your understanding of atomic physics? Explain. Assume the image on this page is about 1,400 pixels across.

☑ INVESTIGATION ASSESSMENT

GO ONLINE for activities that will give you an opportunity to **demonstrate what you have learned:**

☑ **Engineering Performance-Based Assessment** Develop, transmit, and interpret a code.

📄 **Engineering Workbench** Program a rover to carry out a sequence of actions.

🖥 **Career Connections** Learn about how a robotics engineer applies knowledge of physics.

☑ **Investigation Test** Take this test to demonstrate your understanding of information and instrumentation.

☑ **Virtual Lab Performance-Based Assessment** Explore the ability of different technologies to store audio information.

From the Nucleus to the Universe

How did the atoms that make up your body form?

Investigation 14
Nuclear Physics

Investigation 15
Ages of Rocks

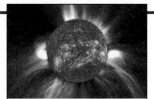

Investigation 16
The Universe

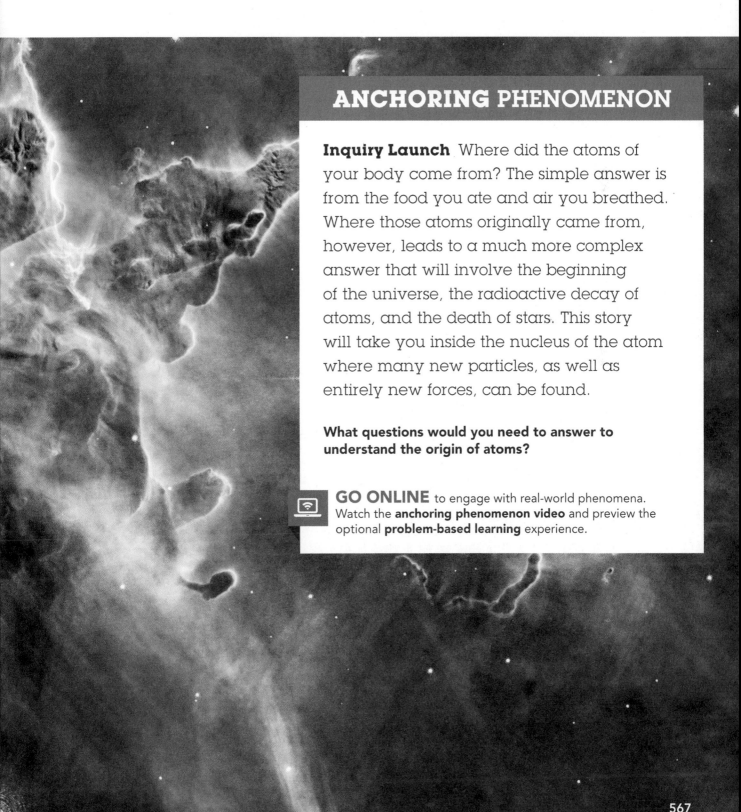

ANCHORING PHENOMENON

Inquiry Launch Where did the atoms of your body come from? The simple answer is from the food you ate and air you breathed. Where those atoms originally came from, however, leads to a much more complex answer that will involve the beginning of the universe, the radioactive decay of atoms, and the death of stars. This story will take you inside the nucleus of the atom where many new particles, as well as entirely new forces, can be found.

What questions would you need to answer to understand the origin of atoms?

GO ONLINE to engage with real-world phenomena. Watch the **anchoring phenomenon video** and preview the optional **problem-based learning** experience.

 GO ONLINE to engage with real-world phenomena by watching a **phenomenon video** and completing a **modeling worksheet**.

How can your electricity come from the fusion of atoms?

Nuclear Physics

Until now, you've learned about forces and energy at either the everyday or atomic scale. All the forces discussed so far represent just two fundamental forces: gravity at very large scales and the electromagnetic force between charged atoms or between electrons and nuclei. Interactions have followed a set of rules that seem familiar and sensible. Mass has always been conserved.

However, things are going to get strange now. In the realm of atomic nuclei, all familiar rules break down, and a new set of rules comes into play. Subatomic particles can collide and entirely disappear, leaving only energy, or pure energy can suddenly transform into particles.

Ideas that once sounded like science fiction are commonplace in the world of atomic nuclei. By mastering them, you will understand how nuclear processes can produce the vast amounts of electricity needed to power the world.

1. **CCC Energy and Matter** Many power plants rely on the chemical process of combustion to generate electricity. During combustion, a fuel such as coal is burned (oxidized) and seems to disappear. What actually happens to most of the mass of the coal?

2. **SEP Ask Questions** Nuclear reactions can be used to generate electricity. List some of the questions you need to ask in order to learn how this happens.

Nuclear Particles

 GO ONLINE to do a **hands-on lab** to model the formation and decay of nuclear particles.

The Nucleus

Before you can understand processes in which atomic nuclei break apart (fission) or merge (fusion), you first have to learn more about the atomic nucleus and its properties. The nucleus consists of all of the neutrons and protons of an atom. The nucleus occupies a very small part of the atom's volume, but it contains nearly all of its mass. Both protons and neutrons are made out of three smaller particles called quarks. As a result, they have similar sizes and masses, so protons and neutrons are often counted together as the **nucleons** of an atom.

Making Subatomic Particles The high-energy collision of an oxygen nucleus with a lead atom produces a burst of 300 particles in a streamer chamber. The paths of 220 electrically charged particles show up as streaks in a photograph of the collision.

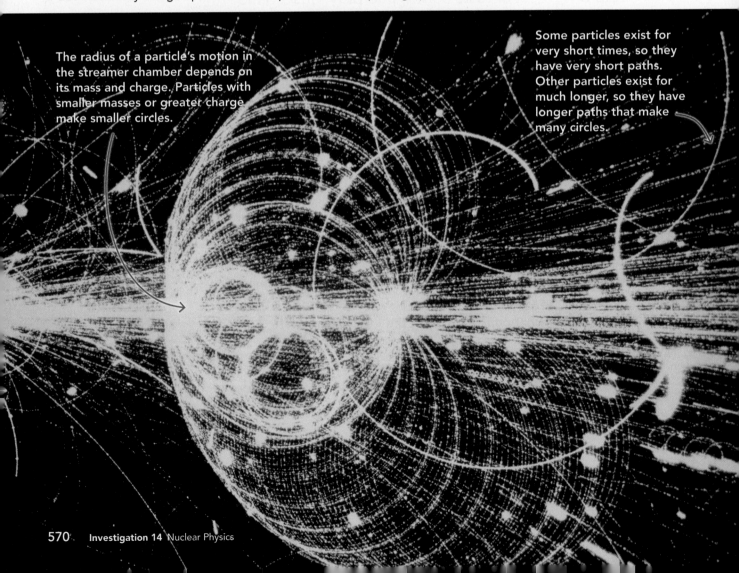

The radius of a particle's motion in the streamer chamber depends on its mass and charge. Particles with smaller masses or greater charge make smaller circles.

Some particles exist for very short times, so they have very short paths. Other particles exist for much longer, so they have longer paths that make many circles.

GO ONLINE to watch a **video** about the atomic nucleus.

Describing Atomic Nuclei You can use the number of protons and neutrons to identify a nucleus. The number of protons is the **atomic number** (Z), and the number of neutrons is the neutron number (N). The sum of these is the **mass number** (A), which is also the total number of nucleons ($A = Z + N$).

Representing Atomic Nuclei The notation $^A_Z X$ is used to represent a nucleus with atomic number Z and mass number A. The X stands for the chemical symbol of the element. The number of protons determines the element, but an element can have different isotopes depending on the number of neutrons. For example, both $^{12}_6 C$ and $^{13}_6 C$ are atoms of carbon because their atomic number is 6, but they are different isotopes because they have different mass numbers and, therefore, different numbers of neutrons. Because isotopes always have the same atomic number, they are often written with only the element name and mass number. For example, $^{13}_6 C$ is the same as ^{13}C and carbon-13.

Carbon Isotopes The nucleus consists of an atom's protons, which are positively charged, and neutrons, which have no charge.

6

C

Carbon

12.0107

The **standard atomic weight** listed on a periodic table, in this case 12.0107, is the mean mass in g/mol, taking into account the relative abundances of all of the isotopes of that element.

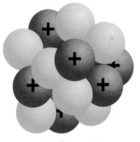

Carbon-12		Carbon-13
6	Number of protons (Z)	6
+ 6	Number of neutrons (N)	+ 7
12	Number of nucleons (A)	13

(3) **SEP Develop Models** Show how you would represent the nuclei of two different isotopes of the element lead (Pb), one with 124 neutrons and one with 125 neutrons.

(4) **CCC Patterns** The most abundant nuclei of the elements helium, oxygen, phosphorus, zinc, cadmium, and mercury are ^4_2He, $^{16}_8O$, $^{31}_{15}P$, $^{64}_{30}Zn$, $^{114}_{48}Cd$, and $^{202}_{80}Hg$, respectively. What pattern do you observe in these nuclei, and what does this say about the relative numbers of neutrons and protons?

Size and Mass of the Nucleus

 GO ONLINE to do a PhET **simulation** that allows you to explore the particles and forces within an atom.

Because nucleons are about 1800 times more massive than electrons, nearly all the mass of an atom is in its nucleus. However, because the electron cloud of an atom is so large, the nucleus takes up almost none of the volume of the atom. The radius of the proton in an ($_1^1$H) hydrogen nucleus is about 8.3×10^{-16} m, but the radius of a hydrogen atom (including the electron cloud) is 5.3×10^{-11} m, about 65,000 times greater.

Unlike atoms, whose electron clouds are quite compressible, nucleons are quite incompressible. Protons and neutrons are always packed together like hard baseballs, making the most spherical shape possible. Because nucleons do not compress, the size of a nucleus can be approximated using the radius of the hydrogen nucleus, which has just the single nucleon.

Radius of Atomic Nuclei
$$R \approx r_0 A^{\frac{1}{3}} = (1.2 \times 10^{-15} \text{ m})A^{\frac{1}{3}}$$
R = radius of nucleus in meters r_0 = a constant A = number of nucleons

The Geiger-Marsden Experiment The existence of the atomic nucleus was shown in 1908 by Hans Geiger and Ernest Marsden, who figured out that the positive charges of an atom were not evenly distributed throughout the atom, as the old Thomson model suggested.

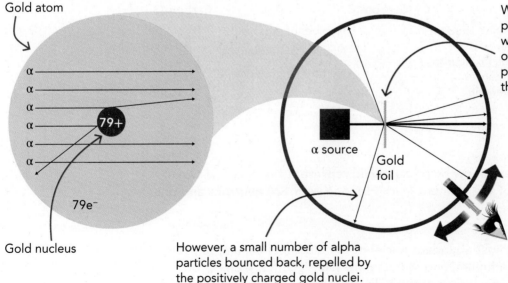

Gold atom

α

α

α

α

α

α

79+

79e⁻

Gold nucleus

α source

Gold foil

When a beam of alpha particles (with a +2 charge) was aimed at a thin sheet of gold foil, most of the particles went straight through the sheet.

However, a small number of alpha particles bounced back, repelled by the positively charged gold nuclei.

(5) **CCC Cause and Effect** Suppose that you carried out the Geiger-Marsden experiment on two equally thin metal sheets of magnesium (Mg) and lead (Pb). From what you know of the properties of these two elements, explain why one or the other would deflect more of the fired alpha particles.

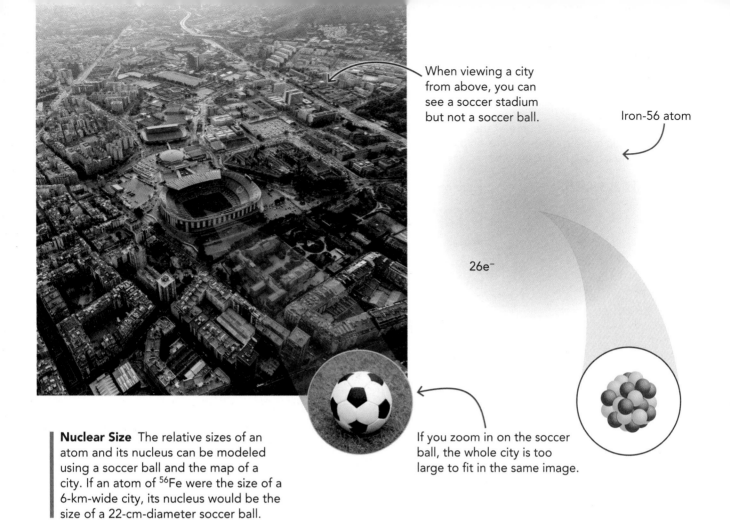

When viewing a city from above, you can see a soccer stadium but not a soccer ball.

Iron-56 atom

26e⁻

If you zoom in on the soccer ball, the whole city is too large to fit in the same image.

Nuclear Size The relative sizes of an atom and its nucleus can be modeled using a soccer ball and the map of a city. If an atom of ^{56}Fe were the size of a 6-km-wide city, its nucleus would be the size of a 22-cm-diameter soccer ball.

Atomic Mass Unit When measured in kilograms, the masses of a proton $(1.673 \times 10^{-27}$ kg) and a neutron $(1.675 \times 10^{-27}$ kg) are extremely small numbers, so a more convenient unit is used. The **atomic mass unit** (u or amu) is defined to be exactly equal to one-twelfth of the mass of a ^{12}C atom that is at rest, at its lowest nuclear and electronic energy levels, and not bound to other atoms. Therefore, 1 u = 1.660539×10^{-27} kg, a proton's mass is 1.007276 u, and a neutron's mass is 1.008665 u. One amu is also the same as 1 gram per mole.

Atomic Densities Because nucleons are very incompressible, the density of nuclei is nearly constant, regardless of their size. The density (because the number of nucleons, A, cancels out) will always be approximately equal to

$$\rho_{\text{nucleus}} = \frac{A \times u}{\left(\frac{4}{3}\right)\pi R^3} = \frac{A \times u}{\left(\frac{4}{3}\right)\pi r_0^3 \left(A^{\frac{1}{3}}\right)^3} = \frac{1.66054 \times 10^{-27} \text{ kg}}{\left(\frac{4}{3}\right)\pi(1.2 \times 10^{-15} \text{ m})^3} = 2.3 \times 10^{17} \text{ kg/m}^3$$

6 **CCC Scale, Proportion, and Quantity** The nucleus of an iron atom (^{56}Fe) has a radius of about 4.6×10^{-15} m. Use this fact and the size information in the figure to determine the size of the entire iron atom.

7 **SEP Construct Explanations** Electron microscopes are better than visible light microscopes for examining things at atomic scales because of the small wavelengths of electrons. Explain why visible light cannot be used to look at atoms, based on what you know about the wavelengths of light.

Nuclear Sizes and Densities

Calculate how many times greater the radius of the nucleus of a $^{238}_{92}$U atom is (the largest stable atomic nucleus) than the proton of the $^1_1$H atom (the smallest atomic nucleus). Then calculate how much denser an atomic nucleus is than a piece of granite (2600 kg/m³).

1. DRAW A PICTURE Sketch a picture of the situation.

2. DEFINE THE PROBLEM List knowns and unknowns and assign values to variables.

Radius of a proton $= 8.3 \times 10^{-16}$ m

Density of granite $= 2600$ kg/m³

The density of a nucleus, ρ_{nucleus}, is known to be approximately 2.3×10^{17} kg/m³ for all nuclei.

3. PLAN AND EXECUTE Use mathematical relationships, the picture, and your definitions to plan and execute a solution.

Find the size of uranium using the equation for the radius of an atomic nucleus.

$$R \approx (1.2 \times 10^{-15} \text{ m})(238)^{\frac{1}{3}} \approx 7.4 \times 10^{-15} \text{ m}$$

Find the ratio of the radii.

$$\frac{7.4 \times 10^{-15} \text{ m}}{8.3 \times 10^{-16} \text{ m}} \approx 8.9$$

Find the ratio of the densities.

$$\frac{2.3 \times 10^{17} \text{ kg/m}^3}{2600 \text{ kg/m}^3} \approx 8.8 \times 10^{13}$$

4. EVALUATE Reflect on your answer.
The radius of a uranium nucleus is about 9 times greater than that of a hydrogen nucleus. An atomic nucleus is about 10^{14} (100 trillion) times denser than a piece of granite.

 GO ONLINE for more **math support**.

▶ **Math Tutorial Video**

📶 **Math Practice Problems**

⑧ How much greater is the radius of $^{16}_8$O, the most abundant isotope of oxygen, than that of $^1_1$H, the atom with the smallest nucleus? How much denser is an atomic nucleus than air (1.2 kg/m³)?

📖 **NEED A HINT?** Go online to your **eText Sample Problem** for stepped out support.

⑨ How does the radius of $^{109}_{47}$Ag, one of two stable isotopes of silver, compare to that of $^{197}_{79}$Au, the only stable isotope of gold?

Nuclear Mass and Energy

Mass by itself is not conserved in atomic interactions, but energy always is, because mass is considered a form of energy. A key concept of nuclear physics is that matter can transform into energy and vice versa through Albert Einstein's famous relation, $E = mc^2$, where E is energy, m is mass, and c is the speed of light (2.998×10^8 m/s). This equation explains how the destruction of small amounts of mass during nuclear fission and fusion releases vast amounts of energy.

When talking about the energies of individual particles, the joule is an inconvenient unit because it is too large. Instead, a unit of energy called the electron volt is used. This smaller unit is much more convenient for discussing the mass-energy of nucleons. In joules, the energy of 1 u is

$$E = mc^2 = (1.66 \times 10^{-27} \text{ kg})(2.998 \times 10^8 \text{ m/s})^2 = 1.49 \times 10^{-10} \text{ J}.$$

EXPERIENCE IT!

Drop a baseball (0.145 kg) from a height of 70 cm. When the ball reaches the ground, it will have gained about 1 joule of kinetic energy. You have just defined a joule. Compare this exercise to the definition of an electron volt.

> **Electron Volt** An **electron volt** (eV) is the amount of kinetic energy, 1.60×10^{-19} J, an electron would gain if it traveled across a capacitor with a potential of 1 volt.

The electron starts out at one plate with no kinetic energy.

Electron

By the time it has crossed between the plates, the electron has gained 1 eV of kinetic energy.

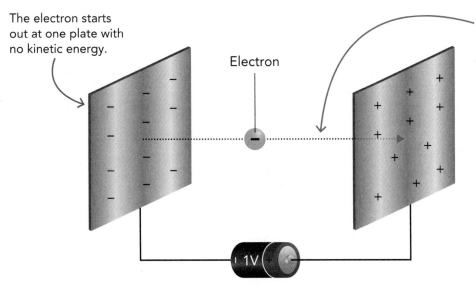

If 1 u of mass is entirely converted into energy, the amount in electron volts is 9.32×10^8 eV. For nuclear reactions, it is common to use units of a million eV (MeV) or a billion eV (GeV). Therefore, the energy of 1 u of mass can also be written as 932 MeV or 0.932 GeV. The eV can also be used to measure small masses, particularly during mass-energy conversions. Because Einstein's equation can be rewritten as $m = \frac{E}{c^2}$, the mass of 1 u can be written as 932 MeV/c^2.

(10) **SEP Use Mathematics** In the diagram, an electron is accelerated across the panels of the capacitor over a voltage of 1 V. Given that the mass of an electron is 9.11×10^{-31} kg, what is the velocity (in m/s) of the electron when it reaches the second panel?

(11) **CCC Energy and Matter** Suppose that a high-energy neutron is traveling at a speed of 18 million m/s. Find its energy in MeV (million eV).

Elementary Particles

Much of science consists of unlearning old models in order to learn new models. This is certainly true for subatomic particles. First, scientists discovered that matter consists mostly of atoms. Then, they learned that atoms consist of electrons, protons, and neutrons. Now, you will see that protons and neutrons actually consist of even smaller particles called quarks.

A newer theory of matter was developed to account for quarks and many other discovered elementary particles. The **Standard Model** organizes these elementary particles into bosons, quarks, and leptons. Bosons are associated with forces. You have already studied photons, which are associated with electromagnetic forces. Quarks and leptons form ordinary matter; quarks make up neutrons and protons, and leptons consist of other particles, such as electrons. Strangely, there are two versions of each quark and lepton: one for matter and one for antimatter.

Standard Model of Elementary Particles Most of these particles are very short-lived and can only be detected by the energies they release during high-energy particle collisions. The Higgs boson was not discovered until 2012.

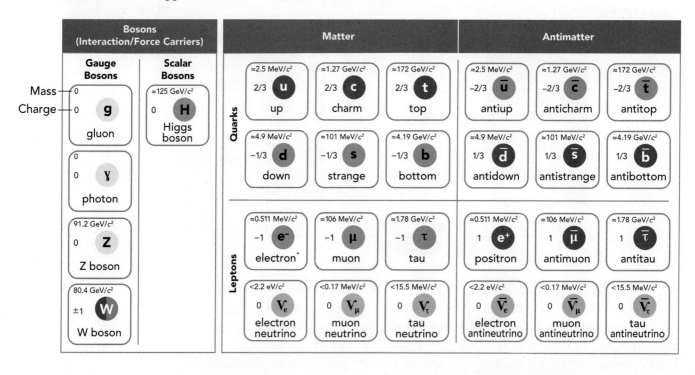

12) **CCC Patterns** Examine the particles in the middle three columns (matter) and the next three columns (antimatter). What pattern do you notice?

13) **CCC Scale, Proportion, and Quantity** An up quark (mass = 2.5 MeV/c^2) is 4.9 times more massive than an electron (mass = 0.511 MeV/c^2). Calculate how many times more or less massive the mass of a Higgs boson, an electron neutrino, and a photon are than the mass of an electron.

Antimatter

Antimatter is matter that is composed of antiparticles. Antimatter seems like something from science fiction—the USS *Enterprise* from *Star Trek* ran on antimatter—but it is very real. All quarks and leptons have matter and antimatter versions. Either version can form naturally during particle interactions such as cosmic ray bombardments or in the lab during high-energy particle collisions. The most common antimatter particle is the positron, which is the antimatter version of the electron and is represented as e^+.

Antimatter is rare in the universe because as soon as an antimatter particle interacts with its matter particle equivalent, they annihilate each other, and their energy converts into other particles, such as photons. This fact makes antimatter difficult to handle. The longest scientists have been able to create and contain antihydrogen atoms (antiprotons) is 17 minutes.

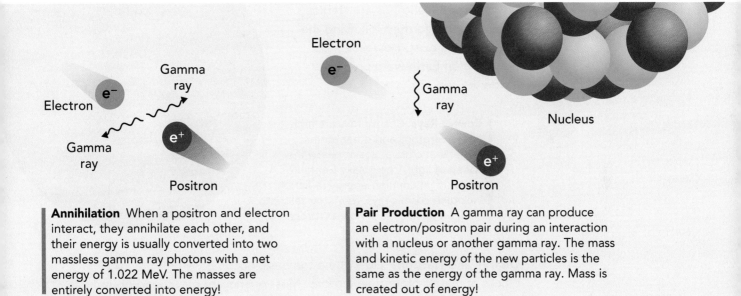

Annihilation When a positron and electron interact, they annihilate each other, and their energy is usually converted into two massless gamma ray photons with a net energy of 1.022 MeV. The masses are entirely converted into energy!

Pair Production A gamma ray can produce an electron/positron pair during an interaction with a nucleus or another gamma ray. The mass and kinetic energy of the new particles is the same as the energy of the gamma ray. Mass is created out of energy!

Large numbers of positrons are formed naturally in Earth's atmosphere. High-energy electrons are ejected from lightning strikes and interact with atoms in the atmosphere to release gamma rays, which interact with other atoms to release electron/positron pairs. The positrons spiral up along Earth's magnetic field lines and have been observed by satellites. Positrons are also important in medical PET body scans. PET stands for positron emission tomography.

14) **SEP Use Evidence to Construct an Argument** When the universe first formed during the Big Bang, there were large numbers of all the elementary particles. How do you know that there were slightly more matter particles than antimatter particles?

15) **CCC Energy and Matter** Develop a hypothesis for why it would be very difficult to build a container to hold antimatter.

Leptons and Quarks

Leptons are elementary particles that that can have a charge of −1, +1 (for antileptons), or 0 (for neutrinos). The most familiar lepton is the electron. Two other leptons, the muon and the tau, also have a charge of −1. However, these leptons are more massive and unstable, only existing for a tiny fraction of a second before decaying into other particles.

Neutrinos are leptons that do not have charge, and they are most curious particles. There are probably about as many neutrinos in the universe as there are protons or electrons (~10^{80}). However, because they have no electrical charge and are nearly massless, they constantly pass right through most matter, including our bodies, without any interactions.

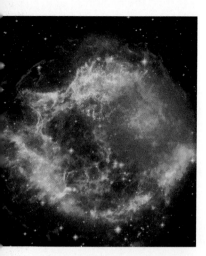

Neutrinos Observations of neutrinos from supernovae have shown that these elusive particles have mass, but their ability to switch from one type to another prevents us from knowing how much.

Neutrinos form in several different ways, including nuclear reactions within stars, radioactive decay, supernovas, and cosmic ray collisions. Neutrinos are stable, and many that formed following the Big Bang still exist. However, most neutrinos on Earth were produced inside the sun.

Cosmic Rays Cosmic rays are high-energy protons and other atomic nuclei that cross space at nearly the speed of light. The galaxy Centaurus A gives off jets of high-energy radiation, including cosmic rays, as matter falls into a supermassive black hole at its center.

Quarks and Hadrons **Quarks** are the basic building blocks of matter other than leptons. Most quarks are only found bound together in twos or threes by gluons. The exception is the enormous top quark, the heaviest of all elementary particles (heavier even than a tungsten atom), which exists for too short of a time (5×10^{-25} s) to bond with other quarks.

Hadrons are particles formed by two or three bound quarks. Hadrons come in two types: **mesons** (formed by two quarks) and **baryons** (formed by three quarks). In each case, the sum of the charges of the quarks adds to an integer: −2, −1, 0, 1, or 2, depending on the kinds of quarks involved.

Neglecting the top quark and its antiquark, there are 150 different possible combinations of quarks in a baryon. Of these, only the proton is stable. This is why protons comprise most of the ordinary matter of the universe. The only other baryon that comes close to being stable is the neutron, which has a mean lifetime (outside of a nucleus) of 14.7 minutes. All other baryons last for only a fraction of a second, and they are observed only in high-energy particle experiments.

Mesons contain one quark and one antiquark. Of the many different possible mesons, the pions (π^+, π^-, π^0) and kaons (K^+, K^-, K^0) are the most common, frequently formed in the secondary particle showers from cosmic ray bursts.

Classifying Elementary Particles

What are the fundamental constituents of matter, and how do they interact?

It's Elementary **Quarks** and **leptons** are elementary particles that **comprise all ordinary matter.** **Bosons,** elementary force-carrier particles, are responsible for the **interactions** among quarks and leptons. Scientists theorize that a force particle for gravity called the graviton exists, but they have yet to find it.

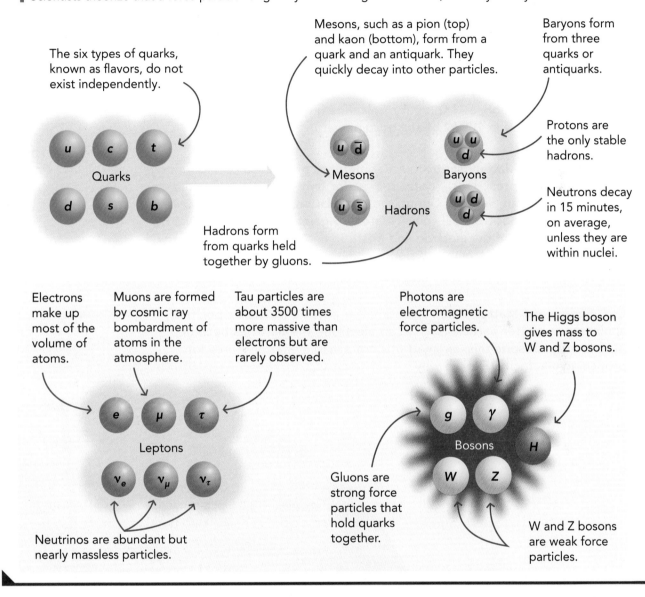

The six types of quarks, known as flavors, do not exist independently.

Mesons, such as a pion (top) and kaon (bottom), form from a quark and an antiquark. They quickly decay into other particles.

Baryons form from three quarks or antiquarks.

Protons are the only stable hadrons.

Hadrons form from quarks held together by gluons.

Neutrons decay in 15 minutes, on average, unless they are within nuclei.

Electrons make up most of the volume of atoms.

Muons are formed by cosmic ray bombardment of atoms in the atmosphere.

Tau particles are about 3500 times more massive than electrons but are rarely observed.

Photons are electromagnetic force particles.

The Higgs boson gives mass to W and Z bosons.

Gluons are strong force particles that hold quarks together.

Neutrinos are abundant but nearly massless particles.

W and Z bosons are weak force particles.

16. **CCC Energy and Matter** If an electron, with a charge of –1, is fired through the magnetic field of a streamer chamber, its path will bend. (Remember that the magnetic force will be perpendicular to the electron's direction of motion.) Describe how the path of a muon through that same magnetic field will be similar and how it will be different. If the muon has the same kinetic energy as the electron, calculate how much slower it is traveling.

17. **CCC Patterns** By looking at the charges of quarks and antiquarks, explain why a meson must always contain one quark and one antiquark and can never contain two quarks or two antiquarks.

INVESTIGATIVE PHENOMENON

 GO ONLINE to revisit your **Investigative Phenomenon modeling activity** with the new information you have learned about Nuclear Particles.

These questions will help you apply what you learned in this experience to the Investigative Phenomenon.

(18) **SEP Use Models** Compared to other leptons in the Standard Model, what two properties of electrons make them good particles for carrying the energy of electricity through power lines?

(19) **CCC Scale, Proportion, and Quantity** Calculate how many electron volts (eV) per second are in 100 W of electrical power.

(20) **CCC Energy and Matter** Positrons are sometimes generated during energy-producing nuclear reactions. Positrons exist for only a short time before annihilating with an electron. During the annihilation, all of the rest mass of the electron and positron will convert into two gamma rays. Use the values of the rest masses of the electron and positron and what you have already learned about the electromagnetic spectrum to show that the photons released are indeed gamma rays.

(21) **CCC Energy and Matter** When an antimatter particle (such as a positron) annihilates a matter particle (such as an electron), the particles become pure energy. Despite this, antimatter is not a viable energy source for producing electricity. Explain why.

 GO ONLINE for a **quiz** to evaluate what you learned about Nuclear Particles.

EXPERIENCE 2

Nuclear Forces

 GO ONLINE to do a **hands-on lab** to model the attraction and repulsion of nuclear particles.

Four Fundamental Forces

Four distinct forces exist in the universe. So far you have studied two: gravity and electromagnetism. Gravity explains things like falling, jumping, rain, rivers, planets, planetary orbits, tides, and the simple fact that people do not fly off Earth into space. Electromagnetic forces explain electricity, magnets, chemical reactions, lightning, collisions, and how atoms are held together. Gravity pulls atoms together to make planets, while electromagnetism gives atoms volume and prevents them from collapsing to a single point.

However, at the level of an atomic nucleus, two new forces come into play: the strong force and the weak force. They control most nuclear processes. Without the strong force, there would be no atoms. Without the weak force, many forms of radioactivity would not occur and fusion within the sun couldn't happen.

(22) **CCC Scale, Proportion, and Quantity** Describe the similarities and differences between electrons orbiting a nucleus and planets orbiting the sun.

Four Fundamental Forces of Nature The strong and weak forces govern interactions within atomic nuclei. The electromagnetic force governs interactions between atoms as well as everyday objects. Gravity dominates at planetary, galactic, and universe-wide scales.

| Strong Force | Weak Force | Electromagnetic Force | Gravity |

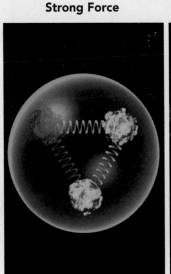   

Strong Force

 GO ONLINE to watch a **video** about subatomic forces.

The **strong force,** also called the strong interaction, is the strongest force at very small distances. It acts between all masses, regardless of electric charge, so it is able to hold protons together against their electrical repulsion. The strong force is even stronger at smaller scales, holding quarks together to make protons and neutrons.

Strong Interaction Among Quarks The strong force holds quarks together in groups of two (forming mesons) or three (forming baryons). At a scale of 1 femtometer (10^{-15} m), the strong force is about 137 times stronger than electromagnetism, a million times stronger than the weak interaction, and 10^{38} times stronger than the force of gravity. For two quarks, the force of attraction is about 10,000 N and, interestingly, does not weaken with distance. The strong force is carried by force particles called gluons.

The strong force has a charge associated with it that is called "color," although it has nothing to do with the colors that you see. This color is analogous to positive and negative electrical charges, except that quarks can have one of three colors: red, blue, or green. The colors of the quarks in a hadron have to balance. Mesons have a color and its anticolor, such as red (+1) and antired (−1), so their color charge is zero. Baryons balance by having a quark of each color.

Strong Force in Baryons The three quarks that form a baryon such as a proton or a neutron are held together by the strong force.

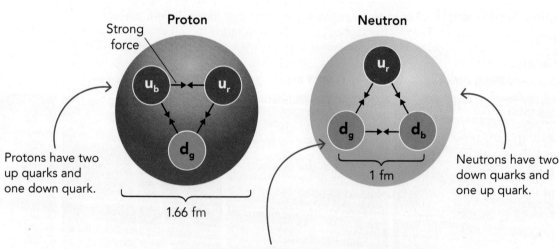

Protons have two up quarks and one down quark.

Neutrons have two down quarks and one up quark.

The three quarks must always have one each of red (r), blue (b), and green (g) colors, similar to balanced electrical charges.

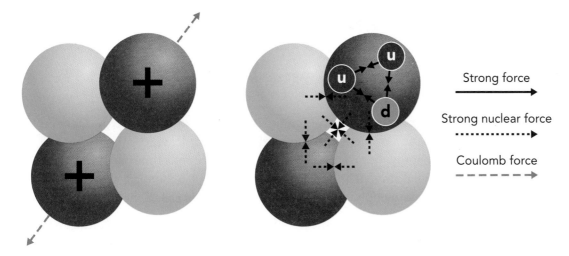

Strong force	→————→
Strong nuclear force	·······▸
Coulomb force	——————▹

Strong Nuclear Force In a ^{4}He nucleus there is just one force pair for the EM repulsion, but six attraction pairs for the strong nuclear force. Each nucleon is also in direct contact with the others, so the strong nuclear force is maximized for each pair. These facts make the ^{4}He nucleus extremely stable.

Strong Nuclear Force Between Nucleons Although the "colors" of the quarks within each nucleon are balanced, some strong force can still be felt outside the nucleon. This manifestation of the strong force, called the strong nuclear force, has a small fraction of the strength it has among the quarks within each nucleon, but it is still strong enough to hold nuclei together. This residual strong force is analogous to the weak electrostatic forces between electrically neutral atoms or molecules.

In a nucleus with many protons and neutrons, the protons strongly repel each other due to their positive charges. The nucleus can exist because the nuclear force of attraction is larger than the electrostatic (Coulomb) force of repulsion. In addition, the strong nuclear force of attraction acts between all nucleons (protons *and* neutrons), whereas the electrostatic force of repulsion only acts between protons.

Unlike the strong force between quarks, the strong nuclear force between nucleons decreases very quickly with distance, much faster than the Coulomb force. This fact means that nuclei cannot get infinitely large. At some size, the force of repulsion among all the positively charged protons overcomes the strong nuclear force, and the nucleus flies apart. This fact is why the largest abundant naturally occurring element is uranium and why there are no stable elements larger than lead. Any atoms larger than lead will undergo a process of decay that will shed protons and neutrons until the atom's nucleus is small enough for the strong nuclear force to hold it together.

(23) **CCC Scale, Proportion, and Quantity** Imagine that the ratio of the strengths of the strong nuclear force to the electrostatic force were slightly smaller than it is. Explain how you think this would affect the number of naturally occurring elements.

Binding Energy

 GO ONLINE to do a PhET **simulation** that allows you to explore the relationship between mass and energy in atomic nuclei.

For all objects, changing position against a force requires energy. Depending on the direction of the force, the particle gains or loses kinetic energy and potential energy. For gravity, we refer to the potential energy of position as gravitational potential energy. For atoms, we call it chemical energy. In all cases, the energy holding the particles together is called the **binding energy.**

When particles come together or "fall" toward each other, they attain a lower energy state, and binding energy is released. This released energy is called a **mass deficit** because mass is a form of potential energy (via $E = mc^2$). For gravitational and electromagnetic interactions, the binding energies are so small that the mass deficits are not usually measurable. You probably never noticed that some mass is always created or destroyed during a chemical reaction or a change in gravitational potential energy.

> **Binding Energy of a Nucleus** An atomic nucleus has less mass than the mass of the separate protons and neutrons. That mass deficit is the binding energy. It must be added to pull nucleons apart and is released when they come together.

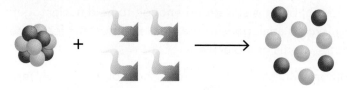

Nucleus (smaller mass)   **Binding energy**   **Separated nucleons** (greater mass)

Binding Energy of a Nucleus
$$B = (Zm_p + Nm_n - m_{nucleus})c^2$$

B = binding energy
Z = number of protons
m_p = mass of a proton (938.27 MeV/c^2)
N = number of neutrons

m_n = mass of a neutron (939.57 MeV/c^2)
$m_{nucleus}$ = mass of the nucleus
c = speed of light

For nuclear interactions, mass deficits are large enough to be observable. Bringing 120 nucleons together releases energy that is equivalent to the mass of one nucleon. This is the source of "nuclear power," where the binding energy is released in the form of the kinetic energy of photons and subnuclear particles. Within protons and neutrons, the strong force holding quarks together is so large that nearly all of the mass of a proton or neutron actually comes from the binding energy, not the rest masses, of the three quarks.

The Scale of Binding Energies

How do the **binding energies** of different **particle interactions** compare?

Big Differences The binding energies for different particle interactions vary greatly depending on the kinds of forces involved and the scales of the interactions.

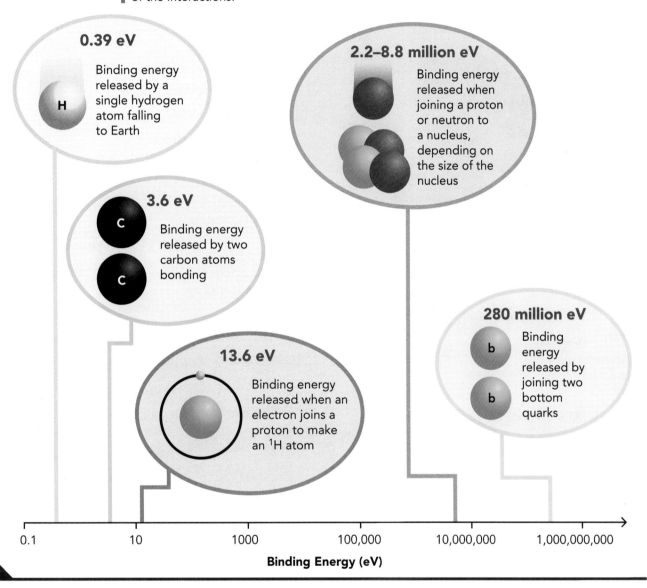

0.39 eV
Binding energy released by a single hydrogen atom falling to Earth

2.2–8.8 million eV
Binding energy released when joining a proton or neutron to a nucleus, depending on the size of the nucleus

3.6 eV
Binding energy released by two carbon atoms bonding

280 million eV
Binding energy released by joining two bottom quarks

13.6 eV
Binding energy released when an electron joins a proton to make an ^{1}H atom

0.1   10   1000   100,000   10,000,000   1,000,000,000

Binding Energy (eV)

---

(24) **CCC Energy and Matter** The rest mass of a neutron is 940 MeV/c^2. It is made of two down quarks and one up quark. The rest masses of the down and up quarks are 4.9 and 2.5 MeV/c^2, respectively. What percentage of the mass of a neutron is its binding energy?

(25) **CCC Scale, Proportion, and Quantity** How is the gravitational potential energy of an object being lifted away from Earth analogous to the binding energy of a nucleus?

Finding the Binding Energy per Nucleon

What is the average binding energy *per nucleon* in the ^{238}U nucleus if the mass of its nucleus is 221,708 MeV/c^2?

1. DRAW A PICTURE Sketch a picture of the situation.

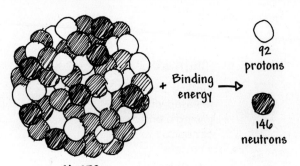

U-238

2. DEFINE THE PROBLEM List knowns and unknowns, and assign values to variables.

$A = 238$

$Z = 92$

$N = A - Z = 238 - 92 = 146$

$m_p = 938.27$ MeV/c^2

$m_n = 939.57$ MeV/c^2

$m_{U-238} = 221,708$ MeV/c^2

3. PLAN AND EXECUTE Use mathematical relationships, the picture, and your definitions to plan and execute a solution.

Find the binding energy of the nucleus.

$$B = (Zm_p + Nm_n - m_{nucleus})c^2 \rightarrow$$
$$B = [(92)(938.27 \text{ MeV}/c^2) + (146)(939.57 \text{ MeV}/c^2) - 221,708 \text{ MeV}/c^2]c^2$$
$$= (86,320.84 \text{ MeV} + 137,177.22 \text{ MeV} - 221,708 \text{ MeV})$$
$$= 1790 \text{ MeV}$$

Divide the binding energy by the number of nucleons.

$$B \text{ per nucleon} = \frac{1790 \text{ MeV}}{238 \text{ nucleons}} = 7.52 \text{ MeV per nucleon}$$

4. EVALUATE Reflect on your answer.
Binding energies per nucleon range from 2.2 MeV to 8.8 MeV. The answer, 7.52 MeV, is reasonable because it lies within this range.

 GO ONLINE for more **math support**.

▶ **Math Tutorial Video**

🖥 **Math Practice Problems**

㉖ What is the average binding energy *per nucleon* in the ^{56}Fe nucleus if the mass of its nucleus is 52,089.80 MeV/c^2?

📖 **NEED A HINT?** Go online to your **eText Sample Problem** for stepped out support.

㉗ What is the average binding energy *per nucleon* in the ^{12}C nucleus if the mass of its nucleus is 11,177.93 MeV/c^2?

㉘ What did you observe about the binding energy per nucleon of the U-238, Fe-56, and C-12 nuclei?

Nuclear Stability

A **nuclide** is a specific combination of protons and neutrons that defines the nucleus of an atom. Despite the infinite possible combinations of protons and neutrons, only 266 nuclides are stable. Most nuclides are not stable and will decay into other nuclides. Nuclides become unstable if they are too large or if the imbalance between the numbers of protons and neutrons is too great.

Force Balance in a Nucleus In nuclei of small or intermediate size, the nucleons remain tightly bound because the strong nuclear force overcomes the electrostatic repulsion between protons. However, the strong nuclear force only operates over very short distances. Each extra proton added to a nucleus feels the combined repulsion of all the other protons in the nucleus, but the strong nuclear force only binds it to the nearest protons and neutrons. At some point, the nucleus becomes unstable. The most stable nuclei occur for isotopes of iron and nickel. The largest stable nucleus is lead-208, or $^{208}_{82}$Pb. The largest nuclide found in nature is plutonium-244, or $^{244}_{94}$Pu.

VOCABULARY

The word **nuclide** has its roots in the word *nucleus*, which is Latin for "inner part," and the Greek word *eidos*, meaning "form." The word *eidos* comes into English as the suffix *-ide*. Therefore, the word *nuclide* refers to the particles found inside the nucleus.

| **Energy Potential** The distance between protons is determined by the combination of the strong nuclear force and the electromagnetic (EM) force. The forces between protons are shown in the graph.

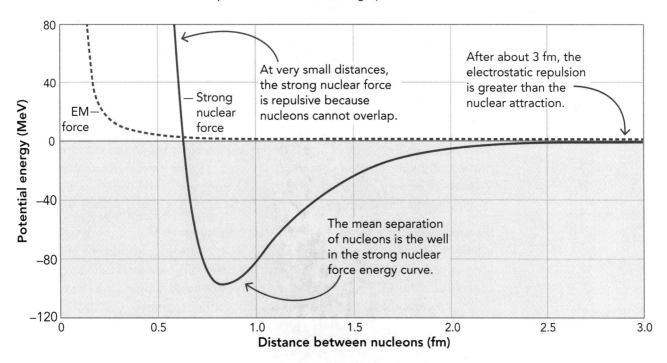

29. **SEP Analyze Data** The net force between two protons is the sum of the two curves: the EM force and the strong nuclear force. Explain how adding them together slightly changes the location of the bottom of the strong nuclear force energy well.

30. **CCC Patterns** How would the graph of the energy potential differ for two neutrons? For a proton and neutron?

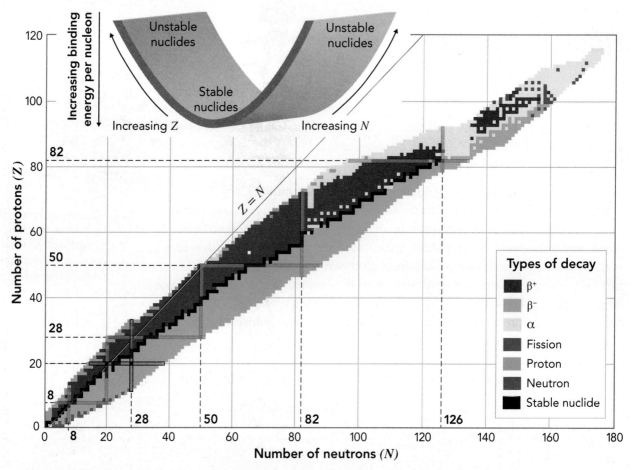

National Nuclear Data Center, information extracted from the NuDat 2 database, http://www.nndc.bnl.gov/nudat2/

Valley of Stability Stable nuclides lie in a valley between unstable nuclides. The magic numbers 8, 20, 28, 50, 82, and 126 indicate values of Z and N that are more likely to have stable nuclides.

Valley of Stability Atomic nuclei become unstable if they have either too many protons or too many neutrons. For each atomic mass number there is a region of maximum stability on a chart of nuclides. Taken together, these regions form a "valley of stability."

Electron shells, or orbitals, have different energy levels that determine how atoms chemically interact. Within the nucleus, neutrons and protons arrange themselves into shells in a similar way, like baseballs packed together in concentric spheres. The arrangement of neutrons and protons in different energy levels within different shells influences the stability of the nucleus. When unstable isotopes decay, they move toward the valley of stability.

As with electrons, nuclei with complete shells of nucleons are more stable. The numbers of nucleons that correspond to these stable states are known as "magic numbers"—8, 20, 28, 50, 82, and 126. Some isotopes that lie relatively far from the valley of stability are stable only when they are "doubly magic," where the number of nucleons is the sum of two magic numbers. For example, $^{48}_{20}$Ca is outside the normal valley of stability, but is far more stable than its position on the graph suggests (48 = 20 + 28).

31 **SEP Analyze Data** Other than hydrogen and helium (which formed during the Big Bang), the most abundant element in our solar system is oxygen. Explain how you might have been able to predict this.

Nuclear Instability

When atomic nuclei are not stable, they change. This change happens by adding particles, subtracting particles, or converting some particles into other particles. If the number of neutrons changes, the element stays the same but a new isotope forms. If the number of protons changes, a new element forms.

Transmutation Scientists now have the ability to change one element into another through high-energy bombardments with other particles. During these high-energy nuclear reactions, particles can be fired into nuclei, knocked out of nuclei, or converted into new particles. These bombardments have allowed physicists to do what the alchemists of old tried for centuries to do without success: convert one element into another. However, the energy required to transmutate elements is enormous, so it is very expensive.

Transmutations take many forms, such as fusing nuclei together (nuclear fusion), splitting nuclei apart (nuclear fission), and adding a single neutron (breeding reactions). Transmutations can also occur through natural means, such as the bombardment of high-energy cosmic rays.

Cosmic Ray Showers When cosmic rays collide with atoms (mostly ^{14}N) in the atmosphere, they trigger a shower of dozens of particles. This process transmutates ^{14}N into ^{14}C. Part of the cosmic ray particle showers includes electromagnetic showers of electrons, positrons, X-rays, and gamma rays. Hadron showers consist of high-energy neutrons, protons, and π and K mesons. Muon showers consist of high-energy muons and neutrinos.

Although phased out of use in 1968, radium was often used in clocks and watches to illuminate the faces in the dark.

Some smoke alarms contain americium, which helps to detect smoke in the air.

These flashlights are illuminated by tritium.

Radioactive Products Radioactive elements have many uses beyond electrical power generation.

Radioactivity The most common forms of natural nuclear transmutations are generally referred to as **radioactivity** because the nucleus emits energy in the form of radiation. This radiation is a combination of particles that usually include photons. There are many different forms of radioactivity, most of which change the composition of the nucleus.

Unstable isotopes that are close to the valley of stability can sometimes exist for years or even millions of years, but isotopes farther away from the valley of stability might exist for just fractions of a second. When radioactivity does occur, the nucleus usually changes in a way that moves the isotope toward the valley of stability. If there are too many neutrons, then a neutron changes into a proton; if there are too many protons, a proton changes into a neutron.

(32) **SEP Construct an Explanation** For years, alchemists tried to make gold, and now people can with transmutation. Explain why it might not be profitable to do so.

Weak Nuclear Force

The **weak nuclear force** (also called the weak force, or weak interaction) governs the decay of subatomic particles and, as a result, plays a major role in nuclear transmutation. The weak force is not only much smaller than the strong force, it also acts over much smaller distances. The weak force acts over distances of about 0.01 fm, which is less than 1% of the size of a nucleus.

Most subatomic particles are not stable; they will decay, or change into other particles, after a short amount of time. Therefore, the weak force is responsible for neutrons and protons changing into each other, the fusion of protons to form helium, the decay of mesons, and most forms of radioactivity.

Beta Decay The lifetimes for particles that decay through the weak force are often very short ($< 10^{-13}$ s). The main exception is a free neutron, which has a relatively long mean lifetime of 14.7 minutes before decaying to a proton and an electron. A neutron is more stable when bound within a nucleus, but it can still easily decay to a proton through a process called beta-minus (β^-) decay. The opposite occurs during beta-plus (β^+) decay, also known as positron emission, when a proton decays into a neutron.

| **Beta-Minus Decay** In β^- decay, a down quark decays into an up quark, turning the neutron into a proton. | **Beta-Plus Decay** In β^+ decay, an up quark decays into a down quark, turning the proton into a neutron. |

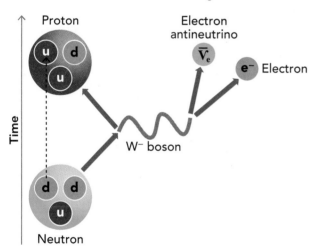

Beta-minus decay

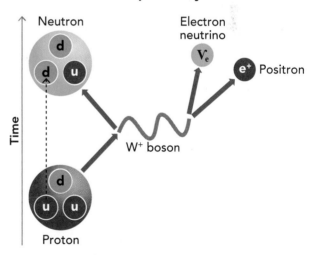

Beta-plus decay

(33) **SEP Develop Models** In beta-plus decay, what will happen to the positron? Given that fact, what will the net reaction products and reactants be of beta-plus decay?

(34) **CCC Energy and Matter** For both beta-decay reactions, show that electric charge is conserved.

The Role of the W Boson In both types of beta decay, the particle decay occurs through force-carrying particles called W bosons. These particles are enormous, with a rest mass of 80.4 billion eV (80.4 GeV), but they last for only 10^{-24} seconds.

It is thought that all of the four fundamental forces have particles that mediate their forces. The strong force is mediated by massless gluons, which bind quarks together within baryons. Electromagnetic interactions are mediated by massless photons. The W bosons play the same mediating role for the weak force, although they do have mass. Only the force of gravity does not seem to have a mediating particle, although some scientists hypothesize that a mediating graviton particle may exist.

Other Types of Decay The weak force can affect all of the fundamental particles of matter and antimatter in the Standard Model. It can cause both stable particles, such as electrons, or unstable particles, such as muons, to decay. For example, both an electron and a muon can absorb a W+ boson and transform into a neutrino.

The weak force can cause the decay of mesons as well as baryons. Mesons, made of a quark and an antiquark, are very unstable and quickly decay to stable particles (such as electrons and neutrinos) and energy. This type of decay commonly occurs during cosmic ray bombardment.

Pion Decay When a cosmic ray hits an atom in our atmosphere, one of the many particles formed is a π^+ meson, also called a pion. The pion is not stable and will quickly decay because of the weak force.

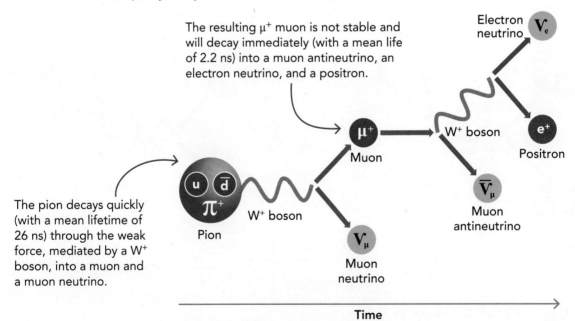

The resulting μ^+ muon is not stable and will decay immediately (with a mean life of 2.2 ns) into a muon antineutrino, an electron neutrino, and a positron.

Electron neutrino V_e

W^+ boson

Positron e^+

Muon antineutrino $\overline{V}_\mu$

μ^+ Muon

W^+ boson

The pion decays quickly (with a mean lifetime of 26 ns) through the weak force, mediated by a W^+ boson, into a muon and a muon neutrino.

u $\overline{d}$ π^+ Pion

Muon neutrino V_μ

Time

(35) **SEP Develop Models** In the pion-plus decay shown in the diagram, what will happen to the positron? Given that fact, what will the net reaction products and reactants be?

(36) **CCC Energy and Matter** Knowing that cosmic rays typically hit atoms at the top of the atmosphere, explain why you are more likely to be hit by a positron than a pion.

GO ONLINE to revisit your **Investigative Phenomenon modeling activity** with the new information you have learned about Nuclear Forces.

These questions will help you apply what you learned in this experience to the Investigative Phenomenon.

37) **CCC Matter and Energy** Electrons are the charge carriers that carry electric power from power plants, some of which are nuclear power plants, to our homes. Describe how electrons can be produced through beta-minus decay.

38) **SEP Use Mathematics** An alpha particle, or ^{4}He nucleus, is the product of nuclear fusion. Binding two electrons to a ^{4}He nucleus to form a helium atom releases 24.6 eV of binding energy. Calculate how many times more is the nuclear binding energy of the ^{4}He nucleus than the atomic binding energy if the mass of the ^{4}He nucleus is 3727.38 MeV/c^2.

39) **CCC Matter and Energy** The direction of electric currents in power lines is defined as the direction of a positive charge moving through the circuit. However, electric currents actually involve negatively charged electrons traveling in the opposite direction. Explain why power lines cannot just have a flow of positively charged positrons instead of the electrons.

40) **SEP Develop and Use Models** From what you know of the magic numbers of nuclear stability, explain why it is not surprising that the isotope lead-208 is the largest stable isotope.

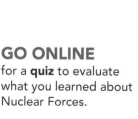 **GO ONLINE** for a **quiz** to evaluate what you learned about Nuclear Forces.

Fission and Fusion

 GO ONLINE to do a **hands-on lab** to build a model to demonstrate how critical mass affects the lifespan of chain reactions.

Converting Mass to Energy

A **nuclear reaction** is a process in which atomic nuclei are transformed by splitting apart or by merging with other nuclei. During all nuclear reactions, energy must be conserved. The energy can take three forms: kinetic energy of masses, electromagnetic radiation, and the masses of particles (via $E = mc^2$).

Three Units of Mass			
Particle	kg	u	MeV/c^2
Electron	9.1094×10^{-31}	0.00054858	0.511
Proton	1.6726×10^{-27}	1.007276	938.27
Hydrogen atom	1.6735×10^{-27}	1.007825	938.78
Neutron	1.6749×10^{-27}	1.008665	939.57

Converting Mass to Radiation When you studied the collision of two large particles, the conservation of energy included the kinetic and thermal energies of both particles, both before and after the collision. With the low-speed collision of an electron and positron, other factors also apply. The conservation of energy now involves the masses of the particles before the collision and the energy of the gamma rays afterward. No mass is left over!

> **Radiation from Electron-Positron Annihilation** If an electron and positron collide head-on (at low speeds, so their kinetic energies are negligible), they annihilate, and their mass is converted into electromagnetic radiation.

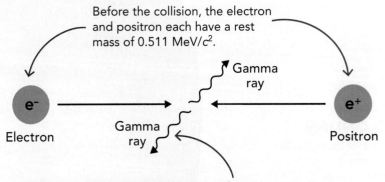

Before the collision, the electron and positron each have a rest mass of 0.511 MeV/c^2.

After the collision, two gamma rays leave in opposite directions. Their energies each equal the energy of the destroyed particles: 0.511 MeV/c^2.

Converting Mass to Kinetic Energy In some nuclear reactions, no gamma rays are created, but the masses of particles before and after the collision are different. In these cases, energy is conserved by having the mass deficit convert into the kinetic energies of the particles.

Collision of ⁶Li and ²H to Form Helium When a lithium nucleus (⁶Li) and deuterium nucleus (²H) collide, the result is two ⁴He nuclei (alpha particles), with 22.2 MeV of mass lost in the process.

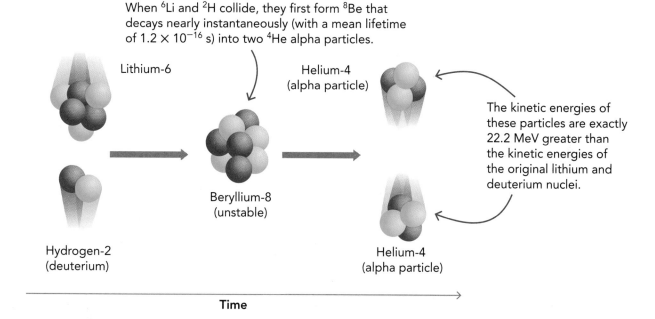

When ⁶Li and ²H collide, they first form ⁸Be that decays nearly instantaneously (with a mean lifetime of 1.2×10^{-16} s) into two ⁴He alpha particles.

Lithium-6

Helium-4 (alpha particle)

The kinetic energies of these particles are exactly 22.2 MeV greater than the kinetic energies of the original lithium and deuterium nuclei.

Beryllium-8 (unstable)

Hydrogen-2 (deuterium)

Helium-4 (alpha particle)

Time

Conservation of Momentum and Charge Although nuclear reactions allow for the creation or destruction of mass, they still obey some of the conservation laws that you encountered earlier. The total electrical charge before and after a nuclear reaction is always the same. Any lost mass is made up for by an increase in kinetic or potential energy. Momentum is also conserved, even when only massless radiation is produced, because photons have momentum (and energy) that is proportional to their frequency.

Conservation of Baryons In addition to the conservation of energy, charge, and momentum, nuclear reactions have an additional conservation law. In any nuclear reaction, the number of baryons (protons and neutrons) remains the same before and after. This even holds true for reactions involving the decay of protons and neutrons. In beta-plus decay and proton decay, a proton converts to a neutron. In beta-minus decay, electron capture, and neutron decay, a neutron transforms to a proton. In every case, the number of baryons stays the same.

41. **SEP Use Mathematics** The momentum of a photon, such as a gamma ray, is equal to Planck's constant (h) divided by the wavelength of the photon (λ). However, you do not need to calculate this to show that momentum is conserved during the electron-positron annihilation shown here. Explain why.

42. **CCC Energy and Matter** Show that the conservation of baryons holds true for the nuclear reaction of ⁶Li and ²H to form two alpha particles.

Curve of Binding Energy

The binding energy per nucleon reaches a peak for nuclides of iron and nickel, which have the most stable nuclei. This stability is a result of the balance between the repulsion of positively charged protons and the attraction of all nucleons via the strong nuclear force. Atomic nuclei smaller than iron and nickel have fewer nucleons, so the net strong nuclear force per nucleon is less. In atomic nuclei larger than iron and nickel, the short-distance strong nuclear force has trouble holding all the protons together.

One way to determine whether a nuclear reaction will absorb or release binding energy is to examine the curve of binding energy per nucleon. Fusing nuclei that are smaller than those of iron results in a nucleus with more binding energy per nucleon, so binding energy is released. Splitting nuclei far larger than iron also results in nuclei with more binding energy per nucleon, so, again, binding energy is released.

Curve of Binding Energy Per Nucleon Any mass difference between the reactants and products is equal (through $E = mc^2$) to the amount of energy that is either released or absorbed by a nuclear reaction.

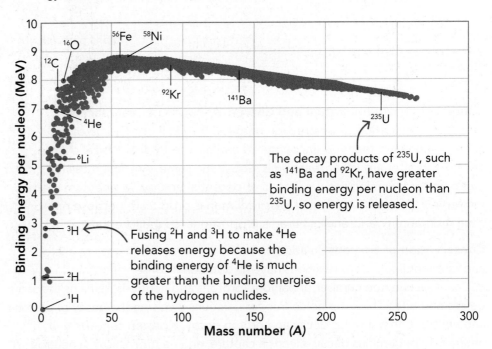

43 **CCC Energy and Matter** Calculate, estimating from the graph, how much energy (in MeV) would be released by the fusion of a ^{4}He nucleus with a ^{12}C nucleus to form an ^{16}O nucleus.

44 **SEP Use Models** Use the Curve of Binding Energy per Nucleon to verify that the collision of ^{6}Li and ^{2}H to form two ^{4}He atoms would release 22.2 MeV of energy.

Nuclear Fission

 GO ONLINE to do a PhET **simulation** that allows you to explore the properties of the products of nuclear fission.

Nuclear fission is the splitting of a large atomic nucleus into smaller nuclei. Certain odd-numbered nuclei, such as uranium-233, uranium-235, and plutonium-239, are **fissile,** meaning that binding one extra neutron to the nucleus provides enough energy (7 to 8 MeV) to overcome the strong nuclear force and cause the nucleus to split apart. It usually splits into two large nuclei and two or three free neutrons, which fly apart at enormous speeds. The nuclear fission of large isotopes is of special importance among nuclear reactions because it has been harnessed (in nuclear power reactors and nuclear bombs) to release huge amounts of energy.

Energy from Fission When a uranium-235 atom splits, the two smaller nuclei have higher binding energies per nucleon, so about 0.1% of the mass of the uranium nucleus is destroyed. On average, this mass is converted into 202.8 MeV of fission energy, most of which (about 169 MeV) is in the kinetic energy of the two new nuclei, which have temperatures of about 2 trillion K. The reaction also releases neutrons with high kinetic energy (about 2 MeV each) and gamma rays (7 MeV). The rest of the fission energy is released later as beta decays of the unstable product nuclei.

| **Nuclear Fission of ^{235}U** The bombardment by a neutron causes the destabilization of a ^{235}U nucleus, which leads to it splitting into two smaller nuclei, releasing energy and free neutrons in the process.

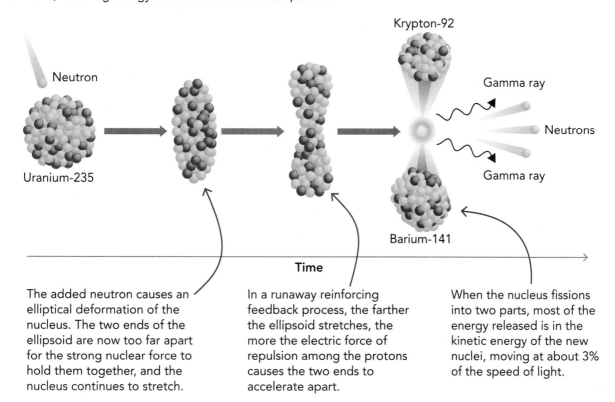

The added neutron causes an elliptical deformation of the nucleus. The two ends of the ellipsoid are now too far apart for the strong nuclear force to hold them together, and the nucleus continues to stretch.

In a runaway reinforcing feedback process, the farther the ellipsoid stretches, the more the electric force of repulsion among the protons causes the two ends to accelerate apart.

When the nucleus fissions into two parts, most of the energy released is in the kinetic energy of the new nuclei, moving at about 3% of the speed of light.

Chain Reactions

EXPERIENCE IT!

Simulate a chain reaction by stacking blocks or playing cards in the shape of a pyramid. Then remove a block or card from the bottom of the pyramid. What happens to the other components of the pyramid?

Nuclear fission releases extra neutrons. The exact number, two or three, depends on the isotope that is splitting and the type and number of products. These neutrons can cause more fissions, releasing more neutrons, and so on, in what is called a **chain reaction.** If the rate of reactions is controlled, as is done within nuclear power reactors using materials that absorb neutrons, then a continuous and steady supply of energy can be released. If, however, the reaction is not controlled, a runaway chain reaction can occur, and all of the fuel fissions at once, releasing an intense blast of energy. This uncontrolled fission chain reaction is what occurs within an atomic bomb.

Nuclear Fission Chain Reaction of ^{235}U The release of extra neutrons by each fission event can lead to a chain reaction that leads to more and more fission events.

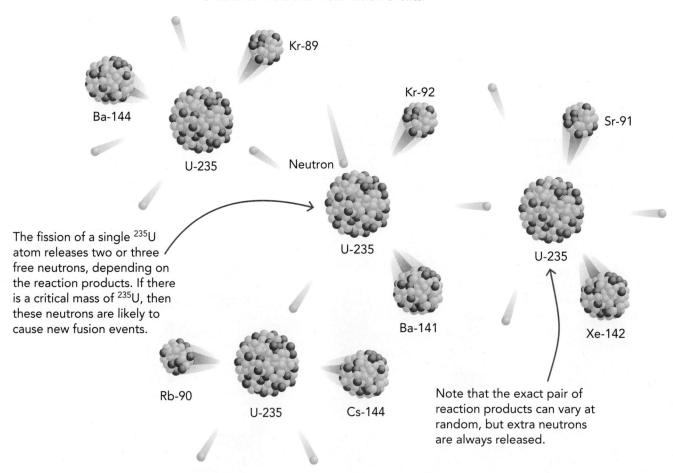

The fission of a single ^{235}U atom releases two or three free neutrons, depending on the reaction products. If there is a critical mass of ^{235}U, then these neutrons are likely to cause new fusion events.

Note that the exact pair of reaction products can vary at random, but extra neutrons are always released.

(45) **CCC Patterns** Compare controlling the rate of free neutrons ejected during a fission reaction to "flattening the curve" of the spread of infections during a pandemic.

(46) **SEP Develop and Use Models** Explain how you can use the two fission products to predict the number of neutrons released by a fission event.

Power From Nuclear Fission

In 2018, nuclear fission power plants provided about 10% of the world's electricity, or about 2500 terawatt hours. There were over 440 civilian fission reactors in operation, with a capacity of about 400 gigawatts. As with fossil fuels, nuclear fission is a nonrenewable form of energy because there are limited geological supplies of uranium and thorium. Once these atoms are split, they no longer exist. However, there is enough uranium and thorium, particularly if extracted from seawater, to run fission power plants for thousands of years.

Applications of Nuclear Fission

What are some of the **practical uses** of **energy** generated from **nuclear fission?**

Nuclear Reactors All nuclear reactors work on the same principle. The **heat from the fission reaction** (from gamma rays and from the kinetic energy and radioactive decay of its products) is used to **turn water into steam in order to run turbines.** These turbines can turn the shafts of electric power generators or the propellers of ocean vessels.

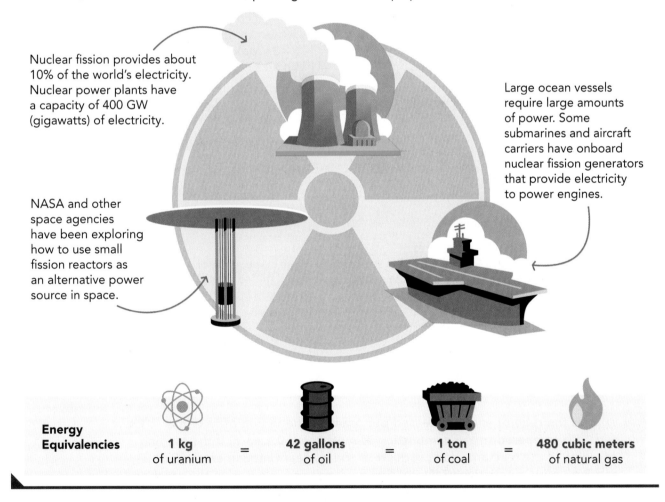

Nuclear fission provides about 10% of the world's electricity. Nuclear power plants have a capacity of 400 GW (gigawatts) of electricity.

NASA and other space agencies have been exploring how to use small fission reactors as an alternative power source in space.

Large ocean vessels require large amounts of power. Some submarines and aircraft carriers have onboard nuclear fission generators that provide electricity to power engines.

Energy Equivalencies

1 kg of uranium = **42 gallons** of oil = **1 ton** of coal = **480 cubic meters** of natural gas

(47) **SEP Defend Your Claim** Considering the output of nuclear reactions, defend an argument for why nuclear fission power could play a role in a country's energy budget at a time when countries are trying to reduce greenhouse gas emissions.

Efficiency of Fuels: Nuclear vs. Hydrocarbon

What is the ratio of energy released per gram by the fission of ^{235}U into ^{141}Ba and ^{92}Kr compared to the combustion of methane (50.1 kJ/g) if the binding energies of the reactants and products of the nuclear reaction are 7.59, 8.33, and 8.51 MeV, respectively?

1. DRAW A PICTURE Sketch a picture of the situation.

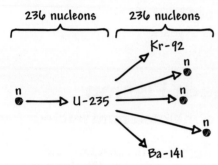

Energy yield = Difference in binding energies

2. DEFINE THE PROBLEM List knowns and unknowns and assign values to variables.

$B(^{235}\text{U}) = 7.59$ MeV

$B(^{141}\text{Ba}) = 8.33$ MeV

$B(^{92}\text{Kr}) = 8.51$ MeV

$E(\text{CH}_4 \text{ combustion}) = 50.1 \text{ kJ/g} = 50{,}100 \text{ J/g}$

$1 \text{ eV} = 1.6022 \times 10^{-19} \text{ J}$

$1 \text{ g} = 6.022 \times 10^{23} \text{ amu}$

3. PLAN AND EXECUTE Use mathematical relationships, the picture, and your definitions to plan and execute a solution.

Find the difference in nuclear binding energy for the reactants and products.	$= 141(8.33 \text{ MeV}) + 92(8.51 \text{ MeV}) - 235(7.59 \text{ MeV})$ $= 173.8$ MeV
Find the difference per amu (per nucleon). Use the total product nucleons (141 + 92 + 3).	$E(^{235}\text{U fission}) = \dfrac{173.8 \text{ MeV}}{236 \text{ amu}} = 0.736 \text{ MeV/amu}$
Convert the energy released by the fission of ^{235}U to joules per gram.	$= 0.736 \text{ MeV/amu} \times \dfrac{6.022 \times 10^{23} \text{ amu}}{1 \text{ g}} \times \dfrac{1.6022 \times 10^{-13} \text{ J}}{1 \text{ MeV}}$ $= 71{,}000{,}000{,}000 \text{ J/g}$
Find the ratio of the fission energy per gram to the combustion energy per gram.	$\text{Ratio} = \dfrac{71{,}000{,}000{,}000 \text{ J/g}}{50{,}100 \text{ J/g}} = 1{,}420{,}000$

4. EVALUATE Reflect on your answer.
The nuclear fission of ^{235}U is 1.42 million times as energetic as the combustion of methane. Because the binding energies in the nucleus are about a million times as great as the binding energies between atoms in a molecule, this answer is reasonable.

 GO ONLINE for more **math support**.

▶ **Math Tutorial Video**

🖥 **Math Practice Problems**

---

(48) What is the ratio of energy released per gram by the fission of ^{235}U into ^{144}Cs and ^{90}Rb compared to the combustion of methane (50.1 kJ/g) if the binding energies of the reactants and products of the nuclear reaction are 7.59, 8.21, and 8.63 MeV, respectively? (Note: two neutrons are released in the reaction.)

📖 **NEED A HINT?** Go online to your **eText Sample Problem** for stepped out support.

(49) What is the ratio of energy released per gram by the fission of ^{235}U into ^{141}Ba and ^{92}Kr compared to the fission of ^{235}U into ^{142}Xe and ^{91}Sr if the binding energies of the products of the second reaction are 8.24 and 8.66 MeV?

Fission Products

The products of nuclear fission are themselves very unstable. This fact is a problem for nuclear power generation because these products are dangerous and must be disposed of carefully.

Radioactive Waste The radioactivity of fission products is a result of the shape of the curve of the valley of stability. Small stable isotopes (such as oxygen-16) generally have equal numbers of protons and neutrons, but large stable isotopes have many fewer protons than neutrons. This occurs because protons repel each other, and having too many protons destabilizes the nucleus. Even though two or three neutrons are ejected when uranium-235 splits, the two products still have too many neutrons: they are far from the valley of stability. As a result, they undergo multiple beta decays (turning neutrons into protons) and gamma decays until they reach a stable nucleus. These decays are the source of most of the radiation from radioactive waste.

Nuclear Fission Reaction Products for Uranium-235 When a ^{235}U atom undergoes fission, it usually splits into two smaller nuclei, but they are quite different in size. This difference is a result of nucleons being arranged in different energy shells within the nucleus. It is entirely random which two reactants result from any given fission.

The other product usually has an atomic mass in the 130–145 amu range.

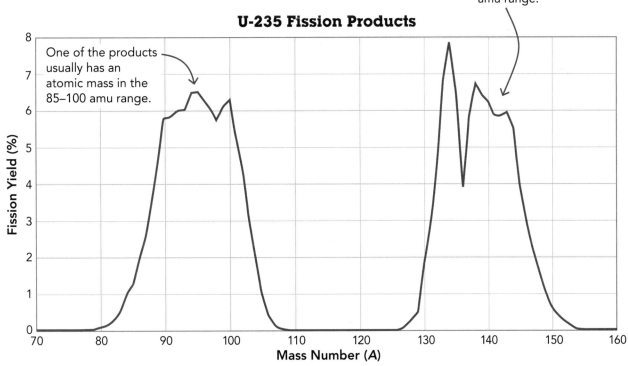

U-235 Fission Products

One of the products usually has an atomic mass in the 85–100 amu range.

50 **CCC Energy and Matter** Suppose that a ^{239}Pu nucleus is bombarded with a neutron and undergoes nuclear fission. If the products are two large nuclei and three neutrons, and one of the large nuclei is ^{103}Zr, use the conservation of baryons to identify the other large nucleus.

Managing Radioactive Waste The waste from nuclear fission is a combination of fission by-products and a variety of actinides (large radioactive elements) that either were part of the original fuel or were produced from the ejected neutrons. As a result, there is a cascade of beta, gamma, and alpha decays that release an enormous amount of energy. Spent reactor fuel rods typically contain about 96% uranium, 1% plutonium, 0.1% actinides, and 2.9% fission products.

For the first 200 years, most of the radiation in the waste comes from the decay of the fission products. After that, lasting for millions of years, most of the radiation comes from the decaying actinides, such as neptunium and americium. In most countries other than the United States, radioactive wastes from commercial nuclear power plants are buried underground.

Breeding Uranium-238, the most abundant naturally occurring isotope of uranium, is not fissile. However, it is "fertile," which means that it can be "bred" through bombardment with a neutron to make plutonium-239, which is fissile. Breeding fertile isotopes can lengthen the lifetime of nuclear fuel and reduce waste.

Radioactive Waste In the United States, no facility to receive and store nuclear waste from commercial power plants exists, so radioactive wastes are stored onsite, often in barrels.

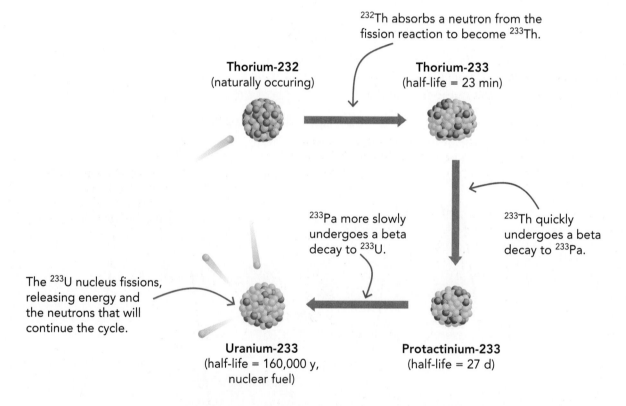

^{232}Th absorbs a neutron from the fission reaction to become ^{233}Th.

Thorium-232
(naturally occuring)

Thorium-233
(half-life = 23 min)

^{233}Pa more slowly undergoes a beta decay to ^{233}U.

^{233}Th quickly undergoes a beta decay to ^{233}Pa.

The ^{233}U nucleus fissions, releasing energy and the neutrons that will continue the cycle.

Uranium-233
(half-life = 160,000 y, nuclear fuel)

Protactinium-233
(half-life = 27 d)

Breeding ^{233}U from ^{232}Th The fissile isotope, ^{233}U, can be bred from the fertile isotope ^{232}Th, and its fission produces the neutrons that continue the breeding. Thorium is much more geologically abundant than uranium, and the fission of ^{233}U also has the advantage of generating less radioactive waste than the fission of ^{235}U or ^{239}Pu.

(51) **SEP Construct Explanations** Explain why, in the breeding cycle of ^{232}Th, the ^{233}U, which is generated from ^{232}Th, is not immediately available for fission reactions.

Fusion

 GO ONLINE to watch a **video** about the difference between fission and fusion.

Nuclear fusion is the combining of two smaller nuclei to make a larger nucleus. For nuclei smaller than iron, fusing them together leads to a more tightly bound nucleus, releasing binding energy in the process. An enormous amount of energy is required to smash small nuclei together so that they overcome the electrical repulsion of the protons. As a result, the only place in the solar system where temperatures and pressures are high enough for this to naturally occur is within the core of the sun, where temperatures exceed 15 million K.

All of the energy that we receive on Earth as sunlight originates from nuclear fusion within the sun's core. This fact means that most of our forms of renewable energy, including photovoltaic solar energy, wind energy, hydroelectric energy, and biomass energy, all of which are driven by sunlight, are ultimately forms of nuclear fusion energy.

Nuclear fusion obeys all of the same conservation laws as nuclear fission. For example, with the proton-proton fusion reaction, which is the initial fusion reaction within the sun, not only is energy conserved before and after, but so is electrical charge and the number of baryons.

VOCABULARY

To help distinguish **nuclear fusion** from nuclear fission, use these reminder words. A fissure is a crack you can use to split something apart. You can fuse objects, such as glasses and metals, by melting them together.

Proton-Proton Fusion The simplest fusion reaction is the fusion of two protons to form deuterium (^{2}H). One of the protons decays to a neutron through β^+ decay.

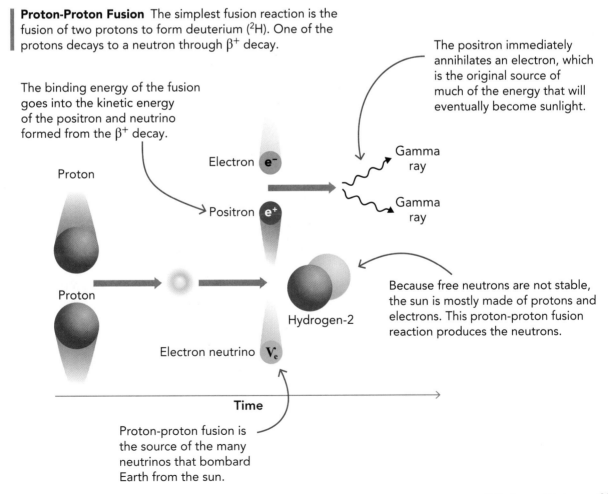

The binding energy of the fusion goes into the kinetic energy of the positron and neutrino formed from the β^+ decay.

The positron immediately annihilates an electron, which is the original source of much of the energy that will eventually become sunlight.

Proton

Electron e⁻

Positron e⁺

Gamma ray

Gamma ray

Proton

Hydrogen-2

Because free neutrons are not stable, the sun is mostly made of protons and electrons. This proton-proton fusion reaction produces the neutrons.

Electron neutrino Vₑ

Time

Proton-proton fusion is the source of the many neutrinos that bombard Earth from the sun.

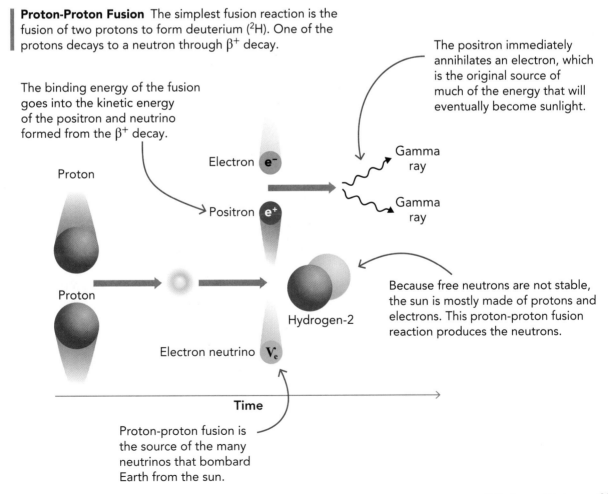

Power From Nuclear Fusion Human-built nuclear fusion reactors can mimic the conditions within the cores of stars and release energy. The strong magnetic fields required to contain the plasma of colliding particles make nuclear fusion much more difficult to control than nuclear fission. Most plans for fusion reactors involve the fusion of two isotopes of hydrogen—deuterium and tritium. Their fusion releases 17.6 MeV of binding energy in the form of the high kinetic energies of the helium and neutron products:

$$^2_1D + ^3_1T \rightarrow ^4_2He \,(3.5 \text{ MeV}) + n \,(14.1 \text{ MeV})$$

Design for a Nuclear Power Plant Engineers are still many years away from being able to build the first commercial fusion power plants.

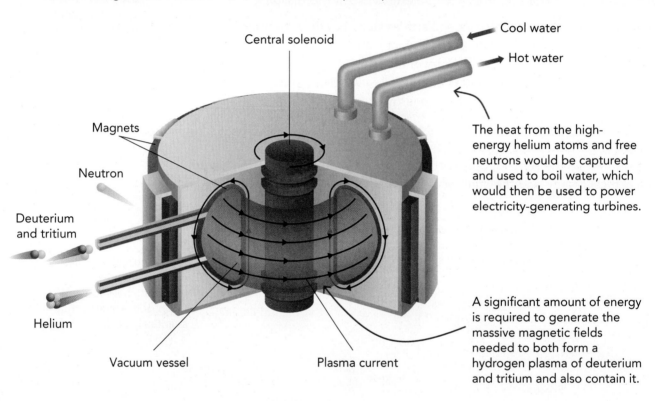

Cool water

Hot water

Central solenoid

Magnets

Neutron

Deuterium and tritium

Helium

Vacuum vessel

Plasma current

The heat from the high-energy helium atoms and free neutrons would be captured and used to boil water, which would then be used to power electricity-generating turbines.

A significant amount of energy is required to generate the massive magnetic fields needed to both form a hydrogen plasma of deuterium and tritium and also contain it.

Unlike electricity generation through nuclear fusion, the technologies required for making nuclear fusion bombs have been mastered for 70 years. These thermonuclear bombs, also called hydrogen bombs or H-bombs because they use the hydrogen isotopes of deuterium or tritium, use a nuclear fission reaction to produce temperatures as high as 300 million K, which then triggers a runaway hydrogen fusion reaction.

(52) SEP Use Mathematics If the mass of a deuterium nucleus is 2.014102 u, use the atomic mass of a proton to calculate the mass deficit produced by proton-proton fusion (in amu) and how much energy (in MeV) is released.

(53) CCC Energy and Matter In the proton-proton fusion reaction, discuss how energy, charge, and baryon number are all conserved.

Comparing Energy Transformations

The world of nuclear reactions is very strange, with forces and particles that are not ordinarily encountered. However, the universe operates with a set of rules that apply across all areas of science. Whether you are working in biology, chemistry, geology, or physics, energy is always conserved in any transformation. For nuclear physics, this requires understanding mass as a form of energy.

Another similarity across scientific fields is that energy transformations will naturally tend toward their lowest energy states. For example, a boulder will roll downhill, not uphill. This fact is the idea behind entropy; the direction of a transformation tends toward objects being more disordered. A tower of blocks falls down, but blocks on the ground don't suddenly leap up and form a tower.

Another way to think of the tendency toward disorder is that time has a direction: toward the lowest energy states. The idea is the same for chemical reactions such as the combustion of wood as well as for boulders rolling downhill. The wood is a more ordered state; the carbon dioxide and ash are a less ordered state. In nuclear physics, the fission fragments are at a lower energy state, a more disordered state, than the uranium atom before it was split.

Entropy Energy is released whenever a system moves toward a lower energy state. The direction of the reactions is driven by entropy and is irreversible. However, some activation energy is always needed to start the reaction.

The activation energy comes from a push. The boulder releases stored gravitational potential energy as it falls.

The activation energy comes from a lit match. The fire releases stored chemical energy as the wood burns.

The activation energy comes from the collision of a neutron. The fission releases nuclear energy when the atom is split.

 CCC Systems and System Models Describe another example of an energy transformation where the system tends to a lower energy state but activation energy is needed.

Revisit

INVESTIGATIVE PHENOMENON

 GO ONLINE to revisit your **Investigative Phenomenon modeling activity** with the new information you have learned about Fission and Fusion.

These questions will help you apply what you learned in this experience to the Investigative Phenomenon.

55 **SEP Construct Explanations** Describe how the electricity that powers your home can come from nuclear fission.

56 **SEP Communicate Scientific Information** For each of the forms of renewable energy in the table, describe how the power of sunlight is ultimately responsible for the energy.

Types of Renewable Energy			
Photovoltaic Solar	Wind Energy	Hydroelectric	Biomass

57 **CCC Energy and Matter** Use the Curve of Binding Energy Per Nucleon graph to explain why the fusion of hydrogen to helium releases more energy per mass than the fission of uranium atoms.

58 **CCC Energy and Matter** Two large isotopes, xenon-137 and strontium-94, are released from an unknown nuclear fission reaction. In addition, three high-energy neutrons are detected leaving the reaction. Explain how to find the unknown isotope that underwent fission. (Remember that it would have absorbed a neutron first.)

 GO ONLINE for a **quiz** to evaluate what you learned about Fission and Fusion.

These questions will help you apply what you learned in this investigation to the Anchoring Phenomenon.

59) **CCC Stability and Change** The human body is about 62% hydrogen. Most of that hydrogen was formed at the time of the Big Bang. However, describe another way that some of the hydrogen atoms in your body may have formed.

60) **CCC Energy and Matter** Iron is a common element in the solar system; it is the single most abundant element within Earth by mass. Your body even contains a significant amount of iron. Use what you know about binding energy to explain why various astrophysical processes might result in the production of large quantities of iron.

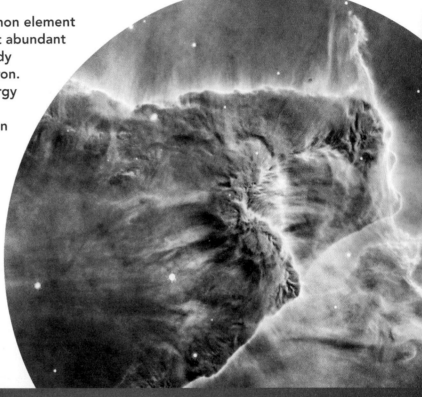

☑ INVESTIGATION ASSESSMENT

 GO ONLINE for activities that will give you an opportunity to **demonstrate what you have learned:**

☑ **Science Performance-Based Assessment** Create and refine a model of the atomic nucleus.

📄 **Engineering Workbench** Compare the energy yield of combusting a mass of fuel versus nuclear fission involving the same mass of nuclear fuel.

💻 **Career Connections** Learn about how a nuclear engineer investigates the nature of matter and its potential for energy generation.

☑ **Investigation Test** Take this test to demonstrate your understanding of nuclear physics.

☑ **Virtual Lab Performance-Based Assessment** Regulate the rate of a nuclear fission reaction inside a nuclear power plant and establish safety protocols to avoid a meltdown.

How did Earth form?

Ages of Rocks

Questions about the formation and age of Earth puzzled scientists for centuries. By counting layers of sediments along the Nile River, which overflowed its banks every year, the ancient Greeks knew that Earth was at least 5,000 years old. Later, scientists measured salts carried to the sea by rivers to calculate how long it would take for the ocean to reach its current level of salinity, or saltiness.

In the 1800s, Lord Kelvin used the rate of heat flowing out of Earth's surface, assuming that Earth had been cooling down since its formation, to determine that the planet was around 20 million years old. This calculation troubled Charles Darwin, who insisted that 20 million years was not enough time for current species to have evolved.

In the 20th century, following the discovery of radioactivity, methods of radiometric dating allowed scientists to pin down Earth's age. In this investigation, you will find that Earth is in fact billions of years old—plenty of time for the evolution of life.

1. **SEP Defend Your Claim** Provide and defend one reason why digging down into the layers of sediments along the Nile River could not give an age of Earth that is billions of years old.

2. **CCC Patterns** Using salinity to determine Earth's age gives a value that is far too low because the ocean's salinity has not changed very much for hundreds of millions of years. Provide a possible reason for this.

3. **SEP Construct Explanations** Not only did radioactivity provide Earth's age, but it also provided the reason why Lord Kelvin's calculations were wrong. Why does the release of heat from radioactivity within Earth make the planet seem much younger than it is?

Radioactive Decay

 GO ONLINE to do a **hands-on lab** to model the half-life of radioactive materials.

Radioactivity

Radioactivity is a general term given to a wide array of processes that involve the release of energetic particles from unstable atomic nuclei. Radioactivity occurs naturally and is either triggered by instability within an atom's nucleus or through the collision of other subatomic particles with it. Radioactivity occurs in many different ways, involving a combination of electromagnetic, strong nuclear, and weak nuclear forces. Radioactivity is very important in geology, as it heats Earth's interior and is ultimately responsible for all interior geologic activity.

Aspects of radioactivity were discovered toward the end of the 19th century by several European scientists, including the Polish-French physicist and chemist Marie Curie. The British physicist Ernest Rutherford first suggested that radioactivity could be used to determine the ages of rocks, which was then proven by Yale University chemist Bertram Boltwood in 1907.

Marie Sklodowska Curie Marie Curie made many discoveries concerning radioactivity. She was the first woman to win a Nobel Prize and the only person ever to win Nobel Prizes in two different fields of science (physics and chemistry).

GO ONLINE to watch a **video** about alpha, beta, and gamma decay.

Ionizing Radiation The particles emitted by radioactive decay travel so fast and have so much energy that they can knock electrons out of neutral atoms, turning these atoms into ions. For this reason, these particles are collectively known as **ionizing radiation.** In other words, they can knock electrons out of atoms so that the atoms become ions. The process of ionization is complicated because high-energy impacts may release not only electrons but also X-rays and other particles. These particles can cause further collisions and more ionization.

Ionizing radiation includes both particles with mass (such as electrons, helium nuclei, and neutrons) and without mass (photons). Only the highest-energy photons in gamma rays, X-rays, and short-wavelength ultraviolet rays are ionizing radiation. Because ionized atoms chemically react with other ions and alter the molecules they are a part of, ionizing radiation is dangerous and damaging to living tissue. The radiation is measured in becquerels (Bq), which is a count of the number of radioactive decays per second.

Three common types of ionizing radiation, called alpha, beta, and gamma radiation, are named after the first three letters of the Greek alphabet. Alpha radiation consists of high-speed helium-4 nuclei. Beta radiation consists of high-speed electrons or positrons. Gamma radiation consists of high-energy (and, therefore, high-frequency) photons.

EXPERIENCE IT!

Use bowling to simulate radioactive decay. Set up pins or blocks and knock them down with a ball. How many rows of pins would it take to absorb all of the kinetic energy of a bowling ball? How many pins would be knocked down? What if you used a tennis ball?

Ionizing Radiation Different ionizing particles interact with matter in different ways.

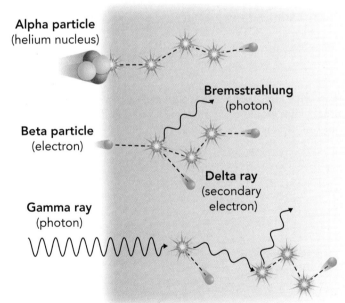

Alpha particles are very ionizing but can be stopped by just a piece of paper or a few centimeters of air.

When beta particles collide with matter, they can release X-rays (known as "Bremsstrahlung") and knock other electrons free.

High-energy photons can ionize matter upon impact. Gamma rays are produced by nuclear processes, whereas X-rays and UV rays are produced by atomic processes outside of the nucleus.

(4) **SEP Develop and Use Models** You have already encountered radiation earlier in the course. Explain how radiation is defined here in a different sense than it was used earlier.

(5) **CCC Energy and Matter** Electrons and helium-4 nuclei are not always considered ionizing radiation. Explain why and when that would be the case.

Exponential Decay

Every unstable isotope decays with a characteristic probability. The decay of a single atom is a random and unpredictable event, but a large sample of that isotope, taken together, will undergo decay at a predictable rate.

One way to compare the decay rates of different radioactive decay processes is to use the half-life, $t_{1/2}$, which is the time it takes for half of the original isotope to decay. The half-lives of radioactive isotopes vary greatly: ^5H has a half-life of just 8×10^{-23} s, but ^{48}Ca has a half-life more than 5.8×10^{22} years.

It is often more useful to work with the mean life (τ) of a radioactive isotope, which is the average time that a single atom will exist before decaying. This time is larger than the half-life because of the large tail on an exponential decay curve. Some atoms exist a very long time before decaying, raising the average. Half-lives and mean lives are related by $t_{1/2} = \tau \ln(2) = 0.693\tau$.

Mean Lives and Half-Lives
$$N = N_0 e^{-\frac{t}{\tau}} \quad \text{and} \quad N = N_0 e^{-\frac{0.693t}{t_{1/2}}}$$
N = number of remaining atoms $\quad$ τ = mean life
N_0 = initial number of atoms $\quad$ $t_{1/2}$ = half-life

Taking the natural log of the equations gives the time required for the initial number of radioactive atoms (N_0) to decay to the current number (N):

$$t = \tau \ln\left(\frac{N_0}{N}\right) = \frac{t_{1/2}}{\ln 2} \ln\left(\frac{N_0}{N}\right)$$

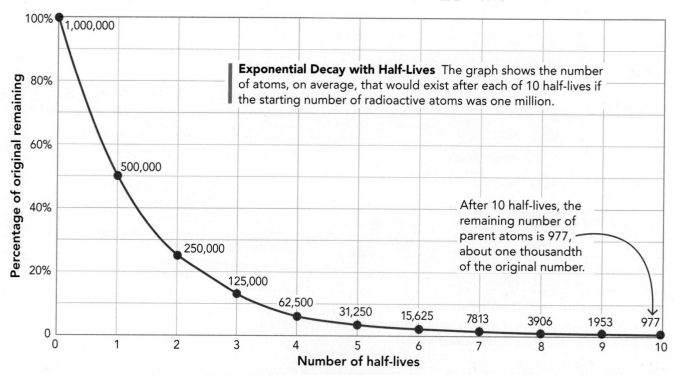

Exponential Decay with Half-Lives The graph shows the number of atoms, on average, that would exist after each of 10 half-lives if the starting number of radioactive atoms was one million.

After 10 half-lives, the remaining number of parent atoms is 977, about one thousandth of the original number.

6 **CCC Stability and Change** The mean life for isotopes of iodine-131 is 11.57 days. What is its half-life (in days and in seconds)?

Exponential Decay

One of the oldest musical instruments yet found was a bone flute made 42,000 years ago. Calculate the percentage of the original carbon-14 that is left in the flute. (The half-life of carbon-14 is 5730 years.)

1. DRAW A PICTURE Sketch a picture of the situation.

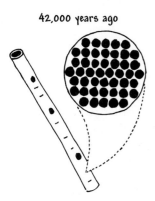

42,000 years ago

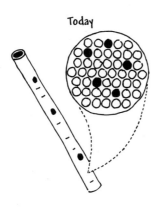

Today

2. DEFINE THE PROBLEM List knowns and unknowns and assign values to variables.

$t = 42{,}000$ years

$t_{1/2} = 5730$ years

$N_0 = 100\%$

3. PLAN AND EXECUTE Use mathematical relationships, the picture, and your definitions to plan and execute a solution.

Choose the correct equation to use to calculate exponential decay.

The half-life of carbon-14 is given, so use:

$$N = N_0 e^{-\frac{0.693t}{t_{1/2}}}$$

Substitute in the known values.

$$N = (100\%)e^{-\frac{0.693(42{,}000\ y)}{5730\ y}} = (100\%)e^{-5.08} = 0.622\%$$

4. EVALUATE Reflect on your answer.

You can round 5730 up to 6000. $\frac{42{,}000}{6000} = 7$, so the C-14 atoms in the flute have decayed about 7 half-lives. The amount is halved after each half-life, so each half-life going back in time would double it. Doubling for 7 half-lives would be $2^7 = 128$, and 1 part in 128 is $\frac{1}{128} = 0.00781$ or 0.781%, close enough to support the answer.

 GO ONLINE for more **math support**.

▶ **Math Tutorial Video**

🖥 **Math Practice Problems**

---

(7) Uranium-235 was part of the material that accreted to form Earth 4.568 billion years ago. Calculate the percentage of the original uranium-235 that is left on Earth today. (The half-life of uranium-235 is 703.8 million years.)

📖 **NEED A HINT?** Go online to your **eText Sample Problem** for stepped out support.

(8) Carbon-11 is an isotope used for positron emission tomography (PET) scans. It has a half-life of 20.4 minutes. If the isotopes arrive in the lab 2 hours after they are made in a cyclotron, how much of the carbon-11 is left?

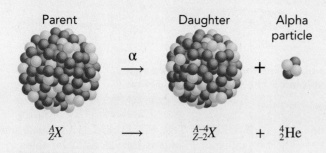

Parent   Daughter   Alpha particle

$$\ce{^A_Z X} \longrightarrow \ce{^{A-4}_{Z-2} X} + \ce{^4_2 He}$$

Alpha Decay Alpha decay removes 2 protons and 2 neutrons, so the atomic mass drops by 4 u and the atomic number drops by 2.

Alpha Decay and Cluster Decay

Alpha Decay The most common form of radioactivity for large atoms is **alpha decay,** where a helium nucleus (α particle) is ejected from a larger atomic nucleus. Nuclei are held together by the strong nuclear force, but during α decay, the strong electrostatic repulsion from the other protons in the nucleus blasts the α particle away at about 5% of the speed of light. Underground alpha decay reactions produce about 95% of the human supply of helium.

Cluster Decay Larger groups of nucleons than α particles can sometimes leave a nucleus during a process called cluster decay. The next most common cluster-decay particle is the carbon-12 nucleus.

Quantum Tunneling in Alpha Decay Alpha emission generally requires a minimum energy of about 25 MeV, but an α particle usually has only 4–9 MeV of kinetic energy, so it can only escape through a process called "quantum tunneling."

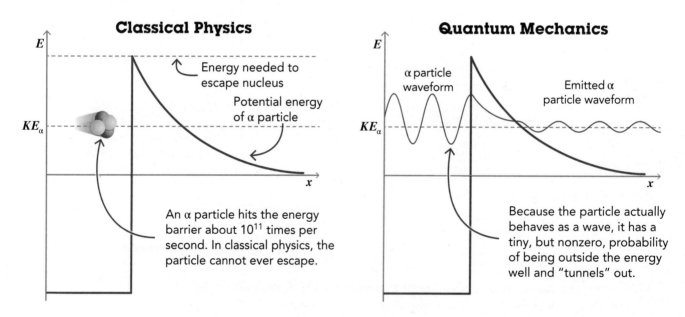

Classical Physics

Energy needed to escape nucleus

Potential energy of α particle

KE_α

An α particle hits the energy barrier about 10^{11} times per second. In classical physics, the particle cannot ever escape.

Quantum Mechanics

α particle waveform

Emitted α particle waveform

KE_α

Because the particle actually behaves as a wave, it has a tiny, but nonzero, probability of being outside the energy well and "tunnels" out.

(9) **SEP Construct Explanations** In theory, an α particle is able to tunnel into a nucleus across the energy barrier as well as tunnel out of it. Explain why tunneling into a nucleus would be much less common.

Beta Decay and Electron Capture

 GO ONLINE to do a PhET **simulation** that allows you to investigate the nuclei of atoms.

Another common form of radioactivity is **beta decay,** when a high-energy electron or positron is ejected from an atom. During beta decay, a quark changes type under the influence of the weak nuclear force. Beta decay has two forms: β^- decay, during which a neutron changes into a proton, and β^+ decay (also called positron emission), during which a proton changes into a neutron. Another type of radioactive decay, called **electron capture,** occurs when an electron is absorbed by a nucleus. The result is similar to positron emission because a proton converts to a neutron.

In all of these decays, the number of baryons, or neutrons and protons, and leptons, or electrons, positrons, and neutrinos, is conserved. (Antiparticles count as –1 lepton.) The result is that the isotope moves closer to the valley of nuclide stability, releasing energy as the kinetic energy of the emitted particles in the process.

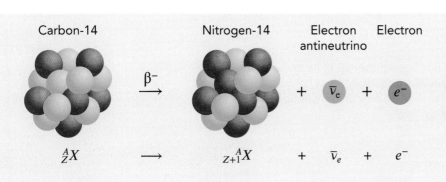

Carbon-14 → Nitrogen-14 + Electron antineutrino + Electron

$$_{Z}^{A}X \longrightarrow {}_{Z+1}^{A}X + \bar{\nu}_e + e^-$$

β^- Decay An isotope with too many neutrons will decay to an isotope with one fewer neutron, emitting an electron and an electron antineutrino.

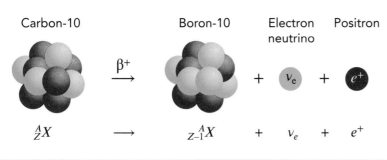

Carbon-10 → Boron-10 + Electron neutrino + Positron

$$_{Z}^{A}X \longrightarrow {}_{Z-1}^{A}X + \nu_e + e^+$$

β^+ Decay An isotope with too many protons will decay to an isotope with one fewer proton, emitting a positron and an electron neutrino.

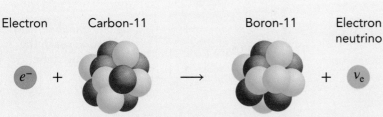

Electron + Carbon-11 → Boron-11 + Electron neutrino

Electron Capture If an isotope has too many protons but not enough energy for positron emission to occur, it will capture one of its own electrons from its lowest electron energy shell.

(10) SEP Develop and Use a Model Write the nuclear equation for the generalized form of electron capture shown in the diagram, in the same manner as the equations for β^- and β^+ decay.

Gamma Decay

Radioactive decay requires only that ionizing radiation be released. Radioactive decay does not require that an atom undergo transmutation, as with alpha and beta decay. The most common example of decay that does not change the composition of an atom is gamma decay, where the nucleus drops to a lower energy state and releases a gamma ray in the process. Gamma rays often ionize atoms that they collide with through the photoelectric effect, which is similar to the process that converts the sun's ultraviolet rays into electricity within solar panels.

Gamma decay often follows an alpha or beta decay, but it can also follow nuclear fission, nuclear fusion, or neutron capture. One example of this process is the two gamma decays that follow the β^- decay of cobalt-60 to nickel-60. The main reaction that occurs most of the time is a three-step process of a β^- decay followed by two gamma decays:

$$^{60}_{27}\text{Co} \longrightarrow {}^{60}_{28}\text{Ni*} + \bar{\nu}_e + e^- (+0.31 \text{ MeV})$$

$$^{60}_{28}\text{Ni*} \longrightarrow {}^{60}_{28}\text{Ni*} + \gamma \ (+1.17 \text{ MeV})$$

$$^{60}_{28}\text{Ni*} \longrightarrow {}^{60}_{28}\text{Ni} + \gamma \ (+1.33 \text{ MeV})$$

Red Forest These trees died due to contamination from the Chernobyl disaster, exposing them to high levels of alpha, beta, and gamma radiation.

Gamma Decay β^- decay does not leave nickel-60 at its lowest energy state. Instead, gamma decays complete the transition. Most (99.88%) of the time, the emitted particles have a relative small amount of kinetic energy and the Ni-60 atom is still at a high energy level.

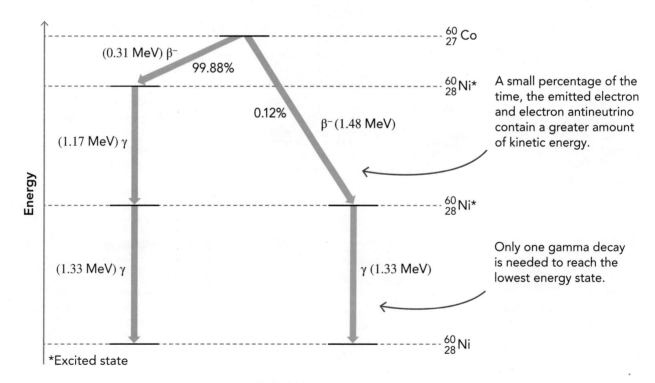

A small percentage of the time, the emitted electron and electron antineutrino contain a greater amount of kinetic energy.

Only one gamma decay is needed to reach the lowest energy state.

11) **SEP Use Models** Prove, using math, that the nickel-60 isotope ends up at the same energy level whichever path the reactions take.

Other Means of Radioactive Decay

How else does **radioactive decay** occur?

> **Other Types of Decay** There are other kinds of decay processes that release energy besides alpha, beta, and gamma decay. **Not all of these processes form a new element.** Most are a result of the weak force.

Neutron emission involves the **loss of one or more neutrons.** It occurs only for very neutron-rich isotopes such as ^{4}H, ^{5}H, ^{5}He, ^{10}Li, etc. These often have **very short half-lives:** the neutron emission of ^{5}He to make ^{4}He occurs with a half-life of only 7×10^{-22} s.

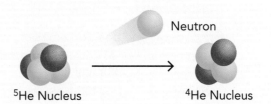

Neutron

^{5}He Nucleus

^{4}He Nucleus

New Element Formed: **NO**

Proton emission is the proton equivalent of neutron emission and occurs only for **very proton-rich nuclei.** It is **very rare and is not observed in nature,** but it can occur within nuclei produced during high-energy bombardment experiments. This was first observed in 1969 for the decay of ^{53}Co to ^{52}Fe.

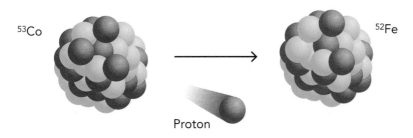

^{53}Co

^{52}Fe

Proton

New Element Formed: **YES**

Spontaneous fission is similar to **nuclear fission,** but it happens naturally for very large actinides such as ^{235}U and ^{238}U. The **half-lives are much longer than for alpha decay,** making spontaneous fission very rare. The spontaneous fission of ^{235}U and ^{238}U atoms leaves defects in mineral crystals, which can be used to help date some types of rocks.

New Element Formed: **YES**

Internal conversion occurs when **an inner electron interacts with the nucleus and attains enough energy to be ejected from the atom.** The hole in the electron shell left by the ejected electron is then filled by an electron from a higher shell, often emitting an X-ray in the process.

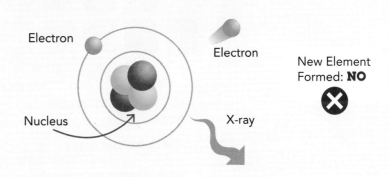

Electron

Electron

Nucleus

X-ray

New Element Formed: **NO**

---

(12) **CCC Energy and Matter** Explain why some of the decays shown in the illustration of other means of radioactive decay will result in a new element and some will not.

Radioactivity and the Valley of Stability

When radioactivity occurs, the ultimate result is to move an isotope either onto or closer to the valley of stability. Isotopes above the valley of stability have too many protons and will usually decay by positron emission (β^+ decay) or proton emission. Isotopes below the valley have too many neutrons and usually decay by β^- decay or neutron emission.

For β^- decay and positron emission, the resulting isotopes are isobars—they have the same number of nucleons (protons and neutrons). These decays happen relatively slowly, with half-lives of milliseconds to millions of years. For neutron and proton emission, however, resulting nuclei are smaller, losing neutrons and/or protons. These reactions occur very quickly, usually in about 10^{-22} s. Half-lives are generally shorter the farther you get from the valley of stable isotopes. Alpha decay is fast for small nuclides and slow for large nuclides.

Decay Paths for Radioactivity Zooming in on the nuclide chart to examine small nuclei shows patterns in the types of decay and half-lives, and it demonstrates how the result of decay is to move an atom toward stable isotopes.

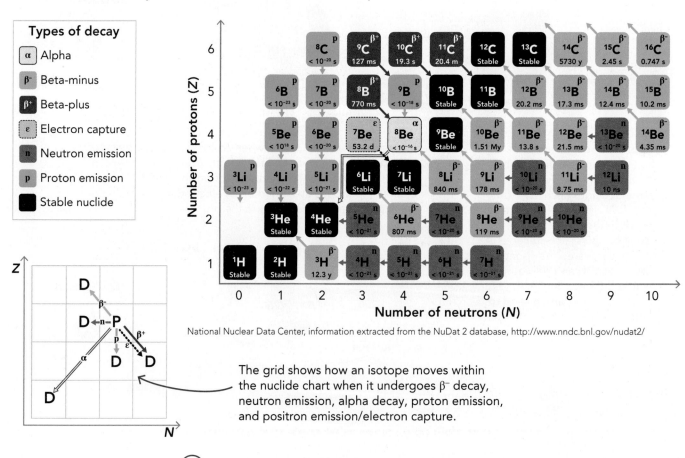

National Nuclear Data Center, information extracted from the NuDat 2 database, http://www.nndc.bnl.gov/nudat2/

The grid shows how an isotope moves within the nuclide chart when it undergoes β^- decay, neutron emission, alpha decay, proton emission, and positron emission/electron capture.

(13) **CCC Energy and Matter** Describe the similarities and differences between the decay paths of carbon-11 and beryllium-11.

(14) **CCC Energy and Matter** Beryllium-12 eventually decays to the stable carbon-12. Determine the particles that are released in this process.

Decay Series for Large Nuclei

The largest stable isotopes are lead isotopes, which all have an atomic number of 82. For isotopes of the actinides, which are large elements with atomic numbers from 89 to 103, stability cannot be reached through a single decay. Instead, a long cascade of radioactive decays, usually combinations of alpha and β^- decays, is required in order to reach a stable isotope.

Many actinide isotopes have more than one decay mode, so there are multiple paths for the decay chain. For example, the decay chain of uranium-238 can take several paths before it ends up as a stable isotope, lead-206.

Decay Chain of Uranium-238 Uranium-238 takes billions of years to decay to thorium-234, but then it undergoes a long sequence of faster decays with half-lives ranging from less than a second to 77,000 years. Each decay releases additional energy, for a total of 51.8 MeV from 8 alpha decays and 6 β^- decays.

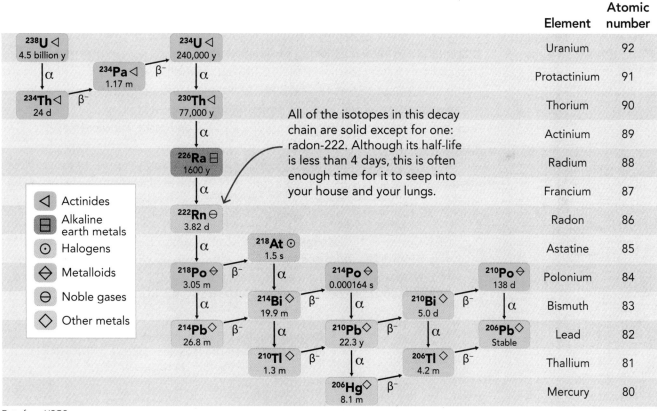

Data from USGS

15) **SEP Use Mathematics** Suppose that a layer of rock containing uranium-238 was deep enough that it took weeks for the radon-222 gas to reach the surface. Explain how some radon could still be leaking into the house.

16) **SEP Develop and Use Models** List out three different decay paths for lead-214 to decay to lead-206. What feature of the path is the same for all three?

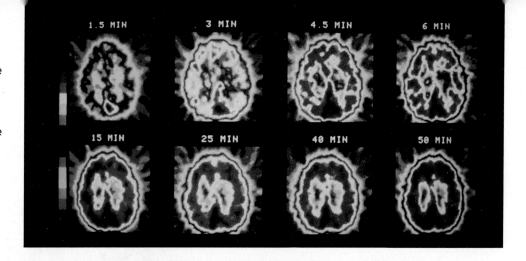

Radioactive Tracer These PET scans of the human brain use a radioactive tracer to show regions that are undergoing active protein synthesis.

Radiation Technologies

Ionizing radiation is hazardous to human living tissue. Sadly, Marie Curie died of aplastic anemia, a result of her long exposures to radioactivity. However, radioactivity also serves important roles in many areas of biology and medicine.

Radiolabeling involves placing radioactive isotopes of certain atoms within a molecule to follow the molecule's pathway through a set of chemical reactions. Molecular imaging uses radiotracers to visualize and quantify various biological processes using either positron emission tomography (PET) or single-photon emission computed tomography (SPECT). PET and SPECT indicate where in the body a radioactive tracer has gone and how much of the tracer has accumulated. Radiation therapy actually uses the deadly nature of radioactive isotopes to directly kill malignant cancer cells, particularly for cancers that are in difficult-to-access places.

17) **SEP Construct Explanations** PET scans rely on isotopes with very short half-lives (minutes to tens of minutes), so they are rushed from the cyclotrons where they are made to hospitals where they are used. Explain why doctors do not use isotopes with longer half-lives.

Radiation Safety This technician can safely perform multiple PET scans because her lead vest absorbs harmful radiation before it reaches her body.

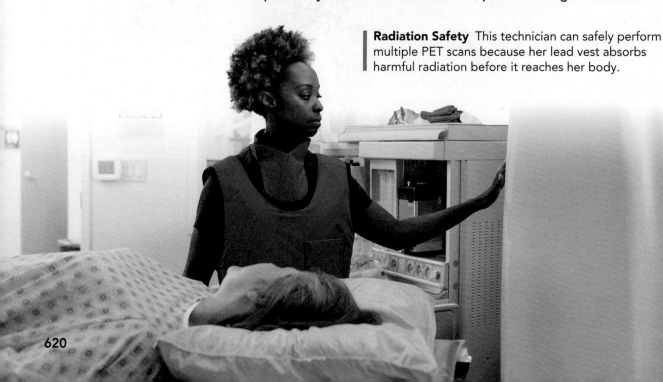

Revisit

INVESTIGATIVE PHENOMENON

GO ONLINE to revisit your **Investigative Phenomenon CER** with the new information you have learned about Radioactive Decay.

These questions will help you apply what you learned in this experience to the Investigative Phenomenon.

18 **SEP Ask Questions** Given what you have just learned about radioactive decay, think about how scientists could use radioactivity to determine Earth's age. What questions do you still need answered?

19 **CCC Energy and Matter** Earth formed with more thorium in its interior than uranium. Thorium is currently about three times more abundant on Earth than uranium. Suppose the radioactive isotope thorium-228 undergoes four alpha decays in a row. Calculate the isotope that results.

20 **CCC Structure and Function** Earth formed with uranium, thorium, and potassium, which decay to provide Earth's interior with the energy for plate tectonics. During beta-minus decay, an atom loses an electron and forms a new element. However, you learned previously that atoms form positively charged ions when they lose electrons, but they do not change type. Explain why the atom becomes a new element in this case but not during the formation of ions.

21 **CCC Energy and Matter** Most of Earth's helium has formed slowly over time from radioactive decay. The Decay Paths for Radioactivity figure shows that helium-4 can form from either helium-5 or lithium-5, but explain why neither of these reactions can explain the slow formation of Earth's helium.

GO ONLINE
for a **quiz** to evaluate what you learned about Radioactive Decay.

EXPERIENCE 2

Radiometric Dating

GO ONLINE to do a **hands-on lab** that models finding the ages of rock layers at an archaeological dig.

Parents and Daughters

If you are trying to determine the age of a rock, the information you have to work with can vary. Sometimes the starting amount (P_0) and the current amount (P) of the **parent isotopes,** radioactive elements before they decay, are known. In those cases, you can use the exponential decay equations that were introduced in the learning experience on radioactive decay.

In other cases, the starting amount is unknown, but the amount of **daughter isotopes,** or radioactive decay end products, is known. If the daughters are stable, then the total number of daughters (D) and parents (P) is equal to the original number of parents ($P_0 = P + D$). If no daughters were in the original material, then the age can be calculated using the following equation.

Age of Material
$$t = \frac{t_{1/2}}{\ln 2} \ln\left(1 + \frac{D}{P}\right), \text{ where } D = P\left(e^{\frac{(\ln 2)t}{t_{1/2}}} - 1\right)$$
t = age of material D = number of daughter isotopes $t_{1/2}$ = half-life of material P = number of parent isotopes

Unfortunately, for most parent-daughter pairs, these equations cannot be used to date objects. For most decays, the daughter isotope is also unstable and quickly decays into other isotopes that may also be unstable. In addition, some isotopes undergo more than one kind of decay, and most radioactive isotopes are extremely rare. As a result, only a small number of radioactive isotopes can be used for determining the ages of objects.

22 **CCC Energy and Matter** One radioisotope of the element samarium (Sm), samarium-147, has a half-life longer than the age of Earth. Explain how you could know what kind of radioactive decay would be responsible for the transmutation of samarium-147 ($^{147}_{62}\text{Sm}$) to neodymium-143 ($^{143}_{60}\text{Nd}$).

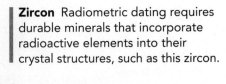

Zircon Radiometric dating requires durable minerals that incorporate radioactive elements into their crystal structures, such as this zircon.

Carbon-14 Age Dating

The best-known form of radiometric age dating is carbon-14 dating. Carbon is plentiful in all living things, so C-14 dating is good for wood, bones, shells, and all other organic objects. C-14 has an excellent half-life (5,730 years) for dating objects as old as 60,000 years. And, C-14 continually forms in the atmosphere by the bombardment of nitrogen-14 from cosmic rays, so new C-14 atoms are constantly being incorporated into living things.

However, atmospheric C-14 formation also presents a problem. C-14 undergoes β^- decay and turns back into N-14. N-14 is abundant, making up 79% of Earth's atmosphere, so parent/daughter relationships cannot be used to determine ages. Either the current amounts of the parent and daughter (P and D) or the current and original amounts of the parent (P and P_0) are needed to find the age. Fortunately, scientists can use the relative abundances of carbon isotopes to calculate the original amount of C-14 (P_0) in a sample.

To determine the age of organic remains, measure the amount of C-12, C-13, and C-14 in an object. The amount of C-14 is the remaining parent isotope, P. The original amount of the parent isotope, P_0, is inferred by measuring the amount of C-12 and C-13, which has remained constant, and dividing the sum by 1 trillion. Then, use the following equation to find the age: $t = \frac{t_{1/2}}{\ln 2} \ln\left(\frac{P_0}{P}\right)$.

| **Carbon-14 Dating** The carbon cycle shows why carbon-14 is ideal for dating organic relics.

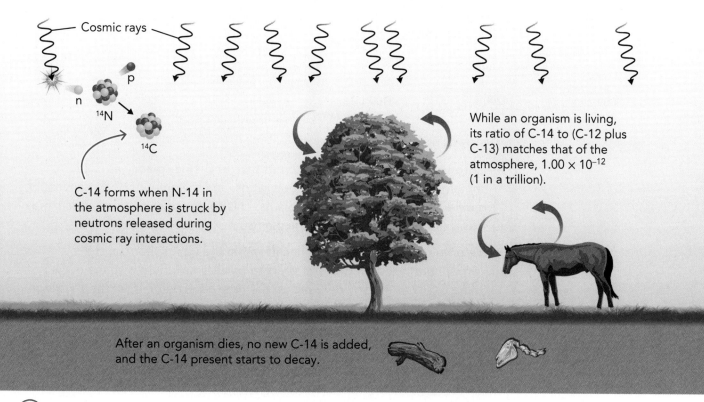

Cosmic rays

^{14}N

p

n

^{14}C

C-14 forms when N-14 in the atmosphere is struck by neutrons released during cosmic ray interactions.

While an organism is living, its ratio of C-14 to (C-12 plus C-13) matches that of the atmosphere, 1.00×10^{-12} (1 in a trillion).

After an organism dies, no new C-14 is added, and the C-14 present starts to decay.

(23) **SEP Construct Explanations** Use the half-life of C-14 to explain why radiocarbon dating is hard to do for objects that are more than 60,000 years old.

Calibrating C-14

Sources of C-14 Dating Errors In practice, carbon-14 dating is much more complicated than plugging numbers into an equation. Many factors can cause the calculated C-14 age to be in error.

- **Atmospheric effects** About a third of the carbon in today's atmosphere is the result of carbon dioxide produced by the combustion of fossil fuels. Because fossil fuels are very old, they contain no C-14, significantly lowering the C-14/C-12 ratio in the atmosphere. Conversely, the testing of nuclear bombs, which peaked in the mid-1960s, doubled the amount of C-14 in the atmosphere. In addition, exposing a sample to today's air, with its differing C-14/C-12 ratio, can contaminate the sample.

- **C-14 production rates** The production of atmospheric C-14 is not constant. Increased periods of solar activity, as shown by the graph, can interfere with C-14 production from cosmic ray bombardment.

Solar Interference Solar wind interferes with the cosmic rays that would normally reach Earth, so periods of greater solar activity reduce the production of C-14.

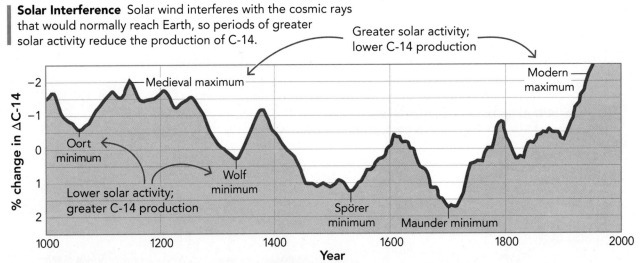

Republished with permission of John Wiley and Sons from Reimer, P. J., et al. (2004), IntCal04 terrestrial radiocarbon age calibration, 0–26 cal kyr BP, Radiocarbon, 46(3), 2004; permission conveyed through Copyright Clearance Center, Inc.

- **Isotopic fractionation** Plants do not take in C-14 as readily as C-12, contaminating their carbon isotope ratios, and the amount of contamination is different for land and marine plants. This source of error also impacts the fossils of the animals that eat the plants.

- **Reservoir effects** C-14 is produced within the atmosphere, and the atmosphere takes hundreds of years to reach equilibrium with the ocean. Some C-14 has already decayed by the time equilibrium is reached, giving ocean fossils a slightly older apparent age.

Calibration Curve To account for all of these sources of contamination, scientists have developed a calibration curve for past atmospheric C-14 levels. Fortunately, there are several different types of data of different ages from which the C-14 calibration curve can be made.

(24) **CCC Systems and System Models** Explain how the burning of fossil fuels has changed the ratio of C-14 to C-12 in the atmosphere.

True Ages The calibration curve provides the accurate true age for a given apparent age determined from the observed C-14/C-12 ratio in an object.

C-14 Calibration Curve The dashed line shows that the true ages are slightly younger than the uncalibrated ages.

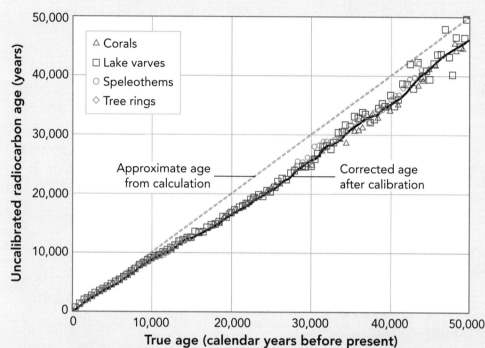

Approximate age from calculation ——— Corrected age after calibration

Data from: P J Reimer *et al.*

Cave formations called speleothems grow a new layer from the annual cycle of rainwater percolating into a cave. They are not organic, but they are made of calcite ($CaCO_3$), which contains carbon.

Corals can grow annual layers that can be counted. In addition, calm oceanic basins can record annual layers of sediments containing fossils.

Trees form a new layer of wood every year. The C-14 calibration curve for the past 12,000 years is largely based on carbon from current and fossilized tree rings.

Lake varves are fine layers of silt that form each year at the bottom of very calm lakes. They contain pollen grains and other carbon-bearing materials that can be analyzed.

25 **Connect to Nature of Science** Explain why it is good practice to include many different data sets and many data points within each set.

26 **SEP Analyze and Interpret Data** Suppose that laboratory radiometric dating gives the age of a bone as 20,000 years. Using the calibration curve, what is the actual age of the bone?

Radiometric Dating of Charcoal

An archaeologist runs a radiocarbon test on charcoal found near the city of Jericho. The results from the mass spectrometer show that for each gram of carbon there is 3.31×10^{-13} g of C-14 remaining from the original amount of 10^{-12} g. How old is the charcoal?

1. DRAW A PICTURE Sketch a picture of the situation.

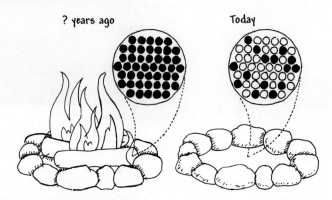

? years ago   Today

2. DEFINE THE PROBLEM List knowns and unknowns and assign values to variables.

$P = 3.31 \times 10^{-13}$ g per g C

$P_0 = 1.00 \times 10^{-12}$ g per g C

$t_{1/2} = 5730$ years

3. PLAN AND EXECUTE Use mathematical relationships, the picture, and your definitions to plan and execute a solution.

Find the apparent age of the charcoal.

$$t = \frac{t_{1/2}}{\ln 2} \ln\left(\frac{P_0}{P}\right) = \frac{5730 \text{ y}}{\ln 2} \ln\left(\frac{1.00 \times 10^{-12} \text{ g}}{3.31 \times 10^{-13} \text{ g}}\right)$$
$$= 9140 \text{ y}$$

Use the calibration curve to find the true age of the charcoal.

The point on the calibrated curve that corresponds to a calculated age of 9140 y is about 11,000 y.

4. EVALUATE Reflect on your answer.
The calibration curve shows that initial calculated ages are younger than true ages. In addition, the current amount of C-14 (3.31×10^{-13} g) is about 1/3 of the starting amount (10×10^{-13} g), so the age should be between one half-life (5730 y), which would have 1/2 of the C-14 left, and two half-lives (11,460 y), which would have 1/4 of the C-14 left. The calculated answer, 9140 y, is in between 5730 y and 11,460 y. The answer makes sense.

 GO ONLINE for more **math support**.

▶ **Math Tutorial Video**

🖥 **Math Practice Problems**

---

27 The results from the mass spectrometer for another sample show that for each gram of carbon there is about 1.40×10^{-14} g of C-14 remaining from the original amount of 10^{-12} g. How old is the fossil horse bone?

📖 **NEED A HINT?** Go online to your **eText Sample Problem** for stepped out support.

28 Consider another fossil. For each gram of carbon there is 6.22×10^{-15} g of C-14 remaining from the original amount of 10^{-12} g. How old is the fossil? Given the data on the calibration curve, discuss the reliability of the calibration age.

Age Dating Older Rocks

Most rocks at Earth's surface are far too old to be dated with C-14. Radioactive isotopes with much longer half-lives must be used to determine their ages. The methods involved also have possible sources of error. For example, the parent and/or daughter isotopes can leach out of rock crystals during metamorphic events with high temperatures, which would result in inaccurate dating.

For many parent/daughter pairs, the starting values of both are unknown. As a result, scientists often use the ratios of both parent and daughter with respect to a stable isotope that does not change. A common example of this is rubidium-87, which undergoes β^- decay to strontium-87 with a half-life of 49.7 billion years. The stable isotope used as an unchanging reference is strontium-86.

Age of Rock Using Rubidium-Strontium Dating

$$t = \ln(m + 1)\tau$$

t = age of rock
τ = mean life of ^{87}Rb, 7.17×10^{10} y
m = slope of the ^{87}Sr/^{86}Sr vs. ^{87}Rb/^{86}Sr graph

Rubidium-Strontium Age Dating To date a rock, plot isotope ratios measured from different samples within a single rock. As the ^{87}Rb decays to ^{87}Sr, the ratios of the three samples will move up and to the left on the graph. The slope of the line will go from flat to sloped, and measuring the slope will give the age of the rock.

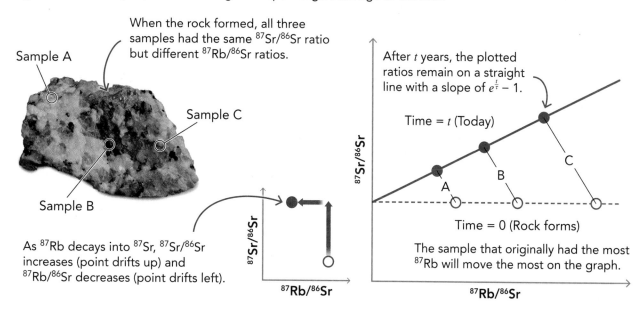

When the rock formed, all three samples had the same ^{87}Sr/^{86}Sr ratio but different ^{87}Rb/^{86}Sr ratios.

Sample A

Sample C

Sample B

As ^{87}Rb decays into ^{87}Sr, ^{87}Sr/^{86}Sr increases (point drifts up) and ^{87}Rb/^{86}Sr decreases (point drifts left).

After t years, the plotted ratios remain on a straight line with a slope of $e^{\frac{t}{\tau}} - 1$.

Time = t (Today)

A
B
C

Time = 0 (Rock forms)

The sample that originally had the most ^{87}Rb will move the most on the graph.

---

29 **SEP Analyze Data** Using the equation for rubidium-strontium dating, suppose that the mineral grains of a rock are analyzed and the current slope on the ^{87}Sr/^{86}Sr vs. ^{87}Rb/^{86}Sr graph is 0.0476. Find the age of the rock.

Uranium-Lead Dating

▶ **GO ONLINE** to watch an Explain **video** about radiometric dating.

One of the most reliable forms of determining the ages of very old rocks is the uranium-lead method. This method simultaneously uses two parent-daughter pairs, $^{238}U/^{206}Pb$ and $^{235}U/^{207}Pb$, which contain long cascades of decays. As the rock containing these four isotopes gets older and the uranium turns to lead, a plot of the two ratios shows an arcing curve called a **concordia.**

The isotopes ^{206}Pb and ^{207}Pb form only from the decay of uranium, so rocks form with neither isotope present. As a result, both the $^{206}Pb/^{238}U$ and $^{207}Pb/^{235}U$ ratios are zero when the rock forms. As uranium decays to lead, these ratios increase at different rates because the half-lives of the uranium isotopes are different, leading to the arcing concordia.

Uranium-lead dating typically uses samples of the mineral zircon, which retains uranium atoms very well. If zircon also retained lead atoms, the age of a rock could be found by simply plotting the ratios on the concordia. However, zircon does not retain lead atoms well, but measurements can still pinpoint the correct location on the concordia using the method described in the diagram.

Uranium-Lead Age Dating You can plot measurements of $^{207}Pb/^{235}U$ and $^{206}Pb/^{238}U$ ratios for different samples of a rock to find the rock's age.

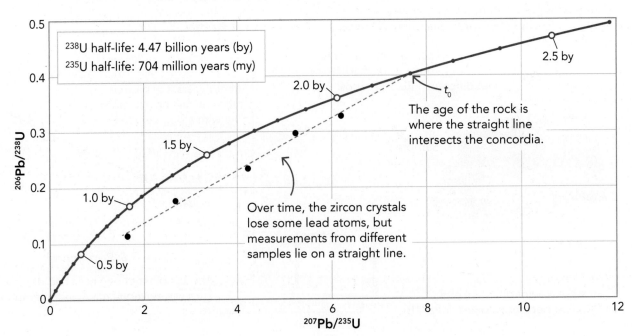

30 **SEP Develop and Use Models** Examine the values on the x-axis and y-axis. Explain how you could approximately determine the half-lives of uranium-235 and uranium-238 from just the concordia curve. (Hint: think about the isotope amounts after one half-life.)

Baffin Island The oldest materials from Earth were found in lavas that erupted on Baffin Island, Canada. Even though the lavas are only 60 million years old, their chemistry suggests that the rock the lava melted from was 4.52 billion years old.

The Oldest Rocks on Earth

Because Earth's geology is so active, finding old rocks is very difficult. Most old rocks have eroded away or been covered by younger rocks. The old cores (cratons) of many continents are sometimes older than 3.5 billion years. These cratons often contain metamorphosed sedimentary rocks, such as the Acasta gneiss in Canada. They may have formed 4 billion years ago, but they contain the sediments of even older rocks. Single crystals have been found elsewhere in the world that are even older, and chemical analyses have found pockets of rock that have been isolated within Earth's mantle for longer still.

The oldest rocks on Earth, however, are not from our planet. They are **meteorites,** lumps of rock or metal that fall to Earth from space and are left over from the formation of the solar system. These meteorites originated in space as meteoroids, where they did not experience erosion, so they are mostly unchanged from when they formed. The most famous of these is a 2-ton meteor that broke up in the atmosphere above the Mexican village of Allende. Its fragments contain small carbon-rich inclusions with ages of 4.567 billion years, marking the time when the solar system formed.

Current Records for Oldest Rocks			
Rock Description	**Dating Method**	**Age**	**Category**
Acasta gneiss	U/Pb, Th/Pb	4.03 by	Exposed rock
Zircon crystal from western Australia	U/Pb	4.408 by	Single crystal
Baffin Island lavas, Canada	Hafnium/tungsten	4.52 by	Rock chemistry
Allende meteorite—Allende, Mexico	Pb-206/Pb-204	4.567 by	Meteorite
SiC crystal in Murchison meteorite	Neon-21	7 by	Pre-solar grain

Acasta gneiss

Allende meteorite

 SEP Construct Explanations Explain why it has been so hard to find rocks more than 4 billion years old at Earth's surface.

Meteorites and Solar Spectroscopy

The oldest meteoroids, called chondrites, not only provide the age of the solar system but also provide its net composition. Their compositions show the relative abundances of the elements that existed at the start of the solar system. This mix of elements was a result of the stellar end-of-life processes that occurred just before our solar system formed. Interestingly, some meteorites also contain pieces of the original dust that came together to form the solar system. These pre-solar grains can be as old as 7 billion years.

The fact that these ancient meteorites represent the composition of the early solar system is supported by the similarity of their composition to the bulk compositions of both Earth and the sun. Earth's bulk composition comes from analyzing large numbers of rocks and making inferences about the composition of the lower mantle and core. The light from the sun's photosphere can be analyzed using spectroscopy to reveal the abundances of elements within that outer layer of the sun.

Compositions of Meteorites and the Sun The fact that most elements fall on the 1:1 line shows how similar the compositions of the sun and meteorites are.

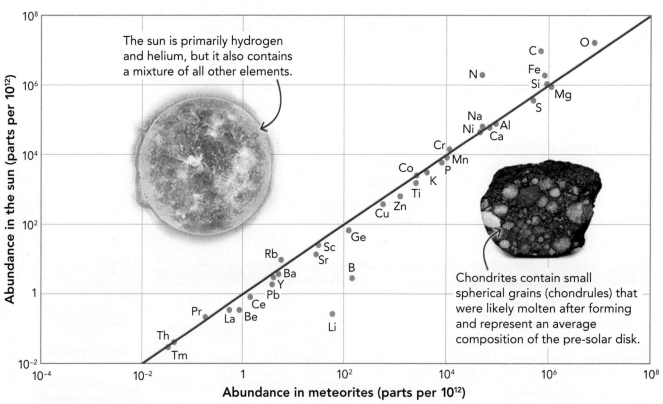

Data from: Table 1, Solar System Abundances of the Elements, H. Palme and A. Jones, volume 1, 2003, Elsevier Ltd.

32) **CCC Scale, Proportion, and Quantity** The rock of Earth's crust and mantle both have levels of iron that are disproportionately low, given that most other elements are similar to the solar and chondrite relative proportions. Provide an explanation for this.

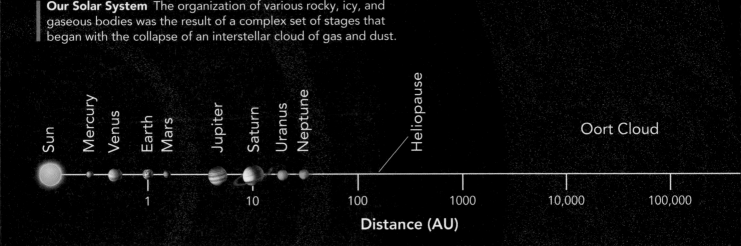

Sun Mercury Venus Earth Mars Jupiter Saturn Uranus Neptune Heliopause Oort Cloud

1 10 100 1000 10,000 100,000

Distance (AU)

Formation of the Solar System

The current theory for how the solar system formed is that it came from a cloud of gas and dust, pulled together by gravity. Parts of this theory are well established, while other parts are more uncertain. The entire process took only tens of millions of years, much shorter than the 4.567-billion-year age of the solar system.

Several lines of evidence support this hypothesis. Most of the solar system revolves around the sun in the same direction, forming a disk called the solar ecliptic. Most large objects (including the sun) also rotate in this same direction. These facts support the theory that everything formed from a spinning disk of gas and dust.

The similarity of cosmic abundances among meteorites, the sun, and Earth also suggests a common origin. However, bulk compositions vary as a function of distance from the sun. This variance can be explained by temperatures in the early stages of solar system formation. Moving outward from the sun, solar system objects change from mostly metal (Mercury) to mostly rock (Venus, Earth, Mars) to mostly gas (Jupiter, Saturn) to mostly ice (Uranus, Neptune, and beyond).

Finally, powerful telescopes provide vast amounts of data about the surfaces and compositions of millions of small solar system bodies. These telescopes have also observed protoplanetary disks forming in other parts of the galaxy.

New Planetary Systems HL Tauri is a young star 450 light years from Earth that shows a protoplanetary disk. This photo was taken by the ALMA Radio Telescope.

The Formation of the Solar System

How did the **sun and planets** in the solar system form?

Nebular Hypothesis Based on astronomical observations, chemical analyses, and computer modeling, the leading hypothesis is that **our entire solar system formed** together from a swirling cloud of gas and dust about 4.6 billion years ago.

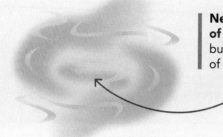

Nebular Cloud Our solar system **begins as part of a large cloud of gas and dust.** The nebula is composed **mostly of H and He gas,** but it also includes some heavier elements ejected by the explosions of older stars.

The force of **gravity** begins to pull the gas and dust together. This may have been accelerated by the shock wave of a nearby supernova.

Pre-solar Nebula A disk forms as **the contracting nebula begins to rotate.** Through the **conservation of angular momentum,** the more the cloud shrinks, the faster it spins.

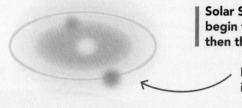

Solar System Bodies The **gas and dust within the rotating disk begin to clump** together, first **through electrostatic forces and then through gravity.** Millions of planetesimals form.

Most of the mass that is not at the center of the disk is swept up into two **gas giants,** Jupiter and Saturn.

Protostar After 99.8% of the solar system's mass becomes **concentrated at the center** of the disk, **the sun forms.** It enters a T-Tauri phase, **blasting clear most of the remaining gas** from the solar system.

Heat from the forming sun prevents **inner planets** from forming with many gases or ices, resulting in mostly rocky planets or, in the case of Mercury, the closest moon, a planet mostly made of metal.

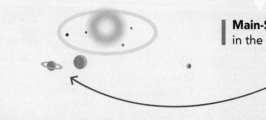

Main-Sequence Star Hydrogen fusion begins in the center of the sun's core. A star is born.

The **resonance** between the orbital periods of Jupiter and Saturn ejects many bodies from the solar system, giving it its current structure.

(33) CCC Scale, Proportion, and Quantity The sun's radius is 109 times larger than Earth's. How much larger is its volume?

Formation of Earth and the Moon

A good scientific practice is to continue to look for ways to refine and improve theories (and the models used to develop, teach, and understand them). Theories, such as of the formation of objects in the solar system, still contain plenty of unanswered questions. In fact, new theories can still replace older ones. This process may be occurring presently for models of the formation of Earth's moon.

In the past, the prevailing model was the impact hypothesis: a Mars-sized planet (called Theia) crashed into Earth, and the moon formed from the parts ejected—most of Theia and some of Earth's crust and mantle. This model made more sense than the capture hypothesis, in which a planet's gravity captures smaller solar system objects into orbit. This process seems to apply only to small moons, such as the Martian moons.

However, a newer model, obtained by combining geochemical evidence with geophysical computer modeling, shows how the moon likely co-formed with Earth. In this model, the early Earth was rotating much faster than it is today. This fast rotation would have pushed hot gas and dust out into a large doughnut-shaped cloud. Gravity could then force part of the cloud to coalesce, eventually forming the moon as it exists today.

Collision Model for the Moon In the traditional model, a planet-sized body (Theia) collided with Earth, melting Earth and ejecting material from both Earth and Theia that coalesced to form the moon.

Co-formation Model for the Moon In the newer model, Earth and the moon formed together from a doughnut-shaped proto-planetary cloud. The moon would have swept up the material in the disk, similar to how Jupiter swept up much of the mass of the outer disk of the early solar system.

 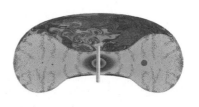 

Republished with permission of John Wiley and Sons, from The Origin of the Moon within a Terrestrial Synestia. SJ Lock, ST Stewart, MI Petaev, Z Leinhardt, MT Mace, SB Jacobsen, Journal of Geophysical Research: Planets 123 (4), 910-951; permission conveyed through Copyright Clearance Center, Inc.

(34) **SEP Construct Explanations** The moon has a very small iron core that is an insignificant percentage of its interior, especially when compared to Earth's iron core, which is 35% of Earth's mass. Describe how both the collision model and the co-formation model can explain this difference.

Impact Craters and Solar System History

EXPERIENCE IT!

Put a small amount of sand in an aluminum pan. Drop a large marble into the pan to form a crater. Remove the marble and then drop a smaller marble on or near the same spot. How can you determine which crater formed first?

When you look at the moon, you see that the crater density, or number of craters in a given area, varies by region. About 85% of the moon's surface is highly cratered. Some dark regions of the moon are large impact basins that filled in with basaltic lava. These regions have many fewer craters on them.

The pattern is similar for other planetary bodies with very old surfaces, such as Mercury and many moons of the outer planets. From these observations and the radiometric ages of moon rocks, scientists have reconstructed the early history of the solar system.

For the first 700 million years, the solar system was a violent place, with many collisions, large and small. About 4 billion years ago, the orbits of Jupiter and Saturn became resonant. Many large bodies were flung out of the solar system during this time, when all the large impacts on Mercury, Mars, and the moon occurred. Since that time, the solar system has been a much calmer place, and cratering rates have decreased significantly.

 SEP Analyze and Interpret Data Assume that the Mare Crisium impact occurred 3.9 billion years ago and that its basalts formed 3.5 billion years ago. Using crater densities inside and outside of the basin, estimate the difference in the cratering rate for the first 1.1 billion years of Earth's history vs. that of the past 3.5 billion years.

Cratering on the Moon Mare Crisium is a younger region with very few craters, formed by lava filling in an impact basin, surrounded by older regions with many more craters.

INVESTIGATIVE PHENOMENON

GO ONLINE to revisit your **Investigative Phenomenon CER** with the new information you have learned about Radiometric Dating.

These questions will help you apply what you learned in this experience to the Investigative Phenomenon.

36 **CCC Scale, Proportion, and Quantity** The half-life of potassium-40 is longer than the half-life of uranium-235, yet it is able to provide radiometric ages that are much younger (50,000 years) than uranium (10 million years). From what you know of potassium and uranium, explain why this might be the case.

Parent	Daughter	Half-life (y)	Effective Range (y)
Potassium-40	Argon-40	1.3 billion	50,000–4.6 billion
Uranium-235	Lead-207	703.8 million	10 million–4.6 billion

37 **SEP Construct Explanations** An old hypothesis for the presence of Earth's moon, the capture hypothesis, suggested that the moon formed elsewhere and Earth's gravity captured it. From what you know of gravity and orbits, explain why this hypothesis is unlikely.

38 **SEP Construct Explanations** What does the fact that pre-solar grains are found in some meteorites say about the conditions during the formation of the solar system?

39 **SEP Construct Explanations** Construct an explanation for how the existence of your body is proof that our solar system formed from the remnants of previous stars.

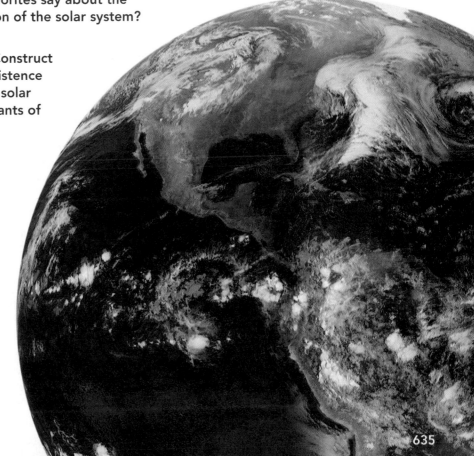

GO ONLINE for a **quiz** to evaluate what you learned about Radiometric Dating.

Geologic Time

 GO ONLINE to do a **hands-on lab** to investigate how plate tectonics has reshaped Earth's surface.

Physical and Geologic Time

To look at a landscape with the "eyes of a geologist" means to imagine what it looked like at different points in the past, or even what it will look like in the future. You can mentally scan back and forth across time as you observe the landscape. The fact that time can be considered the fourth dimension becomes particularly clear when you look at the world in this way.

If you stood on the rim of the Grand Canyon, you might focus on the beauty of the rock layers and the Colorado River. But if you look at the canyon with the eyes of a geologist, you could also look back in time almost two billion years. Each layer gets progressively older as you scan down. These layers mostly formed in the ocean, so you might imagine half a billion years ago, when trilobites ruled the seas, or a billion years ago, before multicellular life. You could see how young the Colorado River is, starting to tear down through these layers only millions of years ago. Geologic processes have operated on Earth for billions of years, and with sufficient experience and training, geologists can picture how regions have changed over this time, with land repeatedly pushed up by plate collisions and eroded away by water and ice.

Grand Canyon The Grand Canyon in Arizona encompasses rock that spans more than 1.8 billion years from the top of the plateau to its bottom.

Physical Time Scales Part of the challenge of science is dealing with vast scales of space and time. Going from the lifetime of W bosons (10^{-32} years) to the age of the universe (13.8 billion years) requires a jump of 42 orders of magnitude. For geologic time, earthquakes rupture the ground in seconds, hurricanes develop over days, volcanic eruptions span months, ground creep takes centuries, ice ages last for tens of thousands of years, erosion operates over millions of years, supercontinents form and break apart over hundreds of millions of years, and continents grow over billions of years. All these processes shape the land simultaneously, but over vastly different time scales.

Geologic Time The time scales involved in geologic time are much longer than time scales in your life. With the Atlantic Ocean enlarging for 200 million years, how can humans, who generally live for less than 100 years, make sense of this time scale? Moreover, 200 million years is only about 4% of the age of Earth. Imagine running a 100-meter race traveling back through Earth's history. You can cover the entire history of the Atlantic Ocean in a few steps. You still have 96 meters to go to reach the birth of our planet.

> **Powers of Ten** A helpful tool for working with time is to put it on a logarithmic scale. When you look at physical and geologic processes by increasing factors of ten, you get a better sense of the great differences in time scales involved.

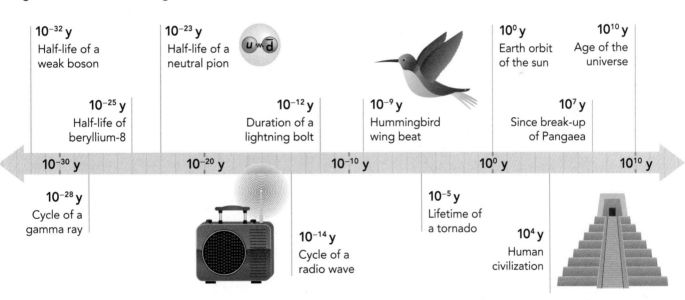

10^{-32} y — Half-life of a weak boson	10^{-23} y — Half-life of a neutral pion
10^{-25} y — Half-life of beryllium-8	10^{-12} y — Duration of a lightning bolt
10^{-9} y — Hummingbird wing beat	10^{0} y — Earth orbit of the sun
10^{10} y — Age of the universe	10^{7} y — Since break-up of Pangaea
10^{-28} y — Cycle of a gamma ray	10^{-14} y — Cycle of a radio wave
10^{-5} y — Lifetime of a tornado	10^{4} y — Human civilization

(40) **CCC Scale, Proportion, and Quantity** Suppose that you stretch out your arm horizontally and that the distance from your shoulder to the tip of your fingernail represents Earth's history. If you take a nail file, how much of the end of your fingernail would you need to remove to erase all of human history? (Assume that the earliest humans lived about 300,000 years ago.)

(41) **CCC Scale, Proportion, and Quantity** The SI unit of time, the second, is defined in terms of the resonant frequency of a cesium-133 atom, which oscillates 9,192,631,770 times per second. About how many times would this atom oscillate over the 13.8-billion-year history of the universe?

Continuous vs. Catastrophic

Modern geologists view geologic time as a continual sequence punctuated by catastrophic events. Geologic forces operate on a spectrum from frequent and small to rare and catastrophic.

For centuries, there were bitter disagreements between geologists who viewed Earth as evolving through gradual and incremental change (uniformitarians) and those who saw Earth as the result of catastrophic changes (catastrophists). This debate also involved viewing geologic time as either linear, tied to the birth-to-death lifespan of the sun, or cyclical, with large-scale processes such as the rise and fall of mountains or sea levels repeating themselves over and over.

As is often the case in such arguments, the answer is somewhere in between. Most Earth processes do occur continuously, but they can also be catastrophic. This is how you should view Earth's geologic history: long stretches of time with slow, gradual change, punctuated by brief periods of intense catastrophic change.

Earthquake Frequency and Energy Earthquakes are an example of a geologic process that is both gradual and catastrophic. The number of earthquakes decreases with each unit increase in magnitude, but the total energy released by all earthquakes of a certain magnitude increases with magnitude.

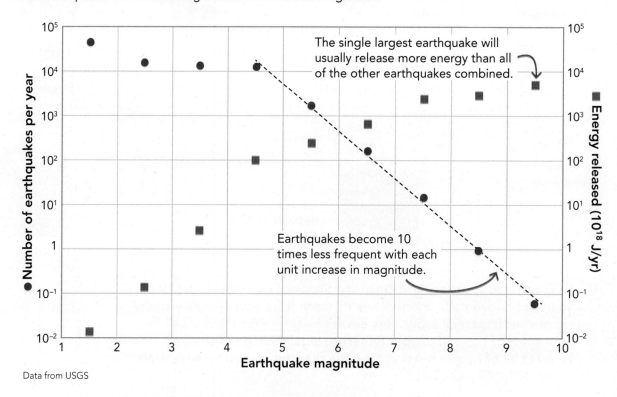

The single largest earthquake will usually release more energy than all of the other earthquakes combined.

Earthquakes become 10 times less frequent with each unit increase in magnitude.

Data from USGS

(42) **SEP Construct Explanations** Explain why you think the earthquake frequency data do not continue to follow the dashed line for very small earthquakes.

Relative Time

Before the development of radiometric dating, geologists could only work in relative time. They could tell if an object was older or younger than other objects based on the layer in which it was found, but they could not determine exact ages. If absolute ages can be determined with radioactivity, then why do geologists continue to work with relative ages?

Unfortunately, radiometric dating is difficult, time intensive, and not always practical. There are also places, such as the surface of Mars, where geologists have access to photographs but not to actual rock samples. In these cases, they can use a few simple rules to interpret the kinds of geologic processes that have occurred. The principles of horizontality, superposition, and crosscutting can be used to determine a sequence of relative ages that allows the interpretation of the geologic history of a region.

- **Horizontality** is the principle that rock layers are horizontal when they form and are usually laterally continuous over great distances.

- **Superposition** is the principle that rock layers form one on top of another, with the youngest layers toward the top.

- **Crosscutting** occurs when a rock body or discontinuity cuts across a layer of rock or another feature. The crosscutting feature is always younger.

VOCABULARY

The prefix *super-* can mean "above," such as in **superposition**, which means "to place above." It can also mean "greater in size," such as in *supernova*.

Layers of Time This rock formation in Salta, Argentina, shows horizontal layers that get younger as you move toward the top.

Finding the Relative Ages of Rocks

How are the relative ages of rocks found?

Rock Rules When trying to **find the relative ages** of geologic features and rocks, geologists use a few simple rules called **the principles of horizontality, superposition, and crosscutting.**

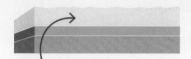  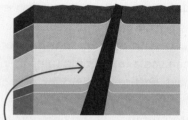

Horizontality Rock layers form **horizontally, continuously, and laterally** over large areas.

Superposition Younger rock layers form over **older** rock layers.

Crosscutting Younger rock or **discontinuities** can sometimes **cut through older layers.**

Using the Rules Using these simple rules, geologists can look at an outcrop of rocks and begin to **interpret the kinds of geologic processes** that have occurred there **over time.**

Fault Tectonic activity can cause the **discontinuity of older rock** layers by fracturing and **shifting the layers out of alignment** with surrounding layers of rock.

Volcanic Dike Rising magma can push through older layers of rock above it, solidifying into "veins" of igneous rock with **characteristics different from the surrounding rock.**

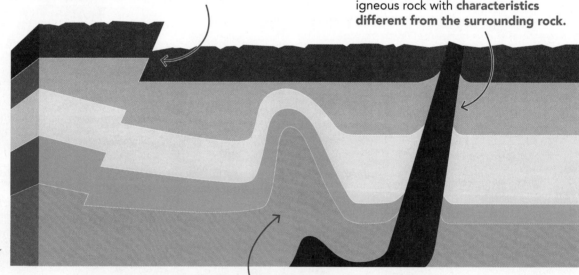

Increasing depth

Folding The **deformation and folding** of rock layers indicates continued **geological activity after the layers of rock originally formed.** In this case, the dike has been deformed by the folding, so the folding must have occurred after the dike formed.

43 CCC Patterns Describe two different situations where the principles of superposition would not apply, such that older rocks would be found on top of younger rocks.

Sea Level Changes

Platform Sediments One of the most important aspects of cyclical geologic time is a broad cycle of sea level rise and fall over hundreds of millions of years. Shorelines are dynamic regions of erosion and deposition. Even though they are very narrow, they are largely responsible for the appearance of much of Earth's land surface.

Most land is relatively flat. A 100-meter sea level rise can cause shorelines to advance inland more than 1,000 kilometers. When the sea level rises, shoreline sediments are deposited inland all across the land. This deposition covers land with layers of sand, clay, and lime, which compress over time to form the sedimentary rocks of sandstone, shale, and limestone. When the sea level falls, shorelines around the world retreat, exposing the land and allowing rock to erode and wash back to the sea.

Over billions of years, repeated shoreline advancements can cover the land with multiple layers of sedimentary rocks. These are known as platform sediments. The beautiful layers of rock at the Grand Canyon are platform sediments. They are largely the result of coastlines moving back and forth over the land many times over billions of years.

History of Sea Level Rise and Fall The global sea level rises and falls according to two main factors: climate and plate tectonics. When climates warm, land glaciers melt, water returns to the ocean, and sea level rises. When tectonic plate motions speed up, the average ocean lithosphere is younger, hotter, and more buoyant. This pushes up the seafloor, causing sea level to rise.

Geologic period

44 **SEP Analyze Data** Examine the data graph of the history of large sea level change episodes. Calculate the mean duration of these broad advancement-retreat cycles.

Unconformities When you look at a sequence of rocks in an outcrop such as the Grand Canyon, the ages of the rocks often do not increase continuously. Often there is missing rock, resulting in a gap in time called an **unconformity.**

You can see this process in action today. In some places, such as the ocean and lakes, sediments are now accumulating. These sediments are future sedimentary rocks. However, most of the exposed land is weathering and eroding, with sediments carried away by water, wind, and ice. This erosion is removing older layers of rock. When the land is flooded again by the ocean and new shoreline sediments are deposited on them, there will be a gap in the geologic record where the eroded rock used to be. This gap will be an unconformity.

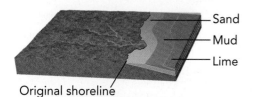

Sand
Mud
Lime

Original shoreline

Grand Canyon Unconformities The layers of the Grand Canyon contain several unconformities. Layers are deposited in units that are part of a single shoreline advance. When the shoreline retreated and the land eroded, time gaps were left in the rock record between consecutive units. The layers of the Grand Canyon contain several unconformities that are difficult to recognize because they are parallel.

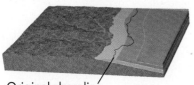

Original shoreline

The Great Unconformity is a gap of 0.7–1.6 billion years between the horizontal layers above and the tilted layers below.

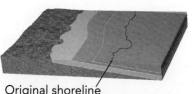

Original shoreline

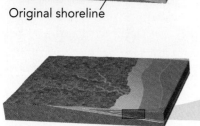

Original shoreline

45 **CCC Stability and Change** Describe how and where on the diagram of the Grand Canyon the next unconformity will form.

46 **SEP Develop and Use a Model** Looking at the diagram of the Grand Canyon, explain how the gap in time across the Great Unconformity can vary from 0.7 to 1.6 billion years depending upon location.

Geologic Time Scales

Fossils In assembling a global geologic time scale from the relative ages of rocks, some of the most important tools are **fossils,** or the remains or traces of ancient life forms. The world's layers of rock contain the history of life in the form of the **fossil record.**

Some fossilized organisms, called index fossils, have characteristics that are useful for rock layer age identification. These species were abundant, lived over wide geographic ranges, existed for a relatively brief period of time, had hard body parts that would fossilize, and are easily recognizable.

Mass Extinctions When fossils and rock layers are arranged in a time sequence, an interesting pattern emerges. The rate of emergence and extinction of species is not uniform. Many times in Earth's past, large numbers of species disappeared from the fossil record. These mass extinctions were followed by rapid expansions in the evolution of other species.

Mass extinctions were triggered by major disruptions at Earth's surface, such as the impacts of asteroids. These extinctions are useful in dividing up periods of the geologic time scale. The best known mass extinction occurred 66 million years ago (mya), when as many as 75% of all species of life, including dinosaurs, vanished. The most devastating event occurred 252 million years ago, when 96% of all marine species went extinct, including all trilobites. These mass extinctions now mark the divisions in the geologic time scale.

Trilobites Trilobites are often used as index fossils. Trilobites were marine arthropods, abundant across the global ocean for almost 300 million years. The last species went extinct during the Permian-Triassic mass extinction.

History of Mass Extinction The course of the evolution of life is not smooth. The numbers of genera (groups of species) over time is punctuated by periods of mass extinctions, identified by the bottom points of the triangles.

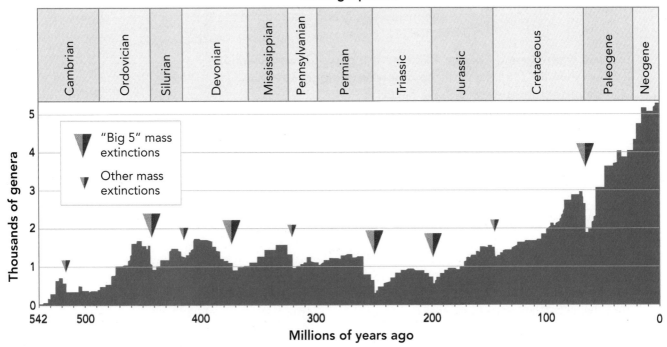

Data from: Sepkoski, J. A Compendium of Fossil Marine Animal Genera (eds Jablonski, D. & Foote, M.) Bull. Am. Paleontol. no. 363 (Paleontological Research Institution, Ithaca, 2002).

Geologic Time Divisions The geologic time scale is subdivided into categories that are themselves divided. Eons are divided into eras, which are divided into periods, which are divided into epochs, which are divided into ages. Nearly all of the time divisions align with periods of mass extinctions.

The geologic time scale was initially constructed entirely from relative age dating. Only toward the end of the 20th century were absolute numbers from radiometric age dating added to the different time divisions. The first four billion years of Earth's history are divided into three eons:

- **Hadean Eon** The oldest and least understood eon of Earth's history, the Hadean eon has largely been reconstructed from extraplanetary evidence such as meteorites and cratering patterns on the moon, Mars, and elsewhere. The end of the Hadean is marked by the solar system impacts of the Late Heavy Bombardment.

- **Archean Eon** Earth began to resemble its modern form during this eon. The early Archean saw the first continents, the early ocean, and the beginning of plate tectonics. It also saw the emergence of single-celled life, which began more than 3.5 million years ago.

- **Proterozoic Eon** Meaning "early life," the Proterozoic eon began with the dominance of photosynthetic cyanobacteria. These ocean bacteria formed the oxygen-rich atmosphere that would later make the evolution of animal life possible. Multicellular life evolved near the end of the Proterozoic.

- **Phanerozoic Eon** Meaning "visible life," the Phanerozoic eon began with a rapid expansion of multicellular life throughout the ocean. It represents only 12% of Earth's history, but it contains most of the subdivisions of the geologic time scale because most of Earth's surface rocks and most species of life are from this eon. The Phanerozoic era saw the assembly and break-up of the supercontinent Pangaea.

Layers in Time A vertical igneous dike cuts through horizontal layers of rock in the Negev Desert in Israel.

(47) **CCC Stability and Change** Examine the geologic cross-section and then list the letters of the different geologic structures in the order that they must have occurred.

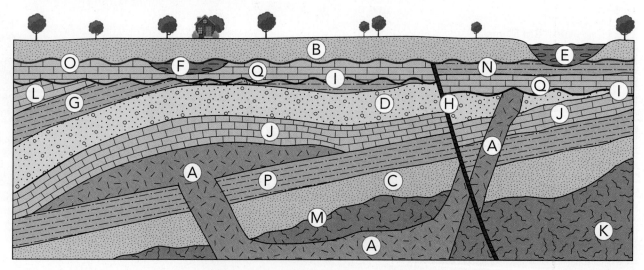

GO ONLINE to watch a **video** about the geologic time scale.

Refining the Time Scale The geologic time scale is not complete. As new fossils are found and radiometric age dating is refined, the times of the divisions continue to undergo slight adjustments. In addition, current events are modifying the time scale. Because of the large numbers of extinctions due to human activities, a new time division called the Anthropocene has been named. Perhaps the impacts of human activities will be great enough to also lead to a new period (Anthropogene) or a new era being classified (Anthropozoic).

EXPERIENCE IT!

On a piece of paper, create a time scale that divides your life into different periods. What distinctions can you use to help you define the different periods?

Geologic Time Scale More recent times have the most subdivisions because of the abundance of rocks and fossils from Earth's most recent history.

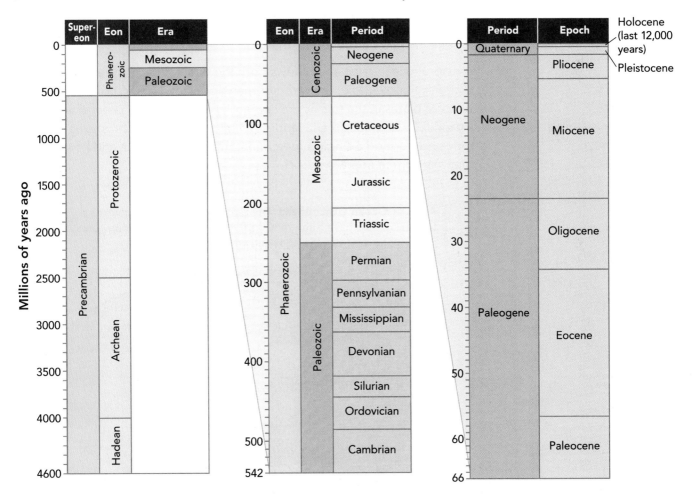

48 **CCC Stability and Change** The state fossil of Ohio is *Isotelus maximus*, a species of trilobite that lived about 450 million years ago and grew to be more than 2 feet long. Explain what this implies about the geologic history of Ohio.

Ages of Ocean Crust

Ocean crust and continental crust have little in common. They have different compositions, thicknesses, and ages, and they are formed in completely different ways. Continental crust has many varieties, but all ocean crust forms the same way: from the cooling of magma and lava at mid-ocean ridges, where tectonic plates pull apart. Both the magma and lava have a basaltic composition, composed of feldspar, pyroxene, and olivine. These minerals are mostly silicon and oxygen with various metals included, usually iron and magnesium.

Seafloor Age New ocean crust forms at mid-ocean ridges and gets older as tectonic plates separate. The farther the crust is from a ridge, the older it is. The western Pacific Ocean has some of the oldest oceanic crust, almost 200 million years old. Usually, however, ocean crust subducts back into the mantle before it gets that old.

A map of ocean crust ages shows both the direction and speed of plate motions. For example, the width of the Pacific age bands shows that tectonic plates in the Pacific are spreading about 3 times faster than in the Atlantic. Tracing back the locations of continents in the past shows that they once formed a single supercontintent called Pangaea and how the they later broke apart.

Ages of Ocean Lithosphere The direction and speed at which tectonic plates have been moving for more than 150 million years can be inferred from the ages shown in this map.

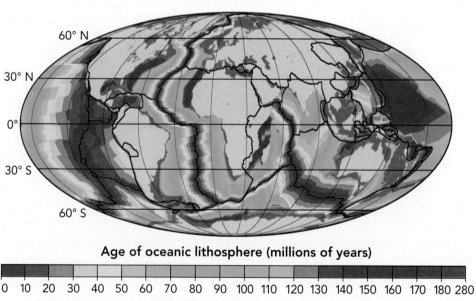

Age of oceanic lithosphere (millions of years)

0 10 20 30 40 50 60 70 80 90 100 110 120 130 140 150 160 170 180 280

Source: National Oceanic and Atmospheric Administration (2008)

Magnetic Field Reversals A timeline of Earth's random magnetic field reversals provides the data to construct an ocean crust age map. Gray areas indicate "Normal" periods when the magnetic field had the same polarity as today. Note how the pattern of reversals is unique—there are no two time periods with the same pattern.

Data from: Hulot, G. & Finlay, Christopher & Constable, Catherine & Olsen, Nils & Mandea, Mioara. (2010). The Magnetic Field of Planet Earth. Space Science Reviews. 152. 159-222

Cenozoic — Q, Neogene, Paleogene
Mesozoic — Cretaceous, Jurassic

0 mya
10
20
30
40
50
60
70
80
90
100
110
120
130
140
150
160
170

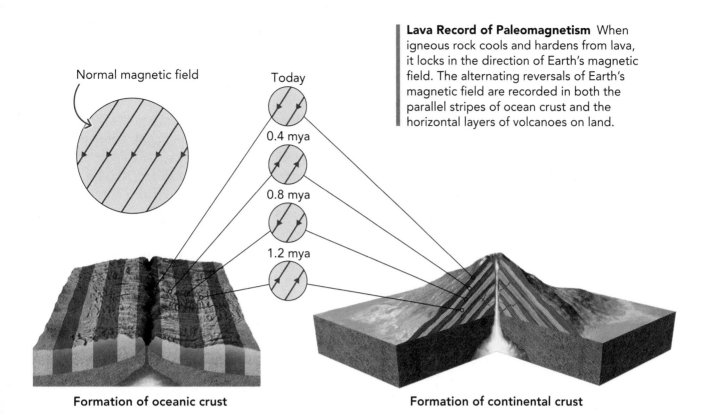

Normal magnetic field

Today

0.4 mya

0.8 mya

1.2 mya

Lava Record of Paleomagnetism When igneous rock cools and hardens from lava, it locks in the direction of Earth's magnetic field. The alternating reversals of Earth's magnetic field are recorded in both the parallel stripes of ocean crust and the horizontal layers of volcanoes on land.

Formation of oceanic crust

Formation of continental crust

📄 **GO ONLINE** to analyze a **set of data** in order to date the ocean floor.

Paleomagnetism Taking direct samples of the ocean floor to determine ages is difficult. It requires drilling under kilometers of water through layers of acculumated sediment than can also be kilometers thick. Fortunately, Earth's core provides an indirect means of determining ocean crust ages.

When iron-rich minerals in basalt cool below a point called the Curie temperature, they lock in and record the direction of the magnetic field. Many ship voyages, zigzagging across the ocean with magnetometers to record the magnetic orientation of ocean floor basalt, have provided a map of the paleomagnetic stripes that yield relative ocean crust ages.

Absolute ages of ocean floor crust are assigned using the history of lava eruptions on land. The rocks formed by cooling lava record the magnetic field from the time they formed, just as ocean rock does. These rocks are much more accessible for drilling and sampling. The rock samples can be analyzed in the lab for both their paleomagnetism and radiometric age. Using many lava flows of different ages from around the world, absolute ages can be assigned to a paleomagnetic reversal record. This record can be compared to the paleomagnetic record of the seafloor to determine ocean crust ages.

(49) **SEP Engage in Argument from Evidence** Fossil evidence suggests that Australia used to be adjacent to Antarctica. Defend this argument using data from the map of ocean seafloor ages.

Ages of Continental Crust

Types of Continental Crust Unlike oceanic crust, continental crust shows no consistent age patterns. It also lacks patterns in its history and composition. Continental crust is an agglomeration of many different rock types of many different ages that result from the unique history of each continent. There are many types and variations of geologic landforms—mountains, canyons, mesas, plateaus, basins, and so on. But most rocks found at Earth's surface can be divided into a few general categories: cratons (including shields and platform sediments), orogens, and accreted terranes.

Continental cratons were the first fragments of continents that crystallized from a molten Earth more than 4 billion years ago. This crust is seen at the surface only in regions called shields. More often, it is covered by platform sediments from times when the ocean flooded the land.

Sometimes, cratons were involved in continent-continent collisions that thrust up long ranges of mountains, such as the Himalayas and Appalachians. These ranges are called orogens, or orogenic belts. Here, the cratonic crust was deformed through folding and faulting, and it was often transformed by high temperatures and pressures into metamorphic rocks.

The edges of continents often consist of accreted terranes. These are continental fragments, volcanic ocean island arcs, or slivers of oceanic crust that have been caught up between continental collisions. They are often dramatically deformed and plastered onto the sides of continents.

Structures of Continents Each continent has a unique age, history, and structure. However, all continents share certain types of crust with similar characteristics and ages.

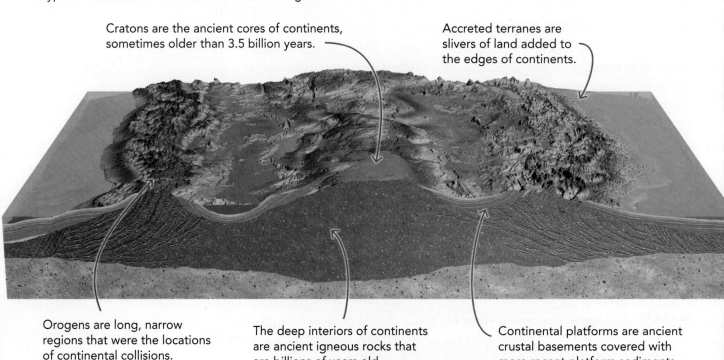

Cratons are the ancient cores of continents, sometimes older than 3.5 billion years.

Accreted terranes are slivers of land added to the edges of continents.

Orogens are long, narrow regions that were the locations of continental collisions.

The deep interiors of continents are ancient igneous rocks that are billions of years old.

Continental platforms are ancient crustal basements covered with more recent platform sediments.

Ages of the North American Crust Centuries of geologic field work have yielded a map of the ages of the continental crust of North America. Several cratons older than 3 billion years old were sutured together by orogenic (mountain building) collisions about 2.3–1.8 billion years ago.

Next, the southern half of North America from Wyoming to Texas formed from a sequence of collisions with ocean volcanic island arcs that triggered a large underground melting of rock. The large granite provinces in the center of the United States formed at that time.

Finally, a set of orogenic events (Grenville, Appalachian, and Cordillera) added numerous accreted terranes to the eastern, southern, and western edges of the continent. These built up through multiple continental collisions as the supercontinents of Rodinia, Pannotia, and Pangaea each came together and broke apart over hundreds of millions of years.

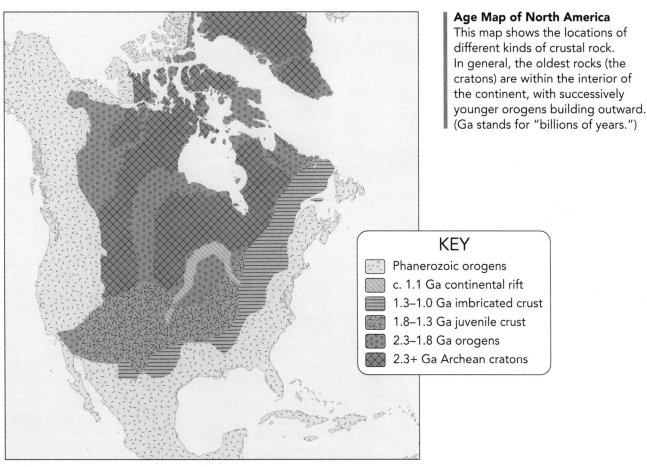

Age Map of North America
This map shows the locations of different kinds of crustal rock. In general, the oldest rocks (the cratons) are within the interior of the continent, with successively younger orogens building outward. (Ga stands for "billions of years.")

KEY
- Phanerozoic orogens
- c. 1.1 Ga continental rift
- 1.3–1.0 Ga imbricated crust
- 1.8–1.3 Ga juvenile crust
- 2.3–1.8 Ga orogens
- 2.3+ Ga Archean cratons

Data from: Hoffman, Paul. (1998). United Plates of America, The Birth of a Craton: Early Proterozoic Assembly and Growth of Laurentia. Annu. Rev. Earth Planet. Sci.. 16. 543-603.

(50) **SEP Construct Explanations** Use a current map to find where St. Louis would be located on the age map of North America. How old are the basement crustal rocks there? The exposed rocks at the surface are mostly sandstones and limestones that are about 400 million years old. Explain what class of rocks these are and how they formed.

INVESTIGATIVE PHENOMENON

GO ONLINE to revisit your **Investigative Phenomenon CER** with the new information you have learned about Geologic Time.

These questions will help you apply what you learned in this experience to the Investigative Phenomenon.

51 **CCC Patterns** Earth's surface formed through a succession of layering events. A disconformity is a kind of unconformity in which, after sedimentary rock layers are eroded down, new ones are deposited on top that are parallel to the ones beneath. Explain why these are difficult to recognize and what they say about the geologic history of a region.

52 **SEP Engage in Argument from Evidence** There was much excitement among paleontologists in 2004, when fossils of a 375-million-year-old, four-legged creature called *Tiktaalik* were discovered. *Tiktaalik* was a "missing link," a transitional fossil between ancient fish and the earliest amphibians. Defend the argument that you would expect many such missing-link fossils never to be found.

53 **CCC Structure and Function** Imagine a geologist 100 million years in the future trying to work out Earth's history, including our current time period. Which of the following current organisms could become good index fossils—lemurs, lettuce, scallops, jellyfish, or earthworms? Explain why.

54 **CCC Patterns** Although magnetic field reversals have always been random, their patterns have changed over time. Describe how the frequency of reversals has changed over time. How do the past 30 million years compare to 85–115 million years ago and to 130–160 million years ago?

GO ONLINE for a **quiz** to evaluate what you learned about Geologic Time.

These questions will help you apply what you learned in this investigation to the Anchoring Phenomenon.

(55) **SEP Ask Questions** Identify three questions you would need to have answered in order to know where the **atoms of your body** were before the formation of the solar system.

(56) **CCC Stability and Change** Explain how it is that some of the atoms in your body did not yet exist at the time of the formation of the solar system.

☑ INVESTIGATION ASSESSMENT

 GO ONLINE for activities that will give you an opportunity to **demonstrate what you have learned:**

☑ **Science Performance-Based Assessment** Determine the ages of rock layers.

📄 **Engineering Workbench** Determine how to examine the composition of a meteorite without contaminating the sample.

💻 **Career Connections** Learn about how a paleontologist uses Earth's fossil record to gain understanding of Earth's history.

💻 **Investigation Test** Demonstrate your understanding of the ages of rocks.

☑ **Virtual Lab Performance-Based Assessment** Determine the history of a region.

GO ONLINE to engage with real-world phenomena by watching a **phenomenon video** and completing a **CER worksheet.**

How will the sun change over time?

The Universe

Depending on your location, you can see thousands of stars on a clear night, each of them like our own sun. You can even see a few galaxies, each filled with many millions of other stars. In writings throughout the history of human civilization, the night sky has inspired people to ask deep questions about the universe and their place in it. What's out there? How and when did the universe form? Will it end? Is there life on other worlds?

Observing the sky with powerful telescopes has revealed that the sun is one of more than 100 billion stars in a galaxy called the Milky Way. The Milky Way is one of more than 100 billion galaxies in a universe that is about 13.8 billion years old.

These discoveries have answered some questions but also introduced many others. When people look up at the night sky, they still face many of the same fundamental unanswered questions: What is our role in the universe, and are there others looking at a different sky and wondering the same thing?

(1) **SEP Ask Questions** Think about different ways the sun could change over time and how those changes would impact life on Earth. What questions do you have about the ways that the sun may change?

(2) **CCC Energy and Matter** The sun gives off light by fusing hydrogen to helium, but even before it first began its fusion, the sun was about 25% helium, by mass. Why do you think the sun began with so much helium?

The Sun

 GO ONLINE to do a **hands-on lab** to model how energy passes through the sun's interior and into space.

Solar Energy

The sun contains 99.9% of the mass of the solar system and is large enough to hold the volume of 1.3 million Earths. However, at a galactic scale, there is nothing unusual about the sun. It is an ordinary, middle-aged, modest-sized star, much like many of the other 100 billion stars in the Milky Way.

Sunlight and Distance The sun is the only star that looks like a disc in the sky because it is so close to Earth, about 150 million km away. This distance is far enough that it takes sunlight more than 8 minutes to reach Earth. However, the next closest star, Proxima Centauri, is 40 trillion km away—so far that its starlight takes 4.2 years to reach Earth. At these scales, a more convenient unit of distance is the **light-year,** which is the distance light travels in a year; 1 ly = 9.461 trillion km. Therefore, Proxima Centauri is 4.2 light-years away from Earth.

The Sun	
Mean distance from Earth	149.6 million km
Mean time for sunlight to reach Earth	8.32 min
Radius	695,700 km
Mass	1.989×10^{30} kg
Composition	74% H, 25% He, 1% other
Mean density	1408 kg/m^3
Mean surface temperature	5800 K
Core temperature	15.7 million K
Luminosity	3.828×10^{26} W
Mean rate of rotation	25.38 days
Distance from galactic center	26,700 light-years
Orbital period around galactic center	230 million years

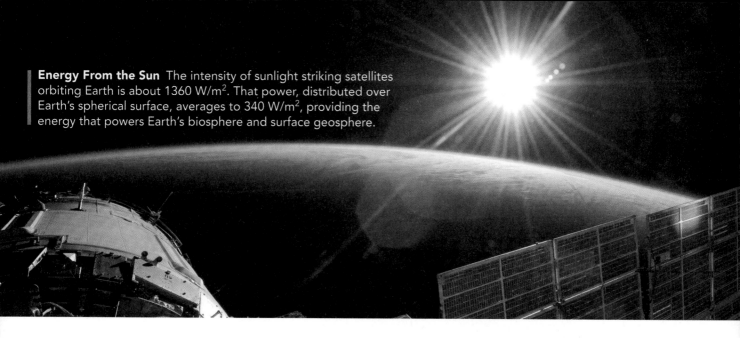

Energy From the Sun The intensity of sunlight striking satellites orbiting Earth is about 1360 W/m². That power, distributed over Earth's spherical surface, averages to 340 W/m², providing the energy that powers Earth's biosphere and surface geosphere.

Fusion and Sunlight Although the sun is an average-sized star, it gives off an enormous amount of energy in the form of electromagnetic radiation, at a rate of 3.828×10^{26} W. The intensity of sunlight is 63 MW/m² at the sun's surface. Because light intensity is proportional to the square of the distance, by the time light gets to Earth, the intensity is just 1361 W/m². By the time it reaches Neptune, it is only 1.5 W/m².

People once thought that the sun was like a giant gas lamp, burning fuel. Scientists now understand that the sun produces energy through nuclear fusion, not combustion. Intense pressures and temperatures exceeding 15 million K at the sun's core make fusion possible.

The surface of the sun is a much cooler 5800 K, with the peak of its radiation output in the visible spectrum. This fact is not a coincidence: The eyes of most animals evolved to see visible wavelengths because they comprise most of the sun's radiation output.

Sunlight and Earth Life on Earth would not be possible without nuclear fusion and sunlight. Nearly all of our energy sources derive from sunlight in some way, so they originally derived from fusion within the sun's core. It is also not a coincidence that life exists in abundance on Earth and not on other planets in the solar system. Planets closer to or farther from the sun get too much or too little sunlight. Only Earth is at the right distance for liquid water to exist continuously at its surface.

EXPERIENCE IT!

Turn a small flashlight on and put it in the corner of an otherwise dark room. Stand in the far corner of the room, opposite the flashlight. Observe how bright it is. Walk to the middle of the room, half the distance to the flashlight. Does the flashlight appear a little bit brighter, twice as bright, or 4 times as bright?

(3) **CCC Scale, Proportion, and Quantity** Suppose that the sun is being watched by an alien on a planet orbiting Alpha Centauri, which is 267,000 times farther from the sun than Earth. Calculate our sun's luminosity there, in W/m².

(4) **SEP Use Mathematics** Explain why the sun's power, as averaged over Earth's spherical surface (340 W/m²), is exactly one fourth of what it is at Earth's distance from the sun (1361 W/m²). [Hint: Think about the areas of circles and spheres.]

The Sun's Fusion

The nuclear fusion occurring within the sun is the proton-proton chain, converting hydrogen to helium. This reaction occurs in several steps and in several different ways, but the net reaction is always the same:

$$4(^1\text{H}) \rightarrow {}^4\text{He} + 2e^+ + 2\nu_e + 26.7 \text{ MeV}$$

Fusion Processes in the Sun

How does the sun produce energy?

Proton-Proton I Reaction Stars with masses similar to or smaller than that of the sun **produce light and energy through a nuclear process** called a proton-proton I reaction. The complete reaction, which occurs over several steps, **releases energy and forms a heavier element** from a lighter one.

Intense gravitational forces deep in the sun's core produce **extremely high temperatures and pressures.**

Conditions in the sun's core **energize hydrogen nuclei (protons) enough to overcome strong repulsive forces and collide.** The collision forms deuterium, composed of a proton and a neutron, and it releases 1.442 MeV of energy as positrons and neutrinos. On average, a given proton must wait 9 billion years before such a collision happens.

The process continues as **deuterium nuclei collide with other high-energy protons,** producing gamma rays and high-energy helium-3 nuclei, each composed of two protons and one neutron. On average, this step happens within just 4 seconds. It releases 5.49 MeV of energy.

Helium-4 and two high-energy protons are produced as the reaction continues with the collision of two high-energy helium-3 nuclei. An average of 400 years will pass before a given helium-3 nucleus collides in this way, releasing 12.859 MeV of energy.

A Powerful Process The **net energy released** from the complete proton-proton I reaction is **about 26.7 MeV.**

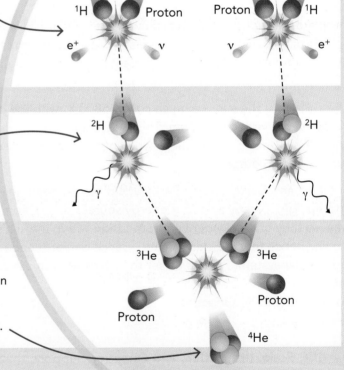

5. **CCC Scale, Proportion, and Quantity** Obtain information to compare the temperatures and pressures in the cores of the sun and Earth. Why does fusion occur within the sun but not within Earth?

Energy in the Sun's Fusion Processes

Calculate how much mass, in atomic mass units (amu), is destroyed per starting nucleon in the proton-proton I chain to make one ^{4}He nucleus. Use 1 amu = 931.5 MeV/c^2 for the mass of a nucleon.

1. DRAW A PICTURE Sketch a picture of the situation.

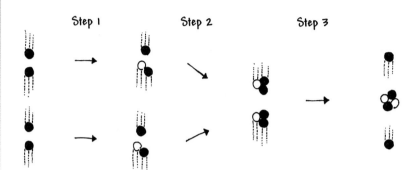

Step 1   Step 2   Step 3

2. DEFINE THE PROBLEM List knowns and unknowns, and assign values to variables.

$$1 \text{ amu} = 931.5 \text{ MeV}/c^2$$

$$E_{\text{step 1}} = 1.442 \text{ MeV}$$

$$E_{\text{step 2}} = 5.490 \text{ MeV}$$

$$E_{\text{step 3}} = 12.859 \text{ MeV}$$

3. PLAN AND EXECUTE Use mathematical relationships, the picture, and your definitions to plan and execute a solution.

Use the diagram and $E = mc^2$ to determine the total mass destroyed to create one ^{4}He nucleus.

$$E_{\text{tot}} = 2(E_{\text{step 1}}) + 2(E_{\text{step 2}}) + E_{\text{step 3}}$$
$$= 2(1.442 \text{ MeV}) + 2(5.490)\text{MeV} + 12.859 \text{ MeV}$$
$$= 26.723 \text{ MeV}$$
$$E = mc^2 \rightarrow m = \frac{E}{c^2} = 26.723 \text{ MeV}/c^2$$

Find the amount of mass destroyed, per starting nucleon, in amu.

$$m \text{ (per starting nucleon)} = \frac{26.723 \text{ MeV}/c^2}{4 \text{ nucleons}}$$
$$= 6.6808 \text{ MeV}/c^2$$

$$6.6808 \text{ MeV}/c^2 \times \frac{1 \text{ amu}}{931.5 \text{ MeV}/c^2} = 0.007172 \text{ amu}$$

4. EVALUATE Reflect upon your answer.
0.007172 amu is about 0.72% of the mass of a nucleon. Therefore, a little less than 1% of the mass of each nucleon is released as energy when four protons fuse to make one helium nucleus.

 GO ONLINE for more **math support**.

▶ **Math Tutorial Video**

🖥 **Math Practice Problems**

---

6. Calculate how much mass, in atomic mass units (amu), is destroyed per starting nucleon in the given proton-proton II branch reactions to make one ^{4}He nucleus. Use 1 amu = 931.5 MeV/c^2 for the mass of a nucleon.

$$^3\text{He} + {}^4\text{He} \rightarrow {}^7\text{Be} + \gamma + 1.59 \text{ MeV}$$
$$^7\text{Be} + e^- \rightarrow {}^7\text{Li} + \nu_e + 0.81 \text{ MeV}$$
$$^7\text{Li} + {}^1\text{H} \rightarrow 2({}^4\text{He}) + 17.35 \text{ MeV}$$

📖 **NEED A HINT?** Go online to your **eText Sample Problem** for stepped out support.

Transfer of Fusion Energy

The conditions inside the sun are well beyond anything in human experience. If you travel just 30% of the distance from the sun's surface to its center, the sun is already too hot for elements to exist as atoms. Instead, matter is a bubbling, frothy plasma of charged particles: protons, larger nuclei, and electrons. If you travel into the core, the pressure is so intense that the mass of the Statue of Liberty would be squeezed enough to fit inside a refrigerator. However, the sun's overall density (1400 kg/m^3) is only about the same as liquid honey.

Internal Activity Because the sun is made of gas and plasma, its interior is constantly moving and shifting in chaotic ways. The sun's core even rotates about its axis faster than its surface. In addition, the sun rotates more quickly at the equator (one rotation in 25 days) than at the poles (36 days).

Because plasma consists of charged particles, the churning interior of the sun generates a magnetic field. The basic structure of this magnetic field is the result of the sun's rotation and large internal convection currents. The sun's magnetic field has a dipolar component, similar to Earth's, but is both more complex and more variable due to the shifting plasma currents. The interior convection patterns change on a 22-year cycle, with the polarity of the magnetic field flipping on average every 11 years.

Solar Pressure and Temperature Because gases are highly compressible, the properties of the sun vary dramatically with distance from the center.

Nearly half of the sun's mass is in its core, which is only about 1.5% of the sun's volume. The sun's temperature reaches 16 million K in the core.

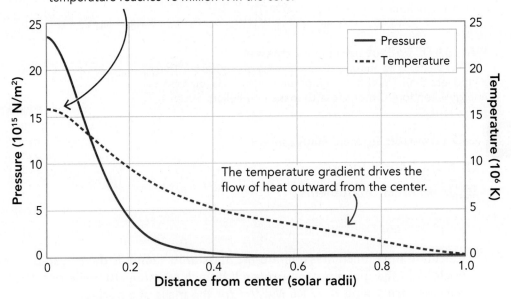

The temperature gradient drives the flow of heat outward from the center.

(7) **CCC Cause and Effect** The temperature and pressure change much more slowly as you travel deeper within Earth than they do within the sun. Explain why this is the case.

Interior Heat Transfer The sun's interior has three layers: the core, the radiative zone, and the convective zone. Because fusion in the sun's core is so slow, it generates only 277 watts per cubic meter, about the same rate of heat generation as a garden compost pile. However, because the sun is so large, that amounts to 3.846×10^{26} watts of total power generation. The sun is nearly in thermal equilibrium, so almost the same rate of energy flow (3.828×10^{26} W) radiates away from the star as electromagnetic radiation.

Most of the heat flowing outward from the core is in the form of gamma rays. In the radiative zone, gamma rays are repeatedly emitted and absorbed by adjacent ions because the plasma in the radiative zone is so dense. Gamma rays take 170,000 years to cross the radiative zone, slowly decreasing in frequency as the temperature cools.

About 70% of the way to the surface, the temperature is 1.5 million K, cool enough for hydrogen atoms to form from protons and electrons. These atoms are more efficient at absorbing radiation, so convection now becomes more efficient at carrying heat. The convective zone is a 500,000-km-thick region of convection cells that transport this heat most of the way to the sun's surface.

Layers of the Sun Heat is generated mostly as gamma rays by core fusion. After following a complex path, it mostly leaves the sun as lower-frequency radiation (X-rays, UV, visible light, infrared).

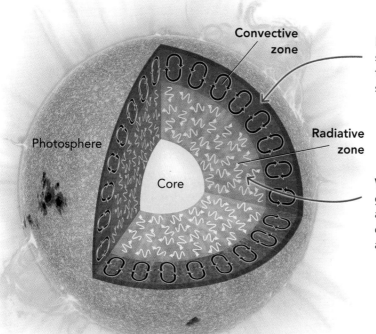

Convective zone

Heat transfer drives a system of convection cells that also generates the sun's magnetic field.

Radiative zone

Photosphere

Core

Within the radiative zone, gamma rays are constantly absorbed and re-emitted, crawling outward at an average of 50 cm per hour.

8 **SEP Develop and Use a Model** As the proton-proton chain continues to fuse hydrogen (protons) into helium, describe how and why the temperature and pressure in the sun's core will change.

Photosphere, Chromosphere, Corona

As a giant ball of gas and plasma, the sun does not have a surface. What appears to be the surface is the **photosphere,** a thin, opaque layer of the sun's atmosphere that is about 5800 K in temperature. Within the photosphere, hydrogen atoms often pick up an additional electron, and these $^1H^-$ ions are efficient at absorbing and re-emitting photons. The layer is so opaque that its radiation spectrum resembles that of an ideal blackbody. This radiation is the sunlight that spreads throughout and warms the solar system.

The **chromosphere,** the layer of the sun's atmosphere above the photosphere, has a density that is 10,000 times less than that of the photosphere. Its thickness is usually 2000 km but can spike to more than 10,000 km in places. Its temperature is cooler, dropping to about 4000 K, which gives it a reddish color. However, across the transition to the corona, temperatures increase to more than 35,000 K.

The **corona** is the sun's outer atmosphere, even less dense than the chromosphere, consisting of wispy high-energy streamers of plasma that can extend for millions of kilometers out into space. Due to their low density, the chromosphere and corona are very faint (the corona is just one millionth as bright as the photosphere) and can be seen on Earth only during total eclipses.

The Sun's Atmosphere These four images of the sun were taken at the same time using filters for different temperatures.

A visible-light image shows the 400-km-thick photosphere, where sunlight escapes the sun.

A UV image showing objects at 2 million K reveals added complexity at the surface. Bright areas show that a concentrated magnetic field is often accompanied by sunspots.

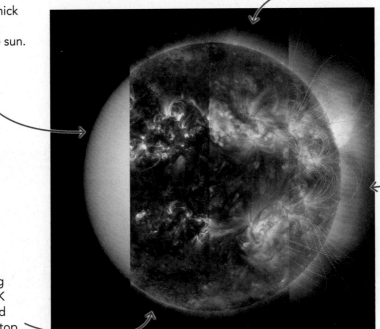

A UV image showing objects at 1 million K reveals the flares and prominences at the top of the chromosphere.

A UV image showing objects at 2 million K also shows the upper atmosphere, the corona, and the regional complexities of the magnetic field.

9) SEP Obtain and Communicate Information Obtain information about the temperatures of Earth's upper atmosphere to identify ways it is similar to that of the sun.

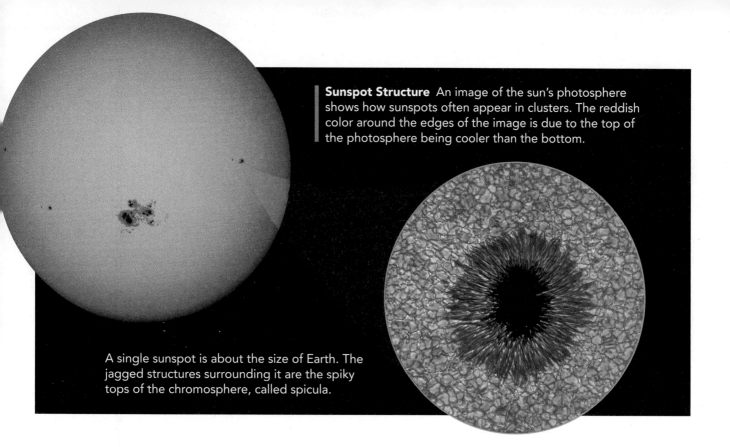

Sunspot Structure An image of the sun's photosphere shows how sunspots often appear in clusters. The reddish color around the edges of the image is due to the top of the photosphere being cooler than the bottom.

A single sunspot is about the size of Earth. The jagged structures surrounding it are the spiky tops of the chromosphere, called spicula.

Sunspots

Since the year 1610, when Galileo first observed sunspots with a telescope, astronomers have been tracking their numbers and patterns. Galileo used sunspots to determine the rate of rotation of the sun. Modern astronomers use them to track the sun's dynamic activity. The presence of more sunspots indicates that the sun's surface is more magnetically and physically active.

Sunspots are not really spots; they are regions of the deep photosphere where temperatures are 1500 K lower than usual. As a result, they give off less radiation and appear darker. Sunspots occur where dense bundles of magnetic field lines protrude up through the photosphere. The fields are so strong that they prevent some of the internal heat from reaching the surface.

Because of the connection between sunspots and the magnetic field, the number of sunspots varies due to the 11-year cycle of the sun's magnetic field reversals. During quiet times, no sunspots may be on the sun's surface. During reversals, the surface can contain more than 200 sunspots. The number of sunspots also varies on longer time scales and correlates with climate changes on Earth.

(10) **SEP Develop and Use a Model** Use the difference in temperature between sunspots and the surrounding regions, along with the model of the photosphere as a blackbody emitter, to show why sunspots emit only 30% of the radiation emitted by other parts of the photosphere.

(11) **CCC Patterns** The sun's 25th documented solar cycle began with a minimum in December, 2019. Estimate when astronomers started documenting the cycles.

Mass Ejections Coronal mass ejections (CMEs) occur every few months. In the span of a few hours, they may blast away as much as a trillion kilograms of superheated gas at hundreds of kilometers per second.

Coronal Mass Ejections, Solar Wind, and Space Weather

The force of gravity at the sun's surface is so great that particles must travel at immense speeds to escape the sun. However, particles are ejected continuously out into the solar system. Particles that escape the sun are called space weather when they reach Earth, and they may pose significant dangers.

Solar Wind Because the sun's magnetic field heats the corona's plasma to millions of degrees, about a million tons of energetic ions escape the sun each second (mostly electrons, protons, and helium nuclei). These ions blast through the solar system at more than 600 km/s. Solar wind forms the plasma tails of comets, which always point away from the sun. Solar wind also erodes the atmospheres of planets that do not have magnetic fields. For example, about one third of the Martian atmosphere has been removed by solar wind.

Solar Prominences Parts of the chromosphere can be pulled up to form giant loops. These loops follow magnetic field lines that are emerging from the sun and reveal their orientation. Solar prominences are most active when the magnetic field is also most active. The entrance and exit locations of solar prominences often coincide with the locations of sunspots.

(12) **SEP Use Mathematics** The escape velocity of an object from the surface of a star is given by $v = \sqrt{\frac{2GM}{R}}$, where G is the gravitational constant (6.67×10^{-11} m^3/kg·s^2), M is the mass of the star (in kg), and R is the distance from the center of the star (in m). Calculate the velocity a particle would need to escape from the surface of the sun.

GO ONLINE to watch a **video** about solar wind and do a PhET **simulation** that allows you to observe star temperatures.

Solar Flares Also related to magnetic activity, solar flares occur near sunspot groups where the magnetic field lines are very compressed. Within minutes, temperatures can rise above 5 million K, and plasma particles and radiation (X-rays, UV, and radio waves) blast into space. The energy of a single solar flare can exceed 10^{25} J, equivalent to more than a billion nuclear bombs.

If a coronal mass ejection or a solar flare is directed at Earth, it can overwhelm Earth's magnetic protection and bombard Earth with high-energy ions. The ionizing energy is not only dangerous to living organisms but can knock out communication satellites. It can also cause power outages by creating surges within electricity power lines due to the connection between electric and magnetic fields. Space weather poses a particular threat to astronauts and a significant challenge for the future colonization of Mars or the moon.

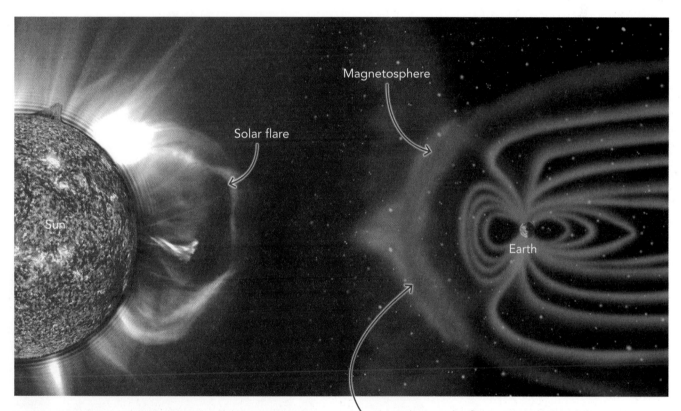

Impact on Earth of Solar Activity Earth's magnetic field generates a magnetosphere that pushes back against the solar wind and other mass ejections. Under normal conditions, the magnetosphere deflects most of the solar wind.

A very large solar flare can push through Earth's magnetosphere, coming in along the magnetic field lines near Earth's magnetic poles. This appears as highly active aurorae (the northern and southern lights).

 CCC Scale, Proportion, and Quantity On March 10, 1989, a coronal mass ejection was observed on the surface of the sun, and the shock front reached Earth 2.26 days later. The solar storm caused spectacular aurorae across North America and knocked out power grids in Eastern Canada. Calculate the mean speed at which the shock wave traveled in km/s and km/hr.

INVESTIGATIVE PHENOMENON

GO ONLINE to revisit your **Investigative Phenomenon CER** with the new information you have learned about The Sun.

These questions will help you apply what you learned in this experience to the Investigative Phenomenon.

(14) **SEP Analyze Data** Examine the graph and describe the connection between solar irradiance and the number of sunspots.

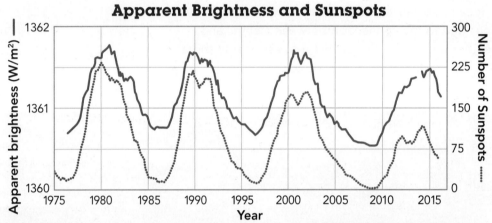

Apparent Brightness and Sunspots

Hansen, J., et al., 2016 Young People's Burden: Requirement of Negative CO2 Emissions. Earth System Dynamics. 8.10.5194/esd-8-577-2017.

(15) **SEP Construct an Explanation** Fusion within the sun's core occurs at a rate of 3.85×10^{26} W, but the sun's luminosity is 3.83×10^{26} W. Explain why these two numbers do not agree.

(16) **SEP Construct an Explanation** Unlike the sun, Earth's magnetic field reverses randomly, not periodically. Geologic evidence shows that when Earth's magnetic field reverses, its total strength decreases by over 90% for more than 1000 years. Explain why this process could pose a danger to humans.

GO ONLINE
for a **quiz** to evaluate what you learned about The Sun.

Stars

 GO ONLINE to do a **hands-on lab** that involves examining the spectra of different types of stars.

Distances to Nearby Stars

In order to make a map of the universe, the distance from Earth to objects in the sky needs to be determined. For nearby stars, astronomers use a method called **parallax,** in which an object's change in position viewed from two different perspectives is used to judge distance. Your brain uses this method to judge the distance to nearby objects using the differing perspectives of each eye.

The distance unit of a **parsec** derives from the process of parallax; it is the distance if the parallax angle θ is exactly one arcsecond, or one 3600th of a degree; 1 parsec = 3.26 light-years.

For distant objects, however, parallax no longer works, because the objects are too far away for them to change position when viewed from different points of Earth's orbit. Imagine a faraway motorcycle coming toward you on a highway. You cannot determine its distance just from the parallax of your eyes. However, you can measure the apparent brightness of the headlight and infer the distance to the motorcycle by how much dimmer the light appears.

EXPERIENCE IT!

Look at a distant object and then close your left eye. Hold one arm straight out in front of your face and raise your thumb. Without moving your arm, close your right eye and open your left eye. Repeat this, moving your thumb different distances from your face. What do you observe?

Parallax of Nearby Stars By using opposite sides of Earth's orbit, astronomers can get a stereoscopic view of nearby stars. They can then use trigonometry to determine the distance d from the parallax angle θ.

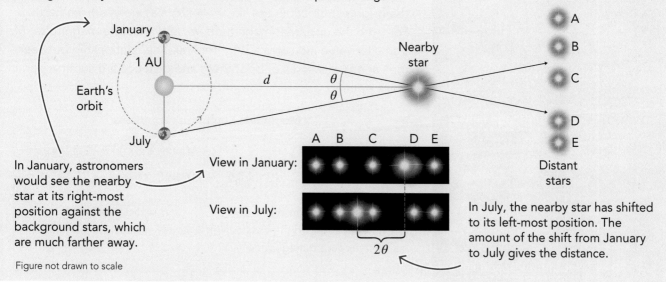

In January, astronomers would see the nearby star at its right-most position against the background stars, which are much farther away.

View in January:

View in July:

2θ

In July, the nearby star has shifted to its left-most position. The amount of the shift from January to July gives the distance.

Figure not drawn to scale

(17) **SEP Develop and Use Models** Redraw the parallax model two more times to show whether the apparent motion of a nearby star against the backdrop of distant stars is larger or smaller depending upon whether the star is farther from or closer to Earth.

Apparent Magnitude of Selected Celestial Objects

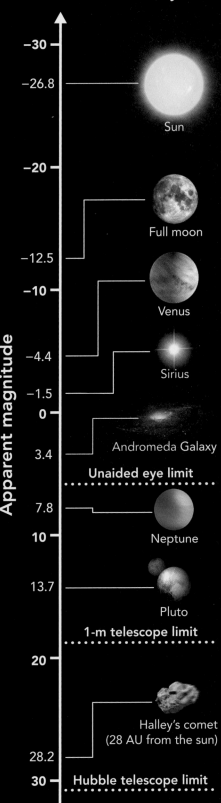

Apparent magnitude

- −30
- −26.8 — Sun
- −20
- −12.5 — Full moon
- −10 — Venus
- −4.4 — Sirius
- −1.5
- 0
- 3.4 — Andromeda Galaxy

Unaided eye limit

- 7.8
- 10 — Neptune
- 13.7 — Pluto

1-m telescope limit

- 20
- 28.2 — Halley's comet (28 AU from the sun)
- 30 — **Hubble telescope limit**

Luminosity, Apparent Brightness, and Magnitude

The most important physical property of a star is its **luminosity (L),** which is the total rate at which electromagnetic energy, or light, is being emitted from the star. Our sun, for example, emits 3.83×10^{26} W, or 383 septillion joules per second. Luminosity is one measure of the brightness of a star. Another is the **apparent brightness (b),** which is the brightness at a given distance in space away from the star. For example, the apparent brightness of the sun observed from Earth is 1,361 W/m². The apparent brightness of a star falls off proportional to the square of the distance.

For nearby stars, scientists can determine the distance from parallax and measure the apparent brightness of the star as seen from Earth. Then they can use the relationship $L = 4\pi d^2 b$ to determine the luminosity of the star.

Because of the wide range of luminosities in stars, scientists find it convenient to compare brightness on a logarithmic scale called magnitude. Every increase of 1 in magnitude corresponds to a decrease in brightness by a factor of 2.5.

The **absolute magnitude (M)** is a log-scale measure of the actual luminosity of a star. This scale is used to compare the brightness of stars assuming they are all being viewed from the same distance, 10 parsecs away. The absolute magnitude of the sun is +4.74, which means it would be barely visible to the naked eye.

The **apparent magnitude (m)** is a log-scale measure of the apparent brightness as seen from a particular location. For our sun, the brightest object in the sky, $m = -26.7$ as viewed from Earth. For both the apparent magnitude, m, and absolute magnitude, M, a smaller value indicates a brighter star. The relationship between the various measures of brightness and distance are summarized in these equations.

Magnitude-Luminosity Equations	
$L = 4\pi d^2 b$	$M = m + 87.447 - 2.5 \log_{10} d^2$
$m = -18.8 - 2.512 \log_{10} b$	$M = -2.5 \log_{10} L + 71.197$

L = luminosity (in W) d = distance (in m)
b = apparent brightness (in W/m²) M = absolute magnitude
m = apparent magnitude

(18) CCC Scale, Proportion, and Quantity Suppose that you are 7.6 cm away from a light bulb releasing 100 W of light. Calculate the apparent brightness, b, and compare this value to the apparent brightness of the sun.

Alpha Centauri

One of the nearest stars to Earth, Alpha Centauri A, is 4.367 ly away. The star has an apparent brightness, b, when seen from Earth, of 2.711×10^{-8} W/m². Calculate Alpha Centauri A's luminosity (L), apparent magnitude (m), and absolute magnitude (M).

1. DRAW A PICTURE Sketch a picture of the situation.

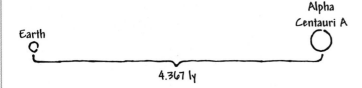

2. DEFINE THE PROBLEM List knowns and unknowns, and assign values to variables.

$b = 2.711 \times 10^{-8}$ W/m²

$d = 4.367$ ly

$\quad = (4.367 \text{ ly})(9.461 \times 10^{15} \text{ m/ly})$

$\quad = 4.132 \times 10^{16}$ m

3. PLAN AND EXECUTE Use mathematical relationships, the picture, and your definitions to plan and execute a solution.

Find the luminosity, L, using the apparent brightness, b, and distance, d.

$L = 4\pi d^2 b = 4\pi(4.132 \times 10^{16} \text{ m})^2(2.711 \times 10^{-8} \text{ W/m}^2)$
$\quad = 5.816 \times 10^{26}$ W

Find the apparent magnitude, m, using the apparent brightness.

$m = -18.8 - 2.512 \log_{10} b$
$\quad = -18.8 - 2.512 \log_{10}(2.711 \times 10^{-8} \text{ W/m}^2)$
$\quad = +0.208$

Find the absolute magnitude, M, using the luminosity.

$M = -2.5 \log_{10} L + 71.197$
$\quad = -2.5 \log_{10}(5.816 \times 10^{26} \text{ W}) + 71.197 = +4.29$

4. EVALUATE Reflect on your answer.
The absolute magnitude and luminosity are close to those of the sun, suggesting that Alpha Centauri A is a slightly brighter star than the sun. However, because it is so far away, its apparent brightness and apparent magnitude are much smaller. At an apparent magnitude of +0.208, Alpha Centauri A is one of the brightest objects in the night sky.

 GO ONLINE for more **math support**.

▶ **Math Tutorial Video**

🖥 **Math Practice Problems**

(19) One of the most distant stars visible with the naked eye, Deneb' is 2600 ly away from Earth. The star has an apparent brightness, b, as seen from Earth, of 9.867×10^{-9} W/m². Calculate Deneb's luminosity (L), apparent magnitude (m), and absolute magnitude (M).

📖 **NEED A HINT?** Go online to your **eText Sample Problem** for stepped out support.

(20) Arcturus is one of the brightest stars in the Northern Hemisphere sky. It has an absolute magnitude of –0.30 and an apparent brightness, b, of 4.295×10^{-8} W/m². Calculate Arcturus's apparent magnitude (m) and distance (d).

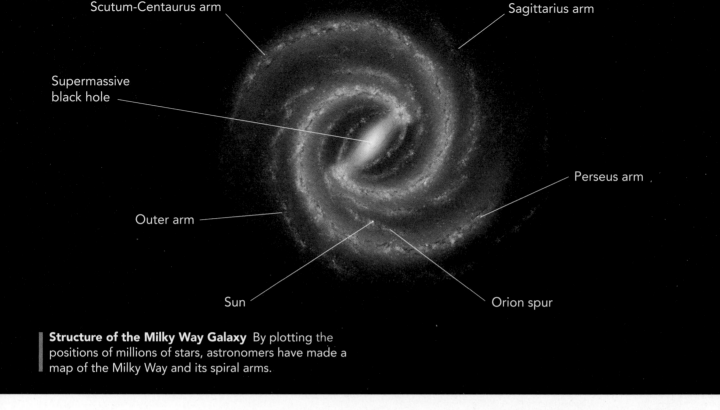

Scutum-Centaurus arm

Sagittarius arm

Supermassive black hole

Perseus arm

Outer arm

Sun

Orion spur

Structure of the Milky Way Galaxy By plotting the positions of millions of stars, astronomers have made a map of the Milky Way and its spiral arms.

Star Distribution in the Galaxy

VOCABULARY

Dark matter, which scientists theorize accounts for a majority of matter in the universe, is referred to as *dark* because it does not interact with an electromagnetic field, meaning it doesn't absorb, reflect, or emit light. Because this matter is invisible, scientists can only infer its existence based on its gravitational interactions with visible matter.

Most stars in the universe are found in large systems called **galaxies.** Galaxies come in many shapes, but they are usually a rotating disk of stars. Galaxies vary wildly in size, containing hundreds of millions to hundreds of trillions of stars. Galaxies are always star factories, with an active cycle of birth, death, and rebirth of stars.

The Milky Way galaxy is a barred-spiral disk 170,000 ly across and 1000 ly thick. The Milky Way contains 100 to 400 billion stars. New stars form along the spiral arms within the disk. Earth is 27,000 light years from the galactic center, which contains a supermassive black hole of 4 million solar masses. The Milky Way has grown in size through the merger of smaller galaxies and will collide with the nearby Andromeda galaxy in about 4.5 billion years.

Our sun takes about 230 million years to make one orbit around the center of the Milky Way, moving at about 828,000 km/h. Rotating galaxies are unexpectedly rigid, resembling merry-go-rounds more than swirling water. Based on this, astronomers surmise that about 83% of the matter in galaxies (and in the universe) is an unknown form of matter called **dark matter** that accounts for the unexpectedly fast orbits of the outer stars.

(21) **SEP Obtain, Evaluate, and Communicate Information** Draw a sketch of what our Milky Way galaxy looks like at night. Explain why it has this appearance and does not look like what is shown in the diagram.

Color and Temperature of Stars

The light from distant stars is the blackbody radiation emanating from their photospheres. For hotter blackbodies, the peak of the spectral radiation curve shifts toward higher frequencies (bluer colors), and the total radiation output increases proportionally with the fourth power of temperature. This relationship provides astronomers with a method for determining the distances to stars that are too far away to be determined by parallax: a star's color is related to its brightness.

More massive stars have more active fusion, hotter photospheres, and a bluer color. Less massive stars have less active fusion, cooler photospheres, and a redder color. Stars change color, temperature, and composition over time, so young and dying stars do not follow this guideline.

Stars in the Milky Way When viewed from space, stars appear in a wide variety of colors.

Color as a Function of Temperature Stars radiate energy according to a blackbody spectrum. The color of a star is an indication of its temperature, which is also an indication of its total luminosity.

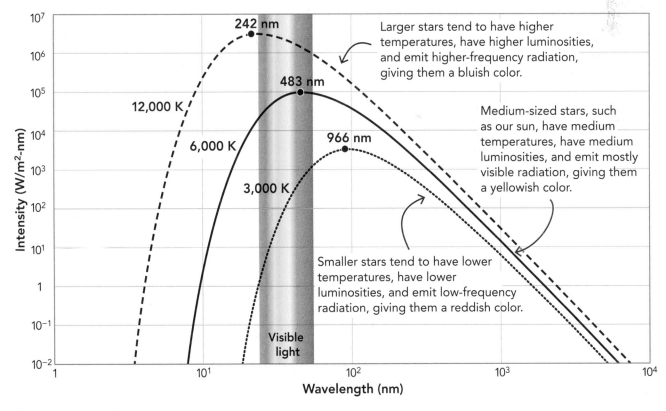

Larger stars tend to have higher temperatures, have higher luminosities, and emit higher-frequency radiation, giving them a bluish color.

Medium-sized stars, such as our sun, have medium temperatures, have medium luminosities, and emit mostly visible radiation, giving them a yellowish color.

Smaller stars tend to have lower temperatures, have lower luminosities, and emit low-frequency radiation, giving them a reddish color.

(22) **CCC Energy and Matter** Because the emission spectra of stars extend above and below the visible spectrum, the visible luminosity doesn't reflect the true luminosity, so magnitudes based just on visible light underestimate the total energy that stars release. Explain for each of the three examples in the graph the impact of this effect.

(23) **SEP Construct Explanations** In a popular series of movies, an alien predator's eyes see in the infrared and not visible spectrum. Explain the kind of star that its species' home planet likely revolves around.

Different Types of Stars

Main Sequence Stars change over the course of their lifetimes, but for most of their existence, they fuse hydrogen to form helium. As they do, stars have characteristic temperatures, luminosities, and sizes that are functions of their masses. This puts each star at a unique location within a plot, called a **Hertzsprung-Russell (H-R) diagram,** which compares stars according to their temperatures and luminosities. The diagonal band defined by the location of the stars in a Hertzsprung-Russell diagram is called the **main sequence.**

As understood from blackbody radiation curves, more luminous stars are bluer and hotter because of the fact that the amount of radiation scales with the fourth power of temperature. Hotter stars are also larger because there is greater radiation pressure pushing outward from their cores due to the greater amount of fusion. Therefore, they have more surface area.

Main Sequence Stars This Hertzsprung-Russell diagram shows four different star characteristics: photosphere temperature (x-axis), luminosity compared to the sun (y-axis), mass (number label), and radius compared to the sun (size of data point).

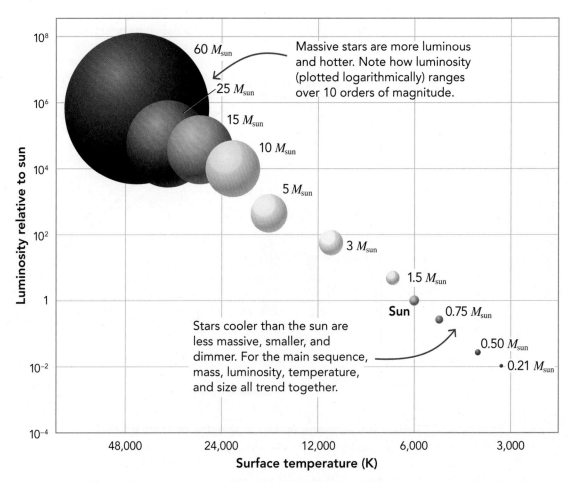

(24) **CCC Scale, Proportion, and Quantity** The radius, R, of a star is proportional to its luminosity, L, and temperature, T, according to $R = \frac{\sqrt{L}}{T^2}$. The star Bellatrix has a luminosity that is 9211 times greater than the sun's and a photosphere temperature that is 3.8 times hotter. Compare Bellatrix's radius to the sun's.

Leaving the Main Sequence Stars move only slightly in an H-R diagram during hydrogen fusion, while their compositions slowly change from hydrogen to helium. However, when a star fuses enough hydrogen such that the pressure is great enough to fuse helium into larger elements, the internal radiation pressure causes the star to expand into a giant or supergiant star. The core temperature increases, but the outer temperature decreases, so that the star leaves the main sequence and moves to the upper right of the H-R diagram.

Earth's sun will follow this evolutionary path, becoming a red giant in about 5 billion years. Then, the sun will shed its outer layers, forming a planetary nebula, and eventually cool and shrink into a white dwarf.

Supergiants do not stay in the upper right part of the diagram very long because post-hydrogen fusion processes use up nuclear fuel quickly. They eventually explode and collapse into intensely hot, dense, and dark neutron stars or black holes, permanently moving far down and to the left, off the diagram.

Star Distribution Along the H-R Diagram A diagram for a neighborhood of stars shows how they are distributed by temperatures and luminosity. The evolutionary path the sun will take is included.

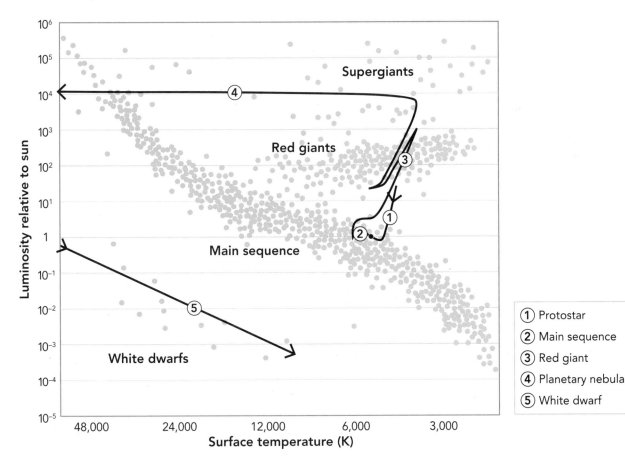

Legend:
1 Protostar
2 Main sequence
3 Red giant
4 Planetary nebula
5 White dwarf

25 **CCC Energy and Matter** Explain why there are very few identified white dwarfs, usually found very close to Earth, even though there should be many more of them in our galaxy.

Life Cycle of Stars

Astronomers have found a fascinating diversity of star types in the universe. This diversity is driven by two main factors: starting mass and composition. Mass is the most important indicator of star type and development, but the composition of the stellar nursery out of which stars form also plays a role.

Life Cycles of Stars

How do different types of stars evolve over time?

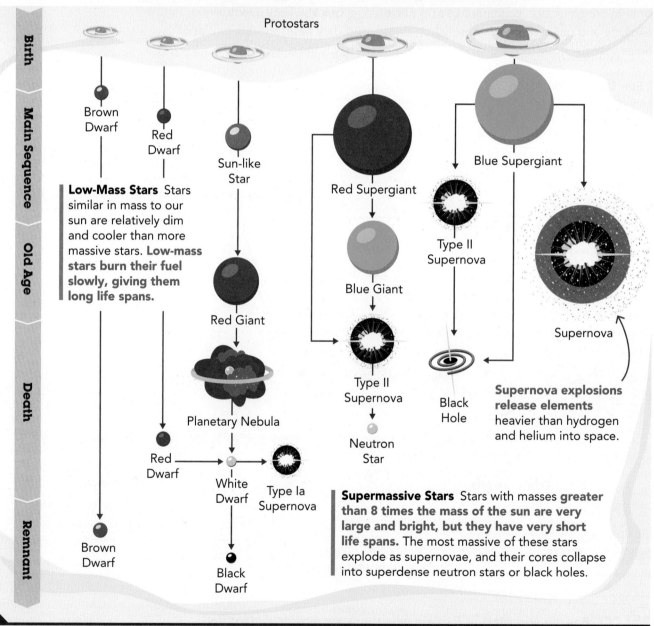

Protostars

Birth
Main Sequence
Old Age
Death
Remnant

Brown Dwarf

Red Dwarf

Sun-like Star

Red Supergiant

Blue Supergiant

Low-Mass Stars Stars similar in mass to our sun are relatively dim and cooler than more massive stars. **Low-mass stars burn their fuel slowly, giving them long life spans.**

Blue Giant

Type II Supernova

Red Giant

Planetary Nebula

Type II Supernova

Black Hole

Supernova

Supernova explosions release elements heavier than hydrogen and helium into space.

Red Dwarf

White Dwarf

Type Ia Supernova

Neutron Star

Brown Dwarf

Black Dwarf

Supermassive Stars Stars with masses **greater than 8 times the mass of the sun are very large and bright, but they have very short life spans.** The most massive of these stars explode as supernovae, and their cores collapse into superdense neutron stars or black holes.

26 **SEP Obtain and Communicate Information** Both sun-like stars and smaller stars end up as white dwarfs, but their evolutions are quite different. Use the diagram to describe the difference between them.

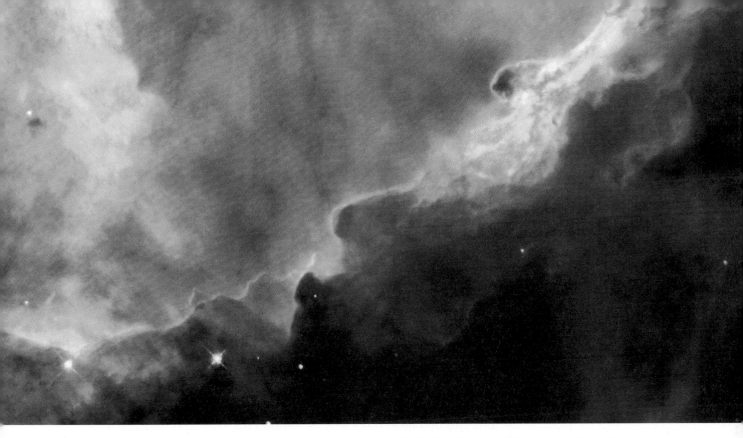

Stellar Nursery This Hubble Space Telescope image of the Swan Nebula shows dust and gas illuminated by newly formed massive stars.

Star Formation

Stars form in different ways from diffuse clouds of gas and dust. Spiral galaxies such as our Milky Way contain a diffuse interstellar medium (ISM) that is mostly hydrogen and helium, with a tiny amount of heavier elements from the deaths of previous stars. In many places, gravity pulls this ISM into slightly denser regions called molecular clouds because they are mostly molecular hydrogen gas. These clouds may contain only 100 particles per cubic centimeter but can be massive (hundreds of thousands of solar masses) and huge (100 ly across).

Molecular clouds do not usually contract because the force of gravity is balanced by the pressure of gas particle collisions. However, clouds can collapse if they collide or if they are compressed by a nearby supernova explosion. A region of molecular clouds triggered by a nearby supernova explosion or other disturbance is called a **stellar nursery,** as tens of thousands of new stars start forming.

As local regions of the stellar nursery collapse under gravity, the centers become denser and hotter and form protostars, which become main-sequence stars when their cores are hot enough for fusion to begin. As a result, stars are usually not found alone in empty space but as part of clusters. Most stars form in systems of two or more stars that orbit each other.

(27) **SEP Construct an Explanation** Construct an explanation for why molecular clouds in regions that have a long history of large stars might collapse more quickly and easily than in regions that have not previously had stars.

Nuclear Fusion Within Stars

Stellar fusion is critically important for two reasons. Stellar fusion produces the elements from which our world and bodies are made. It also provides the energy, through sunlight, that drives the many chemical, geological, and biological processes that involve those elements in many interesting ways.

The relative amounts of the elements of our universe are very uneven, with much more carbon, oxygen, and iron than other similar-sized elements. This distribution is not random but a direct outcome of the particular fusion processes that occur within stars.

Main-Sequence Fusion For stars that are the same size as the sun or smaller, fusion is dominated by the proton-proton (p-p) chain, a set of mechanisms for fusing protons into helium that requires some protons to decay into neutrons. Stars larger than the sun primarily use carbon atoms as catalysts to fuse hydrogen to helium through a set of processes called the **carbon-nitrogen-oxygen (CNO) cycle.**

Both the p-p chain and the CNO cycle have a net effect of converting four protons into one helium nucleus, releasing 26.7 MeV of energy, largely in the form of gamma rays. The energy of these gamma rays heats the star and eventually escapes as starlight.

| Energy Output of Stellar Fusion Processes This logarithmic plot shows the energy release of fusion processes within the cores of stars as a function of temperature.

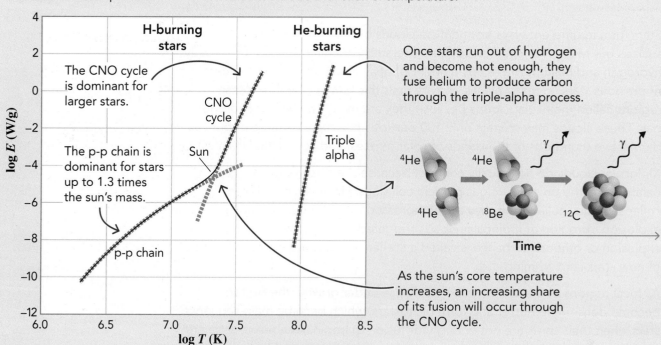

Once stars run out of hydrogen and become hot enough, they fuse helium to produce carbon through the triple-alpha process.

As the sun's core temperature increases, an increasing share of its fusion will occur through the CNO cycle.

Data source: Schwarzschild, Martin (1958) Structure and Evolution of the Stars (Dover edition (1965) ed.), Princeton University Press.

(28) SEP Obtain, Evaluate, and Communicate Information Obtain information about how the CNO-I cycle of stellar fusion works. Explain how a single carbon atom can act as a catalyst, repeatedly converting protons to helium nuclei.

Leaving the Main Sequence When a star begins to run out of hydrogen, the higher density of the remaining helium nuclei causes core temperatures to rapidly increase to more than 100 million K. At this point, the star begins to fuse helium to make larger elements.

Because the helium nucleus is so stable, when two ^{4}He nuclei fuse, the resulting ^{8}Be decays almost immediately through alpha decay back to two ^{4}He nuclei. This quick decay poses a barrier to forming elements larger than helium. When temperatures inside a stellar core finally get hot enough, larger nuclei form.

In the **triple-alpha process,** a ^{8}Be nucleus fuses with a ^{4}He nucleus to produce a ^{12}C nucleus and energy. The energy released causes the star to rapidly expand into a red giant. For very large stars, once there is enough ^{12}C, a ^{4}He nucleus fuses with ^{12}C and then larger nuclei through the **alpha ladder,** a set of nuclear fission reactions in stars that convert helium into heavier elements. Fusion on the alpha ladder happens very quickly and produces an abundance of elements with nuclei that are integer multiples of the ^{4}He nucleus. The larger the star, the higher up the alpha ladder its fusion can go. This process occurs right before the star explodes as a supernova.

> **Alpha Ladder** When a star has enough ^{12}C, the alpha ladder commences. Each alpha ladder fusion reaction releases a gamma ray with 5 to 10 MeV of energy. This burst of radiation keeps the star expanded to a great size.

A set of shells starts to form at the core of the star with different stages of the alpha ladder occurring in each one.

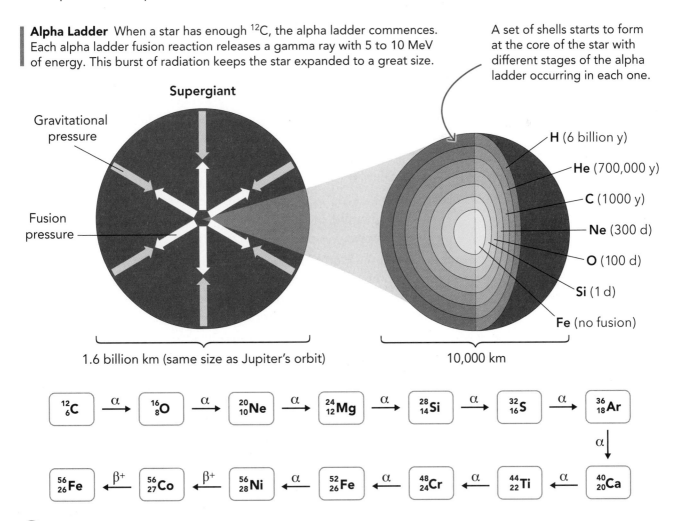

Supergiant

Gravitational pressure

Fusion pressure

1.6 billion km (same size as Jupiter's orbit)

10,000 km

H (6 billion y)
He (700,000 y)
C (1000 y)
Ne (300 d)
O (100 d)
Si (1 d)
Fe (no fusion)

$^{12}_{6}\text{C} \xrightarrow{\alpha} {}^{16}_{8}\text{O} \xrightarrow{\alpha} {}^{20}_{10}\text{Ne} \xrightarrow{\alpha} {}^{24}_{12}\text{Mg} \xrightarrow{\alpha} {}^{28}_{14}\text{Si} \xrightarrow{\alpha} {}^{32}_{16}\text{S} \xrightarrow{\alpha} {}^{36}_{18}\text{Ar}$

$\xrightarrow{\alpha}$

$^{56}_{26}\text{Fe} \xleftarrow{\beta^+} {}^{56}_{27}\text{Co} \xleftarrow{\beta^+} {}^{56}_{28}\text{Ni} \xleftarrow{\alpha} {}^{52}_{26}\text{Fe} \xleftarrow{\alpha} {}^{48}_{24}\text{Cr} \xleftarrow{\alpha} {}^{44}_{22}\text{Ti} \xleftarrow{\alpha} {}^{40}_{20}\text{Ca}$

(29) CCC Energy and Matter Iron-56 is one of the most abundant large isotopes in the solar system. However, two beta-plus decays are needed after the alpha ladder in order to create it. Explain why, using what you know about the valley of stability of nuclides.

Supernova For a small number of stars, a massive explosion blasts ultrahot elements into space in a matter of seconds. Supernovae from supergiant stars can shine with the brightness of 10 billion suns and release as much energy in months as our sun will release over its 10-billion-year lifetime.

The Death of Stars

Nucleosynthesis Processes Stars die in different ways. Most stars are small red dwarfs, which will last for trillions of years, so they are still far from dying. Slightly larger stars, such as our sun, shed their atmospheres, producing planetary nebulae. Even larger stars undergo a variety of fast processes called explosive nucleosynthesis that not only produce all the possible elements but also blast them out into space. These processes occur in the final stages leading up to and during a supernova.

- **s-process** In this slow ("s") process, neutrons cause nuclei to repeatedly undergo neutron capture and β^- decay, moving ladder-like up the valley of stability for thousands of years prior to a supernova.

- **r-process** During the merging of neutron stars, a rapid ("r") succession of neutron captures occurs in seconds, too quickly for β^- decays to occur. This process produces more neutron-rich elements than the s-process and, together with it, most elements larger than iron.

- **p-process** This process is a ladder of proton ("p") captures and β^+ decays. The source of the protons is often high-energy gamma rays knocking protons off other nuclides.

- **rp-process** Like the r-process, this rapid proton ("rp") capture process occurs when part of one star is pulled onto a neutron star and explodes, producing elements up to tellurium.

- **carbon detonation (or carbon deflagration)** If a white dwarf absorbs matter from a nearby star, it can gain enough mass for carbon fusion to occur, and a Type 1a supernova follows, producing elements up to nickel.

30) **CCC Energy and Matter** As an oral presentation, explain why the extra neutrons and protons flying around a star just before and during a supernova are necessary for large elements to form and why they cannot form from radioactivity.

GO ONLINE to watch a **video** on supernovae and do a PhET **simulation** on nucleosynthesis and the origins of elements.

Products of Explosive Nucleosynthesis During a supernova, all of the elements that formed from various stellar and explosive nucleosynthesis reactions are blasted out into space at a few percent of the speed of light. This array of mostly radioactive isotopes can seed a stellar nursery and also trigger the formation of a new star and an accompanying solar system.

Most of these new isotopes are far from the valley of stability, with either too many protons or neutrons, so they immediately undergo a massive set of radioactive decays that take them toward the valley of stability. Many of these decays happen within fractions of a second, releasing vast amounts of radiation that help drive a supernova explosion.

Some radioactive nuclides, such as ^{26}Al, last long enough to make it into newly formed planets, providing the radiogenic heat that allows planets to separate into layers and, in some cases, melt. A few radioactive isotopes have half-lives long enough that they are still around today, such as ^{40}K, ^{232}Th, ^{235}U, and ^{238}U. These isotopes provide the heat that powers the internal convection of a planet and is responsible for plate tectonics, volcanism, and tectonic activity within Earth.

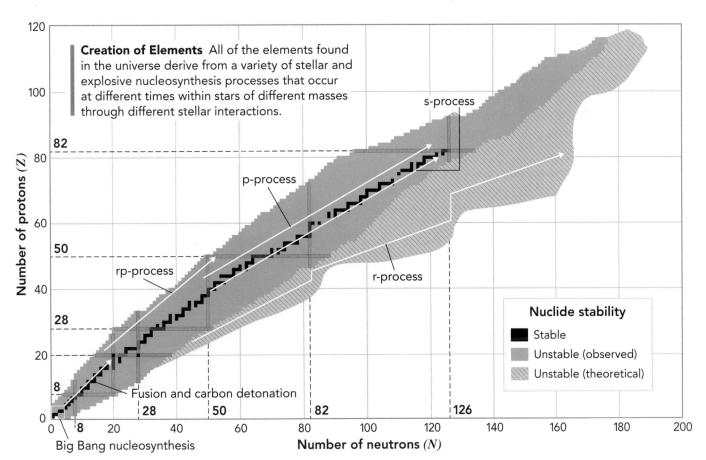

Creation of Elements All of the elements found in the universe derive from a variety of stellar and explosive nucleosynthesis processes that occur at different times within stars of different masses through different stellar interactions.

National Nuclear Data Center, information extracted from the NuDat 2 database, http://www.nndc.bnl.gov/nudat2/

(31) **SEP Develop and Use a Model** For nuclides produced by the r-process, describe in an oral presentation how they are likely to change once a supernova is finished.

INVESTIGATIVE PHENOMENON

 GO ONLINE to revisit your **Investigative Phenomenon CER** with the new information you have learned about Stars.

These questions will help you apply what you learned in this experience to the Investigative Phenomenon.

32) **CCC Scale, Proportion, and Quantity** Astronomers learn about the sun's past and future by comparing it to other stars. Complete the table below about two stars located very close to the sun in the Milky Way.

Star Name	Distance, d (ly)	Luminosity, L (W)	Apparent brightness, b (W/m²)	Absolute magnitude, M	Apparent magnitude, m
Sol (the sun)	0.00	3.83×10^{26}	1361	+4.74	−26.7
Sirius A	8.61	9.72×10^{27}			−1.46
Vega	25.0		2.20×10^{-8}	+0.73	

33) **CCC Energy and Matter** The location of a star along the main sequence determines how it evolves. Barnard's Star is a main-sequence star with a luminosity of 0.35% of the sun's luminosity and a surface temperature of 3134 K. Another such star, Spica, has a luminosity 2254 times brighter than the sun and a surface temperature of 25,300 K. Compute how many times larger the radius of Spica is than Barnard's Star.

34) **CCC Energy and Matter** In an oral presentation, provide two different explanations for why most of the heavier elements of the universe come from the largest of stars.

 GO ONLINE for a **quiz** to evaluate what you learned about Stars.

The Big Bang

 GO ONLINE to do a **hands-on lab** to model the expansion of the universe.

Evidence for the Big Bang

The entire universe, and everything within it, once existed within a single point smaller than the tiniest quark. Not only did all of the mass and energy fit within this point, but so did all the dimensions of space and time. Then, the universe exploded outward at the speed of light, pulling the dimensions and all the energy and matter out with it. The universe is still expanding today as a result of that explosion 13.787 billion years ago.

The concept of an entire universe existing at a single point and then blasting outward is not something that is easily imagined. However, observations of the universe and data collected from it all lead to the conclusion that the universe started with a Big Bang. Currently, no other theories can compete with it. Three primary lines of evidence support the Big Bang theory: the redshift of stars, the cosmic microwave background, and the composition of the universe.

The first line of evidence relies on the Doppler effect. The Doppler effect explains why the wavelength of sound changes depending on whether an object emitting the sound is moving toward or away from you. The Doppler effect also applies to light emitted by stars. The amount that starlight shifts toward the red end of the visible spectrum is called a star's **redshift.**

VOCABULARY

To help distinguish **redshift** from blueshift, remember that **re**dshifted stars are **re**ceding, while **b**lueshifted stars are **b**rought closer.

| **Redshift of Star Color** The redshift, z, is measured as $z + 1 = \frac{\lambda}{\lambda_0}$, where λ is the observed wavelength of a spectral line and λ_0 is its expected wavelength. z ranges from 0 (no shift) to 11 (most distant galaxies).

Star's motion relative to Earth

Moving toward Earth

Stationary

Practically all bright objects in other galaxies are redshifted, revealing that the universe is expanding.

Moving away from Earth

Star's spectrum observed at Earth

Blue-shifted

Stationary

Red-shifted

(35) **SEP Use Mathematics** Calculate how many times larger the observed wavelength of starlight is than the original wavelength for two values of z: if $z = 0.1$ and if $z = 11$.

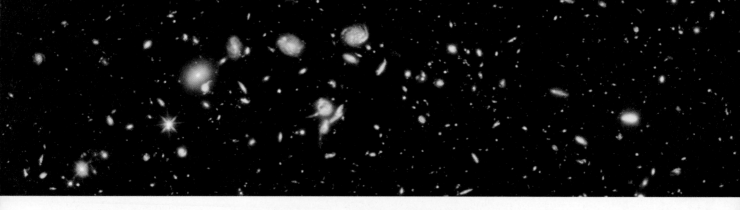

Distant Galaxies Nearly all of the objects in this deep space photograph are distant galaxies. Because light takes time to cross space, telescopes look back in time as well as out into space. Light from the farthest galaxies shows what they looked like soon after the Big Bang.

Expansion and the Age of the Universe

Hubble Constant Except for some very close ones pulled by local gravity, all galaxies are moving away from Earth. A galaxy's redshift can be used to find a galaxy's relative velocity away from Earth.

Galaxies with a redshift of 1.5 or greater would seem to be moving away from Earth faster than the speed of light. Because this is impossible, the redshift of galaxies must be a product of the stretching of the universe itself, called the **cosmological redshift.** As the universe expands at the speed of light, ancient light moving between galaxies gets stretched as well.

A plot of a galaxy's velocity, v, away from Earth versus its distance, d, shows a linear relationship, with a slope called the Hubble constant $H_0 = \frac{v}{d}$. This linear relationship, combined with the concept of a cosmological redshift, demonstrates that every point in the universe is moving away from every other point: the farther the distance, the faster the separation.

Hubble's Law By examining the supernovae of white dwarfs in other galaxies, a linear relationship between a galaxy's distance and its speed away from Earth is evident.

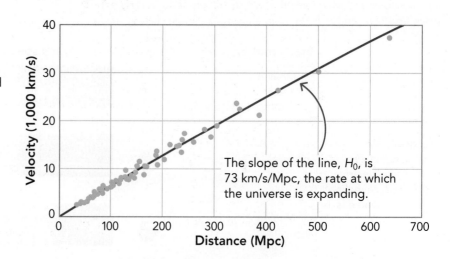

The slope of the line, H_0, is 73 km/s/Mpc, the rate at which the universe is expanding.

36 **SEP Analyze and Interpret Data** Suppose that the supernova of a white dwarf in a distant galaxy has a redshift that suggests that the galaxy is moving away from Earth at 100,000 km/s. How far away is the galaxy in light-years? (1 Mpc = 1 megaparsec = 1 million parsecs)

Age of the Universe Hubble's constant is one of the most important discoveries of the twentieth century because it reveals the age of the universe. If you run time backward until all the galaxies that are now spreading out come back together, then they will collide at a time that indicates how old the universe is.

Because Hubble's constant has units that are s^{-1} (km and Mpc are both units of length), the inverse of Hubble's constant is the time it takes for the universe to expand into its current state. Inverting H_0 yields an age for the universe as 13.4 billion years, which is very close to the current accepted value of 13.787 billion years. The difference, as you will see, is because the rate of expansion has not always been constant.

Structure of the Universe Using the redshifts of supernovae and other bright objects, astronomers can make a three-dimensional map of the positions of nearby galaxies. The result is very strange—galaxies are not evenly distributed but form clusters that themselves form larger linear and planar structures that are similar to the boundaries and walls between frothy bubbles.

EXPERIENCE IT!

Put a generous amount of soap on your hands and wash them vigorously until you create a large amount of bubbles. The three-dimensional surfaces of these bubbles serve as a model of the universe. Describe how the distribution of matter in the bubbly froth is not uniform.

Structure of the Local Universe In this slice through a three-dimensional map of the distribution of galaxies by the NASA Sloan Digital Sky Survey, each dot is a galaxy containing hundreds of millions to billions of stars. Densely clustered points show galaxies made of older stars.

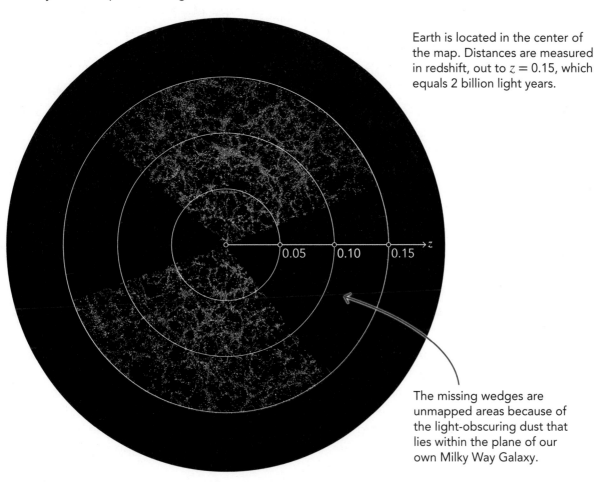

Earth is located in the center of the map. Distances are measured in redshift, out to $z = 0.15$, which equals 2 billion light years.

The missing wedges are unmapped areas because of the light-obscuring dust that lies within the plane of our own Milky Way Galaxy.

37) **SEP Use Mathematics** Suppose that the Hubble constant was 70 km/s/Mpc. Calculate the suggested age of the universe.

A Model of the Big Bang

Imagine a universe on the surface of an expanding balloon. Tiny creatures living on the balloon's surface do not realize that the balloon is three-dimensional; their experience is only two-dimensional. Locally, gravity and electromagnetic forces dominate, and the creatures do not notice any expansion. However, light traveling between distant points gets stretched along with the stretching of the balloon.

The Expansion of the Universe

How can the **expansion of the universe be modeled?**

Balloon Model An expanding balloon covered on all sides with stickers of galaxies can be used to **model the expansion of the universe.** As the universe expands, **the space between galaxies also expands.** However, **due to local gravity and EM forces, the galaxies and the objects in them do not expand.**

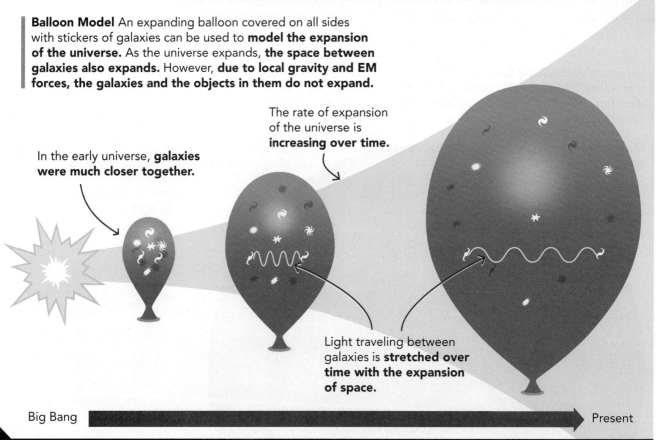

In the early universe, **galaxies were much closer together.**

The rate of expansion of the universe is **increasing over time.**

Light traveling between galaxies is **stretched over time with the expansion of space.**

Big Bang → Present

Now, return to our universe and add a dimension. Galaxies are positioned in three-dimensional space, but our universe is actually wrapped around itself in at least four dimensions. Like the balloon universe, our universe has no edge. The center of the universe is everywhere (including inside yourself), because all of matter and energy was at one point before the Big Bang. The center of the universe is also nowhere, because it is now inside the wrapped universe.

(38) SEP Construct an Explanation Explain why local objects (for example, your body) in this part of the universe are not expanding at the speed of light or why Earth has not expanded over its 4.6 billion-year existence.

Cosmic Microwave Background

An expanding universe explains the cosmological redshift of light from distant galaxies. The more distant a galaxy, the older the light and the greater the stretching in between. The oldest light that can be seen is from 370,000 years after the Big Bang. This **Cosmic Microwave Background (CMB)** radiation, which was once intensely hot and high-frequency, has gotten stretched out so much after 13.787 billion years that its wavelengths are now in the microwave range.

For the Big Bang theory to make sense, a microwave "echo" of the explosion should exist everywhere in the universe. In 1964, researchers at Bell Labs, using a radio telescope, observed a static "noise" that came from all directions and could not be removed from the signals. They had unknowingly discovered the Big Bang's echo, the second major line of evidence in support of the Big Bang.

The microwave photons of the CMB are so plentiful that they outnumber the total atoms of the universe by a billion to one. Every cubic meter of space contains 410 million of these photons. As a result, the temperature of space is not absolute zero, but 2.725 K (which is still very cold).

> **Map of the Cosmic Microwave Background** A map of the CMB by the NASA Wilkinson Microwave Anisotropy Probe (WMAP) shows that the temperature of space is remarkably constant, at 2.7250 ± 0.0002 K, wherever you look.

Different shades show temperature variations of 200 microkelvins, slight variations in the universe's energy distribution 370,000 years after the Big Bang.

Slightly hotter regions show the seeds of future galaxies.

(39) **SEP Evaluate Scientific Information** The observation of the cosmic microwave background at Bell Labs didn't change any of the ideas supporting the Big Bang hypothesis, which had been previously published. Explain why the discovery was still very important.

Recombination and Light

The light observed today as the Cosmic Microwave Background (CMB) originates from a period of time called **recombination,** when the universe expanded and cooled enough for electrons and protons to come together to form atoms. Before then, the universe was a hot plasma of electrically charged electrons, protons, and ^{4}He nuclei. The plasma was so dense that photons would go only very short distances before scattering off charged particles in a process called Thomson scattering. As a result, only photons emitted after recombination survive to this day. This means that there is no visual record, as encoded in photons, of the universe before this time.

At an age of the universe of 370,000 years, electrically neutral hydrogen atoms finally formed (helium atoms had already formed), and photons were now free to move in between the atoms of the universe without being scattered. However, the hydrogen atoms formed with electrons in excited energy states. Recombination also released great numbers of photons into the universe as these electrons dropped into the lowest energy states within the hydrogen atoms. This process, called decoupling, provided most of the photons that are now observed as the CMB. Therefore, recombination is important not only because it produced the light of the CMB but also because it marks the first existence of true atoms in the universe.

Recombination and Decoupling The universe cooled enough 370,000 years after the Big Bang for hydrogen atoms to form with electrons bonded to protons.

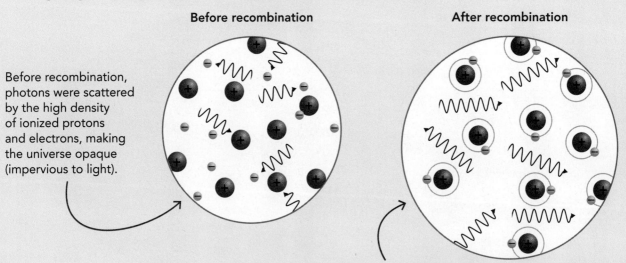

Before recombination

After recombination

Before recombination, photons were scattered by the high density of ionized protons and electrons, making the universe opaque (impervious to light).

Once electrically neutral atoms formed, they no longer scattered light, and the universe became visible. In addition, light that decoupled from the atoms became the light of the CMB.

(40) **CCC Energy and Matter** The cosmic microwave background has the largest redshift of any light in the universe, with $z = 1100$, meaning that the original light waves from recombination have been stretched by a factor of about 1100. If the waves of the CMB currently have a wavelength of 1.9 millimeters, calculate the wavelength of the original light emitted during recombination and use the electromagnetic spectrum to determine what type of radiation it is.

Big Bang Nucleosynthesis

The third major line of evidence in support of the Big Bang is the composition of the universe, which is about 75% ^{1}H and 25% ^{4}He by mass, or 92% ^{1}H and 8% ^{4}He by number of atoms. These values are predicted by the Big Bang theory and verified by the spectroscopy of light from the oldest stars and nebulae.

Protons and neutrons formed within a millionth of a second after the Big Bang and were actively colliding to form deuterium, which is needed by proton-proton chain fusion to make helium. However, the universe was still so hot that photons had more energy than the binding energy of a deuterium nucleus, so deuterium was destroyed as soon as it formed.

By 10 seconds after the Big Bang, however, the universe had cooled enough for deuterium nuclei to survive, and a suite of nuclear fusions and decays began to occur. These reactions did not create nuclei above a certain size for two reasons. First of all, no stable nuclides exist with exactly 5 or 8 nucleons, so fusion reactions that add single nucleons cannot pass beyond these numbers. Second, by the time 20 minutes had passed, the universe had expanded and cooled enough that fusion reactions could no longer occur. As a result, the Big Bang was left with ^{1}H, ^{4}He, and a few other nuclides with seven or fewer nucleons. The rest of the elements of our universe all formed at later times.

Big Bang Fusion and Decay Only these nuclear reactions occurred during the first 20 minutes of the universe. From this point until the birth of stars 300 million years later, the universe was made of ^{1}H, ^{4}He, and negligible amounts of ^{2}H, ^{3}He, and ^{7}Li.

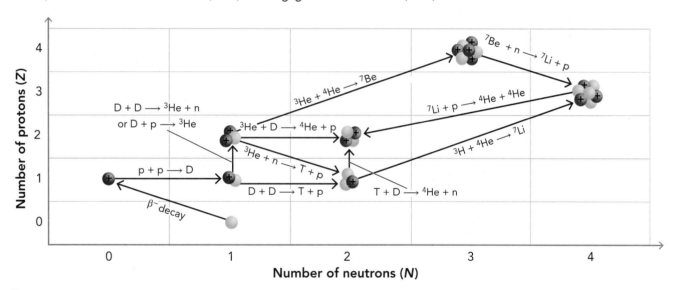

41) **CCC Energy and Matter** The Big Bang theory predicts that after the first 20 minutes of the universe, seven protons would exist for every one neutron. Show how this provides a universe that is H/He = 75%/25% by mass and H/He = 92%/8% by number of atoms, remembering that neutrons survive only if they are bound with protons within a nucleus.

42) **CCC Energy and Matter** Describe the two reactions that formed lithium-7 during the Big Bang, and explain what then happened to most of that lithium-7.

History of the Universe

 GO ONLINE to watch a **video** on the history of the universe from the Big Bang to the formation of the solar system.

People live their lives in linear time, one moment after the next. Stars live in exponential time: a steady state for millions, billions, or trillions of years and then rapid changes at the very end. The universe evolved over logarithmic time: huge changes over the first seconds and minutes, with most everyday physical processes in place for the last 98% of the universe's history.

Force Separation Initially, all four fundamental forces (strong, weak, electromagnetic, and gravitational) were combined as a single unified force.

- **Big Bang** (0 to 10^{-36} s) At a single moment, both the energy and the dimensions of our universe formed. Initially infinitesimally small and infinitely hot, the universe immediately began expanding at the speed of light and cooling. The force of gravity had separated out by 10^{-43} s.

- **Inflationary Period** (10^{-36} to 10^{-32} s) The separation of the strong force from the remaining unified forces drove a period of inflation, with the universe expanding much faster than the speed of light. The first subatomic particles (quarks and leptons) formed from radiation via $E = mc^2$.

- **Boson Emergence** (10^{-32} to 10^{-12} s) Bosons began to form, including the Higgs boson, which provided mass to other particles that were forming. The universe was about 1 AU in size. By 10^{-12} s, all four forces were separate.

History of The Universe
This logarithmic timeline shows the evolution of forces and matter-energy from the Big Bang through the present.

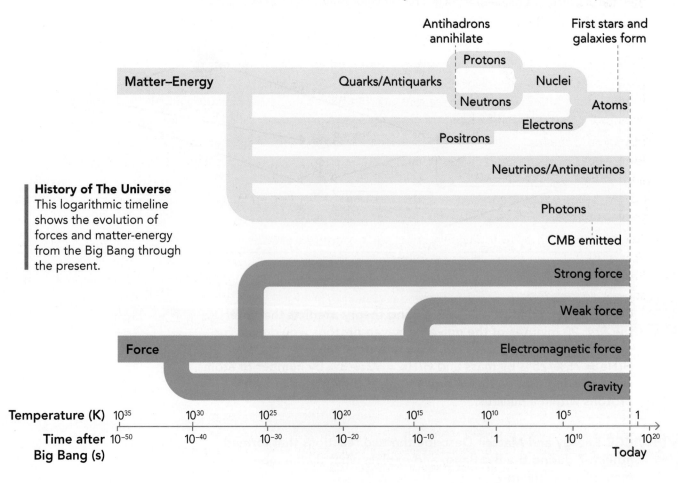

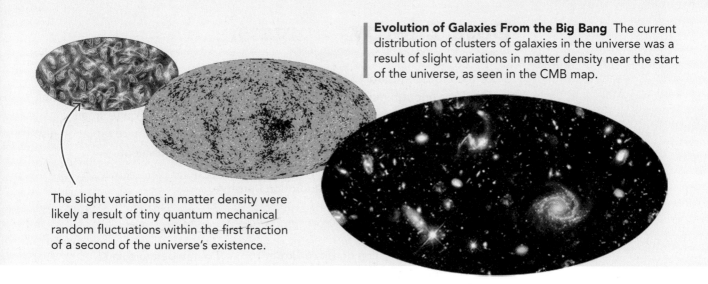

Evolution of Galaxies From the Big Bang The current distribution of clusters of galaxies in the universe was a result of slight variations in matter density near the start of the universe, as seen in the CMB map.

The slight variations in matter density were likely a result of tiny quantum mechanical random fluctuations within the first fraction of a second of the universe's existence.

Matter Condensation After the first trillionth of a second, matter as it exists today started to take shape.

- **Hadrons Form From Quark Soup** (10^{-12} to 10 s) A soup of antiquarks, quarks, and gluons combined to form hadrons (protons and neutrons). These hadrons annihilated any antihadrons that had formed. Collisions of protons and electrons released neutrinos. By 10 s, electron-positron annihilation destroyed all the positrons, leaving only electrons.

- **Nucleosynthesis and Recombination** (10 s to 3 my) Through the first 20 minutes, hydrogen (proton) fusion occurred, resulting in the original nuclear composition of the universe. At 370,000 y, recombination took place and atoms formed, releasing the first light. The universe had a reddish glow.

- **Dark Ages** (3 to 300 my) As the universe continued to expand, the red glow redshifted into the microwave range and was no longer visible, forming the CMB. The universe was dark again, not because it was opaque as before recombination, but because no source of light existed.

- **Stars and Galaxies** (300 my to 9.8 by) The first stars and galaxies began to form, and galaxies formed clusters. High-energy photons from the first stars and quasars re-ionized most of the atomic matter of the universe, which absorbed the photons and kept much of the universe dark until a billion years had passed.

- **Acceleration** (9.8 by to today) The universe's expansion has been accelerating due to the mysterious antigravity effects of dark energy. Because dark energy is still unexplained, the eventual fate of the universe is still not understood.

(43) CCC Patterns Compare the logarithmic history of the growth of the universe to your own body's logarithmic growth from a single fertilized egg cell to who you are today.

(44) SEP Apply Scientific Reasoning The current locations of galaxies might reflect the locations of slight variations of the universe when it was only centimeters in size. Describe something in today's world where a slight variation can manifest itself in a larger way over time.

Dark Energy

Since the Big Bang theory was first developed, astronomers have wondered if the universe has enough mass for gravity to eventually pull everything back together in a "big crunch." The matter density of the universe is actually quite small: 2.4×10^{-27} kg/m³, 83% of which is dark matter. The mass density of radiation also needs to be considered because energy and matter are equivalent.

Radiation Density
$$\rho_{rad} = \frac{4\sigma T^4}{c^3}$$

ρ_{rad} = radiation density (in kg/m³) T = temperature (in K)
σ = Stefan-Boltzmann constant c = speed of light
    = 5.67×10^{-8} W/m²·K⁴   = 3.00×10^8 m/s

It turns out, however, that most of the total mass of the universe is in the form of dark energy (69%), in contrast to dark matter (26%) and ordinary matter (5%). Scientists do not yet know what dark energy is, but it is inherent to the fabric of space, with a constant density of about 7.1×10^{-27} kg/m³. This constant density means that as the universe increases in size, the amount of dark energy is increasing. (Energy is being created!)

Unlike matter, which attracts through the force of gravity, dark energy repels, a form of antigravity. This repulsion means that the universe will likely never have a big crunch, and the expansion of the universe continues to accelerate.

Three Stages of the Universe The energy density of the universe has three components: radiation, matter, and dark energy. The first 50,000 years of history were dominated by radiation, the next stage by matter, and the current stage by dark energy (starting 5 billion years ago).

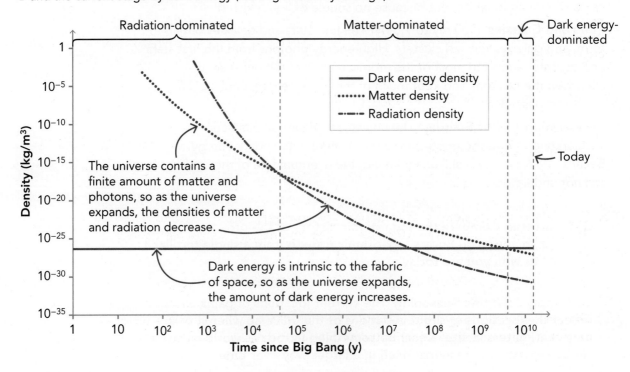

Mass Density of Radiation

Calculate the mass density of radiation in the universe now, with the CMB temperature of 2.725 K, and find its ratio to the matter density of the universe and dark energy density of the universe.

1. DRAW A PICTURE Sketch a picture of the situation.

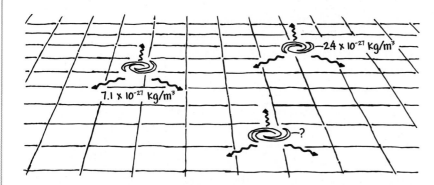

2. DEFINE THE PROBLEM List knowns and unknowns, and assign values to variables.

$T = 2.725$ K

$\sigma = 5.67 \times 10^{-8}$ W/m²·K⁴

$c = 3.00 \times 10^8$ m/s

$\rho_{matter} = 2.4 \times 10^{-27}$ kg/m³

$\rho_{DE} = 7.1 \times 10^{-27}$ kg/m³

$\rho_{rad} = ?$

3. PLAN AND EXECUTE Use mathematical relationships, the picture, and your definitions to plan and execute a solution.

Find the current mass density of radiation in the universe.

$$\rho_{rad} = \frac{4\sigma T^4}{c^3} = \frac{4(5.67 \times 10^{-8} \text{ W/m}^2\cdot\text{K}^4)(2.725 \text{ K})^4}{(3.00 \times 10^8 \text{ m/s})^3}$$
$$= 4.63 \times 10^{-31} \text{ kg/m}^3$$

Find the current ratio of the mass densities of radiation to matter.

$$\frac{\rho_{rad}}{\rho_{matter}} = \frac{4.63 \times 10^{-31} \text{ kg/m}^3}{2.4 \times 10^{-27} \text{ kg/m}^3} = 0.00019$$

Find the current ratio of the mass densities of radiation to dark energy.

$$\frac{\rho_{rad}}{\rho_{DE}} = \frac{4.63 \times 10^{-31} \text{ kg/m}^3}{7.1 \times 10^{-27} \text{ kg/m}^3} = 0.000065$$

4. EVALUATE Reflect on your answer.
Compared to matter, radiation currently accounts for only about one five-thousandth of the ordinary mass density of the universe.

 GO ONLINE for more **math support**.

▶ **Math Tutorial Video**

🖥 **Math Practice Problems**

---

45 Calculate the mass density of radiation in the universe after 1 second, when the temperature was about 10 billion K, and find its ratio to the dark energy density of the universe.

📖 **NEED A HINT?** Go online to your **eText Sample Problem** for stepped out support.

46 The mass of a single hydrogen atom is 1.67×10^{-27} kg. Calculate the current matter density of the universe in terms of hydrogen atoms per cubic meter.

INVESTIGATIVE PHENOMENON

GO ONLINE to revisit your **Investigative Phenomenon CER** with the new information you have learned about The Big Bang.

These questions will help you apply what you learned in this experience to the Investigative Phenomenon.

47 **SEP Apply Scientific Reasoning** Suppose that the fundamental parameters of our universe were slightly different and that all of the hydrogen fused into helium in the first minutes of the Big Bang. What would the stars of the universe be like? Would stars like the sun exist?

48 **CCC Energy and Matter** The temperature of the universe at any particular time is given by $T = 2.725(z + 1)$, where z is the amount of redshift. Use this to find the temperature of the universe when z was 11 (oldest galaxies), 1100 (recombination), and 5200 (the radiation density and matter density of the universe were equal). Compare these values to the surface temperature of the sun.

49 **CCC Energy and Matter** Just as stars like the sun are blackbody emitters, the entire universe at recombination, 370,000 years after the Big Bang, emitted blackbody radiation that peaked in the infrared range close to the visible spectrum. Given what you know about blackbody radiation, explain why the entire universe would have had a reddish glow to it.

50 **SEP Construct an Explanation** According to one story, following a discussion with fellow physicists about the likelihood of life developing on other planets, UFO reports, and the possibility of faster-than-light travel, Enrico Fermi is alleged to have replied, "Well, then where is everybody?" Explain why you think that no alien life form has contacted us.

GO ONLINE for a **quiz** to evaluate what you learned about The Big Bang.

These questions will help you apply what you learned in this investigation to the Anchoring Phenomenon.

(51) **SEP Argue from Evidence** About 60% of the atoms in your body are hydrogen because your body is mostly water, H_2O. Imagine a universe where all hydrogen fused into helium during the Big Bang. Do you think life could exist in a universe without much hydrogen and therefore without plentiful water?

(52) **CCC Systems and System Models** Using the fact that about 60% of the atoms in the body are hydrogen, calculate the mean age of the atoms in your body.

(53) **SEP Use Mathematics** Compare the mass density of your body to the mass density of the universe.

☑ INVESTIGATION ASSESSMENT

 GO ONLINE for activities that will give you an opportunity to **demonstrate what you have learned:**

☑ **Science Performance-Based Assessment** Design a device that can cook food without using electricity or combustion.

📄 **Engineering Workbench** Build a spectroscope that separates light into its elementary colors.

🖥 **Career Connections** Learn how an optical engineer applies physics knowledge.

☑ **Investigation Test** Take this test to demonstrate your understanding of the universe.

☑ **Virtual Lab Performance-Based Assessment** Manipulate the characteristics of a star to see how its brightness and life cycle change.

End-of-Book Resources

APPENDIX REFERENCE TABLES

TABLE 1	
PHYSICAL CONSTANTS	
Acceleration at Earth's surface	$g = -9.8 \text{ m/s}^2$
Astronomical unit (average distance from Earth to the sun)	$1 \text{ AU} = 1.496 \times 10^8 \text{ km}$
Atomic mass unit	$1 \text{ amu} = 1.6605 \times 10^{-24} \text{ g}$
Avogadro's number	$N = 6.0221 \times 10^{23} \text{ particles/mol}$
Boltzmann's constant	$k_B = 1.38 \times 10^{23} \text{ J/K}$
Charge of an electron	$-e = -1.6 \times 10^{-19} \text{ C}$
Charge of a proton	$+e = +1.6 \times 10^{-19} \text{ C}$
Coulomb constant	$k_e = 8.99 \times 10^9 \text{ N·m}^2/\text{C}^2$
Ideal gas constant	$R = 8.31 \text{ L·kPa/K·mol}$
Gravitational constant	$G = 6.674 \times 10^{-11} \text{ m}^3/(\text{kg·s}^2)$
Masses of astronomical bodies	
Earth	$m_E = 5.9722 \times 10^{24} \text{ kg}$
Moon	$m_M = 7.348 \times 10^{22} \text{ kg}$
Sun	$m_S = 1.989 \times 10^{30} \text{ kg}$
Masses of subatomic particles	
Electron (e^-)	$m_e = 0.000549 \text{ amu} = 9.1094 \times 10^{-28} \text{ g}$
Proton (p^+)	$m_p = 1.00728 \text{ amu} = 1.67262 \times 10^{-24} \text{ g}$
Neutron (n^0)	$m_n = 1.00867 \text{ amu} = 1.67493 \times 10^{-24} \text{ g}$
Permeability of free space	$\mu_0 = 4\pi \times 10^{-7} \text{ T·m/A}$
Planck's constant	$h = 6.626 \times 10^{-34} \text{ kg·m}^2 \text{ s}$
Speed of light (in vacuum)	$c = 2.997925 \times 10^8 \text{ m/s}$
Stefan-Boltzmann constant	$\sigma = 5.67 \times 10^{-8} \text{ W/(m}^2\text{·K}^4)$
Wien's displacement constant	$b = 2.90 \times 10^{-8} \text{ m·K}$

TABLE 2

SI UNITS AND EQUIVALENTS

Quantity	SI unit	Common equivalents
Length	meter (m)	1 meter = 1.0936 yards 1 centimeter = 0.39370 inch 1 inch = 2.54 centimeters 1 mile = 5280 feet = 1.6093 kilometers
Volume	cubic meter (m^3)	1 liter = 10^{-3} m^3 = 1.0567 quarts
Temperature	kelvin (K)	1 kelvin = 1 degree Celsius $°C = \frac{5}{9}(°F - 32)$ $K = °C + 273.15$
Mass	kilogram (kg)	1 kilogram = 1000 grams = mass weighing 2.2046 pounds 1 amu = 1.6605×10^{-27} kilograms
Time	second (s)	1 hour = 60 minutes 1 hour = 3600 seconds
Velocity	meters/second (m/s)	1 m/s = 2.2 miles/hour
Acceleration	meters/second squared (m/s^2)	1 m/s^2 = 2.2 miles/hour/s
Frequency	hertz (Hz)	1 hertz = 1/second
Force	newton (N)	1 newton = 1 $kg \cdot m/s^2$
Energy	joule (J)	1 joule = 1 $kg \cdot m^2/s^2$ (exact) 1 joule = 0.2390 calorie 1 calorie = 4.184 joules
Power (also Luminosity)	watt (W)	1 watt = 1 joule/second
Pressure	pascal (Pa)	1 atmosphere = 101.3 kilopascals = 760 mm Hg (Torr) = 14.70 pounds per square inch
Charge	coulomb (C)	1 coulomb = $1/1.062 \times 10^{-19}$ elementary charges
Current	ampere (A)	1 ampere = 1 coulomb/s
Potential (Voltage)	volt (V)	1 volt = 1 joule/coulomb
Resistance	ohm (Ω)	1 ohm = 1 volt/ampere
Electric field	newtons/coulomb (N/C)	1 N/C = 1 V/m
Magnetic field	tesla (T)	1 T = 1 $N \cdot s/C \cdot m$

GLOSSARY

A

absolute magnitude (*M*): a log-scale measure of the actual luminosity of a star (666)

absolute temperature: temperature on a scale that sets absolute zero at zero degrees, such as the temperature on the Kelvin scale (370)

absolute zero: the theoretical temperature at which the individual particles of matter that make up a substance have zero kinetic energy (372)

acceleration: a vector quantity that is the time derivative of velocity (23)

acceleration due to gravity: the constant acceleration towards the center of Earth experienced by a body in free fall near Earth's surface (31)

accreted terrane: a piece of new crust that has been added to the sides of continents through tectonic plate collisions (360)

aeolian system: a system related to the action of wind forces (106)

agonist: a substance that activates a receptor molecule (274)

alloy: a mixture of two or more metallic elements (264)

alpha decay: the most common form of radioactive decay for large atoms, in which a helium nucleus is ejected from a larger atomic nucleus (614)

alpha ladder: a set of nuclear fission reactions in stars that convert helium into heavier elements (675)

alternating current (AC): a type of electric current that periodically reverses direction and changes its magnitude continuously with time (236)

ammeter: a device that measures current in a circuit (426)

amplitude: the maximum distance a particle moves from its starting point in a wave (467)

analog information: information represented by a continuously variable quantity, such as the exact time, or an exact amount of light or sound (540)

angular (rotational) kinetic energy: the kinetic energy associated with the rotational motion of objects rotating about an axis (287)

angular momentum: the product of an object's moment of inertia and its angular velocity (326)

anisotropic: a property of a material that causes it to look different when viewed from different directions (262)

annular solar eclipse: an event that occurs when the moon is farther from Earth, causing a ring of the sun to appear around the moon (138)

antagonist: a substance that fits a cell receptor without activating it (274)

antenna: a rod or wire used to transmit and receive electromagnetic waves (554)

antimatter: matter that is composed of antiparticles (577)

apparent brightness (*b*): a physical property of a star that measures the brightness of a star at a given distance in space away from the star (666)

apparent magnitude (*m*): a log-scale measure of the apparent brightness of a star as seen from a particular location (666)

apparent weight: the upward force on an object that opposes gravity (84)

area vector: a vector that represents an area; the size of the vector represents the magnitude of the area, and the direction of the arrow points perpendicular to the area (233)

asthenosphere: the layer of Earth below the lithosphere consisting of weaker layer of rock that is close to its melting temperature and allows the lithosphere to slide over it (398)

atomic mass unit (amu): a unit used to measure the mass of an atom, equal to 1.660539×10^{-27} kg (573)

atomic number: the number of protons in an atom's nucleus (571)

average kinetic energy: the average translational energy of a particle in an ideal gas (369)

axis of rotation: the imaginary line around which an object rotates (325)

B

back EMF: the potential caused by the operation of an electric motor that acts against the voltage driving the motor (439)

baryon: a type of hadron formed by three quarks (578)

beat: a pulsating sound produced when two sound waves with different frequencies interact (484)

beta decay: a common form of radioactive decay, in which a high-energy electron or positron is ejected from an atom (615)

binding energy: the energy holding particles together (584)

Biot-Savart law: a law of physics stating that the magnitude of the magnetic field is proportional to the current (220)

bit: a unit equivalent to the amount of information needed to specify a choice between binary alternatives, such as dark or light, off or on, yes or no, or 0 or 1 (542)

blackbody: a theoretical object that absorbs all radiation falling on it (532)

blackbody radiation: the electromagnetic waves emitted by a blackbody (532)

brushed direct current motor: a motor design that uses a direct current power source and alternates the direction of the current through a coil of wire using a set of electrically conductive brushes (219)

byte: an array of 8 bits that are read together to give more information than a single bit (542)

C

capacitor: a device that stores electrical energy in the electric field between two parallel sheets (178)

carbon-oxygen-nitrogen (CNO) cycle: a set of processes in which stars larger than the sun primarily use carbon atoms as a catalyst to fuse hydrogen to helium (674)

Carnot cycle: a theoretical or idealized model of a heat engine cycle, consisting of two isothermal processes and two adiabatic processes (388)

center of mass: a point representing the mean position of an object's matter (66)

centripetal acceleration: the acceleration of an object in uniform circular motion (45)

centripetal force: any force that causes an object to move in a circular path (76)

centripetal vector: a vector quantity that is always directed toward the center of a circle (44)

ceramics: a category of materials made from non-metallic substances that are resistant to deformation under stress, can withstand high temperatures, do not corrode easily, and are good thermal and electrical insulators (266)

chain reaction: the sequence of reactions that occur after nuclear fission of a nucleus releases extra neutrons, which can bind to other nuclei, causing more fissions (598)

chromosphere: the layer of the sun's atmosphere above the photosphere (660)

closed system: a system that allows energy in the form of heat or work, but not mass, to be transferred between the system and its surroundings (310)

coefficient of friction: the proportion of resistance two surfaces have to motion with respect to the magnitude of the normal component of the surface force (71)

cold welding: the process of joining two metals together without heat (185)

concordia: the arcing curve in a graph of the ratios of radioactive elements in parent-daughter pairs (628)

conduction: the mechanism that transfers energy through direct physical contact between objects (382)

conductor: a material, such as a metal, that allows electric charges to easily move through it (176)

conservative force: a force for which the work done depends only on the initial and final positions and not the path between those positions (302)

constant accelerated motion: a motion with a constant acceleration (23)

constructive interference: the superposition of in-phase waves that produce a resultant wave with larger amplitude (482)

contact distance: the point where the attractive electric force is balanced by the repulsive resistance to overlapping electron clouds (166)

contact force: the interaction between objects due to direct contact with each other (65)

continental rift: a type of divergent plate boundary where a continent breaks into two or more small tectonic plates (355)

convection: the mechanism by which heat is transferred through fluid flow (383)

convergent boundary: a tectonic boundary where tectonic plates are moving together (351)

converging lens (convex lens): a lens shaped so that all rays entering parallel to the optical axis converge at a single point on the opposite side of the lens (501)

core-mantle boundary zone: the layer of rock that comprises the bottom few hundred kilometers of Earth's mantle; a thermal boundary layer that controls the rate of heat flow out of the core (398)

corona: the sun's faint outer atmosphere, consisting of wispy high-energy streams of plasma that can extend for millions of kilometers out into space (660)

Cosmic Microwave Background (CMB): the oldest light in the universe from 370,000 years after the Big Bang that is now observed as microwave radiation (683)

cosmological redshift: the redshift of galaxies that is produced by the stretching of the universe itself (680)

coulomb: the SI unit for electric charge (157)

Coulomb constant: the constant of proportionality, k_e, in relation to Coulomb's law (158)

Coulomb's law: a mathematical representation of the magnitude of electrical force between two charged objects; $F_e = k_e \frac{|q_1 q_2|}{r_{12}^2}$ (158)

covalent bond: a bond in which at least one electron from the two atoms forming the bond is no longer associated with only one nucleus but instead interacts with both nuclei (252)

crosscutting: when a rock body or discontinuity cuts across a layer or rock or another feature (639)

current density: the amount of current flow through an area (189)

D

dark matter: an unknown form of matter that accounts for the unexpectedly fast orbits of the outer stars in galaxies (668)

daughter isotope: one of the end products of radioactive decay (622)

deformation: a change in shape due to the application of a force (67)

delocalized electron: an electron that is not associated with a single atom or a covalent bond (184)

destructive interference: the superposition of two waves that are out of phase with each other in such a way as to produce a smaller wave or cancelling each other out entirely (483)

diffraction: the bending of a wave around the edges of an opening or an obstacle (494)

digital information: information represented by a discrete variable quantity, usually encoded in bits (542)

discharge: the amount of water that a stream carries (102)

disperse: to separate light into its constituent parts (514)

displacement: the change in position of an object (6)

distance traveled: the total length of the path traveled between two positions (6)

divergent boundary: a tectonic boundary where tectonic plates are moving apart (351)

diverging lens (concave lens): a lens shaped so that all incoming parallel rays diverge away from a single point on the same side of the lens (501)

Doppler effect: the apparent change in frequency caused by either the source of the waves moving, the observer moving, or both moving at different velocities (480)

dot diagram: a motion diagram in which each position of the moving object of interest is represented as a single point (11)

drift velocity: the constant electron velocity resulting from its interactions with the inner electron clouds of metal atoms in a uniform electric field (186)

dynamics: the study of the forces on objects or systems that are in motion (60)

E

eccentricity: the degree to which an orbit's elliptical shape is flattened (143)

Einstein solid: a model of a solid that has atoms connected to their neighbors by springs (70)

elastic collision: a collision within a system in which the kinetic energy of the system remains constant (342)

elastic potential energy: the energy associated with the ability of an object to do work as a result of being deformed from its original shape (296)

elastomer: a polymer with a wide range of uses that display elasticity at ambient temperatures (272)

electric charge: a physical property of matter that causes it to experience an electric force (156)

electric current: the rate at which electric charge passes through an area of wire (187)

electric field: a vector field in which the physical quantity is the electric force per unit charge (172)

electric force: a noncontact interaction between two objects having electric charge (69)

electric generator: a device that converts mechanical energy into electrical energy (435)

electric motor: a device that converts electrical energy into mechanical energy (439)

electric potential field: a scalar field where every point has the value of the electrical potential energy per unit charge; $V = \frac{PE_e}{q}$ (414)

electrical conductivity: a measure of the ability of a material's charge carriers to move through it (259)

electromagnet: a type of magnet where a magnetic field is generated by an electric current (222)

electromagnetic spectrum: the wide range of electromagnetic wavelengths (515)

electromagnetic wave: a wave generated by a disturbance in electric and magnetic fields (512)

electromotive force (EMF): a measure of the energy gained per unit of charge when energy is converted from one form into electrical energy (229)

electron capture: a type of radioactive decay in which an electron is absorbed by a nucleus (615)

electron volt: the amount of kinetic energy an electron would gain if it traveled across a capacitor with a potential of 1 volt, equal to 1.60×10^{-19} J (575)

electrostatic induction: the redistribution of electric charge in an object by the influence of a nearby charge (164)

electrostatic potential energy: the work required to move a charged particle infinitely far away from another charged particle (300)

ellipse: an oval shape described by $\frac{x^2}{a^2} + \frac{y^2}{b^2} = 1$ (142)

encoding: the process of converting data from one form to another (540)

energy: a quantitative property of a system that is associated with the motion of particles and the relative position of particles, measured in the SI unit of the joule (J) (287)

energy bar chart: a visual representation of the changes in a system's energy (289)

entropy: the amount of disorder in a system (384)

equations of motion: equations that describe an object's displacement and velocity when the acceleration is constant; $\Delta d = v_i t + \frac{1}{2} at^2$; $v = v_i + at$ (26, 27)

equipotential surface: a surface that has the same electric potential everywhere on that surface (418)

equivalent resistance: the total resistance of a combination, calculated by adding the resistances (190)

erosion: the weathering and removal of rock (98)

explosive nucleosynthesis: a variety of fast processes in stars larger than the sun that produce all the possible elements and blast them out into space (676)

extensive property: a property that does change with scale (188)

external force: any force exerted by an object outside the system that is acting on the system (81)

F

Faraday's law: a mathematical model used to predict how a changing magnetic field will produce an EMF in a loop of wire; $V_\varepsilon = -N\frac{\Delta\Phi}{\Delta t}$ (230)

ferromagnetic: having the ability to exhibit magnetic effects (201)

field: a region of space where a physical quantity is assigned to every point (171)

field lines: graphical representations consisting of lines directed by and tangent to the field vectors at each point (122)

first law of thermodynamics: the change in a system's internal energy is equal to the amount of work done on the system plus the amount of energy transferred into the system through heating; $W + Q = \Delta U_{\text{int}}$ (376)

fissile: the property of certain odd-numbered nuclei that allows them to split apart after the addition of a single neutron to the nucleus (597)

focal length: the distance from the focal point to the lens, which is determined by the index of refraction and the shape of the lens (501)

focal point: the point from a lens at which light rays converge or appear to diverge (501)

force: the cause of a change in motion or change in shape resulting from the unopposed interaction between objects (54)

force-acceleration equation: an equation based on Newton's second law of motion to represent a system; for static systems, $\Sigma F = 0$; for dynamic systems, $\Sigma F = ma$ (60)

forced convection: a process in which fluids at different temperatures are made to flow past each other so that the thermal energy of the warmer fluid is transferred to the cooler fluid (383)

fossil record: the history of life in the world's layers of rock (643)

fossil: a remain or trace of an ancient life form (643)

free fall: the falling motion of an object without resistance under the influence of Earth's gravity (31)

free-body diagram: a graphical representation of all of the forces and resulting effects on an object or a system, where the forces are drawn at the center of mass (59)

frequency: the number of wave cycles to pass a given point per unit of time (467)

friction: the parallel component of the surface force (71)

G

galaxy: a large system of stars (668)

general equation: an equation that is applicable across a large number of situations but typically requires more analysis (61)

geodynamo: a system that produces and sustains a magnetic field due to electric currents swirling around in Earth's fluid outer core (224)

geographic poles: points on the surface of Earth that are intersected by the axis of its rotation (204)

geologic time: the wide range of time scales that make up the geologic history of Earth (98)

geomagnetic field: Earth's magnetic field (224)

geosynchronous orbit: an orbit with a period of exactly 24 hours (133)

geotherm: the variation with depth of Earth's temperature (401)

glass: a hard, brittle material belonging to a subset of ceramic materials in which the molecular structure is amorphous (266)

gravitational constant: the constant of proportionality used in Newton's law of universal gravitation, known as G (118)

gravitational field: a vector field in which the physical quantity is the gravitational force per unit mass (121)

gravitational force: the noncontact attractive interaction between two objects having mass; also known as gravity (66)

gravitational potential energy: the energy an object has due to its position in a gravitational field (295)

gravity: the noncontact attractive interaction between two objects having mass; also known as gravitational force (116)

H

hadron: a particle formed by two or three bound quarks (578)

heat: the transfer of thermal energy between objects or systems (374)

heat engine: an engine that uses thermal energy to do mechanical work (386)

heat flux: the rate of thermal energy transfer in a given area; often expressed in units of W/m² (400)

heat of fusion: the energy needed to melt or freeze 1 kg of a substance, where the value is negative when freezing occurs (375)

heat of vaporization: the energy needed to vaporize or condense 1 kg of a substance, where the value is negative when condensing occurs (375)

heat pump: a device that moves thermal energy from a cooler region to a warmer region (390)

Hertzsprung-Russell (H-R) diagram: a plot of stars that compares their temperatures and luminosities (670)

Hooke's law: a law that states that the size of a spring's deformation is proportional to the applied force; $F_{SO} = -k\Delta L$ (67)

horizontality: the principle that rock layers are horizontal when they form and are usually laterally continuous over great distances (639)

Huygens' wave model: a model that represents every point on a wave front as a source of semicircular wavelets that spread out in the forward direction at the speed of the wave (494)

hydroelectric power: electrical energy generated by moving water (456)

I

ideal gas: a hypothetical gas made up of randomly moving particles that have negligible volume and no attractive forces between the particles (368)

impulse: the average collision force multiplied by the time the objects are in contact (327)

impulse-momentum theorem: a theorem that states that the change in momentum of a system is equal to the net external impulse acting on it; in vector form, $p_{net,\,i} + J = p_{net,\,f}$ (337)

index of refraction: the ratio of the speed of light in a vacuum to the speed of light in a material (499)

induction: the process of changing the magnetic field going through a loop of wire, which produces an EMF in the loop (230)

inelastic collision: a collision within a system in which there is a loss of kinetic energy in the system (343)

inertia: an object's resistance to a change in motion (53)

instantaneous acceleration: the average acceleration over an infinitesimally small time interval (25)

instantaneous velocity: the average velocity over an infinitesimally small time interval (21)

insulator: a material in which electrons cannot move easily through (183)

integral: the area under a curve on a graph (27)

intensity: a measure of light power per unit area (517)

intensive property: a property that does not change with scale (188)

internal energy: the energy on a microscopic scale associated with the random motion and positions of particles (306)

internal force: any force exerted by an object in a system on another object within the same system (81)

interstitial alloy: an alloy formed from two or more metallic elements whose atoms are significantly different sizes so that atoms of one element cannot fit into the crystal pattern of the other (264)

inverse-square law: a mathematical description of any physical quantity that is inversely proportional to the square of the distance from its source (123)

ionizing radiation: electromagnetic radiation of wavelengths shorter than visible light that has enough energy to knock electrons out of neutral atoms and break chemical bonds in molecules (531, 611)

isobaric process: a thermodynamic process in which pressure remains constant (286)

isolated system: a type of closed system that does not allow energy or matter to be transferred between the system and its surroundings (310)

isostasy: the principle that thicker crust floats more deeply in Earth's mantle and thinner crust floats less deeply (108)

J

junction: a point in a circuit where three or more conductors come together (430)

K

Kelvin scale: an absolute temperature scale that assigns 0 K to the lowest possible temperature and 273.15 K to the freezing point of water (370)

kinetic energy: the energy associated with an object's motion (287)

kinetic friction: the friction between surfaces moving relative to each other (71)

Kirchhoff's junction rule: a rule that states that the sum of the currents entering a junction is equal to the sum of the currents leaving the junction (430)

Kirchhoff's loop rule: a rule that states that, in a complete circuit, all of the decreases in potential from resistance and all of the increases from potential from electromotive force must sum to zero; $\Delta V_{\text{loop}} = \Delta V_1 + \Delta V_2 + \cdots + \Delta V_n = 0$ (428)

L

law of conservation of angular momentum: a law that states that if a system is isolated, the angular momentum of the system remains constant (333)

law of conservation of energy: a fundamental law of physics that states that energy is neither created nor destroyed (309)

law of conservation of linear momentum: a law that states if no external force acts on a system of objects or particles, then the total linear momentum of the system does not change (331)

lens: a piece of glass or other transparent substance with curved sides that is used for concentrating or dispersing light rays (501)

lens equation: a mathematical model used to express the relationship between image, object, and focal point locations; $\frac{1}{d_o} + \frac{1}{d_i} = \frac{1}{f}$ (504)

Lenz's law: a law that states that the induced current and induced magnetic field oppose the change in flux (231)

lepton: an elementary particle that can have a charge of -1, $+1$, or 0 (578)

lever arm: the perpendicular distance from the point of rotation to the line of action (91)

light-year: a unit of astronomical distance equivalent to the distance that light travels in one year (1 ly = 9.461 trillion km) (654)

line of action: the line through the point of application of a force in the direction of the force vector (91)

linear momentum: the product of the mass and the velocity of a body in linear motion, also referred to simply as momentum (322)

linear (translational) kinetic energy: the kinetic energy associated with an object with velocity that is moving through space (287)

lithosphere: the cold, rigid outer layer of Earth forming the tectonic plates that move about Earth's surface (349, 398)

load management: a process that tracks and balances energy supply and demand in power generation networks (450)

longitudinal mechanical wave: a mechanical wave in which the motion of the oscillating particles in the medium is parallel to the direction of the wave (472)

Lorentz force equation: a mathematical representation of the electric and magnetic forces on a charged particle due to electric and magnetic fields as well as the particle's motion (207)

luminosity (*L*): a physical property of a star that measures the total rate at which electromagnetic energy (or light) is being emitted (666)

lunar eclipse: an event that occurs when Earth, the sun, and the moon align in a way so that Earth casts a shadow on the moon (138)

M

magnet: a material that attracts iron and some other metals (198)

magnetic declination: the horizontal angle between true north (the direction to the geographic pole) and magnetic north (the direction a magnetic compass would point) (204)

magnetic domain: a large grouping of similarly aligned magnetic moments in ferromagnetic materials that form naturally (202)

magnetic field: a vector field that describes a material's magnetic influence throughout space (203)

magnetic flux: a measure of the amount of magnetic field that is passing through a given area (227)

magnetic force: the noncontact force that arises between moving electric charges (198)

magnetic moment: a vector that represents the strength and orientation of a magnet (200)

magnetic pole: one of the two regions on a magnet where the attractive and/or repulsive forces are the strongest (198)

magnetic potential energy: the energy associated with the ability of an object to do work due to its position and orientation in a magnetic field; also known as electrodynamic potential energy (301)

magnetization: the process of aligning the magnetic moments in a ferromagnetic material (202)

magnification: the process of making an object appear larger (503)

main sequence: the diagonal band on a Hertzsprung-Russell (H-R) diagram defined by the location of the stars in the plot (670)

mass: a measure of an object's inertia measured in the SI unit kilograms (kg) (53)

mass deficit: the energy that is released when particles come together and attain a lower energy state (584)

mass number: the total number of nucleons in an atom's nucleus (571)

mass wasting: the removal of rock from its location as a result of gravitational forces (101)

mechanical energy: the sum of all the kinetic energies and potential energies in a system (302)

mechanical wave: any wave that results from the oscillation of matter (466)

medium: the type of matter through which a wave's energy propagates (466)

meson: a type of hadron formed by two quarks (578)

mesosphere: the layer of Earth below the asthenosphere with a hotter temperature and high pressure that makes it stiffer than the lithosphere (398)

meteorites: lumps of rock or metal that fall to Earth from space and are left over from the formation of the solar system (629)

moment of inertia: the tendency of an object to resist any change to its rotational motion (325)

momentum: an object's total quantity of motion, defined as the product of its mass and velocity; also known as linear momentum (56)

monochromatic light: light of a single color or wavelength (516)

motion diagram: a diagram that shows an object's position at several equally spaced moments in time (11)

multimeter: a device that can be used to measure several different quantities in a circuit, including voltage, resistance, and current (426)

N

natural convection: a process in which fluids rise or sink because their density decreases as their temperature increases (383)

net force: the vector sum of all of the forces acting on an object (54)

neutrino: a type of lepton that does not have a charge (578)

Newton's first law of motion: a law that states that objects remain at rest or continue with uniform motion in a straight line unless some action causes a change in motion (52)

Newton's law of universal gravitation: the mathematical expression of the gravitational interaction between two objects having mass; $F = G\left(\frac{m_1 m_2}{r_{12}^2}\right)$ (118)

Newton's second law of motion: the mathematical relationship between the net force and the change in motion; $\Sigma F = ma$ (54)

Newton's third law of motion: a law that states that the interaction between two objects can be represented as forces having equal magnitude and opposite directions (57)

no-net-rotation reference frame: the reference frame of the average plate velocity used by scientists to measure tectonic plate motion (350)

nonconservative force: a force that takes energy away from a system and is path dependent (302)

noncontact force: the interaction between objects that are separated by some distance (65)

nonrenewable energy resource: a source of energy that is limited and takes a very long period of time to replenish, such as fossil fuels (447)

nonuniform motion: motion in which the position does not change the same amount in each time interval (12)

normal: the perpendicular component of the surface force (71)

nuclear fission: the splitting of a large atomic nucleus into smaller nuclei (597)

nuclear fusion: the combining of two smaller nuclei to make a larger nucleus (603)

nuclear reaction: a process in which atomic nuclei are transformed by splitting apart or by merging with other nuclei (594)

nucleon: a proton or neutron (570)

nucleus: the small, dense area at an atom's center (246)

nuclide: a specific combination of protons and neutrons that defines the nucleus of an atom (587)

O

Ohm's law: the proportional relation of current and field; $E = \rho J$ and $V = IR$ (189, 422)

ohmic material: a material that follows Ohm's law, with a constant resistance and a linear relationship between voltage and current (423)

open system: a system that allows energy or matter to be transferred between the system and the surroundings (310)

optical axis: an imaginary line that goes through the center of a lens and is perpendicular to the lens plane (501)

orbit: a continuous path of an object going around another object, such as a star, planet, or moon (129)

orbital resonance: a situation in which there are integer ratios among the periods of either revolutions only or of both revolutions and rotations of orbiting bodies (150)

orogen: a long mountain chain generated by continent-continent collisions; also known as an orogenic belt (359)

oscillatory motion: any motion in which an object repeats the same pattern of motion while repeatedly returning to its starting position (47)

P

parallax: a method used to determine how far away a star is, in which an object's change in position viewed from two different perspectives is used to judge distance (665)

parallel combination: an arrangement in which resistors, or other circuit elements, are connected on different paths in a circuit (191)

parent isotope: a radioactive element before it decays (622)

parsec: the distance unit for measuring an object's distance in space; 1 parsec = 3.26 ly (665)

partial eclipse: an eclipse that occurs when Earth or the moon only partly enters the other's shadow (138)

particle model: a representation of light as simple spheres (496)

period: the time it takes for a particle or physical quantity to move through one cycle of oscillation in a wave (467)

permanent magnet: a magnetic material whose atoms have permanently aligned magnetic moments (201)

permeability of free space: a constant that represents the ability of a magnetic field to fill an empty space (220)

phase: a measure of the shift, in radians, of a wave function, typically with respect to another wave (482)

phase angle: a measure of a waveform's shift in time relative to a reference (483)

phase change: a change in the state of matter, for example, from a solid to a liquid (375)

photoelectric effect: a phenomenon in which electrons are emitted from a metal surface when visible and UV light are directed onto it (522)

photon: a particle of electromagnetic radiation, or quantum of light (523)

photosphere: a thin, opaque layer of the sun's atmosphere that is observed from Earth as the surface of the sun (660)

photovoltaic cell: a device that converts energy from electromagnetic radiation into electrical energy (558)

plastic deformation: stress-induced deformation that is not temporary (261)

plate tectonics: the system of tectonic plate motions on Earth's surface (349)

polarized: a property of an electromagnetic wave, where the electric field oscillates in a fixed direction (517)

position: a measure of where an object is at a particular time with respect to some reference point (6)

position graph: a graph showing position as a function of time (also known as a position vs. time graph) (12)

potential energy: the energy associated with the position of an object or the arrangement of a system of objects that exert forces on one another (294)

power: the rate at which energy is transmitted in a system (292)

pressure: the magnitude of the perpendicular component of a force per unit area on a surface (285)

pressure release: a process that occurs when hot rock from the mantle flows upward to take the place of separating plates (354)

projectile: an object that is moving through the air affected only by gravity (38)

projectile motion: the combination of uniform motion parallel to the Earth's surface, and free fall motion (which has a constant acceleration perpendicular to the Earth's surface) (38)

Q

quark: an elementary particle that comprises the basic building block of matter (other than leptons) (578)

R

radiation: the process by which an object heats another object through electromagnetic waves (382)

radioactivity: a common form of natural nuclear transmutation in which an unstable atomic nucleus emits energy in the form of radiation (590, 610)

ray model: a model of waves that uses straight line arrows to represent the direction the wave is traveling (493)

ray tracing process: the process of tracing the path a light ray takes as it goes from an object, through a lens, and out through the other side (502)

real image: an image formed by light rays that actually originate from a point (497)

recombination: a period of time after the Big Bang when the universe expanded and cooled enough for electrons and protons to come together to form atoms (684)

redshift: the amount that a star's light shifts toward the red end of the visible spectrum due to the Doppler effect (679)

reflection: a phenomenon that occurs when a wave or object bounces off an interface or another object (496)

refraction: a phenomenon that occurs when a wave changes direction as a result of a change in wave speed at different points along a wave front (498)

refrigerant: the substance that flows through the system of a heat pump and transfers the thermal energy from the cooler region to the warmer region (390)

renewable energy resource: a source of energy that is readily available or replenished on a relatively short time scale; examples include solar power and hydroelectric power (447)

resistance: a measure of how much a particular object opposes the flow of electrical current (188)

resistivity: a measure of how much a unit amount of material opposes the flow of electric current (188)

resistor: an object added to a circuit in order to increase the resistance in a circuit (190)

resultant: a vector that is the sum of two or more vectors (8)

S

scalar field: a field that has a physical quantity or magnitude at every point but no direction associated with it (171, 414)

scalar quantity: a quantity with magnitude or size, but no defined direction (7)

scanner: a device that converts visual information in a physical format into a digital file (550)

second law of thermodynamics: a law that states that the net change in entropy of a system and its surroundings must always be greater than or equal to zero ($\Delta S \geq 0$); stated another way, heat flows from a warmer object to a cooler object until both objects reach thermal equilibrium (384)

sediment load: the amount of sediment that a stream carries (102)

sedimentation: a process in which rock particles are transformed into new rock (98)

seismic tomography: a modeling process that uses seismic waves from thousands of earthquakes to reveal patterns of internal convection (403)

series combination: an arrangement in which multiple resistors, or other circuit elements, are connected one after another along the same path in a circuit (190)

sidereal month: the amount of time it takes for the moon to make one full revolution with respect to the stars, 27.321661 days (137)

Snell's law: a mathematical model that shows the relation between velocities and directions of light passing from one medium to another; $\frac{\sin\theta_1}{v_1} = \frac{\sin\theta_2}{v_2}$ (499)

solar eclipse: an event that occurs when Earth, the sun, and the moon align in a way so that the moon casts a shadow on Earth (138)

solenoid: a long wire wound into a helical coil that produces a magnetic field when a current flows through it (222)

solidus: the variation with depth of the minimum temperature at which rock melts (401)

space weather: particles that escape the sun and potentially pose significant dangers when they reach Earth (662)

specific equation: an equation that is applicable to the specific problem that concerns you (61)

specific heat: the amount of energy needed to increase the temperature of 1 kg of a particular substance by 1°C (374)

speed: a measure of how much distance an object travels in a specified amount of time (13)

spring constant: a spring's resistance to deformation (67)

stability: the state of an object or system that describes its ability to restore itself to its original static equilibrium after being displaced (92)

Standard Model: a theory of matter which organizes elementary particles into bosons, quarks, and leptons (576)

standing wave: a wave that does not appear to travel, produced when two identical waves interact as they travel in opposite directions (485)

state of matter: a form matter takes on based on particle interactions that can change with temperature and pressure without chemically changing the substance; examples include solid, liquid, and gas (366)

static equilibrium: a condition in which all the forces acting on a system add up in such a way that the object does not move (90)

static friction: the friction between surfaces that are not moving relative to each other (71)

statics: the study of balanced forces on objects or systems that are at rest (60)

stellar nursery: a region of a molecular cloud in which tens of thousands of new stars start forming, triggered by a nearby supernova explosion or other disturbances (673)

strain: the fractional change in an object's length in each spatial dimension as a result of stress (261)

stress: the quantity that expresses the internal forces between particles in an object, the totality of the forces perpendicular to the cross-sectional area, per unit of cross-sectional area; measured in pascals (Pa), which are equivalent to N/m^2 (260)

strong force: the strongest force at very small distances that holds quarks together to form nucleons, acting between all masses regardless of electrical charge; also known as the strong interaction (582)

subduction zones: places on Earth where the tectonic plates sink into the mantle (349)

substitutional alloy: an alloy formed from two or more metallic elements whose atoms are nearly the same size so that atoms of one element can substitute for the other in the crystal pattern (264)

superposition: the principle that rock layers form one on top of another, with the youngest layers toward the top (639)

surface force: the force between two surfaces in contact (70)

sustainability: the ability to maintain ecological balance by not harming the environment or depleting natural resources (458)

synodic month: the time from one new moon to the next new moon, about 29.5 days (137)

system: whatever parts of the universe you are interested in studying (59)

T

tangent line: a straight line connecting a pair of infinitely close points on a curve (21)

tectonic plate: one of the large and small pieces that the lithosphere is broken into (349)

temperature: a measure of the average kinetic energy of particles in matter (369)

tension: the pulling force an object exerts along its length due to being stretched (69)

thermal boundary layer: a region of rapid temperature change that occurs at the boundaries at the top and bottom of Earth's mantle (400)

thermal conductivity: a measure of the ability of a material to conduct heat (266)

thermal conductor: a material that does not resist changes in temperature (382)

thermal energy: the energy, on a microscopic scale, that is associated with the random motions of molecules or other particles and is proportional to temperature (287, 369)

thermal equilibrium: the state of equal average kinetic energies and equal temperatures for objects (381)

thermal insulator: a material that resists changes in temperature (382)

third-law pair: the two related action-reaction forces described by Newton's third law of motion (57)

time derivative: the rate at which the value of a function changes with time (22)

torque: a measure of how effective a force is at producing a rotation; the product of the magnitude of the force and the lever arm (91)

total eclipse: an eclipse that occurs when Earth, the sun, and the moon are perfectly lined up (138)

total energy: the sum of all the energy within a system (310)

total kinetic energy: the sum of any linear kinetic energy and any angular kinetic energy (287)

total momentum: the vector sum of the momenta of all of the individual objects in a system (324)

totally inelastic collision: a collision in which the colliding objects stick together and the maximum amount of kinetic energy is lost (343)

trajectory: the path that a projectile takes (39)

trajectory graph: a two-dimensional motion diagram that shows an object's total trajectory through two different position axes, such as horizontal and vertical positions (39)

transform boundary: a tectonic boundary where tectonic plates are sliding past each other (351)

transformer: an electrical device that increases or decreases voltage by means of sets of wire coils wrapped around a shared iron core (442)

transverse mechanical wave: a mechanical wave in which the motion of the oscillating particles in the medium is perpendicular to the direction of the wave (468)

triboelectric charging: a process in which an object becomes charged after coming in direct contact with another object and then separating from it (163)

triboelectric series: a list of materials ranked according to the tendency to gain or lose electrons (163)

triple-alpha process: a process that occurs in some stars in which nuclei of beryllium-8 and helium-4 fuse, producing nuclei of carbon-12 and releasing energy; the energy released causes the star to rapidly expand into a red giant (675)

U

unconformity: a gap in time in the geologic record caused by missing rock (642)

uniform circular motion: the motion observed when an object travels in a circular path at a constant speed (44)

uniform field: a vector field with evenly spaced field lines and a constant magnitude throughout space (124, 177)

uniform motion: straight-line motion in which the position changes the same amount in each time interval (12)

V

vector component: the projection of a vector quantity along an axis in a coordinate system (7)

vector field: a field in which a vector represents a physical quantity at each point; also called a tensor field (121, 171)

vector quantity: a quantity having both magnitude and direction (7)

velocity: a measure of how much an object's position changes in a specified amount of time (13)

virtual image: an image formed by light rays that appear to originate from a point (497)

viscosity: a measure of the resistance of a fluid to flow, often measured in pascal-seconds or kg/m·s (402)

voltage: the electric potential difference that produces electric current between two points in a circuit (422)

voltmeter: a device used to measure the voltage between two points in a circuit (426)

W

wave front model: a model of waves in which only the moving crests of a wave are shown (493)

wave interference: the phenomenon that occurs when two waves superimpose as they meet while traveling in the same medium (482)

wave speed: a combination of a wave's distance and time properties; represents the speed at which the wave propagates (467)

wave superposition: a process in which the positions of colliding waves are added at each point in time to determine the resultant wave (482)

wavelength: the distance between successive similar points, such as crests, of a wave (467)

weak nuclear force: the force that governs the decay of subatomic particles, also called the weak force or weak interaction) (591)

weight: the downward force experienced by objects resulting from their gravitational attraction to Earth (66)

wireless induction: a process that involves using the constantly changing external magnetic field from a solenoid to induce current in another solenoid (236)

work: a change in a state of a system caused by a force applied along a displacement (283)

work done by: when the system exerts a force on an external object in the direction of the object's displacement (283)

work done on: when an external force exerted by an external object on a system is in the direction of the system's displacement (283)

work-energy theorem: a theorem that states that the total work done on a system is equal to the changes in the system's kinetic energy (288)

Y

Young's modulus: the ratio of stress to strain in a given material; $E = \frac{\sigma}{\varepsilon}$ (261)

The page on which a term is defined is indicated in **boldface** type. Page numbers for appendices begin with *R*.

PHOTOGRAPHY

Photo locators denoted as follows: Top (T), Center (C), Bottom (B), Left (L), Right (R), Background (Bkgd).

Cover: Lightboxx/Alamy Stock Photo; Background: Anatolyi Deryenko/Alamy Stock Vector

FRONT MATTER

iii(a): Geraldine Cochran; **iii(b):** Up Late Creative; **iii(c):** Jason Sterlace; **iii(d):** Up Late Creative; **iv:** Alison Hapka; **vi:** C. Fredrickson Photography/Moment/Getty Images; **viiiL:** Jamie Pham/Alamy Stock Photo; **viiiR:** Jeffrey Coolidge/Stone/Getty Images; **ix:** Matthias Kulka/The Image Bank/Getty Images; **x:** ESA, and M. Livio and the Hubble/NASA

STORYLINES

002: C. Fredrickson Photography/Moment/Getty Images; **112:** Jamie Pham/Alamy Stock Photo; **278:** Jeffrey Coolidge/Stone/Getty Images; **462:** Matthias Kulka/The Image Bank/Getty Images; **566:** ESA, and M. Livio and the Hubble/NASA

INVESTIGATION 1

004: Mostardi Photography/Alamy Stock Photo; **011:** Technotr/E+/Getty Images; **013:** Walter B. McKenzie/Photodisc/Getty Images; **016:** Allard Schager/Moment/Getty Images; **017:** MaxyM/Shutterstock; **020:** Mostardi Photography/Alamy Stock Photo; **025:** Fstop/Photodisc/Getty Images; **031:** Steve Prezant/Image Source/Getty Images; **034:** Mostardi Photography/Alamy Stock Photo; **044:** Wim Van Den Heever/Nature Picture Library/Alamy Stock Photo; **048:** Mostardi Photography/Alamy Stock Photo; **049:** C. Fredrickson Photography/Moment/Getty Images; **047:** Marco Simoni/Robertharding/Alamy Stock Photo

INVESTIGATION 2

050: Mac99/E+/Getty Images; **064:** Mac99/E+/Getty Images; **078:** Mac99/E+/Getty Images; **052:** Roka Pics/Shutterstock; **058:** Rawpixel.com/Shutterstock; **065:** Molishka/Shutterstock; **072:** Ljupco Smokovski/Shutterstock; **079:** Wahavi/Alamy Stock Photo; **080:** David L. Moore—US West/Alamy Stock Photo; **081:** Alexander Kondratenko/Shutterstock; **090:** Anatoli Styf/Shutterstock; **094:** Mac99/E+/Getty Images; **097:** XSA/Shutterstock; **099:** Crystal Hoeveler/500px Prime/Getty Images; **098:** Katrina Brown/Shutterstock; **100TR:** Roberto Sorin/Shutterstock; **100TL:** Kitchin and Hurst/All Canada Photos/Alamy Stock Photo; **100TC:** Eric Phan-Kim/Moment/Getty Images; **100BL:** Andreas Werth/Alamy Stock Photo; **100BC:** Dee Browning/Shutterstock; **100BR:** John MacPherson/Alamy Stock Photo; **102L:** by Paul/Shutterstock; **102R:** David Wall/Alamy Stock Photo; **104:** Boonlert Rutrekha/Shutterstock; **106:** Dmitry Rukhlenko—Travel Photos/Alamy Stock Photo; **110:** Mac99/E+/Getty Images; **111:** C. Fredrickson Photography/Moment/Getty Images

INVESTIGATION 3

114: Don Hammond/Design Pics Inc/Alamy Stock Photo; **121:** University of Texas Center for Space Research/NASA; **127:** NASA; **128:** Don Hammond/Design Pics Inc/Alamy Stock Photo; **129:** World History Archive/Alamy Stock Photo; **133TR, CR:** NASA; **133TL:** Roscosmos/NASA; **133CL:** JPL-Caltech/NASA; **133B:** Goddard/NASA; **141:** Don Hammond/Design Pics Inc/Alamy Stock Photo; **149:** MDF/Wikipedia/NASA's Dawn Mission; **150:** JPL/NASA; **152:** Don Hammond/Design Pics Inc/Alamy Stock Photo; **153:** Jamie Pham/Alamy Stock Photo

INVESTIGATION 4

154: JL Jahn/Alamy Stock Photo; **159L, R:** GIPhotoStock/Science Source; **160:** Gala Images/Alamy Stock Photo; **163:** TaraPatta/Shutterstock; **167:** Danchooalex/E+/Getty Images; **170:** JL Jahn/Alamy Stock Photo; **176:** Arinsaa/Shutterstock; **179:** NC Collections/Alamy Stock

Photo; **182:** JL Jahn/Alamy Stock Photo; **183:** Guenter Fischer/Getty Images; **185:** NASA; **186:** GIPhotoStock/Science Source; **187:** Montu Sutariya/Shutterstock; **190:** Steve Parsons/PA Images/Getty Images; **191:** Bill Brooks/Alamy Stock Photo; **194:** JL Jahn/Alamy Stock Photo; **195:** Jamie Pham/Alamy Stock Photo

INVESTIGATION 5

196: Ersin Ergin/Shutterstock; **201**(a): Charles D. Winters/Science Source; **201**(b): Bokeh Blur Background/Shutterstock; **201**(c): Basel101658/Shutterstock; **201**(d): Aleksandr Pobedimskiy/Shutterstock; **201**(e): Dewin ID/Shutterstock; **201**(f): Natee Photo/Shutterstock; **201**(g): Khak/Shutterstock; **201**(h): Roman Samokhin/Shutterstock; **201**(i): P Maxwell hotography/Shutterstock; **204:** Goddard/NASA; **206L:** Sciencephotos/Alamy Stock Photo; **206R:** New York Public Library/Science Source; **209:** P. Loiez/CERN/Science Source; **211:** Andrew Peacock/E+/Getty Images; **213:** Trevor Clifford Photography/Science Source; **212:** Ersin Ergin/Shutterstock; **219:** Haryigit/Shutterstock; **226:** Ersin Ergin/Shutterstock; **238:** Ersin Ergin/Shutterstock; **239:** Jamie Pham/Alamy Stock Photo

INVESTIGATION 6

240: Peter Casolino/Alamy Stock Photo; **243T:** 1995 Richard Megna/Fundamental Photographs, NYC; **243BL:** 1984 Chip Clark/Fundamental Photographs, NYC; **243BR:** SPL/Science Source; **244T, B:** Charles D. Winters/Science Source; **250:** Peter Casolino/Alamy Stock Photo; **251:** Charles D. Winters/Science Source; **253:** Johnce/E+/Getty Images; **254:** Jetta Productions Inc/DigitalVision/Getty Images; **255:** 4FR/E+/Getty Images; **258:** Peter Casolino/Alamy Stock Photo; **259:** Scotspencer/E+/Getty Images; **261:** Apexphotos/Moment/Getty Images; **266:** JGalione/E+/Getty Images; **267:** Juergen Schwarz/Alamy Stock Photo; **269:** Peter Casolino/Alamy Stock Photo; **271:** Granger Wootz/Getty Images; **272:** Mauro Rodrigues/Shutterstock; **273L:** MaraZe/Shutterstock; **273R:** Monty Rakusen/Cultura/Getty Images; **276:** Peter Casolino/Alamy Stock Photo; **277:** Jamie Pham/Alamy Stock Photo

INVESTIGATION 7

280: LittlePerfectStock/Shutterstock; **282:** Gregg Vignal/Alamy Stock Photo; **284:** James Smith/Alamy Stock Photo; **292:** London News Pictures/Shutterstock; **293:** LittlePerfectStock/Shutterstock; **294:** Balakate/Shutterstock; **296:** Cavan Images/Getty Images; **301:** TPH/AllOver Images/Alamy Stock Photo; **306L:** Chih-Chung Johnny Chang/Alamy Stock Photo; **306R:** Science Stock Photography/Science Source; **308:** LittlePerfectStock/Shutterstock; **309:** SolStock/E+/Getty Images; **310:** Peter Barrett/Shutterstock; **316:** Peter Muller/Cultura Creative/Alamy Stock Photo; **318:** LittlePerfectStock/Shutterstock; **319:** Jeffrey Coolidge/Stone/Getty Images

INVESTIGATION 8

320: Bernhard Lang/Stone/Getty Images; **327L, R:** Ted Kinsman/Science Source; **329:** Bernhard Lang/Stone/Getty Images; **330T:** Wertien/Shutterstock; **330B:** Lovelyday12/Shutterstock; **337:** November27/Shutterstock; **338:** Robert Crum/Shutterstock; **343:** Skynesher/E+/Getty Images; **347:** Bernhard Lang/Stone/Getty Images; **353:** Stocktrek/Stockbyte/Getty Images; **355T:** Roberto Moiola/Sysaworld/Moment/Getty Images; **355B:** Guenterguni/E+/Getty Images; **357:** World History Archive/Alamy Stock Photo; **359:** Alan Morgan Photography/Alamy Stock Photo; **361**(a): Stephan Schramm/Alamy Stock Photo; **361**(b): Stocktrek Images, Inc./Alamy Stock Photo; **361**(c): NASA/RGB Ventures/SuperStock/Alamy Stock Photo; **361**(d): Harvepino/Shutterstock; **361**(e): NASA; **361**(f): Elvishh/Shutterstock; **362:** Bernhard Lang/Stone/Getty Images; **363:** Jeffrey Coolidge/Stone/Getty Images

INVESTIGATION 9

364: LightField Studios/Shutterstock; **366:** Dmitry Gritsenko/Shutterstock; **367L:** SunChan/E+/Getty Images; **367C:** Videophoto/E+/Getty Images; **367R:** Turtle Rock Scientific/Science Source; **372:** Pascal Goetgheluck/Science Source; **376:** Wavebreakmedia Ltd/Alamy Stock Photo; **380:** LightField Studios/Shutterstock; **381:** Indigolotos/Shutterstock; **382:** Photo Researchers/Science History Images/Alamy Stock Photo; **384T:** Photo Researchers, Inc./Science Source; **384B:** Daniel D Malone/Shutterstock; **393:** LightField Studios/Shutterstock; **396:** Michael Thorne; **405:** Gary Glatzmaier; **406:** LightField Studios/Shutterstock; **407:** Jeffrey Coolidge/Stone/Getty Images

INVESTIGATION 10

408: Logoboom/Shutterstock; **410:** Ted Kinsman/Science Source; **418:** Filo/DigitalVision Vectors/Getty Images; **419:** Maskot/Getty Images; **420:** Logoboom/Shutterstock; **421:** IMG Stock Studio/Shutterstock; **422:** Matej_z/Shutterstock; **423TL:** Dja65/Shutterstock; **423TR:** Matej_z/Shutterstock; **423B:** Sergio Delle Vedove/Shutterstock; **424:** Caspar Benson/Getty Images; **426:** GIPhotoStock/Science Source; **427L:** Andrew Paterson/Photographer's Choice RF/Getty Images; **427R:** Quality Stock Arts/Shutterstock; **430:** Joshua Stevens/Dembinsky Photo Associates/NASA/Alamy Stock Photo; **434:** Logoboom/Shutterstock; **435L:** Theodore Clutter/Science Source; **435R:** Monty Rakusen/Cultura Creative (RF)/Alamy Stock Photo; **439:** Dmytro Synelnychenko/Alamy Stock Photo; **442:** GI Photo Stock/Science Source; **444:** Logoboom/Shutterstock; **451:** Rusm/E+/Getty Images; **452L:** Austin Harrison/Shutterstock; **452C:** VanderWolf Images/Shutterstock; **452R:** Kevin Schafer/Alamy Stock Photo; **456:** Spring Images/Alamy Stock Photo; **459L:** Fotos593/Shutterstock; **459C:** FotoKina/Shutterstock; **459R:** Raven/Science Source; **460:** Logoboom/Shutterstock; **461:** Jeffrey Coolidge/Stone/Getty Images

INVESTIGATION 11

464: Andrew McInnes/Alamy Stock Photo; **466:** UfaBizPhoto/Shutterstock; **475:** Lightpoet/Shutterstock; **478:** Andrew McInnes/Alamy Stock Photo; **479:** Sruilk/Shutterstock; **484L:** Peopleimages/E+/Getty Images; **484R:** CapturePB/Shutterstock; **485:** Flinn Scientific; **486:** AGCuesta/Shutterstock; **492:** Andrew McInnes/Alamy Stock Photo; **493L, R:** 2010 Richard Megna/Fundamental Photographs, NYC; **494T:** Roberto Lo Savio/Shutterstock; **494B, C:** 2010 Richard Megna/Fundamental Photographs, NYC; **495:** Ted Kinsman/Science Source; **497:** Danny Green/Nature Picture Library; **501:** ESA/NASA; **503:** Krakenimages.com/Shutterstock; **508:** Andrew McInnes/Alamy Stock Photo; **509:** Matthias Kulka/The Image Bank/Getty Images

INVESTIGATION 12

510: Chad Zuber/Shutterstock; **512:** World History Archive/Alamy Stock Photo; **514:** Yon Marsh/Alamy Stock Photo; **516:** Turtle Rock Scientific/Science Source; **519:** Chad Zuber/Shutterstock; **520:** Cavan Images/Superstock; **528:** Chad Zuber/Shutterstock; **529:** Peregrina/Shutterstock; **530T, C:** H.S. Photos/Alamy Stock Photo; **530B:** Al_Er/Shutterstock; **531:** Guy Viner/Alamy Stock Photo; **535:** Leeborn/Shutterstock; **536:** Chad Zuber/Shutterstock; **537:** Matthias Kulka/The Image Bank/Getty Images

INVESTIGATION 13

538: John Lamb/The Image Bank/Getty Images; **540:** AlexRoz/Shutterstock; **541T:** Junpiiiiiiiiiiii/Shutterstock; **541BL:** Taigi/Shutterstock; **541BR:** Susumu Nishinaga/Science Source; **543:** Davorana/Shutterstock; **545T:** Den Rozhnovsky/Shutterstock; **545CL:** Sashkin/Shutterstock; **545CR:** Bipsun/Shutterstock; **545BL:** Igor Lateci/Shutterstock; **545BR:** Roman

Samokhin/Shutterstock; **548**: John Lamb/The Image Bank/Getty Images; **550**: Mike_shots/Shutterstock; **551**: World History Archive/Alamy Stock Photo; **552T**: SGO/BSIP SA/Alamy Stock Photo; **552B**: Oleksandr Homon/Alamy Stock Photo; **553T**: Mihai_Andritoiu/Shutterstock; **553B**: Voisin/Phanie/Alamy Stock Photo; **554**: Nicholas Rous/Alamy Stock Photo; **556**: John Lamb/The Image Bank/Getty Images; **558T**: Breck P. Kent/Shutterstock; **558B**: Katja Kircher/Maskot/Getty Images; **564**: John Lamb/The Image Bank/Getty Images; **565**: Matthias Kulka/The Image Bank/Getty Images

INVESTIGATION 14
568: Grandriver/E+/Getty Images; **570**: Cern/Science Source; **573T**: Marchello74/Shutterstock; **573B**: DJTaylor/Shutterstock; **578T**: DOE/Fermi LAT Collaboration, CXC/SAO/JPL-Caltech/Steward/O. Krause et al., and NRAO/AUI/NASA; **578B**: NASA; **580**: Grandriver/E+/Getty Images; **581L**: MichaelSvoboda/iStock/Getty Images; **581R**: Photovideostock/E+/Getty Images; **589**: Mark Garlick/Science Photo Library/Alamy Stock Photo; **590TL**: Ted Kinsman/Science Source; **590TR**: Hallopino/E+/Getty Images; **590B**: Radiotec/Shutterstock; **593**: Grandriver/E+/Getty Images; **602**: Evannovostro/Shutterstock; **606**: Grandriver/E+/Getty Images; **607**: ESA, and M. Livio and the Hubble/NASA

INVESTIGATION 15
608: Goddard/NASA; **610**: Bettmann/Getty Images; **616**: Sergey Kamshylin/Shutterstock; **620T**: CNRI/Science Source; **620B**: FS Productions/Getty Images; **621**: Goddard/NASA; **622**: Imfoto/Shutterstock; **625T**: Chris Howes/Wild Places Photography/Alamy Stock Photo; **625BR**: Kevin Schafer/Avalon/Alamy Stock Photo; **625BC**: R Doran/Shutterstock; **625BL**: Billion Photos/Shutterstock; **627**: KAVSS/Shutterstock; **629T**: Ruben M Ramos/Shutterstock; **629C**: John Cancalosi/Alamy Stock Photo; **629B**: The Natural History Museum/Alamy Stock Photo; **630L**: Lukasz Pawel Szczepanski/Shutterstock; **630R**: Matteo Chinellato/Alamy Stock Photo; **631**: Photo Researchers/Science History Images/Alamy Stock Photo; **634**: Damian Peach/Science Source; **635**: Goddard/NASA; **636**: Josemaria Toscano/Shutterstock; **639**: Jeroen Mikkers/Shutterstock; **643**: HSVRS/E+/Getty Images; **644**: Sarit Richerson/Shutterstock; **650**: Goddard/NASA; **651**: ESA, and M. Livio and the Hubble/NASA

INVESTIGATION 16
652: GSFC/SOHO/ESA/NASA; **654**: Jan Wlodarczyk/Alamy Stock Photo; **655**: JSC/NASA; **660**: SDO/NASA; **661L**: SDO/NASA; **661R**: BBSO/UPI/Alamy Stock Photo; **662**: GSFC/SDO/NASA; **663**: ESA/SOHO/LASCO/EIT/NASA; **664**: GSFC/SOHO/ESA/NASA; **668**: NASA Image Collection/Alamy Stock Photo; **669**: NASA; **673**: NASA; **676**: JPL-Caltech/STScI/CXC/SAO/NASA; **678**: GSFC/SOHO/ESA/NASA; **680T**: ESA/NASA; **681**: M. Blanton/Sloan Digital Sky Survey; **683**: ESA/The Planck Collaboration/NASA; **687**: WMAP Science Team/NASA; **690**: SFC/SOHO/ESA/NASA; **691**: ESA, and M. Livio and the Hubble/NASA

TEXT ACKNOWLEDGEMENTS
INVESTIGATION 9
394: Davies, JH, "Global map of solid Earth surface heat flow," *Geochem. Geophys. Geosyst.*, 14, 4608-4622, doi: 10.1002/ggge.20271, 2013, Wiley; **401T**: Graph by Woudloper/Woodwalker, licensed under Creative Commons Attribution 4.0 International Public License https://creativecommons.org/licenses/by/4.0/legalcode. Savvas Learning Company modified the material; **402**: Nicolas Coltice and Grace E. Shephard, "Tectonic predictions with mantle convection models," *Geophysical Journal International*, April 2018, Volume 213, Issue 1, Pages 16–29, by permission of Oxford University Press/On behalf of The Royal Astronomical Society; **403**: Michael Wysession. Based on

"Complex Shear Wave Velocity Structure Imaged Beneath Africa and Iceland," by Jeroen Ritsema et. al., *Science Magazine*, December 1999; **404**: Republished with permission of Elsevier from "A mantle convection perspective on global tectonics," by Nicolas Coltice, Mélanie Géraulta, and Martina Ulvrová, *Earth-Science Reviews*, Vol. 165, 2016; permission conveyed through Copyright Clearance Center, Inc.

INVESTIGATION 12
525: Antoine Weis & Todorka Dimitrova/*American Journal Of Physics*

INVESTIGATION 15
624: Republished with permission of John Wiley and Sons from Reimer, P. J., et al. (2004), "IntCal04 terrestrial radiocarbon age calibration," 0–26 cal kyr BP, *Radiocarbon*, 46(3), 2004; permission conveyed through Copyright Clearance Center, Inc.; **633**: Republished with permission of John Wiley and Sons, from "The Origin of the Moon within a Terrestrial Synestia." SJ Lock, ST Stewart, MI Petaev, Z Leinhardt, MT Mace, SB Jacobsen, *Journal of Geophysical Research: Planets 123* (4), 910-951; permission conveyed through Copyright Clearance Center, Inc.

INVESTIGATION 16
680B: Kirshner, R.P. (2004) "Hubble's diagram and cosmic expansion." *PNAS* January 6, 2004 101 (1) 8-13; https://doi.org/10.1073/pnas.2536799100. Copyright (2004) National Academy of Sciences, U.S.A.